International Trade

TEXTS IN ECONOMICS

Texts in Economics is a new generation of economics textbooks, developed in conjunction with a panel of distinguished editorial advisers:

David Greenaway, Professor of Economics, University of Nottingham
Gordon Hughes, Professor of Political Economy, University of Edinburgh
David Pearce, Professor of Economics, University College, London
David Ulph, Professor of Economics, University College, London

PUBLISHED

International Trade Mia Mikić
Understanding the UK Economy (4th edn) Edited by Peter Curwen
Environmental Economics Nick Hanley, Jason F. Shogren and Ben White
Public Sector Economics Stephen Bailey
The Economics of the Labour Market David Sapsford and
Zafiris Tzannatos
Business Economics Paul R. Ferguson, Glenys J. Ferguson and
R. Rothschild
International Finance Keith Pilbeam

FORTHCOMING

Future Texts in Economics cover the core compulsory and optional courses in economics at first-degree level and will include:

Macroeconomics Eric Pentecost
Econometrics Ian D. McAvinchey

INTERNATIONAL TRADE

Mia Mikić
University of Auckland

St. Martin's Press
New York

INTERNATIONAL TRADE

St. Martin's Press, Scholarly and Reference Division,
175 Fifth Avenue, New York, N.Y. 10010

First published in the United States of America in 1998

This book is printed on paper suitable for recycling and
made from fully managed and sustained forest sources.

Printed in Hong Kong

ISBN 0–312–21311–5 clothbound
ISBN 0–312–21312–3 paperback

Library of Congress Cataloging-in-Publication Data
Mikić, Mia.
International trade / Mia Mikić.
p.   cm.
Includes bibliographical references and index.
ISBN 0–312–21311–5 (cloth). — ISBN 0–312–21312–3 (pbk.)
1. International trade.   2. International trade—Econometric
models.   I. Title.
HF1379.M55 1998
382—DC21   97–44293
                                                         CIP

For my parents and Ella

Contents

vii

List of Figures

List of Boxes

List of Tables

Preface

This book is a self-contained international trade theory and policy text. It is intended for a one-semester course in international trade for undergraduate students with intermediate microeconomics prerequisite. Graduates can use the text as background reading in the basic theory.

The text contains three parts. Part 1 focuses on the development of the positive theory of trade – it seeks to answer the question of what determines the basis and pattern of trade between countries. Part 2 is focused on international trade policy. Part 3 is concerned with topics of regional and multilateral trade liberalisation.

In Part 1, Chapters 1–3 develop models which are centred on the *difference* between countries in technology *or* relative factor endowments as the bases for international trade. Such trade is of an inter-industry type where each country specialises in production and export of distinctly different goods, such as machinery and raw materials. Chapters 4 and 5 discuss determinants of intra-industry trade where each country produces and exports quite similar goods, such as television sets and VCRs. This type of trade is predominantly driven by the existence of *economies of scale* and *imperfect competition*. Irrespective of the actual causes of trade, free trade is found superior to no trade. Chapter 6 considers empirical evidence on the theories discussed in this part. Finally Chapter 7 turns to examining determinants and the welfare effects of international factor flows, such as labour or capital.

In Part 2, Chapters 8 and 9 contain an elaborate discussion of the general and partial equilibrium effects of tariffs, under perfect and imperfect competition, and of non-tariff trade barriers, such as quotas, voluntary export restraints, anti-dumping, export subsidies or environmental standards. Chapter 10 examines the arguments for and against trade barriers including a discussion of the strategic arguments. Chapter 11 is concerned with measurement of the level and the cost of protection. The remaining two chapters of this part deal with 'controversial' topics such as political economy of trade policy and the link between trade policy, reform and development. In Chapter 12 answers are sought to the questions of why trade is not free and why trade policies predominantly aim to restrict trade. Chapter 13 examines the reasons for and results of the adoption of import substitution policies and then looks into the role of trade liberalisation in a transition process.

In Part 3, Chapters 14 and 15 examine the theory and the effects of economic integration in general while Chapter 16 looks at the actual regional integrations in the world. The last chapter considers problems of the coexistence of these regional liberalisation efforts and multilateral trade liberalisation. The significance of the Uruguay Round and the role of the WTO are also discussed.

I am grateful to many people who have directly or indirectly helped in the preparation of this book. I have benefited from comments from David Greenaway, Ed Tower, Geoff Braae, Sholeh Maani, Evanor Palac-McMiken, Martin O'Connor, Ravi Ratnayake, Robert Scollay and an anonymous referee. Very special thanks go to Stephen Rutt, Steven Kennedy, Jane Powell and Sarah Brown at Macmillan Press for their patience, help and encouragement. I am grateful to Keith Povey for his editing, and to an anonymous draughtsperson for re-drawing all of the figures in the book. My students at the University of Auckland, and previously, at the University of Zagreb, provided me with valuable feedback on my international trade courses and convinced me of the need for an international trade book. Special thanks to the Economics Department of the University of Auckland for providing a stimulating environment and collegial and secretarial assistance in the process of writing this book. Finally, special appreciation for my former professors, Gorazd Nikić and Ante Čičin-Šain, who first introduced me to the challenging field of international economics. Any faults that remain in this book are solely my responsibility.

My greatest thanks, however, must go to my family without whose support it would have been impossible for me to complete this task. I am grateful to my mother and my late father for love, support and encouragement through many years during which I seemed to care mostly for international trade theory. But my biggest gratitude of all goes to my daughter Ella. She understood the importance of a deadline, and was able to draw U-shaped Mussa's diagram before she was five. I sincerely hope that all the hours I spent in front of my computer writing this text surrounded by her photographs and drawings will prove to be wisely spent.

MIA MIKIĆ

Acknowledgements

The author and publishers are grateful to the following for the permission to use copyright material: American Economic Association for Table 11.3 from R. Feenstra, 'How Costly is Protectionism?', *Journal of Economic Perspectives*, 6: 3 (1992); Kym Anderson and Richard Blackhurst for Tables 15.1, 15.2 and 15.3 from T. N. Srinivasan, J. Whalley and I. Wooton, 'Measuring the Effects of Regionalism on Trade and Welfare' in *Regional Integration and the Global Trading System*, ed. K. Anderson and R. Blackhurst (1993) Harvester Wheatsheaf, tables 3.3, 3.4 and 3.5; Sayeeda Bano and the University of Waikato, Department of Economics, for Table 6.6 from Bano and Lane, 'Intra-Industry International Trade: The New Zealand Experience 1964–87', Department of Economics: Working Papers in Economics, No. 91/7; Blackwell Publishers for Figure 16.1 from A. Bollard and D. Mayes, 'Regionalism and the Pacific Rim', *Journal of Common Market Studies*, 30 (1992) p. 202; Table 5.1, data from G. D. A. MacDougall, 'British and American Exports: A Study Suggested by the Theory of Comparative Costs, Part 1', *Economic Journal*, 61 (1951), tables I, II and III; Elsevier Science-NL for Table 6.2 from A. V. Deardoff, 'Testing Trade Theories and Predicting Trade Flows' in *Handbook of International Economics*, Vol. 1, ed. R. W. Jones and P. B. Kenen (1984) table 4.1; Institute for International Economics for Table 7.2 from W. R. Cline, *International Debt: Systematic Risk and Policy Response*, 1984, table 1.4, copyright © 1984 by the Institute for International Economics; International Monetary Fund for Table 11.2 from R. Lattimore, 'Economic Adjustment in New Zealand: A Developed Country Case Study of Policies and Problems' in *Economic Adjustment: Policies and Problems*, ed. Sir Frank Holmes (1987) tables 4, 7; Table 10.1 data from *Government Finance Statistics Yearbook* (1990); Kiel Institute of World Economics for Figure 6.2 from H. Siebert, 'A Schumpeterian Model of Growth in the World Economy: Some Notes on a New Paradigm in International Economics', *Weltwirtschaftliches Archiv*, 127 (1991); Organisation for Economic Co-operation and Development for Table 17.3 from A. Hoda, 'Trade Liberalization Results of the Uruguay Round' from *The New World Trading System: Readings,* copyright © OECD 1994; Routledge for Table 6.3 from H. Forstner and R. Ballance, *Competing in a Global Economy*, 1990; Unwin & Hyman for UNIDO, tables 3.6 and 3.8; United Nations Conference on Trade and Development for Tables 6.5, 7.4 and 7.5, data from *World Investment Report 1992: Transnational Corporations as Engines of Growth* (Sales No. E.92.II.A.24); The World Bank for Table 9.2 from T. Hertel *et al.*, *Global Economic Prospects and the Developing Countries* (1995) p. 35; World Trade Organisation for Tables

4.1, 14.1 and Figures 16.1 and 17.1 from *Regionalism and the World Trading System* (1995); Table 17.2 from *Trading into the Future* (1995); and Figure 16.2 and Box 16.3 from *International Trade, Trends and Statistics*, Geneva (1995). Every effort has been made to trace all the copyright-holders, but if any have been inadvertently overlooked the publishers will be pleased to make the necessary arrangement at the first opportunity.

■ *PART I* ■
THE ORIGINS OF TRADE

■ *Chapter 1* ■

Ricardian Model and Extensions

In section 1.1 of this chapter we consider the basic analytical relationships of the Ricardian model. These provide the propositions for the *law of comparative advantage* which states that a country will export that good in which it has relative productivity advantage. This section also deals with the basic propositions concerning the gains from trade. Section 1.2 then considers some extensions of the basic model. It begins by identifying the duality between relative commodity prices and relative wages, looks at extensions through increasing the number of countries and goods, and finally looks at the introduction of transportation costs. Section 1.3 summarises the discussion.

Two appendices at the end of the chapter extend the basic model even further. Appendix 1A (p. 43) provides a generalisation of the principle of comparative advantage. Appendix 1B (p. 46) introduces a different 'basic' model, the Ricardian factor endowment model, in which the coutries are differentiated by their relative endowments of different qualities of labour, rather than productivities of the single labour type as in the basic Ricardian model.

▌*1.1* The basic Ricardian model of comparative advantage

This section focuses on the classical or Ricardian theory of comparative advantage as the means for the simplest examination of the basis for international trade.[1] This model, as any other model, suffers from being bounded by a number of restrictive assumptions (listed below). Some of these assumptions will be relaxed later in this chapter. Even with such restrictions, however, the model proves to be very useful in outlining basic trade theory and production patterns, and in demonstrating the gains from trade. Nevertheless, there are some defects in the model that could cause more or less concern, depending on what we think this model's main aim should be. If it is used with the aim of showing the pattern of international trade, that is, if it is a 'positive' model, then the model suffers from two weaknesses. The first comes from the fact that the model explains the trade pattern on the basis of productivity differences between countries but does not attempt to explain the source of such differences. The second is a problem of indeterminacy of terms of trade or world prices. If, on the other hand, the model is intended for a demonstration of the benefits from trade, that is, as a 'normative' model, then we again encounter some problems. The most important is that the model considers only one single (or one Leontief composite) factor of production, and consequently sheds no light regarding the income distributional effects of trade which have always been the major source of protectionist demands.

The main assumptions on which the very basic model rests are:

(1)   Labour is the only input into production.
(2)   Total amount of labour in each country is fixed and all units of labour are identical (homogeneous quality of work force).
(3)   Labour is perfectly mobile between alternative uses as long as the wage per hour is the same between industries.
(4)   Labour is completely immobile internationally and as a result wages differ between countries.
(5)   Relative labour content is the sole determinant of the relative value (price) of commodities (labour theory of value). That means that a good embodying four hours of labour is four times as expensive as a good embodying only one hour of labour.
(6)   The level of technology is given for both countries, and differs between them therefore providing the sole reason for productivity differences.
(7)   The production function has constant returns to scale. Thus, marginal and average costs of production are constant. In terms of productivity this means that output per labour hour (or labour hours per unit of production of commodity) is constant regardless of number of hours worked (or quantity produced).
(8)   There is full employment.
(9)   Pure (perfect) competition prevails in the internal markets and in international trade.
(10) Transportation costs are zero.

□ The pre-trade economy

Our trade tale begins to unfold in a very simplified version of the real world. We start by first describing production and consumption conditions, and the resulting determinants of relative prices in a pre-trade economy.

Home

Imagine there is a country called Home in which labour as a single input produces just two homogeneous goods, cloth (C) and food (F) under perfectly competitive conditions.[2] The total amount of labour is given as L. In line with the above assumptions all labour is of the same quality, and each worker is indifferent between producing cloth or food as long as both sectors pay the same wage per labour-hour. Furthermore, each worker's output per labour-hour (i.e. average product) is constant and independent of the number of hours worked. Let the symbol a_{LC} (a_{LF}) denote the number of labour-hours that will produce a single unit of cloth (food):

$$a_{LC} = L/Q_C$$
$$a_{LF} = L/Q_F$$
(1.1.1)

Labour's productivity is then given by

$$1/a_{LC} = Q_C/L = AP_{LC} = MP_{LC}$$
$$1/a_{LF} = Q_F/L = AP_{LF} = MP_{LF}$$
(1.1.1a)

Since Home is a one-factor economy, its technology is fully described by each of (1.1.1) in terms of labour content and (1.1.1a) in terms of labour productivity.

Now, by putting together information on quantity of input and technology and by assuming that the requirement for full employment is satisfied ($L = L_C + L_F$), the limits to the production possibilities of Home are given as

$$L = a_{LC}Q_C + a_{LF}Q_F$$
(1.1.2)

where $a_{LC}Q_C$ is labour employed by the cloth sector and $a_{LF}Q_F$ is labour employed by the food sector. The tool that is usually used to examine the production (supply) side in our general equilibrium model is the production possibility frontier (PPF), also known as transformation curve. To draw Home's production possibility frontier, it is useful to have (1.1.2) written as

$$Q_C = (L/a_{LC}) - (a_{LF}/a_{LC})Q_F$$
(1.1.3)

where L/a_{LC} gives the maximum quantity of cloth that can be produced when no food is produced ($Q_F = 0$). Similarly, L/a_{LF} would give the maximum amount of food produced when this economy produces no cloth ($Q_C = 0$). Between these two extreme production points, there are many others; indeed if goods are perfectly divisible the number of their linear combinations is indefinitely large. The locus of all such (full-employment) points is a straight line with a slope of $-a_{LF}/a_{LC}$, and it represents Home's PPF in Figure 1.1. This locus is technologically efficient implying that each point of the PPF satisfies the conditions for *Pareto optimality*.[3]

The special feature of technology illustrated in Figure 1.1 is the constancy of the PPF's slope. The economic meaning of this is that a unit contraction of food production always releases a_{LF} units of labour and *each* unit of this labour always leads to the same increase ($MP_{LC} = 1/a_{LC}$) in the output of cloth (i.e. no diminishing returns to labour). So the total of a_{LF} of labour released will produce a_{LF}/a_{LC} of cloth. In other words, the *opportunity cost* of producing one good (food) in terms of the other (cloth) is constant and equals a_{LF}/a_{LC}.[4]

In our simple economy these opportunity costs coincide with the *relative prices* of goods, that is, a price of one good expressed in terms of the other good. To see how relative prices fully reflect opportunity costs, we turn to the competitive pricing conditions:

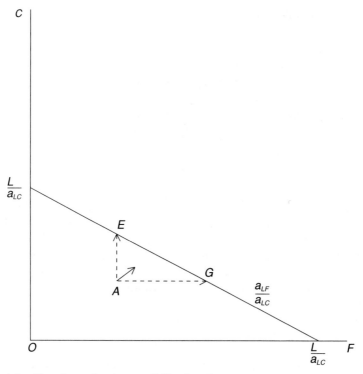

Figure 1.1   *Home's production possibility frontier*

$$MC_F(= AC_F) = a_{LF}w_F = p_F$$
$$MC_C(= AC_C) = a_{LC}w_C = p_C \qquad\qquad (1.1.4)$$

where w is a wage rate. We can also write this as

$$p_F/p_C = (a_{LF}/a_{LC})(w_F/w_C) \qquad\qquad (1.1.5)$$

Since we assume that labour can freely and costlessly shift between two sectors according to which sector is more attractive in terms of wage per labour-hour, it follows that if wages were not equal only one good would be produced in our economy. For instance, if $w_F > w_C$ and the relative price of food is therefore higher than the opportunity cost of producing food ($p_F/p_C > a_{LF}/a_{LC}$), labour will be interested in producing only food, and there will be no incentive to produce cloth at all. Similarly, if the relative price of food were less than food's opportunity cost, workers would have no incentive to stay in the food sector and given their perfect mobility they would all move to the cloth sector. These two situations represent cases where relative commodity prices dictate the complete specialisation in production (where all inputs are utilised to produce only one good). Nothing is wrong with this, as long as such a production structure is acceptable for all in a society (i.e. demand must also be biased towards one good). However, normally we would suppose that many goods and services will be needed to satisfy demand. Therefore, we assume that our model economy will produce as many goods as is defined to be possible (in this case *both* goods) *as long as domestic production remains the only source of supply*.[5] Put differently, being closed for trade means that Home needs to produce some food and some cloth, and in order to do so the relative price of these two goods must not deviate from their opportunity costs, that is

$$p_F/p_C = (a_{LF}/a_{LC}) \qquad\qquad (1.1.5a)$$

So, it is *this* relative price that determines the production pattern. As long as our economy keeps producing both goods, this price is fixed at the level of relative labour contents and does not depend on demand. However demand can affect the relative quantity of goods produced, determining the particular point on the PPF according to the specific taste pattern. However, changes in relative demand (for example, sudden preference for more cloth relative to food) *do not* influence relative price in this model. Therefore, we can say that in this one-factor constant-returns-to-scale economy, it is indeed true that the relative price of food (p_F/p_C) is determined solely by technological factors.[6]

The patterns of production described above are illustrated by Home's supply curve for food in Figure 1.2. If the market relative price for food is less than its opportunity cost, no food is produced and the supply curve is identical to the vertical axis up to the level where relative price corresponds to the opportunity cost. At that level labour is indifferent between working to produce food or cloth, and the supply curve is horizontal. If the market price rises above food's opportunity cost, the production of food becomes L/a_{LF} (with cloth production being stopped altogether); the supply curve again becomes vertical, now at the level of food's potential supply.

At this point we introduce a new concept – the *relative supply* of food (Q_F/Q_C) as a function of the relative price of food (p_F/p_C). We can use Figure 1.2 to trace out relative supply of food. When $p_F/p_C < a_{LF}/a_{LC}$, Home produces only cloth $(QC = L/a_{LC}$ and $Q_F = 0)$ so that relative supply of food is zero. Thus the vertical segment of the food supply curve that coincides with the relative price axis is also the vertical segment of the relative supply curve of food. When $p_F/p_C = a_{LF}/a_{LC}$, Home produces both goods and, as explained above, the relative quantity of goods produced (Q_F/Q_C) can take any value between 0 and L/a_{LF}, which is the maximum quantity of food Home can produce, *ceteris paribus*. Therefore, the relative supply curve of food in a closed Ricardian economy is a horizontal line and corresponds to the flat segment of the supply curve of food in Figure 1.2.

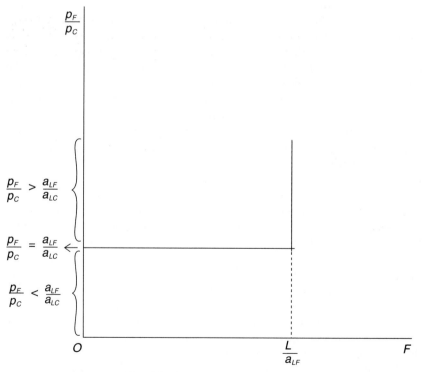

Figure 1.2   *Home's supply of food*

Foreign

Assume now that there is another country, called Foreign (conventionally all variables related to Foreign will be labelled by an *). Foreign's economy is also very simple: it is endowed with L^* of labour which produces same homogeneous goods cloth (C) and food (F). At this stage we allow only a single difference between Home and Foreign, this being in productivity levels. Foreign's technology is described by the following unit labour requirements:

$$a^*_{LC} = L^*/Q^*_C$$
$$a^*_{LF} = L^*/Q^*_F \tag{1.1.1*}$$

For expositional purposes, we will assume that relative labour content in production of food is less in Home than in Foreign:

$$a_{LF}/a_{LC} < a^*_{LF}/a^*_{LC} \tag{1.1.6}$$

Inequality (1.1.6) implies that Home's technology is more efficient in producing food *relative to* cloth than Foreign's technology. In terms of the Ricardian model we say that Home has a *comparative advantage* in producing food over Foreign; conversely Foreign has a comparative advantage in producing cloth over Home. Comparative advantages have great significance when used as a criterion for specialisation in production once countries open themselves to trade. Before going into that, let us emphasise exactly what the concept of *comparative* advantage implies. First, note that in order to determine which of the two countries has a comparative advantage in say, food, we need to have information on *all* four unit labour requirements (or the autarky prices of all goods); that is, we need to know labour content in production of both goods in both countries. It does not suffice to compare labour contents in food production only (e.g. $a_{LF} < a^*_{LF}$) because this gives us an *absolute* advantage, a criterion which is helpful but not the one we want.[7] Also, notice that comparative advantage is a *relative* term. Inequality $a_{LF}/a_{LC} < a^*_{LF}/a^*_{LC}$, meaning that Home has a comparative advantage in food, implies inequality $a^*_{LC}/a^*_{LF} < a_{LC}/a_{LF}$, meaning that Foreign has a comparative advantage in cloth. In other words, in a model of two countries and two goods, once we determine that one country, say, Home has a comparative advantage in one good, say, food, it follows automatically that the other (Foreign) has a comparative advantage in cloth. The fact that one country cannot have comparative advantage in the production of both (all) goods, even while it could have an absolute advantage in production of all goods, is what allows each country to participate in trade and, as we will show shortly, enjoy benefits from it.

According to this *law of comparative advantage*, each country should completely specialise in the production of a good in which it has a comparative advantage.[8] Thus, Home in our example should completely specialise in the production of food. But complete specialisation can be sustained only if countries get involved in mutual exchange of goods that they have stopped producing. In other words, complete specialisation must be accompanied by (free) international trade. What we want to study next then is whether this trade is necessarily gainful to the world and all the countries and individuals involved and also whether the complete specialisation is a precondition for gains from trade. To do this, we need to construct a model of a trading world.

We will start by defining Foreign's PPF. Given our assumptions about Foreign's technology, it is relatively less efficient in producing food than is Home's technology. Hence the slope of Foreign's PPF must be steeper than Home's PPF (keeping food on the horizontal axis). What we do not know is the distance of the PPF from the origin. That of course depends on how much of labour Foreign has. Other things being equal, the larger the country is in terms of labour force, the further its PPF will lie from the origin. Let us assume, at this point, that Foreign is about the same size as Home so that the only significant difference between these two remains in the sphere of technology.[9] Foreign's PPF is illustrated in Figure 1.3. It is a simple matter now to draw Foreign's supply curve of food, and to superimpose Foreign's supply curve on Home's one (Figure 1.4).

In constructing Foreign's supply curve of food we have followed the same steps as for Home. Notice that Foreign's supply curve of food has the same shape as Home's, but lies above it for all prices higher than a_{LF}/a_{LC}. The distance between the horizontal portions of the curves is the difference in the respective opportunity costs, $(a_{LF}/a_{LC}) < (a^*_{LF}/a^*_{LC})$. That is, Foreign can supply the same quantities of food at a *higher relative price* than Home. The reason for this lies, of course, in our assumption of comparative advantage in food being on Home's side. We can note that the region between the two horizontal curves defines the set of relative world prices, say $p^T = p^T_F/p^T_C$ that would motivate specialisations within the two autarkic economies: a region $p_F/p_C < p^T < p^*_F/p^*_C$ is the sufficient condition for trade to occur (note that superscript T always denotes 'with trade'). It turns out that, when trade is allowed, the actual relative price will be in this region. But this also means that it will no longer be possible for the relative prices to be determined on the basis of labour costs only (that is, by technological conditions of the supply side), as it was in closed national economies. Once trade is allowed, we must consider both supply and demand in determination of relative prices. This means that we need to include demand conditions in the model in order to determine the 'terms of trade', p^T.[10]

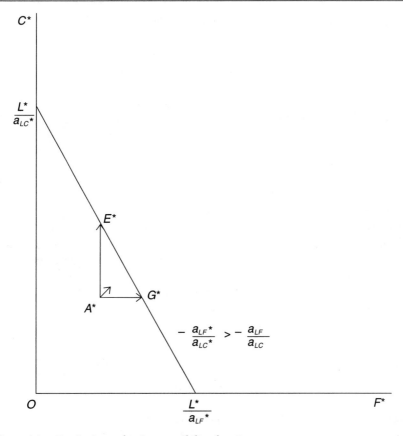

Figure 1.3 *Foreign's production possibility frontier*

☐ World economy: specialisation and trade

Production possibility frontier and prices

We can now take a look at the global picture of world consisting of Home and Foreign. First of all, we will construct the world PPF by adding together Home's and Foreign's production schedules. This is illustrated in Figure 1.5.

In constructing the world PPF we keep in mind the assumption about the international immobility of labour despite its free movements within each country's national borders. Let us begin by supposing that the relative price of food is below food's opportunity cost in both countries, so that both of them produce only cloth. This gives us point A on the cloth axis. If now the relative price of food rises sufficiently to equal its opportunity cost in Home (the lower of the two), Home will start producing both goods

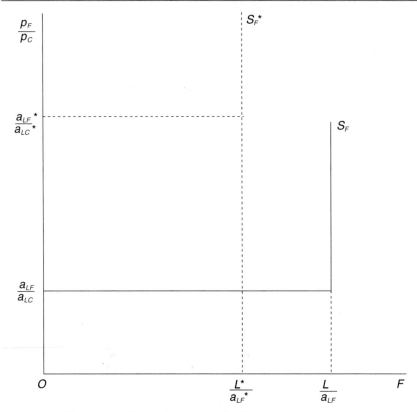

Figure 1.4   *Home's and Foreign's supply of food*

while Foreign labour would still refuse to work in its food sector. Consequently world production could be positioned anywhere along the segment *AR* which corresponds to Home's PPF. If food's relative price is further pushed up so as to exceed its opportunity cost in Home, regardless of how small this difference is, the impact on the production pattern will be quite significant. Home's labour will all shift into producing food. However, as long as p^T is still less than the opportunity cost of the food production in Foreign, all of Foreign's labour will still stay in the production of cloth. Point *R* therefore implies complete specialisation in a production of a comparative advantage good in each country. This point is known as the *Ricardo point* (Dorfman, Samuelson and Solow, 1958). This point is the most Pareto efficient point consistent with full labour use in both countries and given their technologies. It is sustainable with international trade between Home and Foreign for as long as relative price of food does not increase so much as to exceed food's opportunity cost in Foreign. If that happens, Foreign will either produce both goods along *RB*, such as point *G*, (if $p^T = a^*_{LF}/a^*_{LC}$) or specialise in food at point B (if $p^T > a^*_{LF}/a^*_{LC}$).[11]

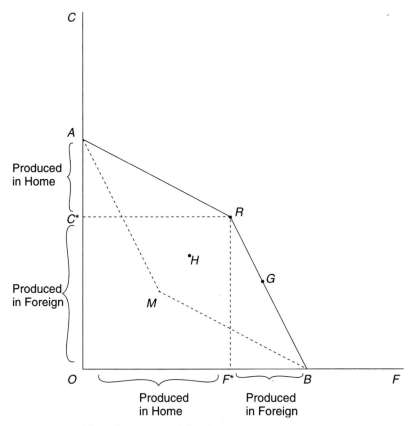

Figure 1.5   *World production possibility frontier*

Determination of the world commodity relative price or the terms of trade depends on where exactly – that is, at which point on the world PPF – these two countries find themselves once they start trading. We have shown that the commodity relative price is easily found within each closed national economy as a ratio of labour content (i.e. marginal rate of transformation or the slope of individual economy's PPF). Accordingly, if for some reasons production ends up along one of the segments of the world PPF that pertain to a national economy's PPF, the world relative price will reflect only the relative labour content of that country. So the world relative price will be determined on the basis of one or other country's labour content, and we still have a kind of labour theory of value in application. However, at point *R* it is impossible to determine world relative price only on the basis of labour requirements in production. Here these relative labour requirements form only the limits for the world price. Namely, for trade to result in an advantage, a country must be able to do better by trade than by relying on home production. This is only possible if for Home $p^T > p_F/p_C$, and for Foreign $p^T < p^*_F/p^*_C$. In other words world relative price lies within the range $a_{LF}/a_{LC} \leq p^T \leq a^*_{LF}/a^*_{LC}$.

To determine precisely the world relative price, we need information about the demand side. This will allow us to determine where on the world PPF the production-with-trade is located, and to determine a price at the Ricardo point R. We can introduce demand into our model in a variety of ways. One way is to assume that the world's preferences can be represented by indifference curves analogously to the preferences of a single consumer, and to map these curves together with the world's PPF (not shown in Figure 1.5).[12] It is quite possible that the highest attainable of such indifference curves will be passing through the point R. A line drawn tangent to such an indifference curve touching the PPF at point R will then indicate the equilibrium relative price (the magnitude of the slope being equal to the marginal rate of substitution) that supports complete specialisation in production according to the principle of comparative advantage. Alternatively, it could happen that tastes are strongly enough skewed towards one of the goods to result in indifference curves sloped in a such way that tangency with the PPF occurs at a point along one of PPF's flat segments. The trade-equilibrium relative price is then, as mentioned above, the same as the slope of that segment, and there is complete specialisation in one country but not the other (see also Box 1.1, p. 23).

The above method of representing 'world demand', however, is not very satisfactory, as implicitly it involves making judgements as to how the two countries' preferences (and individuals' preferences within each country) are weighted relative to each other. This must be solved either arbitrarily through choice of a 'world social welfare function', or within a general equilibrium framework where the terms of trade are solved simultaneously with the optimal affordable bundle for each economy. In what follows we adopt the latter (general equilibrium) perspective, but simplify the analysis by making some (strong) assumptions about similarities of preferences within each economy.

Relative supply and relative demand

In order to represent explicitly the role of each country in determining world demand, it is useful to introduce the concept of *relative demand*. We will construct a diagram where *world relative supply* of food meets *world relative demand* for food. This is done in Figure 1.6.

We derive the *world relative supply curve* of food $(Q_F + Q^*_F)/(Q_C + Q^*_C)$ as a function of world relative price of food p^T from Figure 1.5 (following the same steps as for the derivation of the national economy's relative supply curve). When p^T exceeds opportunity costs in both countries (point A in Figure 1.5), relative supply of food is zero and supply curve coincides with the vertical axis (OA in Figure 1.6). When the relative price reaches the level of the lower opportunity cost (in Home), the

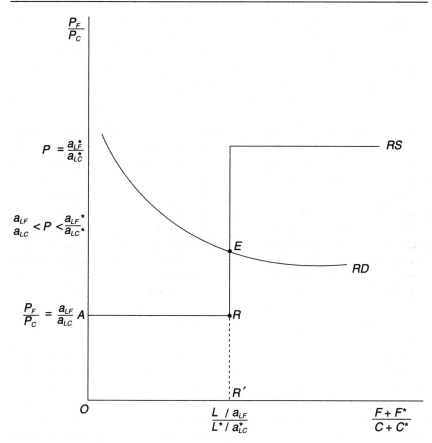

Figure 1.6 *World relative supply and demand*

supply curve is flat (the *AR* segment of the *RS* curve that corresponds to the *AR* segment of the world PPF in Figure 1.5). It becomes vertical again for relative prices that range between Home's and Foreign's opportunity costs. For any such price, relative supply of food is fixed at level *OR'* in Figure 1.6 (where each country specialises according comparative advantage). The last portion of the relative supply curve is again flat, depicting the price that corresponds to the Foreign's opportunity costs and therefore incomplete specialisation in that country. Of course, if price rises so high as to exceed these costs, both countries would produce no cloth and relative supply of food will be infinite (point *B* on the world PPF in Figure 1.5).

The *world relative demand curve* shows the functional relationship between relative price for food p^T and relative quantities of food $(D_F + D^*_F)/(D_C + D^*_C)$, where *D* denotes quantity demanded. In constructing the relative demand curve, for simplicity we assume that tastes are the same in both countries and that income levels do not affect relative demands (income elasticities of demand for each good is 1) giving that in both countries equal and constant shares of income are spent on each good, that is, $p^T_F(D_F + D^*_F) = p^T_C(D_C + D^*_C)$. This gives us a typical downward sloping curve (hyperbolic in this case), and because of our assumptions about income and substitution elasticities the relative demand curve is not sensitive to changes in relative country income or terms of trade.[13]

The intersection of relative supply and relative demand then determines the equilibrium relative price of food. In Figure 1.6, relative demand intersects relative supply somewhere on the vertical segment of relative supply; point E therefore depicts world equilibrium. At such an equilibrium, each country produces only one good (Home produces food and Foreign cloth), but each consumes both goods. Obviously, some 'redistribution' of available goods, called *international trade*, must be happening for that to be possible. The next section describes in detail why this trade brings benefits to all parties involved, and thus why we may suppose it will be voluntarily entered into.

☐ *Gains from trade*

The issue of gains from trade will be addressed at two levels. First, we demonstrate that free trade improves the total world welfare. Secondly we show that a country's overall welfare, under stated circumstances, cannot be made worse through free trade.

Let us first use Figure 1.5, the world PPF, to show that trade maximises the value of total world output. In order to do this, we must carefully define appropriate units of value by which consumption in the two countries can be compared. Before trade, each country has to produce both goods, which places the point of total world production *inside* the PPF (such as at point H). Suppose that trade opens up at some terms of trade p^T lying in between autarkic relative prices. Each country will then completely specialise in line with comparative advantage, shifting the total world production to point R. The movement from point H to point R is a Pareto improvement. It involves a shift from a point inside to a point *on* the world frontier, where the output of each good is now larger.[14]

Suppose for example that, before trade, the point of production was G rather than H. Is trade that involves complete specialisation still preferred to autarky although the total world production now contains less cloth? It is evident that the *value* of world output at point R evaluated with terms of trade p^T, is higher than the value of pre-trade production at G (or H) evaluated at the same p^T. Therefore, taking p^T as a datum, trade must be superior to autarky. That is, trade will always for any admissible terms of trade allow a shift from inside the frontier to the frontier itself, and therefore trade will always bring gains relative to autarky from the world point of view (measured in terms of p^T).[15] It is not necessary that countries *completely* specialise for the gains to be positive because even if one country continues to produce both goods and therefore does not experience any gains from trade, it will not lose either, and the world gains from trade will be identical to the gains of another country (see also Box 1.1, p. 23). However it remains to be shown that each country, considered separately, will evaluate its with-trade situation as unambiguously providing a net gain in value.

It is indeed more plausible to view the purpose of trade not as an improvement of the world welfare but as an welfare improvement for each national economy. Trade should, from this point of view, enable each economy to obtain goods at less cost than domestic opportunity costs. This difference in costs must translate into an increased welfare. That this indeed occurs can be demonstrated in two different ways. First, we can show that trade will enable a country to maximise its 'real income' given its total resources used in production, by which is meant that a larger quantity of one or both goods will be available for consumption with trade compared to autarky. Alternatively, we can show that, through trade, a country can reduce the 'real costs' of production, by which is meant that it can reach the same level of (pre-trade) availability of goods for a lesser physical input of labour.

These gains from trade results will be proved on the assumption that both countries can produce both goods in autarky. In effect the gains are seen as increased allocative efficiency on the basis of global specialisation in line with comparative advantage. This of course includes the case of one country being absolutely less productive, but still being able to enter international trade with the good for which its absolute disadvantage is relatively the smallest. However, there is one extreme possibility that is excluded from our examination by assumptions of our model. This is that one or both of the countries at the time of analysis cannot physically produce one of the goods. Today it is not that Scotland cannot produce grapes, but more that, say, Somalia cannot produce crops of wheat.[16] If we have such a country, then if the assumption is made that 'mixtures are preferred' (as is usually made in neoclassical consumer theory), it will automatically benefit from trade because only through trade can it get that good which it cannot produce itself. Such gains from so-called 'non-competitive imports' are considered to be quite significant (Gray, 1986).[17] Let us, however, focus on the traditional efficiency-raising gains from trade.

In what follows we will concentrate on showing gains from trade for Home only. Gains that accrue to Foreign can of course be derived by symmetry. It must be noted that here we will be concerned only with establishing the aggregate welfare gains from trade even for a country that does not have absolute advantage in any industry, as long as that country trades according to comparative advantage. Because this model works with only one factor of production, there is no mention of distributional issues. We shall first illustrate how Home's real income is unambiguously increased with trade. This is followed by the demonstration of how trade enables Home to reduce the physical quantity of labour used in obtaining the same real income as prior to trade.

Figure 1.7 depicts Home's situation with and without trade and demonstrates neatly the problem of the maximisation of real income in trading equilibrium. Line *AB* represents Home's PPF as given by (1.1.2). We retain the arbitrary assumption that Home has comparative advantage in production of food; by now it should be obvious that such an assumption is not restrictive in any way. Point *P* on the PPF is the point of production in autarky; and in autarky production and consumption are identically equal; $P \equiv D$. The level of Home's welfare derived from this production and consumption is illustrated by the *social indifference curve* I^{18}. The point $P \equiv D$ also indicates the level of real income evaluated with autarky prices. The slope of the PPF reflects autarky relative price, and in this sense the PPF prior to trade is also the country's budget constraint or *consumption possibility frontier* (CPF).

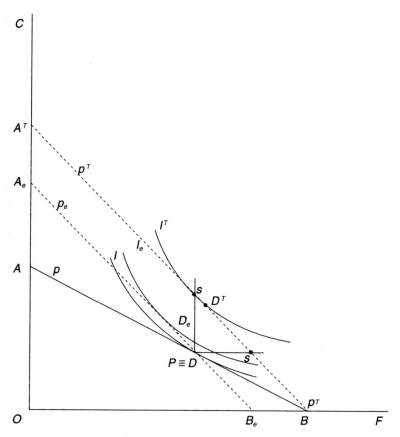

Figure 1.7   *Home's gains from trade*

Formally, point *P* can be considered as the welfare-maximising choice by Home facing autarky relative prices *p* and constrained by budget line *BA*. With trade, Home faces different set of prices p^T (recall that $p^T > p = p_F/p_C$), and also faces a different 'budget constraint'. To identify the new budget constraint with trade allowed at p^T, it suffices to find the maximum feasible value for:

$$Y_r^T = (1/p^T)Q_C + Q_F \tag{1.1.7}$$

where Y_r^T is Home's real income with trade evaluated in terms of food with relative price p^T. For a given p^T, different values of Y_r^T in (1.1.7) give us a family of budget constraints. By setting $Q_C = 0$, it is immediately clear that, with food as numeraire, the maximum 'real income' attainable is equal to the value of Home's maximum production of food, indicated on the graph in Figure 1.7 by quantity *OB*. Through trade with Foreign at terms of trade p^T, this output can be exchanged for an equivalent value of cloth, designated on the vertical axis of Figure 1.7 by quantity OA^T. Since $p^T > p$, we know that A^T is above *A*. So the maximised real income with trade is represented by the budget constraint labelled as p^T and BA^T. This level of real income implies complete specialisation in production of food which is the comparative advantage good for Home. Line BA^T represents Home's consumption possibility frontier with trade; it is the locus of all the combinations of food and cloth Home can consume given the terms of trade p^T and that it produces at *B*.

It is obvious that, assuming convex social indifference curves, Home can now reach a higher indifference curve than in autarky (for example I^T). It is also clear that with-trade consumption can include more of both food and cloth (such as point D^T on I^T). Assuming 'normal' consumer behaviour, namely that more of both goods is preferred to less of both goods, trade therefore provides superior consumption possibilities to autarky. Even if, with trade, the chosen consumption point involves less of one good compared to autarky (such as points lying outside the segment *ss* on p^T), trade is nonetheless gainful since there is a higher budget constraint passing through any such point compared to autarky consumption. In other terms, the *value* of such consumption is the same as the value of a consumption bundle involving more of both goods than in autarky (they both lie on the same budget constraint). Such a value of consumption is not attainable without trade. Finally, it should be noted that any point on the new budget constraint BA^T corresponds to a higher 'real income' than autarky point *P* when the evaluation is done in terms of autarky prices *p*. This completes the demonstration that there is a *rise in real income* whether pre- or with-trade prices are used.

Before turning to cost minimisation, let us make a slight digression. Look again at Figure 1.7 and the autarky point of production and consumption *P* which is the original 'endowment point' of Home, i.e. the quantity of food and cloth produced when outputs are valued at autarky relative prices. If these quantities are now re-valued at terms of trade p^T, Home's new real income is depicted by the line p_e passing through point P. That line also represents consumption possibilities where, however, the country has not fully specialised in production. In other words, if Home continues to produce both goods as under autarky, and then exports the good in which it has comparative advantage, it can increase its consumption possibilities (segment PA_e) although not by as much as if it specialises in production. On the other hand, if Home tries to export cloth, its consumption frontier is limited to PB_e; and alternatively, if it shifts resources into cloth production its consumption frontier shifts down below B_eA_e. This shows that specialisation and trade that do not follow the principle of comparative advantage can be harmful (compared to autarky).

Let us now look at presenting the gains from trade in an alternative way. We said that gains can be expressed as an increase in efficiency or as savings in the physical amount of labour necessary to produce a good if such a good is produced 'indirectly', that is, through trade. The easiest way to show this is to compare amounts of labour needed in direct and indirect production of goods. This is done in Table 1.1. To produce directly one unit of cloth (food), Home uses $a_{LC}(a_{LF})$ of labour. For trade at Ricardo point we have:

$$a^*_{LF}/a^*_{LC} > a_{LF}/a_{LC} \tag{1.1.8}$$

If Home produces food, the good in which it has comparative advantage, and then exchanges it for cloth at $p^T > a_{LF}/a_{LC}$, for each unit of cloth it will use only a_{LF}/p^T of labour which is less than a_{LC} of labour:

$$a_{LF}p^T < a_{LC} \tag{1.1.9}$$

Thus, by producing food and exchanging it for cloth, Home is able to 'produce' cloth with higher productivity than in autarky. See also Box 1.3. It must be then true that if Home produces cloth in which it is relatively inferior, and tries to exchange that for food, it will waste its labour:

$$a_{LC}p^T > a_{LF} \tag{1.1.9a}$$

Table 1.1   *Home's labour content of cloth and food production*

Home's labour content per unit of	Cloth (C)	Food (F)
In direct production	a_{LC}	a_{LF}
In indirect production	a_{LF}/p^T	$a_{LC}p^T$

Although this model cannot be used to discuss important issues of internal distribution of income, it is a useful tool for looking into some questions of the distribution (or rather division) of gains between countries. We have established that the necessary condition for the gains from trade to be positive is the existence of a difference in the autarky relative prices between countries. Now, it can be easily seen in Figure 1.8 that the larger the difference between one country's autarky price ratio and the international price ratio at which trading takes place, *ceteris paribus*, the larger the gains from trade going to that particular country.

The PPFs of both Home and Foreign are brought together in Figure 1.8 where the line *AR* is Home's PPF with respect to the origin 'O' and the line *BR* is Foreign's PPF with respect to the origin 'O*' (this box diagram can be easily constructed from Figure 1.5 – start at the point *R* there and rotate Foreign's PPF by 180° so that point *F** in Figure 1.5 coincides with point O* in Figure 1.8). The dimensions of this box are of course given by the amounts of goods produced in the world if each country specialises completely in line with comparative advantages: *OR*(= *O**Q) is the output of food and *O**R(= *OQ*) is the output of cloth. The initial endowment point from which the division of the total gains from trade evolves is the

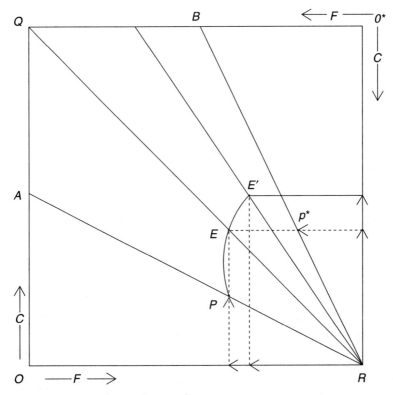

Figure 1.8 *Division of gains from trade*

Ricardo point, R. The total potential gains from trade is indicated by the quadrilateral area $QARB$ between the PPFs of Home and Foreign. It is clear that, *ceteris paribus*, the total gains will be larger the larger this area is; and its size depends on the difference in slopes of the production possibilities for the countries involved.[19] Actual terms of trade give the 'budget constraint' passing through the point of production R and the point of trading equilibrium, such as point E, and divide the area of gains $QARB$ into two areas each of which belongs to one of the countries. The division of total gains by terms of trade RE is shown in Figure 1.8. as exactly symmetrical, i.e. splitting the gains in half for each country. This of course is an atypical result. In more general cases the division of gains from trade is not symmetrical.

Suppose now that terms of trade change from those given by RE, to the ones given by RE':[20]

$$p^T < p^T_1$$

This change illustrates an improvement in terms of trade for Home, since at these new terms of trade Home can get more units of cloth per each unit of food (or in total it could get the same amount of cloth as before by giving less of food). We know that Home will not (cannot) change production structure in response to the terms of trade improvement. The change in world price means that the comparative advantage of Home in production of food has increased, so it ought continue producing food. Since by assumption there is no scope for technology change or labour increase, it cannot produce more than it is already producing at point R. Therefore, the endowment point remains point R and the trading equilibrium now describes the consumption level that, for Home, is superior to the old trading equilibrium $(E_1 \succ E)$. In other words, terms of trade improvement has caused an increase in Home's real income, expanding the consumption possibilities even more. Note, however, two points: (1) gains accrued to Foreign have declined (but are still positive); and (2) exports of food from Home have decreased in volume (but not necessarily in value) and exports of cloth from Foreign have increased in volume (but also not necessarily in value).

■ 1.2 Extensions of the model

Trade economists have enriched the basic Ricardian model in a number of ways in an attempt to bring it closer to the 'real world'. In this section we will incorporate several of the extensions which enable us to gain some useful insights about the structure of international trade and nature of gains from trade.

Box 1.1 *Incomplete specialisation with constant opportunity costs*

In the last section we showed that in the Ricardian world of constant opportunity costs, free international trade typically results in a (complete) specialisation according to comparative advantage, and leads to a maximisation of world production and consumption via an increase in national production and consumption in both countries. However, there is an interesting exception to this when countries differ not only in technology but also in size.

Say that Home again has a comparative advantage in production of food but is now very large relative to Foreign ($L \gg L^*$). The with-trade production and consumption in Home and Foreign is illustrated in Figure 1.9.

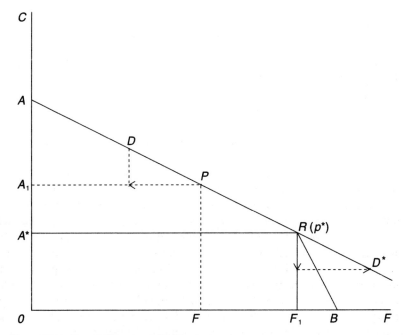

Figure 1.9 *Incomplete specialisation*

The World PPF is given by ARB and the fact that Home is economically much larger is signified by the segment A^*R being much longer than segment F_1B (or $A^*A \gg F_1R$). When Foreign completely specialises in cloth in which it has a comparative advantage, it still cannot meet demand from the much larger Home. Hence Home must produce some cloth itself to satisfy domestic demand (remember there are only two countries in the world!). This situation is represented by a world production point such as P, where total supply of food OF comes from Home but total supply of cloth is combined from two sources: Foreign (OA^*) and Home (A^*A_1).

Note that Home, which is in this case the bigger country, produces a larger number of goods than the smaller country.[21] So, the relative price at point *P* must reflect Home's opportunity costs; and indeed it coincides with Home's autarky relative prices. That leaves Home indifferent towards trade, since it cannot ensure any direct gains from it (with trade, consumption point *D* still sits *on* Home's own PPF), but neither does it lose by trading. All the gains from trade, however, accrue to the small country (consumption is now possible at *D** outside its PPF).

This result has to be regarded with some caution, as it is obtained under the restrictive assumptions of the model. It is often suggested that, in reality, large countries use their economic and political power to appropriate some of the gains from trade that should – under strictly competitive trading – have all gone to smaller countries. But the idea may still be taken from the above result, that the larger the relative size of the country, the less may be the need or opportunity for competitive trade to improve efficiency and/or expand that country's own consumption possibilities.

☐ Trade and wage rate limits

The first extension of the basic Ricardian model is meant to help us deal with one of the common arguments made against free trade. The argument has become popular with trade unions in more DCs, that LDCs use their cheap or low-paid labour as means of unfair competition in international trade. Barriers imposed on such exports should, according to the unions, be welcome since they correct two 'wrongs' at the same time: (1) they encourage fair competition, and (2) they prevent both the underpayment of labour in the less developed world, and the fall of wages in the developed world. We show in this section how misconceived this argument is.

It is obvious that wages will differ between countries in the setup of our model. The assumptions are that perfect competition prevails, that (with constant returns to scale) unit cost of production equals price, and that the sole factor of production, labour, is not mobile internationally. But how different should the wage rates be, and is the difference in any way dependent on exchange of commodities between countries? It is, indeed, and we will see that there is a dual correspondence between wages and commodity prices: at given commodity prices, wages are the maximum earnings for labour, and at given wages, the commodity prices are the minimum unit cost of production.

Let us first express wages in real terms;[22] they can be depicted in terms of goods that are produced in the wage-earner's own country. Since Home has a comparative advantage in food, the real wage must then be expressed as a reward for one labour-hour of work in terms of food:

$$w/p_F = 1/a_{LF} = MP_L^F \qquad\qquad (1.2.1)$$

which is equal to the average and marginal labour productivities in that sector; the higher the productivity, the higher real wage is. Let us suppose that $a_{LF} = 4$; the real wage in Home is ¼ of a unit of food.

Similarly we determine the real wage in Foreign in terms of a good produced in that country (cloth). So we have:

$$w^*/p_C = 1/a^*_{LC} = MP^*_{LC} \qquad\qquad (1.2.1^*)$$

Say that $a^*_{LC} = 2$; the real wage in Foreign is then ½ of a unit of cloth. Although we now know real wages in both countries we cannot yet do much with them since they are not comparable: we cannot compare ¼ of food and ½ of cloth. In order to say something about relative wages in these two countries we must have a *common* unit of measurement. Since we do not want to use money, we must be able to express the real wages in each country in terms of one of these two goods. The problem is that cloth is not produced in Home, and food is not produced in Foreign. However, they can be acquired through trade and commodity terms of trade p^T can be used as a basis for making a comparison of productivities.

Table 1.2 shows 'real' wages in terms of food or cloth produced domestically or acquired through trade. In Home, for one labour-hour workers get paid $1/a_{LF}$ in terms of food which they produce or $(1/a_{LF})p^T$ in terms of cloth which is imported. Likewise, in Foreign labour gets $1/a^*_{LC}$ in terms of cloth or $(1/a^*_{LC})/p^T$ in terms of imported food. By dividing Home's real wages for food (or cloth) by Foreign's, we can get a conversion factor which is than used to determine the range of Home to Foreign wages for *given terms of trade*:

$$w/w^* = p^T(a^*_{LC}/a_{LF}) \qquad\qquad (1.2.2)$$

We can determine Foreign's relative wage in a similar way, which gives the inverse:

$$w^*/w = (1/p^T)(a_{LF}/a^*_{LC}) \qquad\qquad (1.2.2^*)$$

Table 1.2   *Real wages in terms of food or cloth*

Real wage in terms of Countries	Food (F)	Cloth (C)
Home	$1/a_{LF}$	$(1/a_{LF})p^T$
Foreign	$(1/a^*_{LC})/p^T$	$1/a^*_{LC}$

We know that for trade to be beneficial for at least one country (and not disadvantageous for the other), commodity terms of trade must be within the limits given by relative productivities ($a_{LF}/a_{LC} \leq p^T \leq a^*_{LF}/a^*_{LC}$). If $a_{LF}/a_{LC} = p^T$ (when Home produces both goods, and Foreign specialises in cloth), the Home relative wage reduces to

$$w/w^* = a^*_{LC}/a_{LC} \tag{1.2.3}$$

which is in fact the *lower bound* of a relative wage range determined solely by the ratio of the two countries' productivities in cloth production (see Figure 1.10). This particular wage rate ratio allows Home to outcompete Foreign in terms of costs in the production of food, and to be able to produce cloth as well, which costs the same in Home and Foreign. The fact that Home finds it worthwhile to produce cloth despite its comparative disadvantage in that line of production indicates that the real wage rate in Home is lower than in Foreign to exactly the degree required so that the costs of production for cloth are the same in both countries.[23]

Note that it is not possible for the relative wage to fall below the level given by the lower bound (1.2.3) because that would prevent any possibility for trade. Namely, at any relative wage $w/w^* < a^*_{LC}/a_{LC}$, prices of

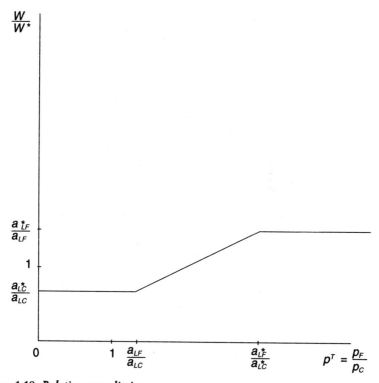

Figure 1.10 *Relative wage limits*

both cloth and food produced by Home would be lower and there will be no benefits from the exchange of goods between Home and Foreign.

Taking the other extreme, for $p^T = a^*_{LF}/a^*_{LC}$ (when Home specialises in food, but Foreign produces both goods) we can get the *upper bound* to the wage ratio:

$$w/w^* = a^*_{LF}/a_{LF} \qquad (1.2.4)$$

implying that all gains from trade go to the Home country. From this, we can write

$$a^*_{LC}/a_{LC} \leq w/w^* \leq a^*_{LF}/a_{LF} \qquad (1.2.5)$$

which gives us the range of Home's relative wages bounded by the ratios of labour productivities for each good.[24] For a numerical example see Box 1.3, (p. 30).

This discussion on the relative wages gives us the basis for defining the so-called 'export condition' (or import condition). By this we mean the cost (or price) advantage that a country must have in order to become an exporter of a particular good. (The import condition, correspondingly, expresses cost or price disadvantage.) In other words, a country will export a good (say, cloth), even if it has an absolute disadvantage in producing it, if and only if its relative wage rate is low enough to offset that disadvantage. That is:

$$p^*_C < p_C \qquad (1.2.6)$$
$$\text{if} \quad a^*_{LC}/a_{LC} < w/w^*$$

even if $a^*_{LC} > a_{LC}$. Obviously, if Foreign's relative wage rate increases by too much, *ceteris paribus*, Foreign's cost competitiveness in exporting cloth will be reduced, while conversely any fall in its wage rate will enhance it.

Let us now return to the argument advocating protection against goods coming from low-wage countries (see Box 1.2, p. 28). We see that the reason for lower wages is in the lower productivity in the country in question, taking account of the feasible terms of trade. In other words, cost or price competitiveness is based on *both* productivity and wage rate levels: if productivity is not high enough, then wages must be lower to enable the country to trade. Similarly, high labour productivity in more DCs permits higher wages relative to less technically efficient countries. Therefore, the complaints from unions in developed (higher-wage) countries about unfair competition are not valid. This competition is not harmful either. The fact that the wages are lower in the exporting country does not in any way prevent the importing country from gaining from free trade. Also, the assertion that protection imposed against such imports would prevent the

Box 1.2   *Comparative advantage and developing countries*

For decades now the concept of comparative advantage and its implications have been misinterpreted and misused for purposes of hampering the idea of 'free' international trade. In most of these instances, developing countries have been invoked either as examples of casualties of ('free') trade or by being accused of themselves causing casualties amongst DCs.

On the one hand we often hear (particularly from journalists and politicians in developing countries) how productivity in the DCs is so much higher than in any developing country, that every developing country would be undercut in all sectors. Therefore it will be quite justified to introduce a protective tariff in the developing country, to enable its producers to compete with those from the developed world. On the other hand, from the mouth and pen of self-appointed experts located in the developed world, we hear that the wage rate in the developing country(ies) is so low that the wage rate for the workers in the developed world would have to be radically reduced in order for their products to compete with the LDCs' ones. Accordingly, protection (tariffs) are needed to maintain the wage rate level and the standard of living unchanged.

The contribution of the concept of comparative advantage here is in showing the fallacy of both arguments. It cannot be denied that in general technological efficiency is higher in the DCs, and that wages are lower in the developing ones. But as shown in section 1.2.1 they are lower precisely in order to offset these countries' lower efficiency (productivity). If the developing countries had both lower productivity and higher wages than DCs, they would have never been able to take part in international trade. And that would harm not only them but also the DCs, because both gain from the mutual exchange of commodities and services. As stated before, the purpose of trade is to obtain imports at less than their domestic opportunity costs of production; whether these lower costs are due to the higher productivity or lower wages, it makes no difference for the fact that such trade is gainful (*even* for the countries that have absolute disadvantage in all lines of production and whose wage rates are much lower than in the rest of the world). Several recent studies have focused on the impact of trade with developing countries on the employment and wages in the DCs. No strong support was found for the claim that increased trade with developing countries causes unemployment (particularly of low-skilled labour) or wage inequality in DCs. Krugman and Lawrence (1993) and Sachs and Shatz (1994), for example, find that not more that 10 per cent of the rise in wage inequality or manufacturing unemployment can be attributed to trade with developing countries.

There is a third common fallacy about comparative advantage and the developing countries. It is often said that these countries are being exploited through trade since by trading they give more units of labour embodied in their export goods then they receive in return through their imports.[26] This is very true; indeed the more different countries are in terms of absolute productivities, the larger will be the difference in labour content in their imported and exported goods. Yet this only establishes one of the reasons (which is *the* reason in the Ricardian model) for trade between them. As a function of the strengths of demand for their commodities, terms of trade will be established which determine the division of gains from trade; and unless these terms of trade coincide with autarky prices in one of the countries, both will gain (see p. 41–2 for more details).

exploitation of labour in the exporting countries is false; as we will show later, such protection will only tend to depress the nominal wages even further, since lowering wages is often the only thing these low-wage countries can do to remain internationally competitive.[25] The other alternative would be to increase productivity, which is precluded in the short run, and often very difficult even in the long run.

☐ *Multiple countries*

The next step we can make in extending the basic Ricardian model is to increase the number of countries to include many countries instead of just two. The presentation in this and next sections becomes simpler if we change notation for countries $(j = 1 \ldots m)$ and for goods $(i = 1 \ldots n)$ when the dimension is larger than 2.

Suppose thus that now we have many countries but that all still produce only two goods, food and cloth. Production in autarky takes place under the same conditions as in the basic model. Let us assume that technologies are as described in the following chain:

$$(a^1_{LF}/a^1_{LC}) \leq (a^2_{LF}/a^2_{LC}) \leq \ldots \leq (a^j_{LF}/a^j_{LC})$$
$$\leq \ldots \leq (a^m_{LF}/a^m_{LC}) \tag{1.2.7}$$

stating that country 1 is relatively the most efficient producer of food, followed by country 2, and so on until country m comes last. In other words, countries are ranked in order of decreasing comparative advantage in the production of food. The necessary condition for a mutual incentive to trade is that at least two countries differ in terms of comparative costs. (It does not matter if some subset of $< m$ countries has the same comparative costs.) This condition is satisfied when in the ordering of the countries as in (1.2.7) at least one of the inequalities is strict. Provided that the sufficient condition, that terms of trade lie strictly between country 1s and country ms autarky prices, is also satisfied, we can propose that country 1 should produce and export food and country m should produce and export cloth. We do not know whether the intermediate countries $(j = 2 \ldots m - 1)$ should specialise in food or cloth, or produce

Box 1.3   *Comparative advantage and the gains from trade – a numerical example*

Consider unit labour requirements for the production of cloth (C) and food (F) in Home and Foreign as given below:

	Cloth (C)	Food (F)
Home	1	1
Foreign	2	6

What is the pattern of specialisation and trade?

To determine pattern of specialisation and trade we need to know countries' comparative advantages. In this example we have:

$$a_{LF}/a_{LC} < a^*{}_{LF}/a^*{}_{LC}$$

or

$$(1/1) < (6/2)$$

This means that Home has a comparative advantage in the production of food and Foreign in the production of cloth. According to the law of comparative advantage, Home should produce more food and import cloth while Foreign should produce cloth and import food.

Home, Foreign and World PPF

Assume that both Home and Foreign have only 60 labour-hours to produce both goods.
Draw their PPFs (put cloth on the vertical axis), draw also the World PPF and explain its shape.
   With 60 labour-hours available to both countries, the maximum outputs are:

	Cloth (C)	Food (F)
Home	60/1 = 60	60/1 = 60
Foreign	60/2 = 30	60/6 = 10

If Home employs all available labour in the production of food, it will produce 60 units of food. On the other hand, if it allocates labour only to the cloth industry, it produces 60 units of cloth. A straight line connecting these two extreme points represents Home's production possibility frontier, PPF. Similarly, Foreign can produce 30 units of cloth or 10 units of food or any other combination of these two goods that lie along its PPF. Next by combining Home's and Foreign's PPFs we can construct the World PPF. The three interesting points on the world PPF are: point F_t where the world production of food is 70 since both countries produce only food; point C_t where both countries produce cloth resulting in the world production of 90 units; point R, resulting from each country specialising in the good with comparative advantage; and the world production of 60 units of food and 30 units of cloth (note that if each specialises in production in which it is disadvantaged, the production structure is 60 units of cloth and 10 units of food, at point r, which is clearly inferior to point R). The shape of the World PPF implies two types of possible results regarding terms of trade, specialisation and trade:

(a) terms of trade settle along one country's autarky relative price with the consequence of that country being indifferent to trade (i.e. not specialising) and not gaining from trade, and

(b) terms of trade lie between two countries' autarky relative prices with both countries specialising and gaining from trade.

Where precisely the terms of trade would settle depends on the demand for cloth and food.

Gains from trade

Suppose demand is such to allow for terms of trade to settle at $p = p_F/p_C = 2$, show that both countries gain from trade.
One way to show the gains from trade is to show that consumption possibilities are enlarged with trade. The consumption possibility frontier has the same slope in each country given by the terms of trade $p = 2$. If each country specialises in production of comparative advantage good, it can enjoy higher consumption level with trade.

An alternative way is to show that indirect production (via trade) is more efficient than direct production:

	Quantities per labour/hour Cloth (C)	Quantities per labour/hour Food (F)
Home (direct production)	1	1
Home (indirect production)	$1p = 2$	–
Foreign (direct production)	$1/2$	$1/6$
Foreign (indirect production)	–	$(1/2)/p = 1/4$

Since for Home $2 > 1$ and for Foreign $1/4 > 1/6$, both countries use their resources (labour) more efficiently if they choose to focus on direct production of goods in which they have comparative advantage and 'indirectly' produce other goods (in which they do not have comparative advantage).

Home's relative wages

Calculate Home's relative wages at terms of trade $= 2$
When $p = 2$, Home will specialise in food and Foreign in cloth. Thus Home relative wage will be given as:

$$w/w^* = p(a^*_{LC}/a_{LF})$$
$$= 2(2/1) = 4$$

What happens if terms of trade increase to $p = 3$?
A change in p can be explained by a shift in demand towards food so that food becomes more expensive. In fact, it is equally expensive now as it was in Foreign prior to trade. Consequently, Foreign loses motivation to engage in trade and will produce both goods. On the other hand, an increase in p reflects even larger gains for Home and that is also expressed through an increase in its relative (real) wage. Thus Home's relative wage reaches its upper bound:

$$w/w^* = p(a^*_{LC}/a_{LF})$$
$$= 3(2/1) = 6$$

where Home's wage rate is six times higher than the Foreign rate. If wage rates were to rise even further (say, ten times Foreign wages), Home would lose competitive advantage in its food industry and Foreign would not be willing to trade at prices that would allow for such relative wages, i.e. if $w/w^* = 10$, it means that $p = 5$, which is outside the mutually beneficial terms of trade.

both. That depends partly on the strength of the relative demand for food, which influences the prevailing terms of trade. If the terms of trade breaks the above chain somewhere in between a pair of countries, all the countries to the left of that point will end up producing and exporting food, and all the countries to the right will produce and export cloth. If demand is such as to result in the terms of trade being identical to the autarky price in one of the countries, that particular country will produce both goods. We can use our relative supply–relative demand diagram to illustrate the possible patterns of trade in case of four countries (Figure 1.11). If it happens that the terms of trade divide *m* countries into groups of exporters and importers of food (cloth), and that none of the countries produces both goods, the situation is almost the same as in the case of two countries. All countries benefit from international trade. We do not know, however, precise bilateral trade flows (which country exports to which), only that total exports match total imports of each good.

In the case where one of the countries does not specialise, we cannot say anything about that country's trade. It could be that it engages in trade or it does not. What we do know is that trade does not bring any gains to this country; but it cannot hurt it either. It depends on world supply and demand of both goods whether that country will be trading or not.

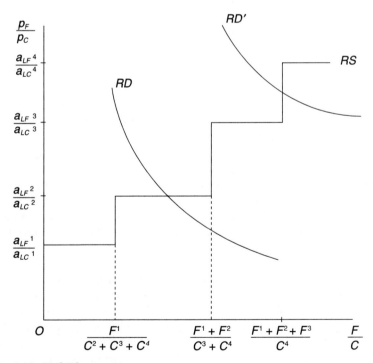

Figure 1.11 *Multiple countries*

☐ *Multiple goods*

It is equally straightforward to extend our model to cover more than two goods ($i = 1 \ldots n$) if we retain our assumption about having only two countries, Home and Foreign. We again use the chain and rank goods according to the relative labour content. Say that all goods are produced in both countries in autarky and that constant relative labour requirements are as below:

$$
\begin{aligned}
& (a^*_{L1}/a_{L1}) \geq (a^*_{L2}/a_{L2}) \geq \ldots \geq (a^*_{Li}/a_{Li}) \geq \ldots \\
& \geq (a^*_{Ln}/a_{Ln})
\end{aligned}
\tag{1.2.8}
$$

Home has the biggest comparative advantage in production of good 1, and the least such advantage in production of good n. In other words, goods are ranked by Home's comparative advantage. Which good(s) are produced in Home is determined again by relative demand. If demand conditions are such as to break the above chain strictly between two goods, all goods to the left of the break will be produced and exported by Home, and all the goods to the right will be produced and exported by Foreign. However, demand conditions could result in one good (but, if the inequalities are strict, only one) being produced by both countries. Whether or not this good will be traded depends solely on demand because it costs the same in both countries; for this good the relative labour content is equal to the terms of trade.

☐ *The model with a continuum of goods*

An alternative way of extending the Ricardian model to many commodities is given in the so called 'Dornbusch–Fischer–Samuelson' model with a continuum of goods.[27] This model is used to consider several real and monetary issues in the Ricardian trading world, some of which we will review here. The supply side of the basic model includes two countries, Home and Foreign, that use only a single input (labour, L and L^*) in production of a very large number (n) of goods. Except for the number of goods produced, the model is built on the same traditional assumptions we have outlined previously: no transport cost, no barriers to trade, labour perfectly mobile domestically but not internationally, etc. The constant labour content per unit of each good z in Home is $a(z)$ and in Foreign is $a^*(z)$; the relative labour content or requirement is defined from the Home country perspective as $A(z) = a^*(z)/a(z)$. All goods are then ranked from the one having the smallest relative labour content to the one having the largest:

$$A(1) > A(2) > \ldots > A(z) > \ldots \tag{1.2.9}$$

That is, ranked first is the good in which Home has the greatest relative productivity or comparative advantage, followed by the goods with lesser and lesser advantage.

The first question this model is then used to address is that of geographical specialisation in production and trade pattern. The identification of the range of goods which will be produced in Home and those which Foreign will end up producing is done by using cost advantage (the export condition) as discussed on p. 27 above. The specialisation of each country will depend on the relative wages because, given the labour productivities, wages determine cost advantages. Home will produce (and export) only those goods whose unit labour cost is not higher than in Foreign. When goods are priced competitively in both countries, we have:

$$p(z) = wa(z) \text{ in Home} \tag{1.2.10}$$

and

$$p^*(z) = w^* a^*(z) \text{ in Foreign} \tag{1.2.10*}$$

where w and w^* are Home and Foreign wages respectively (measured in any common unit). Home then gets to produce/export good z if

$$wa(z) \leq w^* a^*(z) \Leftrightarrow$$
$$a^*(z)/a(z) \geq w/w^* \tag{1.2.11}$$

meaning that:

$$A(z) \geq \omega \tag{1.2.11a}$$

where $\omega \equiv w/w^*$ reflects Home's double factoral terms of trade. The pattern of specialisation in Home and Foreign is illustrated in Figure 1.12. With the goods (z) plotted on the horizontal axis and relative wages (ω) on the vertical axis, the relationship $A(z) = f(\omega)$ is presented as a downward sloping smooth continuous curve. It is downward sloping because the number of goods produced/exported increases as the relative wage drops. The curve is assumed to be continuous because of the very large number of goods. Given the relative wage ω, we can define the marginal or boundary good Z for which $\omega = A(z)$. This good divides the continuum into two groups: all goods to the left of the boundary good Z will be produced and exported by Home, all goods to the right of the boundary good Z will be produced and exported by Foreign. Hence, any specified relative wage is associated with a particular inter-country specialisation of production.[28]

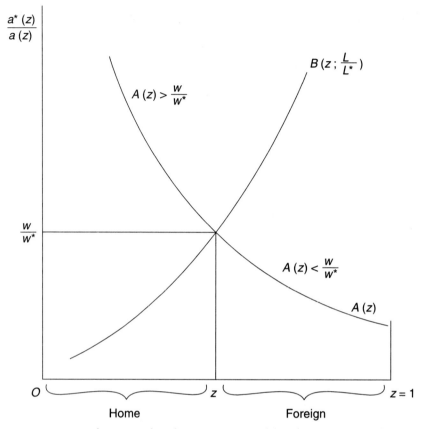

Figure 1.12 *Specialisation and trade pattern in a model with a continuum of goods*

The actual level of the relative wage w depends on the total world demand for each good. This model conventionally assumes that tastes are identical in Home and Foreign and that all consumers in both countries allocate the same share of income to any given good. That constant fraction of income (expenditure share) spent on good z is defined as:

$$b(z) = p(z)D(z)/Y \qquad (1.2.12)$$

where p is price, D demand for good z and Y is total (world) income, and $b(z) = b^*(z)$ by assumption. Now, total world income will be shared among Home and Foreign as a function of the number of goods each produces. Denote the fraction of world income spent on goods produced by Home as $\beta(Z)$:

$$\beta(Z) = b(1) + b(2) + \ldots + b(Z) \qquad (1.2.13)$$

The larger Z is (that is, the larger the number of goods in which Home has a comparative advantage over Foreign), the larger share of world income will go to Home. It follows that the fraction of world income spent on goods produced in Foreign is:

$$1 - \beta(Z) = b(Z) + b(Z+1) + \ldots + b(n) \qquad (1.2.13^*)$$

and of course $\quad 0 \leq \beta(Z) \leq 1$

Total income in this two-country world is the sum of each country's income, which in turn is equal to the amount of total wages paid out to labour in each country: wL and w^*L^* in Home and Foreign, respectively. Thus the total world income is simply the sum of incomes in Home and Foreign, $wL + w^*L^*$. Next, by multiplying world income by the fraction $\beta(Z)$:

$$wL = \beta(Z)(wL + w^*L^*) \qquad (1.2.14)$$

we get the world spending on domestically produced goods (or Home's income) which rearranged gives us

$$\omega = [\beta(Z)/1 - \beta(Z)](L^*/L) \qquad (1.2.14a)$$

therefore defining function $B(.)$ as $B(Z)$ as L^*/L is given.

The $B(.)$ schedule provides the demand side for this model and is represented by the upward sloping $B(.)$ curve in Figure 1.12. This curve demonstrates that for each country the size of income and the wage rate is dependent on the world demand for domestically produced goods.[29] Greater demand for Home's goods (larger Z at the horizontal axis) pushes up the derived demand for labour which in turn raises the wage rate relative to Foreign (higher ω on the vertical axis). The intersection of this curve with the $A(z)$ curve represents the simultaneous determination of the equilibrium relative wages and the accompanying pattern of specialisation/ trade. At equilibrium:

$$\omega = A(z) = B(z) \quad \text{given}(L^*/L) \qquad (1.2.15)$$

The determinants of the above equilibrium relative wages and specialisation pattern are technology, tastes and relative size. In a moment we look at the impact of changes in some of these exogenous variables on the equilibrium. But let us first look at the gains from trade.

Gains from trade in this model are assured by the very requirement for geographical specialisation in production, that is for Home to produce all goods for which $\omega < A(z)$ and for Foreign to produce goods for which opposite is true $\omega > A(z)$. To see how this requirement transfers into the conditions for positive gains from trade, start once again with stating the norms of competitive pricing. In Home price for good z cannot exceed unit production (labour) cost, or:

$$p(z) = wa(z) \tag{1.2.10}$$

and similarly in Foreign:

$$p^*(z) = w^*a^*(z) \tag{1.2.10*}$$

The gains from trade may be interpreted as the savings realised by importation of a particular good(s) rather than domestically producing it(them). Thus the question is: when it is cheaper for Home to import z rather than to produce it domestically? The answer is, when the following is true:

$$wa(z)/p^*(z) = wa(z)/w^*a^*(z) > 1 \tag{1.2.16}$$

or when the domestic cost of production exceeds the Foreign one. That condition can be rearranged into:

$$w/w^* > a^*(z)/a(z) \tag{1.2.11'}$$

or, finally as:

$$A(z) < \omega \tag{1.2.11a'}$$

which is in fact the condition Home follows in determining its pattern of specialisation (recall that according (1.2.11a) Home produces all z for which $A(z) \geq \omega$).

In the original Dornbusch–Fischer–Samuelson article, this model was used as a vehicle for examining how the change in a certain exogenous variable, *ceteris paribus*, affects the pattern of specialisation and trade. As an example we will consider here implications of (1) a change in the relative size of a country, and (2) technological progress in one country.

In Box 1.1 we showed that the difference in countries' size (measured by the relative labour force) has a very important effect on the pattern of specialisation and trade, and on the gains from trade. In our two-country, two-commodity model, the large country was not able to specialise completely in production; and therefore the other (small) country reaped all the gains from their mutual trade. In a model with a continuum of goods the difference in countries' relative size has similar effects. Let us suppose that the relative size of Home, measured by L/L^*, increases compared to the situation depicted by the initial equilibrium. An increase in L/L^* causes a south-west shift of the $B(.)$ schedule in Figure 1.13. At unchanged relative wages this would create an excess supply of labour at Home and an excess demand for labour in Foreign.[30] Therefore, the

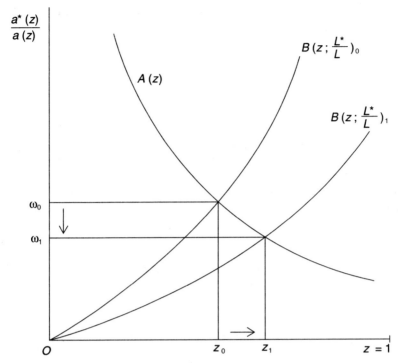

Figure 1.13 *Change in relative country size*

equilibrium relative wage at Home must be reduced, say, to ω_1. The unit labour (production) costs in Home relative to Foreign are now less and Home 'gains' comparative advantage in marginal industries (which means a competitive advantage in terms of the export condition), thus increasing the range of goods produced domestically.

The welfare implications are not difficult to identify. Home's share in the world income (β) has to increase with the increased number of goods Home is producing. However, the real wage in Home is now lower in terms of imported goods (and constant in terms of domestically produced goods), so we can speak of Home being 'worse off' than before the change in relative size. On the other hand, there is an unambiguous improvement of real wages in Foreign. We should also note that analogously to the 2×2 case, a bigger country will end up producing more goods than a smaller country.

Another change we consider is a change in production conditions. Say that Home's technology undergoes an improvement that uniformly reduces unit labour content for domestically producing every good, and thus uniformly improves Home's productivity relative to Foreign. Since this is translated into an increase in $A(z)$ for each good, schedule $A(z)$ will move upwards in Figure 1.14.

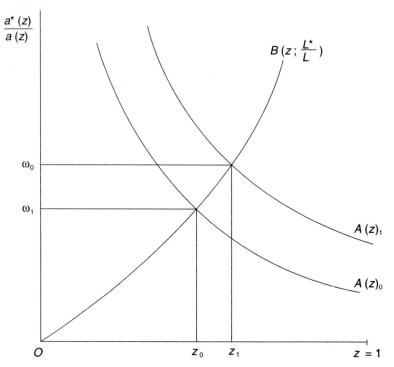

Figure 1.14 **Technical progress in Home**

At the constant relative wage (ω), this reduction in domestic unit labour costs is a source of 'new' comparative advantages, meaning an increase in the number of exported goods by Home. This will result in a trade surplus for Home and as a result its relative wage will have to increase to restore the trade balance. So some of the gains in Home's labour productivity will be offset by the wage increase. But not all the gains are offset. Hence, technical progress in Home makes it better off. What about Foreign's position? It has obviously lost some exporting industries to Home and the relative wage has dropped; does it follow then that technical progress in Home necessarily 'hurts' Foreign? To identify the net effects on Foreign, it does not suffice to look at the nominal relative wage. We must look at the real wage in terms of each of the goods. From Figure 1.14 we see that there are basically three categories of goods. Goods falling in the range Oz_0 are being consistently imported by Foreign both before and after Home's productivity change. Their prices are determined by both productivities and wages in Home:[31]

$$p^{*T}(z) = wa(z) \qquad (1.2.17)$$

and the real wage is then

$$w^*/p^{*^T}(z) = (w^*/w)[1/a(z)] \tag{1.2.17a}$$

As a result of technical progress in Home, w^*/w decreases, but proportionately less than $a(z)$, so that the Foreign real wage in terms of consistently imported goods actually rises.

In terms of goods Foreign exports both before and after the change, it is not difficult to show that the real wage is not changed (remember that there is no technology change in Foreign):

$$p^*(z) = w^* a^*(z) \tag{1.2.10*}$$
$$w^*/p^*(z) = 1/a^*(z) \tag{1.2.10*a}$$

The last category of goods is that of the so-called transitional goods, the ones that Foreign used to export but is now importing from Home. When these goods were produced in Foreign, the real wage expressed in them was $1/a^*(z)$. Obviously, Foreign would not import these goods from Home if it did not gain from it. So it must be that the production cost has risen above the price, or:

$$p^*(z) < w^* a^*(z) \tag{1.2.18}$$

thus implying the increase in real wage:

$$w^*/p^*(z) > 1/a^*(z) \tag{1.2.18a}$$

This leads to the conclusion that technical progress in one economy cannot hurt its trading partners. This is in contrast to the popular view shared among advocates of protectionism in both developing and DCs.

☐ *Transport costs and non-traded goods*

Another interesting use of the model with a continuum of goods is with regard to transport costs and the existence of non-traded goods. So far we have been ignoring the fact that the process of exchange of goods implies some real costs, at least the cost of transportation.[32] Given advances in transport technology, these costs might have been reduced, and significantly so; but they still exist and should be accounted for in our determination of a pattern of trade.

Here we shall only briefly consider the impact of transport costs using the model from the last section. We will start by defining transport costs along the lines of Samuelson's 'shrinkage in transit' model (Samuelson, 1954). The exporter from Home ships one unit of a good worth $wa(z)$ of Home's labour to the Foreign. However, only a portion of that good's worth $[wa(z)]t(z)$, where $t(z) < 1z$, arrives at the destination. In other words, if the exporter wants a whole unit to arrive to the final destination, he must ship more than one unit *in terms of the labour content.* In particular, precisely

$$wa(z)/t(z)$$

must be shipped off. That implies the change in the export condition (import condition) as follows. Home will now produce and export good z if the domestic unit labour cost augmented by the transport cost is less than unit labour cost in Foreign; that is, if:

$$wa(z)t(z) \leq w^*a^*(z) \qquad (1.2.19)$$

thus giving us a modified export condition:

$$w/w^* \leq A(z)/t(z) \qquad (1.2.20)$$

Similarly, Foreign produces and exports all goods for which:

$$w^*a^*(z)t(z) \leq wa(z) \qquad (1.2.19^*)$$

or

$$w/w^* \geq A(z)t(z) \qquad (1.2.20^*)$$

Going back to Figure 1.12 illustrating the pattern of specialisation in the DFS model, we now have two production curves $A(z,t)$ which define bounds indicating the range of goods that have changed their 'character': they are transformed from traded goods into non-traded goods by the existence of transport costs. Put in different terms, all goods for which the following is true:

$$A(z)t(z) \leq w/w^* \leq A(z)/t(z) \qquad (1.2.21)$$

are now produced in both countries, and neither country exports or imports any of them. Note that all of these goods are *tradeable* goods, but they are not traded because comparative advantage in their production has been offset by the magnitude of the transportation costs.

Accepting the obvious fact that, *ceteris paribus*, positive transport costs do reduce the volume and variety of international trade, it can also be pointed out that the existence of transport costs can be a reason for trading to occur. That is particularly true for countries which find costs of internal shipment of some goods to be greater than the costs of shipping them across the national border. An obvious example is the case of two geographically large countries, the USA or Canada, where it can be cheaper to import a good from the neighbouring country than to ship it from another region within the domestic economy, and where moreover it can happen that each country exports one type of good from one region to the neighbouring country, and imports the same type of good from that partner into another domestic region. This is the simplest common explanation for so-called *intra-industry trade*. We will deal later with more complicated explanations that may be given for such trade.

■ *1.3* Summary

This chapter has aimed to provide answers to typical questions asked in the context of international trade while not extending the simple analytical framework too greatly. The questions that are been answered concern the reason for trade, the pattern of trade, and the gains from trade.

The basis for trade is found in productivity differences between countries which are translated into comparative advantage. The *law of comparative advantage* states that each country will export that good in which it has relative productivity advantage and that the world relative trading price will lie in between autarky relative prices. When each country specialises its production according to comparative advantage and then exchanges these goods for the comparative-disadvantage-goods, such trade is found beneficial to all countries.

The basic Ricardian model can be extended in number of ways. This chapter examined the introduction of wages and the increase in number of goods or number of countries, as well as the implications of positive transportation costs.

Two appendices of the chapter provide further extension of the basic model. Appendix 1A is the generalisation of the principle of comparative advantage. Appendix 1B looks into the case of differing labour types and their relative quantities as the basis for productivity differences between countries. This variant of the competitive advantage model provides a link between the basic Ricardian model and the factor endowment model which we discuss in Chapter 2.

▌ *APPENDIX 1A* THE GENERAL VALIDITY OF THE PRINCIPLE OF COMPARATIVE ADVANTAGE

The principle of comparative advantage states that countries will export those goods which have the lower relative autarky price compared to the rest of the world. This statement holds in a strong form in a two-country two-good Ricardian model. An increase in the number of goods, while retaining the assumption of two countries only, does not do a lot of damage to the principle. Given constant opportunity costs and n goods, the pattern of trade can be precisely determined as each country would export goods that were ranked lower in terms of relative cost and import goods that were ranked higher in terms of relative cost. However, since a line must be drawn between exports and imports, and where it is drawn depends on demand, it is possible that a change in demand (or in factors underlying demand structure) will cause a change in the pattern of trade. More particularly, an increase in a number of countries adds to ambiguity. Therefore, when we generalise the principle of comparative advantage to higher dimensions, we are no longer able, in general, to specify the direction of trade of each good. As Deardorff (1980) has made clear, the principal generalisation possible is the result that the value of a country's net trade evaluated in autarky prices is negative (that is, its imports are worth more than its exports at its own autarky prices). The generalised version of the principle of comparative advantage thus states that countries tend, *on average*, to export goods in which they have a comparative advantage. But this allows for the possibility that some particular high-cost goods may be exported and low-cost goods imported, as long as the number and volume of such goods is not sufficient to overturn the average relationship.

In showing this result, it is useful to start with the proof that gains from trade are ensured when countries import goods that are relatively cheaper to import than to produce domestically. Let p and p^T denote the vectors of Home autarky prices and terms of trade (or with-trade prices), D and D^T Home autarky and with-trade consumption vectors, and X and X^T Home autarky and with-trade production vectors. Prior to trade, each country is limited in its consumption possibilities by the production possibilities, so:

$$D = X \tag{A1.1}$$

Trade changes this constraint into the trade balance constraint which requires that the total consumption and total production valued at terms of trade be equal, that is

$$p^T D^T = p^T X^T \tag{A1.2}$$

Gains from trade for Home are ensured if, with trade, it can afford to purchase its autarky consumption vector. This means that Home with trade chooses consumption D^T although it can afford consumption D at the same prices p^T. Equivalently, we can say that Home reveals its preferences for D^T (and the reason it did not choose that consumption prior to trade is that it could not have afforded it). Thus we can write a criterion for the gains from trade as:

$$p^T D^T \geq p^T D \tag{A1.3}$$

Home will experience these gains if it enters international trade following the principle of comparative advantage, that is if it exports those goods whose costs of production are relatively low, and if it imports those goods whose costs are relatively high compared to the rest of the world. Given (A1.3), it must be the case that

$$pD^T > pD \qquad \text{(A1.4)}$$

However, recall that in autarky $D = X$, so it must be true that $pD = pX$; and given profit-maximising behaviour at autarky prices p, the chosen production X must have had greater value than the with-trade production at the same prices. Hence:

$$pX \geq pX^T \qquad \text{(A1.5)}$$

Putting all these together we get:

$$pD^T \geq pX^T \qquad \text{(A1.6)}$$

Let us now define M as the difference between consumption and production in the trade situation, $M = (D^T - X^T)$. Then (A1.6) can be written as:

$$pM \geq 0 \qquad \text{(A1.7)}$$

meaning that imports exceed exports when valued at autarky prices. However we require that at trade prices imports must equal exports and our trade balance constraint (A1.2) can now be written as

$$p^T M = 0 \qquad \text{(A1.8)}$$

If we subtract (A1.7) from (A1.8) we get:

$$(p^T - p)M \leq 0 \qquad \text{(A1.9)}$$

This final inequality says that the elements of the vector $(p^T - p)$ are negatively correlated with the elements of vector M. Translated into our 'comparative advantage terminology', this says that on average, relatively costly goods are imported $(p \geq p^T)$. Although we cannot say anything about any particular good, in the aggregate Home imports goods that are relatively cheaper with trade, and exports goods that are relatively more expensive.

   This exercise confirms our conclusions from the two-country two-good model, that trade is gainful if it follows a pattern consistent with the principle of comparative advantage.

▌ *APPENDIX 1B*   RICARDIAN FACTOR ENDOWMENT THEORY

In the last two sections of Chapter 1 we assumed that the sole input, labour, used in each country was homogeneous and that national differences in productivity resulted from different technologies. Ruffin (1988, 1990) introduces a different basis for productivity differences between countries. He assumes that labour is *not* homogeneous but is, rather made up of various types that differ according to the level of skill. So productivity differences are attributed to the differences between individual workers and are not properties of national technologies.[33] When the skills are different among workers, the quantity and cost of production of each particular good depends also on the availability of the most productive labour type that can be engaged in its production. This model takes account of this fact, and reformulates the principle of comparative advantage. In this model *interpersonal trade* between different types of labour could spill over into *international trade* between countries if the endowment of labour types differs between them.

Let us briefly describe the model which Ruffin (1990, p. 1) names the Ricardian Factor Endowment (RFE) model. The key assumptions are:

(1)   Each person in the world can be categorised as a particular labour type, and labour type is characterised by specific abilities in producing each of the different goods and services).

(2)   Every good or service can be produced with the use of any *single labour type;* and the symbol a_{ij} denotes the labour content of type i used in production of one unit of good j.

(3)   There are constant returns to scale.

(4)   Input coefficients a_{ij} are the same throughout the world (same technology everywhere).

(5)   There is pure competition in internal and external markets.

(6)   Labour cannot cross national borders but the exchange of goods and services is free and absolutely costless. Immobility of labour serves the purpose of differentiating the countries according to their endowments of different types of labour.

(7)   Different labour types have no preferences regarding the employment in various industries as long as those industries pay the same wage (that is, there is no compensating wage differential between occupations). Also workers always work a fixed amount of hours (no leisure–work choice).

We will follow Ruffin (1990) in presenting the simpler (2×2) version of the RFE model. Therefore, assume that there are only two types of labour, unskilled (U) and skilled (S). These labour types can both be used to produce either of the two goods, food (F) or cloth (C). Similarly to the basic Ricardian model, technology is fully described by labour requirements. For example,

$$a_{SC} = L_{SC}/Q_{UC} \qquad (B1.1)$$

shows the amount of skilled labour needed to produce one unit of cloth. Other unit labour requirements we have in Home's economy are: a_{SF}, a_{UC}, and a_{UF} that stand for the unit labour requirements of skilled labour in the food sector and, of unskilled labour in the cloth and food sectors, respectively. So in total we have four input coefficients compared with the two we had in the basic Ricardian model.

Let us next assume that skilled labour has a comparative advantage in production of cloth, or:

$$a_{SC}/a_{SF} < a_{UC}/a_{UF} \qquad (B1.2)$$

which automatically assigns a comparative advantage in production of food to the unskilled labour.[34]

If they are to retain their comparative cost advantage, skilled workers must not be paid more than is allowed by the difference in productivity between them and unskilled workers; otherwise unskilled workers would outcompete them in both lines of production:

$$a_{UF}/a_{SF} \leq w_S/w_U \leq a_{UC}/a_{SC} \qquad (B1.3)$$

This price of cloth is then determined by the cost of production of skilled labour who is the lower-cost producer of cloth:

$$p_C = w_S a_{SC} \leq w_U a_{UC} \qquad (B1.3a)$$

and similarly for the price of food:

$$p_F = w_U a_{UF} \leq w_S a_{SF} \qquad (B1.3b)$$

Because of the dual correspondence between the prices that result from given wages (B1.3a and b) and the wages that result from given prices, the inequality (B1.3) implies that skilled workers could earn their maximum earnings if employed in the production in which they have a comparative advantage:

$$w_S = p_C/a_{SC} \geq p_F/a_{SF} \qquad (B1.4a)$$

and the same goes for unskilled workers:

$$w_U = p_F/a_{UF} \geq p_C/a_{UC} \qquad (B1.4b)$$

This implies then that the following inequality holds:

$$a_{SC}/a_{SF} \leq p_C/p_F \leq a_{UC}/a_{UF} \tag{B1.4}$$

which ensures that both goods are produced.

Let us now suppose that quantities of skilled and unskilled labour are given and fixed:

$$L_S < L_U \tag{B1.5}$$

Using the information in (B1.2) and (B1.5), we can sketch the relative supply curve of cloth following the same steps (not repeated here) as in section 1.1 (p. 8). In Figure 1.15, points A and B indicate the lowest and the highest opportunity costs in producing cloth. We know that these will coincide with two flat segments of the relative supply curve. To determine the equilibrium in this economy we introduce relative demand whose properties are the same as described in section 1.1. The RD curve crosses the RS curve at point E on the vertical segment of the RS (where both types of labour specialise according to their comparative advantage; our economy produces at the 'Ricardian' point). Markets for cloth and food clear at the equilibrium relative price p, and the relative quantity is given by OC.

To transform this closed economy into the trading economy we introduce the second economy, Foreign, which is equipped with the same technology as Home, so that input coefficients are the same and skilled labour has its comparative advantage in cloth production. The difference between the two countries lies in the divergent endowments of skilled and unskilled labour. Let us assume that Home is relatively well endowed with skilled labour, while it is a relatively scarce factor in Foreign:

$$L_S/L_U > L_S^*/L_U^* \tag{B1.6}$$

This difference in relative factor endowments becomes here the necessary condition to generate trade (recall that in the basic Ricardian model it was required that technologies differ for trade to occur). But what can we say about the pattern of specialisation and trade? With identical and homothetic tastes between countries, and no difference in technology, it must be that trade pattern is determined by relative factor endowments. Since Home is relatively rich in skilled labour, and that category of labour has a comparative advantage in the production of cloth, it follows that the relative supply of cloth in Home will exceed relative supply of cloth in Foreign ($OC > OC^*$ in Figure 1.16). That will place the autarky relative prices of cloth for these two countries at two different levels: Home's price will be lower than Foreign's, $p < p^*$ (the result of the requirement that supply = demand). Therefore, when trade opens up, the terms of trade will

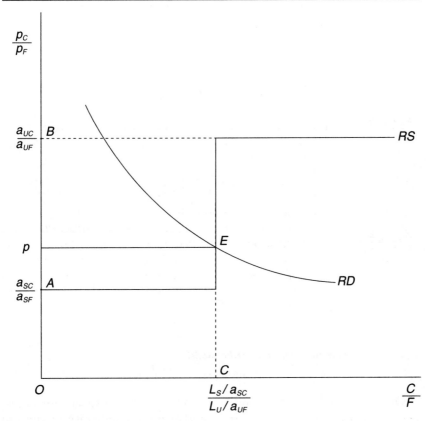

Figure 1.15 *Equilibrium in a closed Home economy*

have to be somewhere in the middle (such as p^T) resulting in *Home exporting cloth* and importing food (and *Foreign exporting food* and importing cloth), with the world equilibrium at point E^T. This pattern of trade, as we shall see in chapter 2, is described by the one of the best known theorems in this field, the Heckscher–Ohlin theorem. Applied to the RFE model with only two types of labour and the same preferences across countries, this theorem states that *each country will export that good in which its abundant factor has a comparative advantage.*

Note, however, the difference in the pattern of specialisation between this and the basic Ricardian model. In the latter, the specialisation in production is (generally) complete, following the pattern of comparative advantages of *countries*. In the RFE model, by contrast, each *labour type* specialises in production but *countries do not*. Each country produces both goods prior to and with international trade; but once trade is allowed, skilled labour in both countries produces only cloth, and unskilled labour in both countries produces only food.

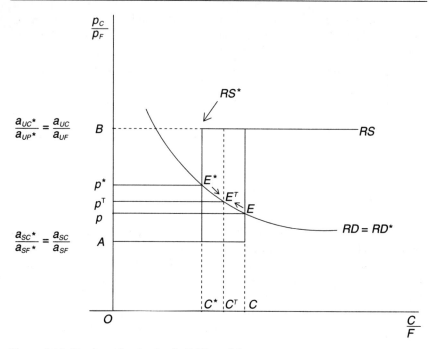

Figure 1.16 Trade and gains in the RFE model

Of course, trade causes the relative commodity prices to equalise across countries, which in our model implies that the relative price of cloth in Home will rise, and in Foreign will decrease to the level of terms of trade p^T. Although the equalisation of commodity prices will lead to the equalisation of wage rates for the same labour type across all countries, the change in internal commodity prices will change the internal distribution of income between skilled and unskilled workers. For this reason, the RFE model allows us to examine some aspects of income distributional effects of trade, and thus to consider the question of gains from trade in a slightly different light. What follows is only a preliminary analysis; Chapter 2 includes a formal presentation.

Each worker's welfare depends on wage and commodity prices. We usually use the concept of real wages to 'measure' consumption levels. Thus for skilled workers we have the wage (or 'income') w_S, which can buy w_S/p_C of cloth and w_S/p_F of food. Using (B1.3a and b, and B1.4a and b) we can express the maximum consumption of cloth and food as:

$$w_S/p_C = 1/a_{SC} \tag{B1.7}$$

$$w_S/p_F = (p_C/p_F)(1/a_{SC}) \tag{B1.8}$$

These can be taken as the two points of the budget constraint for the skilled worker. When trade changes the relative price of cloth (upwards for Home, in our case), the slope of this budget constraint will change: it rotates outwards from the fixed point $1/a_{SC}$ on the cloth axis indicating an extension of the consumption possibilities for this labour type. Therefore, skilled labour in Home is made better off by trade.

In a similar way we can show that unskilled labour in Home experiences a contraction of consumption possibilities as a result of trade. Again using (B1.4a and b) we have:

$$w_U/p_F = 1/a_{UF} \tag{B1.9}$$
$$w_U/p_C = (p_C/p_F)a_{UF} \tag{B1.10}$$

Take these as the two points of the budget constraint for the unskilled workers. The improvement of the relative price of cloth brought about by trade rotates this budget constraint inwards from the fixed point $1/a_{UF}$ on the food axis, indicating a contraction of the consumption possibilities for unskilled labour.

In Foreign the opposite is happening: skilled labour is faced with the contraction in welfare, while unskilled labour experiences higher welfare. In general, we can say that the abundant factor (the one which is used in producing the exported good) benefits by trade while the scarce factor (the one used in producing the imported good) is hurt by trade.[35]

Apart from making an elegant lead into the factor-proportions model of the next chapter, the RFE model can be used to show some other interesting results, one of which is worth a mention here. Recall Box 1.1 (p. 23) and the case of the small country reaping all the gains from trade. In the RFE model, that result will hold only if the small country has a monopoly on the labour type that takes all the gains from the *interpersonal* trade. In other words, if a small country is well endowed with the labour type that gains nothing from the interpersonal exchange, the *large* country will win it all (Ruffin, 1988). Therefore, relative size is not the key determinant of the division of gains; it is the relative endowment of factors that have comparative advantages in goods for which world demand is strong.

■ Chapter 2 ■

Heckscher–Ohlin–Samuelson Model

■ 2.1 Introduction and assumptions

Eli Heckscher and Bertil Ohlin were the first to explore the role of factor endowments as the basis for trade.[1] They laid the groundwork for the developments that substantially changed the nineteenth- and early twentieth-century trade theory. This theory was closely based on the Ricardian explanation of trade, which suffered from some weak points. The more serious weaknesses of the Ricardian model are related to (1) its assumption of a single factor of production and the resulting non-diminishing marginal returns, and (2) the fact that it does not attempt to explain what is behind differences in comparative costs. For example, Heckscher states that '[I]t is a puzzle that until now so little attention has been paid to this basic issue [that is, causes of differences in comparative costs] in Ricardo's theory of foreign trade – a theory that has yet to be successfully challenged' (Heckscher and Ohlin, 1991, p. 47). Then he states that '[T]he prerequisites for initiating international trade may thus be summarised as *different relative scarcity, that is, different relative prices of the factors of production in the exchanging countries, as well as different proportions between the factors of production in different commodities* (Heckscher and Ohlin, 1991, p. 48, emphasis in the original).

Not much of what we today consider to be the Heckscher–Ohlin paradigm can be traced directly to the writings of these two authors, particularly not in the format of the two-factor, two-good general equilibrium model. It was primarily the work of Paul Samuelson that developed and formalised the simple and elegant structure of the $2 \times 2 \times 2$ model, the name of Samuelson is therefore rightly appended to the names of Heckscher and Ohlin.

It has become customary to present the Heckscher–Ohlin–Samuelson (HOS) model through the derivation of its four core propositions or theorems. The first theorem, the Heckscher–Ohlin theorem, determines the pattern of specialisation and trade by comparative advantage based on differing factor endowments. The factor-price equalisation theorem, which follows from the Heckscher–Ohlin theorem, examines how, at common goods prices, factor prices with trade change, and become equalised across countries. The third theorem, the Stolper–Samuelson theorem, describes the relationship between goods prices and factor prices holding a given level of factor endowments constant. The link between outputs of goods and factor endowments, at constant goods prices, is a focus of the Rybczynski theorem, the fourth one of the core. In addition to these, there is also the Samuelson reciprocity condition which identifies the correspondence between the Stolper–Samuelson and Rybczynski theorems. These theorems are subject matter of sections 2.1–2.6, and Appendix 2D.

Although it was not a principal concern of Heckscher and Ohlin to examine the gains from trade, Samuelson has contributed enormously to this topic as well. The later part of this chapter, specifically section 2.7, analyses the welfare effects of (free) trade on a nation as a whole, and on its individual citizens or on homogeneous groups of citizens.

The penultimate section (2.8) considers the issue of stability of the world trading equilibrium. It also includes some useful geometrical techniques. Appendixes A–D discuss the situations in which not all of the restrictive assumptions made at the beginning of the chapter are respected.

The basic HOS model is usually developed for two goods, two factors and two countries (the so called $2 \times 2 \times 2$ model). While these are the smallest possible dimensions of this model, they are also the largest that can be presented geometrically in a clear way. Moreover, as we shall see, most of the central concepts of the model are best illustrated by the $2 \times 2 \times 2$ model.

There are a number of simplifying assumptions in this model, some of which are carried over from the Ricardian framework. These include the assumptions of free trade, no transport costs, perfect competition in all markets, and the international immobility of factors while nationally these factors can move freely and costlessly from one industry to another. In addition it is assumed that:

(1) The production function for each good is homogeneous of the first degree. In other words, this model's production structure retains constant returns to scale. However, it does exhibit diminishing marginal returns to any single factor.

(2)   Technology is shared by both countries, that is, the production function for any particular good is the same in both countries.

(3)   Each good is produced with the inputs of two non-produced factors, for example capital and labour, whose total supplies are perfectly inelastic, and the composition of supply, that is overall capital to labour ratio, is different in each country.[2]

(4)   The production functions for each good within each country are different. This means that goods differ in their factor intensities at all factor prices, i.e. one good is always labour-intensive, the other capital-intensive. Factor-intensity reversals, at least in the simple cases, are ruled out.

(5)   Both factors are completely divisible and are homogeneous within each country. There is also no scope for technological progress.

(6)   Preferences and tastes are identical and homothetic in both countries.

■ 2.2 The pre-trade economy

We first consider an economy (Home), which is closed for international trade, and examine the relationship between commodity prices, factor prices and factor intensities in the two industries of this economy. The conditions for the general equilibrium of this economy are examined on p. 70.

□ *Factor intensity*

At the heart of the HOS theory are the differences in the relative factor supplies with which countries are endowed and the relative proportions of factors used by the industries in producing final goods. In this section we focus on the determination of these relative factor proportions by examining the behaviour of firms in each of the industries in Home.

Factor intensity refers to the proportion of factors used in the production of any one good. In this model factor intensity is a relative concept. This means that the factor intensity of one good is not defined independently from the factor intensity of other goods. For example, factor intensity is simplest to define in the case where there are two factors of production, say capital (K) and labour (L), and two goods, say cloth (C) and food (F). Then, at given factor prices, one good, cloth, is said to be capital-intensive relative to food if the capital to labour ratio is higher in the production of cloth than of food:

$$(K_F/L_F) < (K_C/L_C)$$

If the production technique of each of these two goods was the one with fixed and constant technical coefficients (the so called Leontief technology), the factor intensity of each good would be also fixed, and constant invariably of factor prices. However production with more than one factor of production in general implies some degree of substitution between these factors. If we allow for substitution between factors then more than one production technique becomes possible.[3] The actual technique will then be chosen, given relative factor prices, according to the standard cost minimisation procedure. This, of course, implies that as soon as relative factor prices change, the production technique will have to change to facilitate cost minimisation. As a result the classification of goods according to their factor intensities could become ambiguous. To deal with this problem we assume that there are no *factor intensity reversals*. Thus once a good is classified as being intensive in one factor it remains so at *all* relative factor prices. In fact this requirement is known as the *Samuelson intensity condition*, which assumes that two industries which have different factor intensities do not reverse themselves at any level of relative factor prices. The case when this condition is not satisfied is examined in Appendix 2A (p. 118).

Let us now review the procedure firms take in choosing the cost-minimising techniques of production at given factor prices. We assume the prices for capital (K) and labour (L) are rental (r) and wage (w) rates, respectively. Both factors are used to produce cloth (C) and food (F) in a constant-returns-to-scale perfectly competitive setting.

First, we will examine the behaviour of firms in the cloth industry. They choose their production technique so that costs are minimised, given relative factor prices and the scale of production. If we assume that the quantity produced is one unit $(Q_C = 1)$, our cost-minimisation problem becomes very simple. In general, the cost function to be minimised is given by:

$$C_C = wL + rK \qquad (2.2.1)$$

Since we know that the requirements of labour and capital per unit of cloth are a_{LC} and a_{KC} respectively, we can write the cost function as:

$$C_C = wa_{LC} + ra_{KC} \qquad (2.2.2)$$

The first order condition for a constrained minimum is therefore:[4]

$$\partial a_{KC}/\partial a_{LC} = w/r \qquad (2.2.3)$$

which is to say that the marginal rate of technical substitution in the production of cloth must be equal to the relative factor price.

Figure 2.1(a) illustrates the finding of the least-cost technique to produce one unit of cloth as given by the unit isoquant $Q_C = 1$. Point E on this isoquant shows that the chosen technique is in fact the least-cost one at the factor prices given by (negative of) the slope of the iso-cost line, w/r. The least-cost production technique therefore involves using a_{KC} of capital and a_{LC} of labour, which at factor prices r and w results in minimum cost C_C. This cost can be read directly off the diagram as the cost in terms of capital (equal to C_C/r on the vertical axis) or the cost in terms of labour (equal to C_C/w on the horizontal axis). From the total cost C_C/r in terms of capital, the amount a_{KC} is spent directly on hiring capital services. The difference is equivalent to the hiring of a_{LC} of labour. Similarly, the proportion of direct labour cost in total costs in terms of labour is a_{LC} and the difference to C_C/w is equivalent to the cost of employment of a_{KC} of capital.

The ray drawn through the origin and point E indicates the factor intensity for the cloth industry at given factor prices. This factor intensity, as mentioned earlier, will change as factor prices change. To see this let us draw another iso-cost line indicating lower wages relative to the first iso-cost line. The point of tangency between the isoquant and the new iso-cost line is point E_1. The factor intensity ray is now flatter, reflecting the change of production technique. Given the relatively lower price of labour the

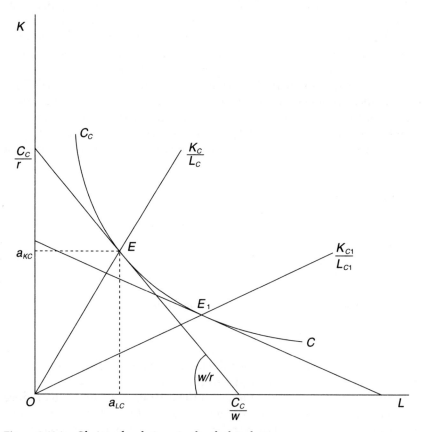

Figure 2.1(a)   *Choice of technique in the cloth industry*

production of a unit of cloth now requires relatively more labour than at point *E*.

The determination of factor intensities in both the cloth and food industries is depicted in Figure 2.1(b), which is also known as the Lerner–Pearce diagram.

Curves *CC* and *FF* in Figure 2.1(b) indicate the unit isoquants for cloth and food industry respectively. Note that these isoquants cross only once, thus assuring that there can be no factor intensity reversals. Following the cost-minimisation procedure, the technique chosen by each industry is given by the point at which the slope of the isoquant (the marginal rate of technical substitution) is equal to the relative factor price:

$$\partial a_{KC}/\partial a_{LC} = w/r \tag{2.2.3}$$
$$\partial a_{KF}/\partial a_{LF} = w/r \tag{2.2.4}$$

Given perfect factor mobility within the national economy, the relative factor prices faced by each industry must be the same, so that their

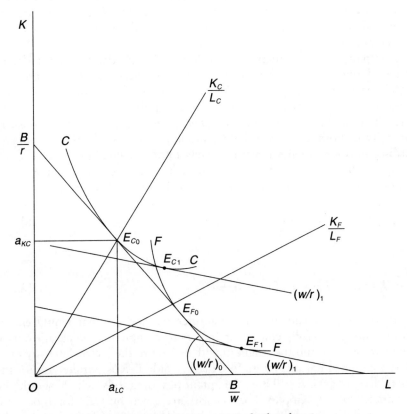

Figure 2.1(b) *Determination of factor intensity in both industries*

marginal rates of technical substitution are also equalised. In Figure 2.1(b) the relative factor price is represented by the slope of the iso-cost line $(w/r)_0$. The tangency of this line and each one of the unit isoquants in accordance with first order conditions is at the points E_{C0} and E_{F0}. The rays through these points can again be used to determine the factor intensity. Since the slope of the ray OE_{C0} is steeper than the slope of the ray OE_{F0} we can say that cloth is *capital-intensive* relative to food, which is relatively *labour-intensive*:

$$(K_F/L_F) < (K_C/L_C) \tag{2.2.5}$$

If the Samuelson intensity condition is to be satisfied, this difference in factor intensities between the food and cloth industries must be kept intact at all admissible factor prices. Thus, if we change the relative factor price in Figure 2.1(b) from $(w/r)_0$ to $(w/r)_1$, we expect that cloth will remain relatively capital-intensive. At the new factor prices the techniques chosen are indicated by points E_{F1} and E_{C1}. Both sectors are using more labour-intensive techniques simply because labour is now relatively cheaper than it was previously. However cloth is still capital-intensive as compared to food; this is again easily read off the slopes of the rays OE_{F1} and OE_{C1}, which are not drawn.

Any pair of factor-intensity rays derived for particular relative factor prices define an area which is referred to as the *cone of diversification* (McKenzie, 1955; Chipman, 1966). It represents the set of overall factor endowments for which the factor market equilibrium conditions will be met. This in fact means that at *given relative factor prices* a positive quantity of both goods will be produced, and the production techniques utilised fully employ both factors. The last point is illustrated in Figure 2.2. Suppose that the total factor endowments are given by point R. This amount will be totally absorbed between the two industries if:

$$K = K_C + K_F = a_{KC}Q_C + a_{KF}Q_F \tag{2.2.6}$$

and

$$L = L_C + L_F = a_{LC}Q_C + a_{LF}Q_F \tag{2.2.7}$$

Geometrically we can find the quantities Q_C and Q_F that would enable both industries to fully employ all factors by completing the parallelogram between point R and the origin O with respect to the factor-intensity rays. The completed parallelogram is OE_FRE_C. Side E_FR is parallel and of the same length as OE_C. Thus the quantities of goods which should be produced to fully employ both factors are given by OE_F for food, and OE_C for cloth. Put differently, only the endowments of factors within the

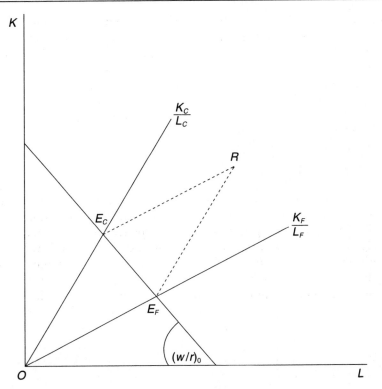

Figure 2.2 *The cone of diversification*

cone of diversification ensure positive production of each good. In the case when the endowment point is outside the cone of diversification, the country must specialise in one of the goods. The possibility and the consequences of the complete specialisation is considered in Appendix 2C (p. 125).

Much of the analysis in this chapter is concerned with the relationships between factor and commodity prices. The tools we have used so far, that is production functions and iso-cost lines, are suited to examine these price relationships only indirectly through analysis of quantities of factors and commodities. It would certainly be helpful if we could analyse price relationships directly. This can be achieved by using the duality techniques.

The dual of the isoquant for good C, $Q_C(K,L)$, represented in Figure 2.1, is given by the *iso-price* curve p_C (w, r).[5] The iso-price curve links those combinations of wage rates, w, and rental rates, r, which are consistent with zero profits at the given commodity price p_C. Therefore, the iso-price curve for cloth industry p_C in Figure 2.3 is a graph of

$$p_C(w, r) = C_C(w, r) \qquad (2.2.8)$$

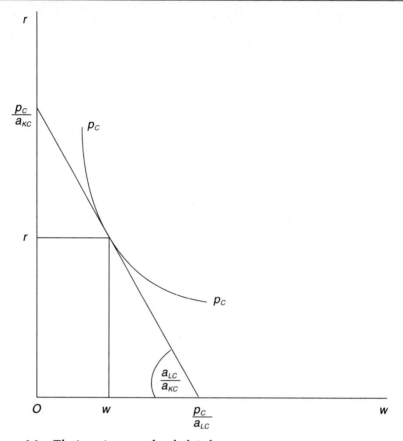

Figure 2.3   *The iso-price curve for cloth industry*

The absolute value of the slope of the iso-price curve gives the capital–labour ratio:

$$dr/dw = -(\partial p_C/\partial w)/(\partial p_C/\partial r) = a_{LC}/a_{KC} \tag{2.2.9}$$

A change in the price of cloth will of course shift the iso-price curve proportionately outwards in the case of a price increase, or inwards in the case of a price decrease.

In Figure 2.4 we add the iso-price curve for the food industry, labelled as p_F and determined as:

$$p_F(w, r) = C_F(w, r) \tag{2.2.10}$$

The two iso-price curves intersect only once. The point of intersection or the competitive equilibrium, E, determines the wage rate w and the rental rate r which are consistent with the given commodity prices of food and cloth. At point E the cloth industry is capital-intensive relative to the food industry because the slope of p_F at this point is greater than the slope of p_C at the same point, or:

$$(a_{LF}/a_{KF}) > (a_{LC}/a_{KC}) \tag{2.2.11}$$

We will now demonstrate that in equilibrium the full employment requirement can be satisfied only if the total factor endowment lies within the cone of diversification. If the economy's factor endowment is not located in the area limited by the two factor-intensity lines, the two industries cannot fully absorb all factors at the given factor prices.

The conditions for the full employment of labour and capital requires that:

$$K/L = (K_C + K_F)/(L_C + L_F) = (K_C/L) + (K_F/L) \tag{2.2.12}$$

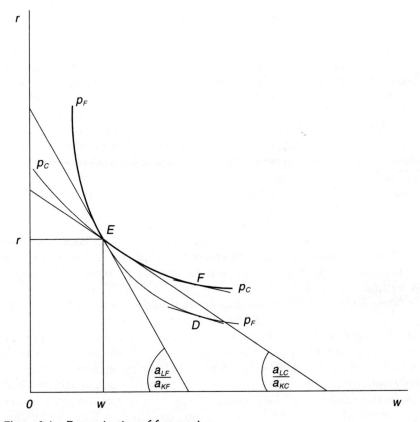

Figure 2.4 **Determination of factor prices**

Multiplying the first term on the right-hand side by (L_C/L_C), and the second term on the same side by L_F/L_F), we obtain:

$$K/L = [(K_C/L_C)(L_C/L)] + [(K_F/L_F)(L_F/L)]$$

We then denote the fraction of the total labour supply employed by the cloth industry L_C/L as λ_{LC}, and the fraction of the total labour supply employed by the food industry L_F/L as λ_{LF} (where $\Sigma\lambda_{ij} = 1$, $i = K,L$; $j = C,F$). Using our earlier result, that for unit isoquants $K/L = a_{Kj}/a_{Lj}$, we can write (2.2.12) as

$$K/L = \lambda_{LC}(a_{KC}/a_{LC}) + \lambda_{LF}(a_{KF}/a_{LF}) \tag{2.2.12a}$$

This proves that the overall factor endowment ratio must be a weighted average of the factor intensities of both industries. To illustrate this suppose that the economy's capital-labour ratio is given by the slope of p_F at point D or, equivalently, by the slope of p_C at point F in Figure 2.4. If factor prices were as determined by point D, the price of food would be equal to the cost of food ($p_F = C_F$), but the price of cloth would exceed the cost of cloth ($p_C > C_C$) because point D lies below the iso-price curve p_C. This in turn means that the producers of cloth would earn positive profits, thus precluding any point, such as point D, from being the equilibrium point. At point F, on the other hand, we have $p_C = C_C$, and $p_F < C_F$. This means that the producers of food will exit that industry and only cloth will be produced (this is one of the reasons for the complete specialisation). Therefore points such as F can represent the equilibrium. An equilibrium that would involve complete specialisation in food production would be represented by a point lying on the iso-price curve for food above the point of intersection, E. Hence we can say that locus of possible equilibria is comprised of those portions of the iso-price curves that are furthest from the origin (plotted as a thick curve in Figure 2.4). This locus is known as the *factor-price frontier*. It consists of the two smooth portions, where the economy produces only one good, and a kink, at which both goods are produced. It is obvious that both goods can be produced only if the total factor endowment ratio lies between the smooth portions of the factor-price frontier.[6]

When the commodity prices change we would expect that factor prices would also change. Figure 2.4 is an appropriate method with which to analyse this relationship. We will, however, do this in detail in section 2.5 when we derive and prove the Stolper-Samuelson theorem which deals directly with the issue of commodity and factor price changes. Here we only indicate that an increase in, say, the price of cloth, would result in conflicting changes in the income of the two factors involved in the production of cloth. The factor that is intensively used will benefit because its price will increase by proportionately more than the price of cloth, while the other factor, labour, will lose through a decrease in its nominal and real reward.

Commodity prices, factor prices and factor intensities

On the basis of the discussion so far, particularly Figures 2.1(a) and 2.4, we can establish that there exists a monotonic and unique relationship between commodity prices, factor prices, and factor intensities (Samuelson, 1948, 1949).

The upper part of Figure 2.5 depicts the relationship between factor prices and factor intensities. The shape of the curves k_F and k_C (where k stands for K/L) depends on the ease with which factors can be substituted for each other in the production of these two goods. When an industry's production function is characterised by an elasticity of substitution greater than 1 it will react to changes in factor prices by changing the factor intensities in its cost-minimising technique more than proportionately. This gives us the shape of K/L as a concave function of (w/r). If both industries' production functions have the same elasticities of substitution (which we assume they have), then the factor intensities of these two industries will always differ at all common factor prices, as shown by Figure 2.5 where for any w/r we have $k_C > k_F$.

The lower part of Figure 2.5 depicts the relationship between factor prices and commodity prices. This relationship is implicit in Figure 2.1(a). When the food industry is always relatively labour-intensive a fall in the relative factor price (w/r) will always lower the relative average cost and the relative price for the labour-intensive good. Thus when w/r decreases, p_F/p_C will decrease as well. To see this we have to refer back to Figure 2.1(a). There each industry's isoquant is tangential to the same iso-cost line. We have established that the cost of producing a unit of food can be expressed as the cost in terms of labour (B/w) or the cost in terms of capital (B/r). The fact that costs can be expressed in this manner is easy to see. The factor requirements for the production of a unit of cloth are a_{KC} of capital and a_{LC} of labour. However a_{KC} of capital is equivalent to $(B/w) - a_{LC}$ of labour. Therefore the total cost in terms of labour is B/w. Following the same procedure to derive the cost of producing a unit of food, given the factor prices as $(w/r)_0$, we arrive at the same amount of labour, B/w. Therefore, at the market place, a unit of food would exchange for a unit of cloth. In other words, *commodity prices can be deduced from the costs of production given the relative factor prices.*

It is simple to demonstrate that the change in the price of one factor would change the price of the commodity that uses that factor intensively in the same direction. Suppose, for example, that the price of labour falls relative to the price of capital so that the new iso-cost line is given by

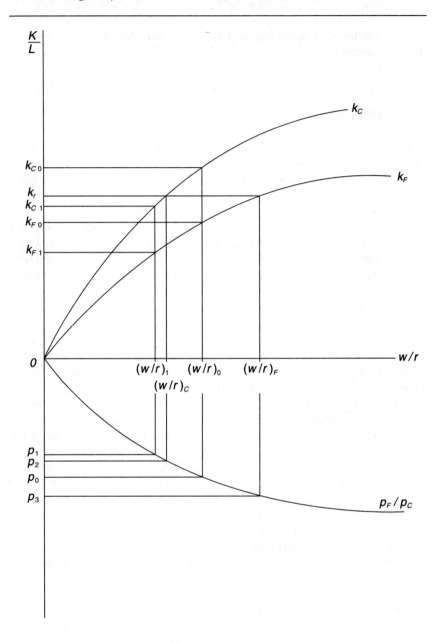

Figure 2.5   *Commodity prices, factor prices and factor intensities*

$(w/r)_1$. The isoquants that can be tangential to this iso-cost line are the old one for the food industry, *FF*, and the new one for the cloth industry (not shown in Figure 2.1(a)) that must necessarily represent a lower quantity of cloth than the old isoquant *CC*. Therefore we have the same amount of food being exchanged for a smaller quantity of cloth. This implies a lower relative price of food, the labour-intensive good. The relationship between factor prices and commodity prices is represented by the monotonic concave curve known as the 'commodity price – factor price correspondence' in the lower part of Figure 2.5.

We can use Figure 2.5 to demonstrate yet another correspondence. We have already shown that incomplete specialisation is possible only when the overall factor endowments lie within the cone of diversification at given factor prices. Now we can show that this requirement is the same as the one which stipulates that at a given overall factor endowment there is a range of feasible relative factor prices at which both goods would be produced. Moreover, for the relative factor prices at either side of this range there would be complete specialisation in production. This is shown very directly in Figure 2.4 with the *factor-price frontier*. However, we can also show it in Figure 2.5. There the point k_r indicates the overall factor endowment ratio. The range of feasible factor prices is then given by $(w/r)_C$ and $(w/r)_F$. We have shown this when we used the identity which states that the economy-wide capital–labour ratio is a weighted average of the two factor intensities (2.2.10a). To illustrate this here suppose that the relative factor price in Figure 2.5 is higher than the one given by $(w/r)_F$. The capital–labour ratios of both industries will be then greater than the overall ratio k_r, which is impossible given the result in (2.2.10a). Similarly, factor-price ratios lower than $(w/r)_C$ are not possible. However, when the relative factor price is *equal* to $(w/r)_C$ [or to $(w/r)_F$], the economy will fully specialise in cloth (food). Note that there is a range of relative commodity prices, p_2p_3, corresponding to the range of relative factor prices. Relative prices outside this range are admissible, although they cannot influence the production structure. Production then takes place at one of the extreme relative factor prices which means that the economy is completely specialised.[7] In such case change in relative prices does not affect production. For example, if the price falls below p_2 the economy will continue to produce only cloth at the quantity that was reached at the level of prices p_2. (This actually implies a change in the terms of trade for this country. We will discuss the welfare effects of the terms of trade changes later in this chapter.)

The allocation of factors and the production possibility frontier

It has already been stated that the economy's overall factor endowments will be allocated between the two industries in accordance with their requirements, that is their factor intensities. Only in this way will both of the factors be completely absorbed in the production of the two goods *at the equilibrium factor prices* (see Figure 2.1(a) and its dual, Figure 2.4).

Here, however, we will examine the allocation of factors using a different method of presentation. This will enable us to look at the allocation of factors from a different perspective. We will be less concerned with market efficiency of allocation and more with technological efficiency. The technique we will use was developed by Savosnick (1958). It enables us to derive the production possibility frontier within the Edgeworth–Bowley box diagram.[8]

In Figure 2.6 the dimensions of the box represent the total supply of the factors of production, K and L, so that along the horizontal axis from the origin O_C we measure the amount of labour used in the production of cloth. Along the vertical axis from the same origin we measure the amount of capital used in the production of cloth. The amounts of labour and capital that are not used in the cloth industry must, by assumption, be used in the food industry. The food industry's usage of factors is measured from the origin O_F along the L and K axis. The diagonal $O_C O_F$ measures the overall capital–labour ratio.

The isoquants for cloth are drawn moving outward from the cloth origin, for example isoquants C_1, C_2, and $\bar{C}$, while those for food are drawn moving downwards from the food origin, for example isoquants F_1, F_2, and $\bar{F}$. The isoquant $\bar{F}$, which indicates the maximum possible production of food, necessarily passes through the cloth origin where

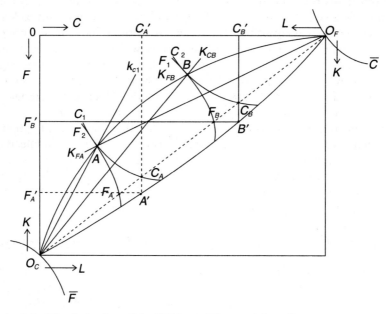

Figure 2.6   *The derivation of the PPF in an Edgeworth box diagram*

$Q_C = 0$. The same applies for the isoquant $\bar{C}$, which shows that the maximum output of cloth is produced when $Q_F = 0$. $\bar{C}$ must therefore pass through the food origin. The locus of tangencies between the food and the cloth isoquants represents the Pareto efficient allocations of factors between these two industries. At each one of these points the slopes of the respective isoquants are the same, indicating that the marginal rates of technical substitution are equalised between industries at the given factor prices. This locus is the contract curve O_CABO_F. Note that it lies completely above the diagonal O_CO_F. This reflects the factor intensities we have assumed to exist in these two industries where factor-intensity reversals cannot occur. The contract curve has the usual property that, if the economy is actually producing at the contract curve, it is impossible to increase the outputs of both goods by merely reallocating resources. Once an economy allocates its factors along the contract curve, a movement along the curve implies an increase in the output of one good and a reduction in the output of the other good. For this reason each point on the contract curve corresponds to a point on this economy's PPF.

This correspondence is best shown by actually deriving the PPF. Because we assume that both production functions are homogeneous of the first degree, we know that if, for example, an isoquant for cloth intersects the diagonal twice as far from the origin O_C as the isoquant C_1 then it represents twice as large an output as C_1. The same applies for the food industry with respect to its origin O_F. In other words, we can measure the output of goods by measuring along the diagonal. By transposing this measuring scale to the axis of the box with the origin O (in the upper left corner), we can derive the PPF. The outputs of cloth are measured along the horizontal axis to the right of the origin O. Similarly, the outputs of food are measured along the vertical axis downwards from the same origin.

Let us now take a point on the contract curve, say point A. The isoquants C_1 and F_2 that pass through point A intersect the diagonal at points C_A and F_A respectively. We will use these intersections to identify the outputs of food and cloth given this particular allocation of factors, A. By projecting the C_A on the cloth axis we obtain point C'_A. We can do this because we know that with the constant-returns-to-scale technology O_CC_A/O_CO_F is equal to OC'_A/OO_F. Likewise, by projecting F_A on the food axis we obtain point F'_A because $O_FF_A/O_FO_C = OF'_A/OO_C$. Hence the quantities produced are OF'_A of food and OC'_A of cloth. These two outputs together determine point A'.

Following the same procedure, we can take any input combination on the contract curve and find a corresponding unique output combination. For instance, point B on the contract curve has a corresponding point B'. By connecting all the output combinations derived in this manner with the points of maximal production of food and cloth, O_C and O_F, we obtain the PPF (see Box 2.1).

Box 2.1   *The shape of the production possibility frontier*

The PPF shows, for a given level of factor availability and technology, the maximum output of one good attainable, for example cloth (Q_C), for a given output of the other good, for example food (Q_F). Thus $Q_C = Q_C(Q_F)$. Defined in this manner the PPF is identified with the locus of efficient production points, where production implies the full employment of all inputs (i.e. 'technological' efficiency).

The shape of the production locus depends upon the interaction of two factors:

(1)   the nature of the returns to scale
(2)   the nature of differences in factor intensities.

If, for example, the capital–labour ratio (K/L) used in the two industries is identical, or if only one factor is assumed so that the influence of the second factor is eliminated, the influence of the returns to scale is easily identified. With constant returns to scale the PPF will be linear, corresponding to the contract curve, which in this case will be identical to the diagonal of the box. Such a PPF is shown as the straight line A in Figure 2.7. Note that this PPF has a constant marginal rate of transformation, meaning that the opportunity costs of these two goods are constant as well.

Other types of returns to scale will result in differently shaped PPFs. Chapter 4 (Box 4.1, p. 160) shows in detail why increasing returns to scale in one of the industries may result in a PPF which is convex towards the origin when only one factor of production is assumed. Other combinations of returns to scale between industries, given the same factor intensities, will also result in differently shaped PPFs.

If, on the other hand, we assume constant returns to scale and allow factors to be used in variable proportions, the PPF will be concave to the origin, provided that there are no factor intensity reversals. This PPF is represented with the concave curve $\bar{C}DE\bar{F}$.

The degree of concavity of the PPF depends, as mentioned earlier, on the differences between the factor intensities in the two industries, and on the ease with which they can substitute between the factors (the elasticity of substitution). If the factors are not easily substituted for each other, different factor intensities will lead to greater concavity along the PPF than would occur in the case of near-perfect substitution between factors. Moreover, the larger the difference in the factor intensities the more pronounced the concavity will be. When this difference is large, the production structure is more sensitive to changes in relative commodity prices. This result occurs because industries (or the firms in each industry) will change factor intensities by a greater proportion than the change in factor prices which occurs following a change in commodity price.

The marginal rate of transformation, or the (absolute) slope of a concave PPF, increases as we move clockwise along it. This means that the opportunity cost of one good, say food, in terms of the other good,

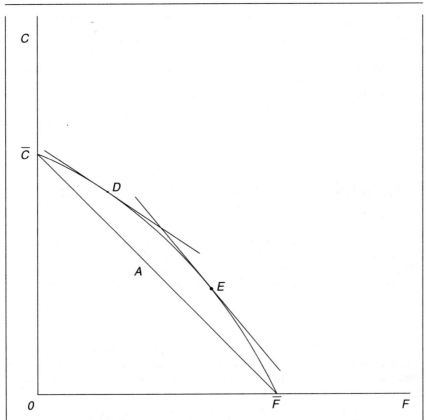

Figure 2.7 *PPF with increasing opportunity costs*

cloth, *increases* as more of the first good (food) is produced. In Figure 2.7 as we move from point *D* to point *E* the tangents at these points become steeper, indicating an increasing opportunity cost of food. Note that the opportunity costs are also given by the ratio of marginal costs of the two industries (or the ratio of their marginal productivities).

The consequence of increasing opportunity costs is twofold. First, it is no longer possible to determine autarkic relative prices. That is, comparative advantage can no longer be determined solely on the basis of supply conditions. To obtain these relative prices we must first determine the economy's autarkic equilibrium. This cannot be done without taking demand conditions directly into consideration. By incorporating demand conditions, equilibrium relative prices are determined as being equal to both the marginal rate of transformation in production and the marginal rate of substitution in consumption. This is illustrated in the next section. We will also see, in Appendix 2B (p. 123), that when the HOS model assumption of the identical tastes is relaxed, demand can play a role in determining comparative advantage.

The other consequence of increasing opportunity costs is that trade typically will not lead to a complete specialisation in production. This model actually requires that both goods are produced with and without trade. However this is what we would expect under increasing opportunity costs. This point can be shown heuristically by demonstrating that goods' relative prices will equalise between two countries which start trading with each other *before* either country reaches the point of complete specialisation. The case when this does not happen, so that one or both countries do specialise completely, is examined in the Appendix 2C (p. 125).

General equilibrium in the 2 × 2 closed economy

In the analysis of this section we have demonstrated the existence of determinate value for relative factor prices, relative commodity prices, outputs for both goods and the distribution of income, given the factor endowments and constant-returns-to-scale technology. To actually determine the values of these variables in a particular equilibrium we need to close our model by specifying the demand conditions.

Much as when we introduced relative demand into the Ricardian world trading model, here too the same questions pertaining to the adequacy of social welfare functions can be raised. However the simplest approach we can take in showing diagrammatically the general equilibrium solution for a closed economy is by using the social indifference curve map. Thus in Figure 2.8 the PPF is superimposed on the social indifference curve map. The autarkic production equilibrium is at point Q, where the price line p_F/p_C is tangent to the PPF. This tangency reflects the fact that in competitive equilibrium the relative price of food must equal the marginal rate of transformation of cloth into food.

The tangency condition can be more formally introduced by stating the first order condition for maximising the value of the national output at given goods prices. This value is usually measured by the national income function of the following form:

$$V = Y(p_C, p_F) = p_C Q_C + p_F Q_F \tag{2.2.13}$$

For our analysis it is more practical to express the value of national output in terms of one of the goods. Thus the value of national output in terms of cloth

$$V_r = p Q_F + Q_C \tag{2.2.13a}$$

is maximised if the small movements along the PPF away from the optimal mix $Q = (Q_F, Q_C)$ cannot change the value of the total output:

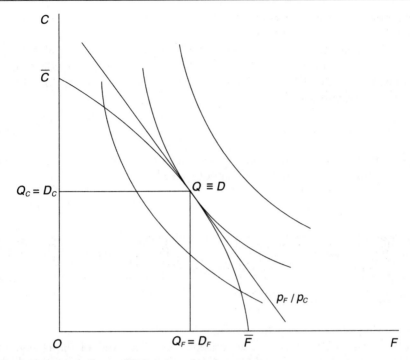

Figure 2.8   *Autarky equilibrium in a closed economy*

$$dV_r = 0 = p\,dQ_F + dQ_C \tag{2.2.14}$$

or

$$-(dQ_C/dQ_F) = p$$

In other words, at the equilibrium production point, the total value of the national output cannot be increased by any feasible change in sectoral outputs. Given the goods prices p, this condition is satisfied at point Q in Figure 2.8. This property of the production equilibrium can be used to examine the effect of the change in the relative commodity price on the value of national output. By differentiating (2.2.13a) and by using (2.2.14), yields:

$$dV_r = Q_F\,dp + p\,dQ_F + dQ_C \tag{2.2.15}$$

or

$$dV_r/dp = Q_F$$

The change in the relative price of food naturally induces a change in the output mix. However, the output response away from the already income-maximising output mix, because of (2.2.14), has no effect on the value of output.

On the demand side, we agreed to ignore any difficulties that might arise from treating a community as an individual. The tastes of the community can be represented by a utility function depending on consumption of two goods, cloth and food:

$$u = u(D_C, D_F) \tag{2.2.16}$$

The community has an income expressed in terms of cloth, and its total expenditure on cloth and food cannot exceed this income:

$$pD_F + D_C = I_r \tag{2.2.17}$$

Consumers therefore face the problem of maximising utility with given income and prices p_C and p_F. The change in utility that results from the change in the amounts of goods consumed is obtained as:

$$du = (\partial u / \partial D_C) dD_C + (\partial u / \partial D_F) dD_F \tag{2.2.18}$$

where $\partial u / \partial D_i (i = C, F)$ are marginal utilities.

We need to introduce a new concept here. The ratio of the change in utility, du, and the marginal utility of cloth, $\partial u / \partial D_C$ – the good in which the community's income is measured – may be defined as the change in *real income*, dY_r. Division by $\partial u / \partial D_C$ then gives:

$$\partial u / (\partial u / \partial D_C) = dY_r = dD_C + [(\partial u / \partial D_F)/(\partial u / \partial D_C)] dD_F$$

where $[(\partial u / \partial D_F)/(\partial u / \partial D_C)] = p$ at the optimum because the movements along the indifference curve sum to zero. Then we can write

$$dY_r = dD_C + p dD_F \tag{2.2.19}$$

(2.2.19) provides the first order condition for expenditure minimisation, that is $dD_C / dD_F = p$, because at equilibrium expenditure cannot exceed income. In other words, at consumption equilibrium the relative commodity price is equal to the marginal rate of substitution of goods. It is obvious that this condition is satisfied at point D in Figure 2.8.

Therefore, in autarky, the community's consumption is limited by the production possibilities (at the upper level), and by the assumption that the total factor income must be spent on the goods produced (at the lower level). Therefore, the total expenditure (equal to income) is the same as the value of national output at the autarkic relative commodity prices p (we assume that these equilibrium prices exist and are unique). Price $p = MRT = MRS$ is said to support equilibrium consumption and production of food $(D_F = Q_F)$ and of cloth $(D_C = Q_C)$. Therefore we can write:

$$pD_F + D_C = pQ_F + Q_C \qquad (2.2.20)$$

which gives the budget constraint for this economy when it does not trade with the rest of the world.

Differentiation of (2.2.20) gives

$$dpD_F + pdD_F + dD_C = dpQ_F + pdQ_F + dQ_C$$

We then subtract dpD_F from each side to obtain:

$$pdD_F + dD_C = dpQ_F - dpD_F + pdQ_F + dQ_C$$

The terms on the left-hand side add to be equal dY_r, so we can write

$$dY_r = -(D_F - Q_F)dp + (pdQ_F + dQ_C) \qquad (2.2.21)$$

Therefore, the two possible sources for the change of the real income are given by the two terms on the right-hand side in (2.2.21). The second term is the price-weighted sum of any change of the production mix; by (2.2.14) it is equal to zero. The first term is the effect of a change in the relative price p. (2.2.21) can be used to assert the gains in terms of the increased real income when a country switches from autarky to free trade (we used a similar expression to express the gains from trade in Appendix 1A, p. 43). More often, however, (2.2.21) will be used to express the changes in real income of an open economy that arise either from the changes in *terms of trade* or the change in the *production*, or both. While it is always the case that free trade brings about a positive change in real income as compared to autarky, there is a possibility for a decrease in real income of an economy already engaged in trade. For example, in the case of a growing economy, the terms of trade effect could be larger than the positive growth effect which would cause real income to fall. This possibility is known as *immiserising growth* (examined in more detail in Box 2.3, p. 104).

There is an alternative way to illustrate graphically an economy's autarky equilibrium by using relative supply and relative demand curves. From the PPF it is simple to derive the relative supply curve for food. The derivation follows the same steps as the derivation of the relative supply curve in the Ricardian model. But because the PPF in the HOS model is subject to increasing opportunity costs, the relative supply curve is upward sloping as in Figure 2.9. Relative demand satisfies the same assumptions as in the Ricardian model. The intersection of RS and RD at point E determines the autarkic relative price of food, p, at which markets for both goods are cleared.

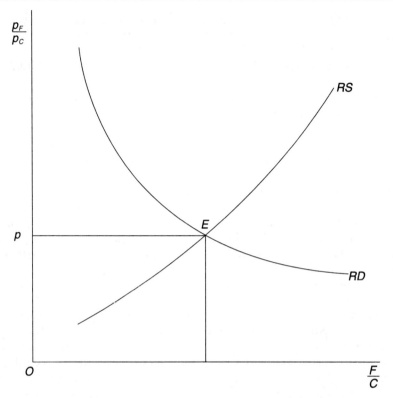

Figure 2.9 *Relative supply and demand and autarkic equilibrium – Home*

■ 2.3 Factor abundance

Given our assumptions with respect to technologies and tastes in the two countries, for trade to take place it is *crucial* that countries differ in factor endowments. The prediction that a country will have a comparative advantage in a good that intensively uses that country's *abundant* factor of production can only be made if countries are endowed with different relative factor quantities. It is important to understand that this require-ment asks for a difference in *relative* factor endowments or factor abundance, not for a difference in the absolute quantity of factors.

There are basically two ways of defining relative factor abundance: the physical definition and the price definition. The physical definition is based on the total amounts of capital and labour (or any other factor) available in national economies. For example, if

$$K/L > K^*/L^* \tag{2.3.1}$$

we can say that Home is relatively capital-abundant compared to the rest of the world (or to the other country, Foreign) who then must be relatively labour-abundant. Equivalently, we can say that Home is relatively capital-abundant if its share of the world's capital stock exceeds its share of the world's labour force (Leamer, 1984, p. 7):

$$K/K^* > L/L^* \tag{2.3.1a}$$

where the world includes two countries, Home and Foreign.

When factor supplies are fixed, as assumed in the model, this physical definition is unambiguous. However, when factor supplies are variable with respect to changes in factor prices, we need to choose a particular equilibrium situation at which we can rank countries according to their relative factor abundance. It is obvious that at different equilibria, different rankings may be obtained. The equilibrium that is typically chosen as the one at which we measure factor abundance is the autarky equilibrium.

The problem which occurs with the reversal of countries' rankings with respect to factor abundance at different equilibria is even worse when we use the alternative, price definition of factor abundance. This definition uses wage–rental ratios and examines factor abundance in terms of the factors' relative scarcity prices. According to this definition Home would be relatively capital-abundant if its autarkic wage–rental ratio were higher than the same ratio is in Foreign:

$$w/r > w^*/r^* \tag{2.3.2}$$

Scarcity prices imply, in essence, that the greater the relative abundance of a factor the lower its relative price. It then follows that the two definitions necessarily correspond. However, this need not always be so because autarkic factor prices are determined by demand as well as supply conditions. For example, it could happen that Home is classified as capital-abundant according to the physical definition but still has a higher rental–wage ratio than Foreign. This is possible if tastes in Home are strongly biased towards capital-intensive goods so that the derived demand for capital pushes its price up relative to the price of labour. In such a case, comparative advantage and trade flows would reflect the difference in autarky factor prices rather than the difference in the physical quantities of factors (see also Appendix 2B, p. 123). This will occur because the link between the commodity price ratio and the factor price ratio is more direct (Figure 2.5) than the link between the commodity price ratio and physical factor endowments.

However the physical definition can be used with equally strong predictive power if we can circumvent the taste complications. The usual procedure is to assume that tastes are identical and homothetic in both countries. In addition to identical production functions, this makes the determination of comparative advantage on the basis of the physical definition of factor abundance equally as valid as the one based on the price definition.

▌2.4 The pattern of trade and the Heckscher–Ohlin theorem

We are now equipped to construct a model in which two countries trade in final goods. This section will therefore examine the determinants of the pattern of trade, and the factor-price equalisation as a consequence of free trade. Section 2.5 will then discuss the consequences of (free) trade for the functional distribution of income within countries (the *Stolper–Samuelson theorem*). The relationship between factor endowments and outputs of goods (the so called *Rybczynski theorem*) is examined in section 2.6. The reciprocity relationship between these two theorems is derived in Appendix 2D (p. 129). The gains from trade are discussed in section 2.7.

At issue in this section is the determination of the patterns of specialisation and trade. Recall that, in the Ricardian model, trade flows were derived from the differences in countries' autarkic opportunity costs. The source of comparative advantage was implicitly assumed in the different technologies available to countries. Demand played no role in determining comparative advantage because of the very special assumptions regarding the cost structure. In the HOS model, countries share identical technology and identical demand conditions. Under constant-returns-to-scale and perfect competition (with no government intervention), the only variable left that can still influence the level of commodity prices is the relative availability of factors. Therefore, the HOS model isolates the difference in factor endowments as the source of comparative advantage and trade. This proposition is central to this model and is known as the *Heckscher–Ohlin theorem*. It states that

> *under the conditions of identical and homothetic preferences, balanced trade and non-reversals of factor intensities, each country exports the commodity which requires for its production the relatively intensive use of the factor found in relative abundance in that country.*

☐ *The world of inter-industry trade*

We assume that two countries, Home and Foreign, comprise the whole world. Each country produces two goods, food (*F*) and cloth (*C*), under the assumptions listed in section 2.1. We further assume that the cloth is relatively capital-intensive good at all factor prices. This assumption is of course completely arbitrary. The theorem's validity is not dependent on which good is intensive in which factor as long as there is no factor intensity reversal. Suppose that Home is the relatively capital-abundant country as given by the physical definition of factor abundance:

$$K/L > K^*/L^*$$

The Heckscher–Ohlin theorem (HOT) proposes that, in this situation, Home would export cloth in exchange for food, which it imports from Foreign.

From our assumptions regarding production in each country it is obvious that the PPFs for Home and Foreign will differ simply because Home is capital-abundant relative to Foreign. The easiest way to show this is to use box diagrams, where the size of the boxes will reflect the difference in factor endowments. That Home is capital-abundant is evident since the height of the box in Figure 2.10 representing the axis for capital is greater for Home than for Foreign, while the quantity of labour measured along the horizontal axis is greater for Foreign. More generally, the slope

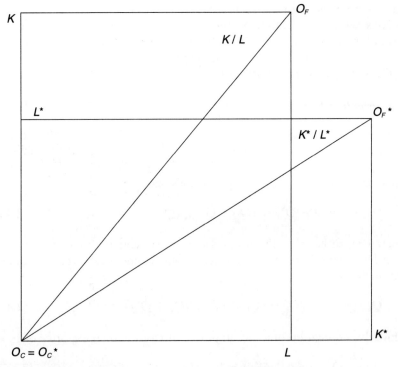

Figure 2.10 *Different factor endowments result in different PPFs*

of the diagonal which measures the overall capital-labour ratio in Home's box is steeper than the slope of the diagonal in Foreign's box, clearly indicating that

$$K/L > K^*/L^*$$

While it is possible to use the Savosnick technique to derive the PPF for each country in its respective box, the graph becomes quite messy and defeats the purpose. Therefore we have derived the PPF for Home and Foreign in separate diagrams (Figure 2.11(a) and (b)). The difference in the shape of the PPFs reflects the direct influence of different factor endowments, since everything else is assumed to be identical in both countries (if necessary, refer back to Box 2.1, p. 68).

From Figure 2.11(a) and (b) it is clear that Home, which is relatively capital-abundant, is able to produce a relatively larger quantity of cloth. Recall that the production of cloth is assumed to be capital-intensive. Equivalently, Foreign's ability to produce the labour-intensive good, food, is larger as compared to Home's. The bias towards the production of a good which uses intensively the abundant factor of production will exist at all commodity prices common to both countries. Combined with the assumption of identical tastes in both countries, this bias in production transforms nicely into the HOT.

Consider Figure 2.11(c). At the same relative commodity price p, the ratio of the production of cloth to food in Home is greater than in Foreign. This is so because the slope of the commodity proportion ray in Home (OP), is steeper than in Foreign (OP^*):

$$Q_C/Q_F > Q^*_C/Q^*_F \tag{2.4.1}$$

However, given the assumption of identical demand, it must be true that at the same relative commodity prices each country wants to consume the same proportions of cloth to food, and in turn that proportion must be equal to the world relative supply of these goods:

$$D_C/D_F = D^*_C/D^*_F = (Q_C + Q^*_C)/(Q_F + Q^*_F) \tag{2.4.2}$$

Therefore, to equalise the proportions of the commodities consumed in both Home and Foreign at the price p_F/p_C, Home must export cloth and import food:

$$Q_C/Q_F > D_C/D_F = (Q_C + Q^*_C)/(Q_F + Q^*_F) \tag{2.4.3}$$

Similarly, Foreign becomes an importer of cloth and an exporter of food:

$$(Q_C + Q^*_C)/(Q_F + Q^*_F) = D^*_C/D^*_F > Q^*_C/Q^*_F \tag{2.4.3*}$$

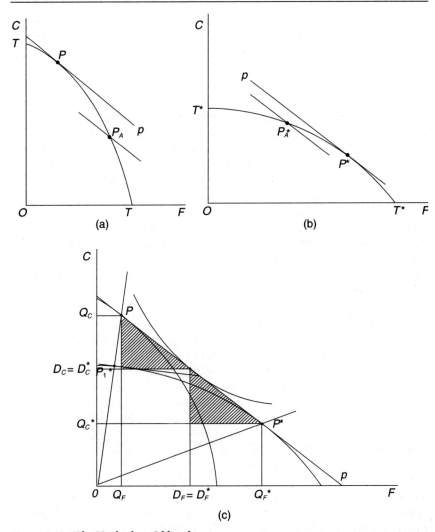

Figure 2.11 *The Heckscher–Ohlin theorem*

This completes the proof of the Heckscher–Ohlin theorem. Note that the theorem was derived using the physical definition of factor abundance. Using the same definition of factor abundance we can demonstrate the validity of the HOT in an alternative way. We use the countries' PPFs as drawn in Figure 2.11(c), but then we compare autarkic commodity prices at the production points which indicate the same proportions of cloth and food in both countries (along any ray from the origin that is common for both countries). For example, take the ray *OP*. The autarkic relative price in Home is equal to the slope of the PPF at point P. The autarkic relative price in Foreign is similarly equal to the slope of its PPF at point P^*_1. From a comparison of these marginal rates of transformation it is apparent that p_F/p_C in Home is higher than in Foreign. This difference in autarky prices is, in turn, translated into comparative advantage. We can therefore say that in this sense Home has a comparative advantage in cloth, the capital-intensive good, while Foreign has a comparative advantage in food, the labour-intensive good.

It is possible to state the HOT by using the price definition of factor abundance. The Heckscher–Ohlin proposition then states that *each country will have a comparative advantage in that good which is relatively intensive in its use of that country's relatively abundant (= cheap) factor.* When using the price definition of factor abundance, thus, it must also be proved that the lower autarkic relative commodity price of any good follows directly from the lower autarkic relative price of the factor intensively used in the production of that good. We have already exhibited the existence of the commodity price–factor price correspondence in Figure 2.5 (p. 64). However, the problem is that in the real world we do not have information on autarky prices. Because of that lack of observability of autarky commodity or factor prices, the price-version definition of the HOT is very difficult, if not impossible, to test empirically (Leamer, 1984).

Regardless of which definition of the HOT one uses, it has been established that *the reason* for trade is still to be found in the difference in nations' characteristics. However, in this model, as compared to the Ricardian model, the main source of comparative advantage is the difference in relative factor endowments, rather than the difference in technology or tastes.

It is important to keep in mind that the process which occurs in each country when it opens up to trade is very complex. We showed in Figure 2.11 that each country will export the good in which it has a comparative advantage in exchange for the other good. Such trade will result in consumption being located on a higher indifference curve in each country; thus implying gains from trade which we will study in detain in section 2.7. We have not said yet what will happen within the production sector of each economy when it faces world commodity prices rather than the domestic commodity price. The world price, or the terms of trade p^T, are determined in this model by the interaction of world relative supply and world relative demand. Unless one country specialises completely, these terms of trade will necessarily lie in between the two countries' autarkic relative commodity prices. In other words, the world relative price of food will have to be higher than Foreign's autarky relative price of food, and lower than Home's autarky relative price of food in order for trade to actually occur:

$$p_F/p_C > p_T > p^*_F/p^*_C \qquad (2.4.4)$$

When the producers in each country face the new relative commodity prices they will adjust the quantities produced: the new higher price for cloth in Home signals that cloth is underproduced at this new price, while in Foreign the same will happen with food. Thus, in Home we expect a movement along the PPF towards the cloth axis to occur until point P is reached at which $MRT = p^T$, while in Foreign we expect a movement along the PPF towards the food axis until point P^* is reached, where $MRT^* = p^T$. This movement, or specialisation in production, will not be as dramatic as it was in the Ricardian model. It will be stronger the higher the elasticity of substitution is between the factors of production. However the increased specialisation implies that factor prices will have to adjust accordingly.[9] In order to increase the output of cloth, producers of cloth will increase their demand for both factors, but relatively more for capital because cloth is a capital-intensive good. The only place these additional factors can be hired from is the food industry, which will release factors as a consequence of the contraction in its production. However, for each unit of food not produced, relatively more labour than capital is released. In combination with the relatively higher demand for capital by the cloth industry (excess demand for capital), this excess supply of labour will cause the relative price of capital to increase until both factors are once more fully employed. The consequence of this will be that the with-trade production techniques utilised in both the food and the cloth industry will be more labour-intensive than they were before trade occurred. As we have seen, this will happen in a country which is relatively capital-abundant. The implication of this will soon become clear; here we can just note that since the opposite process is occurring in the other country, trade will cause the factor prices of these two countries to converge.

So far we have not said much about international trade in this model. One thing that we can mention at this point is that the trade will be of *inter-industry* type. This is similar to what occurred in the Ricardian model. This type of trade implies that countries will specialise in the production of goods belonging to different industries.[10] Thus different countries' product ranges will complement one another, and goods from one sector will be exchanged for goods from another. This is what trade based on comparative advantage is all about. Moreover, we would expect that the more countries are dissimilar in terms of factor endowments, the stronger the inter- industry specialisation and trade will be. In such case the predictive power of the HOT will be even stronger (see Box 2.2, p. 86).

□ *Factor-price equalisation theorem*

Our brief outline of the adjustment process which takes place in response to the opening of a country to trade has demonstrated that, in each country, factor prices will change when each country faces the common free trade commodity prices. The change in factor prices will be such that the abundant factor will become relatively more expensive than it was in autarky. In our example, with Home and Foreign, trade will cause the rental rate in Home (Foreign) to increase (decrease), and the wage rate in Home (Foreign) to decrease (increase). Provided that there are no factor reversals or complete specialisation this process will continue until factor prices are equalised. In other words, factor prices between Home and Foreign will become equal even though factors are not internationally mobile. Commodity trade can thus be seen as a perfect substitute for international factor mobility.

This property of the HOS model is known as the *factor-price equalisation theorem (FPE)*. It states that

> *assuming there are no factor-intensity reversals, there is no complete specialisation, and factors are immobile internationally, free trade in goods will equalise both absolute and the real factor prices across countries.*

One way to illustrate factor-price equalisation is by using a relative supply and relative demand diagram (Figure 2.12). Relative demand for both countries is represented by the same *RD* curve because of our assumption that tastes are identical and homothetic in both countries. World demand thus coincides with *RD*. Each country's relative supply is derived from their respective PPFs. The capital-abundant country, Home, is shown to be capable of producing relatively more cloth per unit of food than the labour-abundant country, Foreign. Hence, the Home's relative supply of food is less than Foreign's at all goods prices: $RS < RS^*$ at all p_F/p_C. Since both countries face identical *RD*, the autarky relative price of food will be higher in Home than in Foreign. The pattern of trade, as predicted by the HOT, will thus include exports of cloth from Home to Foreign and exports of food from Foreign to Home. (See also Box 2.2, p. 86.)

When trade begins the supply of food relative to cloth in Home will increase. We can indicate this by shifting the *RS* curve to the right. The relative supply of food in Foreign will decrease because they will export food and import cloth. Hence the *RS** curve will move to the left. The movements of both countries' relative supply curves will continue until the commodity prices in both countries are equalised at p^T. At this common level of commodity prices both countries will share common factor prices; as illustrated in the left portion of Figure 2.12. We can prove this as follows. Without trade the relative price of food was lower in Foreign than in Home:

$$p^*_F/p^*_C < p_F/p_C \qquad (2.4.5)$$

Free trade is assumed to bring about the complete equalisation of commodity prices. That is:

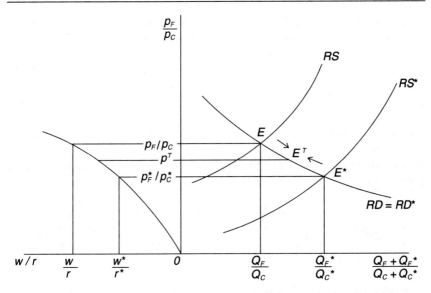

Figure 2.12 *Relative supply and relative demand and factor price equalisation*

$$p^*{}_F/p^*{}_C = p^T = p_F/p_C \qquad (2.4.6)$$

From the commodity price–factor price correspondence, we know that for any relative commodity price there is a corresponding relative factor price. Thus for p^T we can find the relative factor price ω so that:

$$p^T = \omega \qquad (2.4.7)$$

and

$$\omega = w^*/r^* = w/r$$

This formalises the equalisation of relative factor prices.

With the same relative factor prices it must be the case that the factor intensities in each particular industry are equal across countries:

$$K_C/L_C = K^*{}_C/L^*{}_C \qquad (2.4.8)$$

and

$$K_F/L_F = K^*{}_F/L^*{}_F$$

We know that the marginal productivity of labour is a decreasing function of the capital–labour ratio:

$$MP_L = f(K/L)$$

Assuming that the marginal productivities of labour in each particular industry are equal in both countries we have:

$$MP_L^C = MP_L^{*C} \tag{2.4.9}$$

and

$$MP_L^F = MP_L^{*F}$$

At the competitive equilibrium, with mobile factors, both industries must pay the same wages:

$$w = w_C = w_F$$
$$p_C MP_L^C = p_F MP_L^F \tag{2.4.10}$$
$$p_F/p_C MP_L^F = MP_L^C$$

Similarly, in Foreign we have:

$$w^* = w^*{}_C = w^*{}_F$$
$$p_C MP_L^C = p_F MP_L^F \tag{2.4.10*}$$
$$p_F/p_C MP_L^F = MP_L^C$$

implying that

$$w = w^* \tag{2.4.11}$$

provided that commodity prices are fully equalised, as already stated. When cross-country wage rates are equal it follows that rental rates are equal. With this our proof of the factor-price equalisation theorem is complete.

An alternative way of showing factor-price equalisation is to use duality. When Home and Foreign share common relative commodity prices, they must also share the same pair of iso-price curves. Thus we can represent both countries on the same diagram (Figure 2.13, which is almost identical to Figure 2.4). If all the usual assumptions are satisfied, both countries will produce both goods so that both countries' point of equilibrium will be at the point of intersection of the iso-price curves (point E). When countries continue to produce both goods with trade, they necessarily have the same absolute and relative factor prices.

It is important to emphasise that factor-price equalisation depends upon the existence of the unique relationship between factor prices and commodity prices which was shown in Figure 2.5. In addition, for factor-price equalisation to occur it is necessary that the factor endowments of the two

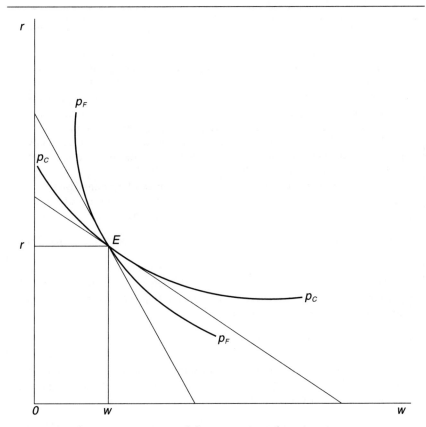

Figure 2.13 *The iso-price curves and factor-price equalisation*

countries are *sufficiently similar*. This in fact requires that the factor endowments of both countries lie within their respective cone of diversification. (More on this in Box 2.2). If the factor endowments for both countries are not in the cone, at least one country (whose endowment is outside the cone) will fully specialise. In this case factor-price equalisation is not possible. Hence, we may conclude that, if the factor endowments of both countries lie within their respective cone of diversification, their factor prices must be equalised (McKenzie, 1955).

Note that the requirement for the factor-price equalisation theorem to hold is exactly opposite from the requirement needed for the HOT to hold: here we require a reasonable similarity between factor endowments, there we wanted them to be dissimilar.

It is also interesting to note that both Heckscher and Ohlin have discussed the possibility of the factor-price equalisation occurring with free trade, 'but only to be refuted on both theoretical and empirical grounds!' (Heckscher and Ohlin, 1991, p. 25).

Box 2.2   *The integrated world economy*[11]

Suppose there is a world without national borders, so that all factors are freely mobile. Also assume that everyone in such a world has identical and homothetic tastes. Furthermore the usual assumptions associated with the production under constant returns to scale and perfect competition are made, so that for any good produced the price equals its unit cost of production. The competitive equilibrium for this fully integrated economy implies the existence of equilibrium goods prices p and factor prices w at which all goods markets are cleared.

The conditions for the integrated equilibrium can be summarised by a set of three equations. The first equation states that pure profits are equal to zero for all goods i that belong in the set of goods I:

$$p_i = c_i(w) \qquad \text{for } i \in I \tag{B2.2.1}$$

where w is a vector of factor prices.

Using Shephard's lemma to define the demand for the factor of production, v, per unit of output of good i, $a_{vi}(w)$, we obtain the second condition that ensures that factor markets clear:

$$\Sigma a_{vi}(w) \bar{X}_i = \bar{V}_v \qquad \text{for } v \in N \tag{B2.2.2}$$

where N denotes the set of inputs, $\bar{X}$ denotes the output of good i, while $\bar{V}$ stands for the available quantity of input l in the integrated economy.

The third condition ensures that goods markets will clear:

$$\alpha_i(p) = p_i \bar{X}_i / \Sigma p_j \bar{X}_j \tag{B2.2.3}$$

where α_i denotes the proportion of the total spending on all goods that is spent on good i.

Suppose that there are two goods, so that $I = \{C, F\}$, where C stands for cloth and F stands for food. These goods are produced with two factors $N = \{L, K\}$, where L and K denote labour and capital, respectively. In this situation our equilibrium conditions take the following form:

$$p_C = c_C(w, r)$$
$$p_F = c_F(w, r) \tag{B2.2.1a}$$

where w denotes the price of labour and r denotes the price of capital. Assuming that cloth serves as numeraire, $p_C = 1$, the price-cost equations (B2.2.1a) can be written as

$$p = c_F(w, r)$$
$$1 = c_C(w, r)$$

where $p = p_F / p_C$. The condition for clearing the factor markets transforms into

$$a_{LC}(w,r)\bar{C} + a_{LF}(w,r)\bar{F} = \bar{L}$$
$$a_{KC}(w,r)\bar{C} + a_{KF}(w,r)\bar{F} = \bar{K}$$

Finally, the condition for clearing the goods markets takes the form of

$$\alpha_C \bar{C} = /(\bar{C} + p\bar{F}) \qquad (B2.2.3a)$$

We now examine whether the same equilibrium allocation of resources achieved in the integrated world economy can be obtained if the factors of production are divided up among countries that can trade in goods, but there is no international factor mobility.

The total quantities of cloth $\bar{C}$ and food $\bar{F}$ produced in the integrated economy can be divided into the outputs produced by the separate national economies, Home and Foreign, so that conditions (B2.2.1a) and (B2.2.3a) are satisfied. It remains to be seen if such a split can also satisfy condition (B2.2.2a). Such a split is possible if and only if factor prices are equalised across these two economies. In other words, the equations

$$a_{LC}(w,r)Q_C + a_{LF}(w,r)Q_F = V_L \qquad 0 \le Q_C \le \bar{C} \text{ and } 0 \le Q_F \le \bar{F}$$
$$a_{KC}(w,r)Q_C + a_{KF}(w,r)Q_F = V_K \qquad '' \qquad ''$$
$$(B2.2.4a)$$

must have solutions in Q_C and Q_F in order for the new resource allocation to reproduce the integrated economy equilibrium. (B2.2.4a) imply that, given identical factor prices, every firm in each country will employ the same production techniques as in the original equilibrium. Thus both countries will experience full employment in the trading equilibrium.

We can write the condition for factor price equalisation in a more general form:

$$FPE = \{V | V = a(\omega)x_i, 0 \le x_i \le \bar{X}_i\} \qquad (B2.2.4)$$

This states that if Home is endowed with factors given by the vector $V(V = \bar{V} - V^*)$, and if the commodity and factor prices, as well as total world output of goods, are determined as in the integrated general equilibrium, factor prices will be equalised between the countries even though factors remain immobile. When factor prices are equalised the trading equilibrium fully reproduces the integrated economy equilibrium.

In such an equilibrium Home and Foreign will combine to produce cloth and food in such quantities so that they sum to the integrated equilibrium totals:

$$Q_C + Q^*_C = \bar{C}$$
$$Q_F + Q^*_F = \bar{F} \qquad (B2.2.5)$$

This concept, the integrated world economy equilibrium and its reproduction through free trade, can be illustrated using the box diagram technique (Figure 2.14).

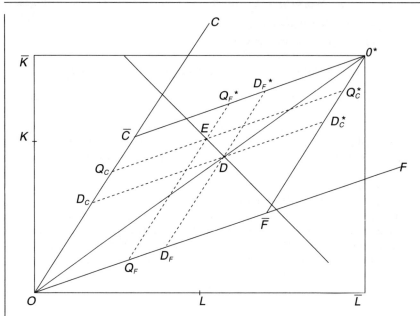

Figure 2.14 *The integrated world economy and the trading equilibria*

The box $O\bar{K}O^*\bar{L}$ represents our given world factor endowments $\bar{V} = \{\bar{K}, \bar{L}\}$. Using equilibrium conditions we can find the integrated equilibrium factor prices (w, r). We can then draw the rays OF and OC along which the factor input vectors for food and cloth must lie. These two rays form the cone of diversification within which the world endowment must be located for both factors to be fully employed. From the full employment requirements we can identify the equilibrium quantities of goods produced along each good's respective factor-intensity ray. Thus the world output of food is $O\bar{F} = a_{vF}(w, r)\bar{F}$, and the output of cloth is $O\bar{C} = a_{vC}(w, r)\bar{C}$. These outputs also represent the total requirements for factors; they sum to point O^*. Note that we would also have arrived at the same equilibrium outputs by starting from point O^* and drawing lines parallel to the factor-intensity lines for food and cloth. Either way we have identified the parallelogram $O\bar{F}O^*\bar{C}$ which represents the FPE set. The diagonal of the box, splitting this region into symmetrical halves, measures world income, OO^*. Any division of this world into two countries where the point of allocation representing each country's respective factor endowments lies inside this parallelogram will result in exactly the same integrated equilibrium.

For example, allow point E to represent the distribution of total resources to Home and Foreign. Home's factor endowment is measured from the origin O, and it consists of OK of capital and OL of labour, while the remaining capital, $K\bar{K}$, and the remaining labour, $L\bar{L}$, belongs to Foreign, whose endowments are measured from the origin O^*. The location of point E above the diagonal OO* implies that Home is relatively capital-abundant. Home will fully employ its given endowments of factors by producing OQ_F of food and OQ_C of cloth. The quantity $(\bar{F} - Q_F) > 0$, being equal to $Q^*Q^*{}_F$, is produced in Foreign. Analogously, since Home produces a positive amount of cloth, $(\bar{C} - Q_C)$, Foreign will produce the remainder $(O^*Q^*{}_C)$.

To determine the pattern of consumption in each country following the division of factors we need to use equilibrium factor prices. They are represented by a negatively sloped line, (w/r), passing through point E. This line intersects the diagonal at point D, dividing the world income into Home's share, (OD/OO^*), and Foreign's share, (DO^*/OO^*). Each country spends its whole income on food and cloth, and the quantities consumed are determined in the same way as the production quantities. Thus the parallels with the factor-intensity rays are drawn through point D to obtain the consumption pattern. Home's consumption consists of OD_F of food and OD_C of cloth, while Foreign consumes $D_F\bar{F}(= O^*D^*{}_F)$ of food, and $D_C\bar{C}(= O^*D^*{}_C)$ of cloth. By comparing each country's production and consumption levels it is clear that Home exports cloth and imports food, while Foreign does the opposite. Such a pattern of trade is exactly the one predicted by the HOT: Home, which is relatively capital-abundant, exports the capital-intensive good, while Foreign, which is labour-abundant, exports the labour-intensive good.

The type of trade that reproduces the integrated world equilibrium is *inter-industry trade*. As mentioned before, this type of trade is associated with inter-industry specialisation based on different relative factor endowments. The more dissimilar countries are in their relative factor endowments, the more pronounced specialisation will be, and the larger the inter-industry trade between these countries will be. This stems from the fact that we have assumed identical and homothetic tastes with the same factor content of consumption (the point D lies on the diagonal which denotes the same factor proportions), while in production countries are endowed with differing factors proportions. Therefore trade in goods actually serves as a means of overcoming the difference in the factor composition of production and consumption in each country. In other words, by exchanging goods, countries are in fact exchanging factor services. Thus in our example Home, which is relatively capital-abundant, exports capital services and imports labour services. For both countries the net extent of this trade in terms of factor content is represented by the vector ED (with the opposite sign for each country). For Home it measures the net export of capital (the net import of labour), while for Foreign it measures the net import of capital (the net export of labour). This interpretation of trade flows is known as the *Heckscher–Ohlin–Vanek theorem*, stating that a country will export the services of factors of production in which it is abundant, and import the services of factors of production in which it is scarce. We will find use for this theorem when discussing the model of trade under imperfect competition.

■ 2.5 Trade and income-distributional effects

In contrast to the Ricardian model the HOS model is constructed in such a way as to facilitate analysis of factor incomes, the distribution of these incomes, and how this distribution is affected by (free) international trade. We have already derived all the elements necessary to discuss the distribution of income with and without trade. We learned how factor prices are determined in a closed economy, what causes them to change (sections 2.2 and 2.3), and in which direction they will change if their domestic economy enters into the international trade (section 2.4). Therefore, we can infer changes in the factor prices from the change in the relative goods prices, and we can state that

> *when both factors remain fully employed, an increase in the relative price of a good will unambiguously increase the real return to the factor of production used relatively intensively in the production of that good, while the real return to the other factor of production will be reduced in terms of both goods.*

This statement is known as the *Stolper–Samuelson theorem* (SST).[12] It forms the third core proposition of the HOS model.

☐ *The Stolper–Samuelson theorem – the proof*

The Stolper–Samuelson argument can easily be illustrated using the factor-price frontier diagram, which is redrawn in this section as Figure 2.15. Home produces both goods at the intersection of the iso-price curves, at point E. Factor prices are indicated as w and r on the wages and rental axes, respectively. Suppose that Home begins trading with the other country, Foreign, at goods prices which reflect the increase in Home's price of the exported good, cloth.[13] This shifts the cloth industry iso-price curve outward to p_C^T by the same proportion as the price increase. We then measure this along the ray through the origin and point E, so that the price increase is given as EE^T/OE. But, since we assume that the price of food does not change, the food industry's iso-price curve does not shift. As a result, the new intersection of the iso-price curves gives us the new competitive equilibrium, point E_1. At this new point, factor prices have changed: the price of capital has increased while the price of labour has fallen. Moreover, the increase in the rental rate is relatively larger than the increase in the price of cloth because $(rr^T/Or) > (EE^T/OE)$.[14] This result – that the price of a factor changes more than proportionately in response to a change in the price of a good intensive in that factor – is what we call the *magnification effect* (Jones, 1965). It is easy to see that, relative to both commodity prices, rental prices have increased while the wage rate has

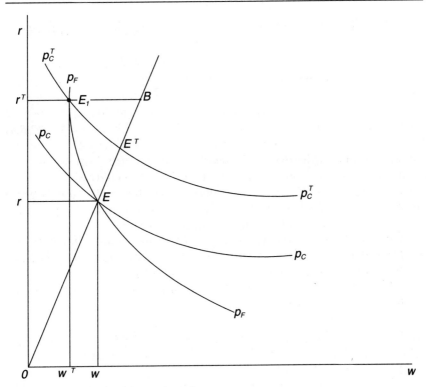

Figure 2.15 *The Stolper–Samuelson theorem*

decreased. This shows the real changes in the rental and wage rates are as predicted by the SST.

Turning to an algebraic proof, we first write the factor-price equations for the cloth and the food industry:

$$p_C = wa_{LC} + ra_{KC} \qquad\qquad (2.5.1)$$
$$p_F = wa_{LF} + ra_{KF} \qquad\qquad (2.5.2)$$

In a competitive equilibrium it must be that the prices of goods are equal to the costs of producing them, so $p_C = C_C(w, r)$ and $p_F = C_F(w, r)$. Keeping this in mind we next totally differentiate (2.5.1) and (2.5.2):

$$dp_C = dwa_{LC} + dra_{KC} + [w(da_{LC}) + r(da_{KC})]$$
$$dp_F = dwa_{LF} + dra_{KF} + [w(da_{LF}) + r(da_{KF})]$$

The last two terms on the right-hand side are the first-order conditions for cost minimisation. They are equal to zero. Dividing each equation by its respective commodity price yields:

$$dp_C/p_C = dw(a_{LC}/p_C) + dr(a_{KC}/p_C)$$
$$dp_F/p_F = dw(a_{LF}/p_F) + dr(a_{KF}/p_F)$$

Performing then some manipulation gives:[15]

$$\hat{p}_C = \theta_{LC}\hat{w} + \theta_{KC}\hat{r} \qquad (2.5.3)$$
$$\hat{p}_F = \theta_{LF}\hat{w} + \theta_{KF}\hat{r} \qquad (2.5.4)$$

where θ_{ij} stand for the shares of rewards accruing to factor $i(i = L, K)$ as a proportion of the total earnings of each industry $j(j = C, F)$. Thus $\Sigma\theta_{ij} = 1$. (2.5.3) and (2.5.4) show that commodity prices are weighted averages of factor prices, and that the changes in commodity prices are also weighed averages of the changes in factor prices.

We can define factor intensity using θ_{ij}. Cloth is capital-intensive if in the total earnings of cloth industry rentals to capital make up for a larger share than wages to labour:

$$\theta_{KF} < \theta_{KC} \qquad (\text{or } \theta_{LF} > \theta_{LC})$$

Suppose that the price of cloth increases relative to food, that is, $\hat{p}^C > \hat{p}^F$. Then from
(2.5.3) and (2.5.4) it follows:

$$\hat{r} > \hat{p}_C > \hat{p}_F > \hat{w} \qquad (2.5.5)$$

And, moreover, if $\hat{p}_F = 0$, the wage rate has to fall:

$$\hat{r} > \hat{p}_C > \hat{p}_F = 0 > \hat{w} \qquad (2.5.5a)$$

From (2.5.5a) it follows that an increase in the price of cloth will increase the absolute and real reward of capital, which is relatively intensively used in the cloth production, and will reduce the absolute and real wage which is intensively used in food whose price has not changed in nominal terms. In more general terms the theorem states that a change in a relative goods price always increases the absolute and real reward of the factor intensive to the good whose relative price has increased, and reduces the absolute and real reward of the other factor.

In this model, it is assumed that each factor of production is owned by a different individual or a group of individuals in a society. In this case, when each individual derives its whole income by selling services of only one factor, the income distributional effects of the change in commodity prices are very strong. A move from autarky to free trade, as shown, involves an increase in the price of the exportable good, and a decrease in the price of the importable good. For example, when Home begins trading, the price of cloth rises, while the price of food falls as compared to autarky prices. Therefore, by the SST, individuals owning the factor intensively used in an exportable industry must gain, because their real income increases in terms of both goods.[16] Conversely, the owners of the factor intensively used in the import-substituting industry are worse off because their income is reduced in terms of both goods. Thus in Home, capital owners will gain from free trade, but workers will lose. This of course generates a conflict between the two groups of factor owners. In our example, workers are likely to resist moves toward free trade, arguing that it will cause a fall of their standard of living. Historically, this was one of the main reasons for granting a protection against imports. Today, the whole issue is more complex, as we will realise in Chapter 12. However, the SST has, in a sense, brought the conflicting effects of free trade into the open.

The SST is relevant to income distribution as long as different groups in society derive income from different factors. If every individual could supply capital and labour services in the same proportion, the same change in a commodity price as above would cause the gains and the loses from trade to offset each other for every individual. In this case, trade would not result in income re-distribution.

But the SST loses its predictive power if factors are owned in different proportions by the same individual. Therefore, we cannot infer the changes in real income resulting from a price change without information on the spending pattern. Let us assume that income primarily comes from the factor whose reward increases, that is, from the factor intensively used in the export industry. Then, if an individual's preferences are strongly biased toward importables, the gains from trade are unambiguous. If preferences are skewed toward exportables, there is a possibility for losses from free trade.

The SST brings to the surface one of the potential sources of the possible losses from free trade, namely that factors used intensively in import-substituting industry are bound to lose. In addition, although with less certainty, we can predict that the potential losers are those with income based on both factors and with strongly biased preferences toward exportables. We will see that there are other sources for losses from free trade for some groups in a society. However, other groups in society gain. In section 2.7 we shall examine how the winners can compensate the losers so that potentially everyone can gain from free trade.

■ 2.6 Endowment changes and output changes

One of the assumptions needed in developing the HOS model was that the economy's overall factor endowments were given and fixed. In this section we examine what happens in a small open economy if we allow factor endowments to change. The analysis can be categorised as comparative statics since it compares the equilibrium arising before the change in endowments with the equilibrium after the change.

Consider first the adjustments an economy must make when it experiences a change in factor endowments. Because we assume constant commodity prices, by the factor-price equalisation (FPE) theorem factor prices must also be constant. When factor prices are constant, producers, in either industry, have no reason to change factor intensities. Therefore the only way to keep all the factors fully employed after they have increased in size is to increase the output of goods. This link between the change in factor endowments and the change in the output of goods is given by the *Rybczynski theorem* which states that

> *at constant commodity and factor prices, and when an economy continues to produce both goods, an increase in one factor endowment will cause the output of the good intensive in that factor to increase by a greater proportion, and will reduce the output of the other good.*

☐ *The Rybczinski theorem – the proof*

Figure 2.16 illustrates the changes in outputs predicted by the Rybczynski theorem. The initial factor endowment point E is on the ray OR. The total amount of capital, K, and labour L, given by E is allocated between the cloth and the food industry according to their requirements for factors. Thus a parallelogram between points O and E is drawn, where the sides correspond to the quantities of goods produced. For example $OQ_F(= Q_CE)$ is the quantity of food, while $OQ_C(= Q_FE)$ indicates the quantity of cloth. Consider the case where both factors increase proportionately so that economy's overall capital-labour ratio stays constant. In Figure 2.16 this change in factor endowments is represented by an outward shift of point E along the ray OR to the point E'. Because neither commodity prices nor factor prices have changed, neither of the factor intensities in which the cloth and the food industry use capital and labour will change. Hence the increased amount of factors results in a larger output of both food and cloth. In this particular case the increase in outputs will be proportionate to the increase in the factors:

$$Q_F Q_F'/OQ_F = EE'/OE = Q_C Q_C'/OQ_C$$

However, if the change in factors is not proportionate, that is if one factor increases at a faster rate than the other, or if one factor does not rise at all, the change in outputs cannot be proportionate either. For example, if this economy experiences a rise in the capital stock, but no increase in the labour force, the new endowment can be represented by a point such as E''.

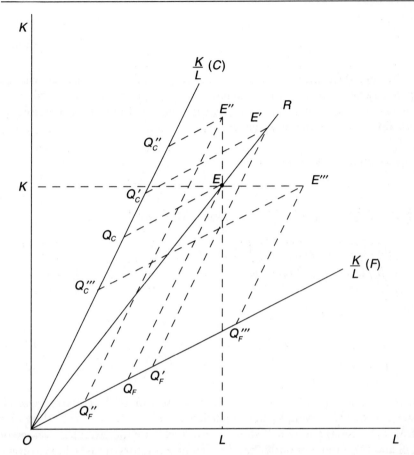

Figure 2.16 *The Rybczynski theorem*

Then, by completing a parallelogram between O and E'', the resulting output of goods changes so that the output of the capital-intensive good, cloth, increases by more than the increase in capital, while the output of the labour-intensive good, food, falls:

$$Q_F Q_F''/OQ_F < O/KE < EE''/LE < Q_C Q_C''/OQ_C$$

Conversely, when there is an increase in the labour force which is not accompanied by a change in the capital stock (E'''), the change in outputs is given by:

$$Q_F Q_F'''/OQ_F > EE'''/KE > O/LE > Q_C Q_C'''/OQ_C$$

To describe these situations algebraically we must first write the full employment equations:

$$K = a_{KC}(w, r)Q_C + a_{KF}(w, r)Q_F \tag{2.6.1}$$
$$L = Q_{LC}(w, r)Q_C + a_{LF}(w, r)Q_F \tag{2.6.2}$$

We then differentiate (2.6.1) and (2.6.2) remembering that if the change in endowments is not large enough to induce specialisation, according to the factor-price equalisation theorem w and r will not alter; therefore a_{ij} remain fixed. We therefore have:

$$dK = a_{KC}dQ_C + a_{KF}dQ_F$$
$$dL = a_{LC}dQ_C + a_{LF}dQ_F$$

By dividing each equation by its respective factor endowment:

$$dK/K = (a_{KC}/K)dQ_C + (a_{KF}/K)dQ_F$$
$$dL/L = (a_{LC}/L)dQ_C + (a_{LF}/L)dQ_F$$

and manipulating we obtain:

$$\hat{K} = \lambda_{KC}\hat{Q}_C + \lambda_{KF}\hat{Q}_F \tag{2.6.3}$$
$$\hat{L} = \lambda_{LC}\hat{Q}_C + \lambda_{LF}\hat{Q}_F \tag{2.6.4}$$

where λ_{ij}, as in (2.2.12a), stands for the proportion of the country's overall stock of factor $i(i = L, K)$ in the particular industry $j(j = C, F)$. Note that $\Sigma\lambda_{ij} = 1$. (2.6.3) and (2.6.4) show that $\hat{K}$ and $\hat{L}$ are the weighted average of $\hat{Q}_C$ and $\hat{Q}_F$, or analogously that the change in factors are weighted average of the changes in output of goods.

We can use λ_{ij} to define factor intensity. Thus cloth will be capital-intensive if $\lambda_{KC} > \lambda_{LC}$ (or if $\lambda_{KF} < \lambda_{LF}$). When a country experiences an increase in its capital stock relative to its labour force, that is when $\hat{K} > \hat{L}$, the change in the output of goods is expressed by:

$$\hat{Q}_C > \hat{K} > \hat{L} > \hat{Q}_F \tag{2.6.5}$$

so that the output of cloth, the capital-intensive good, increases proportionately more than the increase of capital, while the output of food, which is labour-intensive, increases by less proportionately. If, moreover, when the stock of capital increases there is no change in the absolute number of workers, that is, if $\hat{K} > \hat{L} = 0$, then the output of the labour-intensive good food has to fall:

$$\hat{Q}_C > \hat{K} > \hat{L} = 0 > \hat{Q}_F \tag{2.6.5a}$$

Exactly symmetrical results can be derived when the opposite case occurs. When there is a change in the labour force but there is no change in the stock of capital, the output of the labour-intensive good will increase, while the output of the capital-intensive good will fall.

It is instructive to again illustrate the Rybczynski results, but this time in the commodity space. Thus in Figure 2.17 the axes are labelled as cloth (C) and food (F). (2.6.1) and (2.6.2) are represented by the capital constraint, K, and the labour constraint, L, for fixed factor prices and therefore for fixed factor intensities in both industries. The labour constraint line is steeper than the capital constraint line because the cloth industry is relatively capital-intensive. These two lines together determine the production possibilities of this economy, and their intersection defines the equilibrium production point, point E. Let us suppose that, at constant goods prices, this economy experiences an increase in the amount of available capital. It is assumed that the new overall factor endowment still lies within economy's cone of diversification. Therefore, constant goods prices will result in constant factor prices and fixed factor intensities. The effect of the rise in the amount of capital will be in a shift of the K line further out from the origin, such as K_G. In Figure 2.17, the distance EA_G/OE measures this increase in capital, $\hat{K}$. Following (2.6.5a), the new production equilibrium at which both factors are fully employed is at point E_G, where the L line and the K_G line intersect. It is simple to verify the existence of the magnification effect at this new production equilibrium. It comes directly from the comparison of the changes in the output of both goods to the increase in capital:

$$CC_G/OC > EA_G/OE > 0 > F_GF/OF$$

☐ *Factor accumulation and the terms of trade*

The changes on the production side considered prior to this section can be described as production responses to relative commodity and factor prices different from the autarkic ones. These responses were represented by movements along countries' PPFs, leading to increased specialisation, but having no effect on their real incomes. Therefore, the terms of trade effects were the only ones that mattered. But if shifts of the PPF itself are allowed, the real income must be affected not only through the terms of trade effect, but also directly by this growth effect. In the following discussion we examine what total effects on the real income could be expected.

The reasons for the enlargement of production possibilities, represented by an outward shift of the PPF, are usually found in the combined effects of technological progress and an increase in the availability of factors. It is, however, much easier to analyse price changes by looking only at one cause at a time. Since we have just dealt with some aspects of factor

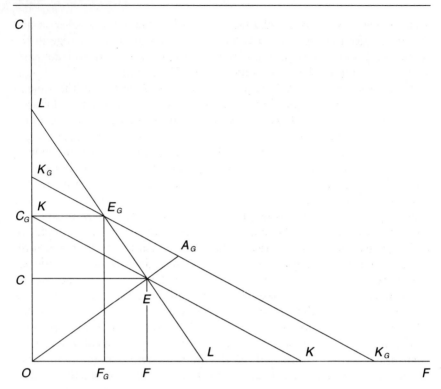

Figure 2.17 *The Rybczynski theorem in commodity space*

endowment changes given by the Rybczynski theorem, it is logical to extend this analysis to cover price changes as well. The effects of technological progress are thus not covered here. Some issues related to technological progress and trade in developing countries (LDCs) will be covered in Chapter 13. For a more detailed coverage, students are referred to the extensive literature on economic growth.

For the purposes of analysis in this section, we have to illustrate the Rybczynski theorem within the commodity space with *variable* factor proportions. Let us then start by showing how factor accumulation affects an economy's production possibilities of the two goods. Recall that the theorem predicts what will happen with the output mix when, starting at some *production equilibrium* $(MRT = p)$, one factor increases in size, relative to the other. The assumptions on which the prediction is based require commodity prices, factor prices and factor intensities to be held constant, *and* both goods to be produced before and after the factor increase. That is, production points both before and after the accumulation must exclude corner solutions. According to the theorem, a new output mix will consist of an increased output of a good whose intensive factor is growing in size, and of a decreased output of the other good. Therefore, we end up with two points of production, one being an equilibrium solution on the original PPF, and a new one presumably lying on the new frontier, at the point where $MRT = p$ as well. We know that this new frontier must lie outside the original PPF because of larger available amounts of capital and the same factor requirements per unit of each good. As for the shape of this frontier, we cannot unfortunately say much.[17]

The factor accumulation effect is illustrated in Figure 2.18, where the initial PPF of Home is given by the curve $\bar{F}P\bar{C}$. The point P is the production equilibrium with relative prices given by $p_0(= p_F/p_C)$. Let us now assume that the amount of available labour increases with no change in the capital stock. Following the Rybczynski result, the only way for Home to fully employ the changed composition of factors $[(\bar{K}/\bar{L}) > (\bar{K}/\bar{L}_1)]$, given no change in prices or factor intensities, is to produce more of the labour-intensive good – food – and to reduce the output of the capital-intensive good – cloth. Thus, while keeping the same factor proportions in both industries, factors are reallocated from the cloth to the food industry so that the new production point, P_1, combines less of cloth and more of food than point P. The line connecting these two production points is known as the *Rybczynski line*. It is possible to trace other points of this locus to which point P_1 belongs following the Rybczynski reasoning.[18] However, note that, strictly speaking, the points of complete specialisation ($\bar{F}$ and $\bar{C}$ in Figure 2.18) do not satisfy the assumptions of the theorem. At such points, only one good is produced, and this fact bars us from applying the Rybczynski result along the axes. At these points the factor intensities in these two industries become the same, that is $K_F/L_F = K_C/L_C = \bar{K}/\bar{L}$. This is the reason why, in Figures 2.18 and 2.19, the new production locus, which is supposed to depict the reactions of output mixes to enlargement in factor(s), is not drawn all the way to the axes.

We can now turn to examining the possible effects of factor accumulation on a country's terms of trade and real income. Let us start with the case of a closed economy, so that Figure 2.18 depicts Home's pre-growth and post-growth autarky equilibria. In this case, production point P_1 is only a hypothetical equilibrium and cannot be sustained unless we assume that cloth is an inferior good. Since we normally do not allow for inferior goods, growth depicted by production at point P_1 will cause an increase in demand for both goods. More specifically, the price line p_1 on which P_1 lies is further from the origin from the price line p_0, representing a higher income at constant prices. The increase in income then boosts the demand for both goods. But because at P_1 the output of cloth actually falls, there will be an excess demand for this good. Analogously, because the demand for food rises by less than its output, there will be an excess supply of food. An excess demand for cloth and an excess supply of food will cause the

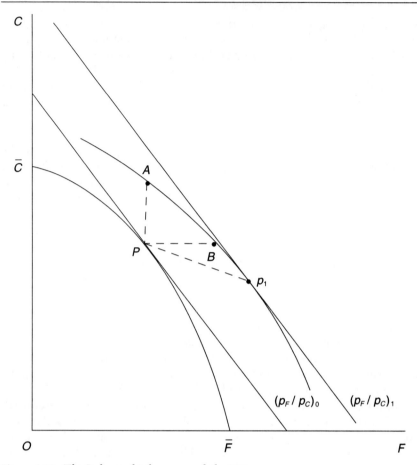

Figure 2.18 *The Rybczynski theorem and the PPF*

relative price of food to fall. Production will then readjust to equalise p and MRT so that more cloth will be produced relative to food than at point P_1. Therefore, in a closed economy, the new production point will be located in the segment AB on the PPF with p lower than at P_1.

Let us now redraw Figure 2.18 as Figure 2.19(a), and also add the with-trade consumption point D. Since consumption at point D consists of more food and less cloth than it is produced at point P, Home must be importing food and exporting cloth at terms of trade p^T. To determine how the terms of trade and real income in Home will be affected by the growth in the labour force, it is necessary to define Home in terms of the economic size and its ability to influence world prices. We first consider the case where Home is assumed to be a large country, and can influence price in world markets.

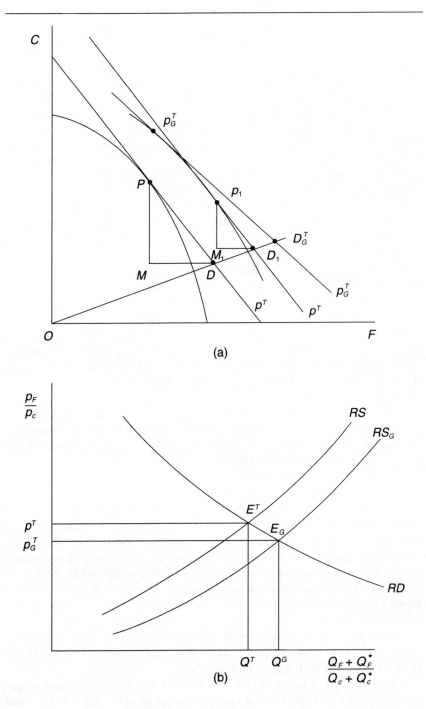

(a)

(b)

Figure 2.19 *Growth and terms of trade in Home*

With the same effect on the output side as in Figure 2.18, that is, with the production point moved to point P_1, Home now experiences a rise in the food supply and a fall in the supply of cloth. It is assumed that there is no growth or demand change in the rest of the world, i.e. Foreign. Therefore, the changes in the world markets for cloth and food are the ones that spill from Home's economy. In Figure 2.19(b), the world relative supply curve of food at the initial price p^T shifts to the right, indicating an increased relative supply of food from Home with fixed relative supply of food from Foreign. Since the relative demand curve does not move, the new equilibrium is at point E_G with prices p^T_G being lower than prices p^T. From the Home's point of view, the fall in p^T represents an *improvement in its terms of trade*. Foreign at the same time experiences a deterioration in its terms of trade. Growth thus has two beneficial effects for Home: it increases its real income at constant terms of trade, and it provides additional gains from the terms of trade improvement.

The above statement requires a qualification about the type of growth Home has experienced. That is, growth which is based in the import-competing industry will have different results from growth located in the exporting industry. Figure 2.19 describes the case of an import-competing industry's growth. To see the difference in the effects of these two types of growth, we shall next examine the effects of export industry-based growth. There are two alternative ways to do this. We could analyse the increase in the stock of capital with no labour growth. Alternatively, we could use the previous example of labour growth, but assume instead that Home is actually exporting food. If we choose to take this second route than we can use the same diagrams, Figures 2.19(a) and 2.19(b), to facilitate our discussion. The only change we have to make is to alter the axes in Figure 2.19(a) so that cloth is on the horizontal and food on the vertical axis, and in 2.19(b) to express RS and RD of cloth in terms of food as the function of the relative price of cloth $(p_C/p_F) = 1/p_T$.

In this setting then, the shift of the production locus and the production point from P to P_1 would imply, at constant terms of trade $1/p^T$, an increase in the production of the exportable good, cloth, and a fall in the importable good, food. It is easily seen that this growth in Home would lead to the same direction of shift in the RS curve in the world market. In particular, the relative supply of cloth would move to the right at constant terms of trade $1/p^T$. Because of the increase in real income, demand for both goods would be rising in the same proportion as income. The new equilibrium point E_G would imply a drop in the world relative price of cloth. This time, however, this would mean that terms of trade for Home have deteriorated to the gain of Foreign.

When a country's terms of trade deteriorate, some of the benefits gained from the pure growth effect at constant terms of trade are offset by this terms of trade loss. Moreover, it is possible for this loss to dominate the positive growth effect. In such a case we speak about *immiserising growth* (see Box 2.3), p. 104. Generally, therefore, we can say that any growth in factor endowments that causes a disproportionate change in the country's production possibilities will create a *bias in production*. Depending on whether the bias occurs in the exporting or the importing industry the resulting change in the terms of trade will be either beneficial or harmful for a country. In particular we can say that *export-biased growth* worsens the terms of trade of the growing economy while resulting in improved terms of trade for the growing economy's trading partner. Conversely, an *import-biased growth* will improve the growing economy's terms of trade at the expense of its trading partners. Therefore, we can add a corollary to the Rybczynski theorem:

> *an increase in the amount of one factor will cause a fall in the relative price of the good that is intensive in that factor, so that the terms of trade will improve or deteriorate according to whether this good is an importable or exportable good.*

This leads to a question whether non-biased growth, that is, *neutral growth*, would leave the terms of trade intact.[19] With no terms of trade effects, a country would enjoy only the benefits from growth. This is what happens to small countries when they grow – since these countries are assumed to be too small to affect world supply or demand, there are no terms of trade effects resulting from the outward shift of their PPF. This is so in the case of any type of growth when the country is small. As a consequence, a small country cannot be immiserised from growth as long as it practises free trade. However, with large countries growth, it is not possible to have constant terms of trade. Even when there is no bias on the production side, growth will result in the change of terms of trade because the sheer size of the country which is growing will affect world relative demand. In such situation the demand factors become important, and the differences in income and price elasticities of demand could be significant.

■ 2.7 Gains from trade[20]

In this section we will address one of the most important issues in the field of international trade: the gains from trade. We start by examining the welfare effects of free trade on a nation as a whole, and then move on to discuss the distributional effects of free trade. We will be able to show that free trade is superior to autarky for a nation as a whole, and moreover that free trade-cum-compensation has a potential to make everyone within a nation better off.

Box 2.3   *Immiserising growth*

Immiserising growth is defined as the strongly export industry-biased growth which worsens the country's terms of trade so badly that the negative effect swamps the welfare-improving effects of growth resulting in a negative overall real income change.

Diagrammatically, the case of the immiserising growth is shown in Figure 2.20.

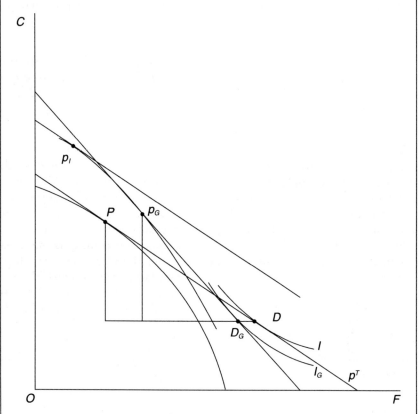

Figure 2.20   *Immiserising growth*

Home's production and consumption with-trade equilibria are given by points P and D at the terms of trade p^T. Let the growth take place in Home's export industry, cloth. It is assumed that this type of growth displaces the production locus much further away from the origin along the cloth axis than along the food axis, so resulting in the Rybczynski output effect. Consequently, Home's output of cloth increases relative to the output of food at all goods' prices. Foreign's production possibilities and its demand pattern remain unchanged. The relative supply of cloth in the world market increases as a result of the growth in Home. Since it is not matched with an equivalent rise in the world relative demand for cloth, the relative price of cloth falls. Moreover, it falls so drastically that the level of real income (I_G) enjoyed by Home after this terms of trade adjustment is lower than real income before growth (I).

For immiserising growth to occur, the following necessary conditions must be met (Bhagwati, 1958):[21]

(1) an economic growth must be very biased in favour of the country's export industry
(2) a growing country must be a large enough actor in the world economy so that the increase in the supply of its export good affects world trading equilibrium
(3) the growth in real income in a country must induce a demand for more imports (high marginal propensity to import)
(4) world (i.e. Foreign) price elasticities of demand for the growing country's export good must be extremely low.

The practical feasibility of immiserising growth is confined to large countries which produce commodities for which demand is inelastic, such as agricultural products, raw materials or some intermediate products. Although some DCs are large producers of these types of products, it is much more likely that a large *developing* country will be affected by immiserising growth.

The theoretical possibility of immiserising growth combined with some empirical findings on the long-term deterioration of the developing countries' terms of trade led to a widespread belief among developing countries governments that growth must be import-biased to be beneficial. Hence many developing countries have experienced two or three decades of the so-called import-substituting strategy of development based on import barriers with investment and other policies being extremely biased towards import-substituting domestic production. Many of these countries unfortunately have not benefited from pursuing this strategy. We examine these issues in detail in Chapter 13. Here we only point out the fact that this strategy of import-biased growth has been advocated across the board to all developing countries, without paying any attention to the crucial assumption on which the welfare-improving effect of this type of growth is based – the size of the country. Only large countries which could influence terms of trade could experience the improvement of the their terms of trade.

☐ Free trade is superior to autarky

We can state the following gains-from-trade theorem:

If a country can trade at world prices which differ from its autarky prices, that is, if $P^A \neq p^T$, then the country is at least as well off under *free trade as under autarky and will be better off unless neither consumption nor production choices are affected by the price changes.*

We shall first prove the theorem and then provide a graphical illustration. Consider first a country under autarky. As shown by (2.2.20) in autarky equilibrium the domestic relative price vector, p^A, is such to equalise aggregate demand, D_A, and aggregate supply, Q_A.

$$D_A = Q_A \qquad (2.7.1)$$

Since the consumer's income arises from the ownership of the output, the expenditure e towards attaining utility u^A is equal to the value of production R:

$$e(p^A, u^A) = R(p^A) \qquad (2.7.2)$$

These two conditions ensure that the consumer maximises welfare while the producer maximises the value of the country's output when the autarky utility level u^A is attained. Given the opportunity to enter free trade, the representative consumer can purchase any consumption vector D^A at world prices p^T given that it is not more expensive than output Q^T at same prices, that is:

$$p^T D^A \leq p^T Q^T \qquad (2.7.3)$$

Naturally, under free trade the representative consumer could choose to consume the same consumption vector as in autarky. But how much would it cost? At world prices the cost of attaining autarkic utility level u^A is *less* than the cost of the autarky consumption vector D^A:

$$e(p^T, u^A) \leq p^T D^A = p^T Q^A \qquad (2.7.4)$$

by (2.7.1).

Similarly the maximum attainable value of output at world prices is certainly as large as the value of autarky production at these world prices since the country can continue to produce what it produced in autarky:

$$p^T Q^A \leq R(p^T) \qquad (2.7.5)$$

As already stated by (2.7.3) under free trade the representative consumer can purchase any bundle with the same value as national income $R(p^T)$. Therefore, the utility level u^T satisfies:

$$R(p^T) = e(p^T, u^T) \qquad (2.7.6)$$

(2.7.4), (2.7.5) and (2.7.6) imply that:

$$e(p^T, u^A) \leq e(p^T, u^T) \tag{2.7.7}$$

The more a consumer spends on goods at fixed prices, the higher welfare is attained. Thus expenditure, e, is an increasing function of utility, u. Therefore (2.7.7) implies that consumer welfare will be at least as high under free trade as under autarky, that is $u^t \geq u^A$. Free trade level of utility will definitely improve over the autarky level if either inequality (2.7.4) or (2.7.5) is strict since then inequality (2.7.7) is also strict, $u^T > u^A$. This will happen if either the production or consumption could alter in accordance with the new signals given by world relative prices. If country is able to relocate its resources under free trade and produce a different bundle so that $Q^A \neq Q^T$, it will be able to enjoy so-called *production gain* from trade because its production increases in value at world prices. Alternatively, if $D^A \neq D^T$ so that consumer benefits from the opportunity to alter the consumption in response to world prices there will be the so-called *consumption gain* from trade. Of course, the gains will be the largest when both production and consumption could alter in view of free trade prices.

Figure 2.21 illustrates the above points. The equilibrium under autarky is given by production and consumption points $D_A = Q^A$, and the utility level attained is U^A. Under free trade the production shifts from Q^A to Q^T which is at prices p^T worth $R(p^T)$. This allows for the expenditure for consumption to be increased so that consumption shifts from D^A to D^T which implies a higher level of utility, u^T. It is obvious from Figure 2.21 that welfare is improved in free trade over autarky. Moreover the distinction between the consumption and production gains from trade is also easy to identify. Given the opportunity to trade at new prices, p^T, even without changing the production bundle, enables this country to achieve higher utility. Any consumption point, such as point D', along relative world price line to the left of (and not including) the point $Q^A = D^A$) will provide this country with higher utility. A further welfare gain is achieved by specialisation in production according to the price signals. With price p^T production moves to Q^T where more of the comparative advantage good F is produced. This increases real income and enables consumer to move to point D^T. In summing up, the total gains from trade $D^A D^T$ can be conceptually divided into the consumption gains, $D^A D'$, and the production gains, $D' D^T$. The above proof of the gains from trade theorem can be extended to the case where the representative consumer sells a vector v of factors to producers in competitive factor markets. We treat these 'factor sales' by consumers as negative purchases of consumption goods and the 'factor purchases' by producers as negative sales of output. In face of prices p^A and factor prices w_A, let $R^*(p^A, w^A)$ be the maximum profits of firms and let $e^*(p^A, w^A, u^A)$ be the minimum expenditure ensuring utility u^A.

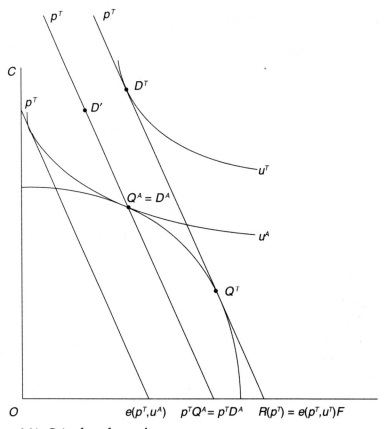

Figure 2.21 *Gains from free trade*

Under free trade the consumer could consume the same consumption vector and supply the same factors as before. Thus, at free trade prices p^T, w^T, the minimum amount $e^*(p^T, w^T, u^A)$ that s/he needs to attain autarky utility level u^A is less than the cost $p^T D^A$ of his/her autarky consumption D^A minus the revenue $w^T v^A$ that would be generated by his/her autarky factor sales v^A.

$$e^*(p^T, w^T, u^A) \leq p^T D^A - w^T v^A = p^T Q^A - w^T v^A \qquad (2.7.4^*)$$

(by 2.7.1).

Similarly at these free trade prices p^T, w^T the maximum profits of firms are certainly as large if they still produce the autarky bundle:

$$p^T Q^A - w^T v^A \leq R^*(p^T, w^T) \qquad (2.7.5^*)$$

Lastly, since the consumer receives all profits, the utility level u^T that can be attained under free trade is given by:

$$R^*(p^T, w^T) = e^*(p^T, w^T, u^T) \tag{2.7.6*}$$

$(2.7.4^*)$, $(2.7.5^*)$ and $(2.7.6^*)$ imply:

$$e^*(p^T, w^T, u^A) \le e^*(p^T, w^T, u^T) \tag{2.7.7*}$$

It follows that $u^A \le u^T$, that is, free trade is superior to autarky.

☐ *Free trade gains with lump-sum transfers*

Let us assume H consumers, indexed by $h = 1, \ldots, H$. From the SST we expect free trade to benefit some consumers and to harm others (by, for example, reducing the returns to the factors they own). In such a case we can describe a system of lump-sum transfers which leaves every consumer as well of under free trade as under autarky. The point is that gainers can be made to compensate the losers. Thus we say free trade has potential to make everyone better off.

Let D^{Ah} and v^{Ah} be consumer h's consumption and factor supply vectors under autarky. Let Q^A and v^A be the aggregate output and factor demand vectors in autarky equilibrium. Then

$$\Sigma D^{Ah} = Q^A \qquad \text{and} \quad \Sigma v^{Ah} = v^A \tag{2.7.8}$$

A country has an opportunity to trade at world prices p^T. Suppose the consumer h receives a lump-sum transfer of income of:

$$T^h = p^T D^{Ah} - w^T v^{Ah} + \{R(p^T, v^T) - w^T v^T - (p^T Q^A - w^T v^A)\}/H$$

where v^T is the aggregate demand for factors and w_T is the vector of factor prices under free trade. The consumer receives sufficient income to finance his or her autarky choices at world prices and in addition receives a share of the 'social surplus' from the move to free trade (note that this social surplus is the difference between maximum profits obtained under free trade and under autarky).

The total transfers are then:

$$\begin{aligned}
\Sigma T^h &= R(p^T, v^T) - w^T v^T - p^T Q^A + w^T v^A + p^T \Sigma D^{Ah} - w^T \Sigma v^{Ah} \\
&= R(p^T, v^T) - w^T v^T
\end{aligned}$$

by (2.7.1).

These transfers merely redistribute the excess of production revenue over factor payments; that is why they are feasible.

We know that autarky production choices (Q^A, v^A) in free trade cannot yield higher profits than the free trade choices (Q^T, v^T). Hence the lump-sum transfers scheme, with v^T and w^T as the free trade factor supplies and factor prices respectively, obtains:

$$R(p^T, v^T) - w^T v^T \geq p^T Q^A - w^T v^A \tag{2.7.10}$$

(2.7.8) and (2.7.9) imply that:

$$T^h \geq p^T Q^{Ah} - w^T v^{Ah} \tag{2.7.11}$$

The lump-sum transfer T^h provides consumer h with a sufficient income to purchase his/her autarky consumption provided that s/he maintains his/her autarky level of factor supplies. His/her optimal choice of consumption and factor supplies under free trade, given the transfers, will be at least as good as his/her autarky choices. Transfers thus leave every consumer as well off as in autarky. Every consumer would be better off if the autarky production revenue was lower than the free trade's so that (2.7.10) and (2.7.11) are strict inequalities.

☐ *Free trade gains without lump-sum transfers*

Lump-sum transfers are not realistically available. Suppose that the gainers can compensate the losers only through the system of taxes and subsidies on goods and factors. We can identify a tax-subsidy system such that no consumer's welfare is worsened by the move from autarky to free trade. This case is also known as Dixit–Norman case, after Dixit and Norman (1980).

In the autarky equilibrium let p^A, w^A be the prices of goods and factors, and let D^{Ah} and v^{Ah} be the choices of consumer h while Q^A, and v^A are the aggregate production and demand for factors. When trade opens we choose commodity and factor taxes so that consumers continue to face prices p^A and w^A even under free trade. We require that they make the same choices and thus attain the same welfare as in autarky. On the other hand we let domestic producers face the world commodity prices p^T and factor prices such to lead them to demand just the quantities v^A which are supplied by consumers in both autarky and free trade. This can be achieved by imposing a vector of commodity taxes $(p^A - p^T)$ as well as factor taxes $(w^T - w^A)$.

Let Q^T be the output vector chosen under this tax scheme. Since both Q^T and Q^A are feasible given factor supplies v^A but Q^T is chosen it must be that:

$$p^T Q^T - w^T v^A \geq p^T Q^A - w^T v^A \tag{2.7.12}$$

By definition of w^T we have that $p^T Q^T = w^T v^A$ so that factor rewards completely exhaust the value of output (note that this is so called Euler's theorem) and we can write:

$$0 \geq p^T Q^A - w^T v^A \tag{2.7.13}$$

The consumers autarky choices satisfy the budget constraint so that:

$$p^A D^{Ab} - w^A v^{Ab} = 0 \tag{2.7.14}$$

The net tax revenue is:

$$(p^A - p^T)\Sigma D^{Ab} + (w^T - w^A)\Sigma v^{Ab} = -p^T \Sigma D^{Ab} + w^T \Sigma v^{Ab}$$
$$= -p^T Q^A + w^T v^A$$
$$\geq 0$$

Each consumer is left with the same consumption and welfare in free trade as under autarky, while the necessary taxes and subsidies produce non-negative revenue collected by the government. In general this revenue can be redistributed to make all customers better off.

■ 2.8 The world trading equilibrium

□ Determination of world prices

Typically we rely on the interaction of demand and supply in determination of price. The world price is no exception. However, since we are more interested in the *relative price* of any good, it is the interplay of the *relative demand* and *relative supply* that will determine such a price. Thus in Figure 2.22 the *RD* and *RS* curves represent world relative demand and relative supply of food as functions of food's relative price. The world price p^T is one that clears both markets for food and for cloth.

An alternative way to illustrate how the world prices are determined is by using the *offer curve*. The offer curve indicates a country's willingness for trade given world prices. More precisely, it indicates the quantity of imports and exports the country is willing to buy and sell at all possible terms of trade.

There are several methods of deriving an offer curve. We will use one that builds on the diagrammatical presentation of an open economy with PPF and social indifference curves. This method is illustrated in Figure 2.23 (a) and (b) where we derive an offer curve for Home. In the part (a) of Figure 2.23 we show Home's trading equilibria for three different terms of trade p_1, p_2, and p_3. As the terms of trade improve from p_1 to p_3, Home's

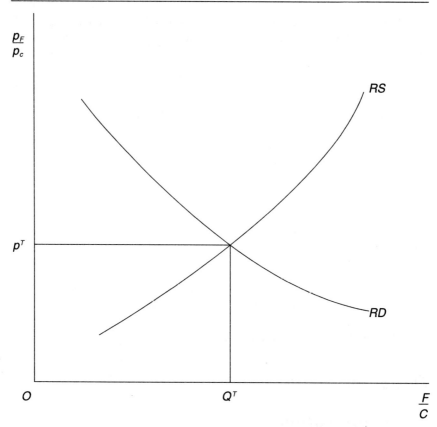

Figure 2.22 *Determination of world price by relative demand and relative supply*

trade volume increases as well. This is represented by larger and larger *trade triangles* whose sides (forming the 90° angle) measure exports and imports at given terms of trade (the slope of the third side). For example, when Home faces terms of trade given by $P_1D_1A_1$ with export of cloth being equal P_1A_1, and import of food equal to A_1D_1. Then when terms of trade improve to p_2, Home specialises even further in the production of cloth, and is willing to trade larger quantities. The trade triangle thus increases to $P_2D_2A_2$.

The information on different trade volumes at different world prices is shown more clearly in part (b) of Figure 2.23 where there is no production and consumption information. Here we consider only quantities of exports and imports. Thus the vertical axis measures Home's exports of cloth while the horizontal axis measures Home's imports of food. The origin in part (b) is treated as the point of production on the PPF in part (a). For instance, prior to trade Home produces at point P_0 where the autarkic

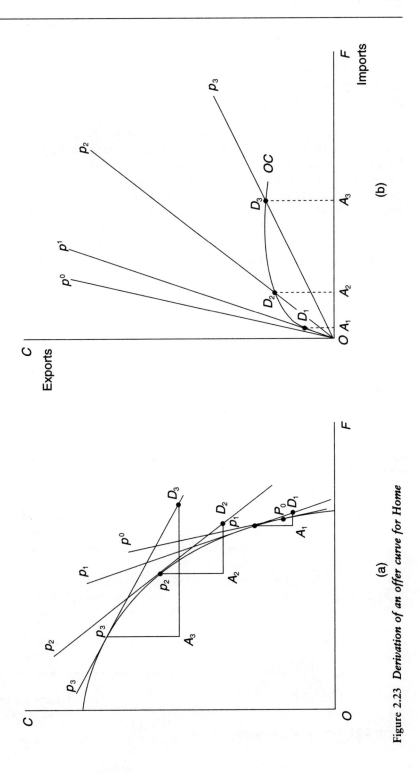

Figure 2.23 *Derivation of an offer curve for Home*

relative price p_0 is tangent to the PPF (part (a)). In part (b) this price line is given by ray p_0 from the origin O which is also both the production and consumption point since Home does not trade. When Home opens for trade at prices p_1, represented by the ray p_1, the exports of cloth $P_1 A_1$ from part (a) is transferred to part (b) as $D_1 A_1$, and the imports $A_1 D_1$ in part (a) are OA_1 in part (b). Thus the first trade triangle in the part (b) is given by $OD_1 A_1$. Next when the terms of trade improve (ray p_2) exports increase to $A_2 D_2$ and imports adequately to OA_2 giving the trade triangle $OD_2 A_2$. Following similar steps, point D_3 is obtained. Joining the origin with points D_1, D_2 and D_3 we generate Home's offer curve. It shows how much cloth Home is *willing* to export in order to obtain various quantities of imported food. It goes without saying that if either production or consumption in Home changes, its offer curve would change in a sense of having different shape and/or position in the cloth-food space.

The offer curve of the Foreign country is derived in a similar manner. It shows Foreign's willingness to export food in exchange for various quantities of imported cloth, at given world prices. Figure 2.24 brings both countries' offer curves together and shows how world equilibrium relative price is determined.

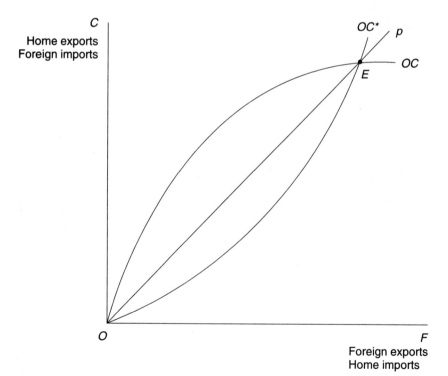

Figure 2.24 *The world trading equilibrium*

Point *E* where the offer curves intersect is the *trading equilibrium* where both markets are cleared: the quantity of cloth that Home country wishes to export equals the quantity of cloth that Foreign country wishes to import, and the quantity of food that Home wants to import equals the quantity of food that Foreign wants to export. The ray going through the origin and point *E*, *p*, is thus the equilibrium relative price or equilibrium relative price or equilibrium terms of trade.

☐ *Stability of the trading equilibrium*

In Figure 2.24 the trading equilibrium *E* is *stable*. We can check that by looking at the changes in quantities demanded and supplied if some other than equilibrium terms of trade *p* prevail. Assume thus in Figure 2.25, panel (a), that the world relative price is given by terms of trade p_1 so that now cloth is relatively more expensive in terms of food. At these terms of trade there would be an excess demand for food in the amount of *XY*, because Foreign would be willing to export less while Home would wish to buy more of food than at the previous terms of trade. Similarly there will be an excess supply of cloth in the amount of $X'Y'$. Thus the relative price of food will have to increase until markets clear again which would happen, given the offer curves, at *p*. The equilibrium is thus stable if an increase in the relative price of a good (in our example, cloth) reduces world excess demand for this good, cloth. The equilibrium in point *E* is not only stable but also is the only one which could exist given the offer curves of the countries. The equilibrium is not always a unique stable equilibrium. Consider panel (b) of Figure 2.25 where the shape of the offer curves indicates that something 'funny' is going on with the elasticities of demand and supply. Assume that the terms of trade are given by p_1. Amount *ZX* then indicates the excess of Foreign country import demand for cloth over Home county's export supply for cloth. Thus the relative price of cloth has to rise until a stable point is found at point *E*. Another stable equilibrium is illustrated by point *G*.

What determines the stability of world equilibrium? In other words, what are the conditions sufficient to guarantee that when the relative price of a good rises, the excess demand for it will fall? The answer is in the so-called *Marshall–Lerner condition* which stipulates that the equilibrium will be stable if the sum of the two countries' elasticities of demand for imports exceeds unity:

$$\varepsilon + \varepsilon^* < 1$$

where $\varepsilon(\varepsilon^*)$ is the elasticity of Home (Foreign) demand for imports.

The proof of this condition for the case of two countries, Home and Foreign, producing two goods, cloth and food, follows. The proof focuses on the responses of each country's demand for imports to the changes in

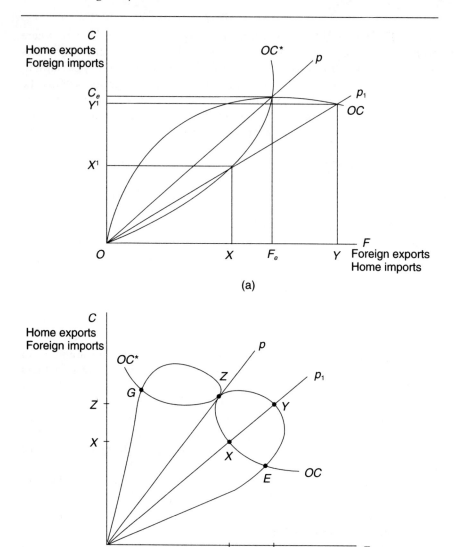

Figure 2.25   *Stability of the world equilibrium*

world price. Stability, as stated above, requires that if the relative price of cloth rises, the world excess demand for cloth drops. The world excess demand of cloth is the difference between Foreign country excess demand for cloth, M^* and Home country supply of cloth. Of course, exports of cloth by Home has an equivalent in imports of food by Home, M/p. Therefore $(M^* - M/p)$ must decrease as p rises. This can be written as:

$$dM^*/dp < d(M/p)/dp \tag{2.8.2}$$

or in terms of relative changes (see Caves, Frankel and Jones, 1993, p. 625):

$$\hat{M}^*/\hat{p} < (\widehat{M/p})/\hat{p} \tag{2.8.3}$$

But $\hat{M}^*/\hat{p}$ is nothing else than the coefficient of Foreign demand for imports ε^*, multiplied by -1, while $(\widehat{M/p})/\hat{p}$ could be written as:

$$(\widehat{M/p})/\hat{p} = \hat{M}/(\widehat{1/p}) = \hat{M}/\hat{p} \tag{2.8.4}$$

or the Home's elasticity of import demand multiplied by -1, ε. Finally by substituting ε and ε^* in the expression for stability we arrive at:

$$\varepsilon^* < \varepsilon - 1 \tag{2.8.5}$$

or

$$\varepsilon^* + \varepsilon > 1 \tag{2.8.6}$$

which is the Marshall–Lerner condition.

■ 2.9 Summary

This chapter covered what has been considered as 'the core' trade theory – the factor endowments based comparative advantage. We started by examining the role of factor endowments on production choices in a closed economy. The fact that a country is able to produce relatively more of a commodity in whose production relatively abundant factor of production is used *intensively*, can easily be extended to include trade. Thus a country will then tend to export those goods that are intensive in the factors in abundant supply. This conclusion is known as the HOT. We then discussed the relationship between relative commodity and factor prices under free trade by deriving two theorems: the FPE theorem, and the SST. The FPE theorem claims that, under certain assumptions, with free trade the complete equalisation of relative commodity prices will result in a complete equalisation of the factor prices. In reality of course we expect only a convergence of factor prices. The SST is a valuable tool for the examination of the income distributional effects of trade. We have shown that free trade may result in some factor-owners being hurt by adverse changes in their factor's reward. But we also showed that despite these strong distributional effects, trade can potentially make everyone better off compared to autarky. We also discussed links between the changes in factor supply and the structure of production (the Rybczynski theorem), the factor accumulation or growth and trade, and the possibility of the immiserising growth. Lastly, we discussed the conditions for the stability of trading equilibrium. Appendices of this chapter provide some extensions by introducing the possibility of factor intensity or demand reversals and of the complete specialisation in production.

APPENDIX 2A
FACTOR-INTENSITY REVERSALS

The Samuelson intensity condition eliminates the possibility of industries reversing their choices of factor requirements when factor prices change. This condition is necessary for the Heckscher–Ohlin theorem (HOT) and the factor-price equalisation (FPE) theorem to hold. In this Appendix we show why a factor-intensity reversal could result in the failure of these theorems.

A factor-intensity reversal refers to the state where one industry uses different factor intensities at different relative factor prices, so that one good, relative to another good, is classified as capital-intensive at one set of factor prices, and as labour-intensive at another set of factor prices. Figure 2.26 demonstrates such a case. We have two isoquants, one for each industry, food and cloth. Isoquants are characterised by a technology which permits reversals. Basically we allow the elasticities of substitution between factors for the two industries to be sufficiently different.[22] When this is the case the isoquants do not intersect only once as in the non-reversal case (recall Figure 2.2(a)). Instead they are tangential to each other, as drawn in Figure 2.26, or, alternatively, they intersect twice (which can be easily shown if the food isoquant is shifted towards the origin as in Figure 2.28, p. 121).

At the relative factor price given by ω_0 the two industries use factors in the same proportion k_r, which is depicted by the slope of the ray Or. This ray is known as the factor-intensity-reversal ray since it divides the factor space into two regions: in the region to the left of the ray the cloth industry will be capital-intensive relative to the food industry at any factor prices $\omega_1 > \omega_0$. In contrast, in the region to the right of the ray the factor intensities of these two industries will be reversed so that food will be capital-intensive relative to cloth for any $\omega_2 < \omega_0$. In this situation it is impossible to classify goods unequivocally by factor intensities.

The implications of this for the HOT are easily established. Recall that the HOT explicitly states that each country exports the good that is produced by using relatively intensively the factor that is in relative abundance in that country. With factor-intensity reversals the structure of trade need not always coincide with the theorem's predictions. Imagine, for example, that the PPFs for Home and Foreign are like those depicted in Figure 2.27 – the PPF for Home, TT, is almost linear, while the Foreign

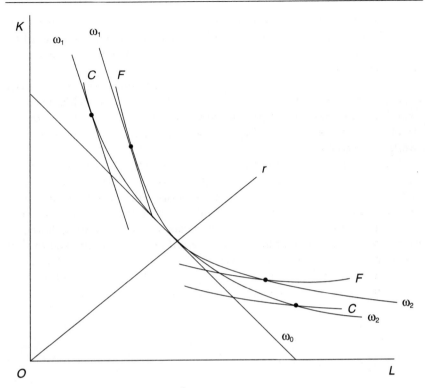

Figure 2.26 *Factor-intensity reversals*

PPF, T^*T^*, is more concave.[23] When the PPFs differ sufficiently in shape they will intersect twice, as in Figure 2.27. We assume that Home is relatively capital-abundant compared to Foreign. Retaining our assumption about the factor intensities of goods we would expect Home to export cloth to Foreign in exchange for food. To determine whether the pattern of trade between Home and Foreign indeed reflects the prediction of the HOT, we first draw a ray from the origin, OR. Along this ray the proportions of cloth to food produced in each country are the same, and we can thus test for the autarkic goods prices. The Home production point is thus point P_R while Foreign's is point P^*_R. The price lines tangential at these points are p_R in Home and p^*_R in Foreign. Since $p^*_R < p_R$ Foreign has a comparative advantage in food, and Home has a comparative advantage in cloth. In this case, therefore, the HOT holds. But to have general validity the theorem should also hold for any other pair of autarkic prices. That this is not the case can be demonstrated by drawing another ray, OS. This ray determines the autarkic production points to be P_S in Home and P^*_S in Foreign. The respective autarkic prices p_S and p^*_S are such that Home ends up with a comparative advantage in food, and Foreign with a comparative advantage in cloth ($p_S < p^*_S$). The pattern of trade is therefore exactly opposite to what the HOT would predict. This makes it clear that if the theorem holds for one situation it cannot hold for the other. Thus, in general, we cannot prove the HOT in the presence of factor-intensity reversals.

As we would expect, a factor-intensity reversal upsets factor-price equalisation as well. This can be seen from Figure 2.28 which is basically the same as Figure 2.26 except that in this diagram the isoquants are drawn so as to intersect. Because they intersect twice, there will be two non-overlapping cones of diversification.

There are now two possible iso-cost lines tangent to both isoquants allowing the production of both goods. If countries' overall factor endowments are in different cones, factor-price equalisation is impossible. For instance, Home's overall factor endowment ratio could be given by k in the cone defined by k_C and k_F with a factor price ratio of ω. Foreign's overall factor endowment ratio is then given by k^* in the cone defined by k^*_C and k^*_F with factor prices given by ω^*. Obviously $\omega^* < \omega$. Therefore,

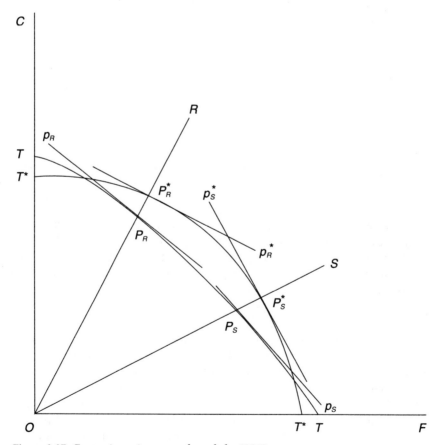

Figure 2.27 *Factor-intensity reversals and the HOT*

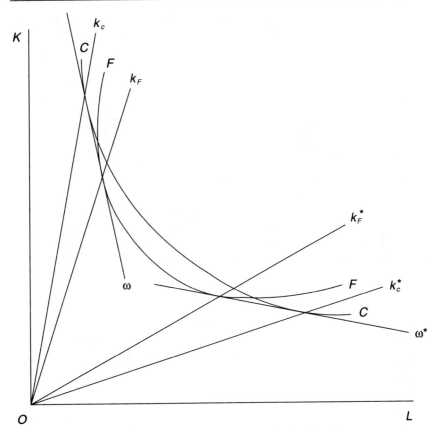

Figure 2.28 A *factor-intensity reversal and the factor-price equalisation*

in this example, factor prices are not equalised. However it is apparent that in this case factor-price equalisation is not ruled out even with factor-intensity reversals. Depending on the location of the overall factor endowment ratios of the two countries, factor-price equalisation is possible. If both countries' factor endowment ratios happen to lie within one of the cones of diversification, goods can be uniquely classified in terms of factor intensities, and factor prices will be equalised.

The case where the factor-price equalisation is violated in the presence of factor-intensity reversals may also be shown using the duality concepts developed in section 2.2. Let us assume that the two iso-price curves corresponding to the free trade prices of cloth and food intersect twice, at points E and F in Figure 2.29. The reason for this is the lower elasticity of factor substitution in the food industry (its iso-price curve is much lower than the cloth industry's iso-price curve). If Home's factor endowment ratio lies between the lines that measure the slopes of the iso-price curves

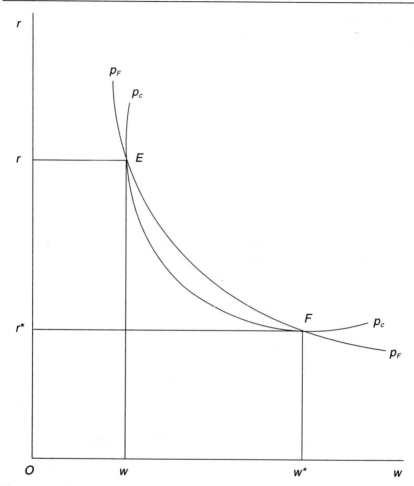

Figure 2.29 *Iso-price curves and factor-intensity reversal*

at point E, under free trade it will move to point E with wage and capital rentals being equal to w and r for both industries. If, on the other hand, Foreign's factor endowment ratio is much lower and lies in the area between the lines measuring the slopes of the iso- price curves at point F, that economy will move to point F under free trade. Foreign's factor prices will then be w^* and r^*, obviously different from Home's factor prices. In summary, then, it should be noted that the existence of factor-intensity reversals creates serious problems for both the Heckscher–Ohlin and the factor-price equalisation theorems. In other words, it could lead to declaring two of the core propositions of the HOS model (generally) invalid. This would certainly be the case if factor-intensity reversals were widely prevalent in the real world. Empirical studies undertaken with the aim of determining the frequency of factor-intensity reversals are not numerous, with almost all of them dating back to the 1960's.[24] These studies concluded that factor- intensity reversal is not a common occurrence. They further concluded that factor-intensity reversals are probably not the reason for either the existence of trade patterns that are inconsistent with the HOT or the non-existence of factor-price equalisation between trading economies in the real world. We shall say more about the empirical testing of the HOS model and its core propositions in Chapter 6.

■ *APPENDIX 2B* DEMAND REVERSALS

Tastes and preferences are assumed to be identical and homothetic in the HOS model even though it is not always necessary. This assumption was required, as shown, for the determination of the autarkic relative prices of goods. Since countries are assumed to produce goods in different proportions, by assuming that the same proportions of goods are demanded by all consumers in both countries, we obtain different autarkic relative prices which then serve as the basis for trade.

However it is also possible to imagine consumers in different countries having different tastes, that is, demanding goods in significantly different proportions. This is known as *demand reversal*. The problems that could arise from demand reversal are described with the help of Figure 2.30. Part (a) of Figure 2.30 illustrates the situation in Home, while part (b) refers to Foreign. The PPFs of the two countries are drawn in such way so as to reveal each country's relative factor abundance defined on the basis of *physical* quantities of factors. Therefore we have capital-abundant Home's PPF having a longer intercept with the cloth axis than with the food axis; the opposite case is shown for Foreign. With these differences occurring on the production side we would expect Home to export cloth and Foreign to export food *provided* that both goods are consumed in the same proportion in both countries. However the indifference curves for these two countries reveal that consumers in Home strongly prefer cloth relative to food, and the consumers in Foreign have strong preferences for food relative to cloth. The interaction of supply and demand results in the autarkic relative prices p_F/p_C in Home and p^*_F/p^*_C in Foreign. From the slopes of these price lines it is obvious that Home's autarkic relative price of food is lower than Foreign's $(p_F/p_C) < (p^*_F/p^*_C)$, leading the capital-abundant Home to *export* the labour-intensive good, food. The same applies to Foreign, which finds itself in the position of exporting the capital-intensive good, cloth, despite being the labour-abundant country.

The pattern of trade shown in Figure 2.30 is therefore exactly opposite to the one predicted by the HOT based on the physical definition of factor abundance – the capital-abundant country is not exporting capital-intensive goods, while the labour-abundant country is not importing them. If, however, the price definition of factor abundance is used, Home's

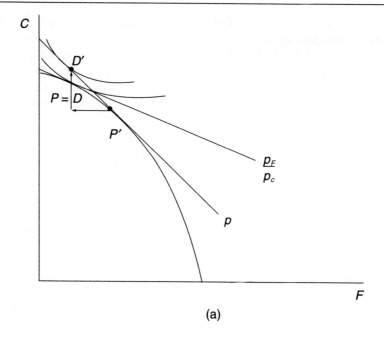

(a)

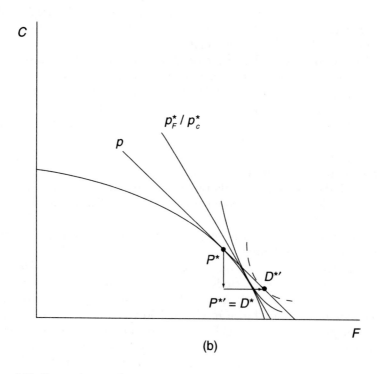

(b)

Figure 2.30 *Demand reversals*

abundant factor becomes labour, while Foreign's abundant factor is capital. This results from the very strong biases in demand in each country which in turn increase commodity and factor prices in such a way as to cause labour to be relatively cheap in Home. In this situation we have the relatively abundant factor, labour, intensively used in the food industry in Home forming the basis for this country's comparative advantage. Therefore this price-version of the HOT would predict that Home, having a comparative advantage in food, would export food, while Foreign, having a comparative advantage in cloth, would export cloth. This is exactly what we find in Figure 2.30.

How important is the case of demand reversals between countries in the real world? The empirical studies on demand patterns show that the strongest demand similarity is between countries that belong to a relatively homogeneous group of countries. Thus, for instance, the DCs of Europe (say the EU countries) will have fairly similar patterns of demand. Even a less homogeneous group of DCs, as Table 2.1 illustrates, shows a high degree of similarity in the structure of consumption. In general this table shows a higher degree of similarity than dissimilarity in the demand structures of the countries that belong to the same income group.

APPENDIX 2C   COMPLETE SPECIALISATION IN PRODUCTION

One of the implicit assumptions used in developing the $2 \times 2 \times 2$ HOS model was the incomplete specialisation in production with or without trade. This is in contrast to the Ricardian model where the existence of constant opportunity costs led countries to completely specialise in production once they opened their economies. The assumption of incomplete specialisation however is more realistic in the sense that most of the countries actually engaged in international trade are not fully specialised. Most of them, apart from some natural resource producers/exporters, do not even have strongly concentrated production. Nevertheless there are several reasons why, at least theoretically, complete specialisation could occur.

One reason for complete specialisation can be found when there are large similarities between two industries in terms of their factor requirements. As already mentioned in Box 2.1, where we discussed the shape of the PPF, a small difference in factor intensities between the food and cloth industries, *ceteris paribus*, will make the PPF less concave. In Figure 2.31 the PPF is almost linear, that is, the opportunity cost of cloth in terms of food is close to constant.

Table 2.1   *The structure of consumption*

	Food	Cloths & Footwear	Rent, Fuel, Power	Medical Care	Education	Transport & Commun.	Other Durable Goods
	Percentage share of total household consumption						
Low-income economies							
India	52	11	10	3	4	7	13
Indonesia	48	7	13	2	4	4	22
Egypt	50	11	9	3	6	4	18
Kenya	39	7	12	3	9	8	22
Zaire	55	10	11	3	1	6	14
Lower middle-income economies							
Philippines	51	4	19	2	4	4	16
Thailand	30	16	7	5	5	13	24
Turkey	40	15	7	4	1	5	22
Poland	29	9	7	6	7	8	34
Chile	29	8	13	5	6	11	29
Upper-middle income economies							
Mexico	35	10	8	5	5	12	25
Brazil	35	10	11	6	5	8	27
Hungary	25	9	10	5	7	9	35
Portugal	34	10	8	6	5	13	24
Korea, Rep.	35	6	11	5	9	9	25
High-income economies							
France	16	6	17	13	7	13	29
Germany	12	7	18	13	6	13	31
Japan	16	6	17	10	8	9	34
New Zealand	12	6	14	9	6	19	34
United States	13	6	18	14	8	14	27

Note: Components may not add to 100 per cent for each country because of rounding.
Source: World Bank (1992), Table 10, pp. 236–7.

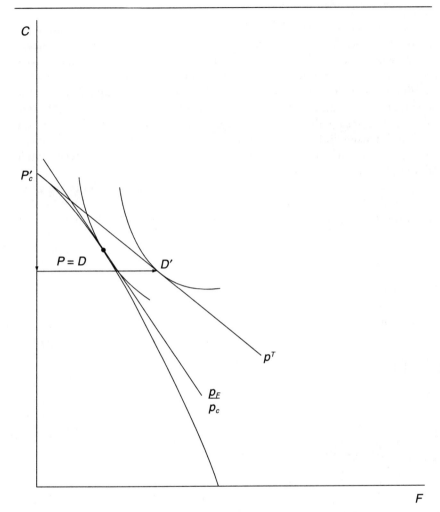

Figure 2.31 *Complete specialisation on the basis of similar factor intensities – Home*

In Figure 2.31, which represents the autarky situation in, for example, Home, the production point, *P*, is determined by the autarkic relative price p_F/p_C. Suppose that the world relative price of food is only slightly lower (that is, the relative price of cloth is just a bit higher) as shown by the price line p^T. This world price will induce Home (Home's producers) to completely specialise in the production of cloth at the point P'_C. The consumption point D' is reached through the exchange of some cloth for food. This consumption point implies gains from trade for this country. Note that the other country need not be specialised in food for trade to take place or for gains from trade to be realised by both countries.

Another possible reason for complete specialisation can be found when there are large differences in factor endowments between two countries. This was mentioned in passing when we discussed the factor-price equalisation theorem and the assumptions required for its validity.

When countries' capital–labour ratios are too far apart, given the assumption of same technologies, their PPFs will have very different shapes. Supposing that Home is capital-abundant, and that cloth is the capital-intensive industry, this very large difference in factor compositions is represented in Figure 2.32 where Home's PPF is very steep, while Foreign's PPF is very flat.

Their respective autarky production-cum-consumption points are given by P and P^*. The price lines tangent to the PPF at each of these points indicate that Home should export cloth and Foreign should export food.

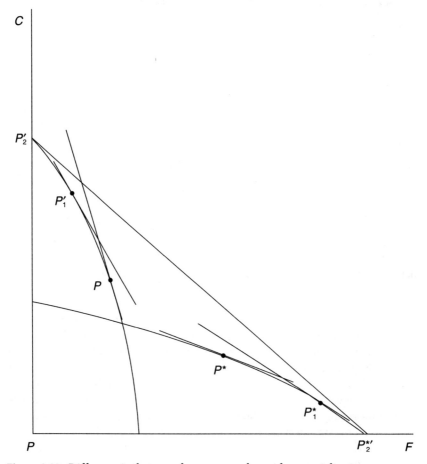

Figure 2.32 *Difference in factor endowments and complete specialisation*

We now allow each of these countries to start producing more of the export good (simultaneously decreasing their production of the other good because of the fixed PPF). As each country produces more of the export good its opportunity cost in terms of the other good increases. Normally these opportunity costs would equalise in both countries before either country could reach the point of complete specialisation. However in Figure 2.32, because of the way the PPFs are drawn, each country completely specialises before the relative prices of goods are equalised. Note that, as in the case above, only one country can end up being completely specialised.

■ *APPENDIX 2D* THE SAMUELSON RECIPROCITY CONDITION

Having established the Stolper–Samuelson theorem (SST) and the Rybczynski theorem it is relatively easy to show that these theorems are *duals* of each other. With cloth being a capital-intensive good then, if an increase in the price of cloth lowers wages, an increase in the labour force (at constant prices) would lower the output of cloth. We recognise the first part of this statement as the Stolper–Samuelson result, and the second part as the Rybczynski result. Put together they imply the Samuelson *reciprocity condition* which states that the effect of an increase in a commodity price on a factor return is exactly the same as the effect of an increase in the corresponding factor endowment on the output of that commodity. This duality between the price and endowment effects is the basic feature of the general equilibrium model.

To prove this dual relationship we follow Ethier (1984, p. 133). The national income function (2.2.13) is rewritten to reflect the fact that production possibilities depend on the availability of factors of production as well:

$$Y = Y(p_C, p_F; K, L) \tag{2.A.1}$$

There are two interpretations of (2.A.1). It can be defined as the maximal income an economy can achieve when facing the commodity prices p_C and p_F, and if the factor endowments are given as K and L. Alternatively, it can be defined as the minimum payments to the factors of production K and L, given that each factor must be paid the value of its marginal product p_C and p_F. Thus (2.A.1) can be also written as:

$$Y = p_C Q_C + p_F Q_F \tag{2.A.1a}$$
$$Y = wL + rK \tag{2.A.1b}$$

Using the definition of Y implied in (2.A.1a) and differentiating Y with respect to each commodity price, yields

$$\partial Y/\partial p_C = Q_C + [p_C(dQ_C/dp_C) + p_F(dQ_F/dp_C)] = Q_C$$
$$\partial Y/\partial p_F = Q_F + [p_F(dQ_FF) + p_C(dQ_C/dp_F)] = Q_F$$

(2.A.2)

where the second terms vanish as a condition of maximisation.
We next differentiate (2.A.1b) with respect to factor endowments to obtain:

$$\partial Y/\partial L = w + [L(dw/dL) + K(dr/dL)] = w$$
$$\partial Y/\partial K = r + [K(dr/dK) + L(dw/dK)] = r$$

(2.A.3)

Finally, differentiating (2.A.2) with respect to each factor, V_j, where $j = L$, K, and (2.A.3) with respect to each commodity price, p_i, where $i = C, F$ yields:

$$\partial^2 Y/\partial p_i \partial V_j = \partial Q_i/\partial V_j$$
$$\partial^2 Y/\partial V_j \partial p_i = \partial v_j/\partial p_i$$

(2.A.4)

where v_j stands for the factor prices and Q_i stands for outputs. Since the left-hand side terms of (2.A.4) are the same, we can write:

$$\partial v_j/\partial p_i = \partial Q_i/\partial V_j$$

(2.A.5)

which is the reciprocity condition saying that the change in a commodity price produces the same effect on a factor reward as a change in the endowment of that factor would produce upon this commodity output. Therefore (2.A.5) links together the SST and the Rybczynski theorem.

■ *Chapter 3* ■

The Augmented Heckscher–Ohlin–Samuelson Model

■ *3.1* Introduction

Despite its 'twoness' (that is, its $2 \times 2 \times 2$ dimensions), the standard HOS model has been typically used in making fairly general statements about the open economy. However these general results are strongly dependent on the assumptions of the free and costless mobility of factors between sectors and their total lack of international mobility, assumptions that are clearly not plausible in the short run. Work on the consequences of a lack of internal factor mobility for the core propositions of the HOS model resumed about two decades ago. On the basis of contributions by Jones (1971), Samuelson (1971), Mayer (1974), Mussa (1974) and Neary (1978) the so-called *specific-factors model* emerged.[1] This model is examined in the next section.

Other models concerned with factor specificity or immobility have also been developed. Two, known as *Krueger's model* (Krueger, 1977) and the *Neighbourhood model* (Jones and Kierzkowski, 1986) are presented in section 3.3. Finally the work which has aimed at increasing the dimensions of the standard HOS model beyond the $2 \times 2 \times 2$ level is summarised in section 3.4. Appendix 3 focuses on an interesting phenomenon known as 'Dutch disease'.

■ *3.2* The specific-factors model

There are many different reasons for the lack of perfect factor mobility between national industries. Factors may have a preference for employment in some sectors, or may even have some preference for specific activities within a sector, as opposed to employment opportunities in other sectors. This is known as *preferential specificity* and usually generates differentiated factor rewards. Limited factor mobility thus becomes a prerequisite for non-specialised production.

Factor immobility may also be policy-imposed. For instance foreign labour could be restricted to working only within particular sectors of the national economy. Alternatively immigration policy may stipulate that foreign factors may be employed only if there are no available domestic factors capable of performing the job. In other cases political considerations may overpower all other considerations so that differentiation of labour which leads to its sectoral immobility could be made, for example, on the basis of political party membership as in the former communist countries.

The most likely reason, however, for factor immobility lies in factors' aptitudes: some factors may have a 'comparative advantage' or the *specialised skills* required to produce some goods but not others. For example, the physical capital installed to produce cars could be hardly seen as appropriate to produce cloth (that is, at least in the short run). Similarly, the human capital currently employed in formulating, say, new trade theories cannot be instantaneously transferred for use as trade negotiators. This 'narrow' specialisation is usually behind the factor immobility used in the specific-factors model which we discuss next.[2]

The basic structure of the specific-factors model is rather simple. There are two sectors, cloth (C) and food (F), and three factors: (1) labour, which is mobile between these two sectors, (2) cloth capital (K_C) which is specific to the cloth sector, and (3) food capital (K_F) which is specific to the food sector. In the short run, neither type of specific capital can move across sectors. Rather each type of capital must first be depreciated in one sector before it may be 're-employed' in the other. This is the only difference in the structure of the specific-factors model and the structure of the HOS model where all (both) factors were perfectly mobile between national industries. In all other aspects the analytical structure of the two models is identical.

The economy above is illustrated in terms of a box diagram which could also be used to derive the production possibility frontier. Figure 3.1 is the Edgeworth box in the context of the specific-factors model. The total endowment of mobile labour is given by the length of the box, $O_C O_C' = O_F O_F'$. The vertical distance $O_C \bar{K}_C$ represents the quantity of capital employable only by the cloth sector. No matter what quantity of cloth is in fact produced, this fixed amount of capital is allocated for use in the cloth sector only. Similarly, the fixed amount of capital $O_F \bar{K}_F$ is used only by the food sector. All solutions with full employment of both types of specific capital must therefore lie on the horizontal line. In the specific-factors model this line is thus the contract curve. In comparison the $\bar{K}_C E G \bar{K}_F$ contract curve of the typical HOS economy would be $O_C E O_F$. If initially the economy produces an amount of cloth and food given by point E in Figure 3.1, any attempt to produce more of either cloth or food will lead to a movement along the horizontal line $\bar{K}_C EGK\bar{}_F$ and to the reallocation of labour between the two sectors. Assume, for example, that more cloth is wanted. This can be accomplished only by using more labour in combination with a fully utilised quantity of specialised capital K_C. This leads to some point to the right of point E, such as point G. Note that this point reflects an increase in the production of cloth $(C_2 > C_1)$, and a reduction in the production of food $(F_2 < F_1)$, which is the trade-off we normally expect. However the amount of cloth produced is less in this specific-factor economy than it would be in the non-specific-factor economy (point J on isoquant C_3). This means that the lack of mobility of cloth-specific capital forces this economy off its long-run contract curve on to the short-run contract curve. The important feature of this contract curve is that it is in fact the locus of the *intersecting rather than the tangential* points of the two sectors' isoquants: points at which the marginal rate of transformation in the two sectors are *not* equal (except at point E). The allocation of resources along this contract curve therefore means a loss in the output of both goods as compared with the long-run (*efficient*) allocation.

From Figure 3.1 it is evident that there is only *one* point common to both contract curves, point E. The PPFs representing the specific and non-specific factor cases will therefore correspond at one point only. This point is given in Figure 3.2 by point E'. In this figure the PPF labelled $HE'S$ is associated with the 'long-run' contract curve O_CEO_F typical for the HOS

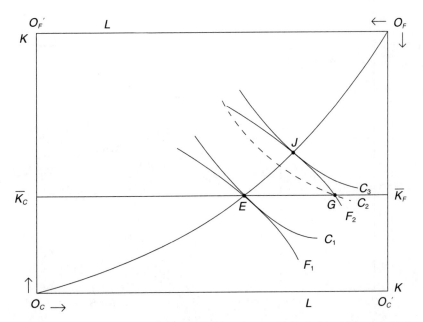

Figure 3.1   *Specific factors in the Edgeworth box*

assumptions of perfect factor mobility. The PPF labelled $ME'N$ is the one reflecting the horizontal contract curve of the specific-factors model. This locus, along which we trace the production possibilities in the *short run*, lies inside the long-run PPF (except for point E') because it is more difficult to transform food into cloth, or vice versa, in the short run given the immobility of both types of specific capital.

The difference between the long run and short run can be clearly seen when an economy opens to free trade. Suppose that initially Home produces at point E' and that the world relative price is given as p^T. In the short run, when capital is immobile, Home can adjust to the opening of the economy only by reallocating labour. Consequently Home's production combination will change from E' to the one given by point E^T on the $ME'N$ locus. E^T is the short-run equilibrium *off* the efficiency contract curve. Only through time, as capital is being scrapped from the food industry and new investment is made in the cloth industry, can Home actually move to the $HE'S$ locus at point E^{T*}.

Both the short-run and the long-run consumption points with free trade $(D^T$ and $D^{T*})$ lie, as expected, outside the PPFs. Home as a whole has certainly benefited from free trade, although less so in the short run than in

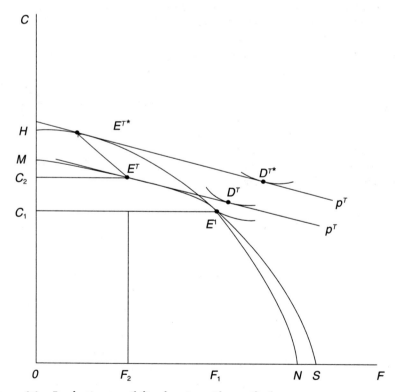

Figure 3.2 *Production possibility frontier with specific factors*

the long run when factors are fully reallocated with respect to marginal productivities. However particular factors experience different welfare changes in the short and long runs. These changes will be discussed in detail in the next section. Here we will just outline the main points. In the long run *all* capital, irrespective of the sector in which it is installed, will benefit from free trade because the relative price of the capital-intensive good, cloth, has risen. In the short run only the capital installed in the cloth sector will gain; the food-specific capital will experience an absolute loss in rents. This model therefore explains why the owners of the food-specific capital are likely to oppose a move to free trade even though it could enhance their returns in the long run. As the specific-factors model may be seen as a more accurate description of the short-run responses in an economy it has provided a framework for studying the dynamic *adjustment* process and stability, as well as adjustment costs (Neary, 1978; Mussa, 1982). In fact the specific-factors model has become an indispensable tool for analysing a variety of trade policy issues.

The second important feature of the specific-factors model is that all factor prices are not equalised between sectors. While wages will be the same in the two sectors since labour can move freely and costlessly between them, the returns to specific factors, except in the one case shown by point *E* in Figure 3.1, will differ across sectors.

To facilitate further discussion on labour allocation, factor returns, and income distribution it is helpful to invoke the U-shaped diagrammatic representation of the specific-factors model used in Mussa (1974). Such a diagram reflecting the autarky equilibrium in, say, Home is given in Figure 3.3. The total amount of labour available to the Home economy is given by the distance $O_C O_F$. The wage rate for the cloth sector is measured along the vertical axis from the origin O_C, and for the food sector along the vertical axis from O_F. The curves $VMPL_C$ and $VMPL_F$ reflect the *value of the marginal product of labour* for each level of labour employment in the two sectors:

$$VMPL_C = p_C MPL_C$$
$$VMPL_F = p_F MPL_F$$

(3.2.1)

where p denotes commodity prices and MPL represents the marginal product of labour. These two curves are drawn with reference to their respective sector origins. Both curves slope downwards, reflecting the fact that the marginal product of labour in each sector declines as more labour is added to a fixed quantity of the specific factor. The position of the curves depends on the technology used in the production of cloth and food, the commodity prices, and the amount of the specific capital in each sector. Higher commodity prices with a fixed amount of factors or a larger amount of specific factors at fixed commodity prices and a fixed

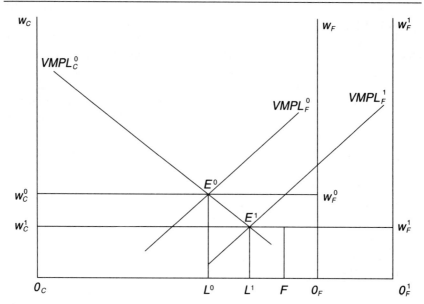

Figure 3.3   *Labour allocation in the specific-factors model*

amount of labour will move the *VMPL* curve upwards. Suppose that the initial situation in Home is described by the curves $VMPL_C{}^0$ and $VMPL_F{}^0$. The equilibrium allocation of labour is determined by the intersection of these curves. Only this allocation of labour equalises the wage rates between the two sectors and we know that perfect labour mobility will not allow for any wage differential. Thus at point E_0 we have:

$$p_C MPL_C = p_F MPL_F = w \qquad (3.2.2)$$

The returns to cloth capital and food capital are given by the triangular areas above this wage rate and below the respective VMPL curve. In general we would expect these returns to differ.

Figure 3.3 could also be used to show another feature of the specific-factors model not shared by the HOS model. We refer to the equalisation of factor prices due to free trade. In the HOS model free trade equalises relative commodity prices which then leads to the equalisation of absolute and relative factor prices. In the presence of specific factors this will not necessarily happen. To see this, assume that Foreign is endowed with equal amounts of labour and food-specific capital but has more cloth-specific capital than Home. When these two countries are opened to trade commodity prices will equalise. However even with identical commodity prices, due to a higher K_C/L ratio the Foreign $VMPL_C$ curve will be positioned above Home's $VMPL_C$. Consequently free trade will fail to equalise factor prices across countries; the wage rate will be higher and the rentals to both types of specific capital lower in Foreign than in Home. In general, whenever we have more factors than goods, commodity prices are not sufficient to determine factor prices. The presence of specific factors may thus serve to explain some of the deviations from the predictions of the HOS model. However, while trade does not equalise factor prices it is likely that it will push them closer together. As will be discussed later the specific-factors model may also explain the observation that some countries export goods that would seem to run counter to their comparative advantage.

☐ *Factors and commodity prices*

One of the properties of the specific-factors model is that it shows a different factor price–commodity price relationship from the Stolper–Samuelson theorem (SST) type of relationships in the HOS model proper. This theorem states that an increase in the relative price of a good will unambiguously increase the real return to the factor used intensively in the production of that good, while the real return to the other factor will be reduced in terms of both goods. The effect of an increase in the relative price of a good in the specific-factors model can be analysed in terms of Figure 3.4. Let us assume that the improved terms of trade shift the $VMPL_C$ curve proportionally upwards to the level of $VMPL_C^1$. At the new equilibrium at point E^1, (1) more labour is now engaged in the production of cloth than before ($L_1 > L_0$), and (2) the money wage for all labour has increased from w^0 to w^1. From the previous analysis we know that this also means a larger output of cloth, and a smaller output of food. But how are the rewards to other factors affected? That is what has happened to the returns to cloth- and food-specific capital, and what has happened to real wages?

As labour shifts from the food sector to the cloth sector, each unit of cloth-specific capital has more labour to work with, and its marginal productivity rises. Since a factor's marginal productivity is identical to the reward to that factor (under our assumptions of perfect competition), this means that cloth-specific capital earns more in terms of cloth and food. Analogously food-specific capital must be earning less in terms of both goods. The real reward to labour is not so easy to obtain. In terms of food, the price of which has not changed, labour now earns more. However in terms of cloth labours' real wages have dropped.

We can use the relations (2.5.1) – (2.5.6) from Chapter 2 to express the relationship between commodity and factor prices more elegantly. The factor-price equations for the cloth and food industry in the specific-factors model have the same form as in the HOS model except that there are two rentals to the capital, r_C and r_F:

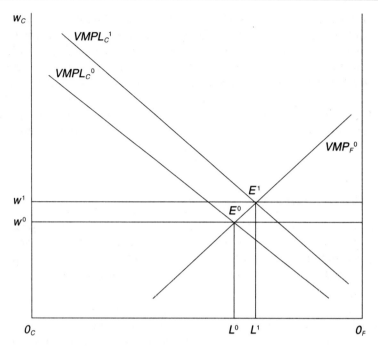

Figure 3.4   Commodity prices and factor prices change

$$p_C = wa_{LC} + r_Ca_{KC}$$
$$p_F = wa_{LF} + r_Fa_{KF}$$

(3.2.3)

When the price of cloth increases relative to the price of food, that is, $\hat{p}_C > \hat{p}_F$, then the factor prices change in the opposite directions:

$$\hat{r}_C > \hat{p}_C > \hat{w} > \hat{p}_F > \hat{r}_F$$

(3.2.4)

From (3.2.4) it follows that the factor which is specific to the sector whose price is rising (cloth-specific capital, in our example) gains absolutely because its money reward increases by more than the price of any good. The factor specific to the other sector, food-specific capital, loses absolutely since its money reward falls by more than does the price of any good. The change in real wage is thus not clear and may depend on the way workers' income is split on the consumption of cloth and food. The real wage might rise if more food rather than cloth, whose price is rising, is consumed. However the opposite could also occur.[3]

Despite the change in the number of factor prices the relationship (3.2.4) again reflects the fact that changes in the price of goods must be sandwiched between the changes in factor prices. The *magnification effect* of commodity prices on factor returns also exists in this model, but not for all factors. There are no such effects for wages, but the returns to both types of specific capital do change by magnified amounts: rental to food-specific capital must fall absolutely, while rental to cloth-specific capital must rise by more than the price of cloth. In contrast to the HOS model where the assumptions of sectorial factor intensities was crucial to the SST results this result is unaffected by the relative factor intensities of the two sectors. This brings us to the important property of the specific-factors model: its ability to at least partially explain the real world phenomena of pro-protection coalitions of both the labour and capital employed by the same sector. This is at odds with the HOS model's expectation that different factors employed by the same sector would be in conflict over the imposition of protection or other income-redistributional measures. As shown in this section within the framework of the specific-factors model both cloth-specific capital and labour are seen as gaining from the increase in the relative price of cloth, for example as the result of introducing tariffs on imported cloth. It is therefore in their collective short-run interest to collude and seek protection, even though this could hurt one of these factors in the long run.

☐ Factor endowments and outputs

This section examines the relationship between changes in factor endowments and the levels of output at fixed-commodity prices. Recall that within the HOS framework this relationship is described by the Rybczynski theorem which states that an increase in the endowment of one factor will cause the output of the good intensive in that factor to increase by a greater proportion and will reduce the output of the other good. Note that for the Rybczynski result to hold it is crucial that both commodity and factor prices are held constant. In contrast the structure of the specific-factors model does not allow for both sets of prices to be held fixed. We must therefore depart from the usual fixed-price assumptions in analysing the relationship between changes in factor endowments and changes in outputs.

Let us first examine the case of mobile labour accumulation (refer to Figure 3.3). An increase in labour, due for example to immigration, for $O_F O_F^1$ stretches the horizontal axis in the U-diagram which automatically shifts the $VMPL_F$ curve and with it the equilibrium point E^0 to the right. At the new labour allocation L^1 both sectors have increased their employment of labour: the cloth sector by $L^0 L^1$ and the food sector by FL^1. Since each sector continued to work with an unchanged quantity of specific capital outputs in both sectors had to rise. However the marginal productivity of labour in both sectors will decline. This means that as a consequence of the influx of labour not only does the money wage rate drop to w_1, but the real wage in terms of both goods also falls. This implies a rise in both the money and real returns to each type of specific capital. Note how these results differ from the Rybczynski results where a small change in the amount of any mobile factor did not disturb the original factor prices.

Turning to the case of specific factor accumulation we can use Figure 3.4 to demonstrate the basic results. Let us assume that only cloth-specific capital accumulates with both food capital and labour fixed. This raises the marginal productivity of labour in the cloth sector since labour has more capital to work with. Looking at Figure 3.4 this is represented as an upward shift of the $VMPL_C$ curve to the level given by $VMPL_C{}^1$. Labour has to transfer from the food sector to the cloth sector in order that the equality between the marginal productivities of labour in the two sectors is restored. Since capital is fixed the output of the cloth sector must rise and the output of the food sector must fall; so far this is in accordance with the Rybczynski theorem. However in the specific-factors model this accumulation of cloth capital also has effects on factor returns. When the MPL_C increases it pulls up the wage rate in both sectors and causes the return to both types of specific capital to fall so that costs are kept in line with the unchanged commodity prices.

The change in factor prices causes a change in the distribution of income. This always creates conflicts between some factors. In the framework of the HOS model it was assumed that income-distributional issues would only be raised through trade of goods or services via the terms of trade change. However the specific-factors model allows for the factor price to change in response to a change in the physical quantity of factors despite changes in outputs. Since the changes in endowment affect factors' rewards in different ways than the terms of trade change, in the specific-factors model we have obtained an additional framework within which to explore the behaviour of political alliances between different factors. According to the specific-factors model it is natural that in the short run all specific factors would vote together when it comes to issues such as a more liberal immigration policy or the free inflow of foreign capital specific to one of the sectors in a national economy. However if there are no changes in factor endowments and the only issue is the terms of trade change through tariffs or similar measures, then the specific factors will be driven apart by conflicting interests. Only one of them will side with labour.

☐ Factor endowments and the patterns of trade

In the HOS model it was possible to extend the effects of factor accumulation on production into a country's trade flows because relative factor endowments were basically the sole determinant of the patterns of trade (recall that demand played no role simply because countries were assumed to have identical and homothetic tastes). The question is, is it possible to infer the patterns of trade from the knowledge of factor endowments and factor intensities in the specific-factors model? Suppose that Home and Foreign, which share identical technology and identical and homothetic tastes, engage in free trade. It is unlikely that the difference in the amount of mobile labour will determine the flow of goods between these two countries. As we have just discussed, the changes in labour causes the outputs of both sectors to move in the same direction. Therefore if Home and Foreign are different only in terms of the amount of labour they have, it will be very difficult to identify their comparative advantage. Of course the country with the more abundant labour force will have lower wages, but this is still insufficient to determine comparative advantage.

However a change in the amount of any specific factor will cause the composition of total national output to change in such a way that the sector whose specific factor is increasing will expand its output while output from the other sector will contract. Thus, if two otherwise identical countries differ in the endowment of any one of the specific factors it is likely that this will determine their comparative advantage and the ensuing trade flows. For example if Home has relatively more cloth-specific capital than Foreign, it will produce relatively more cloth than food. Given identical and homothetic tastes Home must therefore export cloth to and import food from Foreign, which is relatively abundant in food-specific capital. Trade flows are thus fully explained by the difference in countries endowments of specific factors. One should not therefore be too surprised to observe instances where a country exports a commodity that seems to run against the grain of its *total* factor endowments.

■ 3.3 Some other specific trade models[4]

In this chapter we have so far emphasised the opposing effects of trade policy on factor prices that are derived in the HOS model and in the specific-factors model. It would be useful to have a model in which both of the aforementioned effects could appear. Such a model is that of Krueger (1977). She combines the assumptions of the HOS model and the specific-factors models in one construct known as Krueger's model.

This model includes an agricultural sector that employs labour and land, and a manufacturing sector that employs capital and labour in the production of any number of manufactured goods.[5] In other words the model has three factors: mobile labour, agriculture-specific land and manufacturing-specific capital which is mobile among different manufacturing industries. Both agriculture and manufactured goods are tradeable internationally at given prices (i.e. the small country assumption). Constant-returns-to-scale technologies are identical among all countries and factor endowments differ enough among countries to prevent factor-price equalisation, even in the manufacturing sector. No single country can thus produce more than a subset of the total amount of manufactured goods.

Depending on the level of development and the endowment of agriculture-specific land countries may produce and export more or less capital-intensive goods. They will also import some manufactured goods (leading to intra-industry trade!), while countries which have large endowments of agricultural land may import all manufactured goods they consume.

A diagrammatic representation of this model is given in Figure 3.5. This figure combines the Lerner–Pearce unit-value isoquants for determining specialisation in manufacturing in panel (a), and the U-shaped specific-factors diagram for determining wages in panel (b). Together these panels determine the pattern of specialisation and factor prices for a given factor endowments and free trade prices of all goods. Consider first panel (a). With the world prices of three manufactured goods, p_1, p_2, and p_3 the unit-value isoquants are given by M_1, M_2 and M_3 and are connected by common tangents to form the convex hull. This hull acts as the isoquant for the manufacturing sector as a whole. Its slope will therefore give the wage–rental ratio in the manufacturing sector. Along the straight segments of the hull two goods are produced in the manufacturing sector. Given this linear shape it is obvious that along these segments neither the marginal product of capital nor that of labour will change with small changes in the level of their employment. Along the curved portions of the hull, however, only one manufactured good is produced and the marginal products of the factors vary with their employment.

If the level of manufacturing-specific capital is fixed at amount $\bar{K}$, the wage rate will vary with the level of labour employed in the manufacturing sector, L_M. As we move along the horizontal line at $\bar{K}$ to the right, we move in and out of regions of specialisation. For example if less than L_0 of labour is employed by manufacturing the sectoral capital–labour ratio is above the minimum ratio needed for specialisation in M_3. In this region the wage, equal to the MPL_M, is the same as labour's marginal product in producing only M_3. As the allocation of labour to the manufacturing sector increases the capital–labour ratio in M_3 falls, and so must the wage. This is clearly shown by the slope of the w_M curve in this region (panel (b)). When the employment of labour exceeds L_0, another good (M_2) is added to the production undertaken by the manufacturing sector. Factor prices are fixed since the capital–labour ratio in this sector can now fall without influencing the ratio of factors employed in M_2 and M_3. The wage line in panel (b) therefore becomes flat throughout this region of non-specialisation. As the amount of labour employed increases further the sector moves in and out of the region of specialisation and falling wages, and in and out of the region of non-specialisation and fixed wages.

The $VMPL_M$ curve in panel (b) is combined with the curve representing the $VMPL_A$; the wage rate in the agricultural sector. The intersection of these two curves determines the equilibrium allocation of labour between manufacturing and agriculture at point E, where the value of marginal products is equalised across sectors. The pattern of specialisation can then

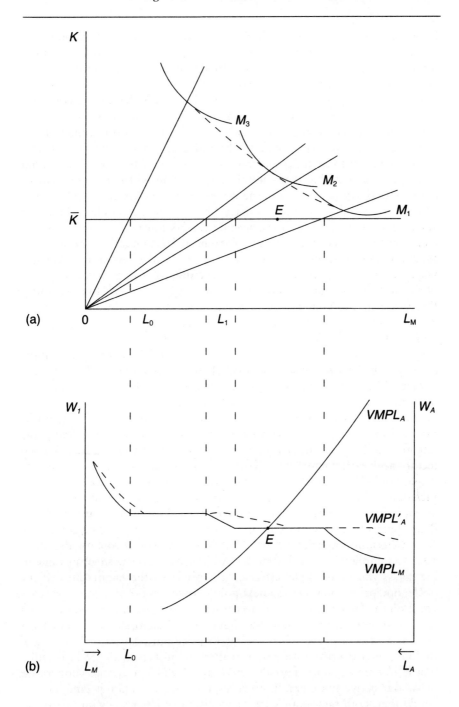

Figure 3.5 *Krueger's model*

be inferred from the segment of the $VMPL_M$ curve in which the intersection at point E occurs. If this is the flat segment of the $VMPL_M$ then the country produces two manufactured goods; otherwise the country specialises in only one manufactured good.

This model is particularly useful for studying how developing countries patterns of trade evolve over time as their endowments change. As the manufacturing sector begins to develop, an increase in the capital stock will cause the $VMPL_M$ to shift to the right. In Figure 3.5 this will then cause manufacturing to completely specialise in M_2. For other initial equilibria it is possible that capital accumulation will not cause changes in the pattern of specialisation, the wage–rental ratio or labour allocation. This is in contrast to the ordinary specific-factors model where the accumulation of any one of the specific factors must cause wages to rise. However in the case when the endowment of land rises the economy will experience an upward shift of the $VMPL_A$ curve. As a consequence manufacturing employment declines, leading to Rybczynski effects on manufacturing outputs. Depending on its endowment of land a country very poor in capital might find itself producing quite capital-intensive manufacturing goods because labour would be attracted into the agricultural sector.

Another specific trade model is the so-called *Neighbourhood Model* developed by Jones and Kierzkowski (1986). This model is distinct from both the HOS and the specific-factors models and has some different implications. The model is quite general because it allows for any number of goods and factors, the only restriction being that the number of goods is assumed to be equal to the number of factors. Diagrammatically the sectors (and factors) can be arranged around a circle as in Figure 3.6. Each sector (and each factor) has two neighbours: each good is assumed to employ only the two factors which are adjacent to it on the circle, while each factor is employable only in the two sectors adjacent to it. For example factor $Vj(j = 1, \ldots n)$ can be employed in the sectors X_{j-1} or X_j. Every pair of neighbours therefore shares one factor, thus making the whole economy interdependent. This fact gives rise to one of the characteristic implications of this model. An increase in the price of just one of the goods causes a 'ripple' effect on the prices of the factors around the circle, one price going up, the next going down, and so on. Moreover, the effect on the factor prices in the sector whose price has increased turns out to depend on whether the number of goods (and factors) in the economy is even or odd. If it is even then one factor price must fall in real terms and the other factor price must rise in real terms, just as in the SST. In other words an even number of goods (and factors) will lead to non-cooperative behaviour between factors. If, however, the number of goods (and factors) is odd then both factors in a sector whose price has risen gain relative to other goods, but one factor must lose relative to the good whose price has risen. This is what happens to the mobile factor in the specific-factors

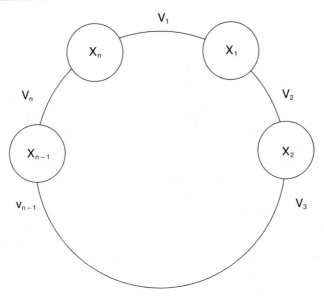

Figure 3.6 *The neighbourhood production structure*

model. In fact the specific-factors model appears to be a simple version of an odd neighbourhood model where the number of factors is greater than the number of goods.

■ 3.4 Higher dimensional issues

The many attempts to generalise the HOS model beyond its standard $2 \times 2 \times 2$ dimensions have given rise to literature too immense and complex to survey in one section. While this section will cover the most important points the interested reader is referred to Ethier's (1984) review of this area which covers the topic in greater detail.

Early efforts to answer the question of what happens to the directions of trade in a trading world of multiple countries, goods and factors became so entangled in arcane mathematical problems (Deardorff, 1985) that the impression was gained that trade theory had little of practical significance to offer. Other work has however succeeded in showing that fairly general results can be obtained without a highly specialised mathematical knowledge (Dixit and Norman, 1980; Deardorff, 1980, 1982). As we discussed in the Appendix to chapter 1 the general proposition of the law of comparative advantage holds in an *on average sense* for any dimensions, even though its predictive power becomes somewhat weakened at higher dimensions. Similarly, trade theory is scrutinised more and more within the framework of the *generalised HOS model*. In this model any number of goods, factors and countries interact in ways that include the standard

HOS model as a special case. The specific-factors and other specific trade models are thus included in this framework.

As in the case of the standard HOS model work on the generalised version has mainly taken the form of attempts to generalise the core theorems of the model. Most attention has been given to the Heckscher–Ohlin (HOT) theorem itself since it is the one which predicts the flows of goods and as such is the theorem most exposed to empirical testing. Deardorff (1982), Ethier (1982a) and Helpman (1984a) have all produced generalised versions of the HOT with various degrees of testability. For instance Deardorff (1982) has shown that both the factor-content and the commodity versions of the theorem are valid in an average sense. More precisely, with respect to the factor-content version of the theorem, it is shown that the simple correlation between the vector of the autarky factor prices of all countries and its factors, and the vector of the net exports by each country for each factor is negative. This weak proposition implies that countries will, on average, tend to be net exporters of their abundant factors and net importers of their scarce factors. With respect to the commodity version the association between three variables: the vector of factor abundance, the vector of factor intensity, and the vector of net exports at world prices, is positive. This means that exported goods must on average use the relatively abundant factors relatively intensively, and imported goods must on average use the relatively scarce factors relatively intensively. Deardorff's result is important because it described long-sought-after generalisation of the HOT. However the result depends on autarky factor prices as the indicators for factor abundance. This version is therefore hard to test empirically.

Theorems other than the factor-price equalisation (FPE) theorem have not attracted much attention in attempts to generalise the HOS model. As Deardorff (1985, p. 9) explains, it is sometimes difficult to see what these theorems can say in many dimensions that is meaningful *and* is not already implicit in their two-dimensional versions. However some of the general statements have made quite important contributions. Unfortunately, they are sometimes based on assumptions that are equally or more restrictive than their two-dimensional counterparts.

The core theorems with many goods and factors[6]

Let us first set the stage for the derivation of the general statements of the core theorems. As with the standard HOS model the general neoclassical assumptions hold with respect to production, factor prices and commodity prices. An economy will have a vector of factor endowments:

$$V = (V_1, V_2, \ldots, V_m) \tag{3.4.1}$$

and a vector of factor prices:

$$W = (W_1, W_2, \ldots, W_m) \tag{3.4.2}$$

The factors combine in the production process to produce a vector of n goods:

$$X = (X_1, X_2, \ldots, X_n) \tag{3.4.3}$$

There will be a vector of commodity prices:

$$P = (P_1, P_2, \ldots, P_n) \tag{3.4.4}$$

The production process depends on the matrix of techniques $A(W)$:

$$A(W) = \begin{bmatrix} a_{11}(W) & a_{12}(W) & \cdots & a_{1n}(W) \\ \vdots & \vdots & \ddots & \vdots \\ a_{m1}(W) & a_{m2}(W) & \cdots & a_{mn}(W) \end{bmatrix} \tag{3.4.5}$$

The input–output coefficients, a_{ij}, are a function of W because the least-cost ratios depend on relative factor prices. Commodity prices depend upon unit factor requirements and factor prices. Thus:

$$P_i = W_1 a_{1i}(W) + W_2 a_{2i}(W) + \ldots + W_m a_{mi}(W), \qquad i = (1, 2, \ldots, n)$$

or

$$P_i = \Sigma W_j a_{ji}(W) \qquad j = (1, 2, \ldots, m)$$

This commodity price vector can be written as:

$$P = WA(W) \tag{3.4.6}$$

Factor usage is similarly related to the input–output coefficients and outputs in the following way:

$$V = A(W)X \tag{3.4.7}$$

We can now discuss how the multiple goods and factors may affect the core theorems.

The factor-price equalisation theorem

Let the number of goods (n) equals the number of factors (m), and each is larger than 2. Suppose then that two countries engage in free trade at an equilibrium commodity price vector, P. If the countries possess the factors V in identical proportions, they will produce goods X in identical proportions, will have identical factor prices W, and will use identical techniques $A(W)$. Each economy will then be identical except for scale. In this case factor-price equalisation is possible but trivial. Of more interest is the case where relative factor endowments are no longer identical. Under these conditions will factor prices still be equalised?

Assuming there is no specialisation in production, we start from the amount of factors necessary to produce all goods:

$$V = A(W)X$$

Let X_1 be some collection of goods, V_1 will then be the corresponding non-negative vector of factors necessary to produce X_1. Similarly, let $V_v = (V_1, V_2, \ldots, V_r)$ be the collection of all vectors V that solve (3.4.7) for the non-negative vector $X_x = (X_1, X_2, \ldots, X_k)$. Thus, if V_H and V_F, the given factor endowments of Home and Foreign, are in the set V_v then both countries can produce all goods at factor prices W. Factor-price equalisation is possible but is it necessary?

Suppose there is another vector W' of factor prices which gives equilibrium at the same commodity prices P, that is:

$$P = W'A(W') \tag{3.4.8}$$

and

$$V = A(W')X' \tag{3.4.9}$$

We know that $A(W)$ is the cheapest technique at factor prices W and technique $A(W')$ is the cheapest at factor prices W'. We can thus write

$$WA(W) = P < W'A(W') \tag{3.4.10}$$

and

$$W'A(W') = P < WA(W') \tag{3.4.11}$$

Therefore it follows from (3.4.10) that

$$WA(W)X < W'A(W)X, \quad \text{or}$$
$$WV < W'V \tag{3.4.12}$$

as $V = A(W)X$. Also from (3.4.11) we can write:

$$W'A(W')X' < WA(W')X', \quad \text{or}$$
$$W'V < WV \tag{3.4.13}$$

as $V = A(W')X'$. However (3.4.12) and (3.4.13) are contradictory – thus if a country has factor endowments in V_v, then given the commodity price vector P equilibrium factor prices are W. In other words, countries need to have sufficiently similar factor endowments for factor-price equalisation to occur. A similar assumption to this was also needed for factor-price equalisation to occur in two dimensions.

Further difficulties can arise if the number of factors is not equal to the number of goods. When there are more factors than goods factor-price determination depends upon factor endowments as well as commodity prices. In general, differences in these endowments prevent factor-price equalisation from occurring. Factor-price equalisation is thus very unlikely. When there are more goods than factors the determination of factor prices depends solely upon the prices of some goods, but it is impossible to know which ones. In general, the addition of more goods does not necessarily change the probability of factor-price equalisation as compared to the two-dimensional case for it should be noted that even with two factors and two goods the most we can hope for in reality is the *tendency* for factor-price equalisation.

The Stolper–Samuelson theorem

Assume that production requires at least two factors. Let the first good be produced in equilibrium, that is, $X_1 > 0$ with $P_1 = C_1(W)$ where C denotes the cost of production. If P_1 increases the cost of production must increase as much as the price of the good increases:

$$\hat{P}_1 \le \hat{C}_1 = \theta_{11}\hat{W}_1 + \theta_{21}\hat{W}_2 + \ldots + \theta_{m1}\hat{W}_m \tag{3.4.14}$$

where $\hat{P}_1$ is the percentage increase in the price of commodity X_1, $\hat{w}_1$ is the percentage increase in the price of factor 1, while θ_{11} is factor 1's share of the total cost of producing good X_1 and $\Sigma\theta_{i1} = 1$. $\hat{C}_1$ therefore represents a weighted average of $\hat{W}_i$ and is bounded by the largest and the smallest of the $\hat{W}_i$. At least one $\hat{W}_i$ must be at least equal to $\hat{P}_1 = \hat{C}_1$.

Now let X_2 be produced after P_1 increases, and let X_2 use the same factors as X_1. Also assume that the price of X_2 does not change, i.e. $\hat{P}_2 = 0$. We can therefore write

$$0 = \hat{P}_2 = \hat{C}_2 \ge \theta_{12}\hat{W}_1 + \ldots + \theta_{m2}\hat{W}_m \tag{3.4.15}$$

From (3.4.14) we know that at least one $\hat{W}_i > 0$ must be at least equal to $\hat{P}_i$, so from (3.4.15) at least one $\hat{W}_j < 0$ (where $i \ne j$). These two conditions imply that $\hat{W}_i > \hat{P}_1$.

The conclusion is that at least one factor gains in real terms (i.e. in terms of all goods) while some other factor loses in real terms. The restrictions on this result are that (1) all goods are still produced after the price of one good increases, (2) this particular good must also be produced before the price increase and (3) all goods require the same factors although not in the same proportions. A further general statement derived in connection to the SST is that a general set of commodity prices changes will on average raise the price of the factors used most intensively by the goods whose prices have risen relative to other goods. Finally note that when the number of factors is larger than 2 the general proposition does not say anything about some of those factors.

The Rybczynski theorem

The method we use in generalising the Rybczynski proposition is the same as was used for the SST. Let V_1 be used in at least two sectors and suppose that its endowment increases, that is, $\hat{V}_1 > 0$. If V_1 is fully employed after the increase and there is no change in factor prices then

$$\hat{V}_1 \leq \lambda_{11}\hat{X}_1 + \lambda_{12}\hat{X}_2 + \ldots + \lambda_{1n}\hat{X}_n \tag{3.4.16}$$

where λ_{11} is the share of factor 1 used in the production of X_1 and $\Sigma\lambda_{11} = 1$. Then V_1 is a weighted average of $\hat{X}_i$, and at least one $\hat{X}_i \geq \hat{V}_1$.

Let V_2 be used in producing the same goods as V_1 and let it also be fully employed. In addition assume there is no increase in the endowment of this factor, that is, $\hat{V}_2 = 0$. Then

$$0 = \hat{V}_2 \geq \lambda_{21}\hat{X}_1 + \lambda_{22}\hat{X}_2 + \ldots + \lambda_{2n}\bar{X}_n \tag{3.4.17}$$

Since at least one $\hat{X}_i \geq \hat{V}_1 > 0$ as factor 2 remains fixed the quantity of some good's j will have to fall; or $\hat{X}_j < 0$. Hence in (3.4.16) at least one $\hat{X}_i > \hat{V}_i$ and at least one $\hat{X}_j < 0$. A general change in factor endowments will also, on average, induce the largest increase in output in those goods that most intensively use the factors whose endowments have increased the most. Note that the restrictions under which these general statements are derived include that the assumption that factor prices do not change with the changes in endowments. However in the case when there are more factors than goods some factor prices must adjust for full employment to be attained. Recall that we also had such a case in the specific-factors model.

The Heckscher–Ohlin theorem

Here we outline the derivation of the factor-content version of the HOT. Recall that in this case we do not need to make assumptions about

demand. However it is important to assume away factor-intensity reversals. In other words, we have to assume that technology is identical across
countries.

Under free trade a country's vector of net imports (M) is equal to the
difference between its total consumption (D^T) and its total domestic
production (X^T):

$$M = D^T - X^T \tag{3.4.18}$$

Note that superscript T denotes variables with trade while A denotes
variables in autarky. We know that the value of consumption with trade at
the autarky prices must exceed the value of consumption in autarky, or

$$P^A D^T \geq P^A D^A \tag{3.4.19}$$

As usual D^T is not available in autarky.

Let M_k denote the factors actually used to produce net imports:

$$M_k = \bar{A}M \tag{3.4.20}$$

where the ith column of $\bar{A}$ represents Home's techniques used to produce
X_i if it is exported $(M_i < 0)$, while it is an overseas technique if the good is
imported $(M_i > 0)$.

Since $D^T = X^T + M$ to produce D^T requires the factors $V + M_k$ (recall
that $V = AX$). In this case the country is in fact forced to abandon the
production of exports and use the overseas technique to produce imports.
This need not necessarily be profitable at autarkic prices. If this is the case,
then:

$$W^A(V + M_k) \geq P^A D^T \tag{3.4.21}$$

and

$$W^A M_k \geq P^A D^T - W^A V \geq P^A D^A - W^A V = 0$$

because of (3.4.19) and the equality of the gross domestic product to the
gross domestic expenditure $(P^A D^A = W^A V)$. Thus we have

$$W^A M_k \geq 0 \tag{3.4.22}$$

For the rest of the world we have

$$W^{A*} M_k{}^* \geq 0 \tag{3.4.23}$$

We know that the requirements for balanced trade mean that $M^* = -M$. The balanced trade constraint could also be written as $M_k^* = \bar{A}M^* = -\bar{A}M = -M_k$. From (3.4.22) and (3.4.23) we obtain:

$$(W^A - W^{A^*})M_k \geq 0 \tag{3.4.24}$$

This result indicates that differences in autarkic factor prices are positively correlated with the factor content of net imports. If $W_i^{A*} > W_i^A$ then the corresponding entry in M_k is positive and the good is imported; if $W_i^{A*} < W_i^A$ then the corresponding entry in M_k is negative and the good is exported. In general, countries tend to export those factors that are relatively cheaper in autarky.

■ 3.5 Summary

This chapter has focused on models of trade that differ from the standard HOS model with respect to model dimensions, that is, number of goods and factors. We began our review by setting up the models which are characterised by number of factors being different from the number of goods, such as the specific-factor model and Krueger's model. The remainder of the chapter was dedicated to the evaluation of the main properties of the factor proportions model in a more general $(m \times n)$ framework.

The section on the specific-factors model demonstrated that changing the dimensions of the model from 2×2 to 2×3 does have implications for its results. These are the most important applications:

(a)   The presence of specific factors affects the relationship between the changes in relative commodity prices and real factor returns. Although the returns to the specific factors remain unambiguously related to commodity price changes, the return to the mobile factor (labour) depends also on the consumption pattern of the workers. However the magnification effect does persist in the context of specific factors which means that the prescription for free trade will have both its advocates and its opponents. What is important here is that the followers of these two groups are classed according to different criteria from the standard model. Here they are industry grouped so that all the factors (specific and mobile) employed in the export sector will favour free trade while all the factors (specific and mobile) in the import-competing sector will oppose free trade. Note that the presence of specific factors does not alter our conclusions with respect to gains from free trade for a country as a whole.

(b)   The relationship between the changes in factor endowments and the production structure is also affected by the presence of specific factors. The Rybczynski-like effects are identified for the increases in a specific factor (note, however, that in this case constant commodity prices do not imply constant factor prices). It is demonstrated that an increase in a specific factor will increase the output of the good which uses this specific factor, while the output of the other good will decline. However, an increase in the mobile factor (labour) will increase the outputs of both sectors, Which sector's output is increased by more depends on the technology of production.

(c)   The presence of specific factors makes the identification of the pattern of trade more difficult. Given the identical endowments of the mobile factor, each country's export will depend on the absolute endowments of the specific factors. If, however, the supply of the mobile factor also differs across countries, the pattern of trade depends on the technology and the relative endowments of specific factors.

(d)   The presence of specific factors makes factor price equalisation even less likely. In fact, even if the prices of commodities are fully equalised, given the larger number of factors than goods, factor-price equalisation is not a necessary result.

The review of the literature on the generalised version of the trade model ($n \times m$) demonstrates that most of the propositions derived from the (2×2) model carry over to the ($n \times m$) model, but in a weaker form. More specifically, the pattern of trade is shown to reflect differences in factor endowments only on average (therefore not really predicting the direction of trade for each individual good). Likewise, the changes in relative factor prices do cause magnified changes in real factor returns, that is, at least one factor will gain in real terms while some other factor will lose in real terms. However, we end up knowing nothing about some factor returns (unless $m = 2$). Similarly, the changes in factor endowments have magnified effects on a country's production structure. A general change in factor endowment will, on average, induce the largest increase in output in those goods that most intensively use the factors whose endowments have increased the most. Finally, factor-price equalisation in the many goods–many factors world is very unlikely. In other words, the addition of more goods and factors weakens the tendency for factor returns to be drawn closer by free trade in the 2×2 model.

An increase of number of goods and/or factors in trade models is not used only in order to demonstrate the general predictions of the standard trade theory. The specific trade model has been found very useful for evaluating as diverse policy issues as the problems of adjustments to trade shocks, lobbying, or distributional issues in general. One of the phenomena that has been studied by using the specific-factor model is the so-called 'Dutch disease', and it is examined in Appendix 3 below.

■ *APPENDIX 3*   'DUTCH DISEASE'

'Dutch disease' is the name given to the phenomenon of *deindustrialisation* or the contraction of the traditional manufacturing (exporting) sector due to the rapid expansion of the extractive sector of the economy. It is called 'Dutch' because this phenomenon occurred in Holland when natural gas extraction in that country grew rapidly, and 'disease' because other sectors of the economy are adversely affected. In addition, the phenomenon was also observed in other parts of the world, for example in Australia, Britain and Norway.

The main features of this phenomenon are easily revealed using the type of analysis implied by the specific-factors model developed in this chapter. To begin, let us assume that a number of industries are producing for the world market at given world prices (i.e. the small country assumption applies). These industries all employ some labour from the common national pool of labour in addition to some type of specific capital. Let us assume that the world price for one of these industries increases. By following the commodity–price factor–price relationship from the specific-factors model we can easily reach the conclusion that an increase in the relative world price of one industry will benefit the factor specific to that sector, while all other specific factors will be hurt. In particular the reward to the specific capital used in the 'booming' industry will rise by more than the price of that industry's output. This is the magnification effect. The rise in money wages will serve to squeeze the rewards to the specific factors used in all other industries whose price has not increased. This, in a simple manner, describes how a 'boom' in one traded sector can cause other sectors of an economy to contract. If these other sectors consist of traditional manufacturing exports the economy may experience the deindustrialisation that Holland did following the extensive extraction of natural gas.

This effect is based on what Corden and Neary (1982) call the *resource movement effect* of the boom. The boom in the extractive sector causes the marginal productivity of labour to rise and therefore attracts labour away from the other sectors. This causes the output in other sectors to contract.[7] In an economy that produces only traded goods this is the only effect of the boom. However it is rare that any economy will produce all goods solely for the exchange in the international market. There is thus a second category of goods: non-traded goods. In the presence of non-traded goods there is a second effect of the 'boom'. This effect is known as the *spending effect*: a higher real income from the boom in the export sector induces greater expenditure on various goods (as usual, we assume there are no inferior goods). While this does not cause the price of traded goods to change, the price of the non-traded goods will increase. This may also cause their outputs to rise. The prices of traded goods cannot adjust to 'domestic' shocks because of the small country assumption. Consequently the rewards to the factors specific to the non-traded sectors might also rise. This second effect thus works in the opposite direction from the first effect.

The total effect of a boom in the extractive export sector will be determined by the sum of the resource movement effect and the spending effect. Depending on the intensity of each effect the output of the non-traded sector can either increase or decrease. What is certain is that the output of the traded goods sector will rise. However in order to analyse the 'Dutch disease' syndrome we must in fact be able to separate the output responses of the various industries grouped together into the traded goods sector. The U-shaped diagram of the specific-factors model can be utilised for this purpose. Without any loss of generality let us assume that there are only two industries in the traded goods sector C: a manufacturing industry A, and an extractive industry B.[8] The non-traded goods sector is called sector N. Goods in industry A are produced by specific capital K_A and some labour from the common pool. Labour from this pool is also employed and combined with industry B-specific capital, K_B, to produce goods B. Sector N also uses labour from the common pool and employs some N-specific capital, K_N. To identify the output changes in these industries following the boom (i.e. the price increase in one of the traded goods) it suffices to examine the allocation of labour. Because labour is the only mobile factor and must be fully employed by the national industries in order to find out whether the output in one industry expands or contracts it is sufficient to find out whether employment increases or decreases in that industry.

Let us consider Figure 3.7, where the horizontal axis $O_N O_C$ represents the total quantity of labour. The employment of labour in the non-traded sector is measured from the origin O_N, while the total employment of labour in the traded sector is measured from the origin O_C. The vertical axes measure the wage rate as expressed in terms of good B. The curves $VMPL_N$, $VMPL_A$, and $VMPL_C$ all represent the value of each industry's marginal product of labour or each industry's labour demand functions at initial world prices. (Note that the $VMPL_B$ is not shown separately to simplify the diagram, it can easily be derived from the total demand for labour of the traded sector and the demand for labour of the manufacturing sector A.) In this initial situation the equilibrium wage is w_0. The allocation of labour is L_0, with $O_N L_0$ employed in the non-traded sector, and $L_0 B$ employed in industry B and $B O_C$ employed in industry A of the traded sector.

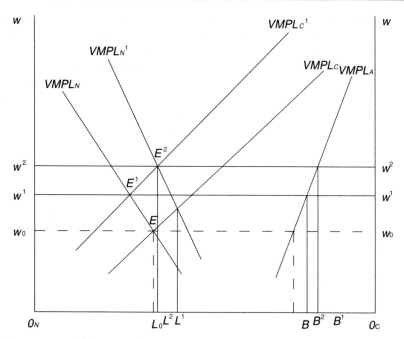

Figure 3.7 *'Dutch disease'*

The boom in sector B is equivalent to an increase in the marginal productivity of labour in that sector. At unchanged prices the $VMPL_B$ will therefore shift, causing the total demand curve for labour of the traded sector, $VMPL_C$, to shift to $VMPL_C^1$. The new equilibrium allocation of labour is given by point E^1 with a corresponding wage rate w^1. In comparison to point E the employment of labour in the non-traded sector has decreased, as it has in industry A of the traded sector, while it has obviously risen in industry B. However this equilibrium is not stable as it takes into account only the resource movement effect. The final equilibrium is reached after the spending effect has caused the price of the non-traded goods to rise. $VMPL_N$ has shifted to the right, for example to $VMPL_N^1$, causing the wage rate to increase even further to w^2. Employment in the manufacturing sector decreases even further. The way our diagram is drawn, the final equilibrium implies an increase in employment in the non-traded sector, implying that its output also expands. However the diagram could also have been drawn in such a way that employment in the non-traded sector did not increase relative to the initial equilibrium. The certain effect that we therefore obtain is that output in the manufacturing industry will contract. This is the phenomenon of deindustrialisation.

In conclusion, let us summarise the effects that a boom in the extractive traded sector will have on the rest of the economy:

(1) Production and employment in the extractive sector itself will rise
     while production and employment in the traditional manufacturing
     sector will decline. Production and employment in the non-traded
     sector may either expand or contract.
(2) The prices of non-traded goods increase. As the prices of traded
     goods are bounded by the terms of trade the spending effect of the
     boom vents itself through the inflation of domestic goods.
(3) The direction in which the real rewards to the specific factors and
     mobile labour will move is indeterminate without further *a priori*
     knowledge.

■ *Chapter 4* ■

Modern Theories of Trade – 1: External Economies of Scale

■ *4.1* Rethinking the reasons for trade

The trade models examined in previous chapters have provided us with an understanding of how *differences* in national resources, technology or tastes lead countries to specialise in production and engage in mutually beneficial trade. On the basis of these models we can expect that:

(1) Countries with the greatest differences in resources, technology or tastes (such as Japan and Ecuador) should trade more heavily than countries that are less dissimilar.
(2) Trade should result in specialisation. Specifically, products being exported and imported by a country should belong to distinctly different product groups or industries (such as bananas and TV sets).

However, the characteristics of actual trade patterns do not conform with the above scenario.

As shown in Table 4.1, the proportion of world merchandise trade that takes place between countries that are similar in resources, technology and tastes (that is, DCs) is, in fact, far larger than the share of trade between these and developing countries. More than two-thirds of world exports in manufactured goods originates in the developed countries, and almost three-quarters of that is destined for DCs themselves. While the developing countries make about a quarter of the world's manufactured goods exports, they still receive only a small portion of the DCs' manufactured exports. Furthermore, as illustrated by Table 4.2, the largest share of trade among the DCs consists of the mutual exchange of machinery and transport equipment and not of distinctly different product groups.

158

Table 4.1 **World merchandise exports, by main areas, 1963–94 (%)**[*]

Origin \ Destination		Developed countries	Developing countries	Eastern trading area	World
Developed	1963	49.9	14.7	2.5	67.1
countries	1973	55.1	12.5	3.3	70.9
	1983	46.2	15.0	2.9	64.1
	1987	55.0	12.3	2.6	69.9
	1994	51.5	17.0	2.0	71.6
Developing	1963	15.2	4.4	1.1	20.7
countries	1973	14.4	3.9	0.9	19.2
	1983	16.3	7.1	1.3	24.6
	1987	13.5	4.8	1.4	19.7
	1994	15.4	9.3	0.3	25.4
Eastern	1963	2.3	1.8	8.1	12.1
trading	1973	2.7	1.5	5.7	9.9
area	1983	3.2	2.3	5.7	11.3
	1987	2.8	2.0	5.5	10.4
	1994	2.0	0.5	0.5	2.9
World	1963	67.4	20.9	11.7	100.0
	1973	72.2	17.9	9.8	100.0
	1983	65.7	24.3	9.9	100.0
	1987	71.3	19.2	9.5	100.0
	1994	68.9	26.7	2.8	100.0

Source: GATT, *International Trade 87–88, Vol. II. WTO, International Trade 1995, Trends and Statistics (Table A2)* for 1994.
Note: * Classification of countries in the GATT/WTO publications has changed. For the purposes of this table 'developed countries' include North America, Western Europe, Japan, Australia and New Zealand; 'developing countries' include Latin America, Africa, the Middle East and Other Asia; the Eastern trading area includes Central and Eastern Europe and the former USSR.

Thus it is obvious that there are other reasons why countries trade, and gain from trade. Both this chapter and the next are concerned with reasons for trade other than those of comparative advantage.

We will start exploring these new reasons for trade with a discussion of the role of *economies of scale* (EOS). It is a fact that trade enables countries to specialise in fewer production lines, hence ensuring that they benefit from economies of scale. The direct implication of the existence of economies of scale for our models is that we must switch from increasing to decreasing opportunity costs. This transforms our production possibility frontier (see Box 4.1, p. 160). But this is not all. Once we allow for economies of scale we must also abandon the assumption of perfectly

Box 4.1   *The shape of the production possibility frontier with EOS*

There are two things that influence the shape of the production possibility frontier (PPF): (1) differences in factor intensities and (2) returns to scale. Different factor intensities, by causing increasing opportunity costs, tend to make the frontier 'bowed out' or concave towards the origin. Similarly, different types of returns to scale will affect the shape of the PPF in different ways. For example, increasing returns to scale (which we are introducing now) tend to make the frontier 'bowed in' or convex towards the origin. The final shape will depend on the relative strengths of these two influences.

For example, when we assume only one factor of production and constant-returns-to-scale, as in the Ricardian model, the PPF is simply a straight line. If we keep the assumption about constant-returns-to-scale, but introduce two factors of production, and assume that two sectors use these factors with different intensities in producing two goods (as we did when we discussed the HOS model), the PPF becomes concave towards the origin. We discussed the reasons for this earlier. Now, if we disregard all differences in factor intensities (and we can easily do that by returning to a one-factor economy) but allow for increasing returns to scale in one or both industries, the PPF can be derived as illustrated in Figure 4.1.

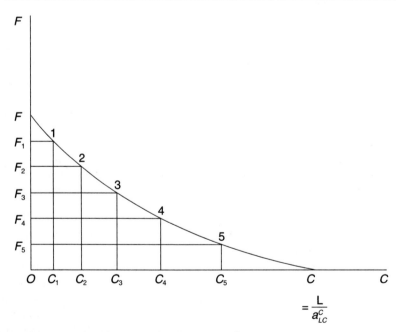

Figure 4.1   *PPF with increasing returns to scale*

Assume that production of good F exhibits constant-returns-to-scale, but that production of C is subject to increasing-returns-to-scale. We can find the end point F of the PPF by allocating the total amount of a sole factor (say, the total amount of labour) to industry F. Let our economy initially produce at that particular point. Then consider a decrease of one unit in the production of F (so that output of F falls to F_1). This means that a certain amount of labour, a_{LF}, is freed to start production of good C. How much of good C will this released labour produce? The quantity of C is equal to a_{LF}/a_{LC} or OC_1, so that the production point of the PPF is point 1. What will happen if the output of F is decreased by one more unit, so realising a further amount of labour of a_{LF} to produce C? Because C is subject to increasing returns to scale, the more of C that is produced, the less labour is needed to produce each additional unit (of course, up to a point). We can say that productivity of labour is an increasing function of output produced, writing this as:

$$a_{LC} = a_{LC}(C) \tag{B4.1.1}$$

where $d(a_{LC})/dC < 0$.
(*Note that we could also have written*

$$a_{LC} = a_{LC}(L_C)$$
$$and \quad d(a_{LC})/dL_C < 0, \; because \; dC/dL_C > 0.)$$

Therefore, when more labour is added to the production of C (so as to increase output to C_2), the unit labour requirement falls, reflecting the increased productivity of labour:

$$(1/a_{LC}^{\,o}) < (1/a_{LC}^{\,1}) < (1/a_{LC}^{\,2}) < \ldots < (1/a_{LC}^{\,C}) \tag{B4.1.2}$$

We can repeat this procedure until we reduce the labour allocated to industry F to zero. Each additional amount of labour released from F will produce more and more of C because of the increasing returns to scale in that industry. In other words, the marginal productivity of labour in that industry increases. With all labour transferred to C, we derive another final point of the PPF, point $C(L/a_{LC}^{C})$.[1]

If we have more than one factor of production the PPF need not be convex to the origin at all, and certainly not necessarily throughout its entire length. The final shape of the PPF will depend on whether or not, and where, the increasing returns to scale effects outweigh factor-intensity effects. (See Kemp and Herberg, 1969, for a more rigorous treatment.)

Table 4.2   *DCs: merchandise trade, 1985–90*

Product groups	1985 (bn $)	1985 (%)	1990 (bn $)	1990 (%)
Total exports	1308.25	100	1965.55	100
Total manufactures	949.45	72.6	1517.60	77.2
Iron and steel	55.10	4.2	63.40	3.2
Chemicals	128.40	9.8	194.60	9.9
Other semi-manuf.	100.45	7.7	170.70	8.9
Machin. and transp. eq.	505.55	38.6	800.60	40.7
Textiles	35.70	2.7	53.10	2.7
Clothing	21.10	1.6	43.50	2.2
Other cons goods	103.15	7.9	191.70	9.7
Total primary prod.	313.65	23.9	388.30	19.7

Source: GATT, *International Trade 90–91, Vol. II*, Table A3, pp. 80–1.

competitive markets in which a large number of firms each produces an identical product. This complicates our analysis because we have to incorporate the non-competitive behaviour of firms in our models. This will be done in Chapter 5. In this chapter, we will see how it is possible to bypass the above problem.

When economies of scale are *external* to the firm, we are not required to abandon the assumption of a perfectly competitive world. Hence, this chapter will study trade, and the effects of trade, in the presence of external economies of scale. The analysis hopes to provide an explanation of how economies of scale alone may give rise to trade and why such a trade, although usually beneficial to all countries involved, could result in losses for some countries.

■ 4.2 Economies of scale

A production process exhibits economies of scale over a particular range of output, per unit of time, if the per unit or average costs (AC) decline over this range as output increases. This type of AC behaviour is usually found in those production processes which entail large fixed costs before production run begin (such as the large amount of R&D expenditure any producer has to invest before beginning production of goods such as aircraft and computers). These fixed costs are very large compared to the consequent costs of actually producing the output, i.e. variable costs, so that AC declines (sharply) as quantity produced increases.

EOS are said to be *external*[2] to the firm, but internal to the industry, when the productivity of an individual firm depends on the size of the industry's output rather than on its own output. For example, the productivity of a New Zealand farm producing butter depends on the size of the dairy industry in New Zealand.[3] This means that the production process of an individual farm exhibits constant-returns-to-scale (i.e. a farm expects that an increase in its output will have no effect on its cost), which is consistent with the perfectly competitive behaviour of every farm in the diary industry.

EOS are often associated with the presence of *increasing returns to scale* (IRS). IRS within a firm are a technological property whereby proportionately increasing all the inputs that a firm uses leads to a more than proportionate expansion of its output. Whenever the production process exhibits IRS it also is subject to EOS. On the other hand, the presence of EOS does not automatically mean the presence of IRS within the firm. IRS can also occur only at the industry level, we then speak of national or industry IRS. In our discussion we will assume that IRS are indeed present in the production process at the industry level, and we will use the terms IRS and EOS interchangeably in this context.[4]

■ 4.3 A trade model with external EOS

Consider now a simple two-country (Home and Foreign), two-good (food and cloth), one-factor (labour) model. The industry that produces food exhibits constant-returns-to-scale in both countries. Cloth production is subject to external economies of scale in both countries. Production of food in a single firm is given by:

$$f = f(l_F) \tag{4.3.1}$$

where f is the output of a single firm and l_F is its input usage.
The maximum production of food in each country is:

$$F = L_F/a_{LF} \tag{4.3.2}$$

where $L_F = L$ (total labour force $L = L_F + L_C$), and a_{LF}, the unit labour requirement in food production, is constant.

Production of cloth for a single firm is given as

$$c = g(l_C, C) \tag{4.3.3}$$

where c is the output of a single firm, l_C is an input used by a firm and C is the output of the cloth industry. The maximum production of cloth in each country is:

$$C = L_C/a_{LC} \tag{4.3.4}$$

where $L_C = L$ (total labour force) and a_{LC} is the unit labour requirement in cloth production which in this case is not constant but depends on the total cloth output by the domestic industry:

$$a_{LC} = g(C) \tag{4.3.5}$$

For example, assume that $a_{LC} = 1/L_a$. Then $C = L_a^2$. Cloth production thus exhibits EOS that are external to the firm and internal to the industry. Figure 4.2 illustrates how unit labour requirement in cloth production varies with the output of cloth. To concentrate fully on EOS as a basis for trade we will assume that our two countries are identical. This means that a diagram such as Figure 4.3, representing a PPF under IRS, applies to each country.

Being identical, in autarky these two countries also have an identical relative price of cloth in terms of food $(p = p_C/p_F)$.[5] The difference between the relative price and the marginal rate of transformation, i.e. the relative price line crossing the PPF, reflects the distortion which occurs because economies of scale are external to the firms (meaning that firms

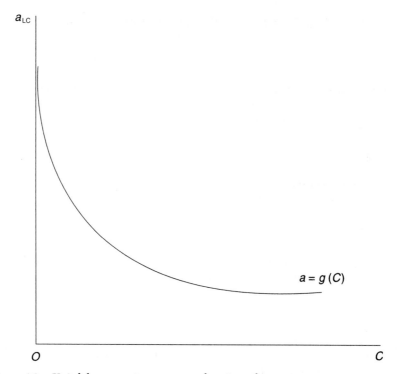

Figure 4.2   *Unit labour requirements as a function of output*

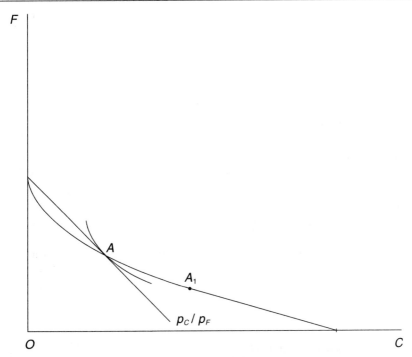

Figure 4.3   *Production possibility frontier under IRS (Home)*

will underproduce cloth). With no difference in relative prices, there is no basis for trade in the sense of comparative advantage. Thus, even if no barriers to trade exist, both countries will produce both goods. This is a free-trade equilibrium (point A in Figure 4.4). However, this equilibrium is not Pareto optimal. That can be easily observed in Figure 4.4. Say that point A, at which both produce and consume in autarky, requires that they divide L evenly between F and C industries. Now if one specialises completely in F (transferring $L/2$ from C to F) and produces at P_F the world production of food will be the same as in autarky. However, the specialisation of another country in C (point P_C) will result in a larger total production of cloth than when both of these countries were producing in autarky (because of EOS). Consumption with trade can be at a point outside the PPF, such as D. *Thus external EOS provide a basis for trade independent of comparative advantage.*

In addition to not being Pareto optimal, the no-trade equilibrium is also unstable. It is sustainable only if both countries produce the same amount of cloth. Any difference in cloth production will lead to the cost advantage in the country with a larger production, which in turn will lead to specialisation and trade. To see this, imagine that Home starts producing more cloth (point A_1), while Foreign continues producing at A (Figure 4.3).

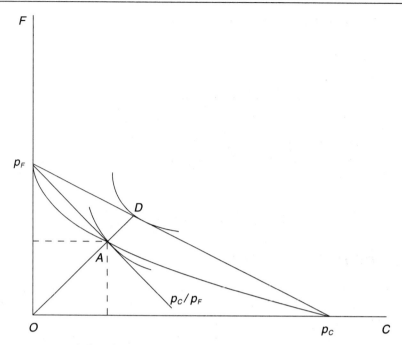

Figure 4.4   *Trade based on EOS*

Then $a_{LC} < a^*_{LC}$, while they can still produce food on equal terms $(a_{LF} = a^*_{LF})$. Because of this wages must be the same in both countries, and consequently, cloth must be cheaper in Home than in Foreign. This will result in a reallocation of resources in both countries. L will shift from food to cloth in Home, and in the opposite direction in Foreign. This process will continue until a new equilibrium is established; where either Home produces only cloth, or Foreign produces only food.

This pattern of production is not the only possible one. A third pattern is easily obtained by reversing the positions of Home and Foreign in the above example. In total we can identify the following stable equilibria in Table 4.3 (cf. Krugman and Obstfeld, 1988, p.129). The actual outcome depends on the strength of the relative demand. If the demand for cloth is not very large, only one country will produce cloth, and there will still be labour left over in this country with which to produce food. If the demand for cloth is large enough, one country will specialise in cloth, even though another country will probably produce it as well.

Thus, even with no comparative advantage, countries end up specialising in the production of different goods. This is because the presence of EOS lead countries to concentrate on a fewer number of tasks. The specialisation is independent of comparative advantage, and there is a tendency towards multiple equilibria.

Table 4.3　*Possible stable equilibria with external economics*

A. Both produce food	
A_1 Home: cloth and food	Foreign: food
A_2 Foreign: cloth and food	Home: food
B. Both specialise	
B_1 Home: cloth	Foreign: food
B_2 Home: food	Foreign: cloth
C. Both produce cloth	
C_1 Home: cloth	Foreign: cloth and food
C_2 Home: cloth and food	Foreign: cloth

☐ *The pattern of trade*

Because EOS lead countries to specialise, they give rise to international trade. As long as both goods are demanded in both countries, they will be interested in trade. The question is, which country will export which good? If the countries are identical, as they are in our example, there is no unique pattern of specialisation and trade. In fact, there is nothing in our model to enable us to predict what the pattern of specialisation and trade will be. Thus we speak of an *unpredictable* pattern of trade. In other words, we cannot use broad national characteristics, as we did in our standard model of trade, to predict which country will export or import which good. Nevertheless, the pattern of trade is determinate in so far as historical or accidental factors, such as 'first mover advantage' (which are not captured by our simple model), play a major role in leading a country to specialise in the production of a particular EOS good. The example usually given is the Swiss watch industry. It started to develop in eighteenth century in Switzerland because the industry was specific-skilled labour-intensive and not natural resources-intensive, and Switzerland, as it happened, fitted those requirements quite well. Not long after that, the established cost advantages were 'locked in', making it impossible for newcomers to take over even if they were well endowed with the necessary resources. Other examples may include the Italian furniture industry, or the Swedish telecommunication industry. What characterises all of these examples is the early achievement of low AC, and the development of technical and other skills which guarantee an advantage that is self-reinforcing. Together with high start-up costs these factors prevent others from successfully competing.

However, the degree of unpredictability is less if countries differ in at least one aspect. Thus, in general, if two countries are of different size, but have identical relative factor endowments and tastes, it can be shown that the large country will specialise in the EOS good, while the smaller country will specialise in the constant-returns-to-scale good.

Consider the two countries from our previous example, but now assume that Home is an economically large country relative to Foreign. Let this be the only difference between these two countries. We can represent their PPFs as in Figure 4.5. Obviously there is no differential resource endowment, and no differential tastes basis for the difference in relative prices. Nevertheless, at the no-trade production points Q and Q^*, relative prices differ: cloth is relatively cheap in Home (large country) and food is relatively cheap in Foreign (small country).[6] The difference in relative prices is due to the assumption that a larger market in Home can support larger production runs, enabling the Home cloth industry to be more productive relative to the Foreign cloth industry. Thus at the free-trade relative price p^T, we have a small country specialising in food and importing cloth, and a large country concentrating on or completely specialising in cloth production, and exporting that cloth.

Does this mean that countries with internal markets small in comparison with the markets of their trading partners can never export EOS goods? Definitely not. It is true that we traditionally see large internal markets as being a prerequisite for an industry to realise EOS benefits; first domestically, and then through exporting. This type of reasoning can be used to explain why small countries such as Japan or Germany have not established themselves as dominant exporters of commercial aircraft as the USA has done, although all three have similar relative factor endowments and tastes. But US producers were able to realise EOS gains even before production for export markets. Nevertheless, small countries, in practice,

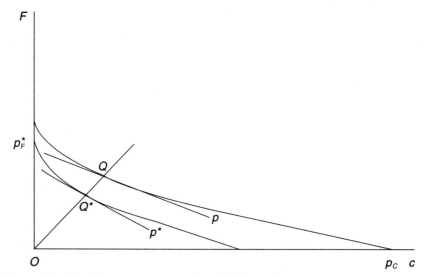

Figure 4.5   *Trade between two countries of different size*

can find themselves in strong exporting positions for EOS goods. What is necessary is some accidental factor that will lead a small country to begin exporting EOS goods. The size of the export market (comparatively much larger than the domestic one) will enable that country to accumulate initial advantage and to establish for itself a permanent export position. Examples include Switzerland (watches industry and pharmaceutical goods), Belgium (standardised manufactured goods such as auto parts), Sweden (telecommunications equipment), Denmark and Italy (furniture), Korea and Taiwan (various standardised manufactured goods) and many more.

☐ *The gains from trade*

The fact that the pattern of trade is unpredictable does not preclude us from determining the gains from trade. To show that trade is beneficial, we can use either of the criteria we have been using so far. We can look at whether trade enables each country to increase overall consumption without increasing its use of resources, or alternatively, we can compare real wage rates before and after trade. If real wages are not lower, or if they increase with trade, we can conclude that a country benefits from trade.

We have already shown (Figure 4.4) that even when two countries are identical, trade based on EOS leads to larger consumption possibilities than in autarky. Let us now consider the example where we have two countries of different size with the same homothetic preferences, so that the difference in commodity relative prices is due entirely to their difference in size. Suppose that with trade Foreign specialises in and exports food, while Home produces both goods and exports cloth (points Q^{*T} and Q^T respectively in Figure 4.6). Both countries gain as they both now consume outside their PPFs (points C^{*T} and C^T). Trade has thus enabled each country to increase their consumption without increasing the overall usage of inputs.[7]

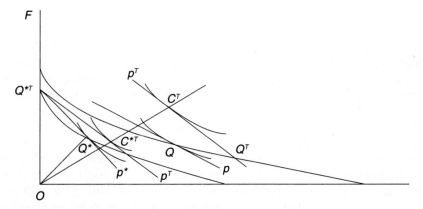

Figure 4.6 *Gains from trade between countries of different size*

Let us now look at the real wage effects of trade. The price of each good is equal to the wage rate times the unit labour requirement. Prices in Home are:

$$p_F = wa_{LF}$$
$$p_C = wa_{LC} = wg(C)$$

Therefore, the real wage rates in Home before trade are:

$$w/p_F = 1/a_{LF} \quad \text{in terms of food, and}$$
$$w/p_C = 1/a_{LC} = 1/g(C) \quad \text{in terms of cloth}$$

Similarly in Foreign:

$$w^*/p^*_F = 1/a^*_{LF} \quad \text{in terms of food, and} \qquad (4.3.8^*)$$
$$w^*/p^*_C = 1/a^*_{LC} = 1/g(C^*) \quad \text{in terms of cloth} \qquad (4.3.9^*)$$

Because with trade Home and Foreign still produce food on equal terms ($a_{LF} = a^*_{LF}$), they must have the same wage rate w^T (where ^{T} means with trade). Since the with-trade price of food $p^T_F = w^T a_{LF}$ is equal to the pre-trade price, the real wage rate in terms of food in both countries is unchanged:

$$w^T/p^T_F = 1/a_{LF} = 1/a^*_{LF} \qquad (4.3.10)$$

But with trade, cloth is produced only in Home. The quantity of cloth Home produces is now larger than before trade ($Q^T_C > Q_C$). Therefore, the unit labour requirement is less ($a^T_{LC} < a_{LC}$), and consequently p^T_C is less than without trade. Thus the real wage rate is higher with trade:

$$w^T/p^T_C = 1/g(C^T) > 1/g(C) \qquad (4.3.11)$$

With no change in the real wage rate in terms of food, and with a higher real wage in terms of cloth, Home is unambiguously better off with trade than without it. But what about Foreign, which is left with no cloth industry? We can determine the real wage in terms of cloth for Foreign despite the fact that it produces no cloth itself. Namely, Foreign exchanges its food for cloth at a lower world price for each unit of cloth than in the absence of trade. Therefore the real wage rate in terms of cloth increases in Foreign as well. Foreign will enjoy a higher real wage in terms of cloth as long as the amount of cloth produced in Home with trade is larger than Foreign would have produced itself in the absence of trade ($Q^T_C > Q^*_C$).

Thus we can say that countries will gain from trade based on external EOS as long as the scale of production with trade in both countries together is larger than would have occurred in any one country in the absence of trade. The source of such gains lies in the with-trade rationalisation (concentration) of the production of goods subject to EOS, which in turn ensures that prices of these goods will fall, benefiting even those countries that do not produce such goods.[8]

However, the gains from trade are likely to be unevenly distributed between the trading countries. To see this, let us first examine what constitutes the total gains from trade. One component is the conventional gains from trade that will accrue to both countries. However, there is a second component of gains that arises from increasing the output of the EOS good. This is reflected in an increased average productivity in the economy which experiences such expansion. Since these gains have attributes of technological progress, the country that does not experience such expansion of the EOS good output is 'less' better off with trade than the other country.

The presence of EOS provides a further source of trade, in addition to the sources of comparative advantage. As shown above, such trade seems to be beneficial to all countries, even though the gains from trade are not necessarily evenly distributed between countries. This begs a question : can this distribution be so uneven as for one country to actually lose from trade? Indeed, it can (see Box 4.2, p. 172). However, this should not come as a surprise. Remember what was said about the non-tangency between the relative price of goods and the marginal rate of transformation in a closed economy: because external EOS constitute an externality (distortion), the country's prices do not accurately reflect the underlying costs of production. Therefore, in a closed economy, the production of the EOS good is suboptimal. The introduction of free trade in such a situation may be welfare-worsening. Specifically, if trade leads to further contraction of an already under-produced good which exhibits EOS, the country is likely, instead of moving towards its optimal production mix (that is, to produce more of the EOS good), to move away from it. However, there is a strong presumption against the inevitability of losses.[9]

■ 4.4 Dynamic economies of scale

The external EOS considered so far refer to the behaviour of industry's costs with respect to its *current* total output at a point in time. If we let this output accumulate in time, and then relate industry's cost to it, we will be dealing with *dynamic economies of scale*. While accumulating this output, unit costs will decrease as a result of increasing experience and knowledge. This process is referred to as *learning-by-doing*. The phenomenon of learning-by-doing is viewed as the process of capability accumulation which results from experience, i.e. learning-by-doing leads to improvements in the skills and capabilities involved in carrying out particular tasks.

This process is often illustrated by the learning curve, as in Figure 4.7. In Figure 4.7 the learning curve L summarises the relationship between the cumulative output of the cloth industry and the unit cost of cloth in Home. Suppose Home is at point A, with the cumulated output of Q_L resulting in a unit cost of c_L. Let Foreign's potential learning curve be L^*. Obviously Foreign has some advantages over Home in that its learning curve lies below Home's learning curve, enabling it to produce Q_L at a lower unit cost, c^*_L. However, Foreign has not started with the production of cloth and incurs start-up costs of c^*_0 before beginning production. Since $c^*_0 > c_L$, the Foreign cloth industry is 'prohibited' from the cloth world market. In other words, by the time potential competitors might appear, Home's advantages have been 'locked-in'; its cloth industry therefore will not be faced with competition.

Box 4.2   *Graham's argument for protection*

Consider a small two-sector economy with a single factor of production, labour. One sector, food, exhibits constant-returns-to-scale and the other, cloth, exhibits increasing returns to scale at the industry level. In other words, the larger the employment of labour and the larger the output of the cloth industry, the smaller the unit labour requirement in that sector. Suppose that the productivity of labour, when fully employed by the cloth industry, is higher than its productivity when fully employed by the food industry. The total product produced in these two cases of complete specialisation can be compared if each case is evaluated at constant prices. Let these prices be the terms of trade. Then, if the terms of trade are such that the value of total product when only food is produced is less than the value of total product when only cloth is produced, we can Pareto-rank these two equilibria by saying that the economy is better off in the latter case.

Let this economy open to international trade. If, with trade, specialisation results in the reallocation of labour from the increasing returns to scale industry (cloth) to the constant-returns-to-scale industry (food), it might happen that a decrease in productivity is such that it cannot be outweighed by gains through trade (i.e. by purchasing the EOS good at a lower price). This possibility was recognised by Frank Graham when he argued that increasing returns to scale might lead to a loss from trade; hence justifying protectionism.[10] Protection would serve as a means of preventing trade from reducing the output of an increasing returns to scale industry, thus preventing the decline of average productivity.

When trade results in losses a country cannot afford to consume its autarky consumption. It is thus forced to consume inside its PPF. This also means that its real wages in terms of both goods have declined in comparison with real wages in autarky.

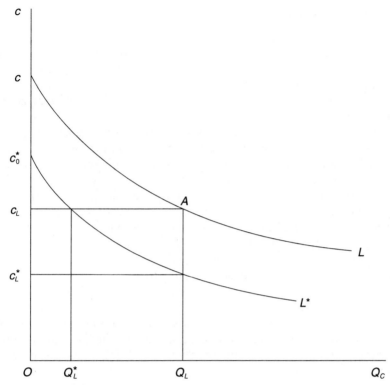

Figure 4.7   *Learning curve*

Suppose that the Foreign government was in a position to foresee such a development in world markets. Accordingly, it could have granted temporary protection to its cloth sector through subsidies or tariffs. Protection would be maintained until the sector had sufficient experience to be 'left alone'. Returning to Figure 4.7, if Foreign's government could neutralise the difference in cost, c^*_0 and c_L, until the Foreign cloth industry reached the cumulated output level of Q^*_L, Foreign producers would be able to sustain their position in the world market because by then they would have 'locked-in' their cost advantage over Home. This type of temporary protection, granted for the sole purpose of enabling young industry to mature in terms of experience and efficiency, is known as the *protection of infant industry*. This is not a new idea. Similar stories advocating the protection of infant industry can be found in the writings of Hamilton (1790) or List (1841). However the revival of the role of dynamic and static EOS within trade theory has given a renewed theoretical strength to modern protectionist arguments as they relate to infant industry. This topic will be discussed at length in Chapter 10.

■ 4.5 Summary

This chapter has considered a reason for countries to trade that arises independently from reasons of comparative advantage. The basic insight gained is that with EOS we do not need countries to be different for trade to exist. Even identical countries will be led to produce different goods, and will trade.

The absence of differences between countries, however, takes away from the model the ability to predict patterns of specialisation and trade. There is a high degree of arbitrariness in our model with regard to identical countries and the pattern of trade. Specifically, we have to accept historical and accidental factors (such as the 'first mover advantage') as determinants of patterns of trade. In the end, three potential patterns of specialisation and trade emerge (excluding the no-trade equilibrium). The first type of trade pattern implies complete specialisation within each country so that one country produces and exports the EOS good, while another country produces and exports the constant-returns-to-scale good. You are quite right to believe that there is no great difference between this outcome and the outcome of the Ricardian model. The second type of trade pattern is the one in which one country specialises in the constant-returns-to-scale good while the other country produces both goods. The implication of this outcome is that there will be equalisation of factor prices between countries. As we will discuss later, in this case trade in goods is a perfect substitute for international factor movements. The third pattern implies specialisation in the EOS good in one country, and production of both goods in the another country. This type of outcome is significant because of its implications for gains from trade, as shown in Box 4.2 (p. 172). However, if countries differ in size, that difference plays a major role in determining the pattern of specialisation and trade. We have shown that countries that differ only in size will specialise in such a way that the large country will export the EOS good and the small country will import it.

EOS have important implications for the gains from trade. Trade in the presence of EOS offers more possibilities for gains than trade based on comparative advantage. However we have also established the possibility of losses from trade. Gains will result if trade increases the production of the EOS good above the level of production that would occur in any country in the absence of trade. Welfare-worsening trade at country level is certainly a new element in our analysis. The implications of this for trade policy are quite significant and we shall return to them later.

Our examination of EOS was motivated by a need to explain the discrepancy between the implications of the standard trade model and the actual characteristics of world trade patterns. Although we gained some insight of how it can happen that similar (or indeed, identical) countries trade, and gain from trade, our simple model was not very successful in explaining why countries would actually exchange similar (or identical) products. On the contrary, the presence of national EOS only enhances the specialisation and trade in products that belong to distinct product groups (see Appendix 4 below, for a discussion of *international* EOS that result in a different type of specialisation). This leads us to the next class of trade models (Chapter 5) where EOS are presented as being internal to firms, and where the assumption of perfect competition is relaxed.

▌ *APPENDIX 4* EOS AND THE INTERNATIONAL DIVISION OF LABOUR

Adam Smith stressed the importance of the economies generated by the division of labour. In his famous example of the pin factory, the division of labour allowed for the production of 4800 pins per worker per day, while without such a division of labour a worker might not have made even one pin in a day. The explanation was that as output expands, labour becomes more productive because of increased specialisation on a particular task in the productive process. The division of labour enhances the productivity of each worker and saves time by making each worker specialise at a particular task. Workers thus do not have to shift from one task to another. This idea has been implemented in numerous production processes that use assembly lines. But such a division of labour is limited by the size of the output produced. Where such a division of labour and resulting EOS are limited by the size of a national market, we have a similar situation as in our examples in this Chapter. Countries will specialise in production of distinct products, and trade between them will be what we call *inter-industry trade* – the exchange of goods that belong to different production groups or industries (like food and cloth).

There is, however, another possibility. Division of labour and EOS could be *international*, i.e. dependent on the size of the world market rather than the size of the national market. Consider the following example. There are two countries, Home and Foreign, both producing food and cloth. They use labour and capital in the production of both goods. Food is a labour-intensive good relative to cloth, and is produced under constant-returns-to-scale. Cloth production exhibits increasing returns to scale at the global industry level, that is, the productivity of each country's cloth industry depends upon the total (joint) production of cloth in both countries. With production of cloth geographically dispersed between Home and Foreign, as the world output of cloth increases, greater degrees of specialisation are allowed so that some components of cloth will be produced in Home and some in Foreign. This increases each country's productivity in cloth production.

The pattern of specialisation and trade is in this case determined by the allocation of resources. If, for example, Foreign is well endowed with labour relative to Home, it will concentrate on the production of food, and will export food to Home in exchange for cloth. Trade will again be of an *inter-industry* character and will be determined by the difference in relative factor endowments, as it was in the HOS model. Nevertheless, small differences in endowments reduce the incentive for such distinct specialisation and inter-industry trade by causing the integrated cloth industry to be divided relatively evenly between Home and Foreign. In the extreme case of identical factor endowments, countries will be self-sufficient in food and it will become a non-traded good. They will, however, gain from exchange of cloth. Trade that will evolve will be *intra-industry* in character – an exchange of goods belonging to the same product group or industry.

Thus, in general, when EOS are international, countries with dissimilar relative factor endowments will specialise in different goods according to comparative advantage and trade will be predominantly inter-industry in character. Conversely, similar countries will have similar patterns of specialisation (i.e. they will not specialise at the industry level) and trade will be intra-industry in nature. It is more likely that such trade will occur in intermediate, rather than in finished (consumer) goods.

This model is reasonably successful in explaining the pattern of trade between DCs and developing countries as illustrated in Tables 4.1 and 4.2.

■ *Chapter 5* ■

Modern Theories of Trade – 2: Imperfect Competition

■ *5.1* New origins of trade

The purpose of this chapter is to further our study into the origins of trade in line with empirical observations of the actual patterns of the world trade. So far we have identified two motivations for international trade: (1) differences between countries that give rise to comparative advantage which leads to specialisation and trade, and (2) external EOS that, irrespective of comparative advantages, give rise to geographical concentration of production, which in turn induces international trade. The models which incorporate either of these two motivations are based on perfect competition – a market structure that is traditionally assumed in trade theory, despite the fact that it became harder and harder to give a real-world justification for this assumption.

One of the main reasons for the persistent use of pure competition in trade models is that other types of market structure are difficult to model in terms as simple and elegant as those which describe perfect competition.[1] The lack of a general model of imperfect competition still prevents us from providing a standard model of non-competitive trade theory (cf. Krugman, 1994). Instead we have several alternative types of imperfect competition, with each type based on a different set of assumptions. Each type therefore requires a customised model of trade. In the last ten years or so, more of those customised models have been developed than it would be suitable to expound in one chapter. Thus we choose to review here the models which have become the representative models for the two particular types of market structure: *oligopoly* and *monopolistic competition*.

177

The model of oligopolistic competition surveyed here is based on the model of reciprocal dumping developed in Brander and Krugman (1983). The Helpman–Krugman model of monopolistic competition is based on Helpman (1981) and Helpman and Krugman (1985). Both of these models have contributed significantly to the quality of explanation of intra-industry trade. They have also caused quite a radical change in how (trade) economists look at important issues such as unilateral protectionism, distribution of gains from trade, growth and trade, and regionalism versus multilateralism. The models based on oligopolistic market structures gave rise to the idea of *strategic trade policy*, which consequently became the theoretical construct upon which revived calls for protectionism were based. The model of monopolistic competition has provided a better explanation of the gains from trade, as well as of the directions and volume of trade. This model also provides the basis for research that is shedding new light on dynamic issues such as trade evolution and endogenous growth.[2]

These trade models incorporate three new elements: internal EOS, imperfect competition and product differentiation. Not all three elements are explicit in each model. In fact, internal EOS is assigned a 'silent role' in causing and sustaining imperfect competition. In such cases the focus shifts from EOS to imperfect competition itself as the main generator of trade. Consequently, we will add two new explanations for trade: (1) brand-specific internal EOS combined with imperfect competition, and (2) the nature of imperfect competition itself. Of course, in the real world these motivations do not act independently of each other. In most cases it will be the interaction of comparative advantage and one or more of the other stimuli that determines the actual pattern of specialisation and trade. Hence, in the model of monopolistic competition presented here two motives are allowed to work together: differences in endowments, and the economies of scale. This model then allows for specialisation at different levels, giving cause to both inter-industry and intra-industry trade.

In this chapter we assume that EOS are *internal* to the firm. They exist when the firm's average cost falls as its own output increases; thus we speak of plant-specific economies of scale.[3] What matters here is the size of the firm, not the size of the industry or country. The existence of internal EOS will inevitably lead to some form of non-competitive market structure. Which market structure will prevail depends largely upon the relative importance of internal EOS.[4] If the minimum efficient scale is relatively large compared with the size of the market, the industry will be able to accommodate a few firms at most, or even just a single firm. The market structure will thus be oligopolistic, or monopolistic, respectively. If, on the other hand, the minimum efficient scale is relatively small, so that the market can support a large number of firms, the market structure will be more in the nature of monopolistic competition.

Our main concerns in this chapter are oligopoly and monopolistic competition. However, the next section will focus on the behaviour of the pure monopolist. In reviewing this most simple type of imperfect competition our goal is to prepare the ground for a discussion of the more complex types of market structure which will occur in the later sections of this chapter.

■ 5.2 Monopoly

Consider a firm that produces a homogeneous good called buses (B), and is the sole supplier to the Home market. In such a situation the downward sloping market demand curve for buses becomes the demand curve that faces the firm. In Figure 5.1 this demand curve is shown as a straight line D to make the exposition simpler. For the same reason, marginal costs (MC) are assumed to be constant. The assumption of the presence of internal EOS are reflected in a downward sloping average cost curve (AC), which indicates that there must be some large fixed costs incurred in producing buses that prevents other firms from entering the industry. More precisely, as the output of this firm increases, its average cost decreases, so that it can

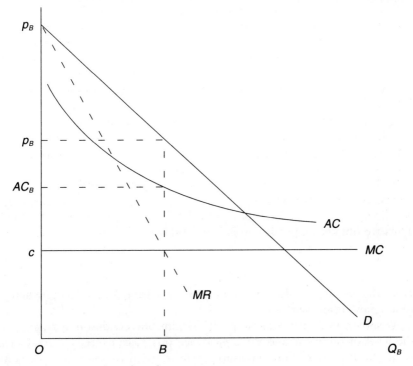

Figure 5.1   *Monopoly and profit maximisation*

always undercut and drive out any smaller producers that try to enter the market. The firm will choose to produce a quantity of buses so as to maximise its profits:

$$\pi = pB - c(w, B) - F \qquad (5.2.1)$$

subject to the production function

$$B = f(V)$$

given the demand function

$$p = p(B), \qquad \partial p / \partial B < 0$$

where B, c, F and V stand for the number of buses, marginal costs, fixed costs and inputs, respectively.

We can rewrite the profit-maximising equation as:

$$\pi = R(B) - C(B) \qquad (5.2.1a)$$

where $R(B)$ and $C(B)$ denote total revenue and total costs. The first order condition then is:

$$\partial \pi / \partial B = \partial R / \partial B - \partial C / \partial B = 0 \qquad (5.2.2)$$

or equivalently

$$MC_B = MR_B \qquad (5.2.2a)$$

which equates marginal costs to marginal revenue at the profit-maximising output.[5] This condition can be rewritten in terms of the price elasticity of demand. Let the price elasticity of demand for buses be $e = (\partial B / \partial p_B)(p_B / B)$. Then marginal revenue can be written as:

$$MR_B = p_B(1 + 1/e) \qquad (5.2.3)$$

Thus we obtain the profit-maximising condition:

$$MC_B = p_B(1 + 1/e) \qquad (5.2.4)$$

Note that a monopolist will produce only where $MR > 0$, i.e. where e reflects an elastic demand.

As shown in Figure 5.1, the profit-maximising condition is satisfied at the level of output B and price p_B. Since this price exceeds average cost AC_B, the firm is earning monopoly profits equal to $(p_B - AC_B)B$. Note that a monopolist charges more and produces less than would a perfectly competitive bus industry. A competitive industry would charge where price equals long-run marginal cost, and would produce at the level of output where $MC = p$ crosses D. However, the monopolist can exploit its monopoly power by restricting output and forcing the price up. Very often (but not necessarily always) this can lead to production that does not correspond to the minimum point on the long-run average cost curve, but is to the left to it. In such a case we speak of excess capacity. This is why a monopolistic market structure is typically described as being inefficient, resulting in the price of a good being higher than the marginal cost of producing it.[6] This inefficiency will be reflected in the distorted relative prices of a national economy, as shown below.

Suppose that there are only two industries in Home: the bus industry B, and the cloth industry C. If both these industries were perfectly competitive, the profit-maximising rule for all firms would be:

$$p = MC \qquad (5.2.5)$$

since $MR = p$.

We can express the relative price of cloth in terms of buses as the ratio of the marginal costs of these two industries:

$$p_C/p_B = MC_C/MC_B = MRT \qquad (5.2.6)$$

(5.2.6) is the familiar competitive equilibrium condition which requires that the relative price line be a tangent to the PPF at the point of the autarkic equilibrium. This is point A in Figure 5.2 (price line not shown). However, with the bus industry being monopolistic as described above, this kind of equilibrium will not prevail in Home. We have established that a monopolist will underproduce and overprice its product, the result being that the unit price of a bus is higher than the marginal cost of producing it. The country's equilibrium condition will therefore become:

$$p_C/p_B(1 + 1/e) = MC_C/MC_B = MRT > p_C/p_B = p_M \qquad (5.2.7)$$

or more simply

$$p_M = p_C/p_B < MC_C/MC_B$$

This implies that relative prices do not accurately reflect opportunity costs, and that the relative price line cannot be tangential to the PPF at the equilibrium point (it is distorted away from the PPF slope). At this point the slope of the relative price line will be less than the slope of the PPF ($= MRT$), as shown in Figure 5.2 by the autarkic equilibrium point A_M.[7] This equilibrium reflects the fact that the monopolist's underproduction causes too many resources to be shifted into the cloth industry, and the monopolist's overpricing distorts the relative prices within the economy. Obviously the level of welfare that can be reached by such an allocation of economy's resources (in the absence of trade) is not the highest possible level. Social indifference curves indicate the level of welfare: in Figure 5.2 we find that $I_M \prec I_A$, saying that the level of welfare in autarky with monopoly is inferior to the level of welfare in perfectly competitive autarky. However, the level of Home's welfare may be increased by allowing free trade. We can show that the welfare effects of free trade with the rest of the (competitive) world will be positive as long as Home is small so that its bus producer cannot extend monopoly power to the world market.

Let us thus assume that Home is small, so that when it opens to trade with the world in which both industries are perfectly competitive, it has to take world prices ($p^T = p_C/p_B$) as given. Suppose that at world prices buses are relatively cheaper than cloth. In other words, Home *appears* to have a comparative advantage in cloth:[8]

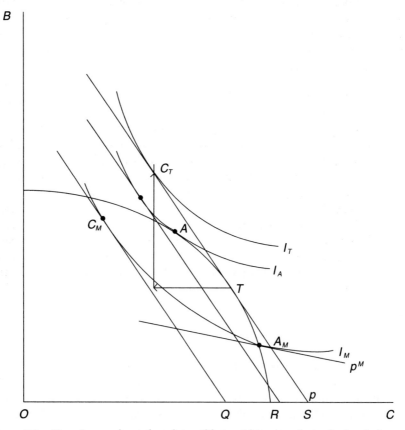

Figure 5.2   *Home's autarky and trade equilibria with monopoly in the bus industry*

$$p_C/p_B < p_C^T/p_B^T = p^T \qquad\qquad (5.2.8)$$

The fact that world prices are given implies that the monopolist cannot follow his previous pricing policy, since the price elasticity of demand for his product becomes infinite (making the demand perfectly elastic with respect to price) and he can only sell at the prevailing world price. The monopolist in Figure 5.2 is therefore forced to *expand* his output. The level of expansion will be dictated by world prices (point T at the PPF).[9] The cloth industry faces the same relative world price and will choose the same point T as the level of production. The with-trade allocation of resources in Home is now consistent with the perfect competition which characterises both industries. The global allocation of resources is also improved provided that Home's comparative advantage in cloth was real; otherwise Home would have started trading in a 'wrong' good.

As shown in Figure 5.2 free trade will cause quite a drastic change in the level and pattern of consumption in Home. The with-trade consumption point C_T lies on a higher social indifference curve I_T. Free trade therefore results in gains to Home, although it implies a decreased consumption of cloth relative to autarky. Moreover, the gains from trade are even larger than they would have been if the bus industry were perfectly competitive in autarky. To see this, it is useful to decompose the total gains from trade (given by the shift from A_M to C_T and amounting to QS in terms of cloth) into two parts: (1) the shift from C_M to A, which results from the removal of the distortion arising under monopoly (QR in terms of cloth), and (2) the shift from A to C_T, which is a consequence of international specialisation (RS in terms of cloth). In other words, only the latter gains constitute the standard gains from trade, while the removal of monopoly constitutes the additional, so-called, pro-competitive gains.

What would happen if the bus monopolist were to become a purely competitive exporter when Home is opened for trade? As shown in Figure 5.3, when faced with the world price p^T the 'monopolist' will expand output from A_M to T. This transformation of a monopolist into a pure competitor in both Home and world markets leads to a decrease in the domestic price of buses (i.e. an exportable good) relative to cloth. This occurs with trade because there is only one prevailing price at both domestic and world markets.[10] Free trade will again result in augmented gains since it will serve to remove domestic monopoly.

To recap, we have shown that when a country with a monopolised industry opens up to trade with the competitive world, trade brings both standard and some *additional* gains, since it increases competition within the domestic market. The pattern of trade was not explicitly discussed here, but it is clear that this is once again determined by the difference in relative autarkic prices.

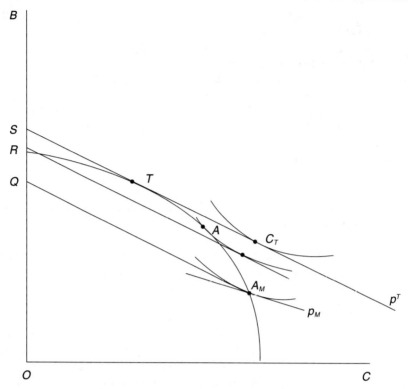

Figure 5.3   *Home's autarkic and trade equilibria when a monopolised industry becomes an exporter*

■ 5.3 Oligopoly: the reciprocal dumping model

We can now discuss our primary interest in this chapter: the implications for trade which arise from certain types of imperfectly competitive market structures. In this section we will consider the case where two monopolies from different countries engage in oligopolistic competition within their respective domestic markets. In fact, since the number of firms is fixed at two, this form of oligopoly is correctly referred to as '*duopoly*'.

Firms can engage in many different types of interactions in duopolies, as well as choosing among several different decision variables. There are thus a number of possibilities to choose from when modelling their interactions. In order to keep our exposition simple, a particular type of behaviour on the part of firms is assumed. This will, of course, make conclusions about trade and gains from trade very sensitive to the special assumptions underpinning our model. Nevertheless, this model of duopoly does help in adding to our understanding of the reasons for intra-industry trade.

□ *A closed economy*

The following assumptions are made in the model:

1. There are only two countries, Home and Foreign, which are identical.
2. There is only one producer of a homogeneous good (for example, buses) in each country. Each firm's objective is to maximise profits (π).
3. These two firms are identical: both have constant MC, while continuously decreasing AC enables each to operate as a monopolist in autarky.
4. Once trade is allowed, each firm perceives each market as distinct, and makes separate decisions about deliveries to each market.

Now suppose that the demand for buses in the Home and Foreign markets is given by the respective inverse demand functions:

$$p = a - b(x + y) \tag{5.3.1}$$
$$p^* = a - b(x^* + y^*) \tag{5.3.1*}$$

where p and p^* are the bus prices in Home and Foreign markets, x and x^* are the outputs of the Home firm sold in the domestic and Foreign markets, and y and y^* are the outputs of the Foreign firm sold in Home's market and in its own market.

To keep things simple, we assume that the total cost functions are linear and symmetrical for both firms. Total costs include a fixed cost K, marginal cost c, and a transportation cost t, which is constant per bus and is positive only when buses are being exported. Then the costs of the Home firm take the form of:

$$C_x = K + cx + (c + t)x^* \tag{5.3.2}$$

and for the Foreign firm:

$$C^*_y = K + c^*y + (c + t)y \tag{5.3.2*}$$

Before trade is begun between Home and Foreign, each firm remains a monopolist in its respective market, and we have $x^* = y = 0$. In this case the price in each market can be easily determined by equating each firm's marginal revenue with its marginal cost. Given our assumption that the firms and markets in Home are identical to these in Foreign, in the analysis to follow we can concentrate on one market only. The other market will mirror what happens in the first.

Consider then the Home market in which, in the absence of trade, total revenue for the Home firm will be:

$$R_x = px = [a - b(x)]x \qquad (5.3.3)$$

and marginal revenue

$$MR_x = a - 2bx \qquad (5.3.4)$$

Since the Home firm does not export, its total costs are equal to $K + cx$, and its marginal costs are equal to c. Thus we have the profit-maximising output determined as:

$$MR_x = MC_x$$
$$a - 2bx = c$$
$$x = (a - c)/2b \qquad (5.3.5)$$

This output is sold in the Home market at the price

$$p = (a + c)/2$$

or

$$p = c + [(a - c)/2] \qquad (5.3.5a)$$

Obviously a firm earns supernormal profits since price exceeds marginal cost. The profits the firm collects from its own market are:

$$\pi_x = Rx - cx - K$$
$$\pi_x = 1/4b(a - c)^2 - K \qquad (5.3.6)$$

The profits the Foreign firm earns in its own market are identical because the price, quantity supplied and costs are the same in both cases. Thus, when both firms operate as monopolists, the price and number of buses supplied to the Home market is identical to the price and number of buses supplied to the Foreign market. In such a situation there is *no advantage based on cost* forming a basis for trade between Home and Foreign.[11] However, if trade does occur, it will have noticeable effects. By focusing on the profit-maximising behaviour of the two firms, a reason for trade is found in that that each of the firms will have an incentive to penetrate each other's market. The incentive is in a form of the mark-up (equal to $(a - c)/2$) that firms charge over marginal cost. If this mark-up is sufficient to cover the cost of shipping buses (t) from one market to another, each firm will try to invade the other's market, hoping to increase total profits. The result will be cross-hauling of buses between Home and Foreign. The type of trade that emerges is an intra-industry trade in identical products.

Before proceeding with our analysis, we should pause to ask what is the point of shipping identical products between two countries and, in doing so, wasting resources on transportation. The cross-hauling of buses instigates increased competition (duopoly instead of monopoly) in each market. This, in turn, reduces distortions (i.e. reduces price and increases deliveries), the result being net social benefits for both countries. There-fore, as we will illustrate, trade that would never have occurred on the basis of countries characteristics, but occurs solely as a result of imper-fectly competitive firms' desire to penetrate each other's market, may lead to gains. Note that we have also derived a simple, but not very realistic, explanation for the phenomenon of intra-industry trade.

☐ *The trading equilibrium*

When each firm begins with delivering to the other firm's market, it must decide upon the quantity of buses it is going to ship abroad. In making this decision, a firm entering the market must take into account the reaction of the firm incumbent in that market. We assume that each firm believes that its own actions will have no effect on the other firm's decision about deliveries for the market those deliveries are assigned for. In other words, we assume that each firm behaves according to the Cournot model of duopoly in each market. Since these markets are symmetric, it is again sufficient to analyse one country only.

Consider then the two firms in the Home market. Setting each firm's perceived marginal revenue equal to its marginal cost in this market, and solving for its deliveries, we obtain the quantity of buses each firm wants to deliver to this market. Thus, to determine the Home firm's profit maximising supply to its domestic market we have:

$$R_x = [a - b(x + y)]x \qquad (5.3.7)$$
$$MR_x = a - b(2x + y) \qquad (5.3.8)$$
$$MC_x(= c) = MR_x \qquad (5.3.9)$$
$$a - b(2x + y) = c$$
$$x = 1/2b(a - c) - y/2 \qquad (5.3.10)$$

Analogously to derive the Foreign firm's profit-maximising supply to the Home market we have:

$$R_y = [a - b(x + y)]y \tag{5.3.7a}$$

$$MR_y = a - b(x + 2y) \tag{5.3.8a}$$

$$MC_y (= c + t) = MR_y \tag{5.3.9a}$$

$$a - b(x + 2y) = c + t$$

$$y = 1/2b(a - c - t) - x/2 \tag{5.3.10a}$$

(5.3.10) and (5.3.10a) for x and y define the firms' reaction functions in the Home market. Reaction functions are conveniently used in Figure 5.4 as reaction curves xx and yy to trace the delivery path of each firm. Each reaction curve plots the profit-maximising level of deliveries for each firm given every conceivable expected delivery which could be chosen by the other firm. Thus, the Home firm's reaction curve (xx) describes how this firm will change deliveries in response to a change in the Foreign firm's deliveries to the Home market. Similarly, the Foreign firm's reaction curve (yy) describes its response to changes in the Home firm's deliveries.

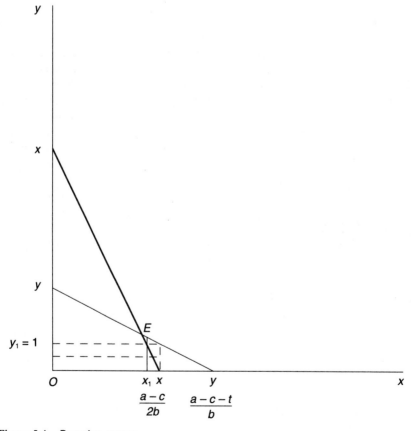

Figure 5.4   *Reaction curves*

With Cournot's behavioural assumptions, and a linear demand function, an increase in the deliveries of the Foreign firm lowers the price both firms will receive from the market. This in turn lowers the marginal revenue received by the Home firm at each level of deliveries compared with its pre-trade marginal revenues. Therefore, for a given marginal cost, the Home firm will reduce deliveries. The Foreign firm responds in the same way. This explains the negative slope of the reaction curves.

The intersection of these reaction curves determines the trading equilibrium.[12] The trading equilibrium will exist if the amount the Foreign firm exports is positive. This occurs only if Home's autarky price is such as to allow for a mark-up larger than the cost of transportation, so that the foreign firm finds it profitable to export to Home. Since we have established that in autarky $[(a - c)/2] > t$, we have assured for a positive exports by the Foreign firm, and a resultant equilibrium that involves exports from Foreign to Home (such as point E in Figure 5.4). Because the Foreign market is symmetrical, the equilibrium there will involve imports from Home, and we will have *intra-industry* trade between Home and Foreign.

By solving the two firms' reaction functions simultaneously we can determine the firms' deliveries in equilibrium. Substituting (5.3.10a) into (5.3.10) yields:

$$x = 1/2b(a - c) - y/2$$
$$x = 1/2b(a - c) - 1/4b(a - c - t) + x/4 \qquad (5.3.11)$$
$$x = 1/3b(a - c + t)$$

Substituting (5.3.11) back into (5.3.10a) yields:

$$y = 1/3b(a - c - 2t) \qquad (5.3.12)$$

It is now apparent that the Home firm's share of the market is larger than the Foreign firm's share:

$$x - y = (1/b)t > 0 \qquad (5.3.13)$$

This result suggests that if there were no transportation costs, firms would divide the Home market between themselves equally. In Figure 5.4 this result would be illustrated by point E, lying on the $45°$ line from the origin. However, with positive transportation costs, the Home firm captures a larger share of the market and that share increases as t becomes larger (i.e. point E is shifted towards the x axis). When t becomes too high, when $[(a - c)/2] < t$, the Foreign firm will cease exporting, leaving the Home firm in a monopoly position, as it was before trade, with the level of deliveries equal to $(a - c)/2b$.

The difference in market share is exactly what makes the trade sustainable. Because the foreign firm has a smaller market share of the Home market, it perceives that market as having a higher price elasticity of demand than its own market. Because of this it is willing to sell buses in the Home market at a lower mark-up over marginal costs than in its own market; that is, while still covering transportation costs. In fact, it is actually *dumping* buses in the Home market, since it is selling buses at a lower net price in Home than in its own market. The Home firm will be in an identical position in the Foreign market. Therefore, the trade that occurs is in fact a dumping of buses by each firm in the other firm's market. This is why this model is called the model of *reciprocal dumping* (Brander and Krugman, 1983).

☐ *The pro-competitive effects of trade*

One effect of dumping is a reduced price of buses in both markets compared with the pre-trade price. The price with trade is:

$$p' = a - b(x + y)$$
$$p' = 1/3(a + 2c + t) \tag{5.3.14}$$

That price is lower than the monopolistic autarky price:

$$p' - p = 1/3(a + 2c + t) - 1/2(a + c)$$
$$p' - p = -1/6(a - c - 2t) < 0 \tag{5.3.15}$$

Since $(a - c - 2t) > 0$ or $[(a - c)/2] > t$, when the Foreign firm exports to the Home market, the with-trade price must be lower than the autarkic bus price. This effect of trade on price is known as the *pro-competitive effect* because it is a result of the increased competition in each market.[13] The lower price of buses reduces firms mark-up over marginal cost. With free trade, price is equal to $p' = c + (a - c + t)/3$ which means that the mark-up falls from $(a - c)/2$ to $(a - c + t)/3$. Trade-induced competition, of course, reduces profits for both firms, although profits remain positive. With-trade profits for the Home firm from its domestic market are:

$$\pi'_x = R'_x - cx - K$$
$$\pi'_x = x[a - b(x + y) - c] - K \tag{5.3.16}$$
$$\pi'_x = (1/9b)(a - c + t)^2 - K$$

Similarly, profits for the Foreign firm from the Home market are:

$$\pi'_y = R_y' - (c + t)y - K$$
$$\pi'_y = y[a - b(x + y) - c - t] - K \qquad (5.3.17)$$
$$\pi'_y = (1/9b)(a - c - 2t)^2 - K$$

Given the perfect symmetry of our model, we have $\pi_x' = \pi^*{}_y'$ and $\pi_y' = \pi^*{}_x'$. That is, in the end, both firms earn the same total profits from both markets. These profits are lower than in autarky because of the lower price. Profits are also negatively affected by the transport cost that each firm incurs. Note that this reduction in profits could lead the firms to engage in collusive behaviour. By forming an *international cartel* firms can try to prevent the establishment of free trade. By doing so they can protect their autarkic level of profits (see Box 5.1).

Box 5.1 *International cartels*

Increased competition leads to smaller profits, tempting firms to enter into some type of market-sharing arrangement. By forming *international cartels*, and agreeing to stay out each other's market (or by apportioning the world market in some other way), firms hope to control the level of output and the price level, and protect their own profits. If they were fully successful in forming such a cartel, firms could in fact appropriate all the potential gains from trade that would otherwise occur as an increase in consumer surplus in the consuming countries. It has always been taught that this is good enough reason for national governments to prevent firms from colluding in such a manner. Since the above-normal profits earned by national firms in world markets have been accepted as a valuable component in the national income, governments are now seen as being supportive of at least some collusive arrangements among firms (and governments). Normally they would accept so-called 'voluntary export restraints' or quotas as an arrangement through which the profits of the domestic firm, and therefore national income, could be increased at the expense of the importing country. Moreover, in an oligopoly structure a quantitative trade barrier may be profit-increasing for both domestic and the foreign firm and therefore could facilitate collusion between them.

Economic theory teaches us that each cartel tends to be *inherently* unstable, because each member has incentive to 'defect' while others are abiding by the rules. Certainly history shows that the majority of international cartels tend to disintegrate rapidly (examples include the attempts to control the world markets of coffee, bauxite, diamonds, tobacco, etc.). The notable exception is OPEC (the Organisation of Petroleum Exporting Countries) which has more or less successfully controlled the world market for crude oil since 1973.

☐ *The gains from trade*

It remains to be shown that this trade can result in net gains for both countries. The simplest way to show this is to examine the sum of consumer and producer surpluses before trade and with trade. If the gains to consumers, due to lower prices, are larger than the losses these lower prices cause producers, gains from free trade are assured.

As Brander and Krugman (1983, p. 317) clearly demonstrate, trade in the model of reciprocal dumping has conflicting welfare effects. This is illustrated by Figure 5.5, which shows the two effects resulting from trade. On the one hand, there is an effect on competition and prices caused by additional deliveries (imports). Total deliveries increase from the autarky level x_A to the level $x + y$. This reduces the price from p to p', and results in the gain shown by the area 12345 (this consists of an increase in consumer surplus 123, and an increase in producer surplus 1345). Since this gain is caused by trade-induced competition it is what we call a pro-competitive gain (i.e. it reduces a deadweight loss of a monopoly). However, trade also causes domestic supply to contract from x_A to x, so that imports equal y. This can be considered as the diversion of production from the lower-cost producer (Home), to the high-cost producer (Foreign), since the latter incurs transportation costs t in addition to c. The sign of this effect is negative (it is a loss of producer surplus) and is represented by the area 4678. The existence of these two opposing welfare effects makes any conclusions about the net welfare effect uncertain. However we can identify two cases in which the welfare effect is not ambiguous. Firstly, if transport costs are so high that they exceed $(p_A - c)$ they will have a prohibitive effect on trade (i.e. they will choke off all trade), and there will be no welfare effects. At the other extreme, if transport costs are zero, trade becomes costless and procompetitive gains rise to 1289 in Figure 5.5, ensuring that trade is beneficial. Thus, when transport costs are sufficiently low, trade is unambiguously beneficial. On the other hand, when transport costs are high, but not prohibitive, trade will cause a reduction in welfare. In this context it might be the case that a frontier measure which would restrict or prohibit trade would keep welfare from falling.

Trade will certainly prove to be beneficial in this type of Cournot model if free entry is assumed (Brander and Krugman 1983; Venables 1985). In such a case price equals average cost (which includes transport cost) and profits are zero. The trade of identical products will not occur if transport costs are too high. However, when trade does take place, it is welfare-improving: it reduces the *AC* and price causing consumer surplus to rise while profits are still zero.

In summing up we can say that the model of reciprocal dumping points to a new motive for trade even when countries produce identical homogeneous goods at the same cost. This motive lies in the market structure

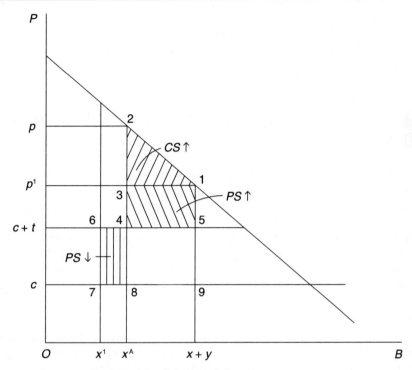

Figure 5.5 *Gains from trade and reciprocal dumping*

itself; trade is initiated because imperfectly competitive firms driven by profit maximisation mutually penetrate each other's domestic market. This results in a new pattern of trade – intra-industry trade. Trade generates pro-competitive gains in terms of reduced price and an increase in quantity. However since trade does not eliminate all monopoly distortions, and because it involves some waste of resources in terms of transport costs for identical goods, the equilibrium we arrive at is not Pareto efficient. Also, the net welfare effect of free trade is ambiguous. It depends on the trade-off between transport costs and the pro-competitive effects. In general, it can be said that the net gains from trade are larger, the smaller the transport costs.

This model provides a simple but powerful example of how trade can be generated solely by imperfect competition. However we must be aware that the model's results are highly sensitive to the assumptions made. For instance, if Cournot behaviour is replaced by Bertrand competition, trade will *not* occur in this model with identical good (Eaton and Grossman, 1983). In Bertrand competition a firm takes other firms' prices as given. When price exceeds marginal cost, each firm will attempt to maximise profits by decreasing price so as to capture the entire market. Suppose, as above, that all firms have the same cost structure and that transport costs are positive. Then each firm will set its price in the domestic market at a level lower than is given by the sum of marginal and transport costs. Hence no trade will occur.

5.4 Monopolistic competition: the Helpman–Krugman model

The section on oligopoly illustrates that trade can occur in the absence of comparative advantage, without EOS playing an explicit role. Note however that EOS implicitly plays a very important role of explaining the oligopoly market structure of our model. In what follows we want to incorporate both comparative advantage and EOS as causes for trade. The model that does this is the Helpman–Krugman model of trade which combines the factor proportions theory of trade with monopolistic competition (following Helpman, 1981; Helpman and Krugman, 1985; Krugman, 1995). This model is capable of depicting a pattern of trade that consists of two different types of trade flows: intra- and inter-industry trade. For example intra-industry trade flows may consist of differentiated manufactured goods, while inter-industry flows may comprise such things as manufactured goods and food. The former are based on specialisation in different varieties due to EOS in the manufacturing sector, while the latter reflects specialisation due to different factor endowments between countries.

Product differentiation and monopolistic competition

The model of monopolistic competition enables us to make yet another step in bringing our models closer to the real-world patterns of trade. We do this by assuming that products are differentiated. We assume that consumers as a whole demand a wide range of varieties of the same basic product, and that firms respond to this demand by producing many differentiated products. By this we mean that products are close but not perfect substitutes.[14] Examples of such differentiated products could include various brands of soft drinks, instant coffee, soap powders, fast food or cold remedies.

There are basically two sources of the demand for differentiated products.[15] First, there are some types of goods of which a consumer will want a small amount of each variety that is available. For example, this may happen with fast food or soft drinks. Secondly, there are examples where each consumer has a very strong preference for only a single variety which suits him or her best. The consumer wants to purchase his or her ideal variety which differs from the ideal variety of any other consumer. An example could be a type of hair style or cold remedy. At present it really makes no difference for our conclusions which source the demand for a variety predominantly comes from. What is important is that there is a taste for variety, with a higher number of varieties increasing average utility. This in turn causes firms to differentiate their products. However, we cannot have a countless number of varieties, as this would imply too great a loss of EOS. Thus we have a large number of firms each producing a slightly different variety of the same basic product. An industry that consists of such firms is characterised by both competition and monopoly power, and is called a monopolistically competitive.[16]

Because products are differentiated, each firm retains some market power (i.e. control over price). This is what gives a monopolistic character to the industry structure. Nevertheless, a firm cannot fully assume the behaviour of a pure monopolist. On the contrary, it must compete in price, as well as in product variety, to attract consumers. Since there are no restrictions to entry, any amount of super-normal profits in the long run will attract new entrants making similar products to those existing in the market. The availability of more varieties will depress demand for the products of the incumbents in the industry, reducing their profits. In the end, profits are competed away, thus giving competitive characteristics to the industry.

An equilibrium position for a typical firm in a monopolistically competitive market is described in the next section.

□ *The firm in monopolistic competition*

It helps to recall the long-run position of a monopoly firm, as shown in Figure 5.1. The firm was making profits since the price charged was above average cost. Let us now assume that instead of producing buses this firm produces a good called manufactures. Potentially there are n different varieties of manufactures. This firm produces only one variety, for example, variety i. Suppose also that there are many other firms, each costlessly producing a different variety ($j \neq i$) of the same basic product. There are no restrictions to entry for these firms. The effect of this is that other firms will enter the industry. In turn, the demand for variety i of the original firm will be more elastic at each and every price. It will also shift the demand curve facing this firm to the left, since the firm will lose market share to the other firms. Entry by new firms will continue as long as there are profits to be made, that is, as long as the price exceeds average cost. In the end all excess profits will be competed away and the original firm, together with the new entrants, would find itself at an equilibrium such as illustrated in Figure 5.6.

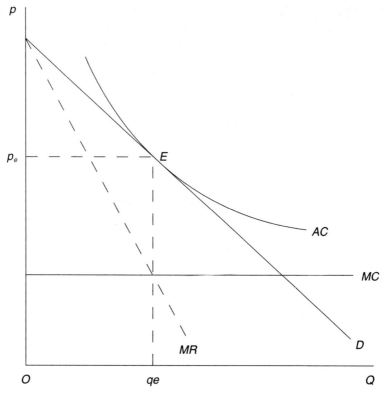

Figure 5.6   *The representative monopolistic firm*

Although each firm makes a zero profit in equilibrium, the equilibrium is Pareto inefficient because price exceeds marginal cost. If output were expanded, efficiency would be increased, the price decreased and consumers would be better off. However each firm is constrained by the downward-sloping portion of the long-run *AC* curve. In other words, each firm operates with an excess capacity. This indicates that there are too many firms in the market. With a fewer number of firms in the market, each firm would be able to increase its output and still satisfy the profit-maximisation requirement. But since each firm can produce only one variety, fewer firms in the market would mean less product variety. This would make consumers worse off since they derive positive utility from increased variety. On the other hand, when they are offered greater variety, they have to pay more, as the increased variety means that many more firms are producing at higher *AC* and charging a higher price.

Consumers in a country such as Home, therefore, where manufacturing industry is monopolistically competitive, ultimately consume fewer varieties than they would wish. Further, there are also fewer varieties available than could potentially be produced. However, these consumers would become better off if the market for manufactures was larger. A larger market, *ceteris paribus*, would support more firms, implying that there would be more varieties. Also, each firm would be able to expand its output, causing a reduction in the price of each variety. Thus, by enlarging the market, more varieties at a lower price would be supplied to consumers (see also Figure 5.7, p. 198).

Remember that one of the functions of trade is exactly this: to enlarge each country's national market. By enabling each domestic firm to supply both the domestic market and an overseas market trade, in effect, creates a larger market for the product in question.

☐ Market size, the number of firms and firm size

Suppose now that the world comprises two countries which share the same technology, have the same factor proportions and tastes, but are different in size. We shall assume that Home is larger than Foreign. The effects of this size differential upon the equilibrium in monopolistically competitive manufacturing industries can be illustrated using Figure 5.7 (Caves, Frankel and Jones, 1993, p. 164, Helpman and Krugman, 1985, p. 155). The number of manufacturing firms (n), which also indicates the number of varieties of manufactures, is plotted on the vertical axis. The output of the individual firm (m), which is a measure of the size of a firm ($m = M/n$, where M is the total manufacturing output), is plotted on the horizontal axis. The curve RC is common to both countries, since they do not differ in either technology or demand conditions. This curve is constructed so that it represents the profit-maximising condition $MR = MC$. In other words, the monopoly power is equal to the degree of EOS, implying that $\pi = 0$ (Helpman and Krugman, 1985, pp. 153–7).[17] Given the characteristics of the RC curve, the various possible combinations of the number of firms (n) and the size of firms (m) in each autarkic country are represented by this curve. As the size of a firm is positively correlated with the number of varieties the RC curve is upward sloping. The further we are from the origin on the RC curve, the larger the total size of the market (represented by M). A larger market necessarily implies a larger number of firms of a larger size (the same effect can be illustrated by the movement down the AC curve in Figure 5.6 because that movement is caused by new entrants into the industry).

Let us now compare the number of firms and their respective autarkic output in Home and Foreign. While otherwise identical, our assumption that Home is larger determines its autarkic equilibrium E to be higher on the RC curve than Foreign's autarkic equilibrium E^*. Each of these particular combinations of n and m must also be lying on the downward sloping curves. These are drawn in such a way that Home's curve is

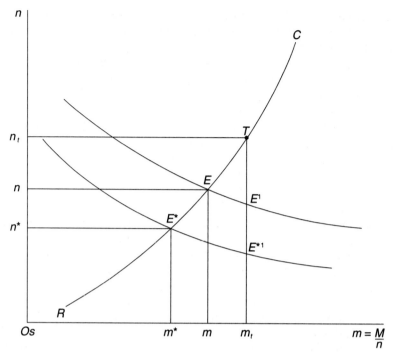

Figure 5.7 *Number and size of firms*

vertically λ times higher than Foreign's, where λ is the difference in country size, and $\lambda > 1$. In autarky, Home's market will support more firms and more varieties, while the output of each firm will be larger, and the price lower than in Foreign. On the basis of this *difference in the autarkic prices* of manufactures, we would predict that Home would become an exporter of manufactures, while Foreign would import them. However, in this model with differentiated manufactures, *this is not what happens*. We will now discuss the pattern of specialisation and trade that may emerge under this construct.

☐ *Trade and trade flows*

Consider first the effects of free trade on the manufacturing sector in both countries. Free trade in manufactures means that there is, in effect, only one market, the world market, for which the manufacturing firms of both Home and Foreign cater. Given the perfect symmetry assumptions, the output of each firm in either country will be the same with trade, while the number of firms will be different. Assume that the downward sloping curves EE' and $E^*E^{*'}$ reflect the possible combinations of n and m, given the internal resource allocation, in each country with and without trade. Then, by vertically summing these curves into $(E + E^*)$, we can illustrate the effects the creation of a single market through free trade has had for manufactures. The equilibrium point T indicates that consumers in each country are offered a higher total number of varieties to choose from with trade then without trade (that is, $n_t > n$, $n_t > n^*$, but $n_t < (n + n^*)$). This is despite the fact that each country experiences a contraction in the number of varieties produced. This is particularly true for the smaller country, Foreign, where the reduction in the number of firms is greater than in the larger country, Home. The trade that takes place between Home and Foreign, therefore, is a two-way trade in manufactures which has the purpose of obtaining for each country those varieties of manufactures that are not produced domestically. Because Home produces more varieties than Foreign, it will be a net exporter of manufactures. However, since Foreign also exports some varieties of manufactures, the lower autarkic relative price of Home's manufactures is thus shown to be an incorrect predictor of the pattern of trade. Note that in this example food is not traded. Each country has the same factor proportions, the same technology is used in the production of the homogeneous good, and demand for that good is identical. There is therefore no basis for trade in food. Thus total trade is *intra-industry* in nature.

From Figure 5.7 it is also clear that each remaining firm, in both countries, is larger in size with trade as compared to autarky. In other words, the output of each variety is now larger ($m_t > m$ and $m_t > m^*; m' = m^*$).[18] A further implication of this model is that each variety is offered at a lower price than before trade. The reduction in the number of firms, and the increase in their size, represents the process of *rationalisation* in the manufacturing sector in each country. We will see that this process contributes significantly to the total gains from trade.

In the above example the only reason for trade is the increasing returns that exist in the manufacturing industry. Although interesting, such a case is rather unlikely in the real world. As mentioned before, it is likely that several factors will interact, generating trade. Accordingly we will modify our model to allow both comparative advantage and increasing returns to act as motivations for trade.

Consider first a world without national borders – the so called 'fully integrated world economy' derived in Chapter 2. Here we again have two factors of production, labour (L) and capital (K), which move freely around the globe, and two industries, manufactures (M) and food (F). The production of food, a homogeneous good, takes place as before, under constant-returns-to-scale. Conversely, the manufacturing industry produces many varieties of manufactured goods, all of which are close substitutes. The production of manufactures is subject to product-specific economies of scale. The technology used in the production of each variety is assumed to be identical. The demand for manufactures is such that the manufactures industry is monopolistically competitive. Capital is used more intensively in the production of manufactures than in the production of food (that is, manufactures are capital-intensive goods).

Assuming that factors of production are perfectly mobile between industries in this world economy, an equilibrium resource allocation is described in Figure 5.8. Total supplies of L and K are given by the sides of the box. The quantities of L and K employed by the manufactures industry are given by vector $OQ(= O^*Q')$ while the quantities of L and K employed by the food industry are given by vector $OQ'(= O^*Q)$. These quantities, when summed, comprise the world endowment of factors OO^*.

Consider now the possibility that world resources are split between two countries.[19] Thus Home has L and K, and Foreign L^* and K^*, of labour and capital respectively. The question is whether international trade can lead to an equilibrium with the essential features of the integrated economy. As we know from Chapter 2, if factors are not divided too unequally, it is still possible for free trade to reproduce the integrated economy equilibrium. This is possible because free trade creates a single market for both manufactures and food, despite the fact that factors cannot freely move between Home and Foreign. However in this case, in contrast to Chapter 2, the nature of trade will be different.

So, let us measure Home's endowment from the origin O, and Foreign's from the origin O^*. A division of world factor endowments between countries is represented by point E. Point E lies inside each country's cone of diversification (i.e. inside the parallelogram OQO^*Q'). We are thus assured that the division of endowments given by point E reproduces the

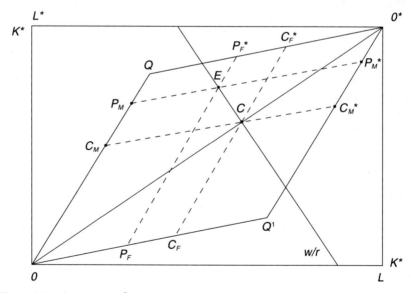

Figure 5.8 *An integrated economy*

integrated economy equilibrium with the same total levels of output, full employment, equilibrium factor prices, and equalised factor prices.

The pattern of production, consumption and trade

The allocation of resources within each country is obtained by constructing parallelograms between point E and each country's origin. Therefore Home allocates OP_M to manufactures and OP_F to food. Similarly, Foreign allocates $O^*P^*_M (= P_M Q)$ to manufactures and $O^*P^*_F (= P_F Q')$ to food. The production of food in Home is $OP_F = F$ and $O^*P^*_F = F^*$ in Foreign. The total production of manufactures in Home is $OP_M = M$ and $O^*P^*_M = M^*$ in Foreign. Each country will produce different varieties of manufactures, however our model cannot determine which country will produce which varieties. Let us just say that Home will produce $n = (M/m)$, while Foreign will produce $n^* = (M^*/m)$. Note that $M + M^* = M$. The sum of Home and Foreign's varieties is equal to the total number of varieties, or $(n + n*) = \bar{n}$, where $\bar{n} M = \bar{M}$ gives the level of output of the world manufacturing sector.

Turning to the pattern of consumption, identical (and homothetic) taste implies that Home and Foreign consume these two goods in the same proportions. Total income is assumed to be spent on these two goods. Each country's income is determined by factor income because there are no profits. Factor incomes are represented diagrammatically by a line passing through E with slope w/r. Point C, where this line intersects with the diagonal, gives us the relative size of each country as measured by its income. Therefore OC is Home's income, and OC/O^*O is its relative size. Similarly CO^* is Foreign's income and C^*O/OO^* is its relative size. Note that according to this unit of measurement Home is larger than Foreign. By completing a parallelogram between C and O and between C and O^*, we can obtain both Home and Foreign's pattern of consumption. It follows that Home consumes OC_M of manufactures and OC_F of food, while Foreign consumes $O^*C^*_M$ and $O^*C^*_F$ of manufactures and food respectively.

To determine the pattern of trade it remains only to compare the patterns of production and consumption in each country. It is obvious that Home consumes more food than it produces, while Foreign consumes more manufactures that it produces. This implies that Home exports manufactures, while Foreign exports food. This pattern of trade is that which would be predicted by the HOS model. Home, which is relatively well endowed in capital, exports capital-intensive manufactures, while Foreign, relatively rich in labour, exports labour-intensive food.

But the trade flow of manufactures does not consist solely of the flow from Home to Foreign. Under our assumptions Home cannot produce all the varieties that are demanded in both Home and Foreign. Some varieties will therefore be produced and exported by Foreign, although Home will remain the net exporter of manufactures. Therefore the trade that emerges will combine two types of flows: *inter-industry* trade of manufactures for food, and *intra-industry* trade in manufactures.

It should be noted that Home, which is assumed to be the large country, ends up being the net exporter of the EOS good. This is not a necessary result of this assumption. Even if Home were the smaller of the two countries, it would be a net exporter of manufactures as long as its capital abundance remained relatively larger than Foreign's. The reason is that once trade occurs, the manufacturing sectors of both countries are catering for the large world market, and it is relative factor abundance that determines the net trade flows.[20]

The same conclusion can be reached by looking at the factor content of trade. First we compare the factor content of aggregate consumption (C) and production (E). It follows that each country 'consumes' factors in proportions different to those it is endowed with. Therefore trade in goods substitutes for the movements of factors by providing a means of equalisation of the factor content in production and consumption in each country (without actually moving any of the factors). The factor content of trade is represented by the vector *EC*. From it we can conclude that Home finds itself in a position of being a net exporter of *capital services*, as embodied in the net export of manufactures. Correspondingly, labour-rich Foreign ends up as the exporter of *labour services* as embodied in the export of food. In conclusion, then, this section shows that it is the difference in relative factor endowments, rather than difference in autarkic relative commodity prices, that serves as the main predictor of trade flows.

☐ *The gains from trade*

A rigorous analysis of the gains from trade when trade consists of both inter-industry and intra-industry flows is not simple. This section provides the main results, without going into the tedium of algebraic proofs. The part of gains pertaining to inter-industry flows is not difficult to establish. They are derived from specialisation along the lines of comparative advantage based on different factor endowments. In the example above, such gains occurred in the trade of food between Foreign and Home.

Although these 'standard' gains from trade can be significant, they are only a portion of the total gains from trade when trade is based on increasing returns, too. From the analysis in Chapter 4 we know that in the case of external economies of scale, larger scale of production will provide additional gains in terms of an increase in real income. However, this result cannot be used directly in the present analysis of gains from trade because here the scale economies are related to products (firms) rather then national or industry markets. Moreover, when we also have differentiated products, we expect that there is yet another source of gains – the degree at which a 'love for variety' in consumption is better satisfied with trade than without trade. Taking this last factor into account, we can say that, in general, a country will not be hurt by trade if the following requirements are satisfied:

(a) the trade-induced change in the number of available varieties to consumers is utility increasing, and
(b) in the trading equilibrium the country can still afford to purchase its autarky consumption vector.

Clearly, by introducing the number of varieties-cum-size of firms as a separate element in establishing the gains from trade, the two models of the demand for differentiated products that we use becomes quite relevant to the results. Thus the Spence–Dixit–Stiglitz model and the Lancaster model now have different implication. From both models it follows that, *ceteris paribus*, consumers would benefit on average from greater variety. In the Spence–Dixit–Stiglitz model this result is derived from the fact that trade adds to the total number of varieties consumers can choose from. However under this model trade may not lead to a change in the scale of production. Thus consumers may not experience gains in terms of lower prices. In this case, requirement (b) may not be satisfied. In the Lancaster model, consumers will unambiguously benefit from trade both in terms of an increased number of varieties and lower prices. Requirements (a) and (b) are both therefore satisfied and gains from trade are assured.

Helpman and Krugman (1985, Chapter 9) provide a detailed and rigorous proof of the *criterion* for the gains from trade in the Helpman–Krugman model. *Trade is beneficial if the world output of the monopolistically competitive goods is larger with trade than any national output of these goods would have been without trade.* Similarly to the criterion used in the case of external economies, here too the only scale of production that matters is the scale of world output; the proportion of output produced by each country is irrelevant.

In concluding this section, it can be noted (anticipating the conclusions derived in Part 2 of this book) that free trade remains the best rule of thumb for trade policy. Free trade based on economies of scale and product differentiation was shown to introduce new sources of potential gains over and above the conventional gains resulting from comparative advantage (when there is no inter-industry trade these additional sources become the only sources of gains because they arise from the intra-industry portion of total trade). The rationalisation effect, that is the reduction in the number of firms and an increase in the output of each remaining firm, ensures that productivity will be enhanced under increasing returns. A further source of additional gains is found in the increased product variety available in each country's market. This directly increases welfare, relative to the closed economy, because it allows consumers, who prefer many varieties, to consume an increased number of varieties. It should also be noted that the overall gains from trade for a country will be larger the larger its trading partner is.

Moreover, it has been demonstrated (Helpman and Krugman, 1985, Chapter 9) that if these additional gains are large enough, and if countries do not differ significantly in factor endowments, trade might not cause income distributional effects. In other words, such trade does not generate conflicts between the owners of different factors of production. Thus at least one of the reasons for protection ceases to exist. However, when trade involves the Lancaster (1980) type of horizontally differentiated products there is a case where a unilateral tariff might be welfare-improving. Free trade typically reduces the number of varieties produced domestically, but the total number of varieties available to consumers increases. An import tariff in this situation will promote domestic entry, in turn increasing domestic variety and decreasing price. However, the increased number of varieties may not be socially acceptable (Lancaster, 1984; Greenaway and Tharakan, 1986).

5.5 Alternative explanations of intra-industry trade

The modern trade theories covered in Chapter 4 and so far in Chapter 5 were developed mostly as a response to the quite obvious discrepancies between the 'then' mainstream trade theory's predictions and the actual real-world trade flows. Some of the mainstream theory's predictions were mentioned when introducing Chapter 4. Contrary to the predictions that the volume of trade between countries will be negatively correlated to the degree of their similarity, empirical observations show that the largest and the fastest-growing trade is, indeed, among the countries that are similar in all three of the broad national characteristics: technology, factor endowments and tastes. Thus trade among developed countries themselves constitutes the major share of the world trade. This type of trade is also growing at a faster rate than the trade between countries less similar in nature, that is between developed and developing countries.[21]

Similarly, with respect to the determinants of the commodity composition of trade, the predictions were that these determinants should reflect comparative advantage so that each country would specialise in what it produced most efficiently. Moreover, each country's line of specialisation would be distinctly different from other countries. The most influential empirical work that tests this prediction is by Grubel and Lloyd (1975). This study also established the fact that the proportion of intra-industry trade grew significantly over time. These empirics, in contradiction to the predictions of mainstream theory, led to a burgeoning literature in search of an acceptable explanation. The explanation set forth by the new trade theory is considered to be revolutionary. However other explanations which have been developed over time should not be ignored. In order to present a balanced view on this issue therefore, we next review some of these alternative explanations.

Geographical location and transport costs

We have already mentioned the costs of transportation as one of the simplest cause or explanations of intra-industry trade which occur between countries that share long national borders, such as Canada and the USA. For goods such as lumber, cement, stone or bricks transportation costs are very high relative to the value of the good itself. Thus it is rational to buy such goods from the nearest supply point, which might mean from a source across the national border rather then from the national supplier. This is what explains the possibility of the same product, say lumber, being exported from British Columbia to California and from Maine to Quebec, which is statistically then recorded as intra-industry trade between the USA and Canada.

However, there is another scenario in which geographical location may play an important role in giving rise to intra-industry trade. This is the case of *entrepôt* trade, which refers to the importing of commodities for the purpose of re-exporting them after they have been repacked and relabelled for the final destination. A large proportion of some countries' trade may actually be entrepôt trade. For example, Singapore, Hong Kong and Macao fall into this category. As reported in the WTO's *International Trade 1995* (Table III.64), 81% of Hong Kong's total export and 40% of Singapore's total export in 1994 was in fact re-export. Such type of trade is also likely to occur within a free trade area and within areas of economic integration where the goods will be imported by one country and then repacked and distributed to other member countries. This will happen because of the attractive geographical location of one country, and this is particularly likely to occur when one country has suitable ports and other necessary facilities compared to other countries. Statistically, however, such trade is recorded as two-way trade in the same type of products between member countries. This will happen because of the attractive geographical location of one country, and this is particularly likely to occur when one country has suitable ports and other necessary facilities compared to other countries. Statistically, however, such trade is recorded as two-way trade in the same type of products between member countries.

Under this heading we can also mention goods that are differentiated in terms of the length of production and consumption. Some goods, such as fresh fruit and vegetables, are not produced in all seasons, but are very often consumed throughout the year; as a consequence a country's trade statistics will record the imports in one season, and the exports in another season. For example, New Zealand exports apples through the months of the South Hemisphere's Fall and imports apples through the months of South Hemisphere's Spring and Winter. This is treated statistically as intra-industry trade. It is however what we refer to as *inter-temporal* function of trade, by which we understand the role trade plays in coordinating and linking production and consumption that occurs at different times. It is obvious that edibles are not the only constituents of this category, but all trade in goods in which consumption or production fluctuates (for example, electricity) is included.

Per capita income levels

Linder's hypothesis (Linder, 1961), which explains the pattern of trade on the basis of different demands, might be a useful tool in explaining trade in differentiated products. Following Linder's view, international trade provides a means of bringing together demand for a number of varieties of manufacturing products and supply of these products. The scope for intra-industry trade comes from the way Linder's hypothesis handles the relationship between income level and demand and supply of differentiated goods. Demand is primarily determined by the level of income: consumers with higher income will demand more expensive goods. Since domestic producers will mostly focus on producing those type of goods that are demanded by domestic consumers, in countries with higher *per capita* income levels, we expect to find a relatively better supply of more expensive goods. If these goods are differentiated, when international trade is introduced it is expected that flow of varieties between countries at the similar level of *per capita* income will be more intensive than between dissimilar countries. In other words, rich countries are expected to mutually exchange varieties of differentiated products in order to satisfy domestic demand.

Trade liberalisation

Grubel and Lloyd's empirical finding is not the only one that does not fit well into the standard predictions. Another one of significance in explaining the growth of intra-industry trade relates to the ease of adjustment following trade liberalisation. It seems that in reality there is no strong link between multilateral tariff cuts and the increased degree of specialisation in developed countries. Thus the high adjustment cost expected by traditional theory in terms of the reallocation of factors has not been observed. Similarly, it was expected that a change in relative commodity prices, brought about by tariff cuts, should have induced conflicts among the owners of different factors. These conflicts were also not particularly apparent in actual cases of trade liberalisation. There are indications from the new trade theory that the adjustment costs and income distributional effects of trade are related to the proportion of intra-industry trade in total national trade: the higher the share of the intra-industry trade, the smaller these effects will be. Since it was mostly intra-industry trade that led the growth of the world trade in the aftermath of tariff reductions, this can explain why countries did not necessarily experience difficult adjustments periods. Alternatively, as some commentators suggest, governments of DCs have deliberately pushed for tariff reductions on goods being exchanged through intra-industry trade between DCs themselves with an objective of minimising the costs of industrial adjustment.

A comparative advantage-based explanation of intra-industry trade

Falvey and Kierzkowski (1987) attempted to explain intra-industry trade without relying on product differentiation. In their model, products are distinguished on the demand side according to perceived quality and on the supply side by the fact that high quality goods' production requires greater capital–labour intensity. The model accounts for trade in differentiated goods in terms of factor endowments, although given its working assumptions it neglects the usual definition of intra-industry goods as goods with similar factor intensity.

Davis (1992) provides an alternative explanation of intra-industry trade based on comparative advantage making the presence of increasing returns not necessary. He does this by introducing the elements of technology differences in the Heckscher–Ohlin model. The key feature of this explanation is the existence of intra-industry specialisation across countries. This specialisation is explained in turn by the substitution possibilities across goods in production which exist because of two things: goods that are traded are produced using similar factor intensities, and there is a large number of goods produced and traded.

■ 5.6 Summary

This chapter has reviewed relatively recent theories that provide an explanation for international trade in similar goods. In contrast to Chapter 4, this chapter focused either solely on the imperfect competition, or on the combination of imperfect competition and increasing returns as the determinants of specialisation and trade.

The simplest model of imperfect competition considered was a case of a domestic monopoly producer. Trade in this situation increases competition and raises the standard gains from trade by the amount of the pro-competitive gains from trade.

The model of oligopoly analysed in this chapter was the one discussed by Brander and Krugman (1983). It is demonstrated that trade in this setting may occur despite the fact that there are no differences between countries. This trade is known as 'reciprocal dumping' which forces each firm to raise its output above the autarky level and thus to reduce the price below the autarky level. Again the gains from trade arise from the pro-competitive effects.

The Helpman–Krugman model includes both the elements of product differentiation and monopolistic competition. In this model international trade enlarges each domestic market and enables the pro-competitive and rationalisation effects to be realised. Thus consumers benefit from an increased number of varieties and from lower prices. Trade in this model might consist of two different flow of goods: inter-industry and intra-industry trade. The former tends to be explained by the relative factor proportion differentials between countries, while the latter reflects the economies of scale. The overall gains from this two-track trade combine the standard gains from trade, that is, the comparative advantage-based gains from trade and the ones resulting from pro-competitive and ratio-nalisation effects. It seems that the income-distributional effects of intra-industry trade are not as strong as the ones predicted from inter-industry comparative advantage-based trade.

Several alternative explanations of intra-industry trade are given. They range from the level of transport costs and seasonal variation to the attempts to account for intra-industry trade through comparative advan-tage models. The message of this last group of models is that increasing returns might not be necessary for the existence of intra-industry trade (Davis, 1992). If so, the implications for trade policy prescriptions are quite different. While the existence of increasing returns and imperfect competi-tion calls for some or other form of trade intervention, when constant returns prevail, free trade remains the strongest candidate for trade policy.

∎ APPENDIX 5   THE $2 \times 2 \times 2$ HELPMAN–KRUGMAN MODEL

∎ The integrated world economy

In the Spence–Dixit–Stiglitz fashion Helpman and Krugman model the demand side using a utility function that treats different varieties of a product separately but symmetrically. Identical consumers each consume a little of each variety and are better off the more varieties they are able to consume simultaneously.

On the supply side we assume a set V of two factors of production (labour, L and capital, K) which must be fully employed, and two sectors, food (F) and manufacturing sector (M). The food sector produces a homogeneous product while the manufacturing sector produces many differentiated varieties of manufactured goods. Assume that the manufactured goods are always capital-intensive relative to food. Production in sector F takes place under constant returns to scale and perfect competition. In the manufacturing sector M every variety is produced with the same increasing returns to scale production function. Each variety is produced by only one firm because each producer competes equally with every other producer. Competition between the producers of the different varieties of manufactured goods will ensure that each variety will have an equal market share and will sell at the same price. Each producer will thus earn zero profits.

We now need to state the equilibrium conditions in the integrated world economy. The first equilibrium conditions are on pricing. Food, produced under constant returns to scale, will be priced at marginal (and average) cost:

$$p_F = c_F(\omega)$$

where $c(\cdot)$ is the unit cost function and ω is the vector of input prices (w, r). Choosing food as the numeraire, we have $p_F = 1$, and the pricing condition becomes

$$1 = c_F(\omega) \tag{A5.1}$$

In the manufacturing sector we have assumed that each variety is produced with increasing returns to scale. We further assume economies of scale to be relatively small so that the sector can accommodate many producers, each of which produces a different variety of manufactured goods. Under this monopolistically competitive market structure every firm chooses a variety and sets its price so as to maximize profits, taking as given the variety choice and pricing strategy of the other producers in the sector. Hence every firm will produce a different variety of the manufactured good.

If the number of firms, $\bar{n}$, is large enough (i.e. $\bar{n}$ is a continuous variable instead of an integer) free entry and exit is expected to eliminate any positive profits as in

$$p = c(\omega, m) \tag{A5.2}$$

where $c(\cdot)$ is the average cost function and m is the output level of a single representative firm. With zero profits in the long run the degree of monopoly power must be equal to the degree of economies of scale, or:

$$R(p, \bar{n}) = \theta(\omega, m) \tag{A5.3}$$

where $R(\cdot)$ is a measure of monopoly power (the ratio of average revenue to marginal revenue) and $\theta(\cdot)$ is a measure of the degree of economies of scale (the ratio of average costs to marginal costs).

Turning to the factor markets we first need to derive unit factor inputs. These can be derived from the unit cost functions. The demand for factor v per unit of output from the food sector and the differentiated manufacturing sector is:

$$a_{vF}(\omega) = \partial c_F(\omega)/\partial \omega_v$$
$$a_{vM}(\omega, m) = \partial c(\omega, m)/\partial \omega_v$$

and the aggregate demand for factor v is

$$a_{vF}(\omega)F + a_{vM}(\omega, m)\bar{M} \qquad \text{for } v \in V$$

Note that we can also express the demand for factor v as the demand by a representative firm in the manufacturing sector as:

$$A_{vm}(\omega, m) \equiv \partial C(\omega, m)/\partial \omega_v \qquad \text{for } v \in V$$
$$\text{and clearly } a_{vm}(\cdot) = A_{vm}(\cdot)/m$$

Our factor market-clearing conditions are therefore:

$$a_{LF}(\omega)\bar{F} + a_{LM}(\omega, m)\bar{M} = \bar{L} \tag{A5.4}$$
$$a_{KF}(\omega)\bar{F} + a_{KM}(\omega, m)\bar{M} = \bar{K} \tag{A5.5}$$

where $\bar{L}$ is the size of the labour force and $\bar{K}$ is the capital stock.

Finally, it remains to state the market-clearing conditions for the food and manufacturing markets. Due to Walras' law it is sufficient that we specify a clearing condition for food only. The share of spending allocated to a particular product is a function of product's prices and the number of varieties available to consumers (Helpman and Krugman, 1985, p. 120). If $\alpha_F(p, \bar{n})$ is the share of spending allocated to food, the market-clearing condition for the food market can be written as:

$$\alpha_F(p, \bar{n}) = \bar{F}/\bar{F}(+p\bar{M}) \tag{A5.6}$$

The final equilibrium condition we need is the one which defines the number of firms in the manufacturing sector (this is given by the fact that the number of firms is identical to the number of varieties):

$$\bar{M} = \bar{n}m \tag{A5.7}$$

Conditions (A5.1)–(A5.7) represent equilibrium conditions that implicitly define equilibrium values for factor rewards (ω), the price and output of every variety of manufactured goods (p, m), the output of food $(\bar{F})$ and manufactures ($\bar{M}$), and the number of firms (i.e. varieties) in the manufacturing sector ($\bar{n}$).

To facilitate the graphical analysis on p. 200, it is useful to define the employment vectors ($\bar{V}_i, i = F, M$) which represent the factor inputs within the two sectors. The allocation of factors in the integrated economy can then be summarized by the set of vectors $\bar{V}_i$.

In Figure 5.8 (p. 200) the quantities of labour and capital demanded by the two sectors of the integrated economy are represented by the vectors OQ and OQ^1, for manufacturing and food respectively. These vectors sum to the world's endowments of factors ($\bar{L}, \bar{K}$) in the vector OO^*. Our assumption about the relative capital intensity of the manufacturing industry is reflected by the steeper slope of the vector OQ relative to the slope of the vector OQ^1. Outputs are measured in units for which $\bar{O}\bar{Q} = \bar{M}$ and $\bar{O}\bar{Q}^1 = \bar{F}$.

■ The pattern of trade in a two-country world

Let us now divide the world into two countries (Home and Foreign). We assume homothetic preferences and a division of consumers such that demand functions in the two economies are the same so that we can concentrate on the supply side. Both countries share the same technology but differ in factor endowments. (If technology differs between countries then it has a prohibitive effect on direct trade in manufacturing goods. In our simple model trade will completely disappear, unless the food industry produces differentiated products as well.) We want to investigate whether this divided world economy can, through trade, reproduce the integrated equilibrium. Sufficient conditions for this to occur are, first, that trade itself involves no costs (i.e. transport costs and trade taxes are zero). Secondly, the equilibrium must be consistent with factor market equilibrium in both countries.

In Figure 5.8 the world's resources are represented by the sides of a box. We measure resources used in Home from the origin O, while O^* is the origin for Foreign. Point E describes the allocation of total factor endowments of these two countries. Since point E is above the diagonal OO^*, Home is relatively well endowed with capital. As mentioned previously, the vectors OQ and OQ^1 show the factor demands of the two sectors in the integrated equilibrium. Home's cone of diversification (at integrated equilibrium factor prices) lies between these sectors, while Foreign's cone of diversification lies between the vectors O^*Q and O^*Q^1. Since E lies inside the intersection of these cones of diversification (i.e. in the factor price equalisation set represented by the parallelogram OQO^*Q^1), there is a division of the sectors between the two countries. This division reproduces the integrated equilibrium levels of output and factor prices, and fully employs factors in both countries. At this point factor prices are equalised in the two countries.

This can be seen by drawing a parallelogram between O and E to obtain points P_F and P_M. Then the integrated equilibrium aggregate output $(\bar{F}, \bar{M})$ is divided between Home $(OP_F = F$ and $OP_M = M)$ and Foreign $(P_F Q^1 = F^*$ and $P_M Q = M^*)$. The same total number of varieties of manufactured goods $\bar{n}$ is produced, but now Home produces $n = M/m$ and Foreign produces $n^* = M^*/m$ (so that $n + n^* = \bar{n}$). Since all firms in the manufacturing industry are symmetric, all firms supply equal shares of all markets.

The pattern of trade can be identified by drawing a negatively sloped line (the slope is given by w/r, where w is the wage, and r is the return to capital in equilibrium) through E. Point C is thus obtained as the point of intersection between this line and the diagonal. It is possible to choose units of measurement so that OO^* is the GDP of the world economy. Point C then identifies relative country size, that is, OC and O^*C represent the GDPs of Home and Foreign, respectively. As we assume that every country spends the same proportion of income on food and on manufactures, and that all income is spent, the aggregate consumption of Home is represented by the parallelogram $OC_M CC_F$. Under this representation OC_F equals Home's consumption of food and OC_M equals Home's consumption of manufactures. From these production and consumption levels it is clear that Home, which is relatively well endowed with capital, is a net exporter of manufactures, which are relatively capital-intensive, and an importer of food. Foreign, which is relatively labour-rich, exports the relatively labour-intensive good food, and is a net importer of manufactures. Each country's after-trade consumption of manufactures thus consists of both domestically produced and imported varieties. Hence the net exports of each country are represented by the difference between the amount of manufactures imported and exported. If s is Home's share of world income $(s = OC/OO^*$ in Figure 5.8), and $s^* = 1 - s$ is Foreign's share of world income, their respective consumption of manufactures is:

$$D_M = s(nm + n^* m) \tag{A5.8a}$$
$$D_M{}^* = s^*(nm + n^* m) \tag{A5.8b}$$

In other words, Home consumes $sn^* m$ of imported manufactures, and exports $s^* nm$ of manufactures (or, Foreign imports $s^* nm$ and exports $sn^* m$ of manufactures). Thus the net exports of manufactures for Home is $s^* nm - sn^* m$ ($C_M P_M$ in Figure 5.8). Foreign's net exports of manufactures is in our case negative (i.e. Foreign is a net importer) and is equal to $sn^* m - s^* nm$ ($P_M C_M$ in Figure 5.8). However the existence of this intra-industry trade does not prevent the inter-industry pattern of trade from being determined by the difference in relative factor endowments between countries, just as in the Heckscher–Ohlin–Samuelson (HOS) model. In other words, information on factor endowments enables the prediction of inter-industry trade patterns: a capital-rich country will be a net exporter of the capital-intensive product, and a labour-rich country will be a net exporter of the labour-intensive product. Moreover, the pattern of trade will reflect the combination of comparative advantage, economies of scale and product differentiation. The last two aspects will exert a stronger influence on the pattern of trade the more similar the countries are in terms of factor endowments and size. In the case of identical relative factor endowments between countries of different size, economies of scale will be the sole incentive for trade and the predictive power of relative factor endowments will disappear.

As shown in Helpman (1981) and Helpman and Krugman (1985), relative commodity prices do not have the power to predict the pattern of trade in the Helpman–Krugman model. The reason for this is that a country's size affects, through economies of scale, relative prices in autarky. In particular, the larger a country is the larger are the economies of scale in the production of differentiated manufactures, and the lower their autarkic price relative to food in that country as compared to another country which has identical relative factor endowments but is smaller in size. Hence, on the basis of the relative pre-trade price of manufactures, we would expect the larger country to export manufactures. However, once trade has begun, both the large and small country will export (and import) manufactures because the identical relative factor endowments will not allow for any inter-industry trade. Moreover, with trade, the price of manufactures relative to food will be lower in *both* countries as compared to pre-trade relative prices. This occurs because trade enlarges the size of each country's market. Therefore, the usual link between the relative prices of traded goods with and without trade is not present when countries have equal factor proportions. The exception to this occurs when relative prices are adjusted for the effects of size. If countries differ in factor proportions and in size, the link between relative prices with and without trade can be reinstated. But the predictive power of the pre-trade relative prices will be weaker the smaller is the difference in factor proportions and the larger is the difference in size. Likewise, relative factor rewards cannot serve as a reliable predictor of the pattern of trade. Therefore, in the Helpman–Krugman model, only the information on factor endowments remains as a solid predictor of the pattern of trade.

Figure 5.8 can further be used to describe the net factor content of trade. Assuming that consumption has an identical composition in both countries, the composition of the factor content of consumption is the same in both countries. Therefore the vector *OC* describes the factor content of consumption in Home. The difference between the factor content of consumption (*OC*) and the factor content of production (implicit in *OE*) reflects the factor content of the net trade flows (vector *EC*). It is clear that

Home is a net exporter of capital services and a net importer of labour services, while the opposite is true for Foreign. Explained differently, each country is a net exporter of services of that factor with which it is relatively well endowed, and a net importer of that with which it is relatively poorly endowed. Note that this model can be modified in such a way that both the food and manufacturing sectors produce differentiated products based on economies of scale. Then intra-industry trade would occur in both sectors. However, with different factor endowments each country would still be a net exporter of the product that intensively uses the services of factors with which it is relatively well endowed.

■ The volume of trade

The volume of trade is defined as the sum of exports across countries. In our case this amounts to:

$$T = s^* p M + s p M^* + (F^* - s^* \bar{F}) \tag{A5.9}$$

where the first component represents the exports of manufactures by Home ($M = nm$), the second component represents the exports of manufactures by Foreign ($M^* = n^* m$) and the third component represents the exports of food by Foreign. Note that, since trade is balanced, we can also obtain the volume of trade by multiplying either country's exports by two. Thus we have:

$$T = 2 s^* p M \tag{A5.9a}$$

or

$$T = 2(s p M^* + F^* - s^* \bar{F}) \tag{A5.9b}$$

In contrast to the standard HOS model, in this model the volume of trade is affected by both factor proportions and the size of the countries. Helpman (1981) and Helpman and Krugman (1985) have established that the volume of trade will tend to be larger when countries differ more in factor endowments and when they are more similar with respect to size as measured by their relative income (given equal factor proportions, the volume of trade is maximized when countries are of equal size). Obviously the importance of the relative size of the country in determining the volume of trade increases as the number of differentiated products traded increases. In addition, as countries become more similar in their factor endowments, trade will increasingly become of an intra-industry character, and the less net trading in factor services will occur. This applies equally to trade in goods, services and factor services (i.e. the cross-hauling of capital).

■ *Chapter 6* ■

Commodit~~y Trade Fl~~ows: Methodol~~ogy~~ ~~Appr~~aisal and th~~e~~

■ 6.1 Introduction

Strict versions of standard trade theories are inclined to be extremely unicausal. The Ricardian model of international trade, for example, tries to explain the existence of trade with reference to a single difference between countries, this difference being in countries' technologies. The HOS model attributes the reason for trade to national differences in factor endowments, while the very basic model of trade, which does not incorporate the production side at all, assigns all trade to different national tastes. This view, that trade can be motivated and sustained by a single factor, is not particularly helpful. It fosters the idea that trade theories are competing with each other in trying to provide an exclusive explanation for real-world trade. However, it seems that real world trade, like any other real-world phenomenon, cannot be fully explained by a single cause. Trade models that are capable of embracing two or more factors that work together in determining the trade patterns among countries should therefore be more useful than the unicausal type, even if they do not prove to be more accurate.

This chapter aims to survey the empirical literature on trade. It is never easy to present an extensive literature within the limits of a chapter. This task is not simplified by the fact that most empirical studies, particularly the recent ones, use quite sophisticated methodology and quantitative analyses. An understanding of the detail of the most of this empirical work would require specialised knowledge and skills. Therefore this chapter aims to cover primarily the general issues involved in the empirical testing of trade theories, without dealing with the topic in depth.

With regard to the new trade theories most of the quantitative work involves measuring the effects of various trade policies under the imperfect market structure, rather than testing how real commodity flows correspond to the ones predicted by these theories. Admittedly the empirical work on the effects of trade policies with imperfect competition is very exciting and significant because it provides (finally?) significant support for the belief 'that free trade is not just a good thing but an important one' (Krugman, 1992, p. 4). In this chapter, however, we will review the tests of trade theories while leaving the quantification of trade policies and trade liberalisation effects to Chapter 11.

The next section selectively reviews the empirical studies in this area. As already mentioned, the volume of literature to be covered here is large, and the studies diverse. We first examine the Ricardian model and the HOS model, the two theories fundamental to explaining inter-industry commodity flows. Following this is a survey of the tests of the new trade theories which are not primarily focused on inter-industry trade flows. Technology-based trade theories are presented as the third and final group of trade theories. The Appendix 6 (p. 239) provides an introduction into the complexities involved in measuring intra-industry trade. It also provides some evidence of the importance of intra-industry trade in the trans-Tasman area.

■ 6.2 Empirical testing

The question of what pattern of trade will evolve if trade is allowed between countries is the one that all fundamental trade theories are concerned with and try to provide an answer to. The basic implication arising from the family of standard models is that commodity trade flows will be of an inter-industry character. Trade leads countries to specialise in production and to export goods that are distinctly different from their imports. For these theories the criterion for specialisation lies in the difference between national autarkic commodity prices. The empirical testing of these theories has therefore been focused on confirming the relationship between autarkic commodity prices and the commodity flows occurring between countries. Specific theories, like the Ricardian model or the HOS model, were referred to only to explain the origin of the difference in autarkic commodity prices.

□ Testing the Ricardian model

One of the major predictions of the Ricardian model is that countries will completely specialise in the production and export of the good(s) in which they have a comparative advantage. Thus we should not find any country exporting a good which is *the* comparative advantage good of some other country. Strictly speaking, Ricardian comparative advantage allows for any good to be exported by only one country: the country with the greatest cost advantage. This means that the existence of comparative advantage is associated with a 100 per cent share of the export market.[1]

The existence of comparative advantage is attributed to international differences in technology, that is, to the differences in productivity across industries.[2] Therefore empirical tests of the Ricardian model have attempted to find a relationship between the level of labour productivity and the pattern of trade.

The first empirical test of the Ricardian model was performed by MacDougall (1951, 1952) who used labour productivity and export data for 25 industries in the USA and the UK in the late 1930s. MacDougall postulated that the US exports should be greater than the UK's exports in every industry i which satisfies the export condition. Recall that the export condition allows a country (say the USA) to export some good i if and only if its relative wage is low enough to offset any absolute productivity disadvantage, or:

$$p^{US}_i < p^{UK}_i \tag{6.2.1}$$

if

$$a^{US}_{Li}/a^{UK}_{Li} < w^{UK}/w^{US}$$

leading to

$$E^{US}_i/E^{UK}_i > 1$$

where E_i is the share of the market of the rest of the world. In other words whenever the ratio of US labour productivity to that of UK labour productivity is greater than the ratio of US wages to UK wages, the US exports should exceed UK exports to the rest of the world. Since US wages were double UK wages, MacDougall argued that the USA would have a comparative advantage only in those industries in which US labour was at least twice as productive as UK labour.

Table 6.1 reproduces some of the results from the MacDougall's tests. Out of the 25 industries tested, 20 industries (covering 97 per cent of the sample by value) confirm the hypothesis that the US exports will be greater than UK exports if US productivity is more than twice UK productivity. However in those industries where the levels of productivity was about the same UK industries' exports exceeded that of US industries. MacDougall (1952) explained this in part by the US 'apparent disadvantage in imperfect world markets'. He referred to the UK reputation for high-quality production, differences in transport costs, stronger commercial ties between Britain and overseas markets, and in general to Imperial Preference.

Table 6.1   *Some results from MacDougall's tests of the Ricardian model*

Industries	US output per worker / UK output per worker	US weekly wage / UK weekly wage	US exports / UK exports
Wireless sets[*]	3.5	na	8
Pig iron	3.6	1.5	5
Motor cars	3.1	2.0	4.3
Glass containers	2.4	2.0	4
Tin cans	5.2	na	3.5
Machinery	2.7	1.9	1.5
Paper	2.2	2.0	1
Cigarettes	1.7	1.5	0.5
Linoleum	1.9	na	0.33
Hosiery	1.8	1.9	0.33
Leather footwear	1.4	1.5	0.33
Coke	1.9	na	0.2
Rayon weaving	1.5	na	0.2
Cotton goods	1.5	1.7	0.11
Rayon making	1.4	na	0.09
Beer	2.0	2.6	0.06
Cement	1.1	1.7	0.09
Men's woollens	1.3	2.3	0.04
Margarine	1.2	na	0.03
Woollen and worsted	1.4	2.0	0.004
Exceptions:[**]			
Electric lamps	5.4	na	0.94
Biscuits	3.1	na	0.23
Matches	3.1	na	0.09
Rubber tyres	2.7	na	0.74
Soap	2.7	na	0.35

Note:
[*]   Radios
[**]   Industries where US productivity was more than double UK productivity but UK exports exceeded US exports to the rest of the world.
na   Not available.
Source: Selected data from MacDougall (1951, Table I, Table II, Table III).

These results were broadly reconfirmed about a decade later by three other tests of US–UK trade.[3] However these results cannot be taken as evidence of the general validity of the Ricardian model, as carefully explained in Deardorff (1984). First, a strict interpretation of the Ricardian model requires complete specialisation. This prevents any comparisons of autarkic price levels – we cannot compare the price of commodity i in two countries if only one country produces it. Since in practice we rarely find countries that completely specialise, there are no practical problems with the observability of prices for the large number of overlapping goods. There is, however, the problem that these prices are not autarkic prices, but post-trade relative prices. We must then assume that these prices reflect the autarkic relative prices to a degree sufficient for the validity of the correlations between comparative advantage and export shares.

Secondly, the results obtained by MacDougall are also consistent with other models (in particular a version of the HOS model) explaining inter-industry commodity flows. This test is therefore deficient as it fails to distinguish between the two models.

Further, we should not, on the basis of these results, reject the Ricardian model either. Although the empirical tests do not support its specific predictions as to complete specialisation based on relative labour productivities, the general conclusion that broad trade patterns will follow comparative advantages does hold. As will be demonstrated in the next section, the pure factor-endowment basis for these comparative advantages cannot be firmly established. It seems that the technological differences between countries are a very strong power generating the trade. Thus there is still scope for the Ricardian type of explanations for trade patterns. More on this will follow on p. 230.

☐ Testing the HOS model

The HOS model is propped up by four theorems: the Heckscher–Ohlin theorem (HOT), the factor-price equalisation theorem, the Stolper–Samuelson theorem (SST), and the Rybczynski theorem. To test the model would thus imply testing all four theorems. In practice empirical studies have focused mostly on the Heckscher–Ohlin theorem and its prediction that trade patterns are explainable by differences in factor proportions.

Testing the Heckscher–Ohlin theorem

The first empirical test of the HOT was conducted by W. Leontief in early 1950s. He compared the capital–labour ratios in the US production of exports and in the production of import substitutes in 1947, finding that the capital intensity in the import-substituting production was higher than the capital intensity in the production of exports. Since by any definition the USA was a capital-abundant country, the results of this test were totaly unexpected. The economic profession at the time trusted Leontief's capacity to perform a correct test. However, the trust placed in the HO approach to international trade was also very deep. This result was therefore called the *Leontief paradox* (see Box 6.1).

Attempted explanations of the Leontief paradox   Leontief's findings were classified as a 'paradox' implying that both his test and the theory he tested were true. Despite this, research and debate following the publication of Leontief's results focused on discovering his error rather than on searching for a new trade theory. The areas in which economists looked in order to reconcile the HOT and Leontief test included: (a) the number of factors and the quality of these factors, (b) the role of trade barriers, and (c) reversals in demand and factor intensities. Much of the research originating in this debate contributed significantly to the clarification of the paradox *and* to the extension of the theory. Some reconciliations discovered are outlined below.

Box 6.1   *The Leontief paradox*

The Leontief paradox is probably the most famous and most troubling empirical result ever found by an economist (the other one being the study by Grubel and Lloyd in 1975). From the time it was formally articulated, the HOS model had been accepted by most economists as *the* model of international trade. Its logical completeness, mathematical elegance and tractability, and the simplicity with which it could be used to study trade issues within the general equilibrium framework made the HOS model widely admissible. In addition, casual observations of international commodity flows seemed to be in accord with the model's predictions. Then a relatively simple empirical test cast long-lasting doubts upon the accuracy of these predictions!

Leontief set out to test what is known as the 'factor-content' version of the HO theorem. If the USA really was, as everyone believed, a capital-abundant country as compared to its trading partners, it was supposed to export the services of capital embodied as capital content in its exported goods. On the other hand, its imports should have consisted of labour-intensive goods reflecting the need for the importation of the services of labour. Leontief used an input–output table (his own invention which, without mentioning the other work he did, earned him a Nobel Prize in 1973) to calculate the factor inputs for a typical $1m of US export production and a typical $1m of US import-substituting production.[4] The result Leontief obtained surprised both himself and the rest of the world. On the basis of 1947 data, the ratios of capital to labour of US exports to US import-substituting production was only 0.77, when it should have been above unity.

The reaction to Leontief's result was not surprising. Many economists, Leontief included, tried to save the HO approach by developing various explanations for the Leontief paradox within the context of the model. As a consequence, a variety of other studies have been produced, some of them leading to theoretical extensions of the HOS model. Table 6.2

summarises the results from several leading empirical studies on US trade. It seems that paradoxical results persisted until the early 1970's when Stern and Maskus (1981) found the capital–labour ratio in export and import flows consistent with what the HOT would predict for a capital-abundant country.

Table 6.2　*Selected results of the factor content of US trade, 1954–81*

Author	Year of trade data & year of input data	Coverage	Capital–labour ratio in exports/ imports $(K_{ex}/L_{ex})/$ (K_{im}/L_{im})
Leontief (1954)	1947 1947	All industries	0.77
Leontief (1956)	1951 1947	All industries Excluding natural resources	0.94 1.14
Baldwin (1971)	1962 1958	All industries Excluding natural resources	0.79 0.96
Stern and Maskus (1981)	1972 1972	All industries Excluding natural resources	1.05 1.08

Source:　Deardorff (1984), Table 4.1, p. 484.

Tests using methods similar to Leontief's were conducted for other countries. The results were similarly paradoxical. Tatemoto and Ichimura (1959) performed the test on Japanese data from the 1950s when Japan was seen as labour-abundant as compared to its trading partners. However Japanese exports were found to be capital-intensive and Japanese imports to be labour-intensive! India's trade with the USA ran against the HO predictions (although India's overall exports seemed to be relatively labour-intensive), as did Canada's. It seems that the only countries whose foreign trade conformed to the HO predictions belonged to the world of developing countries and the then-socialist countries of Eastern Europe and the Soviet Union.[5]

The role of natural resources   Leontief based his test on the 'textbook' two-factor assumption of the HO theorem. Two factors (capital and labour) is, no doubt, a very restrictive assumption when compared to the number of factors used in real-world production processes. Some economists thus raised the issue of the omission of some of the other more important factors from the Leontief test. For example, Vanek (1959) proposed that the USA was actually scarce in the third factor, which he defined as 'natural resources'. He claimed that the USA became a net importer of products from extractive sectors such as agriculture, forestry and mining. He also found a strong positive correlation between capital and natural resource requirements. Thus to produce a unit of an imported good intensive in natural resources would also require a significant amount of physical capital. This led him to conclude that while capital was actually relatively abundant in the USA, a heavy dependence on natural-resource imports would make the capital content in exports relatively less than the capital content in import replacements.

The evidence certainly supports these conjectures, as shown in Table 6.2. When the industries are separated into two groups and the natural resource-intensive industries are excluded from testing, the Leontief paradox largely disappears.

The role of labour skills and human capital   Again on the issue of the number of factors, there were objections to Leontief's aggregative treatment of labour. There are many different categories of labour based on varying skill qualities. Leontief himself was the first to try to explain the paradox in terms of the superior labour productivity of the USA which supposedly made it labour-abundant relative to its trading partners. However his estimates that the effective American labour force would be three times as large as the number of workers actually employed could not be supported by the data.[6] In any case, his attempt also suffered from a more fundamental flaw – he was trying to infer the national factor endowments from the pattern of commodity trade, which is just the opposite of what the HOT states.

Nevertheless the realisation that labour should not be treated as a homogeneous factor provided a strong stimulus for additional empirical research. Keesing (1966) performed one of the first tests which later lead to an examination of the role of *human capital* in the formation of comparative advantages. Human capital is usually described as the combination of education, on-the-job-training, and health embodied in human resources which increases their productivity. In his test Keesing divided labour into eight different categories, the first containing 'scientists and engineers' and the last containing 'unskilled and semiskilled workers'. He then compared the American requirements for each category of labour in export- and import-competing industries with the requirements of 13 other countries. According to his results the US export industries needed relatively more of the first labour category and relatively less of the last labour category. For the import-competing industries the result was just the opposite – the USA was using proportionately less of the highly educated and skilled labour force, and more of the unskilled and semi-skilled labour. Thus, in terms of labour, it seems that the USA was skilled labour-abundant and unskilled labour-scarce. The pattern of trade would then have to reflect this so that exports would contain a high content of skilled labour, while imports (or import substitution) would be largely unskilled labour-intensive. This result certainly goes some way in explaining the Leontief paradox.

Other tests confirmed these results.[7] It is now therefore widely accepted that it is necessary to go beyond the two-factor model in testing factor proportion-based patterns of trade. It seems also that another factor closely related to the category of human capital – research and development (R&D) – has a special role in the formation of comparative advantages in the long run as well as contributing to economic growth in general. This issue will be mentioned again when we review the technology-based trade theories.

The role of factor-intensity uniformity When factor-intensity reversals exist it is not possible to unambiguously rank industries by factor intensities across countries. Thus the HO theorem breaks down. The HOS model takes care of this complication by assuming identical technology for any particular good across countries, as well as equalised factor prices.[8] Thus the same factor intensities will be used in the production of the same good across countries. However if this assumption is relaxed and different production functions for the same industries across different countries are allowed for, the problem of factor-intensity reversals becomes very likely. What are the implications of this for empirical testing?

Minhas (1962) argued that factor-intensity reversals take place and that they can actually account for the Leontief paradox. Specifically, if factor-intensity reversals do occur, then the goods produced in the USA as import substitutes with capital-intensive techniques might still be produced by labour-intensive technology in other countries. The HO would then still be valid for those other countries, but not for the USA. To prove his point, Minhas (1962) tested a number of American and Japanese industries for their factor intensity. He ranked all the industries in the USA and in Japan according to their direct and total capital–labour ratios, and then compared the ranks of industries between these two countries. In the case of direct factor requirements the rank correlation obtained was 0.73, indicating a positive but not very strong association. However when total factor requirement rankings were compared, the rank correlation coefficient fell to 0.33.[9]

These results, although casting doubt upon the HOS model's assumption of identical technology, were largely ignored by the profession. Some testing of factor-intensity uniformity followed shortly after Minhas' work (Leontief, 1964; Hufbauer, 1966) but the conclusions reached were that, even though in the real world we might encounter different technologies for the same industries, the incidence of this happening was not very high. This was meant to be true particularly when natural resource-intensive industries were excluded from the comparisons and when only direct factor requirements were compared.

This wide acceptance of the identical technology assumption led to the general adoption of a single-country technology (most often American) to proxy for the production structure of all other countries. Even Leamer's (1984) comprehensive testing of the Heckscher–Ohlin–Vanek (HOV) theorem assumes non-differentiated technology among countries. However some more recent studies have found that this factor intensity uniformity assumption cannot be justified on empirical grounds (Forstner and Ballance, 1990;[10] Elmslie and Milberg, 1992). Not only does the abandonment of this assumption have empirical implications but it also requires alternative approaches to explaining patterns of trade on the basis of differentiated technologies.

Other testing of the factor content of trade   The Leontief test was the first in the long succession of tests conducted over the last four decades with the aim of either refuting the HOS model (once and for all) or extending its life as the 'core of the international microeconomics' (Leamer, 1993, p. 436). Two major lines of empirical work could be distinguished: one following the HOV approach, and the other focusing on the commodity composition of trade.

Recall from Box 2.2 of Chapter 2 that the HOV theorem is based on the notion that national relative factor abundance is revealed through the factor services embodied in that country's commodity trade flows. This theorem states that a country will export the *services of factors* in which it is abundant in exchange for imports of the *services of factors* which are scarce. Leamer (1980) used this idea to show that the Leontief paradox was the product of conceptual misunderstanding. Recall that Leontief found the ratio of capital to labour of US exports to US imports was less than one. From this it was inferred that the USA might not be as capital-abundant as was widely believed. Leamer showed that this proposition was true only in the case of *balanced* trade. When trade is unbalanced, as was the case with Leontief's and many other tests, the theoretically correct comparison is between the capital per unit of labour embodied in production and the capital per unit of labour embodied in consumption. This is because more of a relatively abundant factor will always be embodied in a unit of production than in a unit of consumption. Using this method on Leontief's data Leamer was able to confirm that US production was relatively capital-intensive as compared to consumption, thus declaring the paradox non-existent.

Leamer later (1984) argued that to properly test one country requires information as to that country's overall factor endowments. When Leontief performed his test he postulated only that the USA was capital-abundant. Leamer (1980) confirmed this postulate. However in his later study Leamer (1984) proposed to simultaneously test many countries by actually *measuring* their relative factor endowments. He again chose the Heckscher–Ohlin–Vanek variant of the theory so that the relationship he tested was between the country's share in the world supply of that particular factor and that country's net exports of goods intensive in that factor. More specifically, if a country has a larger share of the world supply of capital than of the other factors of production, this country should have large net exports of capital-intensive goods.

Leamer based his test on data from 20 developed and 40 developing countries for the late 1950s and 1975. He distinguished among eleven factors and ten aggregative categories of goods. The factors included were one type of capital, three types of labour (professional or technical workers; literate non-professional workers; illiterate workers), four types of land (tropical land; dry-climate land; humid-climate land (A); humid-climate land (B)), and three types of natural resources (coal; minerals, oil). The goods included crude oil and petroleum products; raw materials; forest products; tropical agricultural products; animal products; cereals; labour-intensive manufactures; chemicals and other manufactures. The pattern of trade of six resource-based types of goods can be explained relatively easily by the presence of corresponding resources. Leamer's results are not simple to present in a summarised form. His overall study, however, does suggest that when a sufficiently comprehensive view of nations' factor endowments is taken, the HOV theorem retains considerable explanatory power. In other words net trade (or a large portion of it) can be explained by factor supplies. This is particulary true for categories of goods such as raw materials, agricultural products and labour-intensive manufactures. The net trade in other types of manufactures is not so well explained.

Another test of the factor proportions theory in the context of the HOV theorem was conducted by Bowen *et al.* in 1987 using 1967 data. This test examined twelve different factors in 27 countries in order to determine the net export of factor services and factor abundances. The idea was to first determine each country's share in the world supply of each factor. This proportion was then compared with each country's share of the world income. The HOV theorem predicts that each country will always export those factors for which the factor share is larger than the income share, and import factors for which the factor share is less than the income share. Bowen *et al.* found that, for two-thirds of the factors trade flows were flowing in the opposite direction to that predicted by the HOV more than 30 per cent of the time.[11] These results have led 'some economists to jump up and down and to proclaim the death of the Heckscher–Ohlin model and free trade as well' (Leamer, 1993, p.438). But Leamer (p.439) concludes that in the absence of a clear alternative even these seemingly 'disappointing' results are not strong enough to reject the Heckscher–Ohlin approach to trade.

Regression analysis of commodity composition of trade   The essence of testing the commodity composition of trade flows is to determine the relationship between the net trade of a particular industry and the production characteristics (that is, the factor intensity) of that industry for each country being tested. The information about a country's factor endowments is thus assumed rather than obtained through testing. Many studies have used this method but we will mention only two. Stern and Maskus (1981) tried to explain the US pattern of trade for the period 1958–76. They found that US net exports were positively related to human capital, and negatively related to unskilled labour and physical capital. They also succeeded in reconciling the HOT and the Leontief paradox for the period after 1972.

Harkness and Kyle (1975) conducted another study on the USA following much the same tradition. They were though particularly concerned with the role of natural resources and the quality of labour. They therefore tested resource-based industries separately from all other industries. For the industries that were *not* based on natural resources they obtained the result that physical capital intensity was positively associated with net exports, contrary to the Leontief paradox. They also found that natural resource-based industries were typically import-competing.

Concluding comments on testing the HOT   The HO hypothesis that is being tested states that a country ought to export the good which uses intensively the relatively abundant factor of production. The difficulty with a statement like this lies in its 'multidimensionality'. It is a statement concerning three separately measurable quantities: (1) factor abundance, (2) factor intensities and (3) trade flows. A *correct* test of the hypothesis would begin by measuring all three quantities, and would then attempt to determine to what degree they confirm the HO predictions. Neither simple nor multiple regression tests attempt to do this. They focus on the link between only two of the elements – trade patterns and factor intensities, leaving the quantities of factor endowments to be assumed. The results of these tests cannot therefore be taken as *evidence* on general validity of the HOT. Tests on the factor content of trade, on the other hand, are designed to link together all three quantities and they are managing it reasonably successfully. But they are not very good at identifying what particular goods are being exported and imported.

In concluding this section it should be noted that none of the tests performed was able to refute the HO model. However, neither did the tests provide evidence strong enough to support the universal validity of the model. This is not especially surprising because, as Leamer (1993) has stated, we all knew intuitively that empirical testing was not needed to validate models which we know cannot be perfectly true. Instead, empirical work should be used to show under which particular set of circumstances a specific trade model is most appropriately used. For example, instead of trying to establish the exactness of the HOT, we should be trying to determine more precisely the circumstances under which it will predict trade flows accurately and the circumstances under which its predictive power will be close to nil. As a result of past tests' preoccupation with proving the accuracy of models for which it could not be established, previous empirical results have had little impact on what the economics profession holds as determining comparative advantage or trade patterns in general. Consequently differences in factor endowments retain an important role in our explanations of the determinants of commodity flows. The pure HOS model is not able to fully capture this aspect and must therefore be supplemented by or extended with other theories.

Intra-industry trade and models with increasing returns

Intra-industry trade is usually described as the simultaneous import and export of products that are close or perfect substitutes in terms of production, consumption, or both. Such a phenomenon requires explanations based on economies of scale, heterogeneous products, market power, and consumers' preference for variety. Unfortunately these elements are not found in the standard trade theory in a form capable of explaining the puzzle of intra-industry trade. Thus ever since Balassa (1966) and Grubel and Lloyd (1975) documented large volumes of trade occurring in similar products among relatively similar countries, there has been a need for a new theoretical basis to the empirical phenomenon of intra-industry trade. Grubel and Lloyd's results were often referred to as 'stylised facts in search of a theory'. Without a clear theoretical base discussion on issues arising from intra-industry trade was not possible. A lack of theoretical guidance also meant that further empirical work was limited.

During the past fifteen years we have witnessed the development of a variety of theoretical models aiming to explain intra-industry trade. While not all of these models incorporate economies of scale or imperfect competition (for example, Finger, 1975; Falvey and Kierzkowski, 1987; Davis, 1992) both increasing returns and market power have become the specific feature of intra-industry trade models. Although one of the strongest stimuli for the development of these new models was to search for theoretical explanations of intra-industry trade, a great deal more has been discovered. Recent work on trade models based on imperfect competition, as well as complementing our understanding, has produced new issues such as the costs and benefits of trade policies, the existence of multinational corporations, and the emergence of international technological gaps. While we will concentrate here on theories which provide answers as to why similar countries engage in the trade of similar products, these contributions will be explored in other sections. Because of length constraints studies which focus on the measurement of intra-industry trade without providing additional insights into the determinants of such trade had to be excluded from our survey (see Box 6.2).

It seems that the Helpman–Krugman model based on monopolistic competition provides a plausible explanation for the existence of intra-industry trade. Recall the major propositions of this model:

(a)   the proportion of intra-industry as opposed to inter-industry trade is positively correlated with the degree of similarity between countries' capital–labour ratios

(b)   the more similar countries are in size (or *per capita* income), the larger the volume of intra-industry trade should be

(c)   the larger the proportion of the intra-industry trade in country's total trade, the weaker income-distributional conflicts will be.

While the third proposition might be the most interesting one in terms of policy implications, the empirical work so far has focused more on the first two propositions. Perhaps the best known empirical work is that of Helpman (1987) where he examines the effect similarities in countries' size has on the amount of trade and the amount of intra-industry trade in particular. In contrast to standard theories which ignore the effects of a country's size on the volume of trade, the Helpman–Krugman model predicts that the similarity or otherwise of countries size will play a large role. Helpman tested this hypothesis on a sample of fourteen OECD countries for the period 1956–81. He found that for this group of countries both income similarity and trade intensity have increased throughout the period. This supports the prediction of the model.

Leamer (1992) and Hummels and Levinsohn (1993) have both reviewed Helpman's study. Leamer emphasises that the hypothesis tested in Helpman's study is not very clear. In fact Leamer was able to derive the same proposition that Helpman was investigating by concentrating solely on the consumption side of the model. In particular, Leamer (1992, p. 38) assumes that products are distinguished by their production location (the so-called Armington assumption of consumers preferring diverse bundles of home and foreign goods), that tastes are identical and homothetic, and that trade is balanced. The volume of intra-industry trade will then be positively related to the similarity between countries in terms of their income. If this hypothesis is not supported by the data it means that something is wrong with the basic proposition of identical and homothetic tastes. If this is indeed the case the central role of economies of scale in explaining intra-industry trade is completely brushed aside.

Hummels and Levinsohn (1993) were intrigued by the strong empirical support Helpman was able to obtain for his hypothesis. Using different econometric techniques they tested the same hypothesis obtaining similar support for the model. They then used a different data set and again found that the model explained trade flows remarkably well. However, in the second case they used data from countries for which there was no intuitive reason to expect that they would engage in mutual intra-industry trade.[12] It is obvious therefore that something other than product differentiation and economies of scale must play an important role in generating intra-industry trade.

The Helpman–Krugman model was also tested by Lynde (1992). He performed an econometric analysis of the trade flows of 52 countries for the year 1980, with the aim of comparing the accuracy of the predictions of the Helpman–Krugman model and of the standard HO model. Since both models prediction as to net trade is the same, the comparison had to be made on either the total volume of trade or on the volume of intra-industry trade. Lynde found that correlations across groups of countries for both of these trade volumes were almost uniformly consistent with the predictions of the Helpman–Krugman model. In other words, the more similar the countries size, the larger the volume of trade; the larger the size difference between countries the smaller the share of trade in income; and the more similar countries are in terms of factor endowments the larger the proportion of intra-industry trade. However additional testing of the combined model does not allow for the rejection of either the Helpman–Krugman or the Heckscher–Ohlin model. In fact the author suggests that they should be used as complements in explaining the structure of international trade.

Another interesting econometric study on the determinants of intra-industry trade was conducted by Havrylyshyn and Civan in 1983. They also tested a proposition which, although not explicitly stated in the Helpman–Krugman model, could easily be inferred from its propositions linking levels of income with the levels of intra-industry trade. Their hypothesis was that intra-industry trade was more likely to prevail in trade between DCs than in trade between developing countries. The assumption underlying this proposition is that DCs produce a larger amount of differentiated products than do developing countries. Their findings supported the idea that a higher level of *per capita* income and a higher degree of diversity in manufacturing production will increase the level of intra-industry trade. For developing countries they found that the level of *per capita* income was more important in determining the magnitude of intra-industry trade.

There are a number of difficulties still surrounding the empirical research in this area. Leamer (1992, pp. 33–4) mentioned several, among which were: (1) the difficulty in finding a specific variable to measure theoretical constructs such as the potential for large-scale production; (2) despite the lack of a single composite theoretical model, empirical work tends to create one by including the variables representing each separate theoretical model in a single linear regression equation; (3) null and alternative hypotheses are very difficult to form and are often not clearly stated; (4) it is often problematical to distinguish between determinants originating on the production or the consumption side. It is clear that there remains a large amount still to be accomplished in the empirical investigation on the role of economies of scale and imperfect competition in international trade and there are many interesting and important questions that must be answered in order to complete our understanding of the determinants of trade patterns. This work depends to some extent on the new developments in empirical industrial organisation in general and industry-level modelling in particular. This is even more true with respect to the empirical implementation of these new trade theories. It is particularly important to have at least some empirical evidence when it comes to basing policy prescriptions on models founded on notions of market power.

The theoretical and empirical work on the phenomenon of intra-industry trade which has occurred over the past two decades has certainly brought us much closer to some generalised answers on what has caused the increasing volumes of intra-industry trade. However some recent measurements have indicated that the volume of intra-industry trade has stopped increasing or even decreased in the 1970s (Globerman and Dean, 1990; Scherer, 1992), renewing the intra-industry trade puzzle. If these measurements are correct, it is ironic that just when we have come so close to finding a theoretical explanation for the phenomenon of intra-industry trade it may be losing its practical relevance.

☐ Technology-based trade theories

In response to the Leontief paradox some new theories have also emerged. One strand of these alternative approaches to trade has hinged upon the technology factor and its importance in determining trade patterns. The basic framework was provided by the Ricardian model incorporating technological differences between countries, but with the focus on changes in technology and the resulting patterns of international trade.

Posner (1961) sketched the technology-gap hypothesis in an effort to explain the role of *new* products and production processes in the formation of national comparative advantage. He noted that a country in which an innovative process occurs will have a technological advantage until its trading partners enter into imitative activities. Trade evolves because the imitation gap may be longer than the demand gap; new products will thus be demanded by other countries while they are produced only by the innovating country. The innovating country could therefore find itself exporting the new product even though it has no obvious basis for comparative advantage in terms of factor endowments. Over time though this innovation will be diffused by international trade, diminishing the originator's original advantage. However the dynamic process through which an innovating country *continually* generates new products and processes is seen as a source of long-term comparative advantage.

The central idea of Posner's model is that trade will focus on new products or, less often, new processes. Thus the pattern of trade which evolves in this model is one in which the innovating country always exports new products to the less technologically advanced country, which in turn exports standard or older products. Of course it is possible for trade to occur between two equally advanced countries which are leaders in developing *different* types of new products and processes, and will thus engage in exchange. What is important here is the idea of self-reinforcing technological leadership. The difficulty with this model is that it fails to explain what causes innovation and why production takes place in the innovating country rather than in the country which is best suited, in terms of resources, labour costs or the like, to producing these new products. Factors used to explain the innovative capacity of some countries as compared to others are largely linked to a country's potential for R&D. This activity is in turn primarily determined by the endowment of factors necessary for it to exist. This includes such things as human capital in the form of scientists and engineers, technical equipment, and a high level of savings on which investment into R&D is based. The level of R&D also depends on institutional factors such as patent laws and tax incentives. The existence of markets for the new products or processes and familiarity with these markets is also relevant. Since new products and processes are based on a high content of very expensive factors and involve huge investments, the initial demand, as well as the innovation, will be found in rich countries. The innovating country will have both an absolute advantage and a temporary monopoly in the trade of this new product until other countries imitate it.

It typically takes a long time for the transfer of technology from the innovating country to the least-cost producing country, in most cases a developing country, to happen. This is particulary puzzling in the world of multinationals because they could supposedly transfer the production of new products to the least-cost location with ease. Through this inter-nalisation of production multinationals would increase their profits and prevent (or slow down) the diffusion of knowledge. Vernon (1966) attempted to resolve this problem by developing the *product-cycle hypothesis*. This explanation argues that every product goes through several stages in its 'lifetime' and that the factors needed for its production at any particular stage are different. Production in the initial stage is heavily dependent on skilled engineers and huge outlays on R&D. This stage is also characterised by large degree of uncertainty about production and sales. Production must therefore be located in relative proximity to the demanders. This provides a link between the location of innovation and the location of production. In this initial stage both activities occur in the rich and large economies.

The second stage is entered into as the product matures and becomes standardised. Production in this stage becomes more dependent on physical (rather than human) capital and production tends to shift to other capital-abundant countries. Together with these shifts in production exports to the rest of the world are also changing. The innovating country may actually become a net importer at this stage.

The third and final stage occurs when the product matures enough for the technology of production to become completely standardised and universally available. Production would typically be split into a number of relatively simple labour-intensive tasks taking place at different locations. Most of these would finally end up in labour-abundant developing countries which would then become net exporters. In this last stage the pattern of trade thus resembles the one predicted by the HOT. Figure 6.1 illustrates this three-stage product life cycle and also identifies the position of the innovating country in the evolving patterns of trade. In overview,

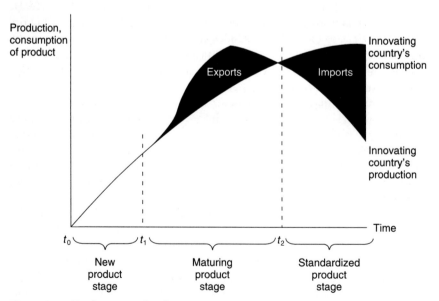

Figure 6.1   *Trade pattern for the innovating country*

the product-cycle theory states that due to the fact that throughout the life cycle of the product its input requirements change, the comparative advantage will shift from one to another country depending on their overall factor endowments and production conditions. In other words it postulates a *dynamic* comparative advantage which is useful for analyzing the evolution of trade patterns over time, something that conventional comparative advantage theory is unable to do. Empirical developments in the pattern of trade between developed and developing countries have been quite consistent with the product-cycle hypothesis.

It should be noted here that Vernon (1979) subsequently modified his original product-cycle theory with respect to the role of multinationals. Because of changes that occured in production conditions in the USA – mostly because of the convergence of labour costs with other technological leaders such as Japan, but also the convergence of the level of income – it seems quite likely that the actual production of new products could take place somewhere else other than in the country in which the research laboratory is. For example, while R&D activities will take place in the multinational's headquarters, usually in one of the more highly DCs, the initial production could easily take place in one of the multinationals subsidiary companies located in a developing country. However, this modification does not bring the product-cycle and the HO trade models any closer together.

Taking into account all the difficulties in measuring technological advantage, the empirical evidence is as favourable toward the product-cycle theory as it could be. A number of studies have incorporated some type of technology-related variables as determinants of the pattern of trade. A comprehensive survey of the many avenues taken in empirical testing is presented by Deardorff (1984). He stresses that all the variables used to explain trade in these technology-based models are related to two things: the 'newness' of the products or processes, and the *special knowledge* possessed by individuals, firms and countries that enables them to develop and exploit available technologies. This leads Deardorff to conclude that it is difficult to distinguish the evidence supporting technology from the evidence supporting human capital and skills as determinants of trade (1984, p. 499).

These initial technology-based models were subsequently elaborated upon by Krugman (1982), Dollar (1986), and, particularly, Grossman and Helpman (1991). They attempted to tie up the new trade models with the long-run growth and development. Grossman and Helpman developed a model where the process of innovation and the diffusion of new knowledge is linked to international trade and is crucial for growth. The structure of the Grossman–Helpman model is neatly presented in Figure 6.2, which is taken from Siebert (1991). In this model there are two factors, human capital and unskilled labour, which are used with different intensities in three sectors – (1) R&D (2) high-technology manufacturing

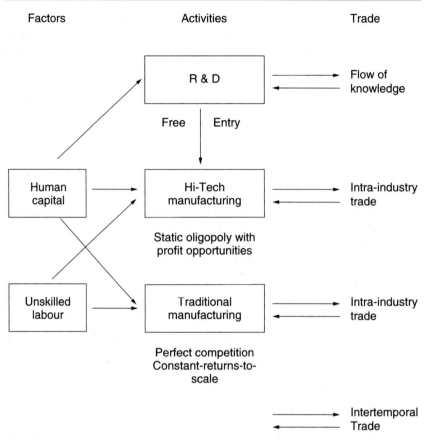

Figure 6.2   *Structure of the Grossman–Helpman model*

which is subject to increasing returns and makes use of the results of the R&D and (3) traditional manufacturing which exhibits constant returns to scale and does not use R&D. There are four types of exchange with other countries through which the knowledge externalities associated with innovative activity could be transmitted:

(a)   The inter-industry trade of traditional manufacturing based on the standard theory of comparative advantage which stems from factor proportions.

(b)   Inter-temporal trade which is also based on comparative advantage and explains capital flows. For example, a country with high savings (or a low time preference rate) will export goods today and import goods in the future.

(c)   Intra-industry trade between oligopolistic firms in high-technology products. Competition here takes place through horizontal and

vertical product differentiation. The knowledge that can be transmitted is contained in the products that are traded or, more specifically, in the products' attributes. Exposure to this competition as well
as the potential rewards from being the first mover in high-technology
activities creates pressure for continuous innovation.

(d)   The international flow of non-rival technical knowledge.

Investment in innovation by the R&D sector can take form of an
expansion in variety or improvements in quality. Whichever form it takes
innovation has the by-product of raising the overall stock of knowledge
capital. Since the knowledge capital is a public good, i.e. it is non-rival and
only imperfectly excludable, the innovations of a specific firm have
positive externalities to other firms and the economy as a whole. Depending on the extent of trade and the international flows of knowledge capital,
other countries may also benefit from these externalities.

The assumption that technological externalities are global in scope is
crucial to extending the theories of trade based on factor proportion.
When the diffusion of knowledge is geographically concentrated within
national borders there is scope for new factors as determinants of the
pattern of trade. Increasing returns arising from local external economies
could generate cumulative advantages, giving history a role to play in
explaining the evolution of trade patterns.

In conclusion it should be pointed out that technology-based trade can
coexist with trade based on factor endowments. As Dollar (1993) states,
technology can be treated as one of the aggregate factors which is a
potential source of comparative advantage. However these two types of
trade will have different effects on factor incomes. In contrast to factor-
based trade, trade based on technological specialisation may accelerate
technical progress across the board, thus increasing real income for all
factors. This last point means that trade is becoming an even more
important factor in developing countries' growth. The picture that emerges
from the empirical research based on these recent technology-based models
is that trade, or rather the liberalisation of trade, has a strong positive
long-run effect on the accumulation of knowledge capital and the rate of
growth.

6.3 Summary: can a trade theory explain the patterns of international trade?

As Leamer (1992, 1993) has repeatedly pointed out, the central issue of
international trade is how, if at all, governments should intervene in
international trade. To tackle this issue we must first have knowledge as to

what determines the patterns of trade and how the benefits from free trade are distributed. Only then can we discuss whether these benefits can possibly be increased if trade is managed or controlled in some way. The trade theories studied in Chapters 1–5 provide the conceptual framework for addressing the question on the determinants of the patterns of trade. In this chapter we have surveyed much of the empirical work which was primarily performed in order to verify how close the theoretical predictions of trade flows are to the ones we actually observe in world trade.

The four broad models of trade that have been the focus of empirical work are: (1) the Ricardian model, (2) the HOS model, (3) technology-based models and (4) a number of models with increasing returns and imperfect competition.[13] Empirical testing was not able to completely discard any of these models although some of them were found to have not very strong predictive power. However it was recognised that each of these models has stronger explanatory power with respect to trade patterns in some specific products or product groups.

Hirsch (1974) and Hufbauer and Chilas (1974) have grouped all manufactured goods into a smaller number of categories which can be associated with existing trade models. Three groups of goods are identified:

(1)   Ricardian goods are those which are traded between countries on the basis of different production conditions. The production conditions for these goods are determined by the endowment of natural resources. This group encompasses all goods which contain a high proportion of domestic natural resources, such as oil, coal or timber, as well as simple intermediate products. The general direction of trade in Ricardian goods is expected to be from developing countries to DCs because most, although not all, natural resources are found in the developing world. This asymmetric distribution of natural resources is seen as being accidental and as often leading into static trade patterns. However trade flows may change under the influence of the discovery of new resources, changes in the quality of original sources, changes in transportation costs, the discovery of synthetic materials, or changes in development strategy or trade policy.

(2)   Heckscher–Ohlin goods are those which are seen as being resource-independent. They consists mostly of so-called 'footloose' manufactures. The important characteristics of these goods is that they are produced with standardised technology without economies of scale or specific factors of production, and the products themselves are highly standardised. In other words, the production of these goods is highly internationally mobile and will search for the right combination of factor endowments (physical capital and labour). The likely

direction of HO goods is similar to the direction of Ricardian goods, but is not so clear cut. Since developing countries are considered to be labour-abundant we expect them to export labour-intensive goods while capital-rich DCs are expected to export capital-intensive goods.

(3)   Technological or product cycle-type goods are those which involve production technologies that are not universally available and change relatively frequently. A proximity to large and affluent markets is also important. The direction of trade will actually depend on the stage of the product cycle the good is in. New products will emanate most from DCs while mature goods will conform to the general HO pattern. However a narrow type of high-technology goods will in fact never mature because the innovating countries (or rather firms) are unwilling to let the knowledge diffuse globally and will use all available barriers to stop information from spreading. This is why knowledge as a specific factor cumulates in these countries and why they are able to retain their position as innovators.

It is particularly in these product cycle-type goods as well as in some HO-type goods, that we expect the most intra-industry trade to occur. This is because product differentiation is easier to obtain in these categories.

Table 6.3   *The pattern of trade, 1970–85 (percentages of total manufactured exports)*

	Ricardian goods			Heckscher-Ohlin goods			Product-cycle goods		
	1970	1980	1985	1970	1980	1985	1970	1980	1985
Developed countries	16.3	14.5	12.1	41.0	42.7	42.2	42.6	42.8	45.7
France	12.5	13.4	12.0	51.5	49.4	46.9	36.0	37.2	41.1
Germany (FR)	5.9	8.9	8.4	43.6	44.9	44.9	50.5	46.2	46.7
Italy	5.3	5.5	6.2	54.9	59.8	56.7	39.8	34.7	37.0
Japan	4.8	3.3	2.1	49.8	48.8	43.1	45.3	47.9	54.8
United Kingdom	9.6	10.5	8.5	42.8	37.9	36.2	47.6	51.6	55.3
United States	15.5	15.5	10.8	28.2	26.5	27.3	56.3	58.0	61.9
Other	30.9	25.1	22.0	37.9	42.7	44.6	31.2	32.3	33.4
Developing countries	46.8	25.6	13.3	43.3	57.7	66.5	11.6	16.6	20.2
NIEs	32.9	16.6	7.4	53.4	55.9	61.6	19.6	27.5	31.0
Second gener. NIEs	80.4	51.2	31.4	17.1	34.2	61.1	2.5	14.6	7.6
Other	47.1	28.7	20.0	43.4	60.4	63.6	9.6	10.9	16.4

Source: Forstner and Ballance (1990, Table 3.6, Table 3.8).

However, as shown by the example of New Zealand–Australia trade in the Appendix (p. 242), intra-industry trade is also possible in resource-based goods (see Table 6.3). Table 6.3 summarises world trade in manufactures over the period 1970–85 on the basis of this three-group differentiation. The numbers paint a very clear picture. In the case of Ricardian goods, DCs remain small net importers while developing countries remain small net exporters. The comparative advantages in HO goods, on the other hand, has changed quite substantially from 1970 to 1985. While the DCs' net exports steadily increased over the 1970s, by 1983 the developing countries had become net exporters. In the case of product-cycle goods, despite some shifts in comparative advantage in favour of developing countries, DCs remain strong net exporters.

In conclusion it should again be mentioned that, except in a very few cases, the empirical work on international trade has not had much influence on how we think about trade. For example, we now have strong evidence that the HOS model cannot explain much of the actual real-world trade. Nevertheless this model is still the centre of most courses in international trade. The reasons for this are several. It has great intuitive power, mathematical elegance, a large scope, and it fits nicely with the neoclassical research programme in general. The ideological reason, that is, its role in supporting the optimality of free trade, is also important. Therefore, despite a number of empirical refutations of the HOS model, it is still in widespread use. While we cannot deny the richness of insights this model provides, it must be recognised that its explanatory power is limited, even in weaker versions of the HO theorem, such as the HOV theorem.

Having said this, we should hasten to add that there is no evidence that the new trade theories have any stronger explanatory power. One exception to this may be in the Helpman–Krugman model which incorporates intra-industry trade into the standard HOS model. In doing this, they have succeeded in keeping some of the characteristics of the pure HOS model, specifically its ideological advocacy of free trade and a good fit with general equilibrium theory, as well as increasing the degree to which the model accurately predicts observed trade patterns. Since this model also makes some new predictions for which there is real data support, for example the positive correlation between the proportion of intra-industry trade in total trade and the similarity in factor endowments between countries, it can be accepted as both a theoretically and empirically progressive shift in relation to the standard theory.

The same cannot be said for other models that belong to this broad group of new trade theories. Nevertheless they are receiving an increasing attention from both trade teachers and trade practitioners. Perhaps this is because of the issues being brought into the open by these new theories are those which could never fit the standard theories well. These issues include the real value of reciprocity, dumping, product differentiation, free entry, or externalities and we will discuss them in Part 2.

APPENDIX 6
ON THE MEASUREMENT OF
INTRA-INDUSTRY TRADE

Despite extensive empirical and theoretical work on intra-industry trade, there are still some unresolved problems in its measurement. The level of intra-industry trade obtained obviously depends on how an industry is defined. However there are still problems concerning the definition of an 'industry', and the level of data aggregation at which this trade is best observed (that is, the problem of categorical aggregation). Other problems are linked to finding a suitable quantitative measure (or formula) of intra-industry trade. Leaving aside for a moment the problems of definition and commodity classification, let us present some of the alternative approaches to the measurement of intra-industry trade.

The formula used most extensively in measuring the level of intra-industry trade for a country as a whole is given by the following index:

$$IIT = \{1 - [\Sigma|X_i - M_i|/\Sigma(X_i + M_i)]\}100 \qquad (A6.1)$$

where IIT stands for the level of intra-industry trade, and X_i and M_i indicate the value of exports and imports of some commodity from category i. This is the abbreviated form of the index known as the Grubel and Lloyd standard measure of intra-industry trade (from Grubel and Lloyd, 1975). This index measures intra-industry trade as the residual from total trade. The value of the IIT index varies between 0 and 100 – the closer the index is to 100, the greater the importance of intra-industry trade, and the closer the index is to 0, the larger the extent of inter-industry trade. Note that the IIT index in (A6.1) is a weighted mean, not a simple arithmetic average.

One problem Grubel and Lloyd had with this measure of intra-industry trade was that it was valid only if the country in question had balanced trade, that is, if total exports equalled total imports. If country experiences a large trade imbalance (surplus or deficit), the measure will be biased downwards, leading to the underestimation of the real extent of intra-industry trade. In other words, with a trade imbalance, the mean IIT will always be less than 100.[14] To deal with this problem Grubel and Lloyd adjusted the formula (A6.1) so as to express each commodity category's exports and imports as a share of total exports and imports respectively. The adjusted formula is given as

$$\begin{aligned} IIT^* =|1 - \{\Sigma|(X_i/X) - (M_i/M)|/\Sigma[(X_i/X) \\ +(M_i/M)]\}|100 \end{aligned} \qquad (A6.2)$$

since the denominator in the above formula must add up to two (100 per cent of exports added to 100 per cent of imports), we can write:

$$IIT^* = \{1 - 0.5[\Sigma|(X_i/X) - (M_i/M)|]\}100 \tag{A6.2a}$$

The values of IIT^* again vary between 0 and 100. The value of 100 is reached when total national trade is of an intra-industry character and the each category's trade is exactly balanced. If overall trade is imbalanced and all trade is of an inter-industry character the value of IIT^* is 0. In general the greater the country's total trade imbalance $(X - M)$, the greater should be the difference between the IIT and the IIT^* measures. To illustrate the difference between these two formulae, let us look at the following example.

Assume a country has just five industries (commodity categories), A–E. Table 6.4 gives the values of exports and imports from each category, as well as the total value of exports and imports.

$$IIT = (1 - 220/600)100 = 63.3$$
$$IIT* = [1 - 0.5(0.57)]100 = 71.5$$

From the above result it is clear that the adjusted formula gives a higher value for intra-industry trade in the case of trade imbalances.

The other various measures of intra-industry trade were also developed primarily to deal with the problem of trade imbalances.[15] However some recent research has suggested that a correction for trade imbalance is not needed after all (cf. Forstner and Ballance, 1990, p. 61).

Until this point we have avoided defining industry i as it appears in the above formulae. The reason is that there is no unanimity as to what level of international trade classification corresponds to an industry and is most suitable for the measurement of the level of intra-industry trade. In practice international trade data is classified according to the so-called Standard International Trade Classification (SITC), Revision 2. Under this classification the more digits that are used indicates a greater level of *disaggregation*. Table 6.5 gives an example of this trade classification. Two, three, or four digit levels of SITC are all used in empirical studies.

Table 6.4   *Intra-industry trade measurement – an example*

Industry	X_i (1)	M_i (2)	$\|X_i - M_i\|$ (3)	X_i/X (4)	M_i/M (5)	(4)–(5) (6)	IIT_i (7)
A	20	40	20	0.08	0.11	−0.03	66.7
B	60	10	50	0.25	0.03	0.22	28.6
C	50	50	0	0.20	0.14	0.06	100.0
D	100	220	120	0.42	0.61	−0.19	62.5
E	10	40	30	0.04	0.11	−0.07	40.0
Σ	240	360	220	1.00	1.00	0.57	

However there is a clear preference for the three digit level of disaggregation with this level more often than not identifying 'industries'.[16] From the example in Table 6.5 it is clear that the three digit level includes products with different characteristics which, in a strict theoretical sense may not belong to the same industry. However using a more disaggregated system is not necessarily better as it may result in the separation of goods that can be close substitutes in production (Balassa, 1979). In fact there is no agreement as to the economic rationale behind the system of aggregation used in international trade statistics. The discussion on this problem went to such extremes that some economists argued that the most intra- industry trade could be explained away by simply changing the level of data aggregation, and that the phenomenon of intra-industry trade was nothing more than a *statistical artifact* (see, for somewhat differing arguments leading to this conclusion in Finger, 1975; Lipsey, 1976; Pomfret, 1985). However, in rebuttal, numerous empirical works have documented the existence of this type of trade only too well (for a good summary on empirical testing see Greenaway and Milner, 1986; Tharakan, 1983 Tharakan and Kol, 1989).

Table 6.5 *An example of the SITC*

		No. of categories in this section	No. of categories at this level in SITC R2
Section 0	**Food and Live Animals Chiefly for Food**	–	10
Division 02	Dairy products and birds' eggs	10	63
Group 022	Milk and cream	34	233
Sub-group 022.4	Milk and cream preserved, concentrated or sweetened	94	786
Heading 022.42	Milk (other than whey) in powder or granulas containing not more than 1.5 per cent by weight of fat	218	1832
Section 7	**Machinery and Transport Equipment**	–	10
Division 79	Other transport equipment	9	63
Group 793	Ships, boats and floating structures	45	233
Sub-group 793.1	Warships of all kinds	158	786
Heading 793.21	Yachts and other vessels for pleasure or sports	385	1832

Source: United Nations (1981).

Box 6.2   *Trans-Tasman intra-industry trade*

In addition to supply-side factors, such as economies of scale and market structures, and demand-side factors, such as preference for variety, which influence the behaviour of intra-industry trade, there is another group of factors which can play an important role. Trade barriers, transportation costs and regional trade arrangements can all be categorised as institutional factors which affect the level of intra-industry trade. It is typically argued that (1) trade liberalisation in general, and membership in free trade areas or trading blocs in particular, stimulates a greater degree of intra-industry trade than would be otherwise, and (2) the costs of adjusting to trade liberalisation are lower in industries characterised by high levels of intra-industry trade. This later idea also implies that the prospects for a successful common market are better in the case of countries with high levels of existing and potential intra-industry trade.[17]

Being a small country specialised in the production and export of agricultural products, New Zealand has tended to examine its trade policy issues in light of the inter-industry framework. However the 1983 free trade agreement with Australia, known as 'Closer Economic Relations' (CER), provides an opportunity to test those propositions linking intra-industry trade and trade liberalisation. The CER agreement, as explained in more detail in Part 3 of this book, has resulted in the phased reduction in tariffs and other non-tariff barriers to trade in all goods between these two countries, so that by 1990 there was free trade in all goods and most services. Thus, if the earlier propositions are true, both countries should have experienced an increase in the volume of mutual intra-industry trade. Further, there should have been less structural change in those industries with a high degree of intra-industry trade. Hamilton and Kniest (1991) have tested these relationships in the CER case. Here we will report their result without dwelling on the actual methods used in the testing. In essence their results provide no support for the proposition that the liberalisation of trade resulting from the CER Agreement has encouraged intra-industry trade. However the intra-industry pattern of new trade, that is, the proportion of trade arising from trade liberalisation, has tended to be different from the pattern of trade established under protection. The evidence thus suggests that in this case trade liberalisation has induced an increase in structural adjustment at higher costs in those industries characterised by inter-industry rather than intra-industry trade (1991, Table 4, p. 365).

In a different type of study, Bano and Lane (1991) examined the changes in New Zealand's trade over the period 1964–87. Table 6.6 summarises their results for intra-industry trade across all industries at the two-digit level for selected trading partners in 1987. Of the 59 industries comprising the total New Zealand trade with the rest of the world in 1987, 15 industries registered an intra-industry trade level of 50 per cent or more, while 21 industries recorded an intra-industry trade figure of greater than 40 per cent. The mean value of intra-industry trade across all industries was around 26 per cent. Intra-industry trade tends to be concentrated in product group 8 (4 of 7 industries), group 6 (3 of 9), and group 0 (3 of 10). This shows that the New Zealand pattern of intra-industry trade is different from most other industrial countries. For these countries it has been established that intra-industry trade prevails in SITC industry groups 5–8. These include those industries[18] which share the typical characteristics of industries involved in intra-industry trade (such as product differentiation, economies of scale, and rapid innovation). New Zealand thus appears to have developed some unusual intra-industry trade relationships. Probably the most significant of these is the high level of intra-industry trade in industry group 0 (food and live animals). Bano and Lane explained this by the fact that New Zealand is still very much specialised in its traditional comparative advantage production (food and food preparation) but has somewhat diversified in a few food products, processing them further.

Table 6.6   *Intra-industry trade of New Zealand by country and industry, 1987*

Country	Average IIT	Industries IIT > 50 per cent	Dominant SITC Groups
World	26.5	15/59	8 (4/7), 6 (3/9), 0 (3/10)
Australia	55.2	28/59	8 (5/7), 6 (5/9), 0 (7/10)
Singapore	28.7	13/56	8 (4/7), 6 (5/9)
Cook Is.	19.7	1/51	8 (1/5)
USA	18.7	12/58	0 (4/10), 6 (4/9)
Thailand	18.3	9/47	5 (3/7)
Canada	17.5	8/53	8 (5/7)
Hong Kong	17.5	11/50	5 (4/6), 0 (3/9)
UK	7.9	5/58	0 (3/10)
EEC	7.6	8/58	0 (3/10)
Philippines	6.8	8/46	5 (3/7)
Japan	5.5	8/56	5 (3/9)

Source: Bano and Lane (1991, Table 3, p. 13).

With respect to trans-Tasman trade Bano and Lane have obtained similar results. High volumes of intra-industry trade in SITC groups 0–3 reflect the closeness of markets, as well as the technological, cultural, political and institutional similarities of these two countries. In fact, in more than two-thirds of the industries defined at the three digit level New Zealand had higher levels of intra-industry trade with Australia than with the rest of the world. In the cases when intra-industry trade with the rest of the world was more important the authors found that two types of products was typically involved. One type of products were those in which either Australia or New Zealand had no exports or imports. In the trade of timber, for example, Australia imports most of its requirements while New Zealand is a net exporter and imports limited quantities of some tropical timber from other countries. The reverse holds for trade in metal ore. The second type of products was those in which one or both countries had a high level of non-discriminatory protection, for example in footwear and textiles, which was transformed into trade diversion by the CER Agreement.

■ *Chapter 7* ■

International Factor Movements and Multinational Corporations

■ *7.1* Introduction

Thus far we have studied the principles behind international trade: what motivates the flows of goods between countries, and what are the welfare effects of these flows to individuals, countries and the world as a whole. Without any doubt international trade is still the major force promoting economic integration in the world. But it is not the only one: the international movements of resources may serve equally as well or, in some cases better, to integrate economies. Our attention now turns to the international flows of the two most used resources: labour and capital.

In section 7.2 we will analyse what motivates *international labour migration* and what the welfare effects are on the three groups of people involved: native labour in the receiving country, the remaining labour in the sending country, and the migrants themselves. In section 7.3 we introduce the concept of *intertemporal trade* which is crucial to an understanding of international borrowing and lending. The welfare effects of well behaved international borrowing and lending are analogous to those of well behaved and free commodity trade flows. But things can go wrong if borrowing and lending are 'badly behaved'. An example is the world debt crisis of the 1980s, which is discussed in detail. Finally, in section 7.4, we change the emphasis from country to the firm level by studying the reasons behind the emergence of multinational corporations and the steady rise in importance of foreign direct investment (FDI).

Before we begin discussing the principles involved in the movements of individual factors let us first discuss the nature of the relationship between international trade in goods and international factor movements in general. Consider the case of two countries which share the same technology on the production side and have identical and homothetic tastes on the demand side but are differentiated in terms of relative factor endowments. In other words, suppose that these two countries fit perfectly into the HOS framework. There are two scenarios on how these countries could become integrated in an economic sense. If these countries become open to the free and costless trade in goods this trade will lead to the equalisation of commodity prices and eventually to the equalisation of factor prices. Given equal factor prices there are no efficiency gains for the world as a whole if factors move across national borders. Moreover, even if factors could cross borders freely and costlessly there is no motivation for them to do so.

The other possibility is that instead of trading in goods these two countries allow their factors to move freely across national borders in response to differences in factor returns. Labour will then migrate to the country in which initially labour was relatively scarce and more expensive, while capital will move from that country into the other country where its return was relatively higher initially. Factor prices will eventually equalise because relative endowments will become identical. Under this theoretical framework with equal factor prices, the same technology and the same demand structure, there will be no reason for trade in goods between these two countries to occur. This means that the trade in goods, and the international movements of factors are actually *substitutes*: if one takes place with no impediments at all, the other cannot exist. Since in reality trade in goods is neither free nor costless it does not usually lead to complete factor-price equalisation. Consequently there is always scope for international factor movements as well. However the two will still be interchangeable; the freer commodity trade is, the smaller will be the need for factor movements.

This view seems plausible as long as we look at international trade as the means by which relatively abundant factors are exchanged for relatively scarce factors. However if trade in goods is driven by other forces, such as technological differences as in the Ricardian model, or by economies of scale, the relation between commodity trade and factor movements may take another form. Suppose that relative factor endowments are identical in both countries – so that we can eliminate this as the cause of trade – but that one country has a much larger national market than the other. Consequently the price of a good produced with, say, external economies of scale will be lower in the large country. That country will then become an exporter of that good. Suppose that labour is used relatively intensively in the production of exports. In the short run exports will drive up the returns to all the factors employed by the exporting industry. The magnification effect means that the factor used relatively intensively in export production will benefit by more. The higher level of wages will attract foreign labour into this *exporting sector*. This will in turn lead to more of the labour-intensive good being produced at a *lower per unit cost of labour*. This then causes the exports of this country to expand even further. In this case, therefore, we can view trade in goods and international factor movements as *complements*. This complementarity between the trade in goods and factor movements is particularly clear if total commodity trade is separated into inter- and intra-industry trade. When relative factor endowments differ between countries and production satisfies the typical HOS conditions the type of trade that evolves is inter-industry trade. However, as we saw above, when we allow for factor movements they will erode the need for trade in goods; factor movements therefore act as a substitute for inter-industry trade. In the other extreme case, when factor endowments are identical and at least one sector is producing under economies of scale, the type of trade that evolves is intra-industry trade. The introduction of factor movements expands this trade. Intra-industry trade and factor movements are therefore complements. Thus, the larger the intra-industry component of a country's total trade the greater the scope will be for factor movements across its national borders.

This background of the complementarity between intra-industry trade and factor movements can be used to briefly raise another issue: the role of foreign direct investments (FDI) in fostering international trade. If FDI serves to increase intra-industry specialisation it is easy to see how it could be detrimental for a country to expand its commodity exports. On the other hand, if FDI flows into a country in response to strong import protection it will serve to minimise commodity trade. Thus, even in the case of intra-industry trade, factor movements could act as a perfect substitute for trade if trade is seriously impeded by import barriers.

■ 7.2 International labour migration

To some extent the effects of labour migration have already been discussed within the context of the Rybczynski theorem under the HOS and specific-factors models (pp. 94 and 140). We derived the effects of an increase in the endowment of labour with the other factor(s) held constant, on the outputs and, in one instance, on the factor prices as well. However the source and nature of the labour increase was not identified as it was not relevant for deriving the results. Although the effects on outputs and factor returns do not differ with respect to the national origin of the additional labour of the same quality, when it comes to implications other than those which are purely economic there is a significant difference between the influx of foreign labour and a simple increase in the domestic population.

The international migration of labour is probably the most sensitive issue of all international flows. Although a large proportion of these labour flows is motivated by purely economic reasons, such as higher earnings or better job opportunities, some migration is motivated by non-economic reasons. Our civilisation is not unused to the huge exodus of people for political or war reasons. The flight of the Jews from Nazi forces in Europe during 1935–45, the flight of many Eastern Europeans from Soviet forces in the years following the end of the Second World War, and the flight of many people of various ethnic origins from the war in the Balkans which has been going on since 1991 are all examples of this. Natural disasters and massive famines such as those that happen so often in Africa, with Somalia in 1992 being the latest example, also cause the relocation of population. These flows of labour that are not motivated by purely economic reasons are less subject to border restrictions because there is no strong political or other opposition to such flows. This is at least true until the numbers of refugees starts to create economic and social tensions, as was the case in Europe in 1992–3. On the other hand, when it comes to 'purely' economic migrants all countries impose regulations which not only limit the inflow of immigrants but prescribe what special characteristics these people must have to gain entry. These characteristics are usually defined in terms of education and training, work experience and health. Through this type of selectivity in terms of quality and quantity governments of receiving countries try to maximise the benefits for their original residents, and possibly for migrants as well, but they are not concerned about the impact such policies may have on the sending countries. Two of the most well known patterns of economic labour migration in our time, the *brain drain* and *Gastarbeiter*, are discussed at the end of this section. Let us first identify the possible effects of labour migration.

We can use the U-shaped diagram of the specific-factors model to identify the immediate effects of an influx of foreign labour on outputs and the distribution of income in both Home and Foreign (Figure 7.1). The horizontal axis OO^* measures the total world labour force. Home's native labour endowment is measured from the origin O, while Foreign's labour endowment is measured from the origin O^*. Suppose that initially in Home there are OL_1 workers. The rest of the world labour force L_1O^* is thus allocated to Foreign. Given different marginal productivities of labour in Home, L_1H, and Foreign, L_1F, this distribution results in different real wage rates. The real wage in Home is Ow_1 while in Foreign it is at a lower level, $O^*w^*_1$. Provided that labour can freely and costlessly move across national borders in response to wage differentials Foreign's workers will begin emigrating to Home. This movement will continue until the value of marginal productivities is equalised at point E. Let us first look at the effects on outputs in each country and in the world as a whole. From Figure 7.1 we see that output increases in Home by an amount given by HEL_2L_1, while it decreases in Foreign by an amount given by FEL_2L_1. It is obvious that the gain in Home's output outweighs Foreign's loss by the area HEF. World output is therefore increased by international labour migration. This result comes as no surprise as labour is redistributed from

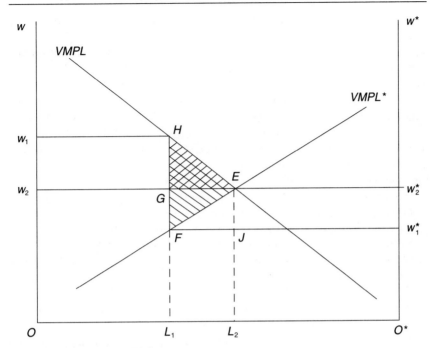

Figure 7.1 *International labour migration*

the country where its marginal productivity is low to the country where its marginal productivity is high. The larger the difference between national wages, the distance *HF*, the larger we would expect the gains to be in terms of increased overall efficiency and world output.

Let us now examine the effects on factor incomes. The new distribution of labour at L_2 is accompanied by a decrease in real wage at Home, w_1w_2, and an increase in the real wage in Foreign, $w^*_1w^*_2$. Migration thus causes wage rates to converge. In Home native labour now receives lower real wages than before. Their loss of income amounts to HGw_2w_1. This income is actually transferred to the owners of capital who now hire the cheaper labour. Their total gain in income is equal to the area HEw_2w_1 which consists of the 'lost' income to native labour and area given by the triangle *HEG*. The latter represents the difference between the additional output created by the migrants, HEL_2L_1, and the income they receive, GEL_2L_1. This difference exists because the average product of the migrants is larger than their marginal product while they are paid only the value of their marginal product. The positive difference *HEG* thus represents the *net gain* for Home.

Migrants, of course, receive higher real wages in the new country; this was one of the motivations behind their migration. The income they 'lose' by emigrating from Foreign is equal to FJL_2L_1, while the income they earn now is GEL_2L_1. They therefore gain the difference which is *GEJF*. Thus, even when migrants are included, the Home country gains from the influx of foreign labour. Therefore, at least on the basis of output and income effects, this analysis could not identify any reasons for preventing foreign labour to migrate to the Home country. However Foreign may wish to stop its labour leaving as it loses absolutely when labour emigrates. The remaining labour will now receive higher wages; the gain in its income amounting to $JEw^*{}_2w^*{}_1$. On the other hand capital now works with fewer workers. This causes its marginal productivity to decline and it in turn receives lower returns. The total loss of income to capital owners is $FEw^*{}_2w^*{}_1$. This leaves a net loss for Foreign of the amount EJF. The income-distributional effects of the international migration of labour are therefore analogous to those of commodity trade: some factors gain and some factors lose despite the fact that the increase in world output should in theory allow everyone to be better off (see Box 7.1, p. 253).

Even though there are strong economic arguments in favour of liberal inflows of foreign labour, many countries have immigration policies which try to restrict the number of workers coming in. The goal is of course to try and maximise the benefits for the country's original residents. Many countries try to be selective in the kinds of immigrants they accept, trying to bias immigration regulations toward high-skilled labour or labour which is accompanied by some investment capital. This is accomplished by awarding more points to those applicants with higher degrees of education and/or with more investment capital (see for example the New Zealand or Australian points based immigration policies). We will next show that for the welfare effects obtained by the original residents it is not unimportant what the relative quantity of capital brought into country actually is.

In Figure 7.2 the original residents own capital and labour in the combination given by point A on isoquant Q_A. This quantity is also the quantity of goods consumed because Home is not engaged in international trade. Relative factor prices are given by the tangent $\omega_A = (w/r)$ to this isoquant at point A. Suppose now that immigration is allowed. Different outcomes can be illustrated with respect to the original residents' gains depending on how much capital the new labour brings in. Let us first consider the case in which new migrants bring in less capital per unit of labour than originally existed in Home. Suppose that the new total factor endowment combination is shown by point B. This enlarged bundle can produce a much larger quantity of output, Q_B. The new wage–rental ratio is also lower than before, $\omega_B < \omega_A$. At the new relative factor prices the *original residents'* factor endowment bundle is worth the same as bundle C. However this bundle can produce quantity Q_C, which is greater than quantity Q_A. The original residents can therefore consume more of this output than before the immigration occurred. A similar result can be obtained for the case when migrants bring in relatively more capital per unit of labour than residents initially have. Interested readers can complete the diagrammatic effects of this case for themselves.

We now turn to the case when migrants bring in with them the same amount of capital per unit of labour as original residents have at bundle A. The new total factor endowment is given by point D on isoquant Q_D. The *community* as a whole can now produce more output, and can by the same token consume more, as compared with the original level of output Q_A. But what is the benefit for the original residents? As we can see clearly from Figure 7.2 there is *none*; at least not in terms of increased consumption of this product. Relative factor prices have not changed and there is no reason why the original residents will gain from this international transaction. Note that this is the same result as in the case where a country cannot gain if it is trading at autarkic relative commodity prices. In short, whenever the immigration of labour causes a change in the wage–rental ratio the original residents should benefit from immigration. Gains from immigration are likely to be the greatest when the disparity between the

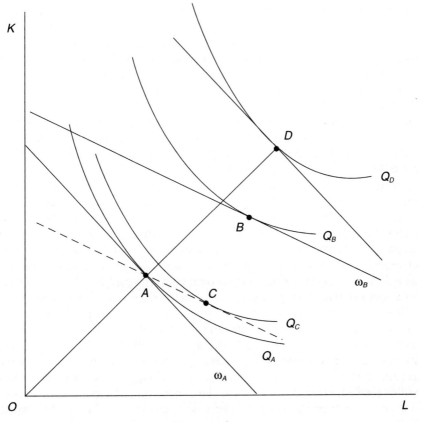

Figure 7.2   *Migrants accompanied by capital*

factor endowment ratio of the original residents and the new migrants is largest. This suggests that relatively capital-rich countries should encourage an inflow of migrants with a relatively low ratio of capital to labour, while capital-poor countries should promote the opposite. By the same token the human capital-rich DCs should benefit the most by pursuing a liberal immigration policy with respect to unskilled labour.

Indeed some empirical research does indicate that a surge of unskilled workers into the USA from Latin America and Mexico did not *significantly* reduce the wage rate for native unskilled labour, nor did it foreclose them from job opportunities. The impact of unskilled foreign labour, which was mostly employed by import-competing industries, did however affect the real incomes of the factors employed in other sectors, particularly the exporting sectors. From our earlier analysis conducted in Chapter 2 we know that an expansion of the import-competing sector through an influx of foreign labour could serve to reduce a country's need for imports, demonstrating how factor mobility can substitute for commodity trade and suggesting that the expansion may have favourable terms of trade effects. In other words the real income of those factors employed in the export sector, such as human capital, may increase due to the immigration of unskilled workers. This also illustrates the fact that in considering the total welfare effects of immigration possible effects on a country's terms of trade should be taken into account (see also Box 7.2, p. 255).

Before we discuss the effects of capital movements let us briefly look at the features of two special types of labour migration. The first one which appeared as a policy in western and northern European countries in the early 1960s is the so-called *Gastarbeiter* or *guestworkers* system. This policy has subsequently been applied by other 'booming' countries, such as some Middle East countries in the years of rising oil prices. The policy is such that workers, typically low-skilled or unskilled labour, are invited to migrate to a receiving country for short time spans to work in industries which are expanding but are experiencing domestic labour constraints. Since these workers are issued with only temporary work permits the receiving country can, in theory, regulate the supply of labour to suit changing macroeconomic conditions. In addition these foreign workers usually face unemployment in their own countries and are thus willing to accept lower than average wages and unwanted jobs in the host countries. Through such policies Germany, Switzerland, and other northern European countries during the 1960s and early 1970s, while they were in an expansionary phase, were able to attract millions of workers from Mediterranean countries and Eastern Europe. Eventually these workers became *de facto immigrants*. The two oil crises and the ensuing worldwide recession created the need for the contraction of economic activities. This had direct implications for the availability of jobs for guestworkers. However what the policy did not take into account was that many guestworkers did not in fact want to leave. It became a problematic and

Box 7.1   *The income* per capita *'paradox'*

In the analysis above we used a simple model in which all labour receives the same real wage before and after migration occurs. Labour is thus assumed to be homogeneous; there are no quality differences between native labour and migrants. In reality however this is not a very likely situation. Migrants typically belong to the category of labour in their native country which receives below-average wages. Once this labour moves to a new country it will again accept wages that are lower than the average native workers' wage, although these are higher than the wage it earned in its former country. When these migrants leave their own country its income *per capita* should therefore rise. On the other hand when workers arrive in a new country that country's income *per capita* should decline since the new labour works for below-average wage. These movements in income *per capita* seem quite correct. But how do we reconcile them with our previous conclusion that the receiving country gains in terms of total real income, while the sending country loses in terms of total real income?

This apparent paradox is actually very simple to resolve. We must not forget to take into account the *diminishing marginal returns to labour*. In their presence, *ceteris paribus*, output in receiving country will grow more slowly than the increase in labour, income *per capita* in the receiving country must therefore fall even though additional output is created. Similarly output in Foreign will fall at a slower rate than the decrease in its labour, leading to an increase in output *per capita* despite the reduction in total output produced.[1]

There is, of course, no doubt in which direction world real income *per capita* has moved. The total world population has not changed but its redistribution between countries has caused the total world output to increase thus leading to a higher real income *per capita*.

costly exercise to compel these workers to return to their original home countries. In fact Germany, France and Switzerland ended up paying *departure grants*. The issue of foreign guestworkers in Germany and other European countries became an even more sensitive issues with the creation of 'Europe 1992' and the virtually unrestricted factor mobility between member countries that accompanied it. These problems were amplified in Germany by reunification and the need to employ former East Germans.

The foreign guestworkers who are, somewhat contrary to many politicians' expectations, also human beings, although benefiting financially from being employed in the host country over a number of years still felt exploited and abandoned. They were the ones who worked for low wages, very often without any security or other benefits when those countries really needed them. Many of them adapted to life in their new country and started to feel very comfortable with the new set of social values and rules. Regardless of these facts they are expected to leave the host country and return to their native countries where they were and still may be unable to find a job or at least one that is equally well paid. However quite a few have decided to leave because their presence combined with rising unemployment has created serious social tensions and an unfriendly environment in which to live.

The other type of labour migration often talked about concerns the so-called *brain drain* phenomenon. It usually refers to the migration of highly skilled labour from poor to rich countries. In contrast to the case of guestworkers this migration is usually considered permanent in character. It became the centre of debate in the 1960s when many of scientists left Europe for the USA. It was also an issues in later years when the flow was from developing countries to DCs in general. Nowadays the largest sources of the brain drain are the states of the former Soviet Union and Eastern Europe. The brain drain occurs because of the better economic and general social conditions that exist for skilled labour in rich countries. The advantages for the receiving countries are typically estimated as large since the receiving country obtains skilled labour and human capital without making any investment. However it is more complex to establish whether the brain drain is actually good for the original residents. First of all we must decide whether the migrants enter into the calculation of welfare effects or not. If they do their welfare gains or losses become an important category to add to the effects on that country's original residents. It is usually argued that *unskilled* migrants will benefit more from migration than skilled ones. Their incremental income would probably be higher than that of skilled migrants. Therefore if the original residents' welfare is not affected differently by the immigration of unskilled or skilled labour, then the immigration of unskilled labour would be preferred. However we cannot expect the effects on original residents to be the same. They will differ because the amount by which the social marginal product of migrants exceeds their private returns will differ for skilled versus unskilled migrants. In fact even within the general category of skilled migrants there may be significant differences in the externalities they can provide for the residents. Those immigrants who provide the greatest net social benefits should therefore be preferred. Immigration policies however rarely go into such details. The arguments for the preference of a general category of skilled migrants over unskilled migrants rest upon the presumptions that skilled migrants will not make heavy demands on public funds and that they will be assimilated into the original group of residents much faster, causing less social and political tension.

On the other hand it may seem that it is much less complicated to determine the economic impact of skilled migration on the sending countries. These typically LDCs are concerned that the skills, and with them potential externalities for growth, in which they have invested are lost forever if they let skilled people leave freely. There have therefore been suggestions that migrants who fit into this category should pay a 'departure tax' to their home country which would cover the costs of their education and training. Although such proposals have many supporters only a few countries have in fact tried to introduce such taxes (for example, communist Romania). In some cases there have also been calls for the receiving countries (mostly DCs) to pay 'compensation' to the sending countries. This of course has no practical significance. However it is possible to make the migrants themselves more 'willing' to help their home country to overcome the losses from their departure. Methods, for example, might include the extension of income tax jurisdiction. In fact this solution, which involves dual citizenship and tax responsibilities, is more realistic with the current change in the nature of the brain drain from permanent to temporary movements of human capital.

Box 7.2 *Immigrant earnings in the USA in recent decades*

The USA belongs to those countries which benefited greatly from a steady influx of immigrant labour in the past. Declining economic performance in the 1990s led to a revival of demands to 'protect national borders' with respect to goods, services and factors coming from other countries. Thus immigration came into the spotlight as one of the forces destroying jobs and national interest. US immigration law has been re-examined and proposals are being made for tougher immigration laws with a view to protecting unemployed natives (Simpson, 1996). But it may happen that the US market for immigrants needs no artificial entry barriers. The one of the most important determinants of migration flows is the level and growth of wages in the recipient countries. If so, the USA is becoming less attractive for new immigrants. Borjas (1995) showed that there was a steady decline in the average wage of immigrants relative to native workers: in 1970 the typical immigrant earned about 1 per cent more than the typical native worker; in 1980 the immigrants earned around 10 per cent less of what natives were earning, and in 1990 this gap had increased to almost 17 per cent. Moreover, the skills of immigrants are continuously declining as compared to native workers. Borjas states that the earning of post-1970 immigrants will not catch up with the earnings of the native workers during their working lives. This is because there is a widening dispersion in growth rates of relative wages for immigrants and natives. The most recent immigrants of 1990s suffer from wage disadvantage of up to 38 per cent.

■ 7.3 International borrowing and lending

As we have established, the difference in prices is an important instigating factor in initiating the movements of goods as well as labour between countries. However in the cases of both commodity trade and labour migration it is not the only reason. Recall that trade in goods based on reasons other than comparative advantage exists and that there are also a lot of political refugees. Similarly, although the interest rates differential between countries is an important motivation behind international capital flows it is not the only motivating factor. Broadly, international capital movements are divided into two types: *portfolio capital flows* and *foreign direct investment (FDI)*. The movements of portfolio capital reflect investments in bonds, securities or firms in one country by residents of another country. These investments are made for purely financial reasons and control rights are not conferred on those who invest in foreign firms. This category of capital movements, as we will see shortly, fits neatly into the analytical framework of trade driven by comparative advantage. On the other hand FDI reflects the purchase of a foreign firm and implies a significant degree of *control* over the management of that firm. In fact the division between portfolio capital and FDI is based on the fact that the latter necessarily implies majority ownership or the exercise of control over the decision making process of foreign firms. This suggests that something other than pure movements of capital is involved in FDI and that something else other than mere interest rate differentials must be the motivating factor. The issues involved in FDI will be discussed in section 7.4.

Note that another category of capital, physical capital or *capital goods*, also flows across national borders. However these movements are not counted as international capital movements. They are typically treated as trade in goods.

☐ *Intertemporal trade*

Although the flows of portfolio capital could be analysed in the same manner as labour migration there are some important distinctions that cannot be captured in this fashion. For example with capital movements it is not necessary, as it is with labour, that the owners of the factor move from one country to another. This complicates the analysis of welfare effects. Also, despite the fact that capital flows are not very tangible, they have very real consequences. They affect both present and future production as well as consumption possibilities and therefore trade. The best way to study the implications of capital movements is to treat them as what they really are: a way for countries to *trade over time*. This special type of trade occurs when a country in effect trades future goods for currently produced goods or vice versa. This is known as *intertemporal trade*. To simplify the analysis we will assume that there are only two time periods, the present denoted by p, and the future denoted by f, and that each country produces and consumes only one good in each period. Thus we speak of present and future goods. Figure 7.3 illustrates Home's PPF. The difference between this PPF and the one we have used extensively thus far is in the nature of the trade-off it represents. In this case the trade-off is between present goods and future goods. The PPF thus shows production possibilities over time. For example if Home's residents decide to produce at point E, and they have no opportunity to trade, they will have the quantity OQ_p of present goods to consume today $(= OD_p)$, and the quantity OQ_f to consume in the future $(= OD_f)$. However they may decide not to consume all of the present production, but rather to invest some of it for future consumption. This decision will depend on how impatient the country's consumers are to consume today. The degree of impatience is measured by the slope of Home's indifference curve which reflects the taste for consumption today versus consumption in the future. More specifically, this slope is called the intertemporal marginal rate of substitution and it reflects the amount of future goods the representative consumer is willing to give up to obtain one more unit of present goods. The common slope of the PPF and the indifference curve at point E in Figure 7.3 therefore reflects the *relative price of present goods in terms of future goods*. As drawn in Figure 7.3 this slope has an absolute value greater than 1. This implies that in order to induce consumers to postpone their consumption present goods must be more expensive than future goods. As is usual when we speak about production and consumption in two different time periods we need to introduce the market rate of interest, i, in order to express relative prices. The price of a unit of present goods in terms of future goods is therefore $1 + i$ (note that i is assumed to be positive). Similarly the price of a unit of future goods in terms of present goods is given by $1/(1 + i)$. The interest rate will be determined by the strength of the demand for and supply of future goods *vis-à-vis* present goods. For example with identical production possibilities a country with less impatience by consumers to consume present goods will have future goods of a higher price, implying that its interest rate is lower.

Using the interest rate we can express the total value of Home's production in terms of present goods over the two time periods (present and future) as:

$$OX = Q_p + Q_f/(1 + i) \tag{7.3.1}$$

(7.3.1) in fact defines the iso-value line. Its tangency with the PPF at point E reflects the maximum value of production given the interest rate. (Note that the value of this country's total production over the two time periods

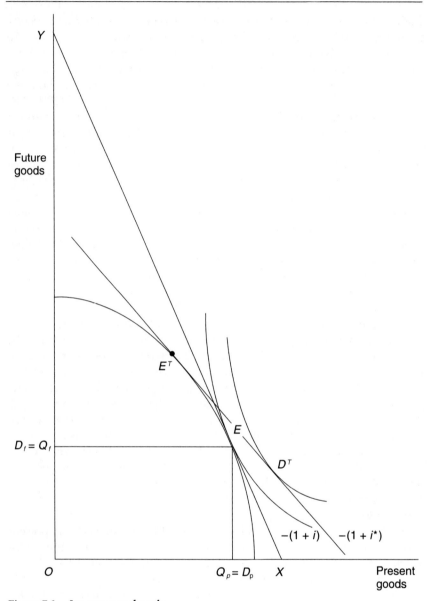

Figure 7.3   *Intertemporal trade*

can be measured in terms of future goods as OY.) The higher the interest rate the steeper the iso-value line will be and the greater will be the tendency to consume today. The total value of consumption over the two periods in terms of present goods can similarly be expressed as:

$$OX = D_p + D_f/(1+i) \qquad\qquad (7.3.2)$$

The left-hand side of (7.3.1) and (7.3.2) are equal, implying that the right-hand sides must be equal as well:

$$D_p + D_f/(1+i) = Q_p + Q_f/(1+i) \qquad (7.3.3)$$

(7.3.3) is the intertemporal budget constraint. This states that the value of a country's consumption in terms of present goods over the two time periods must equal the value of production in terms of present goods over the same two time periods. Therefore if consumption in one period, for example the present, exceeds production in that same period, it follows that consumption in the next period will fall short of that period's production.

We are now equipped to introduce trade in this model. Suppose thus that Home is opened to the opportunities for international capital movements so that it can borrow or land at world interest rates. Assume that this rate is given by $i^* < i$ which means that the relative price of present goods in terms of future goods is less in the world than domestically (that is, foreigners are less eager to consume today and more willing to wait). Therefore the interest rate in the rest of the world must be lower that domestically. Using the terminology developed earlier in the book we can say that Home has a *comparative advantage in future goods* while the rest of the world has a comparative advantage in present goods. With a country having comparative advantage it is always advised to adjust its production structure towards specialisation in the production of the good in which it has that comparative advantage. Having a comparative advantage in either future or present goods should have the same implications for reallocation of resources. When a country has a comparative advantage in future goods it should allocate more of its resources towards producing future goods by borrowing present goods (present consumption) from abroad. This is illustrated in Figure 7.3 by the diversion of resources from the present to the future. If the foreign relative price is a tangent with Home's PPF at point E^T then Home should shift its production to that point. In other words a contraction in the production of present goods and an increase in investment, and thus future production, is required. However because Home at the same time borrows present goods to consume today its consumption combination moves beyond the PPF to the consumption point D^T. This is on a higher indifference curve than in autarky. The gains in terms of enlarged consumption possibilities are obvious.

Let us examine now Figure 7.4 which illustrates the flows of present and future goods for both Home and Foreign. From the way the PPFs of these two countries are drawn it is obvious that Home has a bias toward producing future goods. In terms of trade terminology, Home has a comparative advantage in future goods. Thus given the world relative price of present goods in terms of future goods, Home will 'produce' OQ_p of present goods, and Foreign will produce OQ^*_p of present goods.

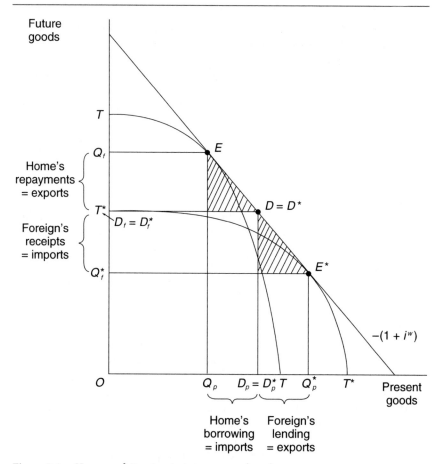

Figure 7.4   **Home and Foreign in intertemporal trade**

However, Home will import via borrowing from Foreign an additional amount of Q_pD_p of present goods and therefore its consumption today will exceed its production (in accordance with its preferences). This constitutes the gains from intertemporal trade. On the other hand, Foreign's consumption of presents goods will fall short of the production by the amount of lending $Q^*_pD^*_p$. In accordance with its preferences this amount will be added to its production of future goods so that consumption will consist of OQ^*_f plus $Q^*_fD^*_f$. In each country the consumption in one of the periods is thus enlarged by trade. A country which consumes more than it produces in the present period runs *current account deficit*. It then has to repay this current account deficit by having to create a *current account surplus* in the future period. A country can do this by selling claims to the production of future goods (that is, country's assets) and thus having to consume less than its production of future goods.

Intertemporal trade is not free from the redistribution effects which accompany trade in commodities within one time period. Although the gains from intertemporal trade are demonstrated for a country as a whole, they will accrue to different generations. For example, while a present generation enjoys an increase of the consumption of the currently produced goods from abroad (financed by running a current account deficit), future generations end up having to repay the debt. The welfare of future generations depends, among other things, on the way the increased amount of present goods (i.e. borrowing) has been used. If it has been used not only to finance an increase in present consumption, but also as investments in improving future production, both present and future generations may benefit from this intertemporal trade. However, if current borrowing is not used productively, future generations may be worse off. This redistributional effect of international borrowing and lending emerged as one of the important issues in the 1980s' debt crisis, to which we turn next.

□ The international debt crisis of the 1980s

The foreign investments process that preceded the world debt crisis in the 1980s was not 'normal' as compared with international lending–borrowing flows in the past. First of all, the supply of capital measured as the share of foreign investments in the income of the source countries was much greater earlier. For example, in early twentieth century Great Britain was allocating between 5 and 10 per cent of its income to overseas investment; France and Germany were investing between 2 and 3 per cent of their income abroad (Fishlow, 1988). By the 1970s foreign investments amounted to hardly 1 per cent of the income of the major industrialised countries. Moreover, the nature of the flows had changed as well. Most of the capital flows, for example flows from Britain at the beginning of the century, were oriented to help development of the receiving peripheral countries and were typically characterised by high returns. In contrast, investments from Germany and France were led not so much by developmental purposes but were more politically driven (these flows were directed to Russia, Eastern Europe and some other African colonies). The returns to such investments were lower and were more prone to repayment difficulties. Borrowing and lending from the 1970s in fact more resembled these latter flows with respect to both lower returns and higher degree of risk. The source of supply of lending capital was thus further narrowed because the recent investments did not generate large returns to be redirected abroad.

Borrowing in the 1970s also accelerated much faster than had historically been the case. For example, the rise in real debt from 1973 to 1982 was at the rate of 12 per cent annually in contrast to a 4 per cent rise earlier. This led to a significant increase in the debt–exports and debt–income ratios for the 'new' borrowers as compared to the borrowers before 1914. All of this became obvious in the 1980s during which period the debt servicing difficulties were the major feature of the international economics.

From the early 1970s onwards for a period of a decade the major portion of all international lending was going to the less developed countries (LDCs), although some of the former socialist economies of Eastern Europe became highly indebted as well. By 1983 the 21 largest borrowers among the LDCs had run up total overseas debts of $514.5 bn. It is no surprise that these two groups of countries also encountered the most difficulties with debt servicing.

Causes and origins of the debt crisis

The simple answer to the question of what caused the debt crisis is that the LDCs incurred too many debts of too large a value. However there are many factors to which the crisis can be ascribed. It would take much space to go into a detailed analysis of all possible factors that contributed to the crisis, but it is possible to group these factors into three broad categories: (a) the global shocks such as oil price increase, inflation and recession, (b) the factors that linked the debt crisis to the behaviour of borrowers themselves, mostly LDCs, and (c) the factors that assigned some of the responsibility to the lenders, mainly financial institutions from the developed countries (DCs) and international financial institutions.[2]

Table 7.1 contains Cline's (1984) estimation of the impact of external shocks on the non-oil LDCs' build-up of debt. Higher interest payments, lower export revenue and a deterioration in the terms of trade amounted to more than $140 bn. In addition expenditures of $260 bn due to the oil price increase contributed to the accumulation of more than $400 bn in external debt. Cline suggested that his estimation of a total debt increase of more than 80 per cent due to external shocks was probably an overestimation. However the fact remains that global causes played an important role in the LDCs' accumulation of debt.

Following the first oil shock of the 1970s changes occurred in the international monetary obligations of the LDCs with regard to the volume and the structure of their commitments. The rate of increase in their external indebtedness should in itself have prompted an increased and improved institutional analysis of the borrowing process. The onset of the ensuing debt crisis is evidence that this did not occur. The growth in the LDCs' external debts was not solely induced by their need to finance their growing oil deficits or because of worsened terms of trade. The persistence of the LDCs' policy of 'indebted industrialisation' where they acquired debts with banks instead of attracting capital in other ways such as FDI was also an important factor in the onset of the crisis. Because of structural changes in their capital flows the LDCs encountered external payments problems. These problems arose because external debt entails the payment

Table 7.1   *Impact of external shocks on non-oil LDCs' debt, 1974–82*

Effect	*Amount US $ bn*
Oil price increase in excess of US inflation, 1974–82 cumulative[a]	260
Real interest rate in excess of 1961–80, 1981, 1982	41
Terms of trade loss, 1981–2	79
Export volume loss caused by world recession, 1981–2	21
Total	401

Memorandum items:

Total debt:	1973	130
	1982	612
Increase:	1973–82	482

Note: [a] Net oil importers only.
Source: Cline (1984, Table 1.4).

of interest whereas with FDI there are no payments until the investments begin to show a profit. Moreover the transition to predominantly bank-based financing, that is, to the flow of capital that creates a debt, was accompanied in the LDCs by the following factors:

(a)   a decline in domestic capital accumulation in exchange for external debts
(b)   the insistence on capital-intensive industrialisation programmes
(c)   poorly designed fiscal, monetary and exchange rate policies, and the postponement of policies designed to restructure and adapt to changes in world demand.

These factors caused many LDCs, in particular some Latin American and Eastern European countries, to accumulate external debts on a scale which far exceeded their repayments potential. For example in a large number of the LDCs the profit from investments financed by external debt was not even sufficient to repay the interest on that debt.

Part of the responsibility for the debt crisis lies with the creditor countries, with banks and with the international financial institutions themselves.[3] A dramatic rise in private bank reserves through the combined effects of the accumulation of 'petro-dollars' and the lack of investment opportunities in the DCs led private banks toward aggressive lending. Private banks' rivalry in the granting of credits to the LDCs was also enabled by the growing liberalisation of international capital markets. These banks tended to 'run with the herd' and in the process they relaxed their checks on the creditworthiness of borrowing countries and ignored the risks associated with lending to them. Following the second oil shock of 1979–80 and the reorientation of most DCs towards restrictive monetary policy, there was a rise in interest rates. The real cost of servicing the debts incurred by the LDCs thus rose rapidly. In August 1982 Mexico first alerted the world to the oncoming crisis by declaring that it could no longer service its debt on the terms previously agreed. The private banks adapted very quickly to the change, switching to short-term credit and generally reducing the supply of credit to the LDCs. The banks which could afford it withdrew rapidly and except for the restructuring and refinancing of existing debts the private financing of the LDCs practically ceased. Faced with a lack of new funds on the one hand, and with a deterioration in their terms of trade and renewed protectionism on the other, the LDCs one after another began to publicly declare that they had problems in servicing their external debts.

At this stage, the international financial institutions became involved, taking a leading role in the creation of a global strategy for solving the debt crisis. Their strategy was based on the IMF's programme for reducing expenditures in indebted countries via individual agreements on rescheduling the repayments of debt, first under the Baker initiative (1985), then on the Brady plans (1989). Although none of these aspects of their global strategy proved fully satisfactory together they did ensure that the crisis did not turn into a world-wide financial collapse.[4]

One of the new concepts that arose from the search for the theoretical explanations of the debt crisis is the so-called economics of *sovereign default*.[5]

The issues of sovereign indebtedness

One of the main features of the lending process of the 1970s was that the capital flows were primarily from private commercial banks to *sovereign* borrowers, the LDCs and the former socialist countries. Even when loans were extended to private borrowers in these countries they were typically government guaranteed. From the point of view of a lender it is immaterial whether it lends to a private firm or a sovereign state as long as neither has difficulties repaying the loan. However when difficulties arise it becomes important who is the bearer of the debt. The difference arises because a country's debt problems are not analogous to those of a private corporation. When a corporation has liabilities which exceeds its ability to pay it is declared insolvent. Such a corporation thus has negative net worth. Bankruptcy laws then provide an institutional framework within which the debtor can give creditors title to the reduced assets of the corporation that has defaulted on its debt. With sovereign debtors there is no analogous international bankruptcy procedure that can be invoked when they have problems servicing their external debts.[6] Are sovereign debtors thus more prone to default on their international obligations? Some answers to this question can be found in the new *willingness to pay* models of debtor behaviour.

The initial assumption in these models is that debtors are inherently *unwilling* to pay and will pay only if there are penalties which will leave them worse off. Because it is difficult or impossible to impose penalties on sovereign debtors the implication is that sovereign debtors lack a good reason to repay their external debts. These models thus reach the conclusion that even when debtors are able to pay they might default simply through unwillingness. In order to fully appreciate the predictions of these models we need to examine both costs and benefits of default.

The possible costs governments may incur when defaulting on international financial obligations include the following. First, assets held abroad may be seized. This primarily entails the foreign exchange reserves or gold reserves of the defaulting country's central bank held by creditors or other central banks. However vessels such as ships and aircrafts in foreign ports, the goods on those vessels, and other assets such as buildings may also be seized. In comparison with the amount of debt accumulated through the years, it is unlikely that the value of seized assets would deter any government from defaulting on foreign debt.

Secondly, countries who default lose reputation as 'good borrowers' and will in all likelihood be excluded from future borrowing. Continuing access to capital markets is important and thus the risk of being left out may well become a serious consideration when making a decision about default. In addition to this financial ostracization, the country could also face political isolation. Moreover, some debtor countries are at the same time creditors and when defaulting they face the risk of retaliation. This retaliation may consist of retaliatory defaults as well as materialising in a decreased volume of international trade with defaulting countries. Not only might the defaulting country's goods be seized by the creditor country, so that the importer from a third country will not receive the goods, but a lack of access to financial markets may seriously restrict their ability to pay for imported goods.

Default on foreign debt may also have repercussions within the domestic financial arena. If a government is refusing to meet its international obligations, its residents may feel that they have the same right with respect to their obligations toward national financial institutions.[7]

Any one of these costs on its own does probably not constitute a sufficiently large penalty to prevent default. However it is likely that two or more of these costs will occur together, imposing significant costs on the defaulting country and deterring a government from that course of action.

However benefits do arise from the refusal to repay foreign debts. The most obvious one is not having to pay the interest and principal owing to foreign banks. The larger the amount of principal and the higher the interest rates, the more the defaulting country will gain. While a country must take into account the costs of potential seizure and international isolation it is likely that defaulting will result in a net gain. This was true for most of the troubled sovereign debtors of the early 1980s. These countries continued to repay their external debts as long as new capital flows were coming into the country. Some therefore suggest that the key to debtor behaviour is found in *net resource transfers*. The net resource transfer from creditor to debtor is a good indicator of the debt burden. It is obtained by taking the difference between the amount of fresh loans from the creditor and the amount of payments towards interest and principal and any other outflow of capital from the debtor country. As long as this net resource flow is positive any government will act in accordance with its international financial obligations even though it could get away with defaulting. In other words as long as creditors continue to supply fresh capital (i.e. new debts), the debtor will be prepared to continue its repayments. Some analysts have suggested that the international debt crisis began in 1982 when most highly indebted countries realised that fresh capital flows had come to a halt. Sovereign debtors' willingness to pay was simply exhausted by the change from positive to negative resource transfers. Because of the nature of sovereign debts there was no further incentive to prevent them from defaulting.

The solutions proposed to resolve the 1980s crisis were accordingly based on the renewal of capital flows to the debtor countries. However this solution is only a temporary as creditors will supposedly continue supplying fresh capital in perpetuity in order to prevent defaults. This result arises from the prediction of the model that as soon as debtors realise that fresh capital flows are declining or stopping the incentive to repay the debt becomes zero. Default in this model is therefore just a matter of time.[8]

One way to enforce sovereign debts is to follow the same lending policies as used when lending to private borrowers. This involves obtaining security or collateral for loans approved. Lindert and Morton (1989) develop a model in which legally enforceable collateral solves the problem of sovereign default. They give examples of countries that have repaid or continue to repay external debts, such as the USA, Canada, Taiwan or South Korea, because their creditors had the means to seize their assets. They also suggest that all those countries which have been regularly repaying debts are in a position of mutual dependence with their creditors through international trade and lending. It seems that this latter provides stronger security to loans than the actual threat of asset seizure. There are also countries that have repaid almost all of their debts, such as Romania, in which neither of these factors has played any role.

In summary the willingness to pay models lead to the conclusion that the bank-led portfolio capital movements which evolved in the 1960s and 1970s are not a sustainable form of capital movement. In particular they are not a sustainable method of financing the development of the LDCs. This type of financing requires an agent which will assume the risk that is placed on lenders when faced with sovereign borrowing. Since it was difficult, if not impossible, to create an international organisation which would act as an umbrella to private banks lending to sovereign debtors other solutions had to be found in order to resume the flow of capital to the indebted countries. Among these solutions was the return to the financing of development through FDI.

7.4 Foreign direct investments and multinationals

FDI is usually defined as any investment in foreign enterprise which is carried out by private companies or individuals as opposed to governments. The companies which play the central role in undertaking these investments are referred to as *multinational companies* (MNCs). The multinationality of a firm has more than one aspect. A firm is multinational if it sells to foreign countries, if it controls and manages production operations in more than one country, or if the firm itself is subject to international ownership. Although all of these aspects of multinationality are important, the one which is most relevant for our present discussion is controlling production activities in more than one country.

In the past it was often the case that the MNC parent company would provide financing for the new foreign subsidiary. In this way FDI was often seen as simply an alternative means of achieving the same results as by international lending. In fact while the proportion of capital flows has declined throughout this century the relevance of FDI has steadily increased. The exception to this trend occurred during the 1970s when the LDCs made a concerted effort to minimise the inflows of FDI and investment in the DCs was almost non-existent because of the recession. Since the mid-1980s multinational activities and FDI have steadily increased although the FDI has different characteristics than before the debt crisis. The most distinct feature of recent trends has been the two-way flows of FDI between the same industries within the DCs. It is only a smaller proportion of FDI that now takes place between DCs and LDCs, or between LDCs themselves. In addition there has been a shift in the sectoral composition of FDI towards services, which are becoming the single largest sector in terms of the inflow and outflow of FDI for most countries. Furthermore it seems that the role of multinationals is increasingly involving control rather than simply the movements of capital. Table 7.3 (p. 270) provides some data on FDI flows in the 1980s while Table 7.4 (p. 270) shows the geographical distribution of MNCs.

Despite the increasing dependence of world economic integration on the activities of MNCs traditional trade theory does not provide a satisfactory analytical background to this phenomenon. Because traditional models consider FDI as merely the movements of capital they can explain only a part of the rationale behind multinational activities. These models, which explain why some goods should be produced by some countries and not by others, are also capable of explaining why multinationals would choose to locate some of their productive activities in one country and some in others. In most cases this *locational advantage* is explained by the difference in resources (akin to the HOS model), the existence of transport costs, and other barriers to the free trade of goods and factors.

The other part of the multinational puzzle concerns the *competitive advantage* of multinationals over locally owned firms. Despite unfamiliarity with local customs, business practices, and regulations, multinationals are renowned for their ability to compete successfully with locally owned firms. Recent contributions to trade theory based on economies of scale and imperfect competition can be used to clarify this competitive advantage (see Box 7.3).

One view suggests that the advantages to the multinational firm from operating productive activities in two or more locations stem from the advantages of horizontal integration. For example these can arise from some property of the technology used in production, such as the existence of multiplant economies. Markusen (1984) has argued that activities such as R&D, advertising, marketing and distribution are non-rival or joint inputs for the firm because they can be provided in one place to support production and sales in other locations. Multinationals thus engage in productive activities in each country but provide joint inputs from a central location.

In a similar manner Helpman (1984) distinguishes between production and 'headquarters services' such as management, accounting, marketing and product-specific R&D. The former is based on product differentiation and economies of scale and is geographically separate from other activities. The latter are highly specialised inputs which must be 'produced' in one country (i.e. the home country of the firm) but can be used to serve product lines in other countries. This approach argues that whenever there are cost incentives for the integration of related activities within a single firm and factor costs or other incentives for the separation of these activities geographically MNCs will emerge. This simple theoretical construct is illustrated in greater detail in Appendix 7.

A related view on the reasons for MNCs' competitive advantage is found in the vertical integration. Helpman (1985) extended his simple theory of a multinational firm to include the possibility of intra-firm trade in inputs other than 'headquarters services', thus making the theory fit more closely with the real-world behaviour of multinationals. This extended theory results in a monopolistically competitive view of trade in differentiated products in which firms with production facilities in more than one country trade in intermediate components, finished goods and headquarters services. A large volume of intra-firm trade is thus predicted.

Box 7.3 *Determinants of FDI into the Australian manufacturing sector*

A substantial share of Australian industry is owned (both direct and joint ownership) or controlled by foreign firms. In 1983, for example, 33 per cent of total industry value added was owned by foreign firms. In terms of employment, foreign firms accounted for 27 per cent. Almost similar shares of value added and employment were controlled by these firms in 1986. It is important to identify the reasons for this relatively high foreign presence in Australian industry. Ratnayake (1993) provides evidence concerning the determination of inter-industry variation of foreign ownership in Australia. He first develops a set of hypotheses incorporating various possible explanations of FDI and then tests them in a simultaneous equation framework. This particular estimation procedure allows for interdependency between foreign ownership and such variables as export intensity, import penetration, trade protection, concentration and profitability.

Determinants which affect the decision of MNCs to engage in FDI in Australian manufacturing include the importance of high technology and high human capital intensity in individual industrial activities, the presence of economies of scale and multiplant operation, profitability, level of import penetration, level of trade protection, and transport costs. Table 7.2 lists all the determinants ranked in order of importance. It seems that foreign ownership of industry in Australia tends to be higher in the human skill-intensive and technology-intensive industries. In addition, high protection seems to be an important inducement for MNCs' participation in Australian manufacturing.

Table 7.2 *Determinants of foreign ownership in Australian manufacturing*

Variable	Importance*
Human capital	Very important
Technology intensity	Very important
Economies of scale	Very important
Industry concentration	Very important
Export intensity	Very important
Nominal rate of protection	Very important
Profitability	Moderately important
Advertising expenditure per unit of sales	Moderately important
Multiplant operations	Less important

Note: * Levels of very, moderately and less important evaluated according to 1 per cent, 5 per cent and 10 per cent degrees of statistical significance.

Table 7.3   *Inflows and outflows of FDI, 1986–90*

Country group	1986	1988	1990	1980–5	1986–90	1980–5	1986–90
		Bn dollars		% share in total		Growth rate	
DCs							
* inflows	64	129	152	75	83	−3	24
* outflows	86	161	217	98	97	−2	26
LDCs							
* inflows	14	30	32	25	17	4	22
* outflows	2	6	8	2	3	1	47
All countries							
* inflows	78	158	184	100	100	−1	24
* outflows	88	167	225	100	100	−2	26

Source: United Nations (1992, Table I.1).

Table 7.4   *The geographical distribution of MNCs*

Country group	Parent corporations	Foreign affiliates	Year
DCs	30,900	73,400	1989
LDCs	63,800	62,900	1989
Cent. and Eastern Europe	300	10,900	1991
World total	35,000	147,200	1990

Source: United Nations (1992, Box I.1, Table 1).

Another approach to explaining the competitive advantage of multinationals is based on the difficulties of trading in intangible assets. One example of such assets is technology, which is broadly defined as any kind of economically useful knowledge. For example, a firm may possess some specific knowledge which results in lower production costs and competitive advantage. While this knowledge may take the form of a patented process it could just as easily be the common knowledge of a group of employees. Trading in those types of assets involves more difficulties than trade in ordinary goods. This is because there are information asymmetries between the buyer and the seller. Because the buyer is not as well informed as the seller (otherwise he would not have a need to buy these assets) it is difficult for him to evaluate the knowledge offered for sale. Further, if the seller tries to fully explain the value of the offered 'package' he would be revealing some of the actual knowledge without receiving any compensation from the buyer. This 'public goods' attribute of intangible assets makes them prone to imitation and other misuses of property rights which are not clearly identifiable.

Apart from the theoretical explanations for the existence of multinationals there are other important related issues. These include the welfare effects of multinationals' activities, problems of tax evasion and transfer pricing, and the role of FDI in regional integration. While this last issue is covered in Part 3 of this book which discusses economic integration, we will briefly outline here the welfare effects of direct investments. When examining the welfare implications of multinationals analysis takes the same general format as the analysis of the welfare effects of resource movements. If MNCs are viewed solely as facilitating capital movements we can safely assume that they will result in increased global efficiency and a larger output. We can also predict that there will be some income-distributional effects, both between countries and within each country. From the point of view of the host country the direct foreign investment can be treated as the accumulation of the factor specific to one of the economy's sectors. The analysis of welfare effects from such an inflow can thus be undertaken in a manner analogous to the analysis of the effects of labour migration performed in section 7.2. For example if we assume that the multinational company in fact transfers capital from home to the host country in response to higher returns in the host country the effect on world output will be positive. This is because the redistribution of capital in accordance with its marginal productivity will increase output in the host country by more than output will contract in the home country.

The income-distributional effects in each country are not very complex. In the host country the inflow of capital will increase the marginal productivity of labour in the industry it has been invested in. Higher wages will attract more labour to this industry, and since labour is assumed to be perfectly mobile these labour flows continue until wages are equalised across both sectors. This will happen at a higher level than before the inflow of FDI. Both types of domestic specific capital will be thus hurt by lower rentals while Foreign capital still earns higher returns than in the home country. The net change in income for the host country will be positive and we can conclude that it gains both in terms of increased output and in terms of income.

In the home country the outflow of capital reduces the marginal productivity of labour in the sector of its origin and labour will shift to another sector. This causes wages in both sectors to fall, while the returns to both types of domestic-specific capital will rise. Home's income increases due to the combined effects of higher income earned by the domestically employed capital and a higher income earned by that capital which has been invested in the host country.

Direct investment thus raises income in both countries as well as world output. However even in this extremely simplified example there are still some very sensitive distributional effects: labour in the home country is hurt by the outflow of capital while the owners of capital in the host country receive lower returns due to the inflow of foreign capital.

In addition to these welfare effects, direct investment has other effects which can directly or indirectly influence the level of welfare in both countries and can cause complex distributional changes. These effects influence both macroeconomic variables such as savings, investment, the balance of payments and similar, and microeconomic factors such as the provision of managerial and technical skills, the realisation of economies of scale, effects on market structure and similar. These welfare effects also depend on the size of the country and whether it is also simultaneously involved in commodity trade. For example in the case of a large country which is host to significant FDI its terms of trade could be adversely affected so that any initial gains from the capital inflow will be reduced. In a special set of circumstances the host country may even become immiserised (Brecher and Choudhri, 1982). This possibility has interesting implications. According to Bhagwati and Srinivasan (1980, p. 298) this result prevents us from asserting that when free international capital mobility coexists with free trade it is mutually beneficial to all freely participating economic agents.

■ 7.5 Summary

This chapter has discussed various aspects of international factor movements. Before looking into the causes and consequences of movements of particular factors, we discussed the relationship between commodity trade and factor movements. These two types of flows in world economy can be substitutes for each other whereby an increased movements of factors will reduce the volume of commodity trade. They also can be complements so that an increased amount of factors moving internationally will be accompanied by rising commodity trade. In both cases, free and unlimited commodity trade or factor movements achieve equalisation of commodity and factor prices.

The welfare effects of international labour migration were examined by looking at three different groups: natives in the receiving country, the remaining people in the sending country, and the migrants themselves. It was shown that the size of welfare effects depends on the type of migration (for example, accompanied or not by another factor of production), but that the natives could not be made worse off by allowing free inflows of migrants. Two special types of international labour flows, *Gastarbeiter* and the *brain drain* were also discussed.

Capital movements were discussed first as portfolio investment movements, and secondly as direct investment movements. For the portfolio capital, an intertemporal trade approach was followed to analyse the causes and welfare effects of such movements. A country with a comparative advantage in future goods is shown to benefit as a whole from an intertemporal trade, that is, exchange of future goods for present goods. Distributional effects are present in this type of trade too, but they relate to intergenerational problems. Since a country which imports present goods in exchange for exports of future goods in fact borrows today and has to repay in the future, the welfare of the future generation depends very much also on how the investment borrowed today are spent. If they are not spent productively, the welfare of future generation might not be maximised. The possible application of intertemporal trade was hinted in discussing the problem of international debt crisis in the 1980s.

The last section of the chapter looked into the determinants of foreign direct investments and multinational companies. The Appendix 7 below presents a new conceptual framework to analyse multinational companies.

▮ *APPENDIX 7* THE SIMPLE THEORY OF THE MULTINATIONAL CORPORATION

The 'new' theory of the multinational firm is based on the trade theory with monopolistic competition, which was discussed in Chapter 5. Here, we will use the same analytical framework of the integrated world economy as developed in Appendix 5 (p. 208). In discussing the basic features of this theory we will also closely follow Helpman (1990).

Consider an integrated world economy which consists of two sectors: manufacturing (M), which produces differentiated products with brand- (or product)-specific economies of scale, and food (F), which produces a homogeneous product with constant returns to scale. Now suppose that in addition to the inputs employed directly in the manufacturing sector, the production of differentiated products requires *headquarters services* (H) that are provided internally by the firm. In this case it is possible to decompose the firm's employment vector $a_m M_m$ into direct employment in manufacturing ($a_{mm}M$) and employment in the provision of headquarters services ($a_{mz}M$). The factor market-clearing condition can be therefore written as

$$V = a_{mm}M + a_z Z + a_f F \qquad (7.A1)$$

where a_{mm} is the input vector per unit of manufactured good, a_Z is the input vector per unit of headquarters services, $Z(= a_{Zm}M)$ is the aggregate output of headquarter services while a_f is the input vector per unit of food.

The key assumption is that manufacturing activities can be divided into those which are directly concerned with production and those which we have called 'headquarters services'. These two activities require different factor intensities. The former could be located anywhere, the actual location being determined by the international differences in factor rewards and the optimisation behaviour of the firm. Suppose, for example, that the available inputs comprise skilled and unskilled labour and that headquarters services are relatively skilled labour-intensive. The cost-minimising firm will then attempt to locate the provision of headquarters services in that country which has the most relatively abundant and cheap skilled labour. By the same token production activities will be located in those countries with a relative abundance of unskilled labour.

Figure 7.5 illustrates how these activities are split. The box supplies us with information on the total quantities of skilled labour (H) and unskilled labour (L) in a two-country world. Home's origin is O and Foreign's origin is O^*. The vector $OQ(QO^*)$ represents the total employment of manufacturing (food) in the integrated equilibrium. The location of the employment vector for the manufacturing sector above the diagonal illustrates that this sector is relatively skilled-labour-intensive. The parallelogram OQO^*Q' is the factor-price equalisation set of endowments *in the case when production and headquarters activities cannot be separated*. Suppose now that it is possible to separate these activities. The vector OQ is now decomposed into OD and DQ where the former represents employment at headquarters and the latter represents employment in direct manufacturing. If the overall factor endowment lies within the area ODQ there will be no factor-price equalisation when headquarters and production activities have to be located in the same country. This results because the former is relatively skilled labour-intensive. However if the firm can keep its headquarters activities in Home but move its production activities to Foreign factor-price equalisation is obtained. The possibility for locating some activities outside national borders thus increases the likelihood of factor-price equalisation.

In this case the pattern of trade resembles the pattern predicted by the HOS model. Home imports the homogeneous good food which is relatively unskilled labour-intensive and is a net exporter of differentiated products. However this is only a portion of total trade. Within the manufacturing sector another flow also occurs, the intra-industry trade of differentiated products. On top of this there is *intra-firm trade* which consists of the exports of headquarters services by a firm (a MNC) domiciled in Home to its subsidiaries in Foreign. The degree of multi-

nationality and the intensity of intra-firm trade increases with the difference in the ratios of factor endowments. By the same token the larger the
difference in factor proportions, the smaller Home's net exports of
differentiated products will be because more products are produced in
Foreign by subsidiaries of Home's MNC.

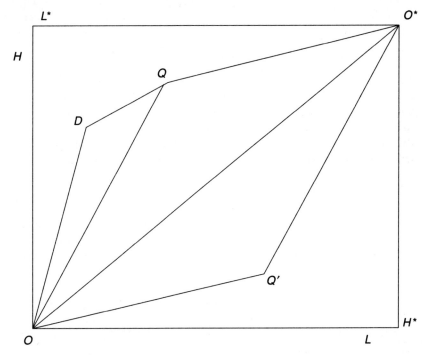

Figure 7.5 *Multinational firm*

■ *PART 2* ■

INTERNATIONAL TRADE POLICY

■ *Chapter 8* ■

Economic Analysis of Tariffs

■ *8.1* Introduction

This chapter's topic is tariffs, one of the many instruments of trade policy. Tariffs used to be the most popular tool utilised by policy makers. However the multilateral negotiations success in targeting tariffs for trade liberalisation has meant that other instruments of regulating trade flows have become relatively more popular. In principle, however, economists still prefer tariffs over other trade policy instruments as tariffs are considered to be the most transparent of all tools. The effects of some of the non-tariff barriers used are studied in Chapter 9.

Section 8.2 of this chapter contains a simple partial equilibrium analysis of tariffs. Section 8.3 broadens the analysis to general equilibrium, examining both the importing and exporting sectors of a national economy. This section's findings differ with respect to the size of an economy. For a small country there is no welfare-improving tariff. However a large country can always find a tariff that will improve its welfare as compared to free trade. A particular tariff which in fact maximises country's welfare is known as the optimum tariff. In section 8.4 we utilise offer curves to discuss optimum tariffs and retaliation. Section 8.5 discusses the Lerner symmetry theorem on the equivalence between taxes on imports and exports. This section includes a discussion on the imposition of a consumption tax and a production subsidy that is equivalent to a tariff. The effects of tariffs when output markets are not perfectly competitive are studied in section 8.6. Finally Appendix 8 (p. 318) looks at some exceptions in the operation of tariffs.

As usual our analysis is based on certain set of assumptions. There are many factors which could influence the results of analysis in different ways. However the most influential factors are probably the size of the country implementing the tariffs, and the nature of the market structure within that country and in the rest of the world. It is customary to begin an analysis with the most simple case, when a country is small and all (input and output) markets are perfectly competitive. After considering this special case we assume that the importing country has the power to influence world prices. We thus introduce the large country assumption while retaining the assumption that all markets are perfectly competitive. Although the nature of this text does not allow for a detailed analysis of situations where the market structure is only partially competitive, we will offer an introductory discussion of these issues.

A tariff is an indirect tax on the imports of a good. This tax creates a wedge between the world and domestic prices of that good.[1] There are basically two different ways in which tariffs may be levied. An *ad valorem* tariff is levied in percentage per unit value or per unit price of the imported good. If the world price of the imported good, for example cloth, is p^*_C and the rate of the *ad valorem* tariff is denoted as t_a, then the post-tariff domestic price $p_C{}^t$ is

$$p_C{}^t = p^*_C(1 + t_a)$$

A *specific* tariff is levied as a fixed amount of money per unit quantity of imports. If t_s denotes the amount of a specific tariff, the domestic price is

$$p_C{}^t = p^*_C + t_s$$

These two types of tariff are equivalent when $t_a = t_s/p^*_C$. The choice between the two methods of levying the tariff will depend on many factors, among which are: the frequency of changes in the world price (p^*_C), the reason for levying the tariff (to grant protection, to decrease imports, collect revenues or a combination of these), and the general conditions in the economy (inflation or recession). From the definitions above it is clear that the amount of *ad valorem* tariffs will depend on the price or value of the goods. In a global inflationary situation, and when the domestic currency is depreciating quickly, the money amount of an *ad valorem* tariff will increase at the same pace, therefore keeping the level of nominal protection constant. However this tariff may add inflationary pressures. A specific tariff under the same conditions will weaken the degree of nominal protection although it could be useful in minimising the practices of underinvoicing and tax evasion. A combination of specific and *ad valorem* tariffs is also often found in practice. For the purposes of our analysis these two tariffs are treated as equivalent and we will, unless otherwise specified, assume a specific tariff at rate t.

■ 8.2 A partial equilibrium analysis of tariffs

□ *A small country*

We begin our analysis by looking at the effects a tariff will have when imposed on the imports of a single good into a small country, called Home. We assume via a *ceteris paribus* clause that a tariff on a single good (call it cloth) has no repercussions for the rest of the domestic economy. In a similar manner the assumption of a small country ensures that the world price of cloth p^*_C is insensitive to changes in trade or any other policy in Home. Figure 8.1 (panels (a) and (b)) illustrates the effects of this tariff on Home's cloth market. In part (a) of Figure 8.1 we assume that the domestic production of cloth in Home is represented by the supply curve S_c. The world supply of cloth is perfectly elastic with respect to price and is given by the horizontal line S_c^*. The domestic demand for cloth is given by the curve D_c. (Note that the domestic supply and demand curves are drawn as linear and normal for simplicity only, not for any other reason.) With free and costless trade under perfect competition the world price p^*_C will also be the domestic price of cloth. The positive domestic excess demand for cloth at this price, equal to q_1q_2, is satisfied by imports of the same amount.

If a tariff is now introduced at a rate t, the world price per unit of cloth remains p^*_C but the price of imported cloth in Home increases to $p_C = p^*_C + t$. This is represented by a vertical shift of the world supply curve for cloth by the amount of the tariff. We also assume that imported and domestically produced cloth are perfect substitutes and that the price of domestically produced cloth does not diverge from the tariff inclusive price of imported cloth.[2] The new equilibrium in the cloth market therefore implies a changed domestic price, changes in the quantities of domestic supply and demand, as well as a changed quantity of imports. In response to the higher price domestic demand has fallen by q_2q_3, while domestic supply has increased by q_1q_4. These two effects jointly cause imports to fall from q_1q_2 to q_4q_3. If the rate of the tariff was higher, more specifically as high as the difference between p^*_C and $\bar{p}_C$, imports would totally cease. This is best seen in part (b) of Figure 8.1 where the curve D_c^m represents the import demand for cloth. It is derived from the underlying domestic supply and demand curves and represents the excess of Home's consumers demand for cloth over what domestic producers supply at various prices. It is obvious that at price $\bar{p}_C$ there is no excess demand for cloth. The demand for imports of cloth is thus zero. The tariff which increases domestic price by an amount so as to equalise domestic demand with domestic supply, thus making imports unnecessary, is called a *prohibitive* tariff.

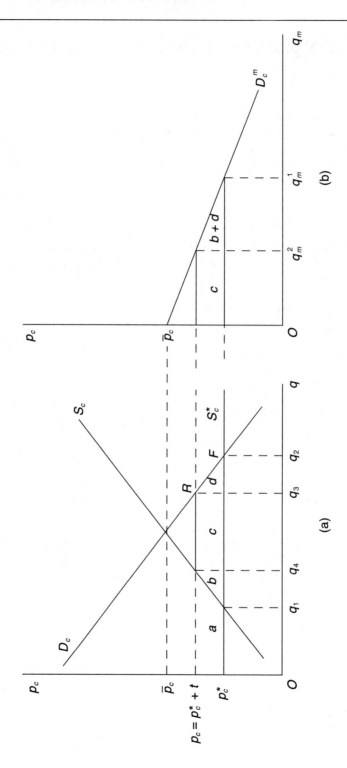

Figure 8.1 *A tariff in a small country with a single sector*

To these price and quantity effects we must add other effects. Two are clearly identifiable from Figure 8.1. The first is the fiscal revenue gained by the government, amounting to the quantity of imports multiplied by the tariff per unit of imports, that is, $(q_4 q_3)t$ in part (a) or $(0q_m{}^2)t$ in part (b) of Figure 8.1. The other effect is known as the redistributive effect. This describes the transfer of income from consumers to producers, both directly through price increases and indirectly through the government. We will determine the size of this effect after we combine the impact of all other effects in determining the so-called *welfare effects* of a tariff. There are basically two effects with opposing signs. On one hand consumers, who now have to pay higher prices for cloth, suffer losses. On the other hand there are gains for both producers, who enjoy higher prices, and the government, who collects the tariff revenue. The price and quantity effects thus impact differently on the different groups in a national economy. In order to identify the net welfare effects for the whole country we need to assign a social worth to the money value of a unit lost or gained by each of these groups. The assumption routinely made by international trade economists is that at the margin the money value of a unit gained or lost by either group has the same social worth. Another assumption commonly made is that the correct quantification of these effects can be obtained through the method based on the concepts of consumer and producer surplus.[3]

The imposition of a tariff on the imports of cloth will move the equilibrium in the cloth market from the free trade point F to the tariff restricted point R. The gross loss of consumer surplus is equal to the sum of the areas $a + b + c + d$. As already mentioned the gains come from two sources. One is the increase in producer surplus which approximates the increased profits. This is equal to area a in Figure 8.1. The other source of gain is the tariff revenue which is represented by the area c. By deducting the loss from the total gains we obtain the net effects of the tariff as:

$$(a + c) - (a + b + c + d) = -(b + d)$$

The net effect is negative thus implying that the tariff imposes costs on society. This net effect is known as the *deadweight* or *efficiency loss*. It consists of two categories. One is the *production distortion cost* (area b) which arises because tariffs distort incentives and lead domestic producers to produce more than would otherwise be 'efficient'. In other words domestic resources are being used to produce cloth at a higher cost (i.e. inefficiently) than in the rest of the world. The other cost is called the *consumption distortion cost* (area d). This arises because tariffs distort incentives in consumption, leading consumers to underconsume this good. This cost can also be seen as a pure consumer loss because it represents the opportunity consumers no longer have to purchase an extra quantity of cloth at the lower world price. The imposition of a tariff on the imports of cloth in Home therefore sends the wrong signals to both domestic producers and consumers whose behaviour then results in welfare losses. In fact under our assumptions there is no price except the world price at which this country can maximise its welfare. Thus for a small open economy, with perfectly competitive markets, the only policy by which it can maximise its welfare is *free* trade.

An approximation of the size of the cost of the imposition of the tariff can be directly observed from the panels in Figure 8.1. In panel (a) the cost is equal to the sum of the areas of triangles *b* and *d*. These triangles are also known as the *Harberger triangles* (Harberger, 1964). In panel (b) the cost is represented by the area of the triangle ($b + d$) under the import demand curve. More formally this area is equal to:

$$\Delta W = 1/2 \, t \, \Delta M \qquad (8.2.1)$$

where ΔW is the change in welfare, ΔM is the change in the quantity of imports, and t is the rate of the tariff. Using the definition of the elasticity of import demand:

$$\varepsilon_m = (\Delta M / \Delta p^*{}_C)(p^*{}_C / M) \qquad (8.2.2)$$

where M is the current level of imports, we can express the change in imports as:

$$\Delta M = \varepsilon_m M \Delta p^*{}_C / p^*{}_C \qquad (8.2.3)$$

Noting that the tariff represents the proportionate change in price between free trade and tariff restricted trade, that is, $t = \Delta p^*{}_C / p^*{}_C$, we can rewrite (8.2.1) to obtain:

$$\Delta W = 1/2 \, (\varepsilon_m M t^2) \qquad (8.2.4)$$

Even though this formula (due to Meade, 1951) only approximates the amount of welfare lost through tariff protection, this method has been widely used in estimating the welfare gains from both complete tariff removal and partial trade liberalisation. We will discuss these and other measurements of the cost of protection later. For now we will mention in passing that most actual estimations of welfare losses due to tariffs (or welfare gains due to their removal) based on the above formula have been discouragingly small in size. Typically these costs amount to approximately 1 per cent of a country's GDP, which is not really high enough to induce any anti-protection lobbying. However later we will show that these measurements based on Harberger triangles underestimate the true costs of protection. When estimates take account of scale economies, market structure effects and the cost of lobbying, they are much higher then when they are based on perfect competition and constant-returns-to-scale. It is somewhat ironic that the models which have enabled us to improve our measurements are also used to lobby for increased protectionism. We will return to this point later.

☐ *A large country*

Let us now (slightly) modify our initial assumptions. Assume that the importing country is 'large', that is, it has some influence over the world price of the imported product. The assumption about all markets being perfectly competitive is retained for now. In part (a) of Figure 8.2 the curve S_c shows the domestic supply of cloth. As before we assume that cloth may also be imported. Suppose that the foreign supply curve S^* is then added to the domestic one so that the overall supply results in a total supply curve S_c^*. Note that the foreign supply curve is less than perfectly price elastic, implying that if we were to draw it, it would also be positively sloped. This means that Home must pay higher prices to induce foreign suppliers to supply more cloth to Home. The demand for both imported and domestic cloth is given by D_c. Given free trade the equilibrium price is $p^*{}_c$. At this price $0q_1$ of cloth is produced domestically, while q_1q_2 is imported. In part (b) this is equal to $0q_m{}^1$ of imports, determined by the intersection of Home's demand for imports curve and Foreign's supply of exports curve.

Let us now introduce a tariff of rate t. The total supply curve will now shift up by the rate of the tariff (shown as S_c^{*t}). The intersection of demand and supply is now at point R. This results in a domestic price of $0p^t{}_C$ while the total demand falls to $0q_4$. Domestic supply has increased by q_1q_3. The rise in domestic supply and the fall in demand due to the tariff combined cause the volume of imports to shrink to q_3q_4. Since Home is large a reduced quantity of imports has an effect on the world price – in the diagram this price has fallen to $p^{*t}{}_C$. The loss of consumer surplus in this example is equal to $(a + b + c + d)$, producer surplus has increased by a, and the government has collected revenue equal to the area $(c + e)$. Except for the additional revenue collected by Home's government these effects are the same as they would have been in the case of the small country. The extra revenue is collected from foreign suppliers who are willing to share the tariff burden with domestic consumers by reducing the price. This effect is known as the *terms of trade gain*. It arises because the tariff induces foreign suppliers to reduce their export prices.

The net effects of a tariff are thus obtained as the difference between the increase in producer surplus combined with the terms of trade gains, and efficiency losses (i.e. the gross consumer loss):

$$(a + c + e) - (a + b + c + d) = e - b - d$$

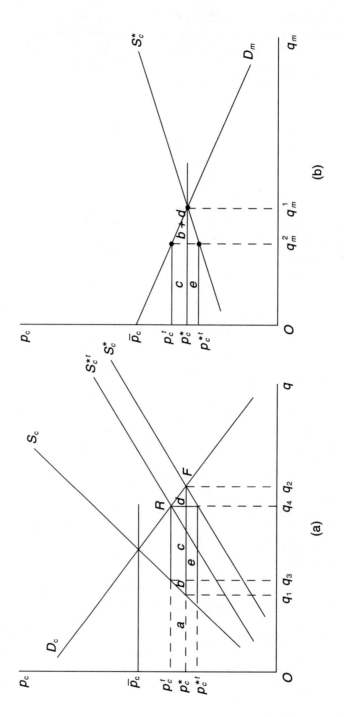

Figure 8.2 *A tariff in a large country with a single sector*

This net result may be either positive or negative. It is important to note that for sufficiently small tariffs the net effect will always be positive. For small tariffs the efficiency loss (the triangles $b + d$) will be always smaller than the terms of trade gains (rectangle e). Thus the result is that a small enough tariff will always *improve* the welfare of a *large* country. For large tariffs, however, it is possible that efficiency losses grow very fast. The trade-off between these losses and the terms of trade gains should therefore be determined carefully. In the process of identifying this trade-off we also obtain an *optimum tariff*. The formula for an optimum tariff is derived in Section 8.3 (pp. 296–8) and we will show that an optimum tariff is always positive for a large country. We will defer discussion on the application of optimum tariffs until section 8.4.

From the analysis so far it should be clear that when a country is small the gains from imposing a tariff will fall short of the losses the tariff causes to consumers (at least under the assumptions made). This translates into the optimum tariff for a small country being equal to zero; a result which has been (over)used to demonstrate the general superiority of free trade over restricted trade. In fact, the conclusion that free trade is best except for, usually irrelevant, cases of optimal tariff application has become one of the maxims of traditional trade policy (Richardson, 1992). Let us now extend our analysis of tariffs.

■ 8.3 A general equilibrium analysis of tariffs

The next assumption we relax is the *ceteris paribus* clause. Although partial equilibrium analysis often is adequate, it can prove useful to have a more complete picture. For example there are cross-market effects arising from protection in one sector which can be picked up by general equilibrium analysis. We will analyse the simplest possible case of a two-sector economy by initially assuming that this economy is small, and then by relaxing this assumption.

□ *A small country*

Suppose Home produces two goods, food, F and cloth, C. Let us assume that food represents exportables while the cloth industry competes with imports from Foreign (the rest of the world). Since Home is small exports and imports take place at given world prices for food, p^*_F and for cloth, p^*_C, $p^* = p^*_F/p^*_C$. In free trade $p^* = p$, the domestic relative price. In Figure 8.3 panels (a), (b) and (c) tell a fairly complete story about what is happening with production, consumption and trade patterns when a country's free trade general equilibrium is disturbed by the imposition of an import tariff in one of the sectors of the economy.

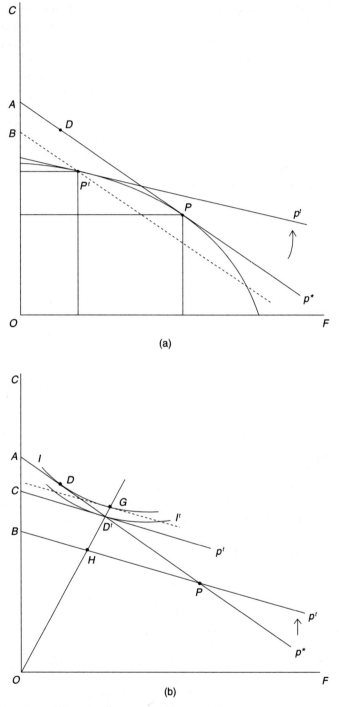

Figure 8.3   *A tariff in a small country with two-sectors*

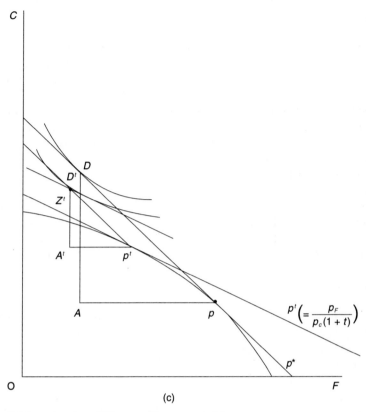

Figure 8.3 (cont.)   *A tariff in a small country with two-sectors*

Let us first focus on the effects of a tariff on the production side of the economy. These effects are shown in panel (a) of Figure 8.3. Production takes place on the PPF at point P, where the ratio of marginal productivities in these two industries is equal to the relative world price. The line indicating this free trade price, p^*, is also the consumption possibility locus or budget constraint for Home. From earlier analysis we know that the consumption point D, at which the price line is tangent to the highest possible social indifference curve (not shown), maximises Home's welfare with the given production and prices.

Suppose now that Home imposes an *ad valorem* tariff on the imports of cloth at rate t. As explained earlier, this cannot affect the world relative price of food $p*$. However food's domestic relative price $p = p_F/p_C$ falls to:

$$p^t = [1/(1+t)]p^* \tag{8.3.1}$$

This is because the domestic relative price of food is lower with taxes on imported cloth than the world relative price of food:

$$p^t/p^* = [1/(1+t)] \leq 1 \quad \text{as long as } t \geq 0 \tag{8.3.2}$$

The effect of this change in the *domestic* relative price of production is obvious from Figure 8.3. The production point at which the marginal rate of transformation of food for cloth is equal to the new relative price of food, p^t, is P_t, where the output of food is less while the output of cloth is higher than in free trade. This is because producers are given incentive by tariff-distorted prices to produce a mix of goods different than in the free trade equilibrium. This new mix of goods is 'wrong' because it results in a reduction of the value of national output as measured at world prices. The value of the post-tariff national output as read from the diagram is OB, which is less than the free trade national income, OA.

It is true that in terms of *domestic prices* production at P_t does indeed maximise the value of national output. However this is accomplished by diverting resources from their most productive uses, for example the production of exportables such as food. This has welfare-reducing consequences. Consequently the move from the free trade production point P to the post-tariff production point P_t represents the production loss due to the tariff.

The changes in consumption are not so simple to analyse. Consumers also face distorted price signals. The tariff, which affects domestic prices, leads consumers to consume a different mix of goods than they would under free trade. Cloth is underconsumed because its tariff-distorted price overstates its cost in terms of food. This is shown in panel (b) of Figure 8.3. In this diagram we focus on the consumption side, disregarding the production-side changes just discussed. In other words we assume for now that production is fixed at point P in both the free trade and the post-tariff equilibrium. In free trade the consumption point is D, at which the world price line is tangential to the indifference curve I. The post tariff domestic price line is given by p^t. This suggests that this is the new consumption possibility frontier. However we must also take into account the fact that the imposition of tariffs also creates revenue. This revenue is part of national income and will be spent on these two goods. More precisely, it is typically assumed that the government redistributes the total amount of revenue back to consumers in a lump-sum fashion. Domestic consumers' total income therefore consists of the value of production at domestic relative prices and the tariff revenue (the tariff rate times imports). As income depends on the amount of tariff revenue, which is in turn dependent on import demand being a function, *inter alia*, of income, it is not an easy task to determine the post-tariff consumption point. We know that the value of production at domestic prices is lower than the value of production at world prices. As the difference cannot be offset by tariff revenue, we conclude that the new consumption point must be on a lower indifference curve than the free trade consumption point.

In panel (b) of Figure 8.3 the consumers' best choice is point D_t on the indifference curve I_t. Note that if consumers could afford the level of spending given by point D on indifference curve I they would have substituted expensive cloth for cheaper food which would have put them at point G on the same indifference curve (i.e. the same level of utility). However because of the production loss they cannot maintain this level of spending. Thus they have to 'fall' to a lower indifference curve. Consumers do not fall all the way to point H on p^t because the tariff revenue (HD_t) allows them to spend more than the value of output at domestic prices. Nevertheless there is still a consumption loss from the imposition of the tariff, shown by the move from D to D_t, and it cannot be offset by the revenue effect.

To summarise, the post-tariff consumption equilibrium point has two features. First, consumers make their choice on the basis of the post-tariff domestic relative prices, not world prices. Secondly, the value of consumption cannot differ from the value of production at world prices. In terms of our diagrammatic presentation it means that the consumption point must lie on both the income-consumption ray, OG, and the world relative price line, p^*.

Finally, panel (c) of Figure 8.3 identifies the effects of a tariff on the volume of trade, in particular on import and export volumes. These effects are obtained by combining the effects on both production and consumption. From the initial free trade equilibrium production and consumption points at P and D, Home's producers are induced by the tariff to produce more cloth and less food while domestic consumers are induced to consume less cloth and more food. This will obviously affect trade volumes. The free trade triangle is DAP, whose vertical and horizontal sides measure imports and exports respectively, while the diagonal is the terms of trade line. The post-tariff trade triangle $D_tA_tP_t$ is much smaller. The amount of imports D_tA_t can be divided in two: the amount that is received directly by consumers, A_tZ, and the amount that is redistributed to them as tariff revenue, ZD_t. However it is important to note that the amount of exports also becomes smaller. Thus the overall effect of protection is to depress the total volume of trade.

This last result is a particularly valuable one. It shows that there are important consequences for other sectors in the economy, most often exportables, if one sector is protected. Thus the costs and benefits of protection cannot be discussed solely on the basis of the effects such protection provides to the sector in question, such as higher production, or higher employment, however desirable these goals could be. We must weigh these 'desirable' effects against those experienced in the rest of the economy. It can easily happen that a job saved in an import-competing industry means a job, or more than one job, lost in the exportable industries. If this is the case the protection is making the small country even poorer.

This is the main conclusion arrived at when considering the case of a small country in a perfectly competitive world: the tariff equilibrium is suboptimal compared to the free trade equilibrium. That the welfare in Home is lower with tariffs than under free trade, despite tariff revenue effect, is obvious from panel (c) of Figure 8.3. This loss of welfare is due to efficiency or distortion losses arising from both the production and consumption sides as has already been shown.[4] Let us show this more rigorously below. Assume initially that we have free trade in which domestic production and consumption responds to the free trade prices for many goods, p^*. The representative consumer has an income or expenditure of e to spend on the vector of goods consumed:

$$e = p^*D \tag{8.3.3}$$

His or her income is equal to the value of the output, y^5:

$$y = p^*P \tag{8.3.4}$$

By spending e the consumer attains a level of utility u^*. Since his/her expenditure cannot exceed the value of output, we have an equilibrium at which both the consumer's welfare and the value of national output are maximised:

$$e(p^*, u^*) = y(p^*) \tag{8.3.5}$$

Let us now assume that Home imposes a tariff on the imported goods which, as we have already described, distorts relative prices. This is shown by:

$$p^t_{imp} > p^*_{imp} \text{ and } p^t_{exp} = p^*_{exp} \text{ so that } p^t < p^* \tag{8.3.6}$$

The representative consumer with an income of e now faces the post-tariff domestic prices. The consumer's best choice now places him on the flatter budget line attaining the level of utility u^t:

$$e = p^t D_t \tag{8.3.7}$$

In the post-tariff equilibrium the consumer receives income from two sources: the revenue from production under tariffs, which is $y(p^t)$, and the revenue from the tariffs. This later amount is given by the tariff rate times the quantity of imports:

$$(p^t - p^*)(D_t - P_t)$$

where the level of imports is given by consumption *minus* production or $(D_t - P_t)$.

The post-tariff utility level, u^t, is therefore determined by the level of expenditure which includes the revenue from the tariff:

$$e(p^t, u^t) = y(p^t) + (p^t - p^*)(D_t - P_t) \tag{8.3.8}$$

The level of utility reached under free trade is at least as high as the level of utility reached with a tariff, $u^t \leq u^*$. We can show this relatively simply by following the same reasoning as we did earlier when showing the gains from free trade in general. We therefore begin with the statement that our consumer can always attain at least the level of tariff-ridden utility by buying the tariff-ridden consumption bundle at free trade prices:

$$e(p^*, u^t) \leq p^* D_t \tag{8.3.9}$$

The balance of payments constraint implies that the value of the bundle consumed with the tariff must be equal to the value of the bundle produced, when evaluated at free trade prices, or

$$p^* D_t = p^* P_t \tag{8.3.10}$$

Similarly, under free trade the maximum attainable value of output at free trade prices is certainly as large as the value of post-tariff production at these same prices since the post-tariff production choice remains feasible under free trade. That is,

$$p^* P_t \leq y(p^*) \tag{8.3.11}$$

Recall that the consumer can spend all his production income to attain the level of utility u^* under free trade:

$$y(p^*) = e(p^*, u^*) \tag{8.3.12}$$

Therefore by (8.13)–(8.16) we have:

$$e(p^*, u^t) \leq e(p^*, u^*) \tag{8.3.13}$$

From (8.17) it follows that $u^t \leq u^*$, that is the level of free trade utility is at least as high as the level of tariff-ridden utility. If tariffs indeed cause distortions on the production or the consumption side as discussed previously, the inequalities (8.3.9) or (8.3.11), or both, would be strict, implying that the level of tariff-ridden utility is certainly less than the free trade utility. We conclude that for the small country under perfect competition free trade is superior to trade restricted by the tariff.

However, it is still true that the trade with a tariff is superior to *autarky*. This is most easily shown by comparing the income available to a consumer to purchase goods in autarky and with a tariff (note that income equals expenditure). In autarky the consumer's income comes only from production. In the post-tariff situation the consumer's income also includes the revenue from the tariff. As long as the tariff revenue is positive the consumer can thus attain a higher level of utility with a tariff than in autarky.[6]

☐ *A large country*

We now assume that Home is a large country. All other conditions remain the same as in our analysis of a small country: cloth represents importables, food represents exportables, and an *ad valorem* tariff is imposed on the imports of cloth. In this case, however, the resulting reduction in the imports of cloth will affect the world price of cloth. Home's terms of trade will thus improve with the tariff. There is also the possibility that the terms of trade gain will be strong enough to offset the tariff-induced efficiency losses, and that Home's welfare will actually be higher with tariffs than it was under free trade. This can be seen in Figure 8.4. The free trade production and consumption equilibria are at points P and D, respectively. The imposition of the tariff on cloth decreases the domestic relative price of food to p^t. This in turn induces producers to increase their production of cloth while consumers will actually consume less cloth. Production shifts to P_t while the consumption point D_t lies on the *improved* world relative price of food, p^{**}, and on the line parallel to the domestic price line, p^t. The extra income gained via the improvement in the terms of trade enables consumers to move to a higher indifference curve I_t. This indicates a higher level of welfare than the free trade equilibrium on indifference curve I.

The possibility of a large country influencing world prices by imposing trade restrictions on its imports (or exports, as will be shown later) is often used as a justification for protectionism in large countries. There are two important points here. First, there is a temptation to believe that for a large country welfare can be continually improved through terms of trade gains. However this is not possible because there is only one tariff level which will result in the maximum level of welfare. We have already mentioned this special tariff level – it is known as the optimum level. If a country sets a tariff higher than this level its welfare will be reduced because efficiency losses outweigh terms of trade gains. Secondly, it is obvious that the large country enjoys its increase in welfare at the expense of the rest of the world. It is thus likely that sooner or later some form of retaliation will

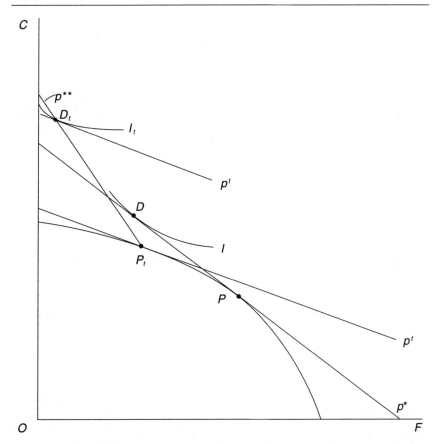

Figure 8.4   A tariff in a large country with two sectors

occur, reducing or completely nullifying the large country's gains. These matters are discussed in section 8.4.

The existence of tariff-induced welfare improvements has given rise to various ideas and postulations about protection-based terms of trade improvements. To experience this effect a country does not have to be large in the literal sense. It is sufficient to have either monopoly power in an export market, or monopsony power in an import market, or be able to create such power through domestic policy in order to influence the terms of trade. By imposing a tariff on imports the government actually gives its exporters the 'power' to influence the terms of trade by restricting both their output and exports. Through this improvement in prices a country can experience welfare gains. We should bear in mind, however, that this constitutes a redistribution of income away from the rest of the world which is made poorer through the deterioration in their terms of trade.

☐ *Tariff and welfare in a large country*

The following analysis of the welfare effects of a tariff is also used to derive an optimum tariff. We shall start with the expression, already given in (8.3.10), stating that at world prices the value of post-tariff domestic consumption vector exactly matches the value of the post-tariff production vector:

$$p^* D_t = p^* P_t \qquad (8.3.14)$$

Total differentiation of both sides and a subsequent addition and subtraction of $p^t dD_t$ on the left-hand side and of $p^t dP_t$ on the right-hand side yields:

$$p^t dD_t + dp^* D_t + (p^* - p^t) dD_t = p^t dP_t + dp^* P_t \\ + (p^* - p^t) P_t \qquad (8.3.15)$$

By using the expression for net imports $M = D_t - P_t$, and by rearranging we obtain:

$$p^t dD_t = -M dp^* + (p^t - p^*) dM + p^t dP_t \qquad (8.3.15)$$

The term on the left-hand side reflects the change in the real income at Home since it gives the change in the consumption vector weighted by the vector of prices. We will denote this as dy. The last term on the right-hand side represents the change in the production vector evaluated at domestic prices. This term approximates zero for the perfectly competitive two-sector economy.[7] Thus the total effect on welfare becomes:

$$dy = -M dp^* + (p^t - p^*) dM^8 \qquad (8.3.17)$$

This total effect can be broken into the two influences a tariff has on a country's utility. The first term on the right-hand side of (8.3.17) shows the so-called *terms of trade effect*. It reflects the change in the world prices caused by Home's imposition of a tariff. This term is necessarily positive for a large country (it is zero for a small country). The more that is imported, the greater the positive impact on the utility of the tariff-imposing country will be. The second term reflects the impact on national welfare caused by a discrepancy between world prices, p^*, and the tariff-distorted domestic prices, p^t. Under domestic prices with a tariff imports are valued more highly by domestic consumers than they are in the world market. Restricting imports thus has a welfare-reducing effect: the *volume of trade effect*. This effect is proportional to the extent of the tariff. Since this effect is induced by the distorted domestic price it is also known as the efficiency loss from a tariff. The total welfare effect will depend on the relative strengths of these two influences. From the various possible outcomes we can state the following conclusions about tariff application in a large country.

(1) In the case when a large country moves from free trade to trade under tariffs, the volume of trade effect vanishes (as the initial tariff rate equals zero), the remaining effect being the terms of trade effect. This effect is, of course, positive. Thus for a large country a tariff is better than free trade. It will be shown below that this applies only for sufficiently small tariffs.

(2) In the case when a country moves from free trade to no trade, with the so-called prohibitive tariff leading to $M = 0$, the only effect of the tariff is the volume of trade effect. Welfare is unambiguously reduced by a prohibitive tariff. A reduction in, but not the complete removal of, a tariff will allow for positive imports and will put the terms of trade effect to work. This will increase welfare. Some trade, even tariff-ridden trade, is thus better than no trade.

(3) In the case when a large country increases the rate of an already existing tariff, various trade-offs between the terms of trade and the volume of trade effects are possible. As long as the terms of trade effect is at least as strong as the volume of trade effect national welfare will be improved by an increase in the tariff rate. However a tariff cannot be continuously increased. Sooner or later the imports of the tariff-ridden good will fall, causing larger and larger efficiency losses. Eventually this will lead to a reduction in welfare. Economists have constructed a formula to determine where the tariff increase should stop so that utility is maximised. The first order condition for utility maximisation is $dy = 0$, so that (8.3.17) becomes:

$$M dp^* = (p^t - p^*)dM \tag{8.3.18}$$

or by using $p^t - p^* = tp^*$:

$$M dp^* = tp^* dM$$

Dividing both sides by $p^* M$ gives:

$$dp^*/p^* = t(dM/M)$$

Here we again use the hat notation to express relative changes:

$$t = \hat{P}^*/\hat{M}$$

or

$$t = 1/(\hat{M}/\hat{P}^*) \tag{8.3.19}$$

This formula shows the tariff rate at which domestic welfare is maximised. This is the *optimum tariff*. The tariff rate is equal to the reciprocal of the ratio of the relative changes in the country's imports and in world prices. The same idea can be expressed in terms of the elasticity of foreign import demand and export supply. We take the world equilibrium condition:

$$p^*M = M^*$$

and then include relative changes:

$$\hat{P}^* + \hat{M} = \hat{M}^*$$

From here $\hat{M}/\hat{P}^*$ equals $(\hat{M}^*/\hat{P}^*) - 1$. Since $\hat{M}^*/\hat{P}^*$ is the coefficient of the elasticity of foreign's import demand along its offer curve:

$$\varepsilon^* = -\hat{M}^*/(1/\hat{p}^*) = \hat{M}^*/\hat{P}^*$$

the formula for the optimum tariff takes the form:

$$t = 1/(\varepsilon^* - 1) \tag{8.3.20}$$

Moreover, from the balance of payments constraint we know that the coefficients of the elasticity of import demand and export supply are related by:

$$\varepsilon^* - 1 = \xi^*$$

where ξ^* is the foreign elasticity of export supply. The formula for the optimum tariff can thus also be expressed in terms of foreign elasticity of export supply as:

$$t = 1/\xi^* \tag{8.3.20a}$$

The optimum tariff rate will be higher the less elastic the relevant Foreign offer curve is, that is the larger effect Home has on its terms of trade. Obviously a small country which faces a perfectly elastic Foreign offer curve has a zero optimum tariff. Under the optimum tariff for a large country, however, the terms of trade gains are just large enough to offset the efficiency loss. If the tariff is increased any further the negative effect will predominate.

From Figure 8.5 it is obvious that when a small tariff is introduced, and its rate is gradually increased, the country's potential welfare (as compared to the free trade level) will at first increase, reach a maximum, and then decrease as the tariff rate further increases. Maximum welfare will be reached at the optimum tariff rate, t^o. As the tariff is increased beyond this rate welfare will eventually fall below the level of potential welfare achieved under free trade.[9]

(4) Although the level of the tariff given as (8.3.20) is optimal in the sense of maximising national welfare, if the tariff is further increased, tariff revenues will be maximised. In other words the revenue-maximising tariff is generally higher than the optimum tariff. This is because at the optimum tariff rate (at which $dy/dt = 0$), because $\varepsilon^* > 1$, the dp^t/dt is still positive.

In Figure 8.5 the rate t^o maximises welfare but not tariff revenue; at this rate the marginal tariff revenue is still positive. Thus by increasing the rate the total revenue will rise until the rate t^r is reached. However

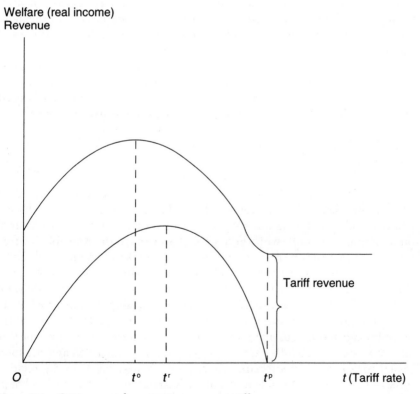

Figure 8.5 *Optimum and maximum revenue tariffs*

beyond the tariff revenue-maximising rate revenue will start to fall and actually reach zero when the rate reaches the level of the prohibitive tariffs at which there are no imports. This occurs at the rate t^p.

8.4 Optimum tariff and retaliation: an offer curve analysis

We defined the optimum tariff as the tariff rate at which the margin between the terms of trade gains and the efficiency losses is the greatest. The terms of trade gains arising from the optimum tariff depend on there being no retaliation by Home's trading partners. In practice, however, it is likely that retaliation will occur as trading partners try to offset at least some of their terms of trade losses. From this point of view retaliation is a rational response. Since retaliation by Foreign reduces Home's initial benefits it is likely that Home will further increase its tariffs in the hope of regaining the lost benefits. This practice may thus start a vicious circle of tariff increases and may result in a tariff war. Such a war has the potential to eliminate all the gains from trade. This insight underlies one of the most important principles built into the functioning of the GATT multilateral trading system: the reciprocity principle (see Box 8.1, p. 305).

This offer curve analysis is particularly useful in examining the ideas of the optimum tariff, retaliation and the reciprocity principle. Let us first recall (from Chapter 2) that Home's offer curve shows how its desired imports of cloth and exports of food vary with the relative prices of these goods. Figure 8.6 illustrates both free trade and tariff-ridden equilibria. Under free trade the intersection of Home's offer curve, given by OO, and Foreign's offer curve, given by OO^*, results in the relative price of food in terms of cloth on the world market being p^E. These terms of trade clear international markets of cloth and food so that OC_E of cloth is offered by Foreign and demanded by Home, while OF_E of food is offered by Home and demanded by Foreign. Let us now assume that Home imposes a tariff on its imports of cloth, while Foreign still adheres to the principles of free trade. The imposition of tariffs in Home will make Home less willing to trade at any given terms of trade. This is why its offer curve, now OO^t, has shifted closer to the axis of its importable good. If the terms of trade were somehow fixed at the level p^E, Home would be willing, as illustrated by its new offer curve, to export only OF_S of food in exchange for OC_S of cloth. Since Foreign's offer curve does not move, at the terms of trade p^E there is an excess supply of cloth (equal to C_EC_S) and an excess demand for food (equal to F_SF_E). This will naturally require an adjustment in the relative price of food so that the new terms of trade are established at the level of p^t where the relative price of food in terms of cloth is higher than before the tariffs. In short the tariff-imposing country, Home, experiences a terms of trade improvement at the expense of its trading partner, Foreign. At the new trading equilibrium, E^t, the volume of trade has decreased for both countries. The total effect on Foreign's welfare is obviously negative. In Home the losses caused by production and consumption distortions may be offset or more than offset, by the terms of trade gains. However Home's welfare will unambiguously improve when it imposes an optimum tariff. This is illustrated in Figure 8.7.

In Figure 8.7 the free trade equilibrium is given by point E, where Home's and Foreign offer curves intersect. At this point Home reaches its *trade indifference curve* TIC^E (which shows different trade situations which would provide a country the same level of welfare). The equilibrium terms of trade, p^E, are tangential to Home's TIC^E at point E. This means that the marginal rates of transformation and substitution of food for cloth in Home are equal to Home's average terms of trade. Assuming that Foreign does not impose any trade restrictions, Home can maximise its welfare by imposing an optimum tariff. The height of this tariff is obtained by identifying the point at which Foreign's offer curve is tangential to

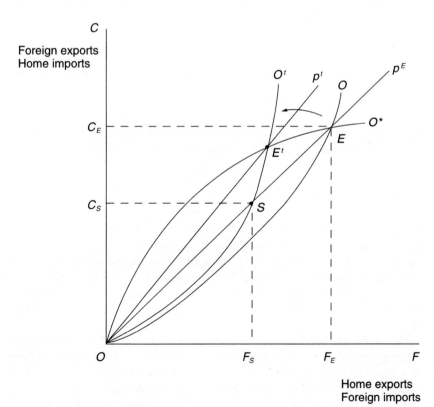

Figure 8.6 *Tariffs with offer curves*

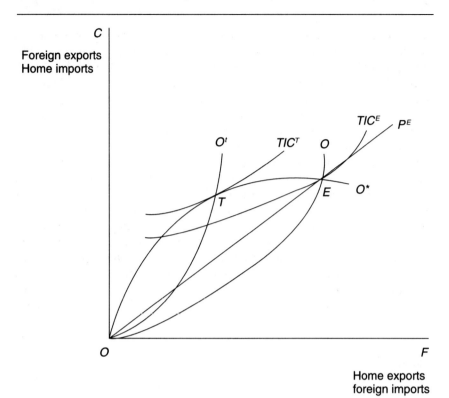

Figure 8.7   *The case of the optimum tariff*

Home's highest trade indifference curve. This occurs at point T, where Foreign's offer curve is tangential to the TIC^T curve of Home. At this point Home's terms of trade are improved to the extent that all efficiency losses are fully offset and welfare is maximised.[10] Note that at this point the slope of TIC^T is given by Home's marginal terms of trade, or the slope of Foreign's offer curve. It is also important to note that at this point we are on the elastic section of Foreign's offer curve. This leads to the conclusion that a country which has the ability to change world prices will always choose to trade along the elastic portion of its trading partner's offer curve. We cannot escape from noticing the resemblance between the behaviour of the large country in international trade and the behaviour of a monopolist who always seeks to operate on the elastic portion of the demand curve it faces.

The optimum tariff case is a good illustration of a Pareto inefficient trading equilibrium from the world's point of view. Although Home maximises its welfare, Foreign is on a lower trade indifference curve which means that its level of welfare is lower than its potential. At this point the slopes of Home and Foreign's trade indifference curves are not equal. Foreign's welfare could thus be improved if it could shift to the indifference curve *tangential* to Home's trade indifference curve. Exactly the same world equilibrium could be achieved by a transfer of real income from Foreign to Home, instead of Home imposing an optimum tariff. However this solution is less politically feasible. Tariffs have always been the politically preferred, although less economically efficient, instrument of world income redistribution. The only constraint in the application of tariffs for this purpose is, naturally, the possible retaliation of trading partners who lose from Home's unilateral action. Figure 8.8 illustrates the effects of Foreign retaliation. Retaliation by Foreign shifts its offer curve to OO^{*t} so that new trading equilibrium is given by the point E^R. At this point Foreign attains a higher trade indifference curve, TIC^{*R}, than before while Home is pushed back to a lower trade indifference curve TIC^{*T}. Needless to say this process of retaliation and counter-retaliation may continue. In fact once begun it is likely that it will continue until one country's trade indifference curve is tangential to the other country's offer curve at a point that already lies on the first country's offer curve. For example point Z in Figure 8.9 is reached by Home's second retaliatory action. However at this point there is no positive tariff which can increase

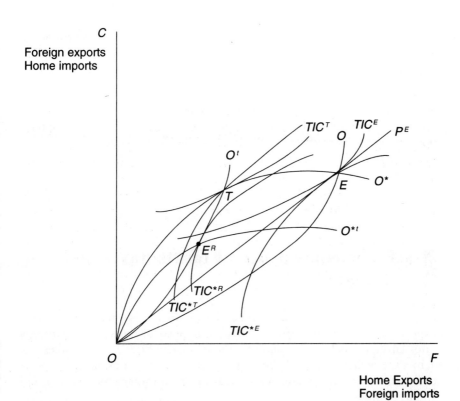

Figure 8.8 *The optimum tariff and retaliation*

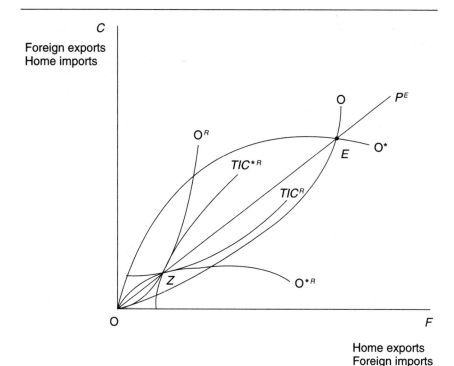

Figure 8.9   *Outcome of counter-retaliation*

Foreign's welfare. Foreign's trade indifference curve TIC^{*R} is already tangential to Home's offer curve at point Z. Foreign thus has no motivation to change its tariff from this level, while Home consequently has no incentive to retaliate. At this equilibrium the volume of trade, although still positive, is significantly reduced from the free trade volume of trade. It goes without saying that both countries gains from trade are being reduced, if not eliminated.[11]

8.5 The equivalence of tariffs, taxes and subsidies

Lerner (1936) showed that in general equilibrium an across the board export tax has the same effect as one on imports of the same *ad valorem* rate. This famous *Lerner symmetry* (theorem) also extends to subsidies. An across the board export subsidy thus has the same effect as one on imports of the same percentage rate. We show below how this symmetry arises and what its limitations are.

Box 8.1 *The reciprocity principle*

The reciprocity, or quid pro quo, principle has been embedded in the GATT rules through the famous *most-favoured-nation* clause, which requires that all contracting parties grant each other terms as favourable as they give to any other country with respect to imports and exports of products. In essence this clause ensures that each party will take part in the reduction of trade barriers because it will expect other parties to 'return the favour', i.e. liberalise their trade as well.[12] Consequently global trade liberalisation can be achieved only by multilateral and cooperative negotiations. Further, although there is a strong theoretical case for unilateral free trade from any individual country, the welfare of the whole world cannot be maximised unless there is universal free trade.[13] Presumably only multilateral negotiations could lead to such a state. One reason for this rests on the fact that reciprocity encourages the formation of interest groups or lobbies in favour of trade liberalisation. These groups combine exporters and consumers against the traditionally strong influences of import-substituting producers, therefore making liberalisation more politically feasible. Another important reason is that these negotiations provide a solution to the 'prisoner's dilemma' problem which is faced by large countries who lose by unilateral free trade and which may lead to a trade war. On the other hand, for small countries, for whom free trade should be the optimum trade policy, the reciprocity principle creates a barrier to their way going all the way to free trade because they want to retain some tariffs as negotiating weapons (concessions) against large countries.

In recent years, however, the term 'reciprocity' has taken on new meaning. It is now used to justify aggressive and unilateral trade actions against one or more countries that are not perceived as playing on a 'level field'. Probably the country which has gone furthest in its application of this new interpretation of the reciprocity principle is the USA when it adopted its infamous 301, Super 301 and Special 301 sections of the Trade Act. They allow it to bilaterally compare its own protection and that of any of its trading partners. If such a comparison demonstrates that the other country is being 'unfair', that is, has a 'higher' overall level of protection against US products than the USA has against its products, it is asked to reduce its protection and make trade 'fair'. If it refuses, the USA retains the right to retaliate by imposing additional protection against that country's imports.

An export tax raises the world price of an exportable good above its domestic price. Suppose that the same *ad valorem* tax is levied on all exportables, while imports are free of taxes. Following our earlier notation the importables are represented by cloth, and exportables by food. The domestic price of importables with no import taxes thus continues to be equal to their world price:

$$p_C = p^*_C$$

However the domestic price of exportables is lower than the world price by the amount of the tax:

$$p_F(1 + t) = p^*_F$$

where t denotes the *ad valorem* export tax rate. The domestic relative price of food in terms of cloth with export taxes is given by:

$$[(p_F/p_C)](1 + t) = (p^*_F/p^*_C) \text{ or}$$
$$p^t(1 + t) = p^* \tag{8.5.1}$$

where p^t is the post-tax domestic relative price of food, and p^* is the world relative price of food. (8.5.1) can also be written in a slightly different way so that we can compare it with the ratio of domestic and foreign relative prices in the case of import taxes (8.3.2):

$$p^t = p^*[1/(1 + t)] \text{ or}$$
$$p^t/p^* = [1/(1 + t)] \leq 1, \quad \text{if } t \geq 0 \tag{8.5.2}$$

Thus (8.5.2) and (8.3.2) are identical. This implies that a general import tax is equivalent to a general export tax: given fixed world prices an import tax on cloth depreciates the domestic relative price of food, while an export tax on food also reduces its domestic relative price. Both instruments are therefore identical in creating a wedge between domestic and world prices. Moreover the level of optimum rate is the same in both cases, tariff and export tax. If the tax revenue is spent in the same manner in both cases, these two instruments should be regarded as being identical in all respects. This means that the effect derived from protecting a domestic import-substituting industry, cloth, could be achieved with equal success by either imposing an export tax on food or by imposing an import tariff on cloth. Alternatively a country wanting to restrict its exports, for example to improve its terms of trade, as in the large country case, could achieve this effect by levying an import tariff. Export taxes and the role of tariffs in substituting for export taxes will be discussed further in Chapter 9. Let us now briefly examine the equivalence between import and export subsidies.

An import (export) subsidy is merely another name for negative import (export) taxes. While we had some freedom with respect to the behaviour of government in the case of trade taxes, in case of trade subsidies we must make specific assumptions. These are that the government raises the amount required for subsidies through some form of general income tax, and that there is no government consumption of any goods produced or traded. We again assume that importables are represented by cloth and exportables by food. The world relative price of food is p^*. If Home's government pays an export subsidy to the food sector at an *ad valorem* rate of s, then the domestic relative price of food would be:

$$p_F(1 - s) = p^*_F$$

The domestic price of cloth will continue to be identical to the world price of cloth:

$$p_C = p^*_C$$

The post-subsidy domestic relative price of food is then given by:

$$p^t(1 - s) = p^*, \text{ or}$$
$$p^t/p^* = [1/(1 - s)] \tag{8.5.3}$$

In the case where Home's government subsidises imports of cloth instead, the exact relationship between the domestic and world relative prices of food obtained in (8.5.3) will exist. Namely the domestic and world price of food will be the same:

$$p_F = p^*_F$$

while the domestic price of cloth will be lower than its world price:

$$p_C/(1 - s) = p^*_C$$

This implies that:

$$p^t(1 - s) = p^*, \text{ or}$$
$$p^t/p^* = [1/(1 - s)] \tag{8.5.4}$$

In the case where there are both export and import subsidies the domestic relative price of food will appreciate as compared to the world relative price of food. Thus, given fixed world prices, an export subsidy to food raises its domestic price, while an import subsidy to cloth will also increase the relative price of food. This is obvious from:

$$p^t/p^* = [1/(1-s)] \geq 1 \qquad \text{if } 0 \leq s \leq 1 \tag{8.5.5}$$

This analysis of the symmetry between tariffs, taxes and subsidies, although having limited relevance for policy applications because of its underlying assumptions, could however shed some light on some real-country experiences. For example, the success of some East Asian countries' economic growth was 'unexplainable' with respect to their inward-looking protectionist trade policies, that is, the high import tariffs they had in the 1960s. We now know that, at least in a simple 2×2 model if import tariffs are matched by equivalent export subsidies, the negative effect of tariffs would be neutralised. This is because of the equivalence between export and import subsidies. Thus the granting of export subsidies at the same time as imposing import tariffs has the same effect as granting import subsidies and imposing import tariffs at the same rate. (Just compare (8.3.2) and (8.5.5). The total protective effect must thus be zero, implying no adverse effects for either production or consumption efficiency.

☐ Production subsidies and consumption taxes

At this point we should comment on the nature of tariffs and their redistributive effects. We can show that the effects of a tariff are equivalent to the simultaneous application of a consumption tax and a production subsidy of the same *ad valorem* rate.

Let us first consider a situation in which producers are protected not by an import tariff but by a production subsidy of the same rate, t. Looking back at Figure 8.1 part (a), the amount of the subsidy, t, given to the producers of cloth is equivalent to the tariff rate t. The subsidy creates a wedge between the free trade price for cloth, p^*_C, which in this case is paid by consumers, and the price p^t_C, which is received by producers. This wedge motivates producers to increase their production of cloth from $0q_1$ to $0q_4$; the same protective effect as occurs under tariffs. In this instance, however, consumers do not suffer a loss in consumer surplus. There is thus no direct consumption effect. The government now spends its revenue on the subsidy. This is the amount of $a + b$. The redistributive effects are given by area a, and the net loss is now only area b compared to area $b + d$ in the case of tariffs.

Consider now the imposition of a consumption tax of the same rate t as the previous tariff. Consumption will decrease to $0q_3$, production will remain at the level $0q_1$, and imports will fall to q_1q_3. The gross loss in consumer surplus is the sum of the areas $a + b + c + d$. However in the case of a consumption tax the total revenue collected would be equal to the areas $a + b + c$; this is larger than in the case of tariff protection where the revenue was only area c. Thus with a consumption tax the net loss is smaller, it is equal to area d. Since a consumption tax has the same effect on consumers as tariffs, it is sometimes referred to as a consumer tax equivalent to the tariff. The revenue collected could be further divided into the pure fiscal revenue effect (area c), and the subsidy-equivalent of the tariff (areas $a + b$). This latter amount is equal to the amount of the subsidy that the government would have to spend to induce domestic producers to produce quantity $0q_4$ at the price p^*_C. Therefore tariffs redistribute income from consumers to producers and to the government by increasing its fiscal revenue. While we assume that this revenue is returned to consumers through a decrease in other taxes or in similar ways, it is clear that this may not actually be the case in reality.

■ 8.6 Tariffs and imperfect competition

The use of tariffs and other trade policy instruments are often justified by the existence of so-called domestic distortions.[14] Domestic distortions involve both product and factor market malfunctions which lead to a difference between private and social costs. This in turn is the basis for the government intervention. Our concern here is government intervention via tariffs.

In a perfectly competitive economy, as demonstrated, tariffs may affect national welfare through both terms of trade and volume of trade effects. The potential effects tariffs have on production were eliminated by our assumption that in absence of distortions small tariff changes would not result in significant shifts along the production frontier. More specifically, when deriving the welfare changes due to tariff changes the term pd^tP_t in (8.3.15) vanished as a condition for maximisation.[15] In other words production was assumed to be efficient in terms of both being on the production frontier and producing an efficient combination of outputs.

Under imperfect competition, which necessarily involves some form of domestic distortion, this reasoning no longer applies. Imperfect competition is reflected in the behaviour of firms which no longer price at marginal cost. This means that although the economy may have production efficient in terms of 'producing on the frontier', the composition of output may be inefficient. Graphically this would mean that the domestic price line is not tangential to the PPF, but cuts it instead. This suggests that tariffs may have an effect on the production mix. An efficient output combination can be obtained when the imperfectly competitive industry, whose prices are higher than marginal costs, expands its production at the expense of the other industry. Our welfare equation must therefore take the influence on the composition of output into account. We shall thus reintroduce this effect in our (8.3.15) so as to show the full impact of a tariff under any type of competitive structure.

Let us reproduce (8.3.15) as (8.6.1):

$$dy = -Mdp^* + (p^t - p^*)dM + p^t dP_t \qquad (8.6.1)$$

where $dy = p^t dD_t$

In imperfect competition prices do not reflect marginal costs. If we denote the vector of marginal costs by c, then in imperfect competition we normally have $p > c$, that is, prices include some mark-up over marginal costs. We have to include this in our equation showing the change in real income. To do this we will utilise the feature of a perfectly competitive economy where marginal costs are proportional to the gradient of the production surface. In such a case cdP_t must be equal to zero.[16] We can thus rewrite (8.6.1) to include marginal costs:

$$dy = -Mdp^* + (p^t - p^*)dM + (p^t - c)dP_t \qquad (8.6.2)$$

The first term on the right-hand side represents the by now familiar terms of trade effect of a tariff: national income increases by the improvement of country's terms of trade. The other two effects on the right-hand side represent the effects of the tariff on efficiency. The first effect is the volume of trade effect: national income increases with the expansion of imports when domestic prices are higher than world prices because of the tariff. The second term is new and applies only in imperfect competition: national income increases by the tariff-induced expansion of output in goods that are priced above marginal cost. This term represents the efficiency gains obtained through the improvement in the composition of output. The net welfare effect therefore depends on the relative strengths of these three effects.

The fact that the tariff results in some type of efficiency gain has important implications for trade policy. If, for example, by the imposition of a tariff or other trade policy instrument we can induce an expansion of the industry with market power, real national income will increase. However this does not provide a blanket justification for protection in all cases of imperfect competition. As Helpman (1989) carefully states, there are 'cases' and 'cases' of market power and almost each one requires a different treatment. The mere existence of imperfect competition does not constitute an automatic justification for trade policy intervention. First and foremost we must differentiate between one-sided and two-sided market power. One-sided market power implies an imperfectly competitive supplier in one market only, while suppliers in this country's trading partners' market are competitive. In this case it matters whether the domestic suppliers have the power or their trading partners have the power. Moreover the number of suppliers who have market power in either market is of crucial importance. If there is more than one supplier the strategic variable suppliers chose to compete on (such as quantity, price, etc.) is also important.

When market power is exhibited by suppliers in both Home and Foreign, we talk about two-sided market power. Each market may have one or more suppliers which again may chose various forms of competition. The number of different combinations is obviously large and it quickly becomes apparent that no government could have sufficient information to engage in risk-free welfare-increasing protectionism, even when it is theoretically justifiable. Despite this fact, literally thousands of pages have been written in the last decade exploring various examples of welfare-increasing or welfare-decreasing protection under imperfect competition (for surveys see Richardson, 1989, 1992; Grossman, 1992). We cannot possibly survey all this literature, which is in places quite technical and complex. In this chapter we will examine the simplest cases of one-sided market power as the basis for protection. We will revisit some of these cases in Chapter 9 where we explain the use of non-tariff instruments and compare the effect of tariffs and quotas or other non-tariff barriers. From that discussion it will become apparent that under imperfect competition different trade policy instruments have very different impacts as compared with their effects under perfect competition. In Chapter 10 we will discuss the case of two-sided market power, probably most famous for providing an environment for the so-called *strategic trade policy*.

☐ One-sided market power: domestic monopoly

With one-sided market power there are two possible locations of power. Either the domestic or foreign producer could exhibit the power.[17] In this section we concentrate on a domestic monopoly. We begin our analysis of tariffs under this market structure by reviewing Bhagwati's famous monopoly example (1965). This example shows how protection creates market power where none would otherwise exist (Helpman and Krugman, 1989, p. 28). Bhagwati assumed that a single firm existed in the import-competing sector of the domestic economy, while the world supply of the commodity is perfectly competitive. The world price is thus fixed. It is also assumed that Home is a small country so that its terms of trade are also given. Moreover domestically produced and imported goods are perfect substitutes. As long as Home is engaged in free trade the domestic firm will not in fact be able to exercise its 'monopoly' power; instead it will be forced into marginal cost pricing. Note that this result implies that the monopolist has no possibility of exporting its product. Figure 8.10 illustrates the free trade and post-tariff equilibria under this market structure. Domestic demand for the firm's product is given by *D*. The corresponding marginal revenue curve is given by *MR*. The firm's marginal cost curve is the upward-sloping curve, *MC*. The world price is constant

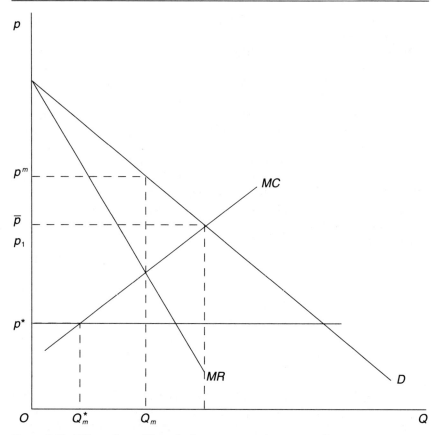

Figure 8.10 *Effect of a tariff on the import-competing monopolist*

at level p^*. The domestic monopolist would chose to produce an output Q_m, where MR equals MC, if it were not for the free trade which prevents him from charging higher price than p^*. At this price the monopolist produces only Q_m^*, where p^* equals MC. The difference between Q_m^* and the total amount demanded at price p^* is of course imported.

Suppose that the government imposes a tariff on imports of this commodity. The effect on both the level of output produced by the domestic firm and the price charged will differ depending on the extent of the tariff. There are three broad price ranges (Helpman and Krugman, 1989, p. 29). One possibility is that the tariff rates are set so as not to push the domestic tariff-inclusive price above the price $\bar{p}$. This price is the one at which import ceases. Recall that this rate of tariff is known as a prohibitive tariff. The level of this tariff-inclusive price is given by the intersection of the demand and MC curves. The second range of prices is given by tariff rates which would put the domestic tariff-inclusive price between this prohibitive price level and the monopoly price level p^m. The third price range is that determined by tariff rates so high that they increase the domestic price above the monopoly price p^m.

If a tariff is imposed at the rate which pushes the domestic price up, say to the level p_1, but not above the level $\bar{p}$, the monopolist will have an incentive to increase its output. The output decision will again be made by equating price, now the tariff-inclusive price, with marginal cost; $p_1 = MC$. The imposition of the tariff has thus not changed the monopolist's behaviour. By applying (8.6.2) we can clearly identify the sign of the effect of tariff. The third term in the equation is zero because the monopolist is pricing at marginal cost, so that $(p^t - c) = 0$. The first term is zero as well since the country is small and its terms of trade are not affected by tariffs. The second term, however, is not zero. It is negative, leading to a welfare loss. Its negative sign arises from the effect the tariff has on the quantity of imports. Imports are reduced when an expansion of imports is required (i.e. when domestic price is higher than the world price).

When the rate of the tariff increases to the level of the domestic tariff-inclusive price, imports will in fact cease. However the monopolist will still not charge and produce the output level at which $MR = MC$. The reason for this is that the threat of import competition still exists. Tariffs with rates in this range (up to p^m) do not lead to any welfare improvement. Looking at (8.6.2) again, the first term remains zero. The second term is also zero because there are no imports. However the third term is now negative because output declines when in fact we would rather have it increased because the price is now higher than marginal cost.

Finally, the tariff rate may increase even further so that the domestic tariff-inclusive price will exceed the profit-maximising price of the monopolist. In such a case the threat of import competition becomes irrelevant and the monopolist may finally behave as one. Output will therefore be Q_m, at which $MR = MC$. The effect of this tariff is therefore to act as a buffer against foreign competition; an import-competing single firm under a high tariff wall is assured of its market power. This obviously reduces welfare.

This effect of a tariff can also be derived for the case when the monopolist faces decreasing marginal costs. The other assumptions are the same as in the previous case of increasing MC. This new situation is illustrated in Figure 8.11. The MC curve for the monopolist is continuously declining, and its AC curve is above its MC curve at all levels of output. The world price is constant at p^*, again reflecting perfectly competitive world supply. Domestic demand is again given by curve D; the corresponding marginal revenue curve is MR. It is obvious from Figure 8.10 that as long as the world price is as low as p^*, the domestic monopolist cannot survive. This price, which leads consumers to demand Q_*, is lower than monopolist's MC or AC and it is not present in the market. The minimum tariff rate necessary to allow this monopolist to

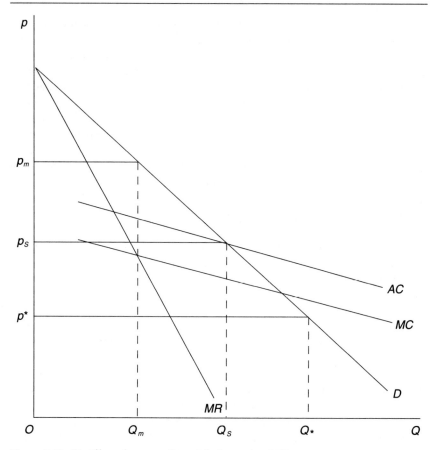

Figure 8.11 *Tariffs and monopolist with decreasing MC*

enter production would be the rate at which the domestic tariff-inclusive price equals the monopolist's *AC*. However as soon as this rate is imposed the monopolist supplies the whole amount demanded by the market at this price! This tariff rate, which allows the monopolist to survive but prevents him from yielding any extra profits, is known as the *made-to-measure* or *scientific tariff* (Corden, 1974, p. 219). If the tariff rate is increased above this level output will be reduced and the price increased until the profit-maximising output is chosen at Q_m. In other words, with decreasing marginal costs it becomes quite apparent that a tariff provides a shelter for the domestic producer from international competition by allowing it to exercise its monopoly power in full.

The impact of a tariff on creating market power in the domestic market is somewhat weakened when we assume that imported products are not perfect substitutes for domestically produced ones.[18] With this assumption the domestic firm can exercise its market power even under free trade.

However protection will make the position of this firm in the domestic market even more powerful.

To sum up, free trade makes markets more competitive and, conversely, protection either gives rise to market power or strengthens already existing market power. We have come to this conclusion by analysing the simplest case of imperfect market structure, monopoly, and by the imposition of the most transparent trade policy instrument, tariffs. In Chapter 9 we will show that quantitative restrictions to trade, such as quotas, can decrease competition even more than tariffs. Thus we are correct in stating that in most cases quotas are worse than tariffs when it comes to restricting competition.[19]

☐ *One-sided market power: foreign monopoly*

Let us now examine the impact of tariffs in the situation where the location of market power is reversed. Perfect competition is assumed in the domestic market while the market power is given to the foreign supplier. Contrary to what we have found in the case of domestic monopoly, a tariff introduced now to protect domestic industry may actually result in some gains. If by such a tariff we succeed in re-extracting a portion of rents the foreign monopolist is getting from domestic consumers, then national income can be increased as compared to free trade. Domestic demand for imports supplied by the foreign monopolist is given by the downward sloping curve D in Figure 8.12. The fact that demand curve is downward sloping demonstrates the market power of the foreign monopolist. From basic microeconomics we know that a monopolist will never produce along the inelastic portion of the demand curve for its product. As long as there is no restriction on imports the foreign monopolist will therefore export Q_e where $MR = MC$. (Constant marginal costs are assumed for simplicity.) Suppose now that tariff is imposed on imports which raises the foreign monopolist's marginal costs by the specific rate of t. At these increased marginal costs, the monopolist reduces exports to Q_e^t where $MR = MC^t$. The price charged is higher, p^t, leading to reduced gains from trade for Home. However Home's government collects revenue in amount of tQ_e^t so that the net effect of a tariff is given as the difference between tariff revenues and losses suffered by consumers. In our example this difference is positive, leading to an increase in national welfare. Moreover with the linear demand curve and for small tariff rates the tariff revenue will always exceed the consumer surplus loss (Brander and Spencer, 1984).[20]

This general result can also be obtained by using (8.6.2) for the change in national income. Out of three terms on the right-hand side of the formula for the welfare effects of a tariff, in the case of foreign monopoly the only term remaining different from zero is the terms of trade effect. The other two terms become equal to zero. The third term vanishes because of perfect competition in the domestic industry which means that $(p^t - c) = 0$. The second term vanishes because initially there was free trade, i.e. $t = 0$. The improvement of the terms of trade is reflected as the change of the domestic tariff-inclusive price of the imported good which increases by less than the amount of the specific tariff imposed. This means that part of the tariff burden is carried by the foreign monopolist. This will happen if and only if its marginal revenue curve is steeper than its demand curve. This condition will always be satisfied for linear demand curves. For non-linear demand curves it may not be satisfied, which implies that in such a case tariffs would worsen the terms of trade and reduce national welfare. In fact to increase welfare in this situation a country should impose a negative tariff, that is, an import subsidy (Brander and Spencer, 1984).

In summary when imports are supplied by a foreign monopolist, domestic welfare will be improved by import tariffs if marginal revenue declines faster than price or by import subsidies if marginal revenue declines slower than price.[21]

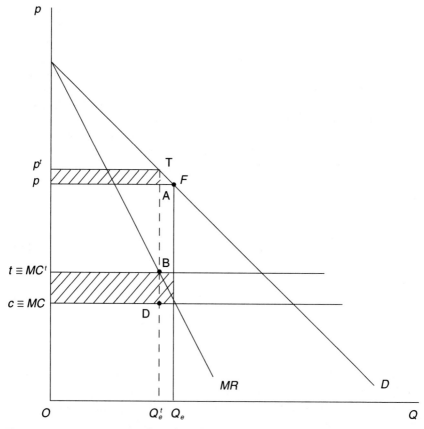

Figure 8.12 *Foreign monopoly and tariffs*

■ 8.7 Summary

This chapter focused on the effects of tariffs on prices, consumption, production, trade volume and gains from restricted trade. The analysis was carried out in both partial and general equilibrium frameworks for both small and large countries. It has been shown that a tariff imposed by a small country which is a price taker in the world markets causes the reallocation of resources in favour of the protected sector so that the production of this good increases at the expense of other sectors, possibly successful export sectors. The tariff therefore redistributes income between production sectors as well as between consumers and protected producers. Since the consumption of this good decreases due to its higher domestic relative price, the volume of trade contracts. The government collects tariff revenue so that national income evaluated at domestic prices increases. This tariff revenue, however, is not sufficient to make up for the efficiency losses and the country's welfare is reduced. As an instrument for redistribution of income within domestic economy a tariff is obviously not the best choice.

When the large country imposes a tariff, the effects are different because of the ability of this country to influence the world relative price. Therefore when this country's production of import-substituting good increases and consumption decreases, the world relative price of this good will fall. Thus the terms of trade of a large country will improve and this might offset the efficiency losses. In fact if a country manages to impose the optimum rate of tariff, which is equal to the inverse of the foreign elasticity of export supply, it is guaranteed to increase its welfare for as long as its trading partners do not retaliate.

Other countries are motivated to retaliate because they are made worse off when Home imposes a tariff. Because their terms of trade worsen, other countries may try to offset these losses by imposing tariffs themselves and so re-redistributing the world income. The possible circles of tariff increases may lead to lower welfare for all. From the world point of view, therefore, tariffs can only be the second best instrument of income distribution between countries and direct transfers of income between countries are certainly superior though politically much less feasible.

It is important to bear in mind that tariffs do not affect only sectors which are meant to be protected by them. Tariffs have effects on other sectors of the economy, and most often adverse effects. Moreover, under certain assumptions, as the Lerner symmetry theorem shows, import tariffs have the same contracting effect on a country's export as would direct export taxes. When the import-competing sector in a small country is monopolised, a tariff will certainly reduce domestic welfare because the tariff serves as the source of market power creation. When however the monopoly is on the foreign supply side, a tariff imposed by Home may increase domestic welfare because via tariffs a portion of rents obtained from domestic consumers may be extracted from the foreign monopolist.

▌ APPENDIX 8   THE METZLER AND LERNER PARADOXES

The Metzler (Metzler, 1949) and the Lerner (Lerner, 1936) paradoxes are the best known anomalous cases with respect to application of tariffs. We will briefly discuss both of them using the offer curve analysis.

The Metzler paradox is described as a situation in which the tariff-imposing country's terms of trade improve by so much that its domestic relative price of importables in fact falls as compared to the free trade level. This of course means that the protection that the tariff was supposed to provide to the import-competing sector is actually granted to the other sector of the economy and at the expense of the import-competing sector. The effects of a tariff in this case will be to increase imports and decrease domestic production of the importable good; this is what is paradoxical.

The Metzler paradox will occur when Foreign's coefficient of import demand elasticity is sufficiently low (less than one). In such a case its offer curve will not be *normal*; it will be negatively sloped at the relevant interval where it intersects the Home offer curve. The negative slope of Foreign's offer curve indicates that Foreign is willing to supply decreasing quantities of its exports in exchange for increasing quantities of imports. This situation is depicted in Figure 8.13. Point E represents the free trade equilibrium at which Home's offer curve OO and Foreign's offer curve OO^* intersect. The tariff imposed by Home shifts its offer curve to OO^t and the new equilibrium is at point M. From Figure 8.12 we can read the tariff rate in terms of the imported cloth as the ratio $MG/C_M M$. With a tariff we normally expect a large country to be able to obtain a larger quantity of imports for the same quantity of exports than without tariffs. In other words we expect its terms of trade to improve. This in fact happens in our example since new terms of trade are $p^t > p^E$. Therefore these new terms of trade represent an improvement for Home's exportable good's prices. What about a degree of protection extended to the import-competing sector? To identify the impact a tariff has on protection we must look at how the tariff influences domestic relative prices. In this case we must add the absolute value of the unit tariff to the terms of trade. With reference to point M, the total amount of tariffs is MG. To obtain OC_M of cloth imports consumers must pay OF_G in terms of the exported good. Thus the domestic relative price is $F_G G/OF_G$, that is the slope of line OG. The domestic relative price p_F/p_C has increased. In fact it has increased by so much that the post-tariff relative price for cloth is lower now than under free trade. This can be seen from the fact that the slope of the ray OG,

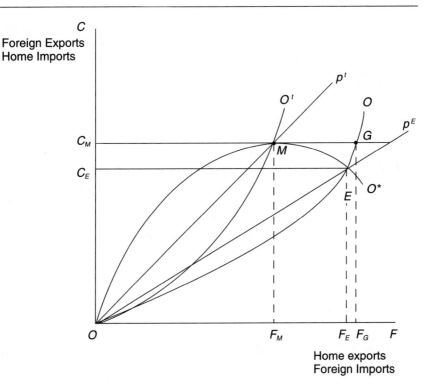

Figure 8.13 *The Metzler paradox*

although less steep than the slope of ray *OM*, is still steeper than the ray *OE*. Thus the cloth sector is actually harmed by a tariff on imported cloth. On the other hand, food sector which enjoys an improvement of terms of trade also experiences an increase in production.

We can stipulate more rigorously conditions under which the Metzler paradox will occur by analysing formally an impact of tariffs on domestic and world prices. To identify the change in world prices, or terms of trade, we must examine the effect of a tariff on the import demand in both countries. We begin again by stating the world equilibrium condition:

$$p^* M = M^* \tag{A8.1}$$

Differentiating this condition we have:

$$\hat{P}^* + \hat{M} = \hat{M}^* \tag{A8.2}$$

From there the change in the foreign imports can be given as:

$$\hat{M}^* = \varepsilon^* \hat{P}^* \tag{A8.3}$$

where ε^* is the coefficient of the elasticity of foreign's import demand along its offer curve. The expression for the change in Home's imports, $\hat{M}$, is less simple to obtain because the tariff increase shifts Home's offer curve in addition to the change that can be observed along the offer curve itself. Home's import are determined by the terms of trade, $p*$, and domestic tariff, t:

$$M = M(p^*, t) \tag{A8.3a}$$

Differentiating and decomposing for the change we have:

$$\hat{M} = -\varepsilon \hat{p}^* + [(\partial M/\partial t)/M]dt \tag{A8.4}$$

where $(\partial M/\partial t)/M$ measures the shift of the offer curve due to its tariff but at the given terms of trade. If we denote this shift as β we have:

$$\hat{M} = -\varepsilon \hat{p}^* + \beta dt \tag{A8.5}$$

Substituting the expressions for $\hat{M}^*$ and $\hat{M}$ into (A8.2) we have:

$$\hat{p}^* = [1/(\varepsilon + \varepsilon^* - 1)]\beta dt \tag{A8.6}$$

This is the effect of Home's tariff on the terms of trade. Note that denominator in the term on the right-hand side is in fact the condition for the stability of the world market. This condition is known as the Marshall–Lerner condition (derived in Chapter 2) which requires that the sum of Home's and Foreign's import-demand elasticities be greater than one. We can simplify (A8.6) by denoting $(\varepsilon + \varepsilon^* - 1) = \Delta$:

$$\hat{p}^* = (1/\Delta)\beta dt \tag{A8.7}$$

The effect of a tariff on domestic prices is simple to obtain from the link between domestic and world prices already used:

$$p = (1 + t)p^*$$

Then

$$\hat{p} = \hat{p}^* + dt \tag{A8.8}$$

or by using (A8.7)

$$\hat{p} = (1/\Delta)(\Delta + \beta)dt \tag{A8.9}$$

From the Marshall–Lerner condition we know that Δ is positive. The sign of β is negative because the increase in tariffs reduces import demand at the given terms of trade. We can prove that by utilising our expression for the elasticity of import demand which was expressed as the sum of the demand substitution elasticity, d, the supply substitution elasticity s, and the marginal propensity to import, or the income effect, m. Thus:

$$\varepsilon = d + s + m \tag{A8.10}$$

If the terms of trade are kept constant there are no changes in real income so that m vanishes from the above equation. Consequently we have

$$\beta = -(d + s) \tag{A8.11}$$

If we use this expression and substitute it in the one for the change in domestic price we obtain:

$$\hat{P} = (1/\Delta)(\varepsilon + \varepsilon^* - 1 - d - s)dt \tag{A8.12}$$

Given the decomposition for ε we have:

$$\hat{P} = (1/\Delta)(\varepsilon^* + m - 1)dt \tag{A8.13}$$

If ε^* is less than $(1 - m)$ we must have the Metzler paradox. The reason is that the foreign import demand elasticity is less than the domestic marginal propensity to spend on the same good (domestic exports) and the price of imports falls in domestic market with tariffs.

The Lerner paradox occurs when the terms of trade of a large country imposing the tariff do in fact worsen. This is contrary to our assumption employed so far about the tariff improving the large country's terms of trade. This case will occur when Home's offer curve is not normally shaped at the relevant region but is positively sloped so that we speak about an inelastic Home offer curve. This case is illustrated in Figure 8.14. Point E represents the free trade equilibrium. Consider the tariff that at constant terms of trade raises domestic prices. For the Lerner paradox to occur it is necessary that a tariff creates an excess demand for imported cloth at constant terms of trade. Geometrically it means that post-tariff equilibrium for Home must be to the right of point E along the constant terms of trade line p_E. Because of that, as shown in Figure 8.14, the new equilibrium terms of trade p^t will worsen for Home. This will always happen when the domestic demand for imports is relatively inelastic. In Lerner's case the domestic demand for imports includes both consumers' demand and government demand as the government is assumed to be spending the whole amount of tariff revenue on the imported good.

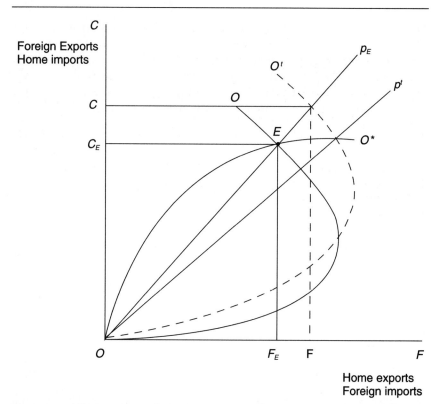

Figure 8.14 *The Lerner paradox*

Both the Metzler and the Lerner paradoxes are similar in that that both imply a stronger income-redistribution effect than a substitution effect. The income redistribution effect arises from the transfer of income from consumers to the government in the form of tariff revenue. Consequently, consumers decrease consumption while the government increases its consumption. If government's marginal propensity to consume imports is greater than that of consumers, which is the necessary condition for the Lerner paradox, this income redistribution will increase demand for imports. This increase then completely offsets the decrease in demand for imports that was the result of the substitution effect. This is in contrast to the so-called 'normal' cases where the substitution effect offsets the income-redistributional effect.

■ *Chapter 9* ■

Economic Analysis of Non-Tariff Barriers

■ *9.1* Introduction

As opposed to a tariff which is a tax imposed on imports, non-tariff barriers (NTBs) are non-tax measures imposed by a domestic government to discriminate against foreign producers and in favour of domestic ones. While tariffs generate revenues, non-tariff barriers can be seen as generating additional costs. The menu of instruments that can be used as non-tariff barriers to international trade is very large.[1] Laird and Yeats (1990, Appendix 4) provide a detailed glossary of non-tariff measures. Table 9.1 follows their exposition. From that list, which is in no way complete, the diversity of non-tariff instruments is immediately apparent. Among the other various economic tools used by governments on an everyday basis we could probably find many more that influence trade in some indirect way, and thus can be classified as non-tariff measures. For this reason it is not possible to produce reliable statistics on the incidence of non-tariff barriers. Estimates made by UNCTAD indicate that for 22 developed countries (DCs) in 1990 non-tariff measures affected 19 per cent of all non-fuel imports (Kelly and McGuirk, 1992, Table 4). This group of countries increased its reliance on non-tariff measures during the 1980s, particularly in the so-called trade-sensitive sectors such as iron and steel, motor vehicles, textile and clothing, footwear, and food items. Out of 20 developed countries, New Zealand, and to much lesser extent Canada, are the only two countries which significantly have reduced their usage of non-tariff barriers since the mid-1980s (Kelly and McGuirk, 1992, Table A8). Data on the extent of non-tariff measures in developing countries is almost non-existent. Greenaway and Milner (1993, Table 2.4) provide summary data of the type and characteristics of trade and exchange rate regimes for a sample of developing countries. It seems that in developing countries the practice of relying on non-tariff measures has moved in the opposite direction from the developed world. As the part of liberalisation and reform processes in the 1980s many non-tariff barriers were dismantled.

It is apparent that a generalised analysis of the economic effects of non-tariff barriers is not possible. Neither is it possible, nor desirable, to discuss each and every measure separately. In this chapter we therefore analyse the effects of selected measures. We begin with the most well known and, until ten or so years ago, the most frequently used non-tariff measure: the import quota. In section 9.3 we discuss the modern equivalent of import quotas, voluntary export restraints. Section 9.4 discusses both the practice of dumping and export subsidies and the effectiveness of anti-dumping and countervailing duties. Section 9.5 turns to a relatively new issue in trade, the use of environmental standards in restricting trade. We also look at the possibility of using trade barriers to protect the environment. Section 9.6 contains a brief discussion on some other residual non-tariff measures such as government procurement policies, administrative regulations, or labour and social standards.

Table 9.1   *Non-tariff barriers for international trade*

Major categories are:

- *Quasi-non-tariff measures*: tariff quotas, seasonal tariffs, increased tariffs due to retaliation or safeguard actions, etc.
- *Quantitative trade restrictions*: import and export quotas, voluntary export restraints (VERs), voluntary import expansions (VIEs), orderly marketing arrangements (OMAs), Multifibre arrangement (MFA), etc.
- *Price–cost trade measures*: variable import levies, production or export subsidies, tax concessions on exports, advanced deposits for imports requirements, anti-dumping duties, countervailing duties, etc.
- *Standards and regulations*: technical standards, health, sanitary and safety regulations, marketing and packaging requirements, restrictions on toxic materials, local content requirements, etc.
- *Other*: government purchasing policies, arbitrary customs procedures, tied-aid programmes, competition and industrial policies, etc.

Source: Adapted from Laird and Yates (1990, Appendix 4).

■ 9.2 Import quotas

Import quotas are the best known quantitative method of restricting trade. By imposing a quota the government stipulates a maximum amount of imports of the good allowed to enter the country during some specified time period (usually one year). Beyond this limit, which can be expressed in volume or value terms, imports are prohibited.[2] Quotas are usually accompanied by a licensing system which controls the allocation of quotas among importers. The government can distribute the quotas among importers in different ways, including the 'first come–first served' basis and the sale of quotas via auctions. The economic effects of quotas differ with respect to the licensing system applied as the system used determines the distribution of the potential revenues from the quota. This is one of the differences between a quota and a tariff since with tariffs it is always the government that collects the revenue while with quotas that is only one possibility. Let us examine the effects of an import quota in the case of a small country. A partial equilibrium analysis of the effects of an import quota in a small country is illustrated in Figure 9.1. The domestic demand for a good, say cloth, is represented by the straight line D. Domestic suppliers, who produce under perfect domestic and international competition, are represented by the supply curve S. Under free trade imported cloth, which is a perfect substitute for the domestic product, is supplied at the price p^*. Total domestic consumption under this free trade equilibrium, at point E, is Oq_2; Oq_1 is supplied by domestic producers, while q_1q_2 is imported.

Suppose that an import quota expressed in terms of the volume of imports restricts imports of cloth to $q_1q_3(= AB)$. Changes in the supply of cloth occur as follows. For prices below the world price, p^*, the supply of goods until the quantity q_1 is from domestic sources. At the price $p*$ the quantity $q_1q_3(= AB)$ is given free access to the domestic market. Any quantity demanded beyond this level must be supplied by domestic producers. The post-quota supply curve thus becomes $SABS_q$. The new equilibrium point, E_q, implies a total consumption of Oq_4 at a higher price, p_q. At this price domestic supply increases to Oq_5 while imports remain limited by the quota to q_1q_3 $(= q_4q_5)$. The same price and quantity effects can of course be obtained by imposing an *equivalent tariff*. This is the tariff rate which reduces imports to the same level as they occur under the quota. In our example the tariff rate which achieves this is $t = p_q - p^*$. This differential between the post-quota domestic price and the world price is also known as an *implicit* tariff for the quota. When the implicit tariff and the explicit tariff rates are identical, there is a full equivalence between a tariff and a quota (Bhagwati, 1965).

The welfare effects of a quota can be identified in a same manner used as in the analysis of the welfare effects of a tariff. The total loss of consumer

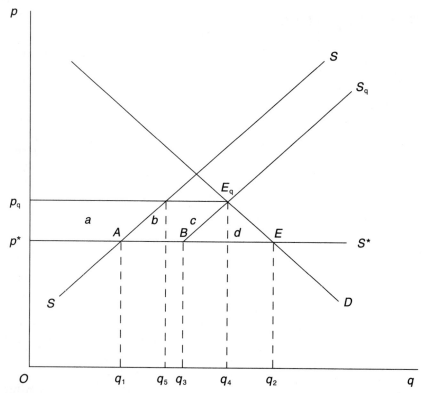

Figure 9.1   *Import quota in a small country*

surplus is the sum of the areas $a + b + c + d$, as it would be in the case of an equivalent tariff. Area a again represents the transfer of income from consumers to domestic producers; it is a source of gains for producers. The rectangular area c, which in the case of a tariff is revenue collected, is now in fact the quota *rent* arising from the price increase caused by the quota. Who receives this rent depends on the licensing system the government uses to allocate import rights. There are two main possibilities. One is that the rent stays in Home; the government itself or the importers can extract this rent, or they can both obtain a share. Another possibility is that rent is pocketed by the foreign exporters. In such a case area c represents a loss for Home. This is in addition to the efficiency loss represented by the areas b and d. These areas also represent the efficiency loss in the case of a tariff. The net welfare effects of a quota are therefore the same as in the case of a tariff except in the case where foreigners extract the rent. However in the case of quotas there are some important redistributional issues which arise from the different possible methods of allocating the quotas.

In a case of a free distribution of licences, on a 'first-come-first-served' basis, the rent goes to these importers who have the facilities to move first and to use up the quota fast (for example, storage facilities and financial ability). Such an importer is in fact subsidised for freezing the resources to build the stock of imported goods. Another way to distribute licences under quota system is to sell them by auction. Australia and New Zealand used to be the only two countries auctioning quota permits in 1980s, and this was done as part of a gradual liberalisation of their protection system which was heavily based on quotas. When import licences are auctioned, importers are expected to bid up the price of the licences to the difference between the domestic price of the imported good and the world price. This difference is equal to the profit (that is, extra profit or rent) they would make if they could import under the quota regime. Perfect competition among importers would therefore transfer the full amount of quota rents to the government (thus equalising the revenue effect of quota to one of the equivalent tariff). The government is able to capture the whole rent also if it decides to sell the whole quota to only one bidder who is paying the highest price. In such a case, the government will create a monopoly. But it may retain the whole quota rent given the assumption that a monopolist-to-be is willing to pay the full difference between the world price and the quota-adjusted domestic price. In case where they are only a few bidders and the government does not want to create a monopoly, the rent will be shared between the government and the importers. Finally, if there is only a single importer existing in the market at the time of imposing a quota, this monopoly importer would be able to obtain the import licences with a minimal bid and government would get only a small portion of the quota rents.

There are other possible methods of allocating licences among importers. Allocation via an administrative body based, for example on historical import share or on productive capacity (for intermediate products) may prevent the creation of monopolies. However this would occur at the expense of passing the rent to the importers. Moreover such an administrative allocation may foster additional inefficiencies through investment in excess capacity, rent-seeking behaviour, and lobbying. Importers may be willing to spend up to the whole amount of the rent (area c) on lobbying for import rights. This reflects a degree of waste of resources. It also opens the way for political corruption and bribery. We will return to issues of rent-seeking and directly unproductive activities in Chapter 12, where we discuss the political economy of trade policy.

Finally the rent, either in full or in part, may be captured by foreign suppliers. The extent of the rent captured would depend on their willingness and ability to collude to raise the export price of the good to the level p_q. The best example of how foreigners can capture the quota rent is in the case when the domestic government bargains for voluntary export restraints; this is discussed in the next section.

From the above it is apparent that the net welfare effect of a quota as compared to a tariff depends on who in fact secures the rent. If it is captured by the domestic government or by importers, the net welfare loss of a quota corresponds exactly to that of a tariff and is equal to the areas $b + d$ in Figure 9.1. However if the rent is captured by foreigners, the net loss to Home from the quota increases to the area $b + d + c$. The world's welfare is reduced in all cases by the area $b + d$, because the rent c is purely a transfer of income between countries.

Although the net welfare loss due to a quota may not be greater than under a tariff, we must not forget that there are additional features of a quota which make it more damaging than tariffs. Three of these features are particularly important sources of additional inefficiencies.

Quotas are rigid

Whatever may happen to the supply or demand conditions in either the domestic or the foreign market, the amount of imports allowed for a specified period of time is fixed.[3] This rigidity typically results in additional price and rent increases. In the case of a tariff the price increase would not occur. There are different scenarios which help in illustrating this point. For example if the domestic demand for cloth rises, under a tariff when foreign supply is perfectly elastic this will simply result in more imports at the same tariff-inclusive price.[4] With an import quota a larger domestic demand for cloth must be satisfied by domestic supply. This is upward sloping, thus implying a higher price as well as increased rent.

A similar result is obtained when there is a change in domestic supply. If domestic costs are increased, for example due to higher wages, domestic supply contracts, pulling the supply curve to the left and leaving a larger quantity of unsatisfied demand at the specified price. Under a tariff this will simply induce more imports, while with a quota there will be both price and rent increases.

Another potential source of change is in the conditions underlying foreign supply. If the price of foreign cloth declines, for example due to technological progress, with a tariff the domestic tariff-inclusive price will also decline. With a quota the price cannot fall while the rent increases even further. The domestic economy therefore does not benefit from the decline in world prices. This also gives rise to the argument that the rigidity of quotas reduces the incentives for domestic suppliers to innovate; they are not forced to be price competitive.

Quotas create or enhance any monopoly power which already exists

To see that this statement is true it is best to examine it diagrammatically. Figure 9.2(a) illustrates the position of a domestic firm which would be a monopoly in the absence of international trade. The demand for cloth is represented by D. Foreign supply is perfectly elastic and corresponds to the world price p^*. The marginal costs of this firm are increasing and are represented by MC. As long as there is free trade, consumers can buy unlimited quantities of cloth at the price p^* and the single firm cannot exercise any of its potential market power. With tariff protection, as seen on p. 311, the firm has some freedom to exercise this power, depending of course on the level of tariff rates. For example if the tariff increases the domestic price to p_t, the quantity produced will still be determined as under free trade by equating marginal cost with the world (tariff-adjusted) price. The resultant quantity is q_t, which is more than the free trade output, q_f. By restricting imports the tariff has given the monopolist an opportunity to charge a higher price, although not as high as would be charged in the absence of any imports.

With an import quota, however, the firm is given a clear message to behave as a 'proper' monopolist. Look at panel (b) in Figure 9.2. Imports are restricted to the level $q_t D_t$ (the level of imports under the tariff). This means that the demand facing our firm shifts to the left. The monopolist supplies such quantities of cloth that satisfy demand now reduced by the import quota. More specifically, the new demand curve, D', has three segments: for prices higher than p^* the monopolist faces a negatively sloped segment of a new demand curve derived from the total demand *minus* the quota. For a price equal to $p*$ the monopolist faces a horizontal segment equal to the quota itself. Finally for prices below $p*$ the new demand is the same as old demand because at these prices there is no incentive for imports. Corresponding to the new demand curve there is a new marginal revenue curve, (MR') also consisting of three segments (not shown in the Figure). The monopolist can now finally apply the '$MR = MC$' rule to determine the quantity–price combination which maximises profits. In Figure 9.2(b) this combination is given by q_q and p_q. The difference between p_q and and p^* is the extent of quota rent per unit of cloth.

A closer inspection of panels (a) and (b) provides some additional insights as to the comparison of tariffs and quotas. The level of imports was equally reduced in both cases; this is where the equivalence of tariffs and quotas under monopoly ends. Under tariffs, domestic production is greater and the price lower than with a quota; with a quota the price–quantity combination is determined on the basis of market power. Conversely tariffs, unless they are excessively high, prevent such behaviour. Under a monopoly market structure in the domestic market the equivalence between tariffs and quotas breaks down. It is clear that a quota creates greater monopoly power than a tariff. Consequently the losses resulting from using quotas in this situation are larger than from using tariffs.

Let us check this conclusion by using our formula for examining the welfare effects of trade restrictions. We reproduce it here in the form as it was given by (8.6.2):

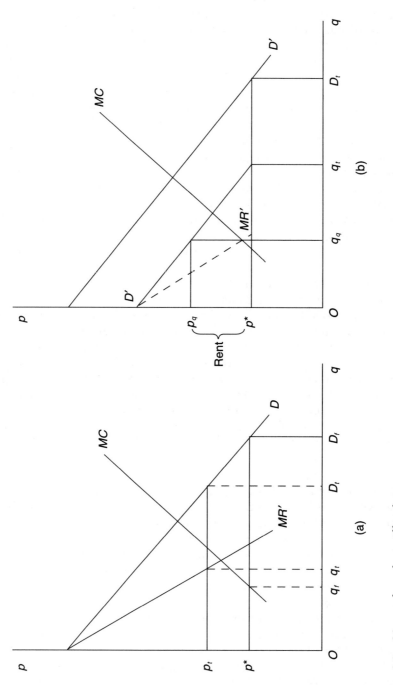

Figure 9.2 *Monopoly under tariff and quota*

$$dy = -Mdp^* + (p^b - p^*)dM + (p^b - c)dP_b \qquad (9.2.1)$$

where $t = b$ to denote any trade barrier such as tariff, quota etc. and p^b and P_b represent the post-barrier price and the production level respectively. Recall what the terms in this equation represent. The first term on the right-hand side is the terms of trade effect. Since we assume that Home is small this term in fact vanishes. The other two terms represent the effects of the trade barrier on efficiency. The first of the two terms is the volume of trade effect: national income increases with an expansion of imports when domestic prices are higher than world prices because trade restriction increases domestic prices. The second term applies only in imperfect competition: national income increases by the expansion in output of goods that are priced above marginal cost. This term represents the efficiency gains obtained through an improvement in the composition of output. This 'improvement', that is, larger production in the protected goods sector at the expense of the unprotected one, should arise from the restriction of imports (this is the so-called protective effect of a trade barrier). What, then, is the difference in income effects when a tariff or a quota is used to protect a single-firm domestic firm in the production of cloth? As mentioned above, the first term equals zero. The second term is negative because imports fall. We can apply an implicit tariff rate that will reduce imports to the exact level of the quota. The size of this term thus need not differ for a quota as compared to a tariff. The whole thing therefore reduces to the difference in the size and sign of the third effect. With a tariff this effect is zero. As we remember from pp. 311–15 with a (small) tariff a monopolist cannot exercise market power and must price at marginal cost. Thus the value of increased output is zero. However when a quota is imposed the firm is granted market power. It therefore *reduces* its production to the level where $MC = MR$. This results in price above marginal cost. A quota thus leads to a perverse protective effect where the monopolist is allowed to reduce production. This affects income negatively. Even if we allow for positive terms of trade effects a quota will have more adverse effects than a tariff. This is because a quota, compared to a tariff, reduces the degree of competition in the domestic market.

Quotas result in a non-transparent protection system

With the extensive application of quotas, and other non-tariff measures, it can become difficult to assess the actual extent of protection.

All in all it is clear that as well as the efficiency losses normally associated with protectionism some extra damages will also result from the imposition of quotas. Most economists would agree that quotas are inconsistent with the public interest. Why is it then that governments prefer quotas (and other non-tariff barriers)? First of all, the main impact of the GATT was to limit the use of tariffs. Therefore the policies left available for governments desiring to extend protection to domestic industries consist mainly of non-tariff measures. It is true that import quotas are used less and less in both developed and developing countries. However the range of other non-tariff measures is so wide that there are still extensive and increasing protectionist actions.

Quotas do provide certainty in terms of restricting imports. This is preferred by both governments and protection-seekers over the relative uncertainty of tariffs. Quotas also greatly advantage producers at the expense of consumers. Because of this by using quotas government can increase a degree of political discretion in granting of protection. In most cases quotas would have effects, particularly in terms of import reductions, much faster than tariffs. This is an important feature if an economy is in balance of payments difficulties and has to reduce imports. It is not therefore surprising that many governments in the developing countries were particularly inclined to use quotas to regulate trade flows.

The GATT rules were drafted in such a way so as to minimise the use of quotas. Article XI prohibits quotas altogether. So-called 'emergency quotas' designed explicitly for balance of payments reasons are allowed by Article XII, but they have to be internationally monitored. However when governments allow foreign suppliers to regulate the quota, there is nothing in the GATT rules to forbid it. This is one of the reasons that some governments resort to this type of protection known as voluntary export restraints (VERs). We discuss this instrument next.

■ 9.3 Voluntary export restraints

A voluntary export restraint (VER) is basically a quota administered by the exporting country government, or exporters themselves. It is typically introduced 'voluntarily' by the exporting country after the importing country threatens it with the imposition of increasingly restrictive direct import controls. In negotiating VERs industries in both countries can also be directly involved.[5]

VERs were invented by the USA in 1935–6 when US and Japanese producers negotiated limits on Japan's textile exports to the USA (see Box 9.1). VERs were almost unused in the post-war period until the early 1970s when the USA sparked the process, first by negotiating VERs with Japan in steel and then, in 1980, VERs in autos, also with Japan. The popularity of VERs increased in the 1980s. The EU has negotiated VERs with quite a few countries in a variety of sectors, including steel, electronics, autos and agricultural products. VERs are one of the major forms of protectionism, presently affecting about 15 per cent of world trade (Kelly and McGuirk, 1992).

In the partial equilibrium framework we have been using with perfect competition, the effects of VERs on domestic prices, production and imports are equivalent to those of tariffs or import quotas. The only difference is in the appropriation of the rents, which in the case of VERs goes to the foreigners. Figure 9.3 (a) illustrates the effects of VERs on the importing country, while 9.3(b) isolates the effects on exporters. For the importing country effects of the VERs are obvious. The domestic demand curve does not shift, while supply is adjusted for the VER. The new equilibrium, E_{VER}, occurs at the higher price, p_{VER}, and with a reduced domestic consumption of cloth. The supply curve with a VER consists of three segments. For prices below p_{VER}, which is the price charged by the foreign exporters, the supply of cloth comes from domestic sources. At the price level p_{VER} the total supply comes from two sources: the amount OQ_2 is domestically supplied while Q_2Q_3 is the voluntarily agreed limit on imports. If the price moved above p_{VER} the additional supply would therefore have to come from domestic sources. The total loss of consumer surplus is equal to the total loss resulting from an equivalent tariff or import quota, that is, the area $a + b + c + d$. Area a is the transfer from consumers to domestic producers. The areas b and d are conventional efficiency losses. Area c is the transfer from consumers to foreign producers and in this case constitutes one of the categories of the net welfare loss. Net welfare loss is thus equal to $b + c + d$. This transfer from consumers to foreign producers arises via an improvement in Foreign's terms of trade. We can identify these effects also by applying our formula for income changes. In the case of perfect competition the third term is not relevant. Also the second term does not apply because the price differential $(p_{VER} - p^*)$ accrues to Foreign. The remaining term on the right-hand side is the terms of trade effect. This is negative from Home's point of view. Its terms of trade worsen, reducing Home's income. Conversely if VERs were

---

Box 9.1   *The most famous VER – the multifibre arrangement*

The Multi Fibre Agreement (MFA) was first negotiated in 1974,[6] applying to fibres made from cotton, wool and synthetics, and covering the export of these products from both developing countries and Japan. The MFA is contrary to GATT principles but has been negotiated under its auspices and is partly administered by it. So far the MFA has been renegotiated and extended four times, the last time in December 1993 when it was extended for only one year in view of the fact that this sector was going to be brought back to the GATT on the basis of strengthened rules and disciplines under the Uruguay Round agreement on textiles and clothing. The MFA as a separate agreement should be phased out by 2005.

The latest version of the MFA is a complex set of clauses and annexes. It encompasses about 3000 bilateral quotas covering various countries and products within the arrangement. These typically freeze market shares, thus depressing the level of trade in these products as the unused quotas are not transferable between countries. The worst affected are the small and potential suppliers in exporting countries, because the agreement creates uncertainties deterring them from expanding or entering the industry, and consumers in the importing countries who end up paying almost twice as much for clothing and other fibre-based products.

Notwithstanding all this, the MFA operates on the basis of quota trade restrictions and quota creates rents. Some commentators claim that the rents generated by MFA may have compensated, at least to some extent, the developing countries for the limited access to markets for textile and clothing of developed countries. Whalley (1994) cites several studies completed in the 1980s and 1990s and estimating the amount of rents which resulted from trade restrictions in textile and clothing. The estimates range from 16.8 per cent level of qouta premium on clothing products (USITC, 1993) up to 300 per cent (Trela and Whalley, 1990). However, these rent transfers were not sufficient to make up for overall cost arising from substantial economic inefficiency caused by the MFA. Therefore it is generally expected that the abolition of the MFA must result in a massive welfare gain for developing countries. Trela and Whalley (1990) show that large numbers of developing countries gain from elimination of MFA restrictions, although the gains are not distributed too evenly. Table 9.2 shows the distribution of gains and losses from the abolishment of the MFA.

Table 9.2   ***Welfare impact of abolishing the MFA by 2005 (constant 1992 $ US bns)***

Region/country	Amount
North America	29.3
EU	27.6
Japan	1.1
NIEs	−6.2
ASEAN	4.6
China	5.4
South Asia	3.0
Sub-Saharan Africa	−0.7
Latin America	−3.7
Rest of world	−10.3

Source: Hertel *et al. (1995),* as cited in the World Bank (1995, p. 32).

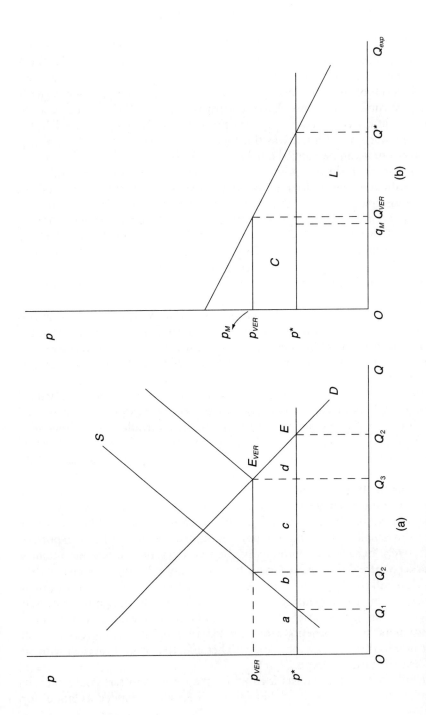

Figure 9.3   *VERs under perfect competition*

to decline, Home's income would be increased because its terms of trade would improve.

The economic effects of VERs obviously go against Home as a whole. While domestic producers benefit due to increased production (they also can get a portion of rent captured by Foreign), domestic consumers are the ones who foot the bill. Since producers are always better represented with the government, it seems that the attractiveness of VERs comes mainly from political considerations. Until the Uruguay Round, the GATT did not say much on VERs, it was thus one of the easiest methods of applying protection. It can be applied quickly on a discriminatory basis which is the most useful if the purpose is to manage import flows sectorally or regionally. Further, it does not provoke retaliation. What about the effects on exporters? From panel (b) in Figure 9.3 it is apparent that the quantity of exports to Home is reduced. Prices are increased, resulting in larger rents.[7] If this rent (area *c*) is greater than the proceeds of lost sales (*L*), gains to exporters are assured. This will always be the case if the domestic demand for cloth is relatively price inelastic. However despite the relative sizes of *c* and *L*, exporters gain, at least in the short run, from exporting to this market because of the rent involved.

The effects of VERs can be different if the form of competition in the domestic or foreign market is less than perfect. In the case of a single domestic firm in the importing country with competitive foreign exporters, the effects of VERs are similar to the effects of an import quota (see Figure 9.2). In both cases the domestic firm and foreign suppliers are permitted to maximise profits by charging a higher price, at which $MR = MC$, than they could under free or tariff-restricted trade. In addition to the efficiency losses arising from trade restrictions, the domestic economy will also suffer a deadweight loss from the monopoly. Consequently the net welfare loss for Home from negotiating a VER under a domestic monopoly is larger than with either an import quota or with tariffs. If market power is on the side of foreign suppliers, that is, if there is only a single supplier or many suppliers form a collusion in response to the VER, the actual amount of cloth exported to Home would be even smaller than the amount negotiated by the VER. If exporters effectively behave as a monopoly they will set the output for Home's market where $MR = MC$. Going back to Figure 9.3 (b), this means that imports fall to OQ_M, and the price rises to an even higher level, p_M, than in case of many competing exporters. In other words foreign firms benefit from operating as a cartel in exporting to Home at the expense of Home's consumers. Some benefits are extended to domestic producers as well because in this last case they enjoy higher effective protection then with an equivalent tariff or import quota.

Until recently economists focused on the rents exporters could capture with VERs. On the basis of these rents, VERs were branded as 'good' for exporters. Are they? To answer this question we must look at the other effects VERs may have on the exporting country. It is obvious from the outset that no general answer can be given. However it is still helpful to discuss at least some of these other effects in order to obtain a more balanced view of VERs. For example, when foreign exporters limit their exports to Home to the level of the VER they do not, at least immediately, adjust their production level. They can thus easily face a production surplus. This in general implies an increased supply to other markets and a potentially reduced price and export earnings from those markets. In addition, the exporting economy experiences general equilibrium effects related to resource allocation. Since the production of the goods under VERs will have to contract, the resources will shift to other sectors, sectors in which they are not as productive as in the restricted sector. This of course leads to efficiency losses for the exporting country which must be deducted from the rents captured when estimating the net effects on the exporting country.

Moreover, if VERs cover all suppliers, exporters can try to collude, for example by forming a cartel. A reduced degree of competition among exporters will benefit higher-cost producers by permitting them to stay in the market. In any exporting country reduced competition may also lead to rent-seeking behaviour, lobbying and wastage of resources (to be discussed in greater detail in Chapter 12). It is also likely that VERs will slow down the growth of exports, at least until other markets are found. Production may even move to the importing country. In addition, slower growth and a smaller scale of exports will reduce the benefits which might have resulted from economies of scale and learning by doing. All in all, the net effects of VERs in an exporting country may not be positive. De Melo and Winters (1993) show how in the case when an exporter under a VERs is a large industry, VERs can result in overall economic losses.

From the importing country's perspective, VERs are implemented to protect specific sectors. See Box 9.2 for a discussion on yet another type of protectionist device. The costs of this action will probably be higher than would occur if protection was granted through some other means. In addition to the conventional welfare losses from trade restrictions, in this case it is likely that the importing country's balance of payments will suffer. This is not only because imports coming from suppliers under VERs will be more expensive, but also because additional imports will be supplied by high-cost suppliers. Furthermore, if VERs are stated in terms of volume, profit-seeking exporters will have an incentive to upgrade their exports in terms of quality and charge an even higher price.

The net welfare effects for the world are the same as in the case of an import quota since the rent represents the inter-country transfer of income. If countries could use direct transfers, the efficiency loss equal to areas $b + d$ in Figure 9.3 could have been eliminated.

Box 9.2   *Voluntary import expansions (VIEs)*

In contrast to VERs, voluntary import expansions, or VIEs, refer to policies, most often quantitative targets set by governments, whereby the imports of specific goods by specific countries are increased.[8] These agreements are also bilateral and discriminatory with the objective being to ease protectionist pressures in export markets. The popularity of VIEs is rapidly increasing, in particular between the USA and successful Asian exporters such as Japan, Korea or Taiwan which have the reputation of using non-transparent and non-border barriers to impede market access to foreign producers. As a tool of breaking down those barriers, VIEs themselves incur high costs in terms of reduced economic efficiency. First, even though VIEs are supposed to increase competition in a market, because they are administered by government they also require (similar to VERs) coordination of (large) firms. This could lead to cartels and an increase in the price of the imported products (Irwin, 1994). Moreover, often VIEs have bilateral character, so the opening of the importing country's market may be only for the producers of the country pressing for VIEs, while producers from the third countries could find their entry being made even more difficult. Thus the effects on third countries is potentially welfare reducing. Furthermore, as the VIEs are instruments of 'export protectionism' (they promote interests of otherwise uncompetitive export producers in the VIEs-seeking countries), by permitting an expansion of those activities they could result in a welfare loss for those economies (Bhagwati, 1988, pp. 82–4). This is particularly so if VIEs become a permanent feature of export promotion policies and if they spread across industries.

Dinopoulos and Kreinin (1990) and Bhagwati, (1988) provide examples of VIEs' impact. Dinopoulos and Kreinin in their study of economic effects of VIEs mention the agreements which committed Japan to increase its imports of semi-conductors, beef, coal, paper and paperboard from the USA. Since this instrument's primary goal is to increase a country's exports its effects are compared with an equivalent export subsidy; the difference is in the administration and consequently in securing the rent. In the case when VIEs is 'voluntarily' employed by the Japanese government, the US captures the rent. However, when the US grants an export subsidy it is Japan which pockets the rent. The two countries could benefit both when Japan employs the VIEs only if the VIE is designed to offset an initial trade restriction in Japan. However, in such case greater benefits will be obtained by direct removal of such import restrictions. In his book, Bhagwati provides examples of discriminatory impact of VIEs (pp. 83–4). For example, the pressure by the USA for the opening of Japan's beef market had an adverse effect of Australia's export to Japan, while the similar pressure applied for opening of Korea's insurance market and import of agricultural products mean a switch from domestic and third country producers to the USA exporters. Instead VIEs, the policy towards closed markets should consist of liberalising trade policy, improving competition policy, enforcement of competition-policy rules, and liberalising and deregulating government procurement practices.

9.4 Dumping, anti-dumping, export subsidies and countervailing duties

Although anti-dumping and countervailing duties belong to the area of rules and disciplines in the GATT (WTO), they are included in this chapter on non-tariff barriers because of the frequent abuse of these measures as non-tariff barriers.

Under the multilateral trade rules, anti-dumping and countervailing duties can be imposed by country members to protect their domestic producers from injury resulting from the dumping of goods by foreign producers or to offset trade-distorting subsidies set by trade partners. The legitimacy of these measures is based on the defence of competition and fair trade. However, in most cases, countries have used anti-dumping and countervailing duties to implement protectionist policies and to the detriment of competition (by protecting a privileged class of competitors, i.e. domestic import-competing firms).

☐ *Dumping and anti-dumping duties*

Dumping is described as selling for less abroad than in a domestic market. Multilateral trade rules include some alternative definitions for cases where domestic market prices do not exist.[9] Price differentials between domestic and foreign markets do not necessarily imply dumping as price discrimination is a profit-maximising strategy implemented by firms operating in segmented markets. Notwithstanding that, the legal definition of dumping is quite elastic and as Finger (1992, p. 122) stated, its operational definition is that 'dumping is whatever you can get the government to act against under the antidumping law'.

Under the multilateral trade rules, *anti-dumping duties* can be used in case dumping is causing, or threatening to cause, material injury to an import-competing industry. The cases of harmful dumping include predatory dumping and intermittent or sporadic dumping. *Predatory dumping* occurs when foreign suppliers set the prices below cost with the objective of driving domestic producers out of business. Once domestic firms are out of business, prices are set at monopoly levels. In practice this type of dumping almost never occurs because the preconditions for predatory dumping to be successful are hard to meet: the foreign producer must have a stable monopolistic position in the world market and domestic firms must face substantial re-entry barriers.

Intermittent or *sporadic dumping* is the disposal of occasional surpluses by exporting them at exceptionally low prices (but not necessarily below cost). The firm that decides to sell at such low prices in foreign markets has no plans to eliminate competition; its production is probably affected by seasonal or other cycles and the firm tries to cover as much of its predetermined costs as possible. Depending on how flexible domestic producers are (and the domestic factor markets as well), some injury might result from sporadic dumping. The question remains, however, about the best policy reaction to it.

There is a third type of dumping which should not cause any concern. It is called *persistent dumping* and it occurs when a producer practices price discrimination between his own and foreign markets with an objective of maximising profits. Thus this type of dumping continues on a long-term basis and does not (under *ceteris paribus* conditions) involve raising prices by a foreign supplier at some later stage. As the reader may recall this type of profit-maximising pricing strategy requires at least three conditions to be met: (1) markets must be separated without the possibility for arbitrage, (2) price elasticity of demand in these markets must be different so that demand is considerably less elastic in domestic *vis-à-vis* foreign markets, and (3) industry must be imperfectly competitive so that firms can set the prices. Figure 9.4 illustrates the case of dumping as the profit-maximising long-term behaviour by a monopolistic producer. In Figure 9.4 we assume that a monopolistic firm produces only in Home but sells in both its domestic market and the export market of Foreign. Demand in its domestic market is given by curve D, the associated marginal revenue curve by MR and the non-constant marginal costs by upward sloping curve MC.[10] Demand in the export market (in Foreign) is infinitely elastic and illustrated by curve D^*. Thus it is coinciding with the marginal revenue MR^* and p^*. In other words, the firm can sell any quantities in Foreign at the price p^*. Given this, firm maximises profits by producing quantity Q_t where MC is equal to marginal revenue in both markets, $MC = MR$ and $MC = MR^*(= p^*)$. It will sell Q' in its domestic market at price p' and the difference $Q_t - Q'$ will be exported to Foreign. Since the domestic price is higher than the export price, the export of this firm is qualified as dumping. Even if the export demand were not infinitely elastic, dumping would occur whenever there was a sufficient difference in price elasticities in demand in the segmented markets, and the price charged would always be higher in the market with less elastic demand. This results from the basic pricing formula $MC = MR$, that is, from the so-called 'inverse elasticity rule':

$$MC = MR = p(1 + (1/\varepsilon))$$
$$(p - MC)/p = -(1/\varepsilon)$$

where ε is the price elasticity of demand. The above relationship says that the difference between price and marginal costs will increase as the demand curve facing the producer becomes less elastic.[11] Since we assume the same marginal costs in both markets, the profit-maximising pricing

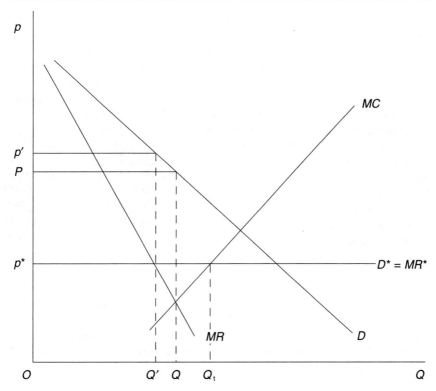

Figure 9.4 *Persistent dumping by Home's producer*

strategy will require the price in the less elastic market to be higher. Following the specific situation in which the price elasticity of demand in Foreign is infinite we may write:

$$p(1 + (1/\varepsilon)) = p^*$$
$$p/p^* = 1/(1 + (1/\varepsilon))$$

For any $\varepsilon < -1$, we have $p > p^*$, that is, price discrimination or, as it is more usually called, dumping.

The consequence of 'dumping' by a monopolistic producer from Home is that consumers in Foreign can obtain this good at a lower price than Home's own consumers (note that consumers in Home have to pay higher price for this product when the firm is engaged in exportation and thus in price discrimination than when there is no trade). The welfare gain to Foreign resulting from consumers being offered a lower price than in no-discrimination case is obvious from Figure 9.4. What cannot be directly shown is the potential or real loss of domestic producers in Foreign; their marginal costs might be higher than the costs of the export supplier's from

Home so that, under free trade, domestic production shrinks and the domestic producer might claim an injury. This is a situation which (in practice) usually calls for an introduction of anti-dumping duties.

An anti-dumping duty is an *ad valorem* tariff imposed specifically on dumped imports. Figure 9.5 illustrates what happens in Foreign's market when this duty is introduced. The demand curve for imports, D^M and the corresponding marginal revenue curve, MR^M are shifted down by the amount of duty, t to the positions indicated by D^M_t and MR^M_t. With unchanged conditions in the exporters's domestic market, he or she now maximises profits by producing a smaller total quantity, and by exporting less of this output, only OQ_t, at the lower price p^t_e. The welfare effects in Foreign that can be identified in Figure 9.5 consist of consumer losses and government gains. Consumers lose area p^tBCp_e. A portion of this loss is captured by the government as part of the tariff revenue collected (p^tBDp_e), and the rest represents the deadweight loss (triangle BCD). The total revenue collected by the government contains this portion of the revenue redistributed from domestic consumers (this is thus internal income redistribution) and the transfer from the foreign producer whose price drops (area $p_eDAp^t_e$ is thus an international redistribution). However the net effect for Foreign is the difference between the areas of the deadweight loss and this international transfer. In this particular case it seems that Foreign benefits from imposing an anti-dumping duty. World welfare is certainly reduced since a monopolist is pushed into producing less. What is not shown in Figure 9.5, however, is the reaction of the domestic producers in Foreign to the introduction of anti-dumping duties. For them this is an opportunity to raise price, thus further redistributing the income and causing some misallocation of resources (see Box 9.3, p. 344).

It is obvious that anti-dumping duties in the case of persistent dumping do more damage than good. Moreover the cases of predatory and sporadic dumping, the traditional ground on which the introduction of anti-dumping duties was defended, can be considered negligible. However advocates of anti-dumping duties have come up with other reasons why anti-dumping should be justified. Three rationales are suggested by advocates of anti-dumping (Leidy, 1995): (1) as a means to help avoid the costs of temporary structural adjustments induced by unsustainably low prices, that is, in the case of transitory dumping; (2) to help to discourage maintenance of the various protectionist policies that segment the markets and thus make dumping possible; (3) as a safety valve to vent protectionist opposition and so take further steps toward greater multilateral trade liberalisation.

All of these rationales have been contested by the opponents of anti-dumping policies. In case of transitory dumping, there are at least two reasons why anti-dumping should not be used. The first reason refers to

the ability of governments to differentiate between temporary and permanent price changes. If governments could do it, private businesses could too
and therefore they would typically not react on those transitory price
movements. The second reason refers to the mis-tailoring of anti-dumping.
If anti-dumping is an appropriate reaction to temporary price movements,
then it should not be used on a prolonged basis as it is current practice.
Leidy (1995) talks about the widespread practice where anti-dumping
duties are used for a decade or more even in the countries whose anti-
dumping laws include five-year sunset provision (therefore limiting
anti-dumping duties to that period). For example, in Canada among
the anti-dumping duties in force on 30 June 1993, 11 of 74 cases had
originated earlier than 1984. In the USA 61 of 268 duties in force in mid-
1993 had original order dates prior to 1984, with a number of measures
dating back to the 1960s. In the EU 12 out of 16 measures reviewed in 1990
and 1992 were renewed.

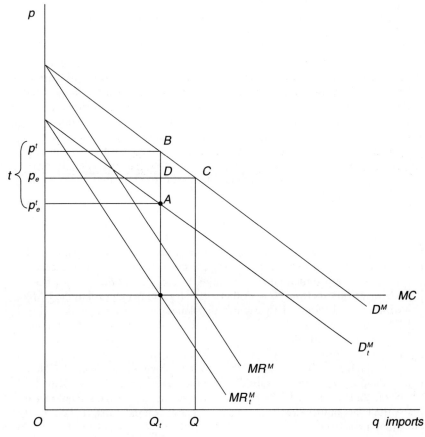

Figure 9.5   *Anti-dumping duty*

Box 9.3   *Are Americans paying more for their kiwifruit?*

'Americans will probably have to pay higher prices for all kiwifruit until the turn of the century if New Zealand is penalised for the single low-priced shipment at the centre of a US dumping dispute' (James Bovard, *New York Times*, 10 February 1992, as quoted in *New Zealand Herald*, 11 February 1992).

This anti-dumping case originated from a late 1990 shipment of kiwifruit diverted to the United States after the Japanese importer changed its mind about buying it. The Californian growers of kiwifruit (The California Kiwifruit Commission) filed an anti-dumping petition before the US Commerce Department and later before the International Trade Commission (ITC) claiming that this shipment sale of kiwifruit at 'give-away prices' caused an injury to Californian growers. In an investigation of the case the Japanese market was used to determine 'the normal value' for kiwifruit because the New Zealand market was considered too small to be used to determine the fair price.[12] Consequently in May 1992 Americans imposed a punitive 98.6 per cent anti-dumping duty on imports of kiwifruit from New Zealand. Before anti-dumping duties, New Zealand was holding 50 per cent of the American kiwifruit market and the USA was New Zealand's third-largest market accounting for 8 per cent of kiwifruit exports. Prices which New Zealand growers were forced to charge after anti-dumping ruling were so much higher relative to competitors' prices (i.e. Chilean and Californian producers) that it was expected that the New Zealand share would drop markedly. Additional losses for New Zealand's growers occurred because the Kiwifruit Marketing Board (KMB) had to divert part of the exports to the European market, thus dropping the price there. Some calculations estimated the losses to be around NZ$500 mn over the five year period 1991–6.

What about welfare effects on the US side? US consumers did certainly not gain by being forced to pay more for New Zealand kiwifruit.[13] With respect to the effects on US producers they both gained and lost. They gained in the sense that they stopped or slowed down an expansion of New Zealand exports. Their losses arose from the fact that New Zealanders also stopped their effort to enlarge the total US market for kiwifruit. Kiwifruit exports from New Zealand have been under control of the KMB which was determined to expand the American kiwifruit market. The KMB was spending a lot of money on advertising until the anti-dumping duties were levied. Given the size of the market, it might have been wiser for the Californian growers to snatch a part of the extra sale generated by a marketing campaign rather than by punishing them. Since the New Zealand growers are not subsidised by the government, their strategy did not include prolonged sales at a loss. Maybe the Californians should have waited for another kiwifruit season in New Zealand to start their anti-dumping action?

As far as the second rationale is concerned, it is hard to see how a protective measure such as anti-dumping duties can discourage maintenance of other protective measures. First of all markets are segmented not only because of trade barriers but also because of other barriers to the flow of goods and services in a form of limited spread of information, speed of transport, regulatory differences, distribution system differences, partial pass-through of exchange rates and similar. Secondly, anti-dumping policy (as any other barrier) facilitates collusive market behaviour. Thus rather than opening the market for other firms, the duties may help the firm(s) accused of dumping to consolidate market power in both domestic and foreign markets and to successfully keep them separated.

While there is a real need for a 'safety valve' to vent protectionist demand in almost all countries, it is a difficult matter to determine which is the lowest cost method of providing one. As a matter of fact, GATT's Article XIX with safeguard provisions is doing nothing else but providing a kind of safety valve. Therefore, there is no need to further the use of anti-dumping duties for this purpose, particularly not as they are implemented currently. It seems that the first best policy of dealing with dumping (persistent or otherwise) is within the framework of a competition policy in which the most important criterion should be the extent of (actual or threatened) injury to competition. Steps toward such a solution were made at the level of two regional integrations. Under the Closer Economic Relations between Australia and New Zealand the competition law was extended to cover trans-Tasman dumping disputes. A similar solution was found in the agreement on the European Economic Area (EEA) between the members of the EU and the EFTA.

☐ *Export subsidies and countervailing duties*

Export subsidies are direct or indirect payments from government to domestic producers–exporters enabling them to sell their goods in export markets at a lower price than in the domestic market. It is presumed that with lower prices exporters would be able to conquer a larger share of the world market. Because they obstruct fair competition, export subsidies are strictly forbidden under the multilateral trading rules set by the GATT/ WTO, except in the case of agricultural goods. Many countries, however, reach for direct and even more frequently indirect export subsidies in hope of gaining a larger share of world markets. Before showing the real effects of export subsidies, let us just mention few examples of the indirect export subsidies that are frequently used. Most often countries use differential credit conditions (in favour of exporters), insurance of certain risks paid by the government, assistance in financing of promotional activities such as trade fairs, advertising, or market research, tax concessions to export-related R&D activities, etc. Subsidising of non-traded activities (that is, subsidising production for local use only) is allowed under the GATT rules.

Figure 9.6 illustrates the effects of a simple export subsidy for a small country case. Partial equilibrium effects are shown in panel (a) while panel (b) shows general equilibrium effects.[14] Panel (a) of Figure 9.6 illustrates the market for some good, say cloth, in Home. Given domestic supply (S) and demand (D), and the world price p^*, the market clears when quantity $q_1 q_2$ is exported. Suppose the government decides to subsidise exporters of cloth in the amount of $p^* p_s$ per unit. Unless domestic consumers are willing to match the price of p_s (and clearly they do not want to do this), it pays to exporters to increase exports at the expense of supply to the domestic market. This will result in price p_s being charged for both exported and domestically sold units of cloth. The change in relative price in domestic market is illustrated in panel (b) by the flatter domestic relative price line (p_s) compared to the previous free trade relative prices (p^*). The change of relative prices in favour of cloth also causes the change in production pattern (the move from P to P_S on the PPF). This shift is normally classified as a distortion of the previously efficient allocation of resources.

Note that the effect on production is symmetrical with the effect an import tariff would have had. Effects on consumption are also symmetrical, that is the quantity of domestically consumed cloth declines. Since the price which consumers have to pay increases, it is clear that consumer surplus is reduced. It is reduced by the area $a + b + c + d$ in panel (a) of Figure 9.6. The total cost of the subsidy is an amount of export times the unit subsidy (this amounts to area $b + c + d$ in our graph). In other words government has to spend money when it engages in subsidising exports; in contrast, import tariffs earn money for the government's budget). Thus consumers are likely to lose twice in this case: once when they have to pay higher price for cloth, and then again if (when) government increases taxes to finance this export subsidy. Similar to tariffs, here also we have a deadweight loss in amount of $b + d$. This waste occurs because the cost of increasing output of the subsidised product exceeds the export revenue. As Richardson (1992) put it, the nation which grants export subsidies is shooting itself in the foot.

Under the multilateral trade rules, export subsidies as well as subsidies that are contingent upon the use of domestic over imported goods are prohibited. Any other production subsidies or supports to cover losses to a domestic industry that have at the same time detrimental effects on other countries may be ruled inconsistent with the WTO obligations. The Uruguay Round Agreement still allows for some subsidies, such as the subsidies on exports of primary products, or the ones supporting research activities or disadvantaged regions.

Similarly to the case of dumping, the country on the receiving end of the subsidised good, although getting it at lower prices, is not overly happy, at

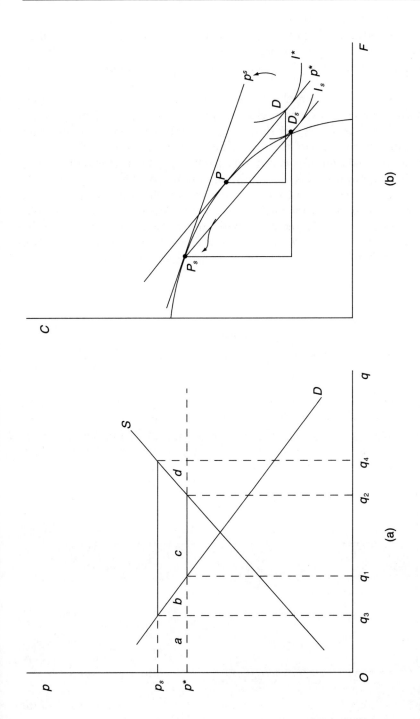

Figure 9.6 *Export subsidy*

least not its producers of the same or similar goods. To offset the impact of export subsidies the importing country has a right to introduce so-called *countervailing duties*. A countervailing duty is a tariff introduced by an importing country with the objective of raising the prices of the subsidised products.

To describe the effects the countervailing duty has let us assume that Home subsidises its export of cloth to Foreign. In Figure 9.7 demand for imported cloth in Foreign is shown by D_m, and the supply of cloth from Home by S (for simplicity we assume perfectly elastic supply). Pre-subsidy price and export/import quantity are p_0 and q_0. When Home grants the subsidy to cloth exporters the supply curve shifts down for the full amount of subsidy (S_s). Given no change in demand for imports, the quantity of imports increases to q_s. Foreign consumers gain an extra consumer surplus (area p_0p_sCA), while Home consumers (government) have to finance the cost of subsidy equal to p_0p_sCD. Therefore, the export subsidy implies a loss across both countries (in a two-country world) of ACD.

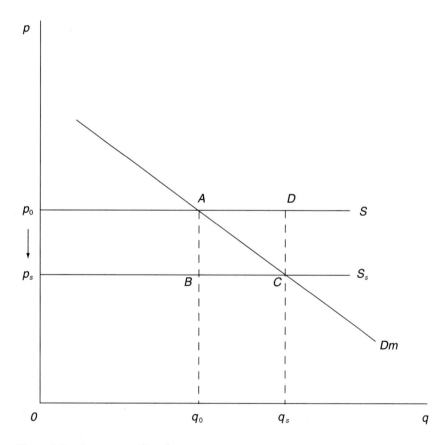

Figure 9.7   **A countervailing duty**

After Foreign introduces a countervailing duty to shift cloth's price back to the pre-subsidy level, its consumers lose all of the surplus gained. They also now demand less cloth. But the Foreign government earns revenue in the amount of p_0p_sBA thus offsetting some of the consumers' loss. However, Foreign as a nation loses ABC. In Home, government 'saves' some revenue: exports are reduced and less money is needed for subsidy. The amount saved is $ABCD$. Adding gains and losses across both countries results in a welfare gain of ABC. This is just sufficient to neutralise the loss caused by the subsidy. Thus the 'world's' welfare is unchanged. However, if we look at the effects of both policies, subsidy and countervailing duty in each country separately it is easy to see that Foreign gains (duty revenue) and Home loses (subsidy bill). In other words, duty in Foreign is effectively paid by Home's taxpayers.

Although the infant industry argument in the case of import tariffs is rarely accepted as fully valid, the infant export industry argument in the case of export subsidies has found quite a few supporters. Leaning on the findings of the 'new' trade theory, advocates of this idea argue that it makes sense to give an export subsidy to the young industry with export potential or to a strategically important industry to help it maintain an excess capacity. However attractive these ideas sound, there is a little evidence from real life about their effectiveness as means of gaining competitive advantage. More importantly, subsidies for this purpose are ruled out by multilateral trade rules. Despite being outlawed by GATT/WTO, predatory dumping and export subsidies, as well as the abuse of anti-dumping and countervailing duties are becoming increasingly popular with governments in both developed and developing countries. Nevertheless the USA and the EU are the most active parties with regard to initiation of anti-dumping investigations.

■ 9.5 Environment and trade

The current international trading rules under the GATT, do not have many explicit references to the environment. Article XX permits protectionist measures if they are taken to protect human, animal or plant life or health.[15] It is presumed that these restrictions will not be 'arbitrary and unjustifiable' methods of discrimination or disguised trade barriers.[16] The same Article allows trade restrictions to be imposed if their purpose is to conserve exhaustible natural resources provided they are primarily aimed at making effective domestic production or consumption restrictions. However Article XX does not allow imposition of trade restriction with the aim of protecting health, safety or resources in other countries. Therefore the US law which banned the import of Mexican tuna caught in nets that killed dolphins was declared illegal by the GATT (needless to say, this boosted the environmentalists' hostility towards 'free' trade and the GATT). GATT rules also allow for the employment of environmental subsidies if they help eliminate serious environmental pressure and if they are the most appropriate instrument (Article XI of the subsidies code). Many environmentalists regard the current GATT rules as inadequate and call for rewriting of the existing rules as well as for addition of many new ones. They require 'greening' of the GATT to reflect environmental concerns. Pro-trade groups, on the other hand, hold that such a revision would open the door for many non-tariff barriers under the guise of environmentalism.[17] Instead, they say, we should 'GATT' the 'Greens' (Esty, 1993). The conflicts between the two groups are often magnified even though there are some legitimate areas of disagreement. To understand these conflicts it is necessary to distinguish between various type of environmental problems and measures that are all carelessly thrown into the basket of 'green protectionism'.

There are two conceptually different groups of problems and related measures in the area of environment and trade. One deals with a stage in the economic process at which environmental damage occurs. Thus we differentiate between externalities that occur when products are being consumed and externalities when products are being produced. Consequently we must distinguish between product-related measures that address consumption externalities and production- and processing-related measures that address production externalities. Current multilateral trade rules allow countries to impose domestic product regulations on imports. They are in general not permitted to impose regulations related to production processes unless similar domestic restrictions exist. The second broad group of problems deals with the geographical locus of environmental damage. There are environmental problems that are domestic in nature and those that are international or transitional (global), such as acid rain, ozone depletion and global warming. While, in a general opinion, a country with local pollution should be left on its own to deal with the damage, in the case of global damage it is suggested that cooperative agreements between polluters and non-polluters might be more efficient than unilateral sanctions imposed on polluters. Let us discuss some of these issues.

With respect to product- or consumption-related concerns it is clear that the sort of measures typically used, that is, technical standards, eco-labelling, recycling and packaging requirements and similar could easily be abused for the purpose of protectionism. Evidence on the intensified use of such measures since the late 1980s (Sorsa, 1995, Figure 1) could be interpreted so as to support this claim or to support the view that governments are becoming more environmentally conscientious in trying to minimise environmental damage (see Box 9.4, p. 353). In the next section under the heading 'Health, safety and other standards' we talk a bit more about the product-related measures.

An important source of green protectionism is the use of trade measures to deal with local and/or global environmental problems. According to Bhagwati (1993a) local pollution which does not cross national borders should not be anybody's concern but the country's where it occurs, and she should deal with it in accordance with her own environmental laws. This is in contrast to the case where a polluted river flows into a neighbouring country – only then does the problem become international. This view, although logical, has been attacked by many who claim that the case of local pollution may have significant impact on international trade and therefore must become an international concern. This problem lies at the bottom of many claims of so-called 'environmental dumping' and we shall explore it a bit further. In order to do that we have to use the concept of comparative advantage which hopefully will not create any special difficulties.

The principle of comparative advantage, which says that a country should export the goods which can be produced relatively more cheaply than abroad, is based on fixed amounts of primary factors of production. The cost of use of these standard factors enters directly into the product prices, or in more general sense we use the concept of opportunity costs as the basket for all kinds of factors and resources used in production. But never in the simple concept of comparative advantage have we included environment as a factor of production. What happens if we do? More recently, trade models have extended the definition of factors to include the environment. The country is thought to be relatively environment-abundant if it has a relatively large *assimilative capacity*. Assimilative capacity is the capacity of the environment to absorb or tolerate pollutants. It reflects the degree to which the environment will be affected by its use or by the production of ecologically damaging products. For instance, the lower the assimilative capacity, the more environmental damage will be caused by the emission of a given amount of pollutants. The level of assimilative capacity is influenced by the physical ability of water, air, and land to absorb damage, but also by the level of pollutants the society is willing to tolerate (Blackhurst, 1977). This tolerance, or a country's preference, with respect to pollution is revealed in the environmental regulations and standards the society chooses to impose. Since countries differ in their environmental preferences (depending mostly on their level of income), the environmental regulations and standards will differ greatly across countries; each country will keep more of the industries whose pollution is relatively more preferred there than in other countries. In general, a LDC would prefer to pollute (that is, produce and grow) now and clean up later, while a highly industrialised country (although having the same assimilative capacity as the poor country) would prefer higher environmental quality. Thus the environmental policy of the poor country (if existent) will be more lax than in the wealthy country, implying also a lower cost of production of the environmentally sensitive goods. In other words, poor countries would end up having comparative advantage in the environmentally sensitive products vis-à-vis DCs. This is what leads some to believe that the 'fairness' of competition in the international arena may be affected. These fears are predominant between businesses and environmentalists in the DCs who claim that lower environmental standards in the developing countries would provide grounds for unfair competition and would ultimately lead to the lowering of standards in the DCs. Thus they insist that standards should be harmonised 'upward' before any further trade liberalisation takes place. Meanwhile they treat the lower environmental standards abroad as 'eco-dumping' and call for countervailing duties to be imposed on such imports from such countries. The welfare effects of such measures have already been discussed.

Although transborder environmental problems seem more complex to deal with than the local problems discussed above, it is likely that the international community will reach agreements on these issues sooner and easier precisely because they concern the welfare of all (Bhagwati, 1993b). Some international agreements have already been reached, such as the Convention on International Trade in Endangered Species (CITES), the Montreal Protocol on Substances that Deplete the Ozone Layer, the London Guidelines for Exchange of Information on Chemicals and the Basle Convention on the Transboundary Movements of Hazardous Wastes. Their impact on international trade and/or the multilateral trade rules has already been felt. The Uruguay Round explicitly mentions the importance of sustainable development and of environmental protection being institutionalised. In the agreement on the WTO it is envisaged that the issues are to be discussed by the Committee on Trade and Environment. At this stage, it is encouraging that the signatories of the Uruguay Round do not perceive the relationship between an open and equitable trading system and environmental protection to be in conflict. However, for the two systems, that is the trading system and environmental protection, to work towards the same objectives, the gap between the short-term perspectives of the trading system and the long-term perspectives of the environmental policy will have to close.

■ 9.6 Other non-tariff measures

From the long list of non-tariff barriers that have not been included in our discussion so far, we shall pick only few to describe in this section. The choice made here has been governed by criterion of practical importance.

☐ *Government procurement policies*

A type of non-tariff protection that is common to all countries, although in differing intensity, is the favouritism of local producers as suppliers of

---

Box 9.4 *Eco-labelling for flowers*

The Netherlands has a long tradition in horticultural exports, in particular exports of cut flowers. However its first mover advantages have been eroded somewhat with the appearance of exporters from developing countries. They may choose a slightly different technique of production than the Dutch growers because they have a relative abundance of natural sunlight and do not have to rely so much on energy-intensive greenhouses. Still the flower industry is predominantly chemical-intensive and polluting. To address demand-driven environmental concerns and also the growing competition from developing countries (in particular from Colombia and Morocco), the Dutch flower industry is encouraging the proliferation of green labels (for example environmental standards defined by flower auction houses). According to the studies reported in Beghin *et al.* (1994, Box 3), one of the new labels is likely to diminish some of the competitive advantages of the developing countries. Starting from 1995 the independent environmental foundation called 'Milieukeur' will award eco-labels for cut flowers. This will be done on the basis of stages in the production process. Importers are allowed to apply for the labels but foreign producers will not have any direct influence on the development of labels. Thus green labelling will create some disadvantage for foreign growers.

---

goods and services for government (local or national) departments. Typically governments are constrained by domestic legislation to buy domestic goods or services even if identical or similar foreign goods cost less (but not if they are substantially cheaper). In addition, governments have at their disposal many techniques aimed at precluding foreign producers from tendering for the supply of goods to the public sector, in particular when it comes to the military (defence) sector. This policy is aimed at supporting domestic production (which can be done also by production subsidy). If the government purchase is small relative to the domestic industry this policy should not cause greater distortion than is present in any government spending (Vousden, 1990, pp. 47–8). However if the government purchases accumulate to a large proportion of domestic industry, distortive effects become significant. The final effect is that the cost of providing public services increases, implying the redistribution of income between domestic consumers (taxpayers) and producers.

The multilateral trade rules of the GATT were amended in 1979 (the so-called Tokyo Code) to restrict these governmental preferences for local suppliers. An agreement was reached (the GATT procurement code) by which countries that signed the code would grant each other equal access to government contracts. However, countries were given freedom to exclude whichever governmental departments they wished from this agreement. Thus although the majority of DCs were signatories to this code, many of their departments were not bound by it.

One of the three agreements signed in Marrakesh in 1994 was an Agreement on Government Procurement, leading some commentators to state that this agreement was likely to be one of the major achievements of the Uruguay Round. Following the Tokyo Code and its revision this agreement continues to be based on the principles of national treatment, non-discrimination and transparency at every step of the national tendering process. It extends the coverage of the initial code to almost all government procurements except that of defence. In addition, the enforcement procedure was also significantly improved. An opportunity is introduced for firms which feel that they are being unfairly treated in the tendering process to protest decisions made by government departments (this procedure is known as 'challenge'). This is the first time the GATT has given an opportunity for foreign firms to be directly involved in enforcement procedures.

☐ Health, safety and other standards

Countries normally have regulations related to the production and distribution of products considered to be hazardous to the health and safety of their citizens. Often, however, these regulations are abused for protectionist purpose.[18] Multilateral trade negotiations so far have done a lot to harmonise differing national standards, thus facilitating freer international trade. Under the Uruguay Round Agreement on sanitary and phytosanitary measures each member will continue to make a sovereign determination of its acceptable level of risk. A country will set its own food safety, animal and plant health standards based on risk assessment and its determination of an acceptable level of risk. Alternatively, countries may use international standards. The Agreement recognises the right of countries to maintain stricter standards than international standards but these stricter measures must be scientifically justified.

Three international scientific organisations are recognised for their expertise in setting standards. One of the long-term goals is to promote harmonisation based on the standards of these organisations. Other important principles are equivalency, risk assessment, and transparency. The principle of equivalency means that if an exporting country's measures ensure the level of health protection desired by the importing country, then those measures should be acceptable even if they are different from those used by the importing country. Risk assessment refers to the technical assessment of the nature and magnitude of risk. Transparency refers to the manner in which health-related measures are formulated and adopted by countries. Countries should make information regarding health requirements available to interested parties and should notify them of any changes that may affect trade.

☐ Formalities of custom clearance and other administrative regulations

With more and more direct and indirect instruments coming under the auspices of the GATT (or now WTO) governments sometimes have to be quite ingenious to come up with a legitimate instrument to restrict imports. Probably the most famous example of the modern times is the French government's success in restricting the imports of Japanese VCRs in the early 1980s by changing custom clearing regulations (this example is fully explained in Box 9.5). Administrative restrictions, if applied strictly, are quite harmful for trade because they effectively make imports non-competitive in the local markets.

☐ Labour and social standards

The interaction between trade policy and labour and social standards came into the focus of international arena once again in April 1994 when some of the DC governments (namely the USA and the EU) insisted on amending the declaration from Marrakesh (the Declaration on the Uruguay Round). They wanted a formal promise that the newly established WTO would get involved into examining the impact of labour standards and working rights on countries' competitiveness.[19]

The USA have been unsuccessfully pushing for the inclusion of labour standards in the multilateral trade talks since the early 1950s. They have been more successful in liking trade to labour standards at the level of bilateral trade arrangements (e.g. NAFTA), and even more so in their trade relations with developing countries. For example, the legislation has been passed (section 301 and 301 super of the Omnibus trade Act of 1988) to enable the USA to condition their presence in the preferential trade schemes, such as GSP or Multilateral Investment Guarantee Agency, on a minimum set of internationally recognised standards of workers rights, known as the *core* labour standards. These include: the prohibition of forced labour, the prohibition of discrimination in employment, the right to freedom of association, the right to collective bargaining, and the prohibition of the exploitation of children in employment (OECD, 1996, p. 4). There is an understanding among the governments of the USA, the EU and many other countries that these core standards should be universally applied (most of these countries have signed and ratified the United Nations and ILO conventions dealing with human rights and

Box 9.5   *The 'Poitiers effect' – a perfect example of administrative barriers*

France (like other developed economies) has been experiencing an increasing influx of Japanese consumer electronics. *The World Bank Development Report* (1987) describes the response of the French government:

> 'In October 1982 the French government decreed that all imports of video-cassette recorders (VCRs) would have to pass through Poitier. . . It is a town hundreds of miles inland from France's northern ports where the VCRs are landed. It has a tiny customs crew that is obviously inadequate to the task of clearing hundreds of thousands of VCRs import. . . Moreover, a particularly long and tedious set of customs regulations were strictly enforced at Poitiers. All the accompanying documents were thoroughly examined and each container opened. A large number of VCRs were taken out of their boxes by the customs inspectors, who carefully checked their serial numbers and made sure that instructions were written in French. Finally, a number of VCRs were dismantled to make sure that they were actually built in their reported country of origin. The regional customs director responsible for Poitiers said of the new regulations: 'Before the new policy, it took a morning to clear a lorry-load of video recorders. Now it takes two to three months. We are still clearing consignments that arrived here [three months ago] when the policy went into effect'. (Lewis, 1982)

As planned, the 'Poitiers effect' severely limited VCR imports into France. Before the use of Poitiers, more than 64 000 VCRs, mostly from Japan, entered France each month for the first ten months of 1981. Afterwards, less than 10 000 VCRs cleared the customs point at Poitiers each month, while the rest of the supply waited in bonded warehouses throughout the town. Exporters did not passively concede to the French barriers. Denmark, the Federal Republic of Germany and the Netherlands, which also export VCRs to France, filed a complaint with the EU Executive Committee in Brussels, which in turn brought charges against France at the European Court of justice for breach of EU free trade rules. Japan brought its complaint to the GATT and then suspended or curbed VCR shipments to France.

It is not clear what the French hoped to gain from the use of the Poitiers weapon. The French electronics firm Thomas–Brandt did not make its own VCRs, but sold Japanese VCRs under its own label. It experienced a shortage of these when the government required all the imports to go through Poitiers. Shortly after the establishment of Poitiers, the EU Commission negotiated a VER limiting Japan's exports to the entire EU. This was followed by an agreement between Thomas–Brandt and Japan's JVC to manufacture component parts in France and later the lifting of the Poitiers restrictions. It is likely that several complex issues concerning intragovernmental and government–industry relations played a role in the Poitiers scheme. Yet, although the motives remain somewhat obscure, the protective effect of it is clear.'

Source: World Bank (1987, Box 8.5, p. 141).

labour standards). There are some other, mostly poorer, developing countries which hold that even the above 'basic' standards do not apply equally to all countries at all times. Instead, the application of any or all of the standards is dependent upon the level of development and capacity of an economy to afford them. This is particularly true in the case of applying some other (non-core) standards such as a minimum wage, limitations on hours of work and occupational safety and health in the workplace. Thus economies at different levels of development may have different preferences about the basic standards, which implies that under *laissez-faire*. The world will continue to have non-harmonised labour standards across countries. Taking that different labour standards only reflect countries' differences in productive resources, we have to conclude that this difference provides yet another source of gains from (free) international trade. Therefore, any attempt to artificially close the gap (by harmonising multilaterally) will reduce opportunities to gain from trade. Instead, free trade should be allowed to provide countries with a growth-friendly environment (see Chapter 13 for more details on the link between trade and growth). At a higher level of development these countries would develop preferences for higher labour standards (and they would be able to afford them) and thus harmonisation at the higher standard level would take place 'naturally'.

A different view on the diversity in labour standards across countries comes from some industries in the DCs which claim that producers in countries where lower standards are permitted enjoy unfair competitive advantages. These complaints are best known as the claims of 'social dumping'. It threatens the working and social conditions in countries with higher standards because these countries could be motivated to reduce the level of their standards thus 'racing the law-standards-countries to the bottom'. Solution is seen in international harmonisation of labour standards at a level acceptable to producers in DCs. Krugman (1997, p. 118) clearly identifies what is the questionable in this request: 'The problem, one might argue, is not that *countries* have an incentive to set standards too low in a trading world. Rather, it is that *politicians*, who respond to the demands of special-interest groups, have such an incentive. And one might argue that this failure of the political market, rather than distortions in goods or factor markets, is what justifies demands for international harmonisation of standards'. Trade policy is only a second best or even a third best policy to remedy many economic ills. There is no particular reason why trade policy should be used in a case of social dumping. In fact, trade intervention is probably the least appropriate response. As always, the choice of instrument depends on the objective. If the goal is higher standards and better working conditions in the poorer countries, then it would be more efficiently achieved by helping these countries to raise their standards of living. If however the objective is to shelter some interest groups in the DCs harmed by foreign competition, this could be done with taxation and direct transfer of income rather than through trade intervention.

■ 9.7 Summary

In this chapter we have reviewed some of the instruments of so-called non-tariff protection. Non-tariff measures comprise all trade barriers other than tariffs, such as: quantitative restrictions or quotas, including voluntary export restraints (VERs), certain government procurement practices, technical standards, rules of origin, subsidies and countervailing duties and anti-dumping. Any discussion of these different types of quantitative restrictions demonstrates strongly that such barriers are more harmful than tariffs. They undermine the functioning of the market by distorting prices and competition, they reduce flexibility in production and consumption decisions, and encourage wasteful rent-seeking behaviour.

The Uruguay Round of trade negotiations has been quite successful in addressing most of the important non-tariff barriers such as those in textiles, agriculture, and many sectors subject to VERs and anti-dumping. Notwithstanding that, there is still much to do in the area of liberalisation of non-tariff restrictions. The problem with them is that new types of these barriers appear as soon as some of the old ones are adequately dealt with. The most recent ones can be found in the two areas that are the important challenge for the trading system in the near future: trade and environmental protection, and trade and labour standards. In both of these areas, free trade does not create any problems; the imposition of a trade policy might. Despite this it seems that there will be a growing tendency towards using all sorts of trade restrictions for the purpose of dealing with seemingly 'unfair' competition.

■ Chapter 10 ■

Arguments for Trade Barriers

■ *10.1* Introduction

Our analysis of Chapter 8 and 9 was quite clear in one respect: except in the case of achieving the terms of trade effects or as safeguard measures, trade barriers cause a reduction in national and world welfare. Our conclusions were reached mostly under conditions of perfectly functioning markets. It should thus not be surprising that in the real world, where markets, in general, do not function perfectly we also find quite an intensive use of trade barriers. As we will show in this chapter it might be legitimate to use some intervention in circumstances of non-functioning or missing markets, but the trade policy instrument will rarely be best policy at hand. Often it will be the 'easiest to use' policy at hand or even the fastest to show results policy, only in a few cases will it be the best policy.

Numerous arguments in favour of trade barriers have been put forward at various times. Some arguments do not lose their strength as times passes; in other words they can always be used to justified one or other form of protection, such as revenue-generating protection. Because of the non-changing nature of these arguments we follow Winters (1993b) and call them *static* arguments. They are discussed in section 10.2. Section 10.3 discuss the arguments on which time makes an impact; they are called *dynamic* arguments. The third group of arguments refers to a new class of arguments called *strategic* arguments; the two most famous representative cases are presented in section 10.4.

■ *10.2* Static arguments for trade barriers

□ *Domestic distortions*

The *domestic distortions* or *market failure* argument for trade barriers is based on the view that the domestic economy does not operate under conditions of perfect competition. Instead the economy is subject to a number of market failures which can be grouped as imperfections in goods' markets, and imperfections in factor markets. When such distortions exist, that is, when market does not allocate resources in a Pareto efficient way, the government should use trade restrictions (so goes the argument) to offset the impact of already existing distortions. This is, put in the simplest possible way, the theory of the second best at work: if there are distortions existing in an economy that prevent it from functioning under perfect competition, then it may be best for the government to use the policies that add more distortions. For a full treatment see Bhagwati (1971) and Bhagwati and Srinivasan (1980).

However it is not necessary for these new distortions to be introduced by trade policies. There are other forms of intervention that might be more efficient in doing the job. In fact, *rarely* would trade policy be the best possible measure. The rule that must be observed in a selection of policy instrument is the so-called *specificity rule*. It says that the most efficient form of intervention to achieve a given objective is the one which attacks the target directly (that is, tackles the problem most *directly*). Such intervention therefore would avoid the unnecessary 'by-product distortions' (such as the consumer loss in case of tariffs imposed to raise domestic production instead of providing production subsidies). In general the best possible response of the government when faced with domestic or other types of distortion would be to remove the existing distortion (such as unemployment in factor markets) instead of mixing it up with protectionist policies. Despite the fact that trade restrictions could ease most of the distortions in an open economy somewhat, they will most likely cause more damage in the long run. In general, whatever a trade barrier can do, some other policy will achieve the same objective more directly and more efficiently.

Going back to domestic distortions, let us start by stating that Pareto efficient allocation involves three aspects of allocative efficiency. One refers to efficiency in the use of inputs and is usually represented by the marginal rate of transformation in production (MRT). The second is related to efficiency in consumption and is represented by the marginal rate of substitution in consumption (MRS). The third is related to social efficiency, implying that marginal social cost equals marginal social benefit for each input or consumption good. In the open economy there is another aspect of allocative efficiency, referring to the marginal rate of transformation through trade (or the foreign marginal rate of transformation) which is given by the world relative prices (p^*). Thus for the efficiency we must have domestic relative prices (p) which will ensure that:

$$p = MRT_s = MRS_s = p^* \qquad (10.2.1)$$

where the subscript s refers to the social marginal rates.

Whenever prices are not what is needed for efficiency, we can talk about market failure or domestic distortions. Then in principle some sort of intervention is possible to correct the market, to bring about a new equilibrium with improved efficiency.

We next turn to two representative cases of such market failure.

Distortions in the domestic goods market

Distortions in the *domestic goods market* imply all those situations when domestic relative commodity prices do not reflect the marginal rate of transformation. This could be assigned to the existence of some form of *imperfect competition* or to the existence of *external (dis)economies* which are reflected in the inequality of social and private marginal costs. Since we have discussed some forms of imperfect competition in goods' markets and the impact of tariffs under such circumstances in Chapter 8, we choose here to discuss the case of externalities. Figure 10.1 provides an illustration. Consider a case where Home has two sectors, an exportable sector of food products, F and importable sector of cloth, C. The PPF reflecting the social marginal rate of transformations is given by PP. However, this economy is plagued by a market failure in that the food sector causes an externality in production which is not reflected in its private cost of production. In other words given the externality the private cost of producing food is lower than the social cost, and the domestic relative prices do not reflect the true (social) marginal rate of transformation in production. In such a case free trade may cause a decline in welfare compared to autarky. Let us see how this outcome is possible. In Figure 10.1, Home is producing and consuming at point P, where because of externality the domestic relative price p is steeper than the marginal rate of transformation. This implies that the relative price of good F is too low, which is not surprising since it does not reflect the social marginal costs. The world relative prices are represented by the line $p*$. Given distorted domestic prices, Home reveals comparative advantage in good F. More specifically,

$$MRT_s < p^* < p_p \tag{10.2.2}$$

where the subscript p reflects private marginal costs. Hence under free trade Home would increase its output of food (say to the point P^*), export some of it and end up consuming at point D^* on the social indifference curve I^* which is lower than under autarky.[1] The externality which caused domestic prices to depart from the social marginal rate of transformation induces Home to specialise in the 'wrong direction', that is in the good in which it does not have comparative advantage. The true comparative advantage is shown by the MRT in production which indicates a need for specialisation in good C.

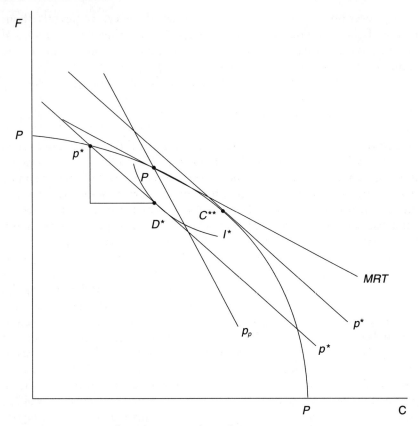

Figure 10.1 *Domestic distortion in goods markets*

The market failure argument for trade barriers suggests that an introduction of a tariff on imports of good C could stimulate production of that good and result in an increase in Home's welfare (compared to free trade with domestic distortion). A tariff (not shown in Figure 10.1) will indeed cause production gain (an increase in output of C) but at the cost of consumers who will suffer consumption loss. In addition such a tariff, even if prohibitive, will never transform good C in an exported product, as long as the externality exists. Thus the more appropriate intervention (first best policy) would be to tax production of F and/or subsidise production of C so that the domestic relative price is brought closer to the world relative price. When these are equalised Home can engage in welfare-improving free trade (point C^{**}).

Distortions in factor markets

There are several kinds of potential *distortions in factor markets*, such as differentials in wages among industries (which are not caused by differences in skills) and unemployment on the labour market side, or rationing in capital markets. Each of these has been seen as a possible justification for some form of protection to domestic production. Whatever the actual cause of distortion, the effects are first to push the PPF inwards, and second to distort relative costs so that even along this inner frontier the private and marginal costs differ. Figure 10.2 illustrates such a case. Suppose that the wage in (manufacturing) sector *C* is different from the wage in an (primary) sector *F*, but both are equal to the value of the respective marginal productivities. As a consequence, Home's production point will not be along its true PPF, *PP*. Instead it will lie at some point on the inner frontier $P'P'$.[2] Given the world relative price p^*, and assuming that the present distortion has no effect on the relative commodity prices, Home will produce at point P' instead at the outer frontier at point *P*. Consequently it will consume at C', on the lower indifference curve I' than is potentially achievable in the no-distortions world. Obviously intervention here is needed to put the economy back to its true frontier. Would a trade barrier do this? Not really. The first best policy is to use a combination of tax and subsidies on the use of factors of production so as to equalise the wage rate.

If this distortion were coupled with the goods' market failure, the level of welfare could be even lower since production would take place to the left of point P' (such as P''). Than a return to the optimum for Home would require first a correction of the wrong specialisation along the inner frontier (this is the case of goods' markets failure) and then the correction of the wage differentials.

☐ The optimum tariff – again

For a large country it is always possible to find a tariff such that this country's welfare is higher than under free trade. This tariff is known as the *optimum tariff*. We have discussed this topic at length in Chapter 8, sections 8.2 and 8.4 and there is no point in repeating the discussion here. As for validity of the optimum tariff argument for protection we remind the reader that it is not without weaknesses, the most important one being the possibility of retaliation. This is probably the reason why we rarely witness the imposition of tariffs solely for the reason of improving a country's terms of trade. However the theoretical possibility of optimum tariffs makes large countries in the world more prone to accept trade liberalisation through multilateral tariff cuts than on a unilateral basis in which case, as the theory says, they lose.

☐ Revenue generation

This is one of the rare 'non-protectionist' arguments for the introduction of tariffs. Both import and export tariffs (taxes) generate revenue to the

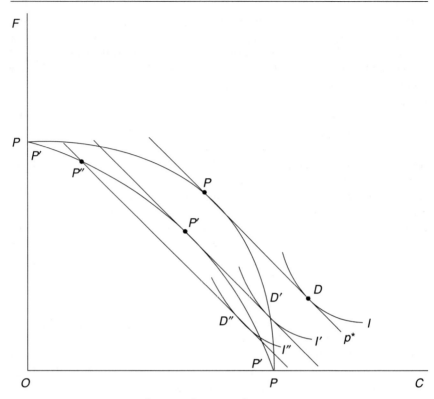

Figure 10.2 *Distortions in domestic factor market*

government and this may be the sole reason for their introduction (see Table 10.1). It does not mean, however, that revenue generation will be the only effect because tariffs can cause protective and other distortionary side effects. But for some governments, in particular in developing countries, the need to raise revenue may outweigh the negative effects. Tariffs are not the optimal instrument for raising revenue. A better policy would be a general income tax or value added tax. Dixit (1985) shows that the same revenue could be collected with a lower efficiency loss by introducing a combination of domestic taxes levied neutrally with respect to domestic and foreign products. The efficiency loss is generated because of the impact tariffs have on domestic relative prices and because of the resulting inward-oriented bias.

It should also be noted that when tariffs are already in place and when revenue generation would imply an increase in tariff rates the total amount of revenue may not increase by much. That will of course depend on the price elasticities of demand and supply. If the import base declines sharply on the increase in the tariff rate, revenue may be only slightly higher with a higher tariff rate as compared to the initial rate. As we discussed in Chapter 8, section 8.3 there is a specific rate of tariff which assures that tariff revenue will be maximised. This rate is called the maximum revenue rate of tariff and in general this rate is higher than the optimum tariff rate, which maximises a country's welfare (refer to Figure 8.5 in Chapter 8, p. 299).

The revenue-generating tariff, despite all its weaknesses, remains very popular as a means of raising revenue in many countries; in developing countries it is probably the most favoured instrument. There are at least two reasons for this. One, and the more important, is that tariffs are easier and less expensive to collect than domestic taxes on consumption and income. Some studies show that administrative cost of levying tariffs, including taxes on exports, is no higher than 3 per cent of revenue collected while the corresponding costs for value added tax and income tax are estimated at 5 and 10 per cent, respectively (World Bank, 1988). This is particularly important for the countries with underdeveloped tax systems (such as transition and developing economies). They may have no other successful means for raising revenue but trade taxes. But it should be emphasised that even in these countries the total economic and social cost caused by trade taxes are certainly much higher than the pure administrative cost and they should be encouraged to switch to domestic taxation as soon as possible. While they may be forced to maintain trade taxes for revenue-generating purposes they are strongly advised to use the lowest possible rate uniform for all sectors so to minimise the bias in the trade regime.

The other reason why some governments may wish to use tariffs to raise revenue is when they think foreigners will pay such tariffs. This is of course again the large country case where it has the market power to change its terms of trade. Even if temporarily successful, this revenue-generating instrument would not be popular with trading partner countries whose income has been used to increase welfare of the large country.

☐ *National security*

National defence is most frequently used as the one of the so-called *non-economic* reasons why a government may want to impose trade restrictions. Other motives belonging to this category of arguments are *national pride* and *national foreign policy*. All of these arguments relate to political rather than economic considerations. With respect to national security, it is usually easy to persuade government (and taxpayers who pay for the protection) that some or other production line is indispensable for the country in case of war. When the production in question is the shipbuilding industry (as it was the case with British mercantilism in seventeenth century) then the reason could be accepted. The problem with this argument for the introduction of trade barriers is that it can easily be

Table 10.1 *Relevance of tariffs and other trade taxes in government revenue*

Country	Year	Percentage
Developed countries		
USA	1989E	1.59
Canada	1988F	3.79[P]
Australia	1988C	4.57[P]
New Zealand	1990B	2.14
Austria	1989D	1.58[P]
Belgium	1988B	0.02[P]
Denmark	1987E	0.06
Finland	1988D	1.09
France	1989B	0.02[P]
Germany	1989E	na
Greece	1981A	3.27
Iceland	1987D	13.50
Ireland	1987A	7.13
Italy	1989A	0.01[P]
Luxembourg	1988A	–
Netherlands	1989A	–
Norway	1989C	0.45
Portugal	1987	3.11
Spain	1987C	2.58
Sweden	1989D	0.54
Switzerland	1984E	7.67
UK	1988C	0.07
Some developing countries		
Botswana	1987	13.75
Cameroon	1989	13.96
Gambia	1982A	68.51
Kenya	1988A	18.16
Lesotho	1986A	55.63
Morocco	1987	12.65
Nigeria	1987	6.59[P]
Uganda	1986	75.32[P]
Bangladesh	1985	42.60[P]
India	1989E	26.46[P]
Indonesia	1988A	5.60
Korea	1990C	10.36[P]
Singapore	1987A	2.56
Thailand	1989A	22.20
Hungary	1988A	5.28
Poland	1988C	6.23
Turkey	1989	6.28

Table 10.1 (cont.)

Country	Year	Percentage
Argentina	1988E	11.40
Bolivia	1988C	10.40
Brazil	1987D	1.64
Chile	1987A	9.87
Mexico	1989C	7.99^P

Note: Letters following a year indicate the percentage of general government tax revenue accounted for by that country's central government, as follows: A:95 and over, B: 90–94.9, C: 80–89.9, D: 70–79.9, E: 60–69.9, F: 50–59.9, G:20–49.9. Superscript p indicates that the data are in whole or in part provisional or projected. na   Not available.
Source: IMF, *Government Finance Statistics Yearbook* (1990).

abused. Thus when protection for 'national security' reasons is sought by producers of shoes, fish netting or even candles, then it must be obvious that the real motivation is strictly protectionist. Trade restrictions (mostly import barriers but sometimes embargoes on exports) introduce distortions in the goods and factor markets and an efficiency loss as well. Thus if some production is really needed for national security reasons and trade cannot survive without government aid, the best aid will be a production subsidy under free trade. In this case the efficiency loss is smaller. In addition the measure is more transparent and the costs to society more obvious than in case of trade restrictions.

National pride as the motivation for protectionism is not so uncommon. Many examples of 'economically irrational' support to automobile, computer or some other high-technology industry existed in the former socialist countries, especially in the Soviet Union, whose political leaders wanted to develop all the industries that existed in the West even at a very high economic cost. A similar syndrome can be found in some developing countries as well. This is comparable to countries competing to host the Olympic Games even when most of them have not the economic means to finance such an event.

The third example of the use of trade restrictions to meet some non-economic objective is foreign policy. Governments often use trade barriers to meet some political objective. The most frequently used restrictions for this purpose are full or partial embargoes to trade with countries on which the government wants to exert some pressure. The most recent and slightly unusual example of the use of trade barriers for non-economic objective was the voluntary (non-government induced) termination of imports and consumption of many French made goods by the wholesalers, retailers and consumers in New Zealand, Australia and some Pacific Islands countries as the response to the French government's decision to continue with nuclear testing in the South Pacific. Such actions hope to cause (significant?) economic losses to French producers who will (it is hoped) press the French government to either provide them with financial aid (which implies additional pressure on French taxpayers) or to stop the testing. In most cases, however, such actions are not very successful; for example it took many years of trade sanctions imposed by almost all countries in the world on the South African government before a more democratic regime was established.

☐ *Other arguments*

It would be impossible to cover all the arguments supporting the imposition of one or other trade barrier. In what follows we provide a rather brief review of some of the arguments, being aware that the reader has plenty of opportunity to read about other arguments in the existing literature. We wish to point the reader to a book called *The Choice* (Roberts, 1994) in which most of the arguments we discuss in this chapter have been brilliantly exposed for what they really are: the requests for income redistribution.

The balance of payments argument

Under the regime of fixed exchange rates when governments were not very keen on changing the value of domestic currency, the means often used to 'cure' external imbalances (that is, current account imbalance) were import tariffs or quantitative import barriers. Import barriers were particularly popular in cases where governments felt that imbalances were only transitory so that other adjustment policies were deemed unwarranted. However it was not uncommon for governments to use import barriers (and export promotion) simply to postpone necessary adjustment policies, therefore causing even more distortions in already unbalanced economic conditions. The important negative consequence of using import restrictions instead of devaluation is an increase in costs for export producers and the reallocation of resources from export- to import-substituting industries (in the longer run). The gains from international trade, and also national welfare, will be reduced.

With the switch to a flexible (floating) exchange rate regime, the effectiveness of import barriers to remedy external balances has been further reduced. Under the flexible exchange rate regime, the reduced imports caused by import barriers will prompt a currency appreciation offsetting the effect of import restriction (with domestic currency having higher purchasing power, imports will again start rising despite tariffs; only in case of quotas will imports be controlled but then revaluation will have effects on the level of domestic prices).

Apart from being restricted by the GATT/WTO, trade barriers imposed for balance of payments purposes do not really work. Thus a country facing an external balance problem should seek a more direct instrument to cure the problem. Usually, fiscal instruments combined with monetary policy will work better. In more difficult cases, restructuring policies will be needed to address the root of the problem.

The income-redistribution argument

This is the proper place to repeat the statement by Edward Leamer (1993, p. 436): 'Every trade barrier that I have ever seen is a device to transfer income from one group to another, or perhaps more frequently to stop the transfer of income that would otherwise take place.' Thus redistribution of income seems to be an subliminal message in all trade instruments irrespective of the declared primary objective assigned to the trade restriction.

The most obvious redistribution taking place when trade barrier is in place is between consumers and producers, with the former being on the losing end. Given this it is hard to accept the usual assumption that the government assigns equal value to all subjects in the country when it designs economic policy. On the contrary, it seems that some or all of the trade restrictions are implemented with the ultimate goal of either redistributing income to the social groups which are 'valued' more by the government or to prevent a redistribution of income that would harm such groups. The hypotheses that are most often used to explain the role of trade policy in distribution of income are:

- Weighted social welfare – that is, the government prefers some social groups over the others. Traditionally the social groups receiving special help from the government were low-paid workers in the textile and clothing industries or similar. In recent times this seems to be changing with more and more governments favouring high-wage industries (hoping for some positive externalities for growth).
- Conservative welfare function – that is, the objective of the government to prevent the income redistribution which would occur under free trade.
- Collective action – that is, the existence of small well organised groups which are able to pursue their interests much better than the rest of the society, and the government finds itself working in the interest of such groups.

Irrespective of what might be the underlying motivation of the government, by applying the specificity rule we know that trade restrictions are not the most efficient instruments to do the job. An income tax (which could be designed to be flat or progressive) is a much better means of redistributing income without causing misallocation of resources. Also it is much easier to control whether redistribution is going into the right direction and not being appropriated by interested groups. In addition, as we know from the application of the specific-factor model, trade protection does not treat factors of production equally in the short and in the long run. While in the short run factors employed in the protected activity will indeed benefit, in the long run these benefits will accrue only to the scarce factor.

The employment and protection of domestic labour argument

Preservation of employment (or reduction of unemployment) together with the need to protect domestic labour from unfair competition from abroad are probably the two most abused of all the arguments for trade restrictions. The level of employment is an macroeconomic issue, depending in the short run on aggregate demand and in the long run on the natural rate of unemployment. Microeconomic policies like tariffs have little net effect on employment. Trade policy should be thus debated in terms of its impact on efficiency, not in terms of numbers of jobs created or lost in a particular sector.

When deciding whether or not to impose a trade restriction, the government should always consider what general equilibrium effects may be caused by protection granted to one sector. Thus when we impose trade restrictions to imports on, say product A, we will create some additional domestic production and employment in industry A and upstream industries. But what happens with industry B which produces an export good, not related to good A (or not upstream to industry A)? The level of activity and employment in that industry will fall. Resources are being attracted to protected sectors which cause a slump in the rest of the economy. Thus what we in fact are doing with trade barriers is redistributing employment within the home economy and exporting some unemployment to trading partners.

A related issue is whether international trade contributes to the demand shift from less-skilled to more-skilled labour. This view is supported only by anecdotal evidence. A more comprehensive analysis finds that neither international trade through the Stolper–Samuelson process nor outsourcing by multinationals are causing a shift in relative labour demand away from the unskilled and toward the skilled and thus causing the wage divergence.

The 1980s have witnessed a revival of the argument originating in the nineteenth century in the USA – the argument based on *'fairness'* or a *'level playing-field'* (Corden, 1987). There are several variants of the basic argument which claim that it is unfair (or even immoral) to import goods which are produced by low-wage labour in developing countries) because that disadvantages producers in high-wage countries *and* supports the exploitation of cheap labour overseas. We have dealt with these arguments in Chapter 1 when discussing the concept of comparative advantage. To accept these arguments means ignoring the principle of comparative advantage and the gains from trade based on them. And as said before, the import barriers to such products will only make it harder for those countries to export, causing a rise of unemployment and fall of wages to an even lower level in those countries. Thus the means of fighting against the substandard labour conditions which may exist in some (not only developing) countries should not include trade restrictions.

Patriotism

'Make New Zealand Work', 'Be American, Buy American', 'Buy British' are only a few examples of advertising campaigns that appear on TV, in the newspapers, or as the stickers on products in these countries. These campaigns are usually organised by government agencies in charge of the economy or in some cases by a producers' association. The messages are meant to 'remind' consumers of their 'patriotic' duty as 'good' citizens to help their country's economy by not spending their income on imported goods.[3] This is a legitimate form of persuasion but still misplaced. Usually consumers do what is best for their country anyway: they buy products whose prices adequately reflect their quality. If there are domestic products satisfying these conditions, they will normally be preferred to imported ones. But if domestic products do not match imported ones, except when they are heavily protected, then it is best for the country not to have such production. When the New Zealand government started its campaign to restrict import consumption of manufactured goods, the producers of agriculture goods (who had almost no protection during the process of economic restructuring) begin their own campaign against government favouritism.

■ *10.3* Dynamic arguments for trade barriers

In contrast to the arguments analysed in the previous section, here we turn our attention to the arguments sensitive to the passage of time. Some of them have been 'in the game of protection' since the beginning of time, such as the infant industry argument, while some are 'newcomers' among the arguments for protection, such as uncertainty. A particularly interesting argument from this class is the so-called *insurance argument*. Examination of these arguments however is not included in this chapter. An excellent coverage of basic issues in this area can be found in Vousden (1990, section 3.3) who also provides further references. We turn instead to examine the infant industry argument in greater detail.

□ *The infant industry argument*

The *infant industry argument* for protection in fact belongs to the domestic distortions type of arguments but for one thing – it is sensitive to the passage of time. This is the reason why it is being considered in this section. The infant industry argument has been the most used argument for protection in practice, at least until the occurrence of strategic policy arguments.[4] Moreover, according to Baldwin (1969), the infant industry argument has long been regarded as the major theoretically valid exception to the case for free trade. The reason for protection arises from the belief that some industries require temporary protection in order to develop into internationally competitive industries. Once these industries are able to face the foreign firms, the protection can and should cease.

Figure 10.3 provides an illustration of the infant industry argument for protection. The PPF of a small country called Home is given by the curve PP. Under free trade and with the world relative prices p^* being tangent to the PPF at point P^*, Home produces a combination of F and C of food and cloth, respectively. By exporting some of food, Home finds itself consuming the combination of F^* and C^* at point D^* on the social indifference curve I^*. Suppose that the government, believing that sector C needs a slight 'push' to become internationally competitive, decides to impose a tariff on imports of cloth. An import tariff changes the terms of trade in favour of the cloth sector (to the position given by p_t) which causes resource movements from food to cloth and a new production combination given by point P_t. Sector F still remains the exportable sector; thus the welfare of Home is necessarily reduced by this imposition of tariffs on imported cloth (not shown in the graph). This is a part of the story that pertains to the short run. In the long run, thanks to protection, there are changes which facilitate a shift of the PPF over time to a new position, given by PP^{**}, further away from the origin. The factors behind the shift range from a newly gained opportunity for the protected industry to achieving the economies of scale necessary to become profitable. Alternatively, a significant improvement in production techniques, or achievement of superior labour and/or management skills (the effect of the learning-by-doing) in the cloth sector could pull the PPF towards PP^{**}. When the PPF shifts outwards, the need for protection ceases and Home again starts trading freely. Supposing that the world relative prices at that point in time are still given by $p*$, Home will be producing at P^{**}, a combination of F^{**} and C^{**} of food and cloth, respectively. This combination of production, given the indifference curve set, implies that Home has remained an exporter of food and an importer of cloth. There is nothing in this argument to prevent Home becoming an exporter of cloth; in fact some would argue that without such a result infant industry argument looses all its potency (see for instance El-Agraa, 1989, p. 142). Anyhow, in our example Home ends up consuming at point D^{**} which, being situated on a higher indifference curve I^{**}, also implies higher welfare for Home. This production-consumption equilibrium is achieved with a decreased volume of international trade, which was the goal of the protection. To sum up, a protection of a young industry is justified because it enables a country to achieve, in a long run, a higher level of welfare than under free trade. This result holds even though protection, in the short run, implies a (temporary) lowering of welfare.

There are several problems with this argument. First, even if protection is justified on the ground that an infant industry is able, if assisted, to grow up, the tariff is not the most appropriate instrument of protection. The *specificity rule* suggests that if other, more direct instruments had been used the decline in welfare which, as it seems has to occur in the short run, could have been smaller. For example, production subsidies, rather than tariffs, could have been provided to the cloth sector with the same protective effect but at a lower cost. The difference is in the amount of deadweight loss; with a tariff such a loss includes both production and

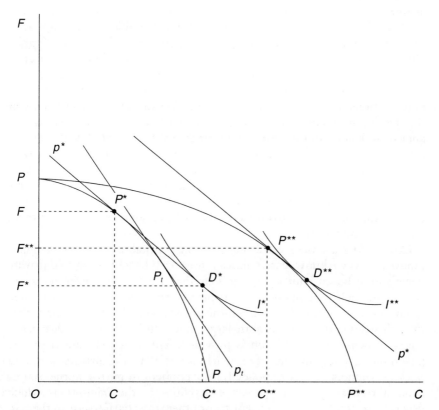

Figure 10.3 *Infant-industry argument for protection*

consumption loss, while with subsidies it includes only the former. Given the range of possible causes of initial inefficiency of infant industries, there are other more direct instruments at government's disposal. But let us first discuss the two most important reasons for the infant industries needing assistance from the government. These two reasons are market failure and externalities.[5]

Market failure refers to the inequality between private and social costs. One of the causes for the two to differ is the *imperfection of the information flow*. More specifically, the private sector may not have all the information about the developments of the macroeconomic situation, investments into infrastructure, changes in the labour and financial markets or education system which may be needed to undertake an investment in the infant industry. Hence such an industry would materialise only if the government provides a signal. In the case of imperfect information the specificity rule would suggest trying to fix the flow of information from the government to the private sector. The imposition of a tariff is certainly not the appropriate instrument.

Imperfection of the local financial (capital) market is often put forward as one of the key reasons for government intervention. When the capital market is not functioning, the private sector is not able to raise capital to finance initial losses for the activity that will potentially become profitable. Given empirical evidence it seems true that in case of industries subject to economies of scale or learning-by-doing the private capital markets are simply not brave enough to make investments. Although capital market imperfections are a more important limitation for private investments in the developing countries, it is not impossible for these imperfections to appear in the developed markets (one of the examples could be the lack of private investment in Airbus Industries). A preferable policy to deal with capital market failures would be to give subsidised loans to the private sector in order to invest in such infant industries. One way to fix this failure is to establish development banks whose objective could be to collect resources from government and private sources and direct them into infant industries.

Externalities are the second source of the profitability-gaining of infant industries. As we know, externalities cause social benefits to exceed private benefits and hence limit investments by the private sector into industries subject to such externalities. When protection to such activities is then given in order to attract resources, the government should be certain that the industries in question generate larger externalities than the industries at whose expense this protection is provided. This is a toll request on the government, implying that it is much better than the private sector in 'picking winners'. A better policy for government to pursue in the case of externalities would be to subsidise activities of the institutions which generate externalities directly. Tariffs or other trade barriers are in the best case the second best policies.

Whatever the basis for the protection, the infant industry must satisfy two tests before government can be certain that protection will produce social benefits too. These tests are *Mill's test* and *Bastable's test*.[6] Mill's test refers to the requirement that the industry eventually becomes internationally competitive. Bastable's test requires the industry to be able to pay back the national losses incurred during the period of protection. An underlying condition in both tests is that protection will have a finite duration. Only when the industry seeking protection is providing enough evidence about passing both tests is there a case for protection. Only under such circumstances will protected activities indeed realise their true comparative advantage. Needless to say, there are not many industries satisfying the above-mentioned tests. In practice, infant industries never grow up; the protection once granted to such industries is only exceptionally removed. Over time, political pressures and lobbying for continued protection (instead of infant industry profitability) increases and it becomes politically unacceptable to remove such protection.

To sum up the case of the infant industry argument for trade barriers, we may say that in economies where distortions in goods and factors markets are rather strong, the basis for infant industry protection may be found. Nevertheless, protection would be more efficient if provided with non-trade measures, such as production subsidies or direct financing by government.

☐ The sunset industry argument

This argument for protection has been raised in the European context where from the 1970s some of the *mature* industries started to show clear signs of lost competitiveness when faced with the 'young' producers from Japan, East Asia and even from the USA. Analysts have been talking about the senility of European industry; the whole phenomenon is known as *Euro-sclerosis*. The industries affected by this disease are mostly labour-intensive industries such as textiles, clothing, and footwear but also the production of steel and steel-based products. The sunset industry argument has been in favour of granting some *temporary* protection to such industries on the ground that given enough time (and resources) they would be able to re-equip and regain competitiveness. Otherwise, the rapid shifts in the pattern of comparative advantage will entail heavy adjustment costs, as labour and capital will be displaced.

There are several objections to this argument, starting from it being a quick fix for the unemployment problem to the political market failure type of arguments. But the strongest objection to the sunset industry argument is similar to the problem arising from the infant industry argument – once support is provided by a trade policy, there is no telling when it will stop. Thus the long-run costs to society of protecting these sunset industries could easily exceed the costs of adjustments in the short run.

■ 10.4 Strategic arguments for trade barriers

A new class of argument for intervention in the trade area is known as *strategic* arguments. They are based on new insights from the theory of trade policy when prices depart from marginal costs. In such cases there is a potential strategic role for government action in shifting the terms of competition to the benefit of domestic firms. The most widely known examples are those in which import protection leads to export promotion and those where export subsidies serve as the means for deterring foreign competition. Let us discuss each case in turn.

□ *Import protection as export promotion*

This case has been developed by Krugman (1984) who exploits the *'learning-by-doing'* phenomenon to justify protection of activities which are likely to become internationally competitive only if granted some support. The special twist to Krugman's case was that a protected activity becomes so competitive that it turns out as an exporter – something completely unthinkable before. In the world of perfect competition and constant-returns-to-scale, import tariffs can never turn the goods from being import substitutes to being exportable goods.[7] Hence Krugman's 'import protection as export promotion' proved to be something very novel and very 'catchy' among the advocates of an active trade policy. They welcomed the Krugman's model as a 'watertight proof' for the benefits in export sectors of a protected domestic market, which supposedly the exporters of the Asian Tigers have enjoyed while their economies were transforming from import-substitution-oriented to export-oriented economies. We will revisit this issue in Chapter 13; now we should turn to examination of the Krugman's model.

Consider two firms, one coming from each Home and Foreign economy. Suppose these firms compete in any number of markets including their own. The markets are fully segmented so that the possibility for arbitrage is excluded, and in each market, Home and Foreign, a Cournot duopoly equilibrium develops. Suppose each firm produces with decreasing costs reflecting declining marginal costs as output rises.[8] Figure 10.4 is used as an illustration of the model. The initial equilibrium E in two markets are shown where reaction curves of Home and Foreign firms intersect. Suppose now the Home government imposes an import tariff. This raises the delivering cost in the Home market for the Foreign firm and shifts its reaction curve downward (panel (a)). The new equilibrium point is at E_1. But this is not the final equilibrium. Since the Home firm's output rises, its marginal costs fall. Similarly the Foreign firm's marginal costs rises because its output falls. This has further repercussions on the reaction

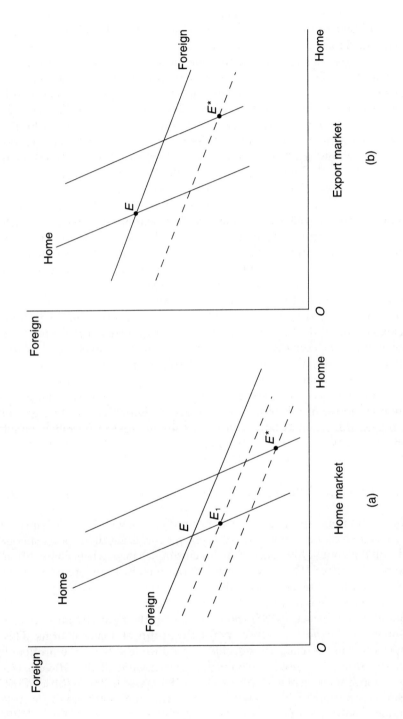

Figure 10.4 *Import protection as export promotion*

curves in both markets: the Home firm's reaction function shifts to the right, and that of the Foreign firm shifts downward. These shifts in turn increase the Home firm's sales and decrease the Foreign firm's sales in both markets. These changes in the volume of sales have repercussions on marginal costs. The Home firm's marginal costs keep declining while the opposite is happening to the Foreign firm. Thus changes in output in both firms continue in the same direction as before. After all these changes have taken place, the reaction functions move into the position shown by the dashed lines with an equilibrium at point E*. At this equilibrium the Home firm has not only reinforced its advantage in the domestic market but it also gained in the export market (panel (*b*)). This is where *import protection* serves as an instrument of *export promotion*.[9] The specific type of industries, which were probably behind the development of this hypothesis are the industries subject to fast 'learning-by-doing'. In such industries any support (including tariffs) which enables them to cumulate large increases in output will enable them to go far down the 'learning-by-doing' curve. This in turn could help them to establish a dominant position in the domestic and, as we see here, in the export markets.

The welfare effects for the Home country are ambiguous. The protected sector has managed to become 'competitive' and to earn higher profits. The expansion of the protected sector however occurred at the expense of other sectors, including previously already competitive export industries. Resources are being drawn to the sheltered sector from other sectors, causing them to contract: thus the existent exports were probably hurt. In addition domestic consumers are being charged higher prices since the monopoly power of the domestic firms has increased. The welfare effects for the world economy are quite clear; an increased concentration of production could only mean a reduction of welfare.

☐ *Export subsidies under imperfect competition*

In the section on export subsidies under perfect competition in Chapter 9 we concluded that a nation who engages in subsidising the exports shoots itself in the foot. How does this conclusion change when competition becomes imperfect? The answer was first outlined by Brander and Spencer (1985) and then extended and added to by many advocates and critics of the strategic trade policy.

Brander and Spencer (1985) show that under the right circumstances, a pre-announced *export subsidy* can raise the profits of domestic firms. This happens because foreign firms decide to produce less. Since the profits of domestic firms are raised by more than the amount of the subsidy, the national income is increased. Although it is increased at the expense of the trading partners, the world benefits because this policy reduces the overall monopoly power. Let us see some details of this case.

An example developed in Brander and Spencer (1985) starts from a duopoly equilibrium in which two firms, H and F, based in two different countries, Home and Foreign, compete for sales in the rest of the world (but not in each other's markets). The whole output produced by these firms is assigned for sales outside domestic markets which simplifies the analysis since we do not have to take into account the effects on domestic consumers.[10] Figure 10.5 illustrates the Cournot equilibrium in the rest of the world market. Each firm's reaction curve shows the preferred outputs of that firm given the outputs of the other firm. The Cournot equilibrium is at point E at which each firm earns positive profits. Since both firms have some market power they are aware of the consequences if any of them increase output. The benefits of the increased output and sales will be offset by the reduction in price. Thus neither firm will change the output level achieved at point E.

If, somehow, the firm from Home could convince the firm from Foreign that it will increase its output what would be the reaction of the Foreign

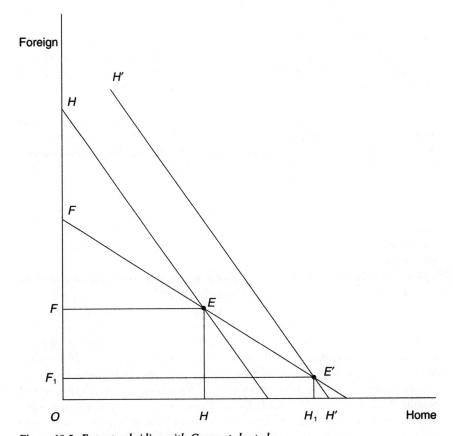

Figure 10.5 *Export subsidies with Cournot duopoly*

firm? It knows that if its own output does not change, the expansion of output by Home firm will reduce the price for both firms. Thus the Foreign firm would reduce its own output in an effort to balance out the output expansion by the Home firm; in such a case, there is a chance that a price decline will not be significant. The only problem which remains is how to make Foreign firm believe that the Home firm would expand. Suppose the Home government offered an export subsidy to its firm. In such a case it would be profitable for the Home firm to maintain a higher output for any given level of output by the Foreign firm. Along the reaction curve marginal costs are equal to perceived marginal revenue. If the export subsidy reduces Home's marginal costs, it can operate with a lower marginal revenue and for any output of the Foreign firm this entails a higher output of the Home firm. This means that the reaction curve of the Home firm will shift out to $H'H'$. At the new equilibrium E', the output of the Home firm is increased, the output of the Foreign firm has been reduced (however by less than the Home firms increase). The profits available at the market have however shifted from the Foreign to the Home firm. This is the reason why such a behaviour was named 'profit snatching' or 'profit shifting'.

The welfare effects for Home include an increase in profits accruing to the Home's firm. That rise in profits is higher than what the Home government spends on subsidy. Since in this example there is no direct effect on consumers' welfare in Home, we can conclude that Home is better off with the subsidy than under free trade. The impact of the subsidy by the Home government was to add credibility to the domestic firm's threat of expanding output. The only rational response by the Foreign firm to this credible threat was to reduce output in order to prevent the market price from falling too much. As a consequence the welfare of Foreign has declined by the amount of profits 'snatched' by the Home firm. Consumers in the rest of the world have benefited because their supplies of the good increased and the price dropped. Adding the welfare effects of all three countries together, we come up with a positive number: the export subsidy has benefited the world as a whole because it has reduced the level of monopoly power.

The case becomes more complicated when domestic consumption is introduced in Home and Foreign markets. In such circumstances, an export subsidy might, because it diverts sales of the domestic firm from domestic to foreign, reduce domestic consumers' welfare. If their loss combined with the subsidy cost is not offset with the amount of shifted profits, Home might find itself with lower welfare. Consumers in Foreign however, would be gaining and depending on their gain being larger or smaller than the profits lost by their firm, the national welfare of Foreign would be increased or reduced. Despite the consumers in the rest of the world again benefiting from this export subsidy, it is not clear what the welfare effects for the whole world would end up being.

■ *10.5* Summary

This chapter has examined three categories of argument for protection. First, a number of static arguments have been presented and examined, ranging from the market failure argument and the preservation of employment in a particular industry to the non-economic objectives for protection. Then we moved into discussing the so-called dynamic arguments for trade policy. We focused our attention on arguments justifying protection for industries in their infancy and their final days. Finally we turned to strategic arguments. These arguments seek to justify protection in cases when the typical assumption of perfectly functioning markets does not prevail and when there is a potential strategic role for government action in shifting the terms of trade to the benefit of domestic firms.

All of these arguments could be also classified as valid or invalid. As invalid we treat those arguments which are based on misunderstanding of the basic principles of trade, such as comparative advantage, or the arguments which fail to achieve the objectives used to justify the imposition of trade barriers in the first place. Although these invalid arguments should not merit serious discussion from the point of view of their logical validity, it is important to examine them because they still are able to attract considerable support among politicians and the general public. Such, for example, are the arguments based on preserving or boosting domestic employment, fairness of competition, or patriotism. Other arguments examined in this chapter could be identified as more or less valid in a sense that trade policy is a valid means to achieve certain economic and non-economic objectives. Despite this, trade policy is never the most efficient instrument. These 'valid' arguments could be further categorised into subgroups. The first contains the arguments for trade barriers in cases where trade barriers have no substitutes in achieving a rise in national welfare. The optimal tariff and some arguments based on imperfect competition belong to this group. Needless to say, validity is preserved by assuming away any form of foreign retaliation. Other trade barriers could be classed as valid but costly. Here we look at the barriers which are successful in achieving the desired objective of, for example, removing domestic distortions, raising government revenue, or changing the pattern of consumption or production. In these cases trade policy intervention is superior to doing nothing, but it is still the second best policy. Following the specificity rule, a more direct policy could be identified to achieve a desired objective, thus shielding a society from unnecessary costs.

In sum, there is only a weak theoretical support that governments could lean on when using trade barriers to achieve the majority of economic and non-economic goals. The real challenge is then to find out why, despite the inefficacy or the second best nature of the most trade policies, trade intervention still remains as the most prevalent and the most popular means of intervention. Some clues to answering this question have been given in the previous chapters but Chapter 12 presents more serious effort to identify the answers.

Chapter 11

The Measurement of Protection

■ *11.1* Introduction

There are two main strands of measurement in the area of protection that we should discuss. One is concerned with the extent of protection provided to a product or an industry. To understand the issue of the extent of protection better we conceptually differentiate between *nominal* and *effective* protection. While the nominal rate of protection is concerned with a single product or industry, the effective rate estimates the level of protection of a single product or industry but taking into account the nominal protection of the activities delivering inputs to the industry concerned. We know from our simple analysis of tariffs that a protection of one industry usually means a 'dis-protection' of others. This happens through (instantaneous and costless) reallocation of resources: factors of production leave other activities and move to the sheltered one. The effects of one industry's protection on all activities of an economy can be estimated by general equilibrium analysis. Such a measure is known as the *true* protection.

The second strand of measurement has traditionally been concerned with how costly protection of one industry is, that is, how large the Harberger triangles are. There have been quite a few attempts at this measurement and almost all of them have come up with disappointing results. According to most of them protection is not costly at all: 1–2 per cent of GDP (or up to 6–9 per cent of GDP for developing countries) is not that much after all. That is why the 'free trade' idea was really never truly accepted by politicians. Only recently, with new findings in the trade and growth theories and the theory of industrial organisation, were economists able to come up with more realistic estimates of the size of the cost of protection. It is now even acceptable to talk about these costs in terms of what they really represent – the gains of trade liberalisation.

In this chapter we describe the basic methods for computing the extent and cost of protection without going into all the problems encountered by the researchers who actually do the measurements. It must be stressed that the measurment of protection has been made more difficult by the existence of numerous non-tariff (i.e. non-price) trade barriers whose effects are hard to estimate. Because each country has its own specific instruments, the level and cost of protection is primarily an empirical question. But some generalisation of methodology and conclusions can be made. This is basically what is done in this chapter. We start with the measures that are limited to one product or an industry. We first explain in section 11.2 how the measures of nominal protection could differ from the rates written down in a customs tariff. Then in section 11.3 we turn to providing a formula and description for measuring an effective rate of protection. The general equilibrium analysis is given in section 11.4 where we mostly deal with the issues of the incidence of protection and true protection. Section 11.5 is concerned with measurements of the cost of protection, that is, gains from trade liberalisation.

■ *11.2* Nominal protection

The nominal rate of protection measures an amount by which protection increases domestic price above world price. For example, a tariff of 10 per cent on imported cloth would increase domestic price of cloth by 10 per cent above the world price of cloth. Thus the rate of nominal protection for cloth is 10 per cent. Following this example it may seem straightforward to compute a nominal rate of protection for any of the given products or activities. One need look only at the *tariff schedule* and read off the nominal rates. But this is only partly true. The rates from the tariff schedule will not tell the whole story because the tariff is not the only means of protection; there are numerous non-tariff instruments as well as other taxes being imposed on imports. The rate of aggregate nominal protection should take into account the effects of all of these instruments. But let us start with tariffs as the sole instrument of protection.

In the case when tariff is an *ad valorem* tariff, and there are no other trade taxes or barriers imposed, the rate of the tariff itself is the nominal rate of protection. If the tariff is expressed in a specific form (in money units per unit of imports), the nominal rate of protection (NRP) can be computed by the following formula:

$$NRP = (p - p^*)/p^* \tag{11.2.1}$$

where p and p^* denote the domestic and world prices, respectively, of the imported good. As already mentioned, the nominal rate of protection based on the tariff schedule does not always give a good indicator of the amount of nominal protection provided to an industry. According to Greenaway and Milner (1993, pp. 64–8) there are several reasons for this. One reason for the divergence of the nominal rates of protection from the schedule is the existence of *secondary tariffs*. These are additional taxes being imposed on imports; they may be called an import surcharge, a statistical tax or a stamp duty, but in effect they are import taxes or secondary tariffs. There are number of possible explanations for the existence of secondary tariffs but most often they are introduced either as a revenue-filling temporary measure or as a 'temporary' import-reducing measure (but is never removed). The practice of having a secondary tariff is widespread in economies that have an underdeveloped protection system and/or an extra need for government revenue (such as the developing countries and former socialist economies). Take, for example, the case of Croatia as the transforming economy. Croatia has inherited the protection system of the former socialist Yugoslavia, based on predominant use of non-tariff measures and administrative regulation of trade flows. Therefore as in any other socialist economy nominal tariffs were not playing an important role; consequently they were quite low for an economy at such level of development. Thus when most of the quantitative barriers and regulations were abolished after the independence of Croatia, the level of protection (and tariff revenues?) based only on the primary tariff rates proved to be too low. There was a need for secondary tariffs. The surcharge taxes in Croatia are well above the primary tariff rates (the ones from the tariff schedule). The average nominal tariff rate in 1994 was only 2.45 per cent, while the average of primary and secondary rates added together was 13.25 per cent.

Another reason for the divergence between the nominal rates and the schedule rates is the existence of exceptions and exemptions to the scheduled tariff. If a country is a signatory to preferential trade agreements, the tariffs actually applying could be significantly lower. The formula for calculating the *actual* tariff for product i is:

$$t_i = R_i/p_iQ_i \tag{11.2.2}$$

where the nominator on the right-hand side is the total customs collections for product i, and the denominator is the total value of imports of product i. This rate of tariff is known as the *ex post* or *implicit tariff* and is often used to illustrate the level of nominal protection. As Greenaway and Milner (1993) state, this measure is also not without problems. In order to pay lower duties importers tend to underinvoice or state the wrong place of origin which results in underestimation of the customs collection and therefore of the rate of implicit tariff.

Tariff redundancy is yet another reason for tariff schedule not being identical to the nominal rates of protection. A redundant tariff is one which has no impact on the level of imports because of some other policy being superior to the tariff. For instance, imports of some good i may be prohibited even though there could be a scheduled import tariff. Or the tariff rate could be so high that it is higher than the prohibitive tariff. (Note that our calculations of nominal and effective protection in fact assume that tariff rates are below prohibitive level of tariffs.) For example, a tariff which brings imports to zero might be 150 per cent. If the tariff is set to 170 per cent, the portion of tariff of 20 per cent is unused or redundant protection (or *'water in the tariff'*). If there is a lot of redundancy in the protection system, the rate of nominal protection calculated on the basis of the tariff schedule would overstate the nominal protection. In such case implicit tariffs should be used for calculations.

But this is still not the end of story on nominal protection. What must be added is the extent of protection due to non-tariff barriers. To do that we must first express non-tariff barriers in terms of *tariff equivalents*. This involves estimation of the effect the non-tariff measure has on the price of the product. For instance, if an import quota raises the domestic price of the restricted import 40 per cent above the world price, then this import quota is considered equivalent to a 40 per cent tariff. In practice, however, the estimation of tariff equivalents is much more complex than could be conceived from our example.

■ *11.3* Effective protection

If the industry concerned were not using any inputs, domestically produced or imported, it would be appropriate to use the nominal rate of protection as the measure of protection provided to it. In practice however this rarely happens. Even the simplest input–output table shows how interdependent productive activities are and that each industry in its production uses intermediate goods (inputs) from other, often quite a few, domestic and foreign industries. In other words, an industry 'adds value' to the inter-mediate goods used. Value added is the difference between the price of the final product and the cost of the intermediate goods used in its production. More formally we say that the value added for a unit of product j, v_j, is equal to:

$$v_j = p_j - \Sigma a_{ij} p_i \qquad (11.3.1)$$

where p_j and p_i are prices of the final and intermediate goods respectively, and a_{ij} is the physical input coefficient. Alternatively we can express value added for a monetary unit (say per US$1 worth) of product j. This implies dividing (11.3.1) by the p_j:

$$v_j / p_j = 1 - (\Sigma a_{ij} p_i / p_j)$$

and by substituting

$$c_{ij} = a_{ij}p_i/p_j$$

we have:

$$v_j = p_j(1 - \Sigma c_{ij}) \tag{11.3.1a}$$

The amount of value added v_j is influenced by protection: it is affected by the protection given to industry j, and by the protection given to the n producers of intermediate goods i. The real effect of protection on value added is revealed through the rate of effective protection. We define the effective rate of protection as the measure of difference between value added in domestic industry and value added at world prices expressed in percentage terms. The extent of the difference is influenced by tariffs (and non-tariff barriers) on both imported inputs and finished goods. Several simple examples should be useful in illustrating this point further.

Suppose that a high-resolution TV set sells on the world market for US$8,000 and the parts of which it is made sell for US$5,000. Suppose also that the domestic TV industry, which is inefficient by world standards, cannot produce a TV set for less than US$5,000. To encourage domestic production, a government grants a 25 per cent tariff on imported TV sets. This allows domestic TV assemblers to charge US$2,000 above the world price, that is, US$10,000. Before the introduction of the tariff, the value added (at world prices) was US$3,000. After the tariff was imposed the value added is raised to US$5.000 or by 66 per cent. Therefore the nominal rate of protection of 25 per cent provides an effective rate of protection of 66 per cent. In general, whenever there is a positive nominal protection to the final product and no protection on inputs, the effective rate of protection will be higher than the nominal rate. This conclusion applies also for the cases when there is a positive protection of the intermediate goods but the nominal rate of this protection is lower than the nominal rate of the protection given to the final good. To check this, suppose that the government adds a second tariff of 20 per cent on imports of television components, raising the cost of components to domestic TV producers to US$6,000. Now the effective rate of protection to the final producer 'drops' to 33 per cent. What if the nominal rates of protection of the intermediate good and the final good are the same, say 25 per cent? Then in our example, the cost of components is raised to US$6,250 with value added being reduced to US$3,750. In other words, the system of protection raises the value added by 25 per cent relative to the free trade level. Therefore, uniform nominal tariffs on inputs and outputs result in equality between effective and nominal protection for output producers.

We can express the concept of effective protection more formally. The basic formula for measuring the effective rate of protection (ERP) for industry j is:[1]

$$ERP_j = (v_j - v_j^*)/v_j^* = (v_j/v_j^*) - 1 \qquad (11.3.2)$$

where v_j is the value added at domestic (post-tariff) prices, and v_j^* is value added at world prices. By using (11.3.1) and (11.3.1a) we can re-write this formula in a more disaggregated form. Under free trade the value added per unit of output j is the price of a unit less the value of intermediate good i used:

$$v_j^* = p_j^* - \Sigma a_{ij} p_i^*$$

where * denotes free trade prices. The value added at domestic post-tariff prices however looks like:[2]

$$v_j = (1 + t_j)p_j^* - \Sigma a_{ij}(1 + t_i)p_i^*$$

where t_j and t_i are applied tariff rates on imports of goods j and i respectively. Then by following basic formula of (11.2.1) we can write:

$$ERP_j = [(1 + t_j)p_j^* - \Sigma a_{ij}(1 + t_i)p_i^*] - [p_j^* - \Sigma a_{ij}p_i^*]/[p_j^* - \Sigma a_{ij}p_i^*]$$

or

$$ERP_j = [t_j p_j^* - \Sigma a_{ij}t_i p_i^*]/[p_j^* - \Sigma a_{ij}p_i^*] \qquad (11.3.3)$$

Alternatively, in terms of cost shares c_{ij} the effective rate of protection is:

$$ERP_j = [t_j - \Sigma a_{ij}t_i]/[1 - \Sigma a_{ij}] \qquad (11.3.3a)$$

One look at (11.3.3) and (11.3.3a) is sufficient to confirm the conclusions we have reached on the basis of numerical examples about the relationship between the nominal and effective rates. With the three determinants of the effective rate of protection, that is, t_j, t_i and a_{ij}, the rate of the effective rate of protection for j will be higher, *ceteris paribus*:

(a)   the higher is the nominal tariff on output,
(b)   the lower is the nominal tariff on input, and
(c)   the higher is the input content.

That the first two conclusions stand were shown earlier through numerical examples but the third, which is also intuitively less obvious, was not. The input content of the production of final goods is very significant in determining the effective protection. The higher the content of inputs, with the nominal rates on outputs and inputs being given, the higher the rate of the effective rate of protection. This is easily checked by using (11.3.3). Suppose that instead of our first case where the input content (in terms of c_{ij}) was 0.625 it now rises to 0.80 and the tariff rates are unchanged. Then we have, by applying (11.3.3a):

$$ERP_{TV} = (0.25 - 0.8 \times 0.2)/(1 - 0.8)$$
$$= 0.45 \text{ or } 45\%$$

With the input content increased to 80 per cent, the rate of effective protection increases from 33 per cent to 45 per cent. Or with an input content of 40 per cent, the rate of effective protection falls to 28.3 per cent. The very high input content (coupled with low protection) is behind some very high effective rates of protection, particularly in developing countries (although the nominal protection may appear very low). A high effective rate of protection in fact means that resources used in adding value in domestic production at final stages are valued at much higher prices than in the world, thus indicating some major distortions in the economy. A high rate of effective protection is typically found in countries with so-called '*cascading*' or '*escalating*' tariff structures. The main feature of such a tariff structure is that rates increase with the degree of processing. This is seen as one of the obstacles for increasing the exports from developing countries to the developed markets (which normally have cascading tariffs) because tariffs make processed exports from the former countries too expensive.

Effective protection may also be *negative*. This happens when the tariff structure is such as to cause an increase in the price of inputs greater than that of output. This will always occur when there is no nominal protection on the final good production of which is based on using inputs having positive nominal tariff protection. A negative effective rate of protection implies that the value added in post-protection conditions is lower than under free trade and this is common occurrence with exporters who do not enjoy any direct assistance but have to use inputs which are heavily protected. In this case the exporter is actually taxed. Let us show this case by using our formula again. Suppose the same producer of high-resolution TVs has no nominal protection, but the producers of the domestically manufactured components have 20 per cent tariff protection. Then with the initial input content of 0.625 we have:

$$ERP_{TV} = (0 - 0.625 \times 0.2)/(1 - 0.625)$$
$$= -0.333 \text{ or } -33.3\%$$

Another but less obvious case is when the domestic producer of the final good (j) displays *negative value added*, that is, when the finished good is worth less than the inputs built into it – both measured at world prices.

This problem is not just a theoretical curriosum, it is being found in empirical investigations especially in the developing countries. It certainly merits some additional explanation.

There are several factors that can provide an explanation for negative value added (Michaely, 1977). First, and probably more frequently, is the inferior production process at home, resulting in extreme inefficiency and huge waste. We have a domestic producer of a final good who transforms imported inputs or their domestic substitutes into an output which at the world market sells for less than the intermediate goods. In other words the production processes in the final stages at home are so inefficient as to result in waste. Another factor explaining the occurrence of negative value added is the existence of transport costs. When there are high transport costs involved in trade of intermediate goods, but not in trade of final goods, the ratio of the price of the imported input to the price of output given the same input coefficients would be much higher at home than abroad (that is, domestic $c_{ij} = a_{ij}p_i/p_j$ would be much higher). In such case it is not hard for negative value added to appear. Michaely (1977, pp. 133–4) gives an example which was quite important in the past – a bulky raw material, coal, imported at a high cost disappears in the production of the final good which sells cheaply at the world market.

There is no doubt about the fate of these final goods producers under free trade – they would not exist or they would be producing with positive value added. The existence of producers with negative value added is possible only under protection. In fact the extent of effective protection in these circumstances is very (infinitely) high.[3]

In the case when production displaying negative value added exists, that is, when inputs cost more than the finished product at world prices, there is a negative impact on national welfare. Welfare could be improved by stopping the national resources from going into the activities displaying negative value added. The solution is hence to close down the industry in question and import finished goods (while paying bounties to maintain the income of displaced primary factors).

From the above account it is obvious that, however simplistic, the effective rate of protection provides important information on the actual degree of protection granted to domestic producers.[4] We have seen that the actual degree of protection could be less than the nominal level, and in some circumstances even negative so that producers are actually penalised by the protection system. In most cases, however, actual protection would be higher than nominal protection showing the inadequacy of the nominal tariff rates for the evaluation of the degree of protection in individual economies or of the scope for further trade liberalisation within multi-lateral trade negotiations. Another important use of effective rates of protection is in determining by how much the trade regime departs from neutrality. The ratio of average effective rates of protection for importables and exportables can be used as an indicator of *trade regime bias*. The system is neutral when this ratio is equal to one. If average protection to importables exceeds average protection to exportables (a ratio higher than one) the system is said to be favouring the import-substituting sector. We will discuss the implications of trade regime bias in Chapter 13.

The formula provided above for estimation of the effective rate of protection looks quite simple. Yet the problems of actually measuring effective rates of protection are onerous. Some of the problems most often quoted by researchers are the following.

(1) *Tariff averaging.* The fact is that any given industry will typically have to face a variety of tariff rates on its different outputs and inputs so that both nominal tariff rates must be measured as tariff averages, which is both complicated and influences the estimates of effective rates.

(2) *Non-tradeable inputs.* There are at least two ways of incorporating non-tradeables into the estimates of effective rates. In the case when they are supplied at constant cost, it is possible to treat them as any other goods with no nominal protection. Alternatively, they can be treated as factors of production if their supply is fixed.

(3) *Non-tariff barriers.* Other instruments, for instance taxes, subsidies, or quotas affect the degree of protection and it is necessary to try to incorporate their influence. The way to do this is to estimate the tariff equivalents of these non-tariff measures.

(4) *Exchange rate effects.* Depreciation (devaluation) raises the prices of all tradeable goods by x per cent and this affects the level of protection. At some exchange rate, the effective rate might be quite high, resulting in a surplus on the balance of payments. This would cause exchange rate to appreciate which in turn would weaken the level of protection for tradeable sectors.

Despite numerous difficulties encountered in measuring effective protection, a lot of work has been done in this area for both developing and DCs.[5] Table 11.1 contains the results from several studies on effective protection in developing countries in the late 1950s–mid-1980s. Since these studies did not use a common methodology, the intercountry comparison is possible only for each study separately.

11.4 The incidence of protection and true protection

As mentioned above the use of nominal and effective rates of protection is not without problems. Most importantly, these concepts only take into account the direct impact of a tariff (or all barriers combined in the tariff

Table 11.1 *Evidence on effective protection*

Country	Year	Average EPR	Range of EPRs
Brazil[1]	1958	108*	17 − 502
	1963	184*	60 − 687
	1967	63*	4 − 252
Chile[1]	1967	175*	−23 − 1140
Colombia[1]	1969	19*	−8 − 140
Indonesia[1]	1971	119*	−19 − 5400
Ivory Coast[1]	1973	41*	−25 − 278
Pakistan[1]	1963–4	356*	−6 − 595
	1970-1	200*	36 − 595
South Korea[1]	1968	−1*	−15 − 82
Thailand[1]	1973	27*	−43 − 236
Tunisia[1]	1972	250*	1 − 737
Uruguay[1]	1965	384*	17 − 1014
Argentina[2]	1969	94	−596 − 1308
Israel[2]	1968	76	−943 − 750
Singapore[2]	1967	6	−1 − 86
Brazil[3]	1980–1	46	−16 − 97
Pakistan[4]	1980–1	60	−799 − 1543
India[5]	1968–9	na	27 − 3354
Mauritius[6]	1980	55	2 − 300
Madagascar[7]	1983	156	−93 − 852
Burundi[8]	1985	na	−4 − 7896

Note: * The sample includes only manufacturing industries.
na   Not avilable.
Source: 1. Krueger (1984, p. 542, Table 3.1); 2. Balassa *et al.* (1982); 3. Tyler (1985); 4. Naqvi *et al.* (1983); 5. Bhagwati and Srinivasan (1975); 6. Greenaway and Milner (1988); 7. Greenaway and Milner (1990a); 8. Greenaway and Milner (1990b); 2–8 as cited in Greenaway and Milner (1993, p. 92, Table 5.4).

equivalents). However the indirect general equilibrium effects that take place in the other sectors, especially non-tradeables, of the economy are not captured by these measurements. To capture the sectoral changes Sjaasted and Clements (1982) have developed the so-called trade policy incidence model. In this model there are three sectors: importables, exportables and a non-traded sector. There are two relative price ratios (importables relative to exportables, and importables relative to non-tradeables) from which the incidence of protection in sectoral terms can be examined. When a trade barrier (say tariff) is introduced, this model can be used to examine the impact of the tariff on the price of importables relative to exportables and relative to non-tradeables. This gives an indication of the so-called *true protection* (see Box 11.1).

Box 11.1   *The incidence of trade protection model*

Consider a simple three-sector model of the economy involving exportables (*e*), importables (*m*) and non-tradeables (*n*). The supply (*S*) and demand (*D*) for non-traded goods may be written as:

$$S = f(p_e, p_m, p_n, \ldots) \tag{B11.1}$$
$$D = f(p_e, p_m, p_n, \ldots) \tag{B11.2}$$

where p_e, p_m and p_n represent the prices of exportables, importables and non-traded goods, respectively. We assume fixed real incomes and total factor endowments. Totally differentiating and dividing both sides by S or D yields:

$$dS/S = (\partial S/\partial p_e)(dp_e/S) + (\partial S/\partial p_m)(dp_m/S) +$$
$$(\partial S/\partial p_n)(dp_n/S) \tag{B11.3}$$
$$dD/D = (\partial D/\partial p_e)(dp_e/D) + (\partial D/\partial p_m)(dp_m/D) +$$
$$(\partial D/\partial p_n)(dp_n/D) \tag{B11.4}$$

By using our familiar hat (^) notation we can re-write (B11.3) and (B11.4) as:

$$\hat{S} = m^s{}_e \hat{p}_e + m^s{}_m \hat{p}_m + m^s{}_n \hat{p}_n \tag{B11.5}$$
$$\hat{D} = m^d{}_e \hat{p}_e + m^d{}_m \hat{p}_m + m^d{}_n \hat{p}_n \tag{B11.6}$$

where the $m^i{}_j$ are compensating supply and demand price elasticities. Market equilibrium requires that

$$\Sigma_i m^s{}_i = \Sigma_i m^d{}_i = 0 \tag{B11.7}$$
$$S = D \tag{B11.8}$$

so that combining (B11.5)–(B11.8) results in:

$$\hat{p}_n = \omega \hat{p}_m + (1 - \omega)\hat{p}_e \tag{B11.9}$$

where the protection incidence parameter is

$$\omega = (m^d{}_m - m^s{}_m)/(m^s{}_n - m^d{}_n)$$

This parameter ω is the proportion of import protection that is an implicit tax on the exportable sector. Likewise $(1 - \omega)$ is the proportion of the explicit export subsidisation that is an implicit tax on the importable sector.

In the case when the sole instrument of protection is a uniform *ad valorem* tariff on imports (t), the true tariff (*T*) is given by:

$$T = (p_m/p_n) \tag{B11.10}$$

and the post-protection prices will differ from the free trade prices (*) by:

$$p_m = p_m^*(1 + t)$$
$$p_n = p_n^*(1 + \omega t)$$

Dividing everything by free trade prices gives:

$$T_i = (p_m/p_n) = (1 + t)/(1 + \omega t) - 1 \tag{B11.11}$$

The true export subsidy (S) in this situation is given by:

$$S_t = (p_e/p_n) = 1/(1 - t) - 1 \tag{B11.12}$$

where $S < 0$ for all S, and $t > 0$.

The industry is said to receive a *positive* true rate of protection if the price of an industry's output is boosted by protection to a greater extent than its input costs. This concept of true protection is the same as the *net protection* described in Corden (1971) which is the tariff *less* the resultant exchange rate appreciation. A positive true rate of protection is called a true tariff if the industry is competing with imports, and a true subsidy or tax if the industry is export-oriented. True protection measures have the advantage of making explicit the actual impact of trade restrictions on different sectors of the economy. Any existing set of nominal tariffs and subsidies can be rewritten as a set of true taxes and subsidies which make explicit the subsidy or tax to the producers of importables, or exportables. True protection will always be less than nominal protection unless the incidence parameter equals zero.

Table 11.2 compares nominal rates of protection in New Zealand's importable and exportable sectors with the average true rates of protection in these sectors for a period of 30 years. Table 11.2 serves as a good illustration of the disparity between the two type of rates. Using an estimate of the incidence parameter of 0.7 Lattimore (1987) shows how trade policy actually worked in New Zealand. Governments had in place two sets of instruments: explicit import duties and explicit export subsidies. Of course these instruments tend to work against each other. Through an impact on non-traded goods both import and export protection ended up being much lower. While this still has provided positive (although more modest) protection to the import substitutes sector, the exportable sector of New Zealand has actually been penalised.

Table 11.2 *New Zealand: nominal rates of protection and average true rates of protection (%)*

Year	Nominal rate of import protection	Nominal rate of export subsidy	True rate of protection – import substitutes	True rate of protection – exports
1955–8	34.2	0.1	14.7	−14
1964–7	53.6	0.5	22.9	−20
1972–3	31.5	1.7	16.4	−10
1978–9	(20.3)[1]	2.3	10.4	−6
1983–4	30.9	11.1	13.8	−3

Note: 1. This rate is thought to seriously underestimate import protection; see a more detailed explanation in Lattimore (1987, pp. 45–6)
Source: Lattimore (1987, Table 4, p. 45; Table 7, p. 52).

The concept of true protection reveals a severe limitation on commercial policy in that while the authorities can grant protection to certain activities by setting up trade barriers or subsidies, the economic consequences are to a large extent unpredictable. This is due to the fact that the *incidence parameter* used in calculating the true rates of protection depends exclusively on the substitutability of demand and supply among various sectors of the economy, i.e. tastes, preferences, and technology.

■ *11.5* The cost of protection

In the final section of this chapter we review some of the methods and results of the estimation of the costs (and benefits) associated with the introduction (or removal) of trade barriers. We can differentiate between partial equilibrium and general equilibrium methods for estimation of the costs of protection. The partial equilibrium methodology is related to estimation of the size of the so-called Harberger triangles, while the general equilibrium analysis is based on the use the so-called computable general equilibrium (CGE) models. Both of these are limited to the conditions of perfectly competitive markets.

The cost of protection in a partial equilibrium framework is defined as deadweight loss of protection. We have already discussed how this loss for a small country might be measured in terms of areas of the Harberger triangles (refer to Chapter 8, section 8.2).[6] In that chapter we derived an approximate measure of the deadweight loss of tariff (or tariff equivalent) as:

$$\Delta W = 1/2\, t\, \Delta M$$

where ΔW is the change in welfare, ΔM is the change in the quantity of imports, and t is the rate of the tariff. Using the definition of the elasticity of import demand: $\varepsilon_m = (\Delta M/\Delta p^*{}_C)(p^*{}_C/M)$, where M denotes the current level of imports, we expressed the change in imports as:

$$\Delta M = \varepsilon_m M(\Delta p^*{}_C/p^*{}_C)$$

Noting that the tariff represents the proportionate change in price between free trade and tariff restricted trade, that is, $t = (\Delta p^*{}_C/p^*{}_C)$, we finally obtained our measure as:

$$\Delta W = 1/2\,(\varepsilon_m M t^2)$$

If the trade barrier in question is not a tariff, we must first estimate the tariff equivalent and then use the above formula to calculate the cost of non-tariff barriers.

Even though this formula only approximates the amount of welfare lost through tariff protection, this method has been widely used in estimating the welfare gains from both complete tariff removal and partial trade liberalisation (see Box 11.2).

It is certainly more interesting to get a general equilibrium estimate of the cost of protection since, compared to the partial equilibrium one, it should have taken into account all the economy-wide effects. Modern computer hardware and software make it feasible to cope with complicated algebraic formulation of the Walrasian general equilibrium. As a consequence CGE modelling has taken over when it comes to estimation of protection cost and/or gains from trade liberalisation. There are many excellent texts where reader can find all the details on the constructing and applying CGE model to trade policy issues.[7]

We should note that one of the important factors contributing to the cost of protection is the phenomenon of rent-seeking or more generally directly unproductive profit-seeking activities. These arise as a consequence of the structure of the existing protection system which allows for additional private benefits to be obtained by lobbying (naturally at the expense of the rest of the society). Or these groups may use lobbying to press government into increasing the level of protection or even imposing new trade barriers. As these activities waste real resources, they raise the cost of protection. We will discuss activities and their welfare implications in Chapter 12.

A growing field of empirical research is related to the welfare effects of protection or removal of protection with imperfect competition. An excellent survey of such research is Richardson (1989). The most important conclusion that Richardson makes on the basis of the empirical studies surveyed is that simultaneous reduction in trade barriers and in the barriers to domestic competition creates sizeable and mutually reinforcing increases in an economy's real income. Although there are exceptions, the rule still remains that trade liberalisation generates significant gains even under imperfect competition with scale economies.

Box 11.2 *Just how cheap is protectionism?*

Feenstra (1992) provides a good example of the magnitude of costs of protection in a large country which by protecting domestic industries generates deadweight losses not only at home but also in trading partners economies. Figures 11.1 and 11.2 illustrate the effect of an import quota on the domestic market in the USA and the effect on the world prices, respectively.

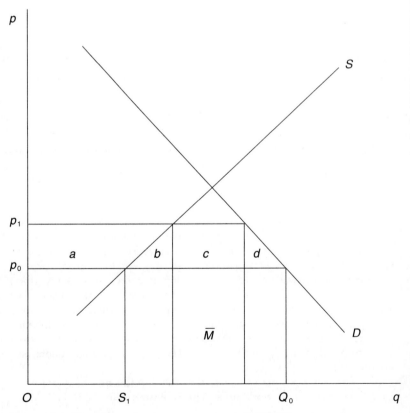

Figure 11.1 *The effect of an import quota on the US domestic market*

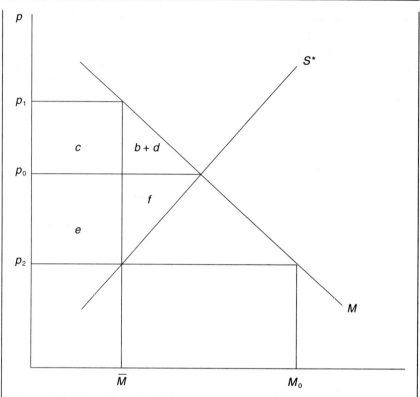

Figure 11.2 *The effect of a US import quota on world prices*

In Figure 11.1 S represents the US supply curve for a particular good, say sugar. D is the US demand for sugar. The pre-protectionist world price of sugar is p_0 and a quantity of M_0 is imported at that price. Assume that the USA introduces an import quota $\bar{M}$ which pushes the domestic price of sugar to p_1. The loss of consumers is given by the area of the loss of consumer surplus: $a + b + c + d$. Part of this is redistributed as the benefit to domestic producers of sugar: this part is given by area a. Area c represents the rents associated with the import quota. As we know, the rents can be captured by domestic importers, domestic government (via auction of quota licences) or by foreign exporters. Assume that it is the foreign governments who allocate the quota to their own exporters. In that case area c is lost for the USA. On top of that, there is a deadweight loss equal to $b + d$. Thus the net loss to the USA from imposing a quota on imports of sugar is $b + c + d$.

It is however plausible to expect that this introduction of quota will have some effect on the world price. This is illustrated in Figure 11.2. M is the US excess demand for imports of sugar and S^* is the excess supply curve from the rest of the world. The pre-protectionist equilibrium price and quantity of imports are p_0 and M_0. If an import quota $\bar{M}$ is imposed, the domestic price rises to p_1. As it is drawn in Figure 11.2, it is possible for the export price of sugar to drop to p_2 since the foreign firms would have be willing to supply sugar to the US market at this lower price. The difference $p_1 - p_2$ is the quota premium per unit sold at price p_2 to the US market, totalling to $\bar{M}(p_1 - p_2)$ or areas $c + e$ in Figure 11.2. How much of this premium transforms into a welfare improvement in the rest of the world? We have to deduct the loss of producer surplus to foreign suppliers equal to area $e + f$. Area f is the deadweight loss to the rest of the world due to the restriction on their exports. Thus the welfare improvement is $(c + e) - (e + f) = (c - f)$. If the import quota is very restrictive it is possible that $c > f$, in which case the rest of the world is a net loser too. The efficiency losses to the world as a whole are combined from the US and foreign losses and amount to $b + d + f$.

Thus the cost of protection facing the USA can be measured by summing the amounts of deadweight loss $(b + d)$ and the amounts of the quota rents (c). The global losses due to the US protectionism can be measured by subtracting the quota rents from the US losses and adding the efficiency losses in the rest of the world. Feenstra (1992) provides a table which is reproduced here as Table 11.3 which carries some estimates of costs of US protection.

Table 11.3 *Annual cost of US protection (bn dollars, c.1985)*

	US deadweight loss $(b + d)$	Quota rents $(c$ or $c + e)$	Foreign deadweight loss (f)
Automobiles	0.2 – 1.2	2.2 – 7.9	0 – 3
Dairy	1.4	0.25	0.02
Steel	0.1 – 0.3	0.7 – 2.0	0.1
Sugar	0.1	0.4 – 1.3	0.2
Textiles & apparel	4.9 – 5.9	4.0 – 6.1	4 – 15.5
Average tariffs	1.2 – 3.4	0	na
Total*	7.9 – 12.3	7.3 – 17.3	4.3 – 18.8

Note: * In diary the quota rents are earned by US importers, and so are not included in the total.
Source: Feenstra (1992, Table 1, pp. 160–9).

■ *Chapter 12* ■

The Political Economy of Trade Policy

■ *12.1* Introduction

The underlying assumption employed in our analysis of the arguments for trade barriers in Chapter 10 was that the government, in setting the level of protection, was benevolent and that it acted to maximise the welfare of the nation via the representative consumer. Under such an assumption, among many trade barriers discussed, only a few can (as the first best or, more often, the *second best* policies) advance the national welfare compared with the free trade situation. These cases of nearly justified trade intervention may include the correction of a distortion (that is, closing a gap between marginal cost and marginal benefit), revenue collection or terms of trade correction. The latter is rightly seen as a 'beggar-your-neighbour policy', thus inviting retaliation from trading partners. In most cases, however, as our analysis clearly demonstrated, protectionist policies result in a net national welfare loss. Why then do, protectionist policies in practice exist? The most common explanation is that the national welfare loss due to protectionist policies is relatively small. Moreover the loss is dispersed across a large number of economic agents (consumers) preventing them effectively making a stand against such protectionist policies. A similar characterisation can be made of those producers who get hurt through the implementation of protectionist trade policies. On the other hand, we find some groups of economic agents (producers) rationally spending resources with the objective of influencing the suppliers of protection, government, in its decision regarding the level and the instruments of protection. In this case we have an *endogenously* determined level (and forms) of protection. To use pure economic theory to try to explain the level of protection, or its specific forms, may then not be sufficient. Given that the protection is determined in a political market, better explanations to this end are provided by examining the interactions of pure economic theory and political actions. Thus there is a need to turn to the field of *political economy*.

In this chapter we discuss how the market for protection functions. In section 12.2 we look at the demand side for protection. In particular we look into the activities of *interest groups* or the private sector through which they attempt to maximise their private benefits arising from the existing trade policies and the activities which are used to modify those policies in order to obtain greater benefits. The common name for these activities is *directly unproductive profit-seeking activities*, and they embrace activities such as revenue-seeking, rent-seeking, tariff-seeking, etc. In section 12.3 we discuss the factors influencing the supply side of protection setting. Section 12.4 examines some of the empirical evidence.

■ *12.2* The demand for protection

Chapter 10 lists many different reasons the various groups in a society might use to seek protection, such as unemployment, a fall in wages, or environmental concerns. As said many times before, most of these reasons are invalid when examined through the looking glass of economic theory. However, some arguments (and probably too many) get accepted because of political pressure. Rarely would any government not bow to the pressure of the employment argument, particularly if the industry in question has some impact on the ethical or moral values of voters. This is, for example, the case with the textile and footwear industries which employ mostly part-time female workers, or with the steel industry which is so important for national defence but also for a national car industry.

Often the original motivation for protection might have been fully valid, as in the case of temporary balance of payments problems. However once the problems are overcome, protection is often not removed. The reason for this is in a strong *lobbying* for the continuance of protection, most certainly motivated by revenue- or rent-seeking. Lobbying for the continuance of protection or for the imposition of a trade barrier is costly. Let us discuss this issue in more detail.

□ *Directly unproductive profit-seeking activities*

Thus far in our discussion we have implied that the resources used in productive activities must result in a positive output. It is not necessary that this output be the maximum output given the resources used (thus implying some technological inefficiency) but the output must still exist. Now we will turn our attention to economic activities of a different type. They are called *directly unproductive profit-seeking activities (DUPs)* and include all sorts of activities which are profitable but do not directly produce any goods or services. They do however use up real resources; since the national product they produce is zero, these activities may be seen as completely wasteful. But what is the objective of such activities? They aim at *redistributing* the existing national product.

It does not come as any surprise that trade barriers necessarily result in a redistribution of national income or product. There are claims that in many cases redistribution is a hidden objective. We have seen how tariffs divert a portion of consumers' income (and, sometimes, of foreign supplier's) to producers, and the rest to the government. It was implied that government works in the best interest of the nation and therefore redistributes those revenues; but this is not what necessarily happens in practice. It is true that, after the administration is paid for its work, a part of the revenue will go on financing social welfare but a large proportion of it will be used to finance subsidies or other forms of assistance to producers. There are many ways in which these resources can be allocated to producers; when producers themselves undertake to obtain some of the revenue and for that purpose use up inputs that would otherwise be used in creation of national product, we have an example of DUPs. Given the number of various trade instruments and the fact that each redistributes national income to the one of the selected groups in society, it is clear that there is a lot of opportunity to increase one's profits by engaging in such socially wasteful activities.

It is customary to differentiate between two basic forms of DUPs. The first type of activities take a (trade) policy as given and focus on redistribution of revenues or rents generated by this policy. These are called *policy-exogenous DUPs*. Examples of such activities are (a) *rent-seeking*, which is a process of wasting resources by chasing politically created scarcity premiums (Magee, 1993); (b) *revenue-seeking*, which is a process of pre-empting of the revenues of tariffs or other taxes; and (c) *smuggling* which includes activities seeking to evade trade policy, such as paying import duty. These activities waste social resources in order to obtain private profits.

The second type of DUPs includes so-called *policy-endogenous* activities. Their objective is to influence government in its decisions with respect to the level and type of protection. This influence could be achieved by *lobbying* and by *strategic behaviour*. These activities are even more harmful for society since, in addition to wasting real resources, they also cause new distortions. Only rarely will these new distortions act as neutralisers of existing distortions thus in fact being cost-reducing. Such cases were known in the former socialist systems where lobbying for additional intervention was in fact correcting a highly distortionary system of quantitative and administered protection (Bhagwati and Srinivasan, 1980).

Next we turn to examining some examples of both policy-exogenous and policy-endogenous DUPs.

Revenue- or rent-seeking

Revenue- or rent-seeking embraces lobbying activities designed to capture rents (scarcity premiums) that accompany most forms of pre-existing protection, such as tariffs and especially quantitative restrictions. In her pioneering article on rent-seeking Krueger (1974) considers the case when the existence of import quotas triggers rent-seeking behaviour. The accompanying instrument of import quotas are import licences which in fact determine who is going to import what. If the government auctions licences, the import quota is captured by the government and this is where the story ends. However if government hands out the import licences free of charge, the rents are there for grabbing for those who manage to get the licence to import the whole or the larger part of the restricted imports. The actual methods of competition for capturing this rent include for instance direct lobbying of politicians, overinvesting in production capacity (to ensure a licence allocated in proportion to productive capacity), over-importation (to ensure a licence allocated in proportion to pre-existent imports), and cost-creating corruption.

Krueger, as many others later, assumed that the value of resources wasted on rent-seeking activities equalled the value of the rent itself. Since in many countries the quota rents can amount to high proportions of GDP, the costs of these activities are quite significant. Going back to the simple world of partial equilibrium analysis, the extent of the social cost arising from rent seeking is shown in Figure 12.1. Assuming that rent-seekers compete for the total amount of quota rents, the costs to society of quota include the usual deadweight loss equal to the sum of areas $b + d$ (Harberger triangles) and the area R (the Krueger rectangle), while the cost of rent-seeking equals area R. As it turns out, the Krueger rectangle is a good long-run measure of the waste of resources by rent-seekers only when (a) there is free entry and exit into and out of the rent-seeking activity, (b) if individuals are risk-neutral or (c) individuals are risk-averse and the rent they capture is not a large proportion of their pre-existent wealth (Vousden, 1990, p. 76).

Let us look at the differences between revenue-seeking and rent-seeking under the general equilibrium framework. First we will consider the case of lobbying for the entire amount of revenue or rent available for capturing. Secondly we will assume that only a part of the revenue or rents is available and that rent-seekers chase that portion.[1]

Entire revenue/rent-seeking   Figure 12.2 should serve as a good illustration in examining the welfare effects of the entire revenue- (or rent-)seeking. We shall start with the case of tariff revenue-seeking. Consider a small economy with two sectors, importable food (F) and exportable cloth (C). The PPF for food and cloth in the absence of DUPs is given by the *PP* curve. Suppose that a tariff is imposed on imports of food. That inserts a gap between world

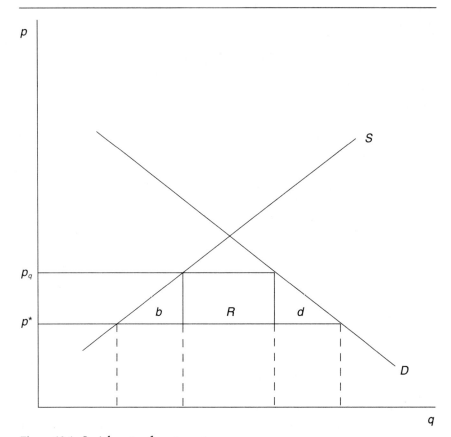

Figure 12.1 *Social costs of quota rents*

prices p^* and domestic post-tariff prices p_t. Tariff-distorted equilibrium involves production at point P_t, and consumption at point D_t on the indifference curve I_t. Given the assumption of one-for-one between the resources spent on revenue-seeking and the value of the revenues available for seeking, it is clear that the amount of tariff revenue will effectively disappear and the factor incomes will be the same as the expenditure on factors evaluated at domestic prices. This implies that once the DUPs are involved the consumption point moves down (along the income consumption path) to the point D_r at a lower indifference curve. Given the small country assumption and that the country could not consume more than it produces, this consumption point must be on the line representing world prices p^*.

Which production combination is related to this consumption point? We know that resources are being wasted on revenue-seeking; this implies that a new production point must be inside the old frontier. Since we know how much resources is wasted, and the tariff-distorted prices are still providing signals to the producer, it is not too difficult to conclude that a

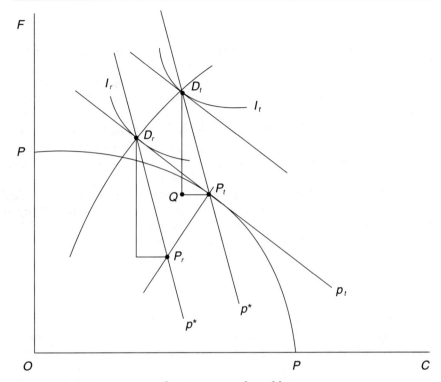

Figure 12.2 *Entire revenue seeking in a general equilibrium*

new production point would lie somewhere along the Rybczynski line which begins in point P_t at the old frontier. In this example the Rybczynski line could be defined as the locus of outputs of food and cloth obtained as factors of production are being withdrawn in the ratio required by DUPs at the given distorted prices. Since the production point must lie also on the world price line p^*, the new production point is found at point P_r.

In Figure 12.2 both consumption and production are reduced after DUPs are introduced into the tariff-distorted equilibrium. This is because in our example the Rybczynski line is positively sloped. It is also possible that, given different factor intensities employed in these two productive sectors and revenue-seeking, the Rybczynski line would be negatively sloped which would result in a different production point (one *closer* to the free trade equilibrium) and therefore have different welfare implications (see Bhagwati and Srinivasan, 1980, for more details on this case of beneficial revenue-seeking). But even with this addition, revenue-seeking could never compensate for the total cost of tariff-induced distortion.

With respect to the social cost of revenue-seeking under the general equilibrium consideration, let us look at the values of tariff revenue and the resources wasted on capturing it. With assumption of a revenue-seeker chasing the whole amount of revenue, the social cost of such DUPs valued at tariff-distorted prices matches exactly the value of the tariff revenue before the DUPs (equal to the horizontal distance between the domestic price lines p_t through D_t and D_r). The actual tariff revenue collected with lobbying is, however, slightly higher; it equals the horizontal distance between the domestic price lines p_t drawn through D_r and P_r. Thus the actual cost of the revenue-seeking can be lower or higher than the tariff revenue, depending on where exactly the world price line cuts the Rybczynski line (Vousden, 1990, p. 79). With this in mind we can conclude that the Krueger rectangle could serve as a reasonable approximation of the true costs of DUPs.

What if the small economy illustrated in Figure 12.2 introduces an import quota instead of import tariff? The imposition of an quota on imports of food means that import licences are in great demand (they are the means for capturing the rents). Let us suppose that quota limits the imports of food to the amount of QD_t (shown in Figure 12.2) which implies the same equilibrium production and consumption as we had when the tariff was introduced. If all the quota rents are sought the consumption point will again move down along the income consumption curve to the domestic price line p_t, tangential to PP. In the case of tariffs this consumption point was supported by larger imports of food (when compared with pre-DUPs). However this is not possible with a quota; a quota is binding instrument and imports could not rise above the allowed quantity QD_t. The consequence is the rise of the relative price of food to the level at which the markets will clear (not shown in Figure 12.2). Thus the case of DUPs is not identical with tariffs and quotas; since a quota implies higher domestic prices, it is reasonable to expect that the factor intensity used in lobbying activities will change appropriately. This in turn will affect the Rybczynski line and the equilibrium point.

Partial revenue/rent seeking   In practice the whole amount of tariff revenue or quota rents is not available for capturing. The government typically uses up a considerable amount of collected revenue and the revenue-seeker does not chase that portion. Or a portion of import licences may be allocated in some pre-defined way immune from lobbying (such as a lottery). Thus that portion does not enter the amount of rents actually sought. Let us first consider the case of partial revenue-seeking followed by partial rent-seeking. Again we will use the small country, two-sector example, illustrated in Figure 12.3. An import tariff is used to restrict imports of food. The tariff-distorted equilibrium, as before, involves production at point P_t, and consumption at point D_t on the indifference curve I_t. However in this case we assume that a portion of tariff revenue is returned back to consumers via lump-sum transfers. Let us discuss what the implications of lobbying are for the rest of the revenue. As before, the sole DUPs result in withdrawing of some of the resources from productive activities. Let us assume that this outflow of factors causes the importable

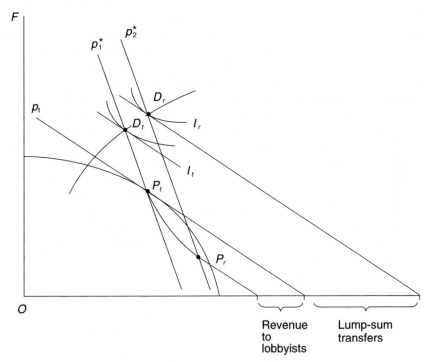

Figure 12.3 *Partial revenue seeking in a general equilibrium*

sector to contract in favour of the exportable sector (moving the price line p^*_1 outwards to the p^*_2). With tariffs, the import quantity is variable, thus imports increase, pushing up the tariff revenue and the lump-sum transfers (and probably the portion of rents captured by lobbying). The increase in income available for consumption places the consumption point (D_r) on a higher indifference curve (I_r). This is the typical case of welfare-improving distortion (lobbying) introduced the second best situation (tariff-distorted equilibrium). The rise in welfare is achieved through a correction in the pattern of production (closer to efficient free trade allocation) which ensures a bigger gain than the cost of revenue seeking.

When an import quota rather than a tariff is applied, again the non-equivalence between quota and tariff comes to the fore. Since an increase in imports under a quota is not possible, the beneficial impact on consumption and production in this case is lost. Once again, an import quota turns out to be hurting the economy more than a tariff.

Tariff-seeking

As said above, protection can be set endogenously by economic agents who by influencing government through lobbying in fact get the level and forms of protection they want. This process is very complex in reality and the illustration we are going to present is by any criterion too simplistic. It will, however, provide some insights in this very important phenomenon (see also Box 12.1). Again we start with a small country whose production possibilities are given by the PPF in Figure 12.4. The world relative prices are given by p^* (thus the free trade equilibrium production is at P^*). Assume that producers of the importable good F join in a lobbying effort for tariff protection. We know already that such lobbying wastes real resources. Suppose that the amount of resources wasted on lobbying shrinks the PPF to $P'P'$. The tariff-distorted prices are given by the line p_t which is tangent at the $P'P'$ at new point of production P_t. By drawing the world price through this point we will obtain a consumption locus with tariff (after the lobbying). Any point of consumption on that locus implies that (a) the tariff-distorted equilibrium is inferior to a free trade equilibrium, and (b) the endogenous tariff-distorted equilibrium may be superior to the exogenous tariff-distorted equilibrium. In other words, an endogenously determined tariff may not as welfare-reducing as the one 'imposed' by the government.

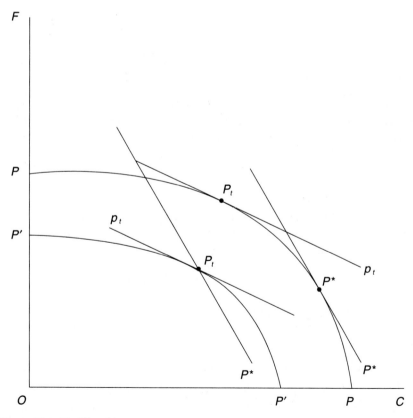

Figure 12.4 *Tariff-seeking*

Is this outcome sufficient to support an endogenous determination of protection as opposed to an exogenous one? Most economists would strongly disagree, the reason of course being that by condoning endogenous protection, we make other possibilities (exogenous protection or free trade) irrelevant and less feasible. Thus it is much wiser to try to change the structure of political pressure and work towards less protectionism in general.

Box 12.1   *Endogenous tariffs in Russia*

Langhammer (1995) examined endogenous tariff making in post-socialist Russia with the aim of explaining the early designs of trade policies during the transformation process. He found that endogenous tariff theory offers a number of useful hypotheses to explain both the level and structure of Russian trade protection during a period of transition. There are several interest groups contributing resources to influence policy making. The obvious group consists of domestic industries facing import competition. Furthermore, there is a group of regions which are net importers of food and consumer goods (such as large cities), a group lobbying for taxing international transactions for revenue purposes, a group lobbying for export quotas to restrict the exports of strategic goods and a group lobbying for more trade between the former republics of the Soviet Union. The objective of all these interest groups is to shift the burden of transformation partly to their trading partners and partly to other groups in the economy, which is consistent with the prediction of the theory. The theory would also suggest a strong preference for quantitative restrictions in line with the legacies of a command economy and central planning in physical units, and this is what is found in practice.

There are some further qualifications which should be taken into account. The collapse of bureaucratic coordination implies a weaker vertical hierarchy and impeded enforcement of policy measures. This in turn means that all lobbying investments are much more uncertain then before. Under uncertainty, lobbying groups might contribute to both actual and potential decision makers and/or to different levels of government. That means that although the lack of institutional order and transparency may help interest groups to obscure their activities and to save costs, it is very likely that the lack of transparency has gone beyond the optimum level and now constitutes a barrier. Furthermore, given that returns to lobbying have to be paid out of the returns of productive activities, there is a tendency to limit the levying of such a 'rent-tax' on the productive use of factors by means of the very low tax base in Russia.

In summing up, Langhammer says that given the status of reforms in Russia, the returns from lobbying are lower than in other more developed and hence more stable economies, while costs are still high, discouraging domestic and foreign investment and fuelling capital flight.

■ *12.3* The supply of protection

The equilibrium level of protection, hypothetically, would be determined by the intersection of the aggregate demand and aggregate supply curves. On the demand side, in addition to legitimate requests for protection (such as, say, infant industry) and the requests for protection based on revenue-seeking, it is necessary to take into account the request of the opponents of protection (the so-called anti-tariff groups) – in other words, those who are certain to lose if protection is granted. The problem is that the individuals or groups who are losing due to protection rarely make an effort to be heard. Thus their preferences rarely enter the demand curve for protection.

On the supply side, we have to identify by which mechanisms the requests for protection are met or declined. Unfortunately protection only rarely (if ever) comes to be determined by a popular vote (for instance, at a referendum). Even if it did, the outcome might not be in favour of free trade.[2] Instead the issues of protection are voted on *indirectly* by politicians, and the process of voting is influenced by other groups in society such as bureaucrats, unions, administrators and similar interest groups. Let us look more closely into the behaviour of these groups.

☐ *Politicians*

Politicians, presumably, want to be re-elected if they are already in office, or they want to come to office. They will thus behave in such a way as to maximise the chance of getting elected. More specifically their behaviour will be determined by (a) the type of voting system, (b) their perception of the intensity of preferences of pressure groups and their ability to impact the voting process, and (c) on the need to obtain the funds for campaigning. This will lead some protection-seekers to postpone their request until the election year, when there is a bigger chance the request will be met.

One needs to keep in mind that protection provides non-budget methods of redistribution, which makes it politically superior to other instruments of redistribution (such as production subsidies and consumption taxes). This explains why, particularly in countries with undeveloped tax systems, trade barriers might be easier to apply. On the other hand, politicians are also known as preferring status quo situations with respect to redistribution (following the conservative social welfare function) which may mean preserving the level of protection even if it reduces overall national welfare.

☐ *Bureaucrats*

Bureaucrats can be an even more important factor in protection supply than politicians, simply because they tend to be longer in power. Bureaucrats' behaviour with respect to supplying protection follows different determinants. Some view bureaucrats as maximising prestige (as opposed to chances for election). To do that they tend to employ an excessive number of staff, or try to emphasise the importance of the sectors they manage. Some, on the other hand, advocate the idea that bureaucrats are more responsive to pressure groups than their political masters. It is common that the existence of particular ministries (such as for agriculture) is in fact an outcome of successful lobbying. It is then logical to expect that such ministries will always 'defend the political entitlements of their clientele to rents and other forms of protection' (Langhammer, 1995, p. 78). Moreover, bureaucrats tend to identify themselves with the interests of the groups they are representing (for example, the Department of Tourism may be captured by the hoteliers' lobby). The implication of this is that bureaucrats offer more protection than politicians.

☐ *Administrators*

The fact is that a large part of protection granted through non-tariff instruments and safeguard measures may be administered on the basis of some existing legislation. We of course refer to anti-dumping and counter-vailing duties which are imposed automatically after a domestic industry succeeds in proving an injury. Unfortunately, this process gets abused with domestic producers starting the injury investigations with the objective of harassing foreign competition and forcing them to weaken their presence in the market. Thus changes in the international trade rules in this area are very welcome.

■ *12.4 Empirical evidence*

There are a number of empirical studies providing stronger or weaker support for some of the hypotheses on protection-setting. These studies have mostly aimed to explain different levels of protection with respect to either different types of activities or different periods of time. Frey and Weck-Hannemann (1996) summarise several studies investigating inter-industry variation of protection in the USA by looking at the demand side (voting on tariffs, non-tariff barriers and voluntary export restraints), and the political equilibrium outcome (the actual level of protection). It is found that tariffs and non-tariff barriers are positively correlated with the importance and degree of concentration of import-competing industries. Higher protection is granted to the industries which exhibit a slow rate of growth and which employ a large number of low-skilled, low-waged employees. The level of protection is negatively correlated, *ceteris paribus*, with the degree of competitiveness and profitability. A relatively strong influence on the level of protection, both tariff and non-tariff, is found for historical continuity and international negotiation, while export-oriented industries and consumers are found to have little or no influence.

With respect to variation of protection through time, it is found that weak macroeconomic conditions, such as slow growth and high unemployment, coincide with high levels of protection. On the other hand, periods of high inflation result in stronger pressure against protection.

Ratnayake (1993) examined the determinants of inter-industry variation of tariff protection to manufacturing in Australia. He found that labour-intensive, low-wage industries tend to be more highly protected even during periods of declining overall protection. Other important determinants included historical tariffs, degree of import competition from developing countries, transport costs and adjustment costs.

Although not all empirical studies support the endogenous tariff-setting theory, there is enough evidence that interest groups do play a significant role in determination of the level and forms of protection in all developed, developing and transforming economies.

■ *12.5* Summary

This chapter has aimed at explaining why different forms of protection still exist although international trade theory clearly proves that a policy of free trade maximises national welfare except in a very limited number of cases. We showed that protection is determined in the political market which is characterised by imperfect competition. On the demand side in this market we had groups of (import-competing) producers very efficiently organised to lobby for protection, and groups of (export-oriented) producers and consumers who try to lobby against. On the basis of the actual levels of protection it seems that the suppliers of protection give greater weight to the pressures of pro-protectionist lobby groups. Although some progress was made in the 1990s when the completion of the Uruguay Round proved that a supplier of protection could stand firm in declining to bow to protectionist pressures, further liberalisation in all countries will require education of all economic actors on the real costs of protection.

■ *Chapter 13* ■

Trade Policy, Transition and Economic Development

■ *13.1* Introduction

As Edwards (1993, p. 1358) noticed rightly, despite the centuries old idea of trade being the *engine of growth*, our 20th century was characterised by long periods of protectionist theories and practice. Everyone is familiar with the rise of protectionism as a response to great depression of 1930s. Then, after the World War II, GATT was established to help this idea on the engine of growth materialise. The then DCs developed countries became more or less faithful to the efforts of GATT by taking part in the rounds of multilateral liberalisation.[1] However, most of the developing countries at that time, chose not to join the trade liberalisation movement. Following the ideas developed by Raul Prebisch and Hans Singer in 1950, they chose to follow the industrialisation policies based on a very limited degree of international openness.[2] These ideas were transformed into the so-called *import substitution industrialisation (ISI)* strategy of development implemented by many developing countries in the 1950s–1970s. This strategy was leaning heavily on to the infant-industry argument of protection and trade policies were designed so to reduce imports and to substitute it by domestic production.

One small group of mostly East Asian developing countries (supported, at that time, by an equally small group of academics) took, however, different road to industrialisation, the so-called strategy of *export promotion*. The focus of this strategy, at first, was on the policies which will encourage exports (both traditional and non-traditional exports). With time this strategy has adopted a *neutral* stance of trade and other policies towards export- and import-substitution.

The export promotion strategy, which in the meantime also changed the name in the outward oriented strategy, gained a popularity firstly among academics, and then quickly among policy-makers in the developing countries in the 1980 when it became clear that more open and outward-oriented economies have outperformed economies which followed an ISI strategy, mostly from Latin America (see Table 13.1).[3]

Since the 1980s, economists and policy-makers in most developing countries have embraced the development strategies based on more liberal trade policies and less regulation within domestic sector. This U-turn in the developing countries' strategy was not caused but certainly was helped by the International Monetary Fund, the World Bank and other multilateral economic and financial institutions all of which began to insist on the market oriented reforms and trade liberalisation as conditions for loans and development finance. It is thus not surprising that this wide recognition of the outward-looking trade regime's central place in development and transition has become known as the 'Washington consensus' (Williamson, 1994).

The DCs themselves have, on the other hand, only half-heartedly joined this march in honour of free market philosophy. Most of them have continued to take part in the multilateral trade liberalisation under the Uruguay Round. But the commitment to 'free trade' has been weakened by the long period of unemployment and adjustment problems in those countries. Thus their attachment to liberal trade policy was effectively balanced with an active industrial policy and the tendency to form regional clusters of free trading, such as NAFTA and the European Economic Area (EEA).

At the turn of the decade, the third group of countries appeared at the scene. These were the countries from behind the Iron Curtain; former socialist countries going through both political and economic revolutions at the same time. As planned economies these countries' views on trade were even more negative than of the countries which followed ISI strategies. Self-sufficiency was the ultimate objective of most of the planned economies. When these planned systems collapsed in the late 1980s, they collectively embraced the ideas of free trade and no government regulation as the fundamental premises of the new systems to be built. Thus they embarked onto the *transition* focusing on the opening of their economies.

This chapter looks into the role trade has in both transition process of the former socialist countries and development of the 'ordinary' developing countries. In Section 13.2 we first review the main features of the import substitution industrialisation and the reasons for its relative failure. It might look unnecessary to pay attention at something which, as it looks now in mid-1990s, has long lost on its importance in practice; but having in mind that ISI strategy is based on the infant industry argument students should recognise that this class of economic ideas die hard and that they can get revived very successfully. Section 13.3 is dedicated to the role of trade policy in the transition of the former socialist economies. Some

Table 13.1 *Growth and export of Latin America and East Asia: 1965–1989 (%)*

Country	Annual rate of growth of real GDP		Annual rate of growth of manufacturing		Annual rate of growth of exports	
	1965–80	1980–89	1965–80	1980–89	1965–80	1980–89
A. Selected Latin American countries						
Argentina	3.5	–0.3	2.7	0.6	4.7	0.6
Brazil	8.8	3.0	9.8	2.2	9.3	5.6
Chile	1.9	2.7	0.6	2.9	7.9	4.9
Colombia	5.8	3.5	6.4	3.1	1.4	9.8
Mexico	6.5	0.7	7.4	0.7	7.6	3.7
Peru	3.9	0.4	3.8	0.4	1.6	0.4
Venezuela	3.7	1.0	5.8	4.9	–9.5	11.3
Latin America and Caribbean (average)	6.0	1.6	7.0	1.5	–1.0	3.6
B. Selected East Asian Countries						
Hong Kong	8.6	7.1	na	na	9.5	6.2
Indonesia	8.0	5.3	12.0	12.7	9.6	2.4
Korea	9.6	9.7	18.7	13.1	27.2	13.8
Malaysia	7.3	4.9	–	8.0	4.4	9.8
Singapore	10.1	6.1	13.2	5.9	4.7	8.1
Thailand	7.2	7.0	11.2	8.1	8.5	12.8
East Asia (average)	7.2	7.9	10.6	12.6	10.0	10.0

Source: World Bank (1989, 1990) as cited in Edwards (1993, p. 1360).

experience with trade liberalisation from the selected Central European countries is given. Finally section 13.4 provides a brief review of the trade liberalisation in New Zealand, a rare case of a DC undertaking dramatic economic reforms including trade liberalisation.

■ *13.2* Trade policy as an input to development

□ *Import-substituting industrialisation strategy*

An import-substituting industrialisation (ISI) strategy may be defined as a set of policies which as a common objective have a reduction of imports and their substitution by domestically produced goods. This strategy is also know as the inward looking or inward oriented strategy of development. The more formal definition of the ISI strategy is given in terms of the *bias of the trade regime*. This bias is commonly measured by looking at the difference in price incentives with respect to home and foreign markets. Thus the ratio of the effective exchange rate for importables and the effective exchange rate for exportables provides an acceptable measure of a bias (see also Bhagwati, 1987). When the ratio is equal to one, trade regime is *neutral*, implying that the trade regime is not favouring either market in particular. Ratio exceeding one means that incentives result in home market producing more revenues than exports which classifies the regime as favouring import-substituting activities or as being biased against exports. Likewise, a ratio below one implies that a bias against exports thus not exists; rather price incentives are such to favour exportables over importables. Figure 13.1 illustrates how this price incentives affect the structure of production. As said in the introduction the ISI strategy was formed around the ideas by Raul Prebisch and Hans Singer. They contented that developing countries' terms of trade suffered from long-term deterioration and that the low standards of living in those countries at the time were attributable to their dependence on production and exports of primary commodities (Krueger, 1997). More specifically the main premises were that: (1) the developing countries will never be able to close the gap between them and the rich countries without *industrialisation* because of the secular deterioration of the terms of trade for the primary products (this is the famous *Prebisch-Singer hypothesis*); (2) industrialisation will not be successful without protection because the manufacturing sector of the developing countries was too inefficient, although potentially sound, to compete with the imports from DCs. This is familiar infant industry argument for protection at its best; 3) DCs would not be able to absorb the increased exports of primary products from the developing countries and hence the latter will not be able to grow (if they had no other sectors in the economy able to grow). This is the so-

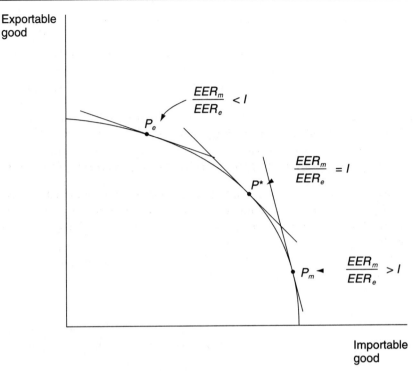

Figure 13.1 *Bias in the trade regime*

called old *export pessimism* argument. There is also the new export pessimism argument based on fears of losing access to the developing countries' markets due to raising import barriers to the products from developing countries (see also Box 13.1); (4) set of premises related to the productivity and availability of labour and capital in the developing countries. It was widely accepted that marginal productivity of agricultural labour was in the proximity of zero (from either side!), allowing for unskilled labour to be treated as free good. Moreover, it was held that industrial workers and entrepreneurs had a higher propensity to save and invest than workers employed in the agricultural sector, particularly the type of agriculture found in poor countries in the 1950s. Hence it was desirable to shift income distribution in favour of the former and this was most easily done by shifting the relative prices of industrial and agriculture goods. Of course, direct assistance to the industrial sector in the form of subsidised loans, tax reductions and similar have helped a lot in redistributing income.

On the basis of those premises, ISI received a widespread support and 'became the hallmark of development strategies for manufacturing and the underlying rationale for trade policy' (Krueger, 1997, p. 4) during the long period 1950–80.

The problems that most countries adopting the ISI experienced include:

- The too high dependence of the manufacturing sector on the imported intermediate goods (because of the cascading protection structure).
- A strong anti-export and anti-primary-sector bias which inhibits growth.
- A protection structure with a very wide tariff rate dispersion and with overall level of tariff rates being high.
- A reliance on administrative and quantitative controls which distort signals to producers and consumers.
- A high technological inefficiency with producers mixing their inputs in a wrong way given their true availability (in other words, appearance of capital-intensive techniques in labour-abundant economy).
- A non-ability to reach economies of scale because of the small size of the domestic market.
- An increased inequality in income distribution; and rising unemployment with low capacity-utilisation rate.

The list of problems caused by the ISI is impressive. Moreover, it is the fact that countries which applied the ISI strategy lagged behind other countries in terms of growth of GDP, manufacturing production, and exports (as shown in Table 13.1). But it is also true that countries such the United States, Germany, Japan, Korea, and Taiwan went through a phase of import substitution in their early stages of industrialisation. Admittedly a success of their ISI and the one which was applied for instance by the Latin American countries is not comparable. The question is what did make this difference? Why some economies seem to be able to gain from ISI while others lose? Among several available answers, probably the closest one is that what make difference is an ability to *switch* from the ISI strategy to outward oriented strategy at appropriate stage of development. For this transition to be successful it is necessary that the ISI which was used in the early stages of development did not go to far in its anti-export bias and in causing the distribution of income to become too inequitable. With respect to accommodating the protection structure to a new strategy, there is a view that a sudden jump from IS-biased to neutral would cause too large a shock for the economy. Instead, parallel to the existing protection system, a system of export subsidies should be introduced in order to neutralise the adverse effects of the ISI on the export industries. With the subsidies in place, the export sector will face almost the same incentives as under free trade and country would be able to correctly use its comparative advantages. The problem with this scheme is that it requires quite a deep knowledge on the part of government on the extent of needed subsidies which rarely any government has. Moreover, it could result in new incentives for lobbying.

☐ *Export-led growth or growth-led export?*

Since the 1960s there has been a debate among trade and growth economists on the definition and attributes of the so-called export-led growth strategy. The agreement could not be reached on the existence of a bias of the incentive regime in this strategy. As Krueger (1990) put, there was almost an agreement on what export-led strategy was not: 'a set of ad hoc, specific policies encouraging designated industries that are highly protected in domestic market to sell some . . . fraction of their output abroad . . .' (p. 68, n. 4). Most economists would agree that an export-led growth strategy must be free from a bias in favour of production of import substitutes. In Bhagwati's terms, export-led is close to be synonymous with neutral with respect to relative incentives for domestic and export markets. In such case, export-led growth strategy is consistent with static optimal resource allocation achieved in free trade. This is one possible explanation to why higher income growth rates are found in countries recording fast growth of exports, such as East-Asian countries (see also Table 13.1).

Other commentators believed rather, that export-led strategy implied quite a strong bias in the incentive regime in those countries, and, more importantly, that governments in those countries played a leading and heavily interventionist role in the process of the economic development (see in particular Wade, 1990). There is some evidence that governments of these countries have pursued very active industrial policy and that they have in fact guided the market and not followed hands-off approach. Nevertheless, the growth in this case again follows from the dynamic gains associated with the export-led strategy.

The focus of debate nowadays has switched from how biased export-led growth strategy is to the causal relationship between export and growth. What is clear without doubt is that 'trade has been a friend of economic development and growth, not an enemy, as many policymakers and economists feared in the immediate postwar period' Rodrik (1995, p. 101). But what is far less clear is whether a rise in exports was the most important determinant of growth or just one of its facilitators. An OECD report (1993) examines in some detail this relationship between exports and growth. It proposes that the evidence from fast-growing economies of East Asia in fact support the view that strategies actually led in those countries were building up national internal competitiveness which resulted in dynamic growth *and* then in an increased supply of exports. In this sense it is correct to talk about *growth-led exports* and not export-led growth. This idea is a result from recent developments in growth theory which are focused on the role of increasing returns to scale, technology strategies, knowledge absorption process and investment in generating dynamic economic growth. This growth is then the source of rapid growth in the export of manufactures.

Box 13.1   *The flying geese paradigm*

Have you ever seen geese flying? They use an arrow formation, with a goose in front having an important task of breaking the air so that geese in the back can use the advantage and follow in the slipstream of the leading goose. The leader is expected to stay in front only for a limited time after which it leaves that position for the second goose to fill. The former leader slips back until its time comes to lead again. Meantime, the geese take turns in leading the formation, while all the time co-operating and taking care of each other. In this way geese can travel huge distances ensuring their own survival. How does it apply to trade and development?

Recall the export pessimism hypothesis holds that there is a limited absorptive capacity of the DC's markets for the products exported by developing countries. As a consequence of the DC's markets saturation, relative price of these products would fall sufficiently enough to prevent the new exporting countries (so-called second-tier newly-industrialised economies, NIEs) to reproduce the fast export and overall growth rates achieved by the first-tier NIEs and Japan. Yet the development experience of Asian countries shows that this is not what is happening. If anything, the second-tier NIEs are growing at least as fast as their predecessors. The explanation is found in the *flying geese* paradigm. The upgrading from resource-based and low-skill, labour-intensive production to more sophisticated, capital-intensive and skill labour-intensive manufactures by the lead economies (first Japan, and then Korea and Taiwan) enabled them to leave the 'top' position in those particular less-sophisticated industries and by doing so to open up opportunities for less-developed economies in the region (Malaysia, Indonesia, Thailand) to begin exporting these goods. This pattern of succession is mirrored in foreign trade and investment linkages. The countries which developed first retain their leading position by moving up the trade hierarchy and by exporting more advanced products in which they gain a comparative advantage. FDI, by transferring technology and skills, provides an important vehicle for recycling of comparative advantage. The metaphor of flying geese has been used to describe the shift of industries from one country to another with the inverted arrow-shaped curves representing the evolution of the same industry in different countries over time. This paradigm was originally formulated by K. Akamatsu in early 1930s for Japan. Most of his writings are published in Japanese, but there is one on this subject available on English (Akamatsu, 1962).

■ *13.3* Trade policy as an input to transition

A *transition* is typically defined as a progression from a socialist planned economy to an open market-oriented economy. It is a complex process of building a new system for the generation and allocation of goods and resources. Although there are some general principles underlying transition, each individual country must design its own transition programme based on the country's unique political and economic features and the current international economic environment.[4] One of the common features of all transition programmes is the placement of trade liberalisation among the fundamental ingredients of an early phase of transition process.[5] The reasons for this central role of trade liberalisation are linked to both external economic considerations and the potential domestic economic impact (OECD, 1994, pp. 15–16). From the external perspective, trade liberalisation is expected to upgrade the technological level of the national economy. In addition to broadening and redirecting of imports, it is hoped that trade liberalisation will bring about an increase in exports therefore helping in building up demand for domestically produced goods. Furthermore, the key role of trade liberalisation is found in price reform and competition (anti-monopoly) policy.

The role for free trade in the transitional economies can be summed through the following static effects of free trade:

(a) introduction of a set of rational economic prices for traded goods essential for efficient resource allocation
(b) introduction of the competitive pressures that keep monopoly inefficiencies in check in small economies, and that push domestic producers to achieve the highest potential efficiency
(c) the introduction of better and more appropriate inputs and technology through access to foreign investment, equipment imports and the demonstration effect of imported goods.

Moreover, recent theory of endogenous growth suggests that free trade can make a significant contribution towards a permanent increase of the growth rate (as opposed to the level of GDP) of an economy.

This section discusses those aspects of trade policy most important for the transition process. We first deal with the meaning and design of trade liberalisation for the economies in transition. Then we list the potential benefits of trade liberalisation, and discuss the role of transitional trade protection, and export promotion. Finally we examine the experience that some countries in central Europe have had with trade liberalisation.

☐ *Trade liberalisation design*

Trade liberalisation involves a movement from too much and the wrong kind of government intervention to more reliance on markets in the external sectors.[6] Usually it is said that trade liberalisation implies a reform of a trade regime towards an '*outward orientation*'. However outward orientation could mean at least three things (Dean, Desai and Riedel, 1994). One is a move towards more *neutral* trade regime. Secondly it could mean a move towards a more *liberal* regime (free trade). Thirdly it could imply greater economic *openness*.[7]

Greater neutrality of a trade regime (defined as equating incentives between the exporting and import-competing sectors) could be achieved in several ways. One is to reduce import barriers without changing export incentives. Another is to reduce import barriers and/or improve export incentives. Alternatively, less costly instruments of protection could be substituted for more costly instruments. Any one of those three methods will bring *relative prices* of exports and import-competing goods towards more neutrality. However, they may have unfavourable effects on the degree of liberality of a trade regime which is measured by a degree of intervention. For example, the first method used, the reduction of import barriers alone, will also imply increased liberality of a regime. On the other hand an introduction of export subsidies may very well increase a degree of intervention. In other words, a more neutral regime does not necessarily imply a more liberal regime.

Openness on the other hand does not have to be related to neutrality and/or liberality of trade regime. Openness is determined by the ratio of foreign trade to national GDP. The higher such a ratio, the more open economy is. Thus the size of national economy is most relevant in determining a degree of openness: typically small economies would have higher ratio of trade to GDP than large economies.

Most experts agree that both neutrality and liberality of trade regime are the necessary qualities to be incorporated into the new 'outward oriented' regimes of transitional economies. This implies both correcting the effects of distortionary interventions that protect domestic industry against competition from imports and result in an anti-export bias, and reducing the degree of government intervention so that markets and prices are allowed a greater role.

There are three elements which must be taken into account in designing trade liberalisation: optimality, feasibility and credibility of trade liberalisation (Dean, Desai and Riedel, 1994). Optimality is concerned with maximising the present value of net welfare gains to the economy. Feasibility is concerned with political sustainability of reform. Credibility implies widespread belief among all economic agents into the political will that the liberalisation will be carried through. In what follows we focus on the first element of the optimality of trade liberalisation program. There is (almost) a consensus about the optimal design of trade liberalisation: *tariffication* and then *reduction of tariffs* followed by an introduction of *uniform tariffs* (Papageorgiou, Michaely and Choksi, 1991; Thomas and Nash, 1991). Let us deal with each one in turn.

The process of tariffication implies conversion of quantitative restrictions (QRs) into tariff-equivalents. The idea is to provide an equivalent degree of protection without being price distortive. This move will certainly improve both neutrality and liberality of trade regime even though it may cause a (temporary) increase in average nominal tariffs.[8] There is no doubt about the benefits from dismantling of QRs. In addition to improved neutrality and liberality, there are positive effects in terms of higher tariff revenue, less lobbying and rent-seeking, more competition and less uncertainty with a regime based on price instruments. Despite these benefits there are some arguments for temporary retention of QRs or at least for very gradual elimination (tariffication) of them. These arguments mostly deal with feasibility of reform (Dean, Desai and Riedel, 1994, p. 6). One of the methods for transforming QRs into tariffs that appeals the most is through the introduction of tariff-quotas by which the difficulties of calculating the tariff-equivalents are avoided and the advantages of QRs are retained (Takacs, 1990).

Regarding the lowering of the level of tariffs there is a choice between several methods of reduction: equal absolute reductions in the size of tariffs, equiproportional reduction in tariffs, concertina reductions, or extended concertina reductions. The concertina method implies reduction of the highest tariff rates to a specified level, while leaving all lower rates intact. This is repeated until the tariffs are lowered to a predetermined level (but different from zero) and are uniform. By applying this method the dispersion of tariff rates are being narrowed at every step of tariff-cut. Because concertina method focuses on cutting the highest rates, the reduction of deadweight loss is thought to be greater with this method. The extended concertina method is similar except that it in addition to cutting the highest rates also raises the lowest tariff rates towards the predetermined minimum level (thus the average tariff is falling). Given this, the extended concertina method is likely to generate even larger welfare gains than the simple concertina reduction.

There are potentially several problems with concertina methods. 'Water in the tariff' could mean that a very significant drop in tariff rates would have to be made before any effects on import side to be felt. Another possible side effect of extended concertina method could be an anti-export bias caused by an increase in tariffs on previously duty-free imports (often raw materials and intermediate and capital goods used for export production). In addition the problem with concertina methods as with all partial reduction in barriers is that it is a typical 'second-best' exercise and could lead to a reduction in welfare. The conditions for both simple and extended concertina methods to raise welfare is if at each stage of cuts or increases the goods subject to the highest or lowest tariffs are net substitutes for all other goods.

Since it is generally true that an equiproportionate reduction in tariffs raises welfare, many commentators argue for a combined application of this and concertina methods. The aim is to achieve the more uniform tariff structure with much lower average tariff rates. To this end, in addition to tariff reduction, tariffs must be rationalised (i.e. number of rates should shrink), dispersion of rates must be narrowed, and number of exemptions must drop significantly.

☐ *Potential benefits of trade liberalisation*

In case of transitional economies, the system of trade controls used in the past relied on implicit barriers and administrative regulations. Until early 1990s in almost all of the transitional economies state was the only 'economic entity' allowed to engage in foreign trade activities. Traditional price-based trade controls played little or no role in influencing foreign trade flows. It was the central authorities who were determining the value, the volume and often the geographical pattern of trade flows through the bilateral trade arrangements. The insulation of the domestic economy from the influences of the world prices was almost complete; it was achieved through the complex system of taxes and subsidies (known as the equalisation mechanism). Since most of the instruments of trade protection were not price-based, the measurement of trade liberalisation in transitional economies is even more complicated than in the typical market economies. The methods normally used in the later countries rely on the so-called 'Harberger's triangles'. By calculating static costs of protection in a partial equilibrium, these methods give a crude estimation of the benefits of trade liberalisation. However, a renewed interest in 'outward orientation' during the last decade has produced some new insights with respect to the size and types of effects of trade liberalisation. For the countries in transition the most important findings are that cost of protection do not automatically transfer into the benefits from liberalisation and that these benefits are larger:

(a)   when there is a movement from high tariffs (or other barriers) to low ones
(b)   in presence of pro-competitive effects, scale efficiency and technology gain
(c)   with an opportunity to import new technologies (i.e. knowledge) thereby fostering economic growth (import-led growth *à la* Romer).

The most important effects of trade liberalisation can be expected in the following areas.

Effects on consumers

In the markets that are functioning, trade barriers (tariffs and non-tariff barriers) raise the prices of both imported goods and domestically produced goods. The share of consumer surplus left to consumers is thus smaller with trade barriers then without them. However, in economies where the majority of trade barriers are not price-based or their effects are not allowed to influence domestic prices, the utility of consumers is more affected through the implicit trade controls which limit the variety of products and/or quality of products available. Such protection most often result in a creation of the black market for the imported goods with prices affecting their scarcity. When trade is liberalised, consumers face lower prices of both imported and domestically produced goods which gives them more utility out of their income. In transition economies consumers utility is also positively affected by the fact that freer imports also means the end of forced substitution in consumption. In addition, the new relative prices signal to consumers to demand different structure of goods which will have positive impact on resource allocation in general.

While traditional trade theory dominantly focused on final homogeneous goods, the beneficial effects of trade liberalisation could be enhanced by including final differentiated goods.[9] With respect to final consumer goods, the availability of broader list of (imported) final differentiated goods will lead to better match with consumers' preferences for variety (*à la* Spence–Dixit–Stiglitz or *à la* Lancaster) resulting in an improved welfare.

Effects on producers

Irrespective of the type of the system, producers of the sheltered sectors obviously think they cannot be adversely hit by protection (otherwise they would not seek it). When protection is provided by one or more price-based measures, the most apparent effect is an increase in producers surplus due to a higher price producers can charge for their products. However there are other effects of protection which could influence producers' costs and therefore the amount of surplus they actually manage to appropriate through protection may not be large at all. Protection limits access to the international market (though it saves the bigger chunk of domestic market for domestic producer), therefore it could prevent producers achieving economies of scale. (Of course if a national market is a very large market, protectionism works the other way around; however, there are few national markets large enough to support economies of scale of modern production facilities.) Furthermore, protection limits competition by barring foreign producers to enter local market. Non-exposure to competitive pressures allows producers to lag behind the world leaders in terms of innovations, cost-saving investments, etc. At the level of the whole economy protection prevents or limits the extent of structural changes necessary to increase efficiency and productivity. Another negative effect is a creation of less stable and predictable environment and certainly less effective environment for investment, domestic or foreign. The effects that operate on the cost side should be subtracted from the gains in terms of increased producers surplus to obtain the net effect (which very well may be negative). Moreover the effect on the rest of producers, not 'fortunate' enough to enjoy protection but have to foot the bill together with consumers, should be taken into account as well.

Thus the gains for producers from removing protectionist measures arise from greater availability of inputs and technology, greater domestic competition and rationalised market structure, availability of favourable growth externalities and 'a Schumpeterian environment especially conducive to growth' (Dornbusch, 1992). Regarding intermediate goods, today we know that a greater variety of inputs does more for production than a greater quantity of a narrow range of inputs (Romer, 1989). Trade liberalisation allows freer access to a variety of imported inputs and technology at a lower cost which has similar effect to technological progress – it shifts the production frontier outward. In other words trade liberalisation enhances productivity. Other gains result from scale economies and economies of scope that arise in larger (international) markets. Competitive pressure from imports (and foreign direct investment) leads to a much more economically rational market structure.

According to Dornbusch (1992, pp. 75–7) opening up of the economy expose producers (entrepreneurs) to a great intensity of change (e.g. new goods, new methods of production and management, new markets etc.) which is the source of productivity growth. Thus trade liberalisation has a potential to 'shake an economy out of a slow-growth trap' placing it at the higher growth path. There is however no evidence that trade liberalisation can provide a source for a sustained increase in growth in the longer run. Long term sustainable growth is, as the recent literature on growth suggests, rather the matter of investments in human capital and equipment.

Effects on fiscal revenue

Even though socialist countries did not rely on tariffs to regulate the trade flows, they imposed high trade taxes (such as import, export and foreign exchange transactions surcharges) so that revenue collected from trade taxes was not negligible. With trade liberalisation, most of these surcharges have disappeared while the level of tariff rates has been reduced to very low levels (see Table 13.2). There are potential losses and gains to the fiscal revenues from trade liberalisation. The losses could be broken down to direct and indirect ones. The direct losses arise from the reduction in the level of trade taxes. The indirect losses arise due to the structural changes in production. Without protection many industries contract or stop production all together which affects their tax payments and also employees' income taxes. On the other hand, there is a potential for fiscal gain if economy following liberalisation starts to grow faster so that the volume of taxable transactions in the traded and domestic sectors increase. Unfortunately, the massive drop in output following opening up of the former socialist economies meant that the gains were far smaller than the losses. According to the World Bank *Development Report 1996* (p. 118), transition economies collect only one-third of the revenues from trade taxes collected by the DCs in 1994. This fall in trade taxes revenue adversely affected economies' ability to finance transition and made a big pressure on their fiscal deficits. It is obvious that with liberalisation and deregulation the proceeds from tariffs and other trade duties have become one of the more important sources of budget revenue, because trade taxes are a more convenient and politically more acceptable method of raising revenue than, for example, from an economist's point of view, the more desirable consumption and income taxes. It is plausible to argue for an introduction of temporary and low across-the-board import taxes which would serve as the least-cover revenue filler (cf. Tanzi, 1991 and Falvey, 1994). Some countries in the region like Poland, Hungary, Slovenia and Croatia have had to impose additional but temporary uniform import surcharges to help their public finances with a positive impact on their growth rates. See also discussion on transitional protection on p. 428.

Effects on employment

Probably the most misused argument for adoption of trade barriers is the one claiming that protection from foreign competition saves domestic jobs. The fact is that protectionism may save some domestic jobs only in the short run, and only at the expense of other domestic and foreign jobs. Therefore the costs of a job saved are much higher than they would be if an appropriate adjustment policy had been used – protectionism is an inefficient means of sustaining employment. With trade liberalisation it is important to look at the general equilibrium effects. In theory an expansion of export sector, and higher growth of an open economy should be able to absorb an excess of labour from the previously sheltered sectors. In practice we cannot deny the possibility of transitional unemployment, particularly in former socialist economies which have always experienced very low mobility of factors and rigidity of wages. This problem can be helped by introduction of some measures to speed up flow of factors and to foster adjustment.

Effects on the balance of payments

Although trade liberalisation almost always goes hand in hand with exchange rate devaluation, it is not surprising that balance of payments (or at least current account) might deteriorate during the transition process. The problem in most cases is in determining the 'correct' exchange rate – it is not a rare case for the rate to be too little devalued. When the borders are opened, the combination of an overvalued domestic currency and a higher relative domestic inflation causes the imports to grow faster than exports. Increasing current account deficit is in the most countries perceived as a serious problem – a threat to macroeconomic stabilisation. It is common that in such circumstances a country reaches for the trade barriers to ease the pressure on its current account and the balance of payments. Even the GATT and the WTO rules make provision for this. In the case when exchange rate cannot be used to correct balance of payments problems, and the trade policy is the only alternative, the least-cost instrument of trade policy is again uniform tariff. However, as tariffs are not the first-best instrument to sort out balance of payments problems, the prolonged protectionism for this macroeconomic stabilisation purpose cannot be justified.

☐ *Transitional protection and export promotion*

Regarding the reduction of tariffs in transitional economies there are views that tariffs in fact should either decrease very gradually or even increase in the early phases of transition. Three main reasons for this view are being brought forward: (a) government revenues, (b) balance of payments, and (c) a modified version of infant industry protection.

Tariff revenue is a significant source of financing government expenditure in transitional economies. A lowering of tariff rates however does not necessarily mean lower level of revenues. As known from the trade theory there is a revenue-maximising tariff rate. In economies that are normally relying on the price-based trade instruments, it is likely that the level of tariff rates prior to reform are well above those revenue-maximising rates given their elasticities of demand for the imported goods. Thus in fact lowering these rates would increase level of revenues. This is not necessarily the case in the economies which used almost no price-based instruments but relied on the quantitative or some other administrative barriers to regulate trade flows. On the contrary, given the state of tax systems in the transitional economies, an introduction or an increase of the existent trade taxes (import and export tariffs) could constitute the main and the most stable source of the government revenue. As long as tariffs and other trade taxes used to collect revenue are uniform, distortions should be minimal and therefore acceptable as a temporary budget revenue filler. If however tariffs are tailored to fit the special needs of some of the sectors (or consumers), and are varied according to these needs, this would only open the door for rent-seeking and bureaucratic meddling. The costs of raising revenue through 'made to measure protection' would be much higher than in the case of uniform tariffs. Particularly dangerous could be an attempt to 'pick winners' since this task is likely to end up in failure which would be costing taxpayers dearly in terms of even higher trade and consumption taxes in future.

Tariffs or trade barriers in general should not be used to protect balance of payments. Theory states that devaluation supported by appropriate fiscal and monetary policies provide a neutral instrument to do the job. Devaluation is considered to be competition-enhancing instrument as it makes domestic exports less expensive. However it is also true that devaluation might have an adverse effect on exports (and thus on the balance of payments in a round about way) by pushing up the prices of all goods, including intermediate and capital goods used in export production. Thus, as argument goes, tariffs (or QRs) on selected goods would defend balance of payments more effectively. We must note that a country's balance of payments problem could only be seriously tackled if the measure addresses the root of the problem. In the transition economies this means that both devaluation and tariffs would provide only temporary balance of payments relief since the imbalance in the external sector has the roots in a relatively low efficiency of domestic production. Thus the 'correct' policy would necessarily lean on microeconomic restructuring.

With respect to the 'infant industry protection' argument the transition economies are in a way similar to the economies of the European Union (EU). Namely, more developed economies in the EU had to use a modified 'infant industry argument' in order to install and keep protection of industries and activities that would otherwise close down in face of free foreign competition not because they are young but because they are too old (the so-called Euro-sclerosis). How valuable is a temporary high(er) protection for the most vulnerable activities? This is the core of the idea of the *'transitional protection'* (Corden, 1990; McKinnon, 1991; van Brabant 1994). It centers on the fact that a rapid trade liberalisation of a rigid economic system such as of the former socialist countries, may lead to a destruction of much of the productive capacity (as experienced in ex-GDR). This would add to unemployment and worsen other macroeconomic imbalances with a result of the weakened public support for reform. Consequently it may pay to institute trade barriers on a precommitted temporary basis. All trade barriers should be first expressed in *ad valorem* tariffs structured into several cascading categories in a form of a 'hard tariff path' (Corden, 1990). It is namely vital that a declining tariff rate path is established and committed to in advance. In this way the initial absolute level of protection would be left unchanged. Tariff structure of this nature would provide largest protection to the 'negative value-added' activities forestalling the collapse of the massive portions of production in these economies. This 'transitional protection' will then allow for gradual change of economic structure thereby reducing the costs of reform.

This idea, however attractive is problematic because of the traditionally low credibility of central authorities in the transforming countries to stick to the 'hard tariff path'. Namely, the likelihood that the predeclared phasing-out of tariffs will not materialise is high. Not sticking to the predefined conditions of transitional protection (i.e. reverting to 'soft tariff path') could seriously hinder other reform policies. Here the membership in an international trade body such as the WTO could help to some extent because it could exercise an external pressure to continue with the liberalisation.[10]

There is however a set of activities that might be a legitimate candidate for an extra temporary protection: infant *export* industry sector. There are several reasons why these activities might deserve some additional support; the most important one is that nearly all of the transitional economies (particularly in Central Europe) have to find an alternative but stable market for their industrial goods, which they used to export to the countries of the CMEA. In order to get a share of the Western import market, the transitional economies' products must be both price and quality competitive. While exchange rate policy could improve (temporarily) price competitiveness, other policies are needed to better the quality competitiveness.

The role of government is not diminished by the need to liberalise and deregulate economies in transition. In particular, its role with respect to trade liberalisation can be divided into two stages. First stage is the phase of trade liberalisation itself. The role of government is in managing the liberalisation process which includes two types of activities: identification of the objective of liberalisation, and facilitation of transition by establishing a social safety net, by reducing the constraints to the allocation of resources and by engaging in multilateral and bilateral trade negotiations. At the later stage, in a liberalised economy, government still has an important role. Its responsibility is to assure a stable and clear legal framework, to maintain a stable macroeconomic environment including a realistic exchange rate and possibly to engage in some elements of industrial policy, particularly in export promotion activities.

As already mentioned, an active exchange rate policy can help in improving price competitiveness of export activities, but other policies are needed to upgrade quality of the products and services and prepare producers to compete at the world market. Some of the policies on a disposal are export credit policy, fiscal policy, wage policy, and measures concerning direct foreign investment. More direct export supporting policies, such as subsidies, should be kept as a measure of last resort.

Struggling to conquer new markets, producers have to rely on the functioning export credit insurance and financing agency. This need was indeed realised very early in the process of trade liberalisation. Consequently, most of the countries have established export credit agencies but they are not fully operational due to the lack of foreign currency funding (OECD, 1994, pp. 46–7). Although the needs for foreign currency can be somewhat reduced by using modern financing techniques and by bilateral swap agreements, due to no experience these techniques are rarely used. The problem of lack of experience is somewhat relaxed by technical assistance from OECD export credit agencies. The problems with export credit insurance is in relatively weak demand for it since exporters are still to be taught to use this facility. The weak demand also arises from weakening of export growth.

Apart from export credit financing, other policies can be used to support export without being very distortive for the other activities. These primarily include services providing assistance to firms for sales promotion, exhibitions, market definition and the implementation of a sales network abroad (OECD, p. 47).

☐ First experiences with trade liberalisation

In the 'core' transitional economies (that is, Central European countries) trade liberalisation progressed quickly modifying their trade regimes into rather liberal and neutral even by international standards. Table 13.2 provides a comparison of the level of protection between transition and other economies. Current trade regimes in these countries rely on instruments that are typically used in all market economies: tariffs, some quantitative restrictions, an active exchange rate policy, and a set of incentives for direct foreign investments (see also Table 13.3). In some of these countries the initial tariff regimes were too liberal for the type of economies they were (Poland, Hungary and the Czech Republic are the best examples). In fact, the exceptionably strong (system inherent and implicit) protection provided to producers under planned system was removed abruptly without giving any consideration for the type of the overall macroeconomic and microeconomic conditions in those economies. The initial effects of such move on the trade balance were better than expected. In trade with OECD countries these three countries achieved small trade surplus in the first year of the liberalisation (OECD, 1994, p. 43). However the developments in their trade balances in the subsequent years showed clearly that the work on reform is far from finished. Although the primary causes for the deterioration in trade balances of these countries are different, they all resorted to (re)introduction of the protection of domestic production from foreign competition.[11] Some countries (such as former CSSR or more recently Hungary, Croatia and Slovenia) have opted for increase in tariffs or for an introduction of additional import duties. Other countries chose to adopt less direct instruments such as tightening quality control or changing sanitary and technical standards. All in all these steps may indicate some reversal of the liberal trade policies which prevailed in most countries in the early stage of transition.

In summing up this section we have to agree that trade liberalisation plays a strategic role in the transition process. While by dumping cheaper foreign goods on domestic markets, trade liberalisation helps in controlling

Table 13.2 *Post-Uruguay Round most-favored national tariffs on non-agricultural products for selected countries 1/(rates in per cent)*

	Transition economies	United States	European Union	Australia, New Zealand	East Asia	Latin America	Africa	South Asia
Forestry products	1	0	0	0	3	13	16	10
Fishery products	6	1	11	1	7	21	21	4
Mining	2	1	1	1	5	11	12	19
Textiles	8	8	7	15	16	22	35	56
Clothing	11	15	11	35	8	29	41	64
Lumber, pulp and paper	4	0	1	4	6	10	21	19
Petroleum	5	1	1	1	8	20	13	34
Chemicals	6	3	4	8	10	15	15	34
Primary Steel	6	0	1	2	6	15	15	35
Primary non-ferrous metals	4	3	6	6	9	14	22	59
Fabricated metals	6	3	3	13	12	21	26	60
Transport equipment	12	5	6	20	15	22	20	25
Other machinery	7	2	3	9	11	17	13	30
Other manufactures	6	2	3	7	10	18	21	35

Source: Francois *et al.* (1995) (IDB),1/Tariffs are weight-averaged, based on MFN trade as reported in the IDB.

inflation, its role is perhaps even more important in microeconomic restructuring. On the other hand, trade liberalisation may have some adverse effects on the other reform's objectives (at least in the short run) such as reduction of current account deficit, budget deficit or unemployment rate. These are exactly the areas of concern in the most 'advanced' transitional economies at present time, Hungary, the Czech Republic, and Poland. All of them, as well as most other transition economies, followed the widely accepted 'principles of trade liberalisation' starting with abolishment of state trading, introduction of traditional trade policy instruments, and finally ending with radical opening and liberalisation. It is clear now that some of the countries could have reduced the costs of transition by moving down the road of trade liberalisation at a slightly slower speed. We are not advocating a strong dosage of protectionism as oil for the brakes. Rather it has to be a carefully chosen mixture of exchange rate policy, tax policy, wage policy, and of course trade policy. One thing is however sure. The prescription to 'liberalise as fast and as much as possible' without taking into consideration macroeconomic and microeconomic circumstances of an individual economy is *not* the best advice money can buy.

13.4 Trade liberalisation as an input to reform: the case of New Zealand

Today New Zealand is the single developed economy going through radical trade liberalisation and other economic reforms with an aim of strengthening the role of free markets in the economy. This section focus on the segment of reforms dealing with trade liberalisation. According to Wooding (1987) there are six main phases of trade protection in New Zealand. The first lasting from late 1880s until mid-1930s was marked by tariffs changing their function from revenue generating to protecting domestic industry. In addition the initial tariff scheme moved away from almost uniform tariff to a differential one giving more and more protection to manufactured goods. The second phase that ended in late 1940s is best described as switch from tariff-based protection to quantitative controls. In 1938 across-the-board import licensing, along with exchange controls were introduced as temporary measures to shelter primarily depleted overseas reserves and secondly the manufactured sector. However even after the foreign exchange crises was passed, the licensing remained a central trade instrument for over half a century. The third phase, taking place during the 1950s, is significant only because some of the import licences were removed, mostly on raw materials in 1950–1 only to be reintroduced in 1957 when New Zealand experienced a sharp worsening of its terms of trade.

Table 13.3 *Trade policy and export performance in CEE and the NIS*

Country group	Trade policy			Export performance average annual contribution of export growth to GDP (in %)[b]			
	State trading, 1994	Quantitative restrictions, 1994	Years of current account convertibility by end-1995	Manufacturing exports to OECD, 1994 (in % of GDP)[a]	Exports to OECD only, last year before transition to 1994	Total exports, last year before transition to 1994	Total exports, first year of transition to 1994
Group 1 Poland, Slovenia Hungary, Czech Rep., Slovak Rep.	Very small	No	4	24.5	2.3	2.1	3.0
Group 2 Estonia, Lithuania Bulgaria, Latvia, Albania, Romania Mongolia	Very small[c]	No[c]	2	18.1	1.4	−3.1	3.7
Group 3 Kyrgyz Rep, Russia Moldova, Kazakstan	Moderate[d]	Yes[d]	1	3.3	0.2	−11.2	0.5
Group 4 Uzbekistan, Ukraine Belarus, Tajikistan Turkmenistan	Extensive	Yes	0	4.4	−0.1	−14.4	0.3

Table 13.3 (*cont.*)

Regional tensions group					
Croatia, FYR Mac. Armenia, Georgia Azerbaijan	Extensive	Yes	0	3.7	..	..

.. Not available

Note: Data are simple averages for each country group

a. For Albania, Mongolia, and Slovenia, data are for total exports

b. The last year before transition was 1989 for Poland, 1990 for the other CEE countries, and 1991 for the NIS.

c. Mongolia was the only Group 2 country with significant state trading and quantitative restrictions by 1994.

d. The Kyrgyz republic was the only Group 3 country that had essentially eliminated export restrictions by 1994.

Source: Kaminski, Wang, and Winters (1996); IMF (1995); EBRD (1995); World bank staff calculations as cited in World Bank (1996, Table 2.2, p. 31).

The fourth phase, from late 1950s to late 1970s, could be labelled 'the import replacement' phase. New Zealand has developed a comprehensive protective structure, aiming to protect finished manufactured goods. Although it is not possible to calculate the extent of protection in that period, because of the complex scheme of import licensing, it is believed to be very high compared with OECD averages. By that time it was recognised, by both governments and private sector, that a change in trade policy orientation, from inward to outward looking is desirable and necessary. It was not until late 1970s that trade liberalisation began in a more significant way. Additional pressure on the abolishment of the import licensing system came from the signing of the Closer Economic relation Agreement between Australia and New Zealand (ANCERTA or CER) in 1983. By the early 1980s the licensing dripped to cover only 18 per cent of the value of the imports (it was around 75 per cent in the mid-1960s). However this 18 per cent included virtually all import-competing goods produced locally (Duncan, Lattimore and Bollard, 1992). During that period, because of the difficulties in exporting caused by Great Britain's joining the EEC, some compensation to exporters (of primary products) were offered in a form of export tax incentives and preferential access to import licences.

The final phase, the phase of trade liberalisation, started in 1984. The export incentives were eliminated virtually overnight. The import licences were eliminated fully in 1988. Distortionary types of tariffs (such as specific and compound tariffs) were removed. The goods which are not made in New Zealand were identified and they were given duty-free status. In 1987 a five step tariff reduction programme (1988–92) was introduced with an aim to lower tariffs and make them more uniform. To meet this objective the so-called 'Swiss formula' method of tariff reduction was used. By this formula high tariffs are reduced more quickly and more radically than low tariffs achieving the structure of more uniform tariffs at the lower level. In 1990 the post-1992 tariff programme was announced according to which most tariffs would fall to a maximum level of 10 per cent by 1996. However this particular programme was never implemented since the Labour party lost the 1990 election. The National government which came into office modified the program, slowing down tariff reductions by only one-third (and not less than 5 per cent), while textile, apparel and carpet tariffs will continue to receive individual treatment (but still to be reduced over time). The 1996 coalition government in their 1997/98 Budget goes ahead of the scheduled 1998 tariff review and proposes a rapid phase down of tariffs on remaining 'highly' protected sectors such as car assembly. Thus duties on imported cars are due to be cut from 25 per cent to 15 per cent by 1 July 2000.

Given that only twenty years ago the biggest part of the New Zealand's protection was based on quantitative controls, it is fair to say that in its overall economic reforms New Zealand is unmatched within the OECD in the distance it has travelled in opening its borders to trade (Hazledine, 1993, p. 23). However, this is not the most important achievement of the New Zealand trade liberalisation. In contrast to other countries which are normally led by multilateral or bilateral liberalisation agreements, New Zealand ventured the *unilateral* liberalisation (although supported by the CER agreement). But what is the score with respect to the impact liberal trade policy had on the production, and trade structure? In other words, have the promised gains of liberalisation (efficient allocation of resources in production, higher welfare level, more competitive exports, etc.) been materialised? Unfortunately the lack of comprehensive empirical investigation precludes us from giving very clear and founded answer to this question. But from evidence there is the initial disappointing effects have been turning to more promising ones (see for more details Dalziel and Lattimore, 1996). It is undoubtful that consumers are paying now lower prices and are obtaining greater variety of goods. Thus their consumer surplus had to increase. On the other side (in contrast to our simple theory) most of them were working in the activities that had to be eliminated in this open economy. The unemployment rate is still relatively high and therefore being the continuous but not serious threat to the continuation of the reform process.

■ *13.5* Summary

Three interrelationships were explored in this chapter. The first was the role of trade and trade policy in development and growth. Import-substituting industrialisation was discussed in detail, not because it is the one prevailing in modern economies but because there is a need of exposing the dangers of blindly adopting such a strategy. We also mentioned that the debate is still not resolved on the causality between exports and growth. Empirical evidence shows that countries, such as the East Asian NICs, record both high growth rates of GDP and high growth rates of exports. While the orthodox view is that free trade orientation (or export-led growth) is responsible for fast and sustained economic growth in those countries, the new growth theory suggests that the causality runs from growth to exports, and not vice versa.

The second relationship examined was between trade and trade policy and transition of the former socialist economies. Issues such as the design of trade liberalisation and transitional protection were discussed. On the basis of experience from early phases of transition, it is suggested that a very fast and general trade liberalisation could be too costly in terms of the collapse of output, fiscal revenues, unemployment and reduction in social security.

Finally, the relationship between trade and trade policy and the economic reform of the DC was examined on the basis of New Zealand's case. Prior to the reform of 1984 New Zealand's domestic markets were highly protected by high tariffs and by numerous quantitative and administrative restrictions. Nowadays, New Zealand is one of the most open economies in terms of liberal flows of goods, services and factors between national market and the rest of the world. The effects of this change in incentives has to still be reflected in the economy's performance in the long run.

■ *PART 3* ■

ECONOMIC INTEGRATION

■ *Chapter 14* ■

The Theory of Economic Integration

■ *14.1* Introduction

The term *economic integration* does not have a single meaning. It is used to describe interdependence among national economies which are engaged in international trade. It also refers to any group of national economies which are fully unified in an economic sense. Economic integration may be understood as a *process* leading to the complete abolition of all discrimination between economic units belonging to different national economies, or as a *stage* in such a process. Seen as a stage, this process is often confused with the various forms of economic integration. Before we began examining these different forms of integration let us note that there are also other terms used to describe economic integration whose main defining characteristic is geographically-discriminating trade policy. Some of the most frequently used terms include regional trading arrangements (RTAs), regional integration agreements (RIAs), trading blocs, regionalism, preferential trading arrangements (PTAs), regional trade liberalisation, and preferential tariff reduction. Even though these terms do not have identical meanings they are used interchangeably to refer to both the process and the state of affairs known as economic integration. In fact these terms predominate in the renewed debate over the virtues of multilateral trade liberalisation. While integrative processes used to be seen as implying that economic integration would lead towards multilateral trade liberalisation, nowadays we tend to see *regionalism* as being a threat to the multilateral trade liberalisation which has evolved through the GATT in the post-war period. We will discuss this issue in Chapter 17.

In this chapter we focus on the welfare effects of economic integration. Economic integration can be broadly defined as the discriminatory removal of all trade impediments between participating nations, often accompanied by the establishment of certain elements of cooperation and coordination such as the partial or full harmonisation of economic policies in one or more areas. Economic integration can take many different forms. The types usually considered by the theory of economic integration are defined below.[1]

(1) *Free trade areas* are where tariff import restrictions among participating countries are removed but each country retains its own national tariff barriers against non-members. The best known real-world example of a free trade area is the European Free Trade Association (EFTA). More recent examples include the Closer Economic Relations (CER) agreement between Australia and New Zealand and the much talked about free trade area between Canada and the United States, CUSTA.

(2) *Customs unions* involve the suppression of all intra-area trade barriers among member countries and the establishment of a common set of external tariffs on imports from non-members. The European Economic Community (EEC) began as a customs union.

(3) A *common market* transcends a customs union as it also entails the free movement of labour, capital and other factors of production as well as the free movement of enterprises among member countries. A real-world example of this type of integration is the present form of the European Union (EU) as elucidated in the 'Europe 1992' framework.

(4) *Economic union* is a common market where national economic policies such as trade, monetary, fiscal and welfare policies are harmonised. The Benelux economic union, comprising Belgium, Luxembourg and the Netherlands, is seen as the initial step that led towards the establishment of the EU. More recently EU members have ratified the Maastricht Treaty which entails this type of integration.

(5) *Total economic integration* implies the full unification of national economic policies as well as the establishment of a central authority whose decisions are binding for all member countries. When this central authority extends its coverage to matters other than purely economic ones, member countries in effect become one state. The integration then takes the form of *complete political integration*.

The various types of economic integration actually established do not perfectly correspond to the above classification. Some real-world integrations include features from two or more of the theoretical forms. For example the CER agreement between Australia and New Zealand does not include the common external trade barriers, making it a 'primitive' type of integration, but it does allow for the free mobility of labour and for almost free capital mobility. This latter characteristic pertains to more complex types of integration such as a common market or economic union. One of the reasons for the confusion surrounding the types and stages of integration is that when countries follow their initial plan and form a particular *type* of economic integration, for example a FTA, they are often pressured by either the success or failure of the initial form of integration to proceed or evolve into a more complex type of integration such as a customs union or a common market. Countries therefore move in stages through the integrative process.

☐ A brief history of regional integrations

Economic integration is not a new phenomenon. It can be traced back to the early formation of customs unions which were driven by the political will to abolish internal tolls and tariffs and form nation-states.[2] This was the case with France in the late eighteenth century and with various states in central Europe that about the same time were divided by more than 1800 customs frontiers. One of these states, Prussia, moved to form an economic union which culminated in the formation of the *Zollverein* in 1834 when most member states, later to comprise Germany, adopted Prussia's external tariffs. It was only in the mid-nineteenth century that Switzerland and Italy abolished internal tariffs. The weakening of trade with colonies together with the establishment of sovereign states in Europe were the primary factors which led to the many treaties containing a 'most favoured nation' (MFN) clause. This in turn resulted in major tariff reductions both in Europe and around the world. The period from the mid-nineteenth century until the First World War thus stands as the first period of multilateral trade arrangements. Irwin (1993, pp. 91, 99–100) finds that in some respects this period is superior to the multilateralism of the present GATT system.

In contrast, the inter-war period was marked by the establishment of protectionist bilateral arrangements and discriminatory trading blocs. The performance of the world economy in this period, including the Great Depression and a significant fall in world growth and trade, is typically used to emphasise the adverse consequences of bilateralism. However, as we discuss in Chapter 17, there is no such thing as either universally bad bilateralism or universally good multilateralism. The effects of each depend on the particular set of circumstances. Moreover it has been recently argued that our belief in how the bilateralism of the inter-war period distorted the pattern of international trade is not based on strong empirical evidence (Eichengreen, 1993). In fact it can be argued that if countries had not turned to this form of trade, the contraction of world trade and the depression would have been even deeper.

The first wave of post-Second World War interest in regional economic integration occurred in the 1960s. This interest was initiated by the establishment in 1957 of the first major customs union of sovereign states, the European Economic Community (EEC).[3] Following the EEC the European Free Trade Association (EFTA) was formed in 1960, and on the other side of the world the Australia–New Zealand Free Trade Area (ANZCERTA or CER) was established in 1965. There have also been a number of attempts among LDCs to organise various types of economic integration. These attempts have almost all failed. These aspirations towards regionalism among LDCs will be examined in Chapter 16, where we also discuss the more successful cases of economic integration. It seems that the first wave of post-war regionalism was followed by an interlude when the world trading system, formulated under the GATT, was at its peak. The second generation of preferential trade agreements began to occur in the 1980s in the form of increased membership of the EC and continued with the creation of CUSTA, and stronger commitment to free trade in the CER, ASEAN and APEC. The movement to liberalise trade within the Asia–Pacific region has become known as *open regionalism* being based on non-discrimination and market integration. Table 14.1 illustrates how intra-regional trade has been increasing even faster than the world trade.

The rising interest in regionalism in the 1990s came from the loss of momentum in the multilateral trade negotiations of the GATT Uruguay Round. It has been increasingly argued that countries can achieve the goal of reviving world trade much sooner through bilateral than through multilateral negotiation. For example the bilateral agreements of the inter-war world economy are not believed to have led to a slowing of world trade, but rather were actually motivated by this slower growth and by recession. Countries have thus turned to bilateral agreements in the

Table 14.1   *Share of intra-regional trade (exports and imports) in a region's total trade, 1928–93*

	1928	1948	1963	1973	1983	1993
Western Europe	50.7	41.8	61.1	67.7	64.7	69.9
Central and Eastern Europe and the former USSR	19.0	46.4	71.3	58.8	57.3	19.7
North America[*]	25.0	27.1	30.5	35.1	31.7	33.0
Latin America[*]	11.1	20.0	16.3	27.9	17.7	19.4
Asia	45.5	38.9	47.0	41.6	43.0	49.7
Africa	10.3	8.4	7.8	7.6	4.4	8.4
Middle East	5.0	20.3	8.7	6.1	7.9	9.4
World	38.7	32.9	44.1	49.3	44.2	50.4

Note: [*] Mexico is included in Latin America.
Source: WTO (1995a, Table 3, p. 39).

expectation of mitigating the reduction in world trade. This may be occurring currently when the world trading system based on GATT's multilateralism is compared to the potential development of the trade system based on the triad of the EU, North America and East Asia. Chapter 17 examines the key issues in this heated debate.

The next section will proceed by discussing the basic theory of customs unions. Our attention will then turn to a comparison of customs unions with free trade areas, and finally we will introduce the basics of the theory of common markets.

■ *14.2* The basic theory of customs unions

While this section focuses on the effects of the formation of customs unions most of the analysis is also applicable to other types of economic integration. Countries grouped in a customs union abolish trade restrictions within the union and implement a unified trade policy towards non-members including a common external tariff (CET) on imports. It may seem that a customs union will necessarily lead towards an improvement in welfare as by creating a free trade enclave it represents a step towards the ideal of world-wide free trade. This notion that total world welfare can be improved by the elimination of trade restrictions within a group of countries was behind GATT's Article XXIV which provides an exception to the non-discrimination code for customs unions, free trade areas, and interim agreements which lead to either type of integration.[4] However, as we know from the theory of the second best, it may not in fact be the case that partially free trade in the form of a customs union or other type of regional integration will necessarily bring about an improvement in welfare. It was Viner (1950) who made the initial contribution to a more complete examination of the welfare effects of customs unions. He studied the effects of formation of a customs union on the production of member countries. Viner found two possible production effects with contradictory welfare implications. To describe these effects he coined the terms *trade creation* and *trade diversion*. From then onwards, the core of customs union theory has been the notion that the net effect of a customs union is dependent on the relative strengths of the trade-creation and trade-diversion effects. Ethier and Horn (1984) refer to this idea as the Vinerian description.

☐ *Trade creation and trade diversion*

Viner argued that a formation of a customs union creates trade between member states in response to the mutual elimination of tariffs on each other's goods. Trade diversion shifts the trade flows from non-member countries to member countries in response to the tariff discrimination produced by the union's formation. The presumption is that trade creation is beneficial while trade diversion is harmful. This is because trade creation represents the substitution of inefficient (higher-cost) domestic production by efficient regional partner-country production. This raises the welfare of the members and the world as a whole. However trade diversion has a welfare cost since it involves inefficient regional partner-country production substituting for efficient third-country production.

While this analysis considers only the production effect of the union a proper evaluation of welfare effects must also take into account the consumption side as the trade creation and trade diversion effects occur there in the form of increased or decreased consumer surplus. When consumers are able to substitute cheaper foreign goods imported from a member country for more expensive domestically produced goods their surplus will increase. Conversely, if they are forced to consume more expensive goods which originate within the customs union rather than non-member countries' cheaper goods they will suffer a loss of consumer surplus. The total trade creation and trade diversion effects should thus take account of both the changes in production and consumption.

Following Robson (1987) these two effects can be illustrated in the partial equilibrium framework (Figure 14.1). Figure 14.1(a) depicts Home's domestic demand (D_H) and supply (S_H) for a certain good. Figure 14.1(b) depicts Foreign's domestic demand (D_F) and supply (S_F) schedules for the same good. These two countries are considering establishing a customs union. In panel (b), in addition to the domestic supply and demand curves, we therefore also include a second supply curve $(S_F + M_{H,F})$ which combines the domestic supply of Foreign and the excess supply of Home $(M_{H,F} = S_H - D_H)$. This curve represents the total supply of this good in Foreign's market originating within the customs union. The price p_w indicates the price for the same good on the world market. We assume a perfectly elastic world supply. The welfare effects of the formation of a customs union between Home and Foreign primarily depend on the pre- and post-union tariff positions. Two cases are discussed here: (1) when the pre-union tariffs in both Home and Foreign were prohibitive and there was no trade, and (2) when before the union only Home had a prohibitive tariff while Foreign's imports from the rest of the world were positive.

(1)   Suppose that before the customs union both countries had prohibitive tariffs. The prices were thus p_H in Home and p_F in Foreign. Both countries had created an artificial self-sufficiency in this good as the tariff equalised domestic supply and demand in each country. After forming a union both countries levy a CET on imports of this good. Usually, but not necessarily, this tariff is determined as an average of the pre-union rates. In Figure 14.1 the level of this tariff-inclusive price is given by p_{CET}. This price allows for an increase in demand in Foreign, to OS, but also results in a contraction of Foreign's product-

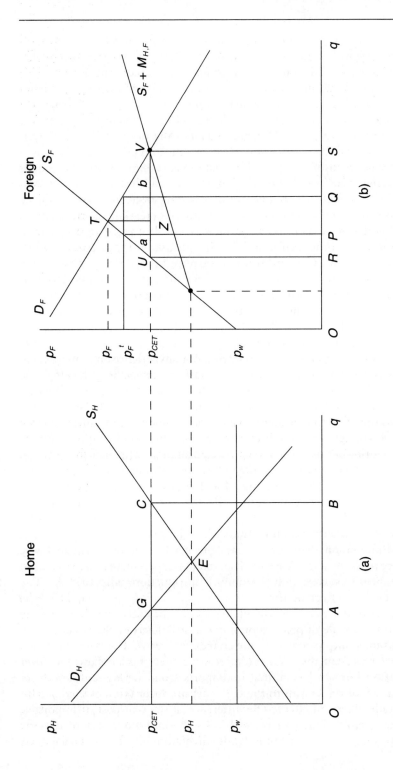

Figure 14.1 *Trade creation and trade diversion*

ion to OR. On the other hand in Home demand falls to OA while production expands to OB, the difference being exported to Foreign.

For Foreign this trading equilibrium thus implies trade creation. To see this we will use the concepts of producer and consumer surplus. The total increase in consumer surplus amounts to $p_{CET}VTp_F$. The loss in producer surplus is $p_{CET}UTp_F$. The net benefit is given by the triangular area TUV. This gain includes the original Vinerian trade creation, or the production effect of the union (TUZ). This is a decrease in costs due to the fact that the cost of importing the good is less than the cost of producing it domestically. However it also includes a gain in consumer surplus arising from the substitution of imports for other goods (TZV). With the creation of the customs union Home experiences an increase in the price of this good. Consumers thus suffer a loss of the amount p_HEGp_{CET} while producers enjoy an additional surplus of p_HECp_{CET}. Since the increase in producer surplus outweighs the consumers loss, Home is clearly better off with the customs union than it was without it.

With respect to the rest of the world there are no welfare effects in this particular example because neither of the countries traded before creating the customs union. The total welfare effects of the union are thus confined to these two countries. Both experience an improvement in welfare due to the trade creation effects outweighing the effects of trade diversion. The static impact-effect analysis of this specific case thus suggests that the creation of customs unions should be welcome.

(2)   A second case to consider is when only Home has a prohibitive tariff while Foreign's tariff is lower and allows some trade with the rest of the world. Let us assume that Foreign's initial tariff inclusive price is $p_F{}^t$ which results in the volume of imports from the rest of the world being given by PQ and allows for domestic production of OP. The Foreign government would collect a revenue in an amount of $PQ \times p_w p_F{}^t$.

For simplicity, assume that when Home and Foreign form a customs union their CET clears the markets at the tariff-inclusive price p_{CET}. In such a case the demand in Foreign increases to OS, as in the previous case, while domestic production falls to OR. The production effect of the tariff reduction in Foreign is equal to the area of triangle a. This triangle represents the costs saved because the inefficient scale of production is decreased. There is also a net gain in consumer surplus equal to the triangular area b. Together these two areas represent the total trade creation effect for Foreign. However because Foreign has shifted its imports from the low-cost producer (the rest of the world) to the high-cost producer (Home) there is also a trade diversion effect. The difference in the unit cost of imports is now $p_w p_{CET}$. This cost multiplied by the initial quantity of imports PQ is equal to the total trade diversion effect for Foreign. A comparison of the magnitudes of the trade creation and trade diversion effects then reveals the net static-impact effect of a customs union on Foreign's welfare. In this particular example the formation of a customs union did not result in an improvement of welfare as the trade diversion effect outweighed the trade creation effect.

The Home country experiences the same beneficial effects of participating in the customs union with Foreign as in the previous example. The rest of the world will also be affected in the case where trade diversion occurs. However these welfare effects are not observable in Figure 14.1 since we have drawn the world supply curve as perfectly elastic.

To sum up, in this partial equilibrium framework, with constant costs, there will be a net welfare gain if the amount of trade created multiplied by the difference in unit costs between the home and partner countries exceeds the amount of trade diverted multiplied by the difference in unit costs between the partner and the non-member countries.

☐ *Trade modification*

In addition to the trade creation and trade diversion effects there is a third effect on trade flows, but one that is not due to the discriminatory tariffs introduced by the union. As Ethier and Horn (1984) discuss, the change in the pattern of trade with the outside world, due to the replacement of one set of tariffs with another, is termed *trade modification*. This effect is different from the trade diversion effect. The trade diversion effect is based on price discrimination and as such has to have a negative sign, that is, it contracts the amount of trade with the outside world. The trade modification effect does not evolve from price discrimination and it can assume either a positive or a negative sign. It can therefore either increase or decrease trade with the outside world.

Following Ethier and Horn (1984) we will consider the example of three countries; Canada, Japan and the USA. Initially the USA and Canada trade automobiles between themselves and independently with Japan. After forming a customs union Canada and the USA set a CET on cars imported from Japan. The union formation causes a contraction in the trade with Japan and a trade diversion effect will occur. Suppose next that cars can be divided into two broad categories, for example, large and small. Let the USA and Canada trade large cars with each other and small cars with Japan. The customs union will result in an increased trade of large cars between the USA and Canada. The trade pattern between Canada, the USA and Japan is thus again modified. The welfare effects are the same as in the pure case of trade diversion because Japan produces a substitute for the good produced within the union. Suppose however that the car industry is a unified world industry with the USA importing engines from

Japan and car bodies from Canada. With a customs union between the USA and Canada there will be no tariffs on car bodies. An expansion of imports of car bodies from Canada will thus result. This will in turn increase the imports of engines from Japan, even though they incur a tariff because engines are complementary to car bodies. This effect, increased trade with Japan, is trade modification with a positive sign.

As is obvious from the above example, a degree of substitutability and complementarity between goods is crucial in determining how much the trade modification effect will differ from the trade diversion effect. The conclusion we can draw is that the larger the proportion of the customs union countries' trade that is based on differentiated products which are complements rather than substitutes, the more important will be incorporation of the trade modification effect in addition to the trade diversion effect. Both effects must therefore be considered when studying the welfare effects of a customs union.

☐ *Factors influencing welfare effects*

This partial equilibrium analysis is not the type of analysis from which we can usually derive general conclusions about the potential welfare effects of customs unions. However in this area general equilibrium analysis has not been fully worked out (Lloyd, 1982, 1992) and, rather problematically, we have to rely on what our partial analysis indicates about which factors will determine the welfare effects of the union. There are several factors the impact of which should be taken into account when considering the sign of the welfare effects of a customs union.

(1)   The larger the share of domestic goods and the smaller the share of goods imported from non-member countries in total consumption, *ceteris paribus*, the greater the likelihood that the formation of the customs union will be beneficial for all members. This is based on the fact that the substitution of member country products for domestic products entails trade creation and their substitution for goods originating in non-member countries entails trade diversion. Thus, as Lipsey (1960) correctly argued, the lesser the relative importance of non-member goods, the larger the chances for strong trade creation effects will be.

(2)   The more competitive (overlapping) the production structures of the member countries are the greater the chance will be that those countries' welfare will increase following the formation of a customs union. This is based on the assumption that there is more scope for trade creation among countries with similar production structures because these countries tend to replace less efficient domestic production with imports from member countries. Moreover the greater the

cost difference in production for similar goods the greater will be the gains from the customs union. This is because such a cost difference will enhance the possibilities of resource allocation and trade creation. On the other hand if countries' production structures are complementary the formation of a customs union will lead to the substitution of member countries goods for lower-cost goods originating in non-member countries.[5]

(3) The height of the tariffs certainly affects the strength of the trade creation effect. High pre-union tariffs against future member countries enhances the likelihood of trade creation and hence benefits from the creation of the customs union. Analogously a low level of tariffs against future non-member countries acts in the same direction by reducing the chances for trade diversion and reducing welfare losses. The reason is that low tariffs against imports from the rest of the world imply that locally produced goods are already competitive and the costs of trade diversion from the rest of the world to the member countries will be correspondingly low. This proposition does not apply to countries that were members of GATT prior to forming a customs union. In particular these countries must observe the most-favoured-nation (MFN) clause of GATT which means that they can not levy differentiating tariffs against imports from different counties. However the level of the CET against the rest of the world after the unions formation is also important; the lower this tariff the smaller the scope for trade diversion.

(4) The greater the size of a customs union in terms of area and number of countries the larger is the probability that trade creation effects will outweigh any trade diversion effects because the larger is the probability that the least-cost producing country will be included in the union. In the extreme case of a customs union encompassing the entire world the result would be completely free trade with no trade diversion effects. Related to this idea is the proposition that small countries will gain more from becoming a member of a union than will larger countries (where size is defined as market size). This result follows from the impact the size of the market has on the possibilities for the reallocation of production as well as the extent of economies of scale. The role of economies of scale will be discussed in a separate subsection on the dynamic effects of customs unions.

(5) Transportation costs also play a role in determining the total welfare effects. The lower the transportation costs are among member countries, *ceteris paribus*, the larger will be the benefits from their customs union. It is therefore expected that neighbouring countries have better chance of forming a beneficial customs union than faraway countries. Transportation costs and other communication costs are the main factor in what is known as the formation of '*natural*' trading blocs (Krugman, 1993). The presumption is that the

freeing of trade in such types of blocs will result in large intra-
regional trade flows thus enlarging the gains from forming the bloc.

To sum up, trade creation can, in general, be expected to be high when the
union is characterised by members who are at similar levels of development, incur low transport costs, have an already high share of intra-
regional trade and have a low level of common external protection.

⬜ The customs union and unilateral tariff reductions

The reason why the formation of a customs union is seen as beneficial is
due to the trade creation effect which occurs in response to the reduction
of tariffs and other import barriers amongst member countries. Because
pre-union tariffs act as distortions their removal must be welcomed as it
presumably enables a country to switch from second best to first best
equilibrium. This is true only when a country does not establish new
external protection against non-member countries. Since the formation of
customs union involves exactly this, it ought to be seen as a second best
exercise where one distortion merely replaces another. Cooper and Massell
(1965) and Johnson (1965) have developed this argument further, suggesting that a country's participation in a customs union is inferior to the
unilateral elimination of tariffs. Under this latter policy trade creation
would occur without any accompanying trade diversion. This result must
be modified if the unilateral policy does not completely eliminate tariffs
but only reduces them. In Figure 14.2 we compare the effects of unilateral
tariff reduction with participation in a customs union where the reduction
in tariff rates is the same in both cases.

As discussed in Figure 14.1 the impact of Foreign's participation in a
custom union comprises the elimination of tariffs on imports from Home
and a decrease on tariffs for imports from the rest of the world. The
common tariff-inclusive price is p_u. The trade creation effect is therefore
$a + b$ while the trade diversion effect is d. In the case of a unilateral tariff
reduction from $p_F{}^t$ to p_u the effect in terms of an increase in the demand for
and a decrease of the domestic supply of this good is the same as in the case
of a customs union. However, imports from the rest of the world will now
increase to RS and the tariff revenues collected by Foreign government
equal $p_w p_u \times RS$, or the areas $e + d + f$. The areas labelled e, d and f
represent the gains to Foreign from implementing a unilateral tariff
reduction rather than forming a customs union with Home. This gain
consists of the tariff revenue to Foreign's government. This gain thus
remains in the country while in the case of entering into a union it will be
lost in the form of revenues to the exporters from Home. Foreign thus
gains from being able to buy this good at a lower cost (p_w) than in the

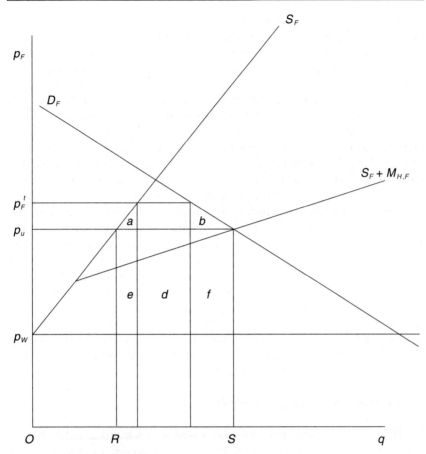

Figure 14.2 *Unilateral tariff reduction versus customs union*

union (p_u). Of course Home loses because its exports to Foreign cease as trade is diverted to the rest of the world, the rest of the world being the lower-cost producer.

There are, however, other sources of gain for Foreign if it forms a customs union with Home. In the case of the customs union formation Home's market will be open to all kinds of Foreign products, and not only the one that we focus on in Figure 14.2, and will possibly earn higher export revenues. Dynamic gains are also possible (see p. 455). In terms of static effects the superiority of a unilateral tariff reduction thus depends on the relative strength of the gains through the lower import costs and the losses through export revenues forgone. The gain in terms of export revenues will be higher the higher is the pre-union tariff in the member countries. Revenues will be also affected by tariffs in non-member countries. This is because Home producers will try to avoid paying tariffs in non-member countries if they can export tariff-free to member countries.

This issue of the superiority of unilateral tariff reduction has been examined in the context of pursuing non-economic objectives by forming a customs union. Cooper and Massell (1965) and Johnson (1965) have identified one of these objectives as the goal of developing industrial capability (that is, a preference for industry). It is assumed that this development is easier to realise if the national economy has the support of a larger market obtained under a customs union than if it remains on its own. Johnson argued that a preference for industry may reflect nationalistic aspirations and rivalry with other countries – the intent of industrial firms and workers (unions) to increase their incomes; or the belief that industrial activities involve beneficial externalities. In the case of large beneficial externalities resulting from the creation of a customs union there is no need to introduce any non-economic objectives when establishing the superiority of customs union versus unilateral tariff reduction. Wonnacott and Wonnacott (1981) demonstrate that if the preference for industry does not exist then a customs union may not be superior to unilateral tariff reduction. However countries may opt for the union solution because it may be a more viable political option than unilateral action. However, the formation of a customs union may evolve in a more complex form of economic integration with positive impacts on potential member countries. Theoretically this could lead to a more liberal policy toward multilateral trade liberalisation although the developments in the opposite direction favouring a 'fortress mentality' are also likely.

☐ *Terms of trade effects*

So far we have assumed that the establishment of a customs union has no effect on the terms of trade. In the real world, however, we should expect that terms of trade will change both among the countries within the union and between member and non-member countries. Even in the case of constant terms of trade with the outside world when the members' terms of trade are affected within the union the changes will have an impact on the welfare distribution among members countries. Unless the union is small its creation will have an impact upon the terms of trade with non-member countries. In such a case the trade diversion effect, which involves a welfare loss to member countries, should be adjusted for possible improvements in the terms of trade. Depending on the magnitude of the change in the terms of trade the negative welfare effects of trade diversion may be offset by the gains achieved through improved terms of trade. By the same token, while we assumed no change in the welfare of the outside world under constant terms of trade, when the outside world experiences a deterioration in its terms of trade the formation of a customs union must adversely affect its welfare.

The possibility of terms of trade improvements may thus be a potential motivation for establishing a customs union. This may also explain why such an option may be preferred to unilateral tariff reduction: in the latter case the impact on a country's terms of trade is negative. However even if an improvement in the terms of trade is indeed a part of the motivation for the union, this improvement will not be realised if the union is not large enough. In general, the larger the union, *ceteris paribus*, the larger the chances are for positive terms of trade changes and for losses to the rest of the world. This result is based on the elasticity of the union's offer curve: the larger the union the more elastic its offer curve. This high price sensitivity means that the union will be unwilling to buy the outside world's products unless the relative price of their goods falls. In other words, the larger the union the lower the elasticity of the rest of the world offer curve.

Another factor which influences the probability of post-union changes in the terms of trade relates to the level of tariffs before and after the creation of the union. Vanek (1965) has shown that it is possible for member countries to realise gains without imposing a loss on non-member countries. This can occur if the post-union CET is sufficiently less than the pre-union tariffs of the member countries. Vanek's proposition has been extended by Ohyama (1972) and Kemp and Wan (1976). According to Ethier and Horn (1984), the second basic notion of the theory of customs union is due to all four of those authors: Kemp, Vanek, Ohyama and Wan. The post-union external tariffs can be set at levels which lead member countries to trade exactly the same aggregate collection and quantity of goods that they traded with the rest of the world prior to the union. In this case the establishment of a customs union will have no effect at all on the rest of the world while member countries must benefit in the aggregate because of the freeing of mutual trade. The setting of the CET to such level would require the manipulation of tariffs so that in the end the union experiences only trade creation and all trade diversion is eliminated. This in fact would require a small deterioration in the union's terms of trade. The Kemp and Wan proposition thus states that by an appropriate choice of external tariffs and lump-sum transfers among member countries, any customs union can guarantee that no countries in the world lose, and that some gain with union formation. Seen in this way, the formation and further extension of a customs union represents a welfare-improving 'stepping stone' towards free trade at a world level. This idea has become more relevant with the re-examination of the merits of regionalism than the Vinerian description and is naturally at the heart of the arguments of the advocates of regionalism.

☐ Dynamic effects

Besides the static-impact effects already discussed, the establishment of a customs union also has *dynamic effects*. Balassa (1961) views these dynamic effects as one of the many ways through which a customs union, or any other form of integration, may influence the rate of growth of those countries participating. Some of the ways in which integration can affect the rate of growth is through economies of scale, increased competition, the stimulation of investment, and stimulating technical change. These dynamic effects are not easy to analyse systematically and a degree of controversy still surrounds them. In this section we will discuss the effects of economies of scale since these can be analysed in an orthodox manner.

Economies of scale

We have already established (Chapters 4 and 5) that the existence of economies of scale provides an additional source of gains from free trade, and by the same token one more argument for the liberalisation of trade. This also makes economies of scale a relevant factor in determining the welfare effects of regional trade liberalisation which takes the form of a customs union or some other type of economic integration. Economies of scale can be viewed from the firm level (internal economies of scale) or from the industry or country level (external economies of scale). Following Corden (1972) we will focus on the economies of scale internal to the firm. The analysis applied here is very simple and even though we imply internal economies of scale, we shall assume there are no effects on the market structure. Figure 14.3 provides a framework for analysing the effects of the formation of a customs union in the presence of economies of scale. Suppose there are two *small* countries, Home and Foreign, which form a customs union. In each country industry A experiences falling average costs. However, as we assume there is no market power, the pricing strategy of this industry in both countries is to price at average cost. The world price is given by p_w. Note that neither country's average cost in the production of good A falls as low as the world price. This means that neither country can exploit its economies of scale to such a degree that it becomes internationally competitive. As we will see later, this factor is quite important. Given the cost structures in Home and Foreign, and the world price as illustrated in Figure 14.3, there are several possible scenarios. In one scenario we can assume that both governments provide *made-to-measure* tariff protection so that prior to union both countries produce good A. Other scenarios would allow for the production of A in only one of these two countries, or in neither if there is no government protection. Let us focus on two of these possibilities. The interested readers can work out for themselves the effects in the other two.

In the first scenario made-to-measure protection implies that in each country the tariff will be just high enough to encourage domestic production at a level at which average costs are equal to price. This level of protection does not therefore give rise to any monopoly profits. Consequently the tariff-inclusive price in Home will be p_H which generates output Oq_H. The tariff-inclusive price in Foreign will be p_F which generates output Oq_F. The Foreign industry A is more efficient, which is

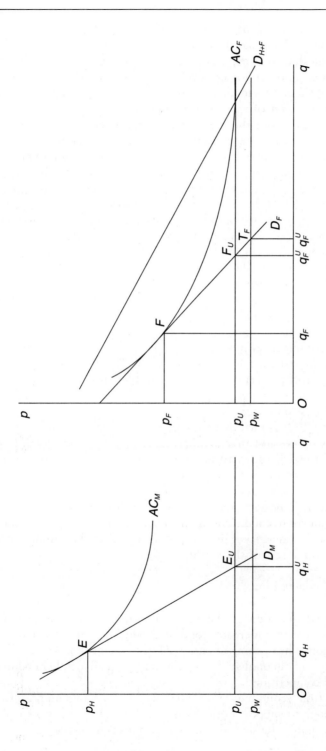

Figure 14.3 *Cost-reduction and trade suppression effects*

reflected in the need for a lower tariff maintaining domestic production. After Home and Foreign form a customs union, the entire production of good A will shift to Foreign as the cheaper producer. The expanded output q_u requires a much lower level of support in the form of a CET: $p_u = p_w + CET$. In Home the production of good A has ceased. This represents the part of the trade creation gain which relies on the shift to cheaper supply from the member country. The other part of the trade creation gain is on the consumption side. The quantity consumed has expanded to the level of $q_H{}''$. The total trade creation gain in Home is thus equal to the area $p_H p_u E_u E$. In Foreign consumption has also expanded to the level of $q_F{}''$, the consumption part of the trade creation generating a gain equal to $p_F p_u F_u F$. However Foreign also benefits from the reduction in average costs as its output expands following the formation of the union. This effect is known as the *cost-reduction* effect.[6]

The second scenario implies that prior to the formation of the union only one country produces good A. Suppose that in our example only Home, the less efficient producer, was producing good A with the made-to-measure tariff while Foreign was importing it tariff-free from the rest of the world. Post-union Home experiences the trade creation gains described above: domestic production will cease and the lowering of tariffs will create a consumer surplus. However Foreign will experience a different effect. Its domestic producers will now find that they can produce good A under the tariff protection umbrella. Cheaper supply from abroad is thus replaced by more expensive domestic supply. This effect is known as the *trade-suppression* effect.

Corden (1972) argued that the cost-reduction effect is likely to outweigh the trade-suppression effect so that the economies of scale will lead to net benefits from the formation of the union. However this conclusion depends on a set of special assumptions including made-to-measure tariffs, average cost pricing and a CET lower than any individual tariff prior to the union. It is nevertheless obvious from this simple analysis that with these production conditions in member countries it is not possible to achieve such efficiency gains in production that the union becomes an exporter to the rest of the world.

Increased competition

It is argued that one of the most important aspects of regional trade liberalisation is that it creates conditions which will result in more effective competition. The opening of national borders contributes to a loosening of monopoly and oligopolistic market structures in all member countries. The increased competition in terms of a larger number of firms will not reduce the gains from economies of scale because the increased market size will be large enough to support both. As well as leading to improvements in cost efficiency more intensive competition also leads to increased technological progress. In particular, increased competition may stimulate research activities aimed at developing new products or new production techniques. In addition, those types of integration which free up factor movements increase the transmission of technological knowledge.

From our discussion in Part 2 it follows that the gains from increased competition and economies of scale may also be obtained through unilateral trade liberalisation. This is true. However there are additional gains which stem from free access to member countries markets that cannot be obtained through unilateral trade liberalisation.

■ *14.3* Customs unions versus free trade areas

Until recently most attention focused on the theory of customs unions while free trade agreements were almost ignored. However the negotiation of the free trade agreements between Canada, the USA, and latterly Mexico, has led recent attention to centre on the effects of free trade areas. Recall that the feature which distinguishes a free trade area (FTA) from a customs union is that each participating country in the FTA retains the power to erect their own separate protection against imports from the rest of the world. It is thus very likely that countries will maintain different tariffs and other barriers on products coming in from outside the FTA. This raises the possibility of *trade deflection*. Trade deflection will occur if imports enter the FTA through the participating country which has the lowest tariff. Of course, this assumes that transportation costs and other costs related to imports do not outweigh the difference in tariff rates. The consequences of this trade deflection are therefore equivalent to the adoption of a CET equal to the lowest tariff for each commodity in any of the participating countries. Under the assumption of constant terms of trade the trade deflection effect will therefore limit the extent of trade diversion and will have welfare-increasing effects in member countries. However if the terms of trade change there will be an impact on distribution of welfare between member countries and the outside world. Trade deflection will reduce both the terms of trade gain for member countries and the terms of trade loss for the outside world as compared to a customs union, *ceteris paribus*.

In addition to trade deflection, an FTA creates the possibilities of *production deflection* and *investment deflection*. Production deflection occurs if the producers of products with an imported intermediate input content shift production to countries which have the lowest tariffs on those inputs. To this statement must be added the provision that this will occur only if the tariff differential outweighs the difference in the costs of production. The production deflection will have an adverse impact on welfare because it causes the reallocation of resources contrary to what each country's comparative advantage would a *priori* indicate. This inefficient allocation may in turn cause a change in the pattern of investment. *Ceteris paribus*, investors will tend to invest in the member countries with the lowest tariffs on imported inputs or with the highest tariffs on finished products. This leads to so-called *tariff factories*. The welfare effects of investment deflections are of course negative. These deflection effects are actually unintended aspects of FTAs. To avoid them member countries of FTA usually impose *rules of origin*. These rules restrict the freedom of intra-area trade in products which incorporate certain proportions of imported products or undergo certain transformation process in member countries. However these rules tend not to be very effective. In order to limit deflection effects member countries are thus encouraged to reduce their own tariffs towards the level of the lowest tariffs in the FTA.

Recent research motivated by the advent of new FTAs shows that rules of origin are the source of an important protectionist bias inherent in the FTA which is not present in customs unions (Krueger, 1993). More specifically, the rules of origin extend the protection accorded by each country to producers in the other free trade agreement countries. As such, the rules of origin may enhance the degree of economic inefficiency in the FTA as compared to a customs union.

There are arguments typically used to defend the establishment of the FTA rather than a customs union.[7] However at least some of them can also be turned upside down to facilitate the argument against FTA superiority. For example, it is widely thought that the formation of an FTA does not result in the escalation of tariffs in member countries. This is in contrast to the case of customs union formation where a CET usually allows for some countries with low pre-union tariff levels to raise their tariffs.[8] The FTA is thus preferable to a customs union. Nevertheless when a customs union is formed, the country with the lowest tariffs, if it is the dominant country within the union, could force other member countries to lower theirs, arguing that this would increase the likelihood of welfare improvement by the union. Thus a customs union may end up as having larger welfare-increasing effects and also as resulting in lower costs for the outside world.

It is similarly argued that because the FTA allows the member countries to retain their own tariffs against the rest of the world they have a greater opportunity to pursue trade policy reforms while in customs unions countries with tendencies for such reforms may have to abandon them because of the requirement of CET. In the extreme case of strong lobbying groups in the least efficient country of the union, the whole union could be pushed towards a high CET. As the counter-argument it should be mentioned that lobbying can be made much more effective and less costly within national borders than within the union so that the formation of the union may lead to the weakening of the interest groups' power and the lowering of tariffs as compared to the each individual country's tariff level within the FTA.

Box 14.1 *Rules of origin and the WTO*

Rules of origin is a set of laws and regulations applied by government trade authorities to determine the country of origin of goods. They affect different aspects of trade because the origin of the goods has a direct bearing on the administration trade measures such as quota systems, tariff preferences, or anti-dumping and countervailing duties. For example, if a countervailing duty is to be applied by an importing country to the VCRs of a country C, it is necessary to determine whether a particular import of VCRs coming from country C should be considered to be the product of country C. If country C has used the components and parts of several other countries to assemble VCR for selling it in the importing country's market, the matter of imposing countervailing duties could become quite complex. In the past countries typically had two sets of rules: general rules applicable to all countries, and some special rules (often not very transparent) for preferential trade, and for regional arrangements. In many cases that allowed for a use of rules of origin as protectionist devise. In order to make the rules of origin simpler, more uniform and stable, the Uruguay Round considered desirable to prepare a harmonised set of rules of origin to be adopted by all countries. However, the Agreement on Rules of Origin (one of the WTO agreements) signed in Marrakech in 1994 had to postpone harmonisation (at best, for three years until the Committee on Rules of Origin finishes its work). Meantime, this agreement 'requires WTO members to ensure that their rules of origin are transparent; that they do not have restricting, distorting or disruptive effects on international trade; that they are administered in a consistent, uniform, impartial and reasonable manner, and that they are based on a positive standard' (WTO, 1995b, p. 31).

■ *14.4* The basic theory of common markets

Our analysis of regional economic integration has so far focused on those types of integration which assume immobility of factors of production outside national borders. A *common market* differs from these types of integration in that it involves the full integration of both product and factor markets. The former is achieved through regional trade liberalisation, just as in a customs union. The latter is achieved through the elimination of obstacles to the free movements of factors of production among the member countries. The full integration of factor markets cannot be achieved without some harmonisation in the regulation of the markets for labour, capital and enterprise. The description of a common market thus specifies the harmonisation of regulations pertaining to the free movement of factors of production as well as tax and other related policies.

A proper evaluation of the addition of fully integrated factor markets to the customs union should include both static-impact effects and dynamic effects as well as the impact which perfect factor mobility is likely to have on the autonomy of national macroeconomic policies and national taxation and social security policies. The following section introduces just one aspect of a full evaluation: it is concerned with the additional costs and benefits from the inclusion of integrated factor markets to an already integrated goods' markets. Other aspects of this analysis can be found in Robson (1987).

Behind the idea of international trade is the idea of achieving Pareto efficiency in resource allocation throughout the world (in other words, the goal is an increased real income for all participants). One way to achieve this is through the perfectly free trade of goods and services provided that the equalisation of commodity prices leads to factor-price equalisation. Alternatively, perfectly free international factor movements will lead to the equalisation of factor prices. The common market involves a variant of both of these processes. Trade between member countries is liberalised but is not fully free of distortions. Factor prices therefore cannot be equalised through trade alone. Any degree of factor price differential between member countries will result in a call for the introduction of increased factor mobility to bring the factors' marginal productivities closer together. Led by price differentials this reallocation of factors within the common market results in gains analogous to the gains from international factor movements studied in Chapter 7. There we had mobility of factors not limited by the boundaries of regional integration, while here factors are free to move only within one integrated area. However this difference does not have any bearing on the basic analysis of the gains from factor mobility.

Figure 14.4 utilises the by now familiar U-shaped diagram to illustrate the main features of production in two countries, Home and Foreign, which have created a customs union but have not yet established the free flow of factors. For simplicity we focus on the movements of a single factor, for example capital. The usual assumption of production of a single good under perfectly competitive conditions with no distortions is retained. The amount of capital is given and fixed so that Home initially has $O_K K_u$ of the total capital stock and the rest, $K_u O^*_K$, comprises Foreign's capital stock. Each country uses another factor, for example labour, in production. The amount of labour is also given and fixed. Moreover it will not be allowed to move between countries. Prior to the creation of a common market the rewards to capital in Home and Foreign are different: in Home capital earns less (r_u) than in Foreign (r^*_u). The effects of the introduction of capital mobility on outputs, national incomes, and the distribution of income in Home and Foreign are identified as in Table 14.2.

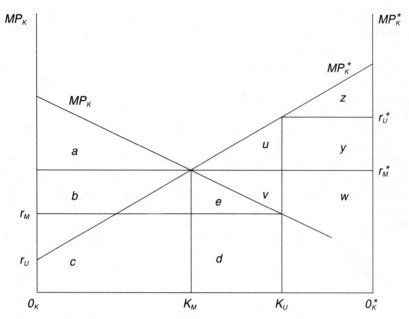

Figure 14.4 *The effects of capital mobility in the common market*

Table 14.2 *Introduction of capital mobility*

	Home	Foreign
A customs union		
Capital stock	$O_K K_u$	$O^*_K K_u$
Output	$a+b+c+d+e$	$z+y+w$
Capital's share (profits)	$c+d$	$y+w$
Labour's share (wages)	$a+b+e$	z
National product[*]	$a+b+c+d+e$	$z+y+w$
A common market		
Capital stock	$O_K K_m$	$O^*_K K_m$
Output	$a+b+c$	$z+y+w+d+e+v+u$
Capital's share (profits)	$b+c$	$w+d+e+v$
Labour's share (wages)	a	$z+y+u$
Remittances[**]	$v+e+d$	$-(v+e+d)$
National product[*]	$a+b+c+v+e+d$	$z+y+w+u$
Change in national product	v	u

Note: [*] National product is total output increased by remittances.
[**] Remittances are positive for inflows and negative for outflows.

The static effects of factor mobility in response to the creation of a common market between Home and Foreign are an increase in Home's national product compared to its domestic product by an amount v, an increase in Foreign's national product as compared to its domestic product by the amount u. The total net gain is thus $v + u$. This gain reflects the improvement in allocational efficiency across the common market as compared to the customs union.

In addition to these allocational effects there are also distributional effects within each country. In Home, which experiences an outflow of capital, labour's marginal productivity falls. Labour in Home consequently receives lower wages. In other words labour loses and capital owners win from the creation of a common market which incorporates capital mobility. In Foreign an addition to the stock of capital improves labour's marginal productivity, increasing its wages relative to the customs union level. Labour is thus relatively better off compared to capital owners. Needless to say this would change if the creation of the common market was to imply labour rather than capital mobility. In the case when both or all factors are able to move freely, an analysis of this type is not capable of capturing all the possible effects. The value of the above analysis is thus seriously restricted by the assumptions built into it. In addition, many important aspects of factor mobility are ignored in this type of analysis. It is really capable of shedding some light only on the resource allocation efficiency effects. In order to make any judgement on the preferability of common markets *vis-à-vis* other types of economic integration, *dynamic effects* should also be considered. Most of these dynamic effects relate to the possibility of non-parallel growth in the different regions of the common market following factor mobility. An example of this is *polarisation*, the accentuation of regional differences due to the interregional migration of factors. Polarisation concerns the fear that both capital and skilled labour may be attracted to the more advanced regions of the integration. In such a case production will concentrate in these advanced regions, causing growth rates to diverge between the different regions of the integration. Unemployment and other social problems may correspondingly be accentuated in the lesser developed regions of the common market. On the other hand there is a chance that the positive dynamic effects will occur even if growth is centralised in one or a few regions. This possibility is known as the presence of *spread* or *trickle-down effects*. These effects involve the diffusion of technology and externalities throughout the integration because the fast growth of the centre increases the demand for other regions' products, thus leading to higher growth in those areas as well. Most authors believe that polarisation effects will predominate. Such a presumption creates a need for strong regional policies and income transfers from the more advanced regions to those regions which lag behind. In turn this requires a strong and elaborate institutional framework which forces the common market to move to even more complex forms of integration.

■ *14.5* Summary

More than half of world trade takes place within free trade agreements or among countries that have decided to achieve free trade by a certain date. 40 per cent of world trade is affected by the liberalisation process taken so far in just two regions of the world, Europe and North America. It could be then an understatement to say that the importance of the regionalism has increased. Several commentators in this field in fact share a concern that a continuous increase in regionalism may diminish the efforts of nations to persevere in global integration (see, for example, Bhagwati, 1993). We address this particular concern in more detail in Chapter 17. In this chapter we have focused on examining the theory behind the formation of various types of regional integration agreements. Basically, two questions were asked: how does regional integration affect the welfare of integrating countries, and what is the effect on the rest of the world? RIAs result in two static welfare effects: trade creation through which welfare is enhanced, and trade diversion which reduces welfare. No conclusions on the net welfare effect can be made without looking also at the dynamic effects, such as realisation of economies of scale, increased competition, or increased investment and technology flows. The presumption is that RIAs generate welfare gains for the participating countries with small and possibly negative spillovers onto the rest of the world (Baldwin and Venables, 1995).

■ *Chapter 15* ■

Empirical Analysis of the Effects of Integration

■ *15.1* Introduction

There have been many empirical studies that have attempted to measure the effects of economic integration. While most of these studies tried to estimate the growth of trade attributable to the formation of the integration *per se*, others attempted to measure the changes in welfare. The main goal of such measurements has always been to provide an empirical foundation on which to base discussions as to whether economic integrations are 'good' or 'bad'. The problem is that the results obtained were not conclusive enough to provide strong support for either view. While in the last decade or so the techniques available for studying economic integration have improved significantly with the usage of computable general equilibrium models (CGE), it is still difficult to obtain reliable results. Today it is more important then ever to have these results in order to solidify the discussion on regionalism. However not many new studies look at the effects on non-members' welfare. For example most of the studies completed on the effects of CUSTA or NAFTA were concerned with changes in the patterns of trade and the welfare of members rather than the welfare of non-members. The prospects of Western Hemisphere Free Trade Area (WHFTA), and any defensive or retaliatory bloc in the Pacific are seen as detrimental for world welfare (see for example Bhagwati, 1993, p. 161) but there are no reliable empirical results to support such a claim. While this chapter cannot survey all the issues involved in the empirical analysis of the effects of economic integration, we do summarise the main features of the methods used in empirical measurement, and outline earlier research.

■ *15.2* Basic methods: a description

The theoretical focus when discussing the effects of integration has been on the changes in the pattern of trade in terms of trade creation and trade diversion effects. The Vinerian proposition (as we saw in Chapter 14) is that the overall effect of the integration is the net effect of the two. Net trade creation is thus obtained from the combined production and consumption effects. A net change in trade flows then results from an increase in consumption due to lower prices within the integration and from a decrease in production in response to increased imports. However this change in trade flows is not a reliable predictor of the welfare consequences of integration. The (static) change in welfare is given by the areas of the two triangles corresponding to the consumption and production effects. These are the so-called 'Harberger triangles'. Since we assume that domestic prices fall by the full amount of the external tariff the total welfare effect equals one-half of the amount of net trade creation multiplied by the extent of the external tariff. Note that this assumption that consumers receive the entire benefit of the price fall is quite restrictive. In fact the evidence actually suggests that consumers do not receive the full amount of the tariff reduction. This in turn implies that one of the variables needed to determine the welfare changes, the change in price, is not always known. A further difficulty, and one which is perhaps even larger, is to determine the exact magnitude of the trade creation which can be attributed to the integration.

The two basic approaches used to determine the magnitude of net trade creation, ex ante and ex post studies, differ with respect to their time perspective. *Ex ante* studies aim to predict the effects of trade liberalisation on prospective integrations or existing integrations which are to be enlarged. In either case the necessary data on the pre-integration situation exists. However the results are still somewhat weak because they are dependent on demand and supply elasticities which are also estimated and vary in their reliability depending on the time period under study. Moving from the short run to the long run elasticities tend to increase. If the study of the effects of the integration is for a longer period of time but is based on the short-run estimation of elasticities it is obvious that the results will be affected. *Ex post* studies aim to evaluate the effects of integrations already in existence. The problem with those type of studies is their need to create a so-called 'anti-monde' (counterfactual) world in order to obtain a result. This method involves examining the changes in trade patterns which have taken place as a result of a integration and comparing them with a hypothetical situation where the integration does not exist. The difference in results is then attributed to the existence of the integration. This method therefore implies that the only important factor in the period under study was the integration; such an assumption is certainly naive. There are further difficulties with this method. The methods used to construct an anti-monde are fraught with problems while the distinction between static and dynamic effects is also problematic.

There are three basic methods used to create a hypothetical world: the direct method, the indirect method, and the survey. The direct method is based on a precise analytical model whose parameters are estimated econometrically. Simulations are then used to produce alternatives. The indirect method has been more popular but is applicable only in *ex post* studies. It involves projecting pre-integration trade flows into the post-integration period, and then calculating the effects of the integration as a residual between the actual and the projected flows. The survey method involves the assessment of the views of experts and entrepreneurs on the conditions of particular sectors and industries and the extent to which they think integration has affected or could affect them. In general this method implies case studies, it may thus provide a valuable means of generating statistical data for broader studies.

Most of the methods described above have been used in partial equilibrium studies which focus on the effects of terms of trade changes and changes in trade flows. The general equilibrium models based on perfect competition have reaffirmed the important role of the terms of trade changes (Whalley, 1985). These models have more recently also incorporated economies of scale and imperfect competition. They have been used to measure the effects of unilateral liberalisation (Harris, 1984) and to estimate the effects of prospective integrations, such as 'Europe 1992' or CUSTA (Smith and Venables, 1988; Brown and Stern, 1988). These models stress the importance of real income changes on the overall effects of integration. While empirical models with an imperfectly competitive structure ought to have a special place in evaluating the relative merits of integrations, their results are very sensitive to variations in specifications. Their results should thus be taken as indications of possible effects rather than predictions.

15.3 Empirical measurement: the record so far[1]

This section charts some of the major studies of regional integration agreements, indicating the methodology used and the results obtained. The studies are classified into three broad groups. The first groups comprises the so-called *ex post* studies. These studies focus mainly on European integration and were in vogue in the late 1960s. The second and third groups perform a more model-based counterfactual analysis of integration. The second group comprises models based on constant-returns-to-scale and perfect competition, while the third group consists of models incorporating imperfect market structures and economies of scale. Both these types of models involve either partial or general equilibrium modelling. The majority of these studies are conducted on an *ex ante* basis.

Table 15.1 identifies some of the more prominent *ex post* studies of the economic effects of integration. These studies perform simple econometric

Table 15.1 *Ex post studies of RIAs, 1967–75*

Study	Approach	Data	Main conclusions
Balassa (1967)	A partial equilibrium study primarily focusing on the determination of income elasticities of import demand before and after formation of the EC.	The pre-formation period is 1953–9 and the post-formation period is 1959–65. The data used is broken down into seven major commodity groups.	The results show trade creation for manufactures, no trade diversion for raw materials, and trade diversion for foodstuffs due to the formation of the EC. The gain to the EC was estimated to be an increase in the real GNP growth rate of 0.1 per cent per year.
Aitken and Lowry (1972)	A partial equilibrium cross-sectional econometric study of trade flows for the LAFTA and CACM regions. The study attempts to measure the increase in trade among member countries.	The data used are from 1955–67. For each of these years a set of trade flow equations is estimated.	Neither CACM nor LAFTA had significant trade-diverting effects, but they did have significant trade-creating effects.
Truman (1975)	A partial equilibrium econometric study of trade shares for the EC-6 and EFTA before and after the formation of these regional trading blocs. Hypothetical import shares are calculated after integration and compared to the actual import shares. Two different methods for calculating import shares are used.	The pre-formation period is 1953–60. The year of comparison between hypothetical and actual import shares is 1968. Eleven manufacturing industries are examined.	Using the first method, in 37 per cent of the commodity cases, trade shares decrease for non-member countries, 43 per cent of the cases see trade shares increase for non-member countries, and in 20 per cent of the cases trade shares fall for both member and non-member countries. The first method gives an $11bn trade increase, of which the extra-regional trade increase is $2bn. The second method gives a $1bn trade increase, including an extra-regional trade fall of $2.3bn.

Source: Adapted from Srinivasan, Whalley and Wooton (1993, Table 3.3, p. 63).

analyses on data pertaining to intra- and extra-regional trade flows, and are not capable of providing any conclusions on welfare effects. These studies typically find some evidence for trade creation in the case of the EC and EFTA in the 1960s. For the integrations in Latin America, weak evidence was found for trade creation while there was no evidence of trade diversion.

The models based on constant-returns-to-scale and perfect competition are summarised in Table 15.2. An early example of the static partial equilibrium calculation of the effects of a preferential tariff agreement is a study by Verdoorn (1954) on the OECD countries. In this study intra-regional trade was shown to increase by 19 per cent after tariffs on manufactured goods were eliminated. This positive effect was accompanied by a much weaker trade diversion effect.

The first comprehensive general equilibrium analysis of a regional integration was conducted by Miller and Spencer (1977) on the effects of Britain's entry into the EC. This study, like almost all studies, uses the so-called *Armington* assumption or structure. The Armington structure assumes that otherwise 'identical' products are imperfect substitutes for one another only because they are produced in different countries (for example US, European and Japanese cars). This assumption is necessary in order to remedy some of other problems which occur in general equilibrium models, such as the existence of complete specialisation or the cross-hauling of the same or similar products. The Miller and Spencer study defines five regions, the UK, the EC, Commonwealth countries (Australia and New Zealand), the USA, and the rest of the world. Its results show relatively small welfare effects following Britain's entry into the EC, where transfers are more than offset by Britain's contributions to the EC budget. The price effects obtained in this study are relatively large. This is particularly so with respect to agricultural product prices in the UK. Associated with these price changes are large trade effects, except, somewhat unexpectedly, for Britain's imports from the Commonwealth which decreased by only 0.8 per cent.

A later general equilibrium study with a similar goal to Miller and Spencer's was conducted by Hamilton and Whalley (1985). Although examining more blocs and more goods, this study also produces results showing relatively small welfare effects and somewhat larger trade effects. Similar results are obtained by Harrison, Rutherford and Wooton (1989) who looked at the various welfare effects occurring when countries left the EC. Their results found small welfare losses for the countries leaving the Community, except for Ireland where such losses approached 8 per cent of its GDP, and some gains for the USA, a country outside the Community.

Harris and Cox (1984) conducted one of the earliest studies of regional integration agreements incorporating both economies of scale and imperfect competition. The major studies of this type are presented in Table

15.3. Harris and Cox focus primarily on the effects of the trade agreement between Canada and the USA, although they also look at the effects of the multilateral and unilateral trade liberalisation. The main differentiating feature between the Harris–Cox type of study and the competitive general equilibrium studies is the magnitude of welfare effects. In the Harris–Cox type of imperfectly competitive study the welfare effects are much larger, because in addition to the usual Harberger 'welfare triangles' they also take into account an increase in welfare occurring through economies of scale.

More sophisticated studies of this type have investigated the effects of Europe 1992 (see Table 15.3). In principle they obtain positive welfare and trade effects, the magnitude of which vary greatly. Other than to state that there are positive welfare effects from regional integrative processes, it is therefore difficult to generalise their findings. This is particularly so for the European integration, and now 'Europe 1992' and the EEA, while other regional integration agreements also seem to be producing small welfare and trade effects.

■ *15.4* Summary

Given the number and variety of empirical studies on economic integration it is impossible to offer one general result. However it is fair to say that the prevalent sentiment about the integrative processes is that it produces some trade creation. However it is unknown what the actual contribution of all the regional integration agreements in the post-war periods has been to world economic welfare. It is equally hard to predict what the effects of the proposed agreements or the agreements which are being established now will be. According to Srinivasan, Whalley and Wooton (1993) the impact of these new blocs is even harder to estimate because some new factors are not captured by empirical studies. The most important among these factors are the changed goals and focus of the new *vis-à-vis* 'old' blocs, such as the search for safe-haven, the support for domestic policy reforms by smaller countries, and the frustration by bigger countries with the multilateral liberalisation. Notwithstanding this inability to capture all the effects of integration it is easily seen that quantitative predictions tend to overstate the impact of regionalism on the world economy. If future regionalism orientates towards liberalising the dynamic component of world trade involving the most rapidly growing economies we may end up praising it for fostering trade and overall growth. It seems that much will depend on the strength of the new multilateral trading system which emerged from the Uruguay Round (see Chapter 17). However one thing is certain. We have to learn to accept regionalism as one of the features of the world economy, and by doing so de-emphasise its influence.

Table 15.2 *Competitive counterfactual studies of RIAs, 1954–89*

Study	Approach	Regional scenarios	Main conclusions
Verdoorn (1954)	A static partial equilibrium study. Assumes consumption elasticities of substitution between imports and domestic production of −0.5 and between different country's exports of −2.	Tariffs between 10 OEEC countries are eliminated on manufactures. A common tariff is then imposed by all countries after formation of the preferential tariff agreement.	Assuming unchanged exchange rates, total world exports increase by $400mn (or 2.6 per cent of 1952 total world exports). Intra-bloc exports increases by $1b (or 19 per cent of 1952 intra-bloc exports), of which $600mn (or 6 per cent of 1952 intra-ROW exports) is diverted from the rest of the world.
Johnson (1958)	A static partial equilibrium calculation. Calculates maximal potential welfare gains to the UK through the impact of lower tariffs or prices received by UK exporters and paid by UK importers.	Tariffs between the UK and EC are eliminated on manufactures. A common tariff is imposed after the formation of the integration.	Trade gains accrue to the UK of between £62mn and £192mn (or 0.8 per cent and 2.4 per cent) on the export side and £31mn (or 0.3 per cent) on the import side. The minimum of these welfare gains is roughly 1 per cent of GNP for the UK in 1970.
Scitovsky (1958)	A static partial equilibrium study. Assumes that the difference in marginal costs between countries in an industry is due to the import tariff of the importing country. The gains from the integration are thus the resource gains from equalisation of marginal costs.	Uses trade data from Verdoorn (1954), assuming that exchange rates appreciate to get the same trade balance as before the customs union, to calculate welfare effects of West European integration.	Europe gains $74mn, the amount lost by the rest of the world. This is a gain from increased specialisation and represents less than 0.05 per cent of European GNP. Europe gains $465mn from a favourable terms-of-trade improvement.

Miller and Spencer (1977)	A static general equilibrium model. Uses an Armington structure with two final goods per country, constant returns to scale and perfect competition.	There are two scenarios for the UK joining the EC, both involving the abolition of mutual tariffs and the imposition by the UK of the EC's common tariff. The first involves the UK transferring 90 per cent of its tariff revenue to the EC, while the second does not.	The UK gains from a small terms-of-trade gain on entry. This is more than offset by the transfer to the European budget on entry. The price of agricultural goods compared to manufactured goods rises by 22 per cent for the UK. Under the no-transfer scenario, the UK increases its manufactured exports and imports to the EC by 50 per cent in both cases. Also the UK increases its agricultural imports from the EC by 72 per cent and decreases its imports from the Commonwealth by 0.8 per cent.
Hamilton and Whalley (1985)	A static general equilibrium model, with 8 world blocs and 6 goods per country, 5 of which are tradable. The Armington assumption is used. There are constant returns to scale and perfect competition.	The first scenario looks at agreements between the US and each of the other 7 blocs. Then 3 RIAs involving EC and Japan, the industrial countries and the developing countries are examined. Finally a more-intensive examination of a RIA between the US and the EC is made.	Industrial countries always gain from a RIA with the USA, but the developing countries lose. The second scenario sees the first two RIAs increasing all of the members' welfare but the NIEs losing in the third RIA. Only the RIA of the USA and the EC is examined in detail, with US exports rising by 9.7 per cent to the EC, and EC exports rising by 5.8 per cent to the USA. The USA exports less to, and imports more from, other areas whereas the reverse is true for the EC. These effects are small.

Table 15.2 cont.

Study	Approach	Regional scenarios	Main conclusions
Harrison, Rutherford and Wooton (1989)	A static general equilibrium model. There are 11 regions and 6 goods, all of which are tradeable. The Armington assumption is used. There are constant returns to scale and perfect competition. There are non-tariff barriers (as well as tariffs, subsidies, etc) of 40 per cent between non-EC countries and 20 per cent between EC members.	1. Eight cases of various countries leaving the EC (with CAP remaining in place). 2. Eight cases of each country leaving the EC (no CAP).	In both scenarios, all EC countries would have welfare reductions on leaving the EC. The USA would have a small welfare gain in all cases. The highest loss is for Ireland (8 per cent of GDP) and the smallest for France and Italy (0.9 per cent of GDP).

Source: Adapted from Srinivasan, Whalley and Wooton (1993, Table 3.4, pp. 64–5)

Table 15.3 *Imperfectly competitive counterfactual studies of RIAs, 1984–92*

Study	Approach	Regional scenarios	Main conclusions
Harris and Cox (1984); Harris (1984)	A static general equilibrium model is used to study various regional trade regimes involving Canada. Assumes 9 constant-returns-to-scale (CRS) perfectly competitive industries and 20 increasing-returns-to-scale (IRS) non-competitive industries. The IRS firms have constant per-unit variable costs as well as fixed costs. Canada takes import prices as given, but it can affect export prices. The Armington assumption is used. There is a representative agent who maximises utility.	Unilateral free trade (UFT) where Canada sets all of its tariffs to zero; multilateral free trade (MFT) where Canada and the rest of the world set their tariffs to zero; selective tariff cuts in 12 of the 20 IRS industries; bilateral free trade (BFT) with the USA; and sectoral free trade (SFT) with the USA in textiles, steel, agricultural machinery, urban transport equipment and chemicals.	Canada receives welfare gains of 4, 9, 9 and 1.5 per cent of GDP under scenarios UFT, MFT, BFT and SFT. Canada's trade volumes with the world increase by 55, 90, 88 and 15 per cent with UFT, MFT, BFT and SFT respectively. Canada's trade volume increases by 99 and 14 per cent with the USA under BFT and SFT. Real-wages in Canada rise by 10, 25, 28 and 6 per cent under UFT, MFT, BFT and SFT.
Smith and Venables (1988)	A static partial equilibrium model is used to study the effects of lower non-tariff barriers on various sectors in the EC. 10 sectors are considered, each of which has firms which use IRS technology. The firms each produce a differentiated product and the Armington assumption is used. The rest of the economy is modelled as a perfectly competitive industry with CRS technology in each case.	Sector-by-sector trade barrier reductions of the order of 2.5 per cent of the base value of intra-EC trade are analysed in eight different cases. Segmented and integrated markets when barriers are removed are studied with Cournot conjectures and constant and variable numbers of firms, and Bertrand conjectures and constant and variable numbers of firms.	Under Cournot conjectures, welfare effects for segmented markets and barrier removal range from −0.01 per cent of consumption for cement, lime and plaster to 1.3 per cent for office machinery. Under integrated markets, increases under barrier removal range from 0.2 per cent in cement, lime and plaster to 5.6 per cent in artificial and synthetic fibres. Under Bertrand conjectures, the segmented markets' welfare results change insignificantly,

Table 15.3 cont.

Study	Approach	Regional scenarios	Main conclusions
	All products are tradeable. The trading regions considered are France, Germany, Italy, the UK, the rest of the EC and the rest of the world. The home country consumer has a preference for domestic goods over foreign goods.		whereas integrated markets increase the range from 0.04 to 1.2 per cent in the respective industries. Trade changes under Cournot range from a 78 per cent decrease for cement, lime and plaster under integrated markets to an increase of 164 per cent in the same industry under segmented markets. Bertrand conjectures result in considerably smaller absolute changes.
Mercenier (1992)	Both partial and general equilibrium analyses are used to study the integration of segmented EC markets in 1992. There are 4 CRS and 5 IRS sectors. The Armington assumption is imposed for the CRS sectors. There is a single representative consumer who maximises utility. Capital and labour are only domestically mobile in the short run but capital is internationally mobile in the long run.	Both Bertrand and Cournot conjectures are used. Sector-by-sector integration is analysed as is complete EC integration. The short run fixes the number of firms while the long run allows the number of firms to vary.	For partial integration, there are small welfare increases for EC countries, with mixed results for the rest of the OECD. Output generally rises and the number of firms and average costs of firms fall. For complete integration, there are also small welfare gains for the EC countries, with the rest of the OECD experiencing virtually no change. The terms of trade generally increase for all of the EC countries and fall for the rest of the OECD. No trade effects are reported.

Haaland and Norman (1992)	General equilibrium study of effects of EC integration on EC, EFTA, Japan and USA. Model is similar to Smith, Venables and Gasiorek (1992). There are 11 IRS and 1 CRS tradable goods and 1 CRS non-tradeable good for each region. Factors of production are skilled and unskilled labour, capital and intermediate goods. There is a single representative agent in each region. EC and EFTA each consist of 6 separate, but identical, countries and submarkets. Firms are assumed to be symmetric in each industry within a region.	Four scenarios: (1) trade costs between segmented EC markets are reduced by 2.5 per cent of the initial value of EC trade, with initial trade costs assumed to be 10 per cent within EC and EFTA and 20 per cent between Europe, Japan and the USA; (2) trade costs are reduced and EC markets are integrated; (3) trade costs in Europe (including EFTA) are reduced, as in (1) scenario; and (4) same as scenario (2), except now for all Western Europe.	For scenario (1), EC gains a 1 per cent increase in welfare. EFTA, USA and Japan have declines in welfare of 0.3, 0.02 and 0.02 per cent respectively. For scenario (2), EC experiences welfare gains of 1.9 per cent but there are falls in EFTA, USA and Japan by 0.4, 0.4 and 0.6 per cent respectively. For scenarios (3) and (4), EFTA experiences positive welfare gains while the EC gains in welfare are smaller than in scenarios (1) and (2). The welfare losses for Japan and the USA are smaller.
Baldwin (1992)	A small dynamic general equilibrium model of the dynamic gains of trade for the EC. Single infinitely lived representative consumer and IRS technology for firms in each country. Discount rate, inter-temporal elasticity of substitution and capital share of income are assumed to be 0.05, 0.1 and 0.3. Divergence of social and private returns on capital due to IRS is the key assumption.	Integration of EC markets is assumed to lower non-tariff trade barriers, and static gains calculated by Cecchini, Catinat and Jacquemin (1988) are assumed. These are then dynamised.	Dynamic welfare effects from trade liberalisation increase welfare from between 15 and 90 per cent of the static gains.

478

Table 15.3 cont.

Study	Approach	Regional scenarios	Main conclusions
Smith, Venables and Gasiorek (1992)	General equilibrium study of gains from lowering non-tariffs trade barriers and the integration of segmented markets in the EC in the spirit of earlier Smith and Venables (1988) work. There are 14 IRS and 1 CRS sectors. Factors of production include four types of labour, capital and intermediate goods. There is a single representative consumer. For each country and industry, firms are symmetric.	Markets are either segmented or integrated. Firms use Cournot conjectures. There is a short run with a fixed number of firms and a long run with a variable number of firms.	Welfare increases range from 0.2 per cent of GDP for Germany in the short run, to 1.4 per cent for the EC South in the long run under segmented markets. For integrated markets, the range is an 0.2 per cent increase for Germany in the short run, to 2.9 per cent for the EC South in the long run.

Under segmented markets, changes in exports by the EC to the ROW range from a decrease of 0.4 per cent in banking and finance in the short run, to an 8.3 per cent increase in transport equipment in the long run. Import decreases range from −0.8 per cent for banking and finance in the long run, to −20.2 per cent for transport equipment in the long run. Under integrated markets, the absolute value of these effects is increased by roughly a factor of two. |

Source: Adapted from Srinivasan, Whalley and Wooton (1993, Table 3.5, pp. 68–70)

■ *Chapter 16* ■

Economic Integration in Practice

■ *16.1* Introduction

In this chapter we briefly survey the attempts at economic integration since the Second World War. While a fairly large building could be filled with the titles on the various economic integrations in this period our main purpose is to provide some basic information about some (more viable) economic integrations keeping in mind that our central interest lies in trade patterns. More comprehensive and issue-based discussions on most of the integrations mentioned in this chapter are available in the publications edited by Anderson and Blackhurst (1993) and de Melo and Panagariya (1993).

Europe is the location of the oldest and the most successful of all integrations: the European Union (EU). Bearing in mind the likely growth of regionalism and the likely attempts to imitate the EU there is much to be gained from a close appraisal of the EU's performance. Several such appraisals have been undertaken (see for example Winters, 1993a; and Sapir, 1992 and the bibliographies listed therein). Due to the nature of this book and limitation in space these studies are not reviewed except in passing. The other integrations in the European region, the European Free Trade Area (EFTA), the now former Council for Mutual Economic Assistance (CMEA), and the new regional initiatives are also mentioned. Going westward we briefly summarise the two free trade areas in North America, the Canada–United States Free Trade Agreement (CUSTA) and the North American Free Trade Agreement (NAFTA). The many attempts at integration among the developing countries in Latin America and Africa are well presented in Nogues and Quintanilla (1993), Foroutan (1993), and de la Torre and Kelly (1992). These are not covered here. Instead we review the integrations in Asia and the Pacific. A brief coverage of the free trade agreement between Australia and New Zealand (CER) is also provided. Appendix 16 (p. 503) lists 34 integrations with their members.

■ 16.2 Europe

□ *The European Union*[1]

The European Union (EU) has both 'deepened' and 'widened' considerably since its inception under the Treaty of Rome in 1957 (see Box 16.1). It has deepened in the sense that from a simple customs union it developed first into a common market, through the implementation of 'Europe 1992', and most recently into an economic union, through the Maastricht Treaty. The widening of this integration has occurred at many different levels. First the number of full members has doubled from the original six – Belgium, France, Germany, Italy, Luxembourg, and the Netherlands – to fifteen with Great Britain, Ireland and Denmark acceding in 1973, Greece in 1980, Portugal and Spain in 1986, and Austria, Finland and Sweden in 1996. The European Economic Area (EEA) was created by joining with the members of EFTA. The third layer of widening consists of the extension of preferential trading arrangements to include various Mediterranean countries, some African, Caribbean and Pacific (ACP) countries and most recently seven Central and Eastern European countries and three Baltic states. The geographical influence of the EU is thus hardly confined to Europe.

The share of intra-regional trade in total trade can be used as a proxy for the extent of regionalisation. The share of intra-area exports has steadily increased since the Treaty of Rome, jumping from less than 40 per cent in 1958 to nearly 55 per cent in 1970. In the period 1970–85 intra-regional exports were almost constant at a level of around 55 per cent. Since then the percentage has jumped again, reaching over 60 per cent in 1995. Similar movements are observed for intra-area imports (Sapir, 1992, pp. 1492–4). This significant increase in EU intra-regional trade must be viewed with some caution because other factors, including external trade policies and competitiveness, could have exerted a significant influence.

The impact of the EU on the pattern of European and world trade, and the welfare effects thereof, are typically obtained by considering the static effects of trade creation and trade diversion. Measured in this way, at least in the area of manufactured goods trade, the impact of the EU has been positive. The EU has significantly expanded trade amongst both members and non-members. Explanations for this success are usually related to the historically high growth of this region at the time and the succession of very effective trade negotiation rounds. A high growth rate

Box 16.1   *The EU – the world's leading trader*

According to the WTO (1995) report on International Trade, the EU was the world's largest merchandise trader accounting for around 43 per cent of world merchandise exports and imports in 1994. Its intra-trade alone exceeded one-quarter of world merchandise exports. The share of intra-EU trade is close to two-thirds of the EU's total trade. In 1995 the EU retained its position as the largest world trader. Moreover, even when intra-EU trade is excluded, the EU was still accounting for 19 per cent of world trade.

During the first half of 1995 the intra-regional exports of the EU were up by 14.2 per cent compared to the same period of 1994 (see Figure 16.1). Most significant increases were recorded by the Netherlands (24.4 per cent) and Portugal (20 per cent), while Greece (6.8 per cent), the UK (7.1 per cent) and Italy (8.8 per cent) had the lowest growth. All countries also recorded an increase in intra-EU imports. Those rose by 12.5 per cent in the same period. Lowest rises were for Greece (2.6 per cent) and the UK (5.6 per cent), highest for Portugal (19.7 per cent), Denmark (18.7 per cent) and Spain (18.3 per cent). During the first six months of 1995, intra-EU trade accounted on average for 63.8 per cent of the member states' total trade flows. Germany, Italy and the UK had the lowest ratios of intra-EU trade. Austria, Portugal, Belgium and Denmark had the highest proportion of intra-EU imports in their total imports, and Portugal, the Netherlands, Belgium and Ireland had the largest share of intra-EU exports in their total exports.

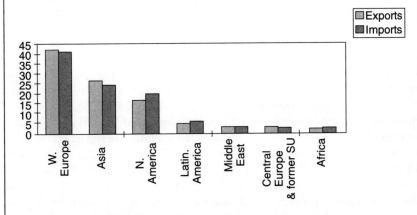

Figure 16.1 *Regional shares in world merchandise strange, 1994*
Source: WTO (1995); *European Union News* 14, p. 7.

of members' economies following the formation of the integration (close to 5 per cent in the 1960s) presumably helped create an increased demand for manufactured goods imports from both members and non-members. The source of this impressive growth is found in the formation of the integration itself, although other sources of growth may also exist.

Another source of trade expansion is related to the EU contribution towards the substantial multilateral trade liberalisation which has occurred in industrial goods. Sapir (1992, 1993) insists that the formation of the EU was the main driving force behind the Dillon and Kennedy rounds of GATT which both resulted in substantial tariff cuts. Average tariffs in the EU, for example, fell from 13 per cent to 6.6 per cent after the Kennedy Round (1992, p. 1500). Conversely Winters (1993a, p. 210) argues that tariff cuts by the EU itself were not that significant. He does accept that when the liberalisation of other countries is taken into account these Rounds have led to trade liberalisation. The question therefore remains as to whether or not the Dillon and Kennedy Rounds (and multilateral trade liberalisation in general) would have occurred without the formation of the EU. Some hold that the USA felt threatened by the possibility of trade diversion resulting from the establishment of the EU and consequently pushed for the multilateral trade liberalisation which has produced high growth in world trade. Others argue that at that time the USA was the strongest world power and was therefore not likely to have needed the EU as an excuse to start pressing for liberalisation if it wished to do so. The truth probably lies somewhere in between. In the contemporary situation, with a changed relationship between the EU and the USA, and with several other large actors in the world economy, it is even more difficult to establish the extent of the impact the EU has on the world trading system. Almost equal in economic size and political power, the EU and the USA are now able to threaten each other equally with retaliation and with the capability to attract other smaller countries to join them, thus potentially encouraging regionalisation in the world economy.

One area in which the EU is rightly accused of causing increased protectionism and net trade diversion is in trade in agricultural products. The Common Agricultural Policy (CAP) was adopted in 1962. This policy involved high guaranteed domestic prices supported by variable levies on imports. Huge agricultural surpluses and high storage costs in turn required export subsidies. In short, this policy is ineffective and costly. Its trade-diverting effects became progressively larger as the EU increased from six to twelve members. In the 1980s the extent of costs of trade diversion finally prompted discussions on this policy, both inside and outside the EU. As a result trade in agricultural products was placed on the agenda of the Uruguay Round for the first time in GATT history, with expectations of achieving major liberalisation in this area. However trade in agricultural products has proved to be the single largest obstacle to concluding this round of trade liberalisation.

In total, as far as static effects are concerned, the EU has had a beneficial effect on non-members. This is despite the welfare-deteriorating effects of the CAP. There is a broad consensus of opinion agreeing that the EU lowered external trade barriers enough to satisfy the requirement that the outside world was not made worse off (the Kemp–Wan theorem). In addition dynamic effects have increased the demand for imports of manufactured goods, allowing non-member countries to expand their exports to the EU. However, not all countries were equally successful in using the growth of the EU as a platform for export expansion. Countries whose income elasticity of exports to the EU was low benefited the least, and countries who depended on the exports of temperate agricultural products almost certainly lost. On the whole, however, it appears that the EU in its pre-Single market form has benefited most non-member countries.

The effects of the formation of the Single Market, or 'Europe 1992', have been popularised by the Cecchini report (Cecchini, 1988).[2] One of the conclusions of this report, which has become the most commonly cited one, relates to the growth effect of the Single Market: the Report states that the 'Europe 1992' programme will result in a 5 per cent increase of EU GNP. The source of this growth is to be found in the removal of the broad arsenal of non-tariff barriers which cause economic losses. These barriers include border formalities, disparate technical standards, public procurement biases, restrictions on the entry of firms into certain sectors, and many others. The elimination of these barriers should both improve market access and increase competitiveness, both of which have welfare-improving effects. Another set of barriers which are concerned with regulatory standards, for example trade marks and the prudential regulation of banks and professional qualifications, would require the harmonisation of national regulations, but at a less restrictive level. It would be based on the mutual recognition by member states of each other's regulations rather than through the imposition of common regulations (see Box 16.2). A full implementation of this programme affects EU trade with non-members in several ways. As feared by many current exporters to the EU a reduction in internal transaction costs will cause trade diversion. Moreover, tougher internal competition in addition to the exploitation of economies of scale will make EU producers more competitive in world markets. This could force the incumbents out of the market, thus creating effects similar to those of strategic trade policies. On the positive side, the creation of 'Europe 1992' will, as mentioned above, increase EU income, thus creating trade for non-members as well as members. This trade-creating effect will hopefully offset the trade-diverting effects.

In conclusion, the role of the 'new' EU on world trade will depend on how the process of regionalisation in the world economy continues to evolve. If tripolarisation indeed takes deeper roots, 'Europe 1992' may react by pursuing a more aggressive trade policy, for example through anti-

Box 16.2   *The single market – more work is needed*

The Single Market is not working properly as yet and member states will have to put a lot of hard work in order to make it work. That, in short, is the message of the latest assessment of the Single Market. The European Commission examined for the first time the implementation of all the measures concerning the Single Market, and not simply those set out in the White Paper on the '1992' programme. As many as 173 national measures are still missing. These are measures which should have been taken by the member states implementing the 221 European laws provided for in the 1985 White Paper on the Single Market. As of 15 May 1996 the EU-15 had translated 92.6 per cent, on average, of these measures into national law. The translation rate ranged from Denmark's 99.5 per cent to Austria's 80.4 per cent. In the case of all 1308 of the European directives which are relevant to the Single Market – they include the 221 laws mentioned above – the average rate of translation stands at 89.7 per cent, with a maximum of 96.6 per cent for Denmark, and a minimum of 77.4 per cent for Finland. A number of problem sectors still remain. The problem sectors include public procurement, with just 74 per cent of the measures transposed into national law; intellectual and industrial property (71 per cent), consumer protection (79 per cent) and energy (73 per cent). Several member states have failed to translate insurance directives correctly and the free movement of persons, particularly as regards the recognition of professional training is also not without problems. The Commission has announced accelerated infringement proceedings and adjustments to the Single Market to take account of technological change.

Source: Frontier Free Europe (June 1996, p. 3).

dumping legislation. This in turn may trigger non-cooperative actions by all blocs, with detrimental consequences for all. If the Uruguay Round is successfully implemented and multilateralism regains its strength, 'Europe 1992' is likely to play a cooperative game, thus benefiting the world at large.

☐ *The European Free Trade Association*

In 1960 seven countries not wishing to join the EU established the European Free Trade Association (EFTA). These countries were geographically dispersed throughout Europe: from the UK in the west, Portugal in the south, Denmark, Norway, Sweden and Finland in the north to Austria and Switzerland in the centre of Europe.[3] These relatively small countries had every right to feel threatened by the formation of the EU. One logical response to such a threat was to establish an alternative regional trading arrangement. By creating the free trade area they opted to form a much looser type of integration than the EU. However EFTA's primary distinction from the EU is that EFTA has never been concerned with any form of integration other than a purely economic one. The initial goal was to eliminate all tariffs on trade in manufactured goods by 1967. This was seen as a realistic goal since all members already had relatively low tariffs on manufactured goods. However because tariffs were already at low levels there was reason to believe that although the effect of tariff removal would be positive it would also be quite small. At this point it is pertinent to recall that the height of pre-integration tariffs plays an important role in determining the welfare effects. However transportation and other trading costs also play a role. Since these countries are dispersed over a wide area they experienced higher trading costs, which certainly had some adverse effects. As expected, rules of origin had to be introduced to prevent imports entering through the country with the lowest external tariffs. The initial tariff removal goal was achieved on time well before the size, and to some degree the nature, of the EFTA changed in the 1970s. In 1973 the UK and Denmark left EFTA and joined the EU. With the addition of Iceland and Liechtenstein, and after losing Portugal to the EU, EFTA ended with eight members. However the change in the membership was not the most important factor in the destiny of the EFTA. The agreement to remove trade barriers on all manufactured goods between the EU and the EFTA began the process of these two integrations merging. In 1991 they signed an agreement relating to the formation a new common market under the name of the European Economic Area (EEA). This area opened up the free movements of goods, services and factors of production after 1993. In addition Sweden, Finland, Austria and Norway formally opened accession negotiations in early 1993. Those negotiations were successfully concluded in 1994, and Austria, Finland and Sweden became members on 1 January 1995. While Norway again voted against membership in the EU, it will continue to pursue its interests within the EEA. Most of the gains expected from full membership for Austria, Finland and Sweden should stem from liberalisation of services and agriculture while there is not much scope for large gains in the area of trade in industrial goods (Winters, 1993a; Norman, 1991).

The European Economic Area

Even before the agreement on the European Economic Area (EEA) took place, free trade in goods had existed between the EU and EFTA since the creation of the free trade area in 1972. What this new agreement does create is the freedom for capital, people and enterprises to move without restrictions throughout Europe. This will encourage further integration at the production level.[4] Under the framework of the EEA, EFTA countries will participate in a number of EU regional programmes and projects, such as those in research and development (R&D), the environment and education. However they will not participate in some key policy areas. Most importantly they will not adopt a common trade policy or a common development coordination policy, nor will they participate in the coordination of economic, fiscal and foreign policies. EFTA members will also be excluded from the CAP and the fishery policies of the EU.

A significant effect of the creation of the EEA is the freeing of capital movements because all the remaining restrictions and regulations relating to payments, investments, capital market flows, and other types of capital movements are to be removed. It is estimated that the formation of the EEA will raise the EFTA's GDP by up to 5 per cent.

☐ *Eastern Europe and the former Soviet Union*

Regional trading arrangements involving the countries in this region have been in a state of flux since the beginning of the 1990s. The most comprehensive regional arrangement, the Council for Mutual Economic Assistance (CMEA), was formally disbanded at its 46th and final meeting on 28 June 1991. Other trading groups and industrial cooperation agreements have also disintegrated, the countries of this region being currently engaged in a reorientation process. This involves making new links with Europe and with Asia and the Middle East. The fact that these countries still cannot reap the many benefits from the multilateral trade negotiations has prompted them to initiate a number of new regional arrangements. These will be reviewed after we discuss the CMEA.

Council for Mutual Economic Assistance

The Council for Mutual Economic Assistance (CMEA) was set up in January 1949.[5] At its peak it had ten full members: the Soviet Union, Bulgaria, Czechoslovakia, the GDR, Hungary, Poland, Romania, Mongolia, Cuba and Vietnam. Albania was a member from 1949 to 1961 (although the membership was never formally revoked) while the former Yugoslavia was the only 'limited participant'.[6] It joined the CMEA in 1964 under partial associate status and was relatively active in most of the standing commissions and other organs of the CMEA. It has always been claimed that the CMEA was set up as a political response to the Marshall Plan for the reconstruction of Europe and to counteract the economic integration emerging in the Western world (the OEEC, or what is today the OECD). The rationale behind the CMEA explains to a large extent why it had only a negligible integrative effect until a revised charter on economic and technical cooperation was passed in 1959. It was then that the CMEA really started to affect members' production and trade patterns. Compared to the EU, the CMEA was a more intergovernmental and less supranational organisation. The former Soviet Union was the dominant state in the integration, leading many observers to conclude that the real purpose of the CMEA was to ensure Soviet hegemony in Eastern Europe.

The integrative mechanisms of the CMEA basically comprised two components (Brada, 1993). The first was the trade regime while the second was the effort to promote the so-called 'socialist division of labour'. Let us examine these two components in turns.

Trade amongst the members of the CMEA was conducted on the basis of bilateral agreements and until the introduction of transferable rouble (TR) in 1963 was cleared through bilateral accounts. The TR was an accounting currency only and was never actually convertible into any of the individual currencies. The main aim of introducing the TR was to transform the CMEA into a true economic integration with 'multilateral' trade and payment flows among its members. This was never achieved and the TR lost its accounting role even before the official demise of the CMEA. However the bilateral character of trade among the members of the CMEA did not continue to predominate solely because of the failure of the TR. There are other factors stemming from the very nature of planned economies that create continuous pressures for bilateralism. Firstly trade is much easier to handle administratively when it is conducted on a government-to-government basis. This usually meant five-year agreements and annual protocols that fix the quantities and prices of the goods exchanged. Secondly, because of their non-convertible domestic currencies, individual countries (or their trade negotiators) aimed as much as possible for balanced bilateral trade. The so-called 'commodity inconvertibility', the lack of convertibility of national currencies into traded goods, meant that unplanned surpluses or deficits could not be used to finance trade with other members.[7]

The most important element in intra-CMEA trade relations was the price-setting mechanism. Soon after the formation of the CMEA it adopted the principles of uniform pricing based on adjusted world market prices.[8] Because of the inherent biases towards industrial goods, particularly in favour of heavy industry, and because of the difficulties involved in obtaining world prices for industrial as opposed to primary products, the structure of relative prices in intra-CMEA trade tended to differ from that found on world markets. More specifically the relative price of manufactures in CMEA trade consistently tended to exceed their relative prices on world markets (Wolf, 1988). This created another form of bilateralism; structural or *commodity bilateralism*. Commodity bilateralism existed because the prevailing structure of prices could not clear all bilateral markets in the region. This gave rise to the phenomenon of trade in 'hard' and 'soft' goods. 'Hard' goods were those goods which the CMEA price system undervalued relative to world prices. These goods could be easily sold on, or purchased from, the world market for convertible (hard) currencies. Examples include foodstuffs, oil and raw materials in general. 'Soft' goods were the opposite case of overvalued goods. These goods could not be sold on the world market. Examples include most manufactured goods, obsolete machinery and equipment. CMEA members had an incentive to avoid delivering 'hard' goods to each other and in cases where they did trade 'hard' goods that trade had to be balanced. Often 'hard' goods were sold only if the importer would agree to buy some quantity of 'soft' goods as well. In geographical terms the pattern of trade within the CMEA was a radial one, with the former Soviet Union as the major supplier of oil and raw materials.[9]

This pattern of trade also reflected the 'socialist division of labour', the other component of the integrative mechanism of the CMEA. This was imposed by the Soviet Union from the early years of the CMEA, leading to complementary elements in the industrial structure of the Soviet Union and each Eastern European country. The objective was to achieve a high degree of specialisation in order to exploit economies of scale. However this idea backfired in that it removed any incentive to create either a sufficient variety of product or goods of quality. Consequently much of the production structure of the Eastern European countries specialised in the production of low-quality obsolete industrial goods adapted to Soviet standards. On the other hand there were many cases of parallel facilities with the same function. The reason for this is found in the fact that individual members required their 'just' share of industrial production irrespective of their ability to produce such goods on a competitive basis. The division of labour thus degenerated into a process of parcelling out new areas of production among all members, leading in the end to a very broad range of products produced by each country (Brada, 1993, p. 321). Despite much rhetoric, so-called specialisation agreements, and complex programmes of cooperation and development, there were almost no significant joint investments or flows of capital between members.

From today's perspective the CMEA can be evaluated as being more 'successful' in the trade arena than in fostering specialisation in production. The success in trade is measured by the intra-regional trade which evolved to a much greater extent than it would have done in the absence of the integration. Due to the reduction in the transaction costs of intra-CMEA trade, its share of trade increased relative to trade with the outside world. This conclusion remains valid even after correcting for the over-valued TR, which originally overstated the extent of intra-regional trade (Pohl and Sorsa, 1992, p. 53).

With regard to this 'overtrading' among CMEA members, from their point of view it might be desirable to decrease the level of such trade to its 'normal' level. However the question of how fast this trade should be allowed to decline so as not to cause serious problems for the CMEA economies came too late because with the formal break-up of the CMEA as an integration, the trade flows amongst its former members fell drastically. This collapse of intra-regional trade coincided with a sharp drop in the output of most of the ex-CMEA countries. The fall in output ranged from 7 per cent in Hungary to 20 per cent in Bulgaria for 1991 (Brada, 1993, p. 326). Initially it was thought that trade disruption was the main cause of the fall in output. However it is also likely that the collapse in intra-regional trade was also a consequence of the contraction in output which happened because of stabilisation and other reforms. A crucial role was also played by the loss of the Soviet market, both as the main supplier of the oil and raw materials and as an importer. The other factors that played a role in the decline of intra-regional trade included the change to dollar payments, the introduction of customs duties, and the liberalisation of trade with the outside world. Although some of the lost intra-regional trade will redevelop more efficiently under a different system it is unlikely that these countries will try reforming as a trading bloc. However some of these countries, particularly most of the states of the former Soviet Union could, at least in the near future, try to minimise further negative shocks on output and employment by continuing an economic integration of some sort.

Recent regional initiatives

After the collapse of the CMEA trade and payments system, a wide range of other regional initiatives developed. This section briefly reviews some of the main achievements in this area. It is based on the report on Regional initiatives by the EBRD (1992).

Arrangements with Western Europe   The *Europe Agreements* (or the *Associations Agreements*) aim to further the relationship between the Central and Eastern European countries and the EU by establishing a framework for cooperation and assistance in the areas of trade, legislation, science and technology, and technical assistance. The main goal of these agreements it to *asymmetrically* establish free trade in industrial goods over the period of ten years. This means that the EU is expected to reduce its protectionist measures much faster than the signatories on the other side. So far, these agreements have been signed with all Central and Eastern European economies: Poland, Hungary, the Czech Republic, Slovakia, Romania, Bulgaria, Slovenia, and with three Baltic states: Latvia, Lithuania and Estonia (Box 16.3). The associations established by the Europe Agreements will help these countries achieve the final objective of becoming members of the EU.

The *Partnership and Cooperation Agreements* are envisaged to encompass all the states of the former Soviet Union. These agreements are weaker than Europe Agreements in that issues of future membership cannot be addressed. However, they will cover trade, technical assistance and aid in a manner similar to the Europe Agreements.

In addition to the above agreements with the EU, agreements with EFTA are also being negotiated. The Czech Republic, Slovakia, Hungary, Poland and Romania have already signed trade agreements with EFTA. These

Box 16.3   *Trade between the EU (12) and the countries of Central and Eastern Europe and the former USSR*

According to the WTO International Trade (1995a) report the most dynamic regional component of trade of the EU in the whole decade has been its trade with the region comprising the countries of Central and Eastern Europe and the former USSR.[10] At the same time, the demise of CMEA and the political and economic transition have led to a significant reorientation of these countries' trade away from mutual trade to trade with DCs, especially with the EU (see Figure 16.2).

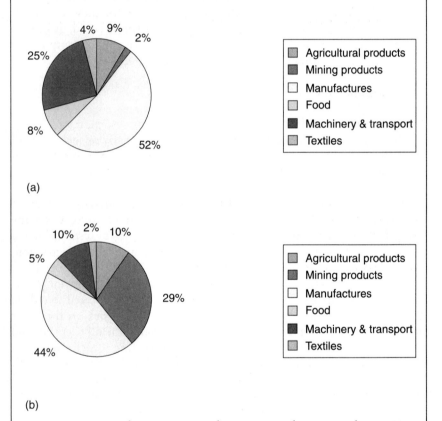

(a)

(b)

Figure 16.2   *Commodity composition of EU exports and imports to the transition economies*
Source: WTO (1995) (Geneva: WTO, p. 8).

While the value of total merchandise exports and imports of the EU expanded between 1991 and 1994 by 11 and 5 per cent respectively, merchandise exports to Central and Eastern Europe and the former USSR increased by 47 per cent and merchandise imports from this region increased by 40 per cent. By 1993,

Central and Eastern Europe and the former USSR had become the third most important regional trading partner (out of six) for the EU, after Asia and North America. At the same time, the orientation of transition economies towards the EU was dramatic. In 1994, the EU purchased close to half of the exports of Central and Eastern Europe and the former USSR, and supplied about half of their imports; for all of Western Europe, the shares were 60 per cent and nearly 70 per cent, respectively.

The transition economies export to the EU mainly agricultural products, products of mining and low value added manufactures. The commodity structure of the EU's exports to the transition economies is more or less similar to the overall structure of its total exports dominated by manufactures (about 80 per cent), particularly by machinery and transport equipment and by chemicals. The exceptions have been the large shares of agricultural products (food in particular) and of textiles. Agricultural exports to the transition economies accounted for almost 15 per cent of total merchandise exports of the EU in 1994 compared to 12 per cent in total merchandise exports. Moreover, the share has increased considerably since 1990 when agricultural exports accounted for less than 10 per cent of merchandise exports to the transition economies. The expansion of exports of textiles was equally fast as a result of far-reaching subcontracting arrangements with firms in the transition economies.

agreements in fact mirror the Europe Agreements as they both aim at encouraging free(er) trade and broader economic integration between signatories. Since July 1992 free trade agreements have been implemented with all of these countries except Romania.

Intra-regional arrangements The demise of the CMEA trading system was followed by a sharp decline in trade among former socialist countries and also a radical reduction in their output. This led to a revival of proposals to establish new regional trading agreements with the aim of preventing further falls in mutual trade and creating incentives to restore economic cooperation in this region. Initially such proposals were met with strong political resistance and criticism based on past experience with the CMEA and hopes for rapid access to the EU (ECE, 1994). In the end the *Visegrád framework for cooperation* was initiated by Poland, Hungary and the former Czechoslovakia. These countries agreed to coordinate their approach to the EU to further their mutual aim of eventually becoming full members. One of their main goals was to form a free trade zone as a way of gaining entry into the EU. After some problems caused by the splitting of Czechoslovakia, the four countries finally concluded the *Central European Free Trade Agreement* (CEFTA) which entered into force on 1 April 1993. Slovenia joined CEFTA in late 1995 also, stating that membership represents a better starting point for that country's ultimate objective – membership in the EU.

There are two basic objectives of the agreement. The first relates to the elimination of trade barriers among the member countries, while the second attempts to eliminate the discrimination that has evolved against intra-Central European trade compared to trade between these countries and the EU. The elimination of trade barriers is planned in several steps. The agreement provides for a list of products (List A) subject to no tariffs at all from the date the agreement came into effect. A second list (List B) includes products whose trade should be liberalised fast, while the liberalisation of trade in sensitive products will have to wait until after January 2001. The liberalisation of trade in agricultural products will take place under separate regime and will remain restricted by quantitative restrictions for some time to come. The initial effects of the preferential agreement within CEFTA were disappointing. However in 1994 most bilateral trade between the members countries did increase, typically by larger margins than the total trade of these countries (ECE, 1994).

Other arrangements have also been contemplated or revived. These include:

- The *Central Europe Initiative*, which is a loose agreement of cooperation between Hungary, Poland, the Czech Republic, Slovakia, Croatia, Slovenia, Italy and Austria.
- The *Council* of the *Baltic Sea States* links the states of the Baltic Sea, covering political and economic affairs, trade, the environment, and energy and transport.
- The *Black Sea Economic Cooperation Agreement* involves eleven countries around and near the Black Sea and aims to increase cooperation in six main areas: banking and finance, the environment, trade and industry, infrastructure, statistics, and the private sector.
- The *Economic Cooperation Organisation* is a 27-year-old cooperation agreement initiated by Turkey, Iran and Pakistan. It has been reactivated and now includes the Central Asian countries and Azerbaijan.
- The *Caspian Sea Cooperation Zone* links Iran, Azerbaijan, Russia, Kazakhstan and Turkmenistan with the aim of increasing cooperation in the fields of shipping, fisheries, and oil and gas exploration and extraction.

■ 16.3 North America

The Canada–United States Free Trade Agreement

The idea of establishing a free trade area between Canada and the USA is at least 100 years old. Apart from a brief period of free trade in the nineteenth century, from 1854 to 1866, and the successful Auto pact signed in 1965, until recently there have been no other serious attempts to form an economic integration. This changed in 1988 when an agreement setting up a free trade area was actually signed. The process of negotiation was initiated by Canada, apparently in an attempt to safeguard its share of the US market from the aggressive expansion of Japan and other countries. Other reasons for the Canadian initiative also existed, not the least important being a need to foster competition in the Canadian market.

The objectives of the Canada-United States Free Trade Agreement (CUSTA) include the elimination of barriers to trade in goods and services, the facilitation of fair competition within the area, the liberalisation of investment conditions, and the establishment of joint mechanisms to resolve trade disputes. The complete abolition of tariffs and other trade barriers is planned to happen over a period of ten years. However the agreement also contains separate sectoral arrangements which could undermine the actual extent of trade liberalisation. At any rate the elimination of tariffs is expected to have only a small economic impact since at the time of the signing the average US tariff on Canadian exports was only 1 per cent, and almost 80 per cent of Canadian exports were eligible for duty-free entry (Whalley, 1993). The agreement thus also focused on other measures, such as the anti-dumping and countervailing duties covered by Chapter XIX. In short, while not all the possible restrictions to trade are taken care of, the agreement provides a foundation for the expansion of bilateral trade between Canada and the USA. While this trade is already substantial, constituting 21 per cent of total US trade, geographical proximity means that liberalisation of trade could make it even larger. Numerous studies have already estimated many of the possible economic effects of CUSTA. These include the impact on trade flows, sectoral impacts, the effects on investment flows, effects on the labour market, etc. Most of these studies were performed while CUSTA was not yet operational. They are thus categorised as *ex ante* studies. CUSTA has now been in operation for several years and new studies capturing the actual effects of CUSTA are beginning to emerge.

From our knowledge of the welfare effects of regional trade liberalisation, we would presume that the larger effects would be on Canada, the smaller of the two countries. This is for two reasons. First, as the smaller country Canada would benefit from trading at the newly established prices which will be closer to the original US prices than Canadian prices. Whichever country's after-trade prices are further away from its autarky prices benefits more from the freeing of trade (recall this from Chapter 1). Secondly, the opportunities to produce for a larger (combined) market will enable Canadian firms to exploit economies of scale to a much larger extent than previously. Given Canada's already established reliance on the US market the economies of scale argument also explains why it is better for Canada to have a trade deal securing access to the US market than to rely on multilateral liberalisation. Since the change in relative prices within Canada is expected to be larger than in the USA it is reasonable to expect that any adjustment shocks and costs there will also be larger.

The *ex ante* studies projected exactly these gains: placing the Canadian annual real income gains in the region of 9 per cent while the USA was expected to experience gains of less than 1 per cent. However studies completed after three years of the agreement could not confirm these gains. It seems that so far CUSTA has generated little new liberalisation in the sectors which needed it most: agriculture, textiles, apparel and steel. Nor did investment flows increase by much over the first three years. At the same time exactly the opposite trends have been apparent with respect to bilateral trade and investment flows between Mexico and the USA. It looks as if trade had shifted to the cheaper source partner country (even before the formal implementation of the FTA).

□ North American Free Trade Agreement

In February 1991 the United States, Canada and Mexico agreed to begin negotiations on a free trade agreement. In August 1992 they announced that an accord had been reached in the form of the North American Free Trade Agreement (NAFTA). It took another year for this agreement to be ratified by all three governments. All the formal obstacles to the agreement taking effect as planned on 1 January 1994 were thus removed. However there are still many concerns yet to be resolved. Similarly to CUSTA, NAFTA was initiated by the smallest partner – Mexico, thus confirming its commitment to trade and investment reforms. In essence this agreement is an improved version of the CUSTA because its agenda includes issues that were only partially solved in the previous FTA – issues such as the protection of intellectual property rights, rules on local content, and export performance requirements. Moreover NAFTA takes the FTA one step further by addressing cross-border environmental issues.

As already noted US–Mexican trade expanded rapidly even before the agreement was finalised, leading some observers to argue that other factors, such as domestic Mexican policy reform and consequent economic growth, influence bilateral trade more than a trade agreement could. However it can also be argued that Mexico would not have been able to implement these reforms if it were not for expectation of the trade deal with the USA.

Much of the trade growth came from the *maquiladoras* (see also Box 16.4). The expansion of the *maquiladoras* was driven naturally by differences in labour costs, but also by reforms in Mexico. The fate of the *maquiladoras* under NAFTA is not yet certain, although the further growth seems likely. On one hand it seems plausible for US firms to

Box 16.4   *The* maquiladora *programme*

Initiated in 1965 by the Mexican government in response to the cancellation of the previous programme that had allowed Mexican workers to cross the American border for seasonal work the *maquiladora* programme allows a firm located in Mexico for the purpose of manufacturing products for exports to be 100 per cent foreign owned. Recent adjustments to the programme have also meant that a portion of production could be also sold in the domestic market. Only the value added in Mexico (labour costs and parts) is subject to import tariffs upon re-entry. The textile industry was the first to use the *maquiladora* programme. It was then joined by other labour-intensive industries such as electrical components, furniture and transport equipment. By 1990 470 000 workers were employed in *maquiladoras*. While most are US owned there are also some Canadian, Japanese and European operations. The *maquiladora* industry is one of the most dynamic sectors of the Mexican economy and has developed into the second most important sector of foreign exchange, the first still being crude oil.

NAFTA is not likely to alter the future development of the *maquiladora* programme. Although now with NAFTA all Mexican exports can enter the USA duty-free, the *maquiladora* programme is likely to continue growing. Hanson (1996) provides an explanation. The pre-NAFTA pattern of border trade between Mexico and the USA reveals that the USA has a comparative advantage in components production, while Mexico's advantage, given its cheap labour, is in assembly. As Mexican assembly plants expand under the free trade arrangement, it is likely that demand for US made components will grow, contributing to manufacturing employment and growth of border American industries.

relocate even more production under these programmes with the FTA than without it. On the other hand, the FTA will increase Mexican growth. This will have opposing effects. Its wage costs will increase, reducing one of the most important elements in the moving of production to Mexico. Secondly both income and purchasing power will increase and producers may want to move production closer to the source of demand. The other factor influential in the location decision was used extensively in the arguments opposing NAFTA: the relatively lax environmental laws in Mexico. Some view these laws as having even more influence over the decision to move production to Mexico than the lower costs of labour. However these arguments, as yet, lack any empirical support.

A number of general equilibrium studies of the potential effects of NAFTA are summarised in Waverman (1992) and in the US International Trade Commission (1992). As *ex ante* studies, they show only weak evidence of the possibility of significant trade diversion effects against non-members, at least from the US imports perspective. Moreover, the agreement, although welfare-improving for all three members, is not shown as leading to large overall gains for the two DCs, the USA and Canada. Mexico is seen as capturing most of the benefits but also as being the source of most of the problems still existing in the implementation of the NAFTA, such as lack of adequate infrastructure, lack of qualified workers, and the level of green and blue (environmental and labour) standards.

With respect to the institutional structure of the NAFTA everything has been implemented as required by the agreement. This means that the preconditions have been created to establish the North American Development Bank, a NAFTA Information Centre, a Secretariat for Labour Market Issues, and local offices of the US Environmental Authority. The NAFTA secretariat will have its headquarters in Toronto.

The expansion of trade volume after the implementation of the agreement has also been recorded. According to the US Bureau of Economic Analysis, in the first six months of NAFTA implementation US exports to Mexico increased by 16.7 per cent and to Canada by 9.6 per cent compared with the same period of the previous year. Imports from Mexico increased by 20.3 per cent and from Canada by 10.2 per cent. The high increase in American exports to Mexico is linked to the high demand for American cars. There is still a considerable doubt whether these developments can be strongly correlated to the NAFTA agreement. For now, we have strong evidence only that NAFTA is not hurting trade relations among the member countries, that it is not causing massive unemployment in the USA and that Mexico has found a use for it as an anchor for its restabilisation and growth.

There is some concern that NAFTA may be used as a stepping stone to create a broader Western Hemisphere Free Trade Area (WHFTA) or Free Trade Area of the Americas (FTAA) comprising the North and South Americas. This initiative could be seen as quite a beneficial one since it should contribute to increased prosperity on the American continents via liberalisation of trade, promotion of investments and debt reduction. From the US perspective, extension of free trade to the WHFTA level could achieve an increase in exports of US$ 36 bn and an increase in imports of US$ 28 bn which is attractive enough for the current Clinton administration to try and begin the extension by widening NAFTA to include Chile. If any real pressures for the creation of a rather closed WHFTA occur, the rest of the world, and in particular Asia and the Pacific, may find themselves in a position where they need to counteract or even retaliate. The creating of a more formal (i.e. closed) economic integration in the Asian Pacific would then become inevitable, thus fragmenting the world economy into three large blocs and some excluded countries.

■ *16.4* Asia and the Pacific

Geographically this region is vast. It includes developed market economies such as the USA, Canada and Japan, and economies which have just recently begun to develop market-based systems, such as China. To discuss regionalism from the whole region's perspective would be neither easy or useful. In what follows we will therefore focus on those countries which comprise the core of the Asia–Pacific region.[11] This subregion is the world's fastest-growing region, in terms of both GDP and trade. Another characteristic of this region is that it, so far, contains only very weak formal trading arrangements. Extra-regional trade has always been more important for this region than intra-regional trade (see also Figure 16.3). This lack of regionalisation is not solely the result of intensive extra-regional trade linkages, but is also due to the fact that there is no obvious need to 'go regional'. The diverse nature and interests of the countries in the region, combined with the region's geographical size, have also been a factor in the low priority placed on regional trading arrangements.

The main thrust of this region's trade policy has been based on the multilateral trading system and is on balance outward-oriented. Notwithstanding this fact, some of the fastest-growing Asia–Pacific countries have also been seen as the most active practitioners of 'strategic trade policies', aggressive subsidies and non-border policies. The rest of the world, notably the USA and the EU, have fought this 'outward orientation' by introducing anti-dumping defences, voluntary export restraints (VERs) and, most recently, special bilateral, sectoral and structural negotiations over trade and industrial policies (Richardson, 1992). Recently this region's

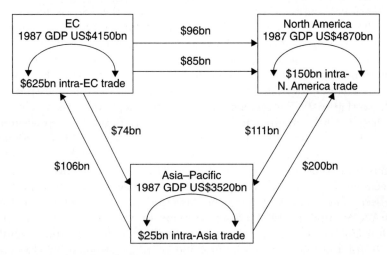

Figure 16.3 *Trilateral trade flows (1988)*

Source: Bollard and Mayer (1992), fig. 1, p. 202.

inclination towards regionalism has strengthened primarily because of the need to counteract activities in the 'Western Hemisphere'. While a formal framework for this regionalism has yet to occur, a non-discriminatory regional integration is considered necessary in order to maintain the high growth potential of the region. The attractiveness of establishing a 'local' economic integration will be enhanced if the Uruguay Round fails to revitalise multilateralism and the open trading system.

The oldest and most successful regional grouping in the Asian Pacific region is the Association of Southeast Asian Nations (ASEAN). An overview of this group's efforts in the area of regionalism is given in the next subsection. The other subsections discuss the possibilities which relate to the rise of the Chinese economic area and the role and significance of the Asia–Pacific Economic Cooperation (APEC).

□ *The Association of Southeast Asian Nations*

ASEAN, the Association of Southeast Asian Nations, was formed by Indonesia, Malaysia, the Philippines, Singapore and Thailand in 1967. Brunei joined in 1984, and Vietnam in 1995. The founding document of ASEAN, the Bangkok Declaration, although including announcements of active collaboration and mutual assistance in the field of economics, focused primarily on political and security issues. Thus, until the present day, the ASEAN organisation has had little impact in terms of stimulating economic growth through intra-regional trade and investment. Despite this, all members except for the Philippines have experienced strong economic growth.

The slow progress of economic cooperation in the ASEAN region may have been the only realistic way of integrating a group of countries characterised by historical and cultural heterogeneity and even political disputes. In its first decade ASEAN existed only as a symbol. However communist takeovers in Vietnam and Kampuchea brought the ASEAN countries closer together. This had spillovers in the economic sphere as well, so that in 1977 a preferential trade agreement was signed. This was the first major commitment towards the liberalisation of intra-regional trade. Unfortunately the amount of trade covered by this agreement provided few opportunities for intra-ASEAN trade growth. The increase in this trade that occurred in the early 1980s was in fact unrelated to the agreement. It was mostly composed of an increase in the petroleum trade between Indonesia, Malaysia, and Singapore (Imada, 1993). The third ASEAN Summit in 1989 addressed some of the reasons for the poor performance in strengthening intra-regional trade and investments links, giving for the first time clear direction to trade cooperation. This was accomplished by setting a goal of extending the preferential trade arrangement to cover 50 per cent of the value or 90 per cent of all items traded. A five-year time frame was set for this goal (seven years for Indonesia and the Philippines). Mutual tariff preferences to ASEAN members were also increased and the exception lists were restricted to 10 per cent of all items traded. Somewhat disappointingly even this move was unsuccessful in increasing trade among members. A renewed commitment to economic liberalisation was again expressed at the fourth Summit in early 1992. This led to an agreement to transform the old preferential trade agreement into the ASEAN free trade area (AFTA). The time frame set was the next fifteen years. This is seen as a huge step forward, especially after so many years of resisting stronger regional integration.

AFTA is to be formed under common effective preferential tariff scheme which will include all manufactured products (including capital goods) processed agricultural products, and those products which fall outside the definition of agricultural products. Another method of ensuring progress in liberalising trade is through pre-setting a schedule for tariff reductions. However many details are yet to be worked out before this scheme can be implemented. Notwithstanding the above we already have several studies which estimate the potential effects of AFTA. These estimates vary in magnitude from moderate to significant increases in intra-regional trade, but it seems that there exists a consensus as to the direct impact of AFTA on the region's total trade and production – it is likely to be small. On the other hand, the indirect effects of the AFTA, especially the improved international competitiveness, are estimated to be more substantial. However even taking into account these positive effects it seems that the ASEAN countries will need to continue to push their exports to other markets in order to retain their high growth potential.

☐ The emergence of a Chinese Economic Area

This area centres on Hong Kong and includes China's Special Economic Zones (SEZs) and Taiwan. It has developed rapidly since the middle of the 1980s. The driving force of this subregion was the ending of the Cold War which reduced the amount of restrictions on trade and investment which predominated over that period. With a more open economic system adapted by China the natural trade and investment linkages among China, Hong Kong and Taiwan have been revived. According to Jones, King and Klein (1992) the 1989 incident in Tiananmen Square actually accelerated China's growing economic links with Hong Kong and Taiwan. This occurred because the developed Western countries reduced their foreign investment and lending to China and because the reduced authority of the central government allowed regional governments more freedom in implementing economic reforms and expanding foreign trade.

There is no doubt that a *de facto* economic integration among China, Hong Kong and Taiwan is emerging. This is revealed through the intensification of trade flows, direct foreign investment, other financial flows and renewed transport links. The increase in intra-area trade is impressive: it grew from 10 per cent of the total trade of these three countries in 1978 to over 35 per cent in 1990. Such a growth in intra-regional trade volume has not been achieved by any of the free trade agreements formally established outside the OECD countries in the after-war period. As discussed in the previous section, even the ASEAN countries which experienced enviable increases in trade with the rest of the world have managed only modest increases in their intra-regional trade. What is most impressive of all about this rise in intra-regional economic cooperation is that it occurred without a formal agreement. In fact this *de facto* trading bloc has resulted in some political discussions between the three countries. This runs counter to the 'normal' path of discussions and agreements which usually precede economic integration. In the case of the Chinese Economic Area it may happen that a formal agreement will follow.

It is not always necessary for an integration to be policy-led. We have already mentioned that FDI can also successfully be the driving force. In the case of the Chinese Economic Area it seems that policy was involved, but in rather indirect way. It was not the result of Taiwanese or Hong Kong policy, as neither made any adjustments to their systems. In fact, Taiwanese policy has actually impeded trade in the past. Rather, it was the Chinese policy of economic reform which was important. It opened the way for entrepreneurs to seek the expansion of business with partners outside China proper but still within a region of natural extension.

Three factors are identified by Jones, King and Klein (1992, pp. 16–20) as having provided the basis for the growth of trade up to now and providing great prospects in the future. They are Taiwanese capital and technical–managerial expertise, Hong-Kong's services as middleman, and China's cheap labour and abundance of natural resources. They contend that a continuation of this economic integration for just one generation will result in major changes in both the world economy and in global trading patterns. Their prediction is that this integration's share of world exports, even excluding their intra-regional exports, will exceed that of Japan's by the end of the 1990s.

☐ Asia–Pacific Economic Cooperation

Asia and the Pacific is a vast region comprising so many different economies that a single economic integration or trading bloc is unlikely ever to be established. In addition, even with the potential for success of some subregional groupings, such as NAFTA, AFTA or the Chinese Economic Area, the region's over-riding interest is still in a more open global trading system. The most these countries have ever considered was a very loose institutional framework for economic cooperation. This has been provided in a formation of the Asia–Pacific Economic Cooperation (APEC) group. This was launched in Australia in 1989 with twelve original members: the six members of ASEAN, the USA, Canada, Japan, South Korea, Australia and New Zealand. In 1991 they were joined by China, Hong Kong and Taiwan. This group of diverse but complementary economies accounts for more than half of world GDP and almost 40 per cent of world trade. Intra-group exports approached 65 per cent of their total exports. In 1992 a ministerial forum established a permanent APEC secretariat in Singapore. APEC's guiding principles specify that coopera-tion should be outward-looking, participation open-ended, and regional trade liberalisation promoted in accordance with GATT rules and not detrimental to other economies. This policy of *open regionalism* makes APEC significantly different from other regional blocs, in particular the EU, whose main thrust is discriminatory. The phenomenon of open regionalism stems from this region's higher propensity to trade extra-regionally than intra-regionally.

So far APEC has been confined to attempts to supporting the imple-mentation of the Uruguay Round and the WTO and some general discussions on the proliferation of regional trade agreements. Some work has also been done on regional information exchange and technical cooperation. However more work is needed to address the practical means of reducing transactional costs in the flow of goods and services within the region and to lay the groundwork for future policy decisions. It is hoped that APEC will be able to escape from the 'regionalism' trap and will continue with its main aim of strengthening the multilateral trading system. However if the Uruguay Round fails to improve the international environment of this region's market access, they may decide to use their joint bargaining power both to open other markets and to create a wider market of their own. This solution is something the world should view with apprehension.

16.5 The Australia–New Zealand Closer Economic Relations Agreement

This agreement, known as ANZERTA or CER, has been in force since 1983 and has had two major reviews, in 1988 and 1992.[12] It is seen as a hybrid between a free trade area and a common market. Its free trade area features stem from the removal of tariffs and quantitative restrictions for all products traded across the Tasman which have 50 per cent Australian and/or New Zealand content and for which the last process of manufacture takes place in either Australia or New Zealand. Free trade in goods has been achieved in a relatively short period of time, over the years 1983–90, primarily because the 1988 review pushed hard for the acceleration of the process of goods trade liberalisation.

Another major achievement of the 1988 review was the commitment of both partners to attempt to complete a single, internal market *à la* the EU although without its bureaucratic superstructure. This involved extending the scope of CER to include the free movement of capital and labour and free trade in services. Thus, in addition to bilateral free trade in most services as well as goods, CER is characterised by some important single markets features. These include: the replacement of anti-dumping and countervailing duties with harmonised competition guidelines for fair business practices, the attempt to establish common business law and common rules on standards and technical specifications, disciplines over non-border subsidies to industry, and cross-country standing for each country's regulatory authority to investigate and enforce the new agreements.

There is thus a close resemblance between the type of issues discussed in Europe 1992 and in the reviews of CER, although it is unlikely that CER will go as far as monetary or political union. However there will be a need for greater harmonisation of these two economies, for example in taxation, in order to provide for truly free capital mobility. The scope for independent policy actions by each partner will consequently be reduced. The possibility of increased political coordination, although unlikely, is therefore not excluded. Over the period of CER's existence trade and investment between Australia and New Zealand has expanded significantly. Each country has become the other's largest market for elaborately transformed manufactures, which account for half the total bilateral trade. However, because CER still only accounts for a small proportion of each country's total trade, the rapid progress made towards more complete regional integration has not undermined the efforts for unilateral trade liberalisation in either country. Indeed this is the secret of CER's success – barriers to bilateral trade in all goods and almost all services have been eliminated, producing positive welfare effects, while trade restrictions against non-member countries have also been substantially liberalised, thus ensuring zero (or minimum) negative welfare effects. The CER agreement is thus hailed as the best model for how a GATT-consistent trading bloc can contribute to regional trade and at the same time strengthen the open multilateral trading system.

▮ *APPENDIX 16*   REGINAL TRADING ARRANGEMENTS

▮ *Europe*

☐ *European Union (EU)*

Members: Austria, Belgium, Denmark, Finland, France, Germany, Greece, Ireland, Italy, Luxembourg, Netherlands, Portugal, Spain, Sweden and Great Britain.

Authority: The European Union is founded on three treaties: the Treaty Establishing the European Coal and Steel Community (ECSC), 18 April 1951; the Treaty Establishing the European Economic Community (EEC), 25 March 1957; and the Treaty Establishing the European Atomic Energy Community (Euratom), 25 March 1957. The framework to form the internal free market ('EC 1992') is established by the Single European Act, which entered into force 1 July 1987, and an economic and monetary union on the Maastricht Treaty from 1992.

☐ *European Free Trade Association (EFTA)*

Members: Iceland, Norway, Switzerland and Liechtenstein (associate member).

Authority: Convention Establishing the European Free Trade Association, 4 January 1960

☐ *Lomé Convention*

Members: The EU and its former colonies in certain African, Caribbean and Pacific nations (ACP): Angola, Antigua and Barbuda, Bahamas, Barbados, Belize, Benin, Botswana, Burkina Faso, Burundi, Cameroon, Cape Verde, Central African Republic, Chad, Comoros, Congo, Côte d'Ivoire, Djibouti, Dominica, Dominican Republic, Equatorial Guinea, Ethiopia, Fiji, Gabon, Gambia, Ghana, Grenada, Guinea, Guinea–Bissau, Guyana, Haiti, Jamaica, Kenya, Kiribati, Lesotho, Liberia, Madagascar, Malawi, Mali, Mauritania, Mauritius, Mozambique, Namibia, Niger, Nigeria, Papua New Guinea, Rwanda, St Kitts & Nevis, St Lucia, St Vincent & the Grenadines, São Tomé e Principe, Senegal, Seychelles, Sierra Leone, Solomon Islands, Somalia, Sudan, Surinam, Swaziland, Tanzania,

Togo, Tonga, Trinidad & Tobago, Tuvalu, Uganda, Vanuatu, Western Samoa, Zaire, Zambia and Zimbabwe.

Authority: Lomé Convention, 28 February 1975; 1979 Great Britain and as amended Lome Convention IV, 15 December 1989.

Central European Free Trade Agreement (CEFTA)

Members: Czech Republic, Hungary, Poland, Slovakia and Slovenia.
Authority: Free trade agreement signed 21 December 1992.

Czech and Slovak Republics Customs Union

Members: Czech Republic and Slovak Republic.
Authority: Customs union agreement signed 28 October 1992 and established following dissolution of the Czech and Slovak Federal republic.

■ Africa

African Economic Community (AEC)

Members: Algeria, Angola, Benin, Botswana, Burkina Faso, Burundi, Cameroon, Cape Verde, Central African Republic, Chad, Comoros, Congo, Côte d'Ivoire, Djibouti, Egypt, Equatorial Guinea, Ethiopia, Gabon, Gambia, Ghana, Guinea, Guinea-Bissau, Kenya, Lesotho, Liberia, Libya, Madagascar, Malawi, Mali Mauritania, Mauritius, Mozambique, Namibia, Niger, Nigeria, Rwanda, São Tomé e Principe, Senegal, Seychelles, Sierra Leone, Somalia, Sudan, Swaziland, Tanzania, Togo, Tunisia, Uganda, Zaire, Zambia and Zimbabwe.
Authority: Treaty Establishing the African Economic Community (under the auspices of the Organisation of African Unity), 3 June 1991.

Central African Customs and Economic Union (UDEAC)

Members: Cameroon, Central African Republic, Chad, Congo, Equatorial Guinea and Gabon.
Authority: Treaty Establishing the Customs and Economic Union of Central Africa, 8 December 1964, entered into force 1 January 1966.

☐ West African Economic Community (CEAO)

Members: Benin, Burkina Faso, Côte d'Ivoire, Mali, Mauritania, Niger and Senegal.

Authority: Agreement establishing the West African Economic Community, January 1974.

☐ Economic Community of West African States (ECOWAS)

Members: Benin, Burkina Faso, Cape Verde, Côte d'Ivoire, Gambia, Ghana, Guinea, Guinea–Bissau, Liberia, Mali, Mauritania, Niger, Nigeria, Senegal, Sierra Leone and Togo.

Authority: Treaty Establishing the Economic Community of West African States, 28 May 1975.

☐ Preferential Trade Area For Eastern and Southern African States

Members: Angola, Burundi, Comoros, Djibouti, Ethiopia, Kenya, Lesotho, Malawi, Mauritius, Mozambique, Namibia, Rwanda, Somalia, Sudan, Swaziland, Tanzania, Zaire, Zambia and Zimbabwe.

Authority: Treaty for the Establishment of the Preferential Trade Area for Eastern and Southern African States, 21 December 1981, entered into force 30 September 1982.

☐ Economic Community of Central African States (CEEAC)

Members: Angola, Burundi, Cameroon, Central African Republic, Chad, Congo, Equatorial Guinea, Gabon, Rwanda, São Tomé e Principe and Zaire.

Authority: Treaty for the Establishment of the Economic Community of Central African States, 19 October 1983, entered into force 1 January 1985.

☐ Mano River Union (MRU)

Members: Guinea, Liberia and Sierra Leone.

Authority: Treaty of Malema, 3 October 1973.

☐ Economic Community of the Great Lake States (CEPGL)

Members: Burundi, Rwanda and Zaire.
Authority: Agreement Establishing the Economic Community of the Great Lake States, 20 September 1976.

☐ Southern African Development Coordination Conference (SADCC)

Members: Angola, Botswana, Lesotho, Malawi, Mozambique, Namibia, Swaziland, Tanzania, Zambia and Zimbabwe.
Authority: First meeting held in Arusha, Tanzania, July 1979.

☐ South African Customs Union (SACU)

Members: Botswana, Lesotho, Namibia, South Africa and Swaziland.
Authority: Agreement Establishing the South African Customs Union, 11 December 1969.

■ The Middle East

☐ Cooperation Council for the Arab States of the Gulf (GCC)

Members: Bahrain, Kuwait, Oman, Qatar, Saudi Arabia and the United Arab Emirates.
Authority: Charter of the Cooperation Council for the Arab States of the Gulf, 25 May 1981 and 11 November 1982.

☐ Arab Common Market

Members: Egypt, Iraq, Jordan, Libya, Mauritania, Syria and Yemen.
Authority: Resolution of the Council of Arab Economic Unity (CAEU), August 1964.

☐ Union of the Arab Maghreb (MAGHREB)

Members: Algeria, Libya, Mauritania, Morocco and Tunisia.
Authority: Agreement Establishing the Union of the Arab Maghreb, 15 February 1989.

☐ *Economic Cooperation Organisation (ECO)*

Members: Iran, Pakistan and Turkey.
Authority: Established as Regional Cooperation for Development by the Treaty of Izmir, 21 July 1964.

■ *Asia*

☐ *Association of Southeast Asian Nations (ASEAN)*

Members: Brunei Darussalam, Indonesia, Malaysia, the Philippines, Singapore and Thailand.
Authority: Bangkok Declaration, 8 August 1967.

☐ *ASEAN Free Trade Area (AFTA)*

Members: Brunei Darussalam, Indonesia, Malaysia, the Philippines, Singapore and Thailand.
Authority: Formation proposed on 8 October 1991, and furthered by the Singapore Declaration of 1992, 28 January 1992, and the Agreement of the Common Effective Preferential Tariff (CEPT). Scheme for the ASEAN Free Trade Area (AFTA).

☐ *Closer Economic Relations Agreement (CER)*

Members: Australia and New Zealand.
Authority: Australia and New Zealand Closer Economic Relations Trade Agreement, 1 January 1983.

☐ *Asia Pacific Economic Cooperation (APEC)*

Members: ASEAN members (Brunei Darussalam, Indonesia, Malaysia, the Philippines, Singapore and Thailand), Australia, Canada, China, Hong Kong, Japan, New Zealand, South Korea, Taiwan and the USA.
Authority: Proposed by Australia as an annual forum in 1988.

☐ East Asia Economic Group (EAEG)

Members: ASEAN Members (Brunei Darussalam, Indonesia, Malaysia, the Philippines, Singapore, and Thailand), Hong Kong, Japan, South Korea and Taiwan.
Authority: Proposed by Malaysian Prime Minister Mahathir Mohamad, December 1990.

■ The Americas

☐ Canada–United States Trade Agreement (CUSTA)

Members: United States and Canada.
Authority: The United States–Canada Free Trade Agreement Implementation Act, 1988.

☐ North American Free Trade Agreement (NAFTA)

Members: United States, Mexico and Canada.
Authority: North American Free Trade Agreement, 12 August 1992.

☐ Caribbean Basin Initiative (CBI)

Members: Anguilla, Antigua & Barbuda, Bahamas, Barbados, Belize, Costa Rica, Dominica, Dominican Republic, El Salvador, Grenada, Guatemala, Guyana, Haiti, Honduras, Jamaica, Nicaragua, Panama, St Lucia, St Vincent & the Grenadines, Surinam, Trinidad & Tobago, Turks & Caicos Islands, British Virgin Islands, Montserrat, Cayman Islands, Netherlands Antilles, St Kitts & Nevis.
Authority: Caribbean Basin Recovery Act, 1983.

☐ Caribbean Community (CARICOM)

Members: Antigua and Barbuda, Bahamas, Barbados, Belize, Dominica, Grenada, Guyana, Jamaica, Montserrat, St Kitts & Nevis, St Lucia, St Vincent & the Grenadines and Trinidad and Tobago.
Authority: Treaty Establishing the Caribbean Community, 4 July 1973.

☐ Organisation of Eastern Caribbean States (OECS)

Members: Antigua and Barbuda, Dominica, Grenada, Montserrat, St Kitts & Nevis, St Lucia and St Vincent & the Grenadines.
Authority: Agreement Establishing the East Caribbean Common Market, 11 June 1968; Treaty Establishing the Organisation of Eastern Caribbean States, 18 June 1981.

☐ Central American Common Market (CACM)

Members: Costa Rica, El Salvador, Guatemala, Honduras and Nicaragua.
Authority: Formed ancillary to the General Treaty of Central American Economic Integration, 13 December 1960.

☐ Mexico Central America Free Trade Agreement

Members: Mexico, Costa Rica, El Salvador, Guatemala, Honduras and Nicaragua.
Authority: Currently under negotiation.

☐ Andean Common Market (ANCOM)

Members: Bolivia, Colombia, Ecuador, Peru and Venezuela.
Authority: Agreement of Cartagena, 26 May 1969.

☐ Latin American Integration Association (LAIA)

Members: Argentina, Bolivia, Brazil, Chile, Colombia, Ecuador, Mexico, Paraguay, Peru, Uruguay and Venezuela.
Authority: Treaty of Montevideo, 12 August 1980, entered into force 18 March 1991.

☐ Common Market of the South (MERCOSUR)

Members: Argentina, Brazil, Paraguay and Uruguay.
Authority: Treaty Establishing a Common Market (Treaty of Asuncion), 26 March 1991.

Note:

This listing excludes certain trade preferences between the EU and such Mediterranean nations as Malta, Cyprus, Turkey, Lebanon, Egypt, Syria, Morocco, Algeria and Tunisia and also between the EU and Central and Eastern European countries and the Baltic States.

■ *Chapter 17* ■

Regionalism and Multilateralism

■ *17.1* Introduction

The ratification of the North American Free Trade Area (NAFTA) agreement in the US Congress was seen by many as a further sign that the new wave of regionalism was turning the world away from the multilateral trading system established by the GATT. It is certainly true that the renewed interest in regionalism of the 1980s and 1990s has its roots in the weakening of the multilateral trading system. The length and complexities of the preparatory phase of trade negotiation following the Tokyo Round indicated that the GATT-based trading system might be losing its vitality and momentum. The multilateral trade negotiating game has changed significantly. The number of players involved has increased substantially over the years: more than 120 countries participated in the Uruguay Round. With such a large number of players the extent of free-riding and the likelihood of not reaching an agreement was quite high. The leading player in the multilateral negotiations, the USA, changed its stance from being strongly in favour of the multilateral approach to one which is only mildly supportive. In fact, as many commentators in this area claim, the US official position with respect to multilateral trade negotiations has helped to establish the view that regionalism may be seen as an *alternative* to the multilateral trading system rather than a complement to it. Moreover, regionalism is seen as inextricably linked with the global integration of foreign direct investments and production (see also Balasubramanyam and Greenaway, 1993 and Box 17.1, p. 513).

The widening of the European Community (EC) in the 1980s, the creation of the European Economic Area (EEA) in 1992, the deepening of the EU through the creation of the Single Market '1992' and the creation of CUSTA all have led to the perception that regionalism is indeed establishing strong roots. The vision of a *tripolar trading system* based on the trade blocs centred around three poles – the USA, the EU and Japan – has become an important element in this new trend of regionalism.

Many of the developing countries have become involved in this second generation of regionalism in a different way from how they were involved in the first wave. Following the major role developing countries in general played in the world debt crisis of the 1980s, such countries have been urged to switch from inward- to outward-looking development strategies. International economic institutions and the governments of the developed countries both believe that the developing countries should implement comprehensive economic reforms in order to create more open economies. One of the important factors believed to have enhanced the rate of such reforms was a change in the treatment of the developing countries in international preferential trading arrangements. There was a noticeable switch from *non-reciprocal* to *reciprocal* treatment in agreements between developed countries and developing countries. This has caused developing countries to concentrate less on the multilateral trade negotiations and to expect less from the GATT. In turn, this has contributed to the general feeling that multilateralism is losing its strength and should be replaced by regional trading arrangements.

In this chapter we address some of the issues raised in the renewed debate on regionalism versus multilateralism. The following section discusses the basis for the claim that the world economy is becoming increasingly regionalised. These claims seem to be motivated by fear and there is only weak evidence that the world is being driven into three regional integrations. However the available evidence is imperfect and we need to take into account the possibility that regionalisation will become stronger in the future. In section 17.3 we discuss whether or not it is possible for regionalism to coexist with multilateralism. Finally, in section 17.4, we focus on the institutional issues and the means by which the newly established World Trade Organisation (WTO) can ensure that regionalism is a complement to rather than a substitute for multilateralism.

▌ 17.2 The extent of regionalisation in the world economy

Almost all the comments on regionalism in the world economy take for granted the premise that the extent of regionalisation in the world economy has increased in recent decades. However here we are inclined to adhere to Lloyd's opinion that the actual extent of regionalisation is an open question and that claims of increased regionalisation should be treated as a testable hypothesis (Lloyd, 1993, p. 42; 1992, pp. 14–23).

Box 17.1 *Regionalism and FDI*

The world economy has been pressured by two apparently divergent forces since the 1980s. One is *globalisation*, or the global integration of the world economy through multinational companies and FDI. The other trend has been the *regionalisation* of the world economy through the apparent increase in the importance of regional trade arrangements. These two processes have for some time now coexisted happily. However some commentators speak about FDI themselves becoming more regionalised, creating an additional source of growth in the regionalisation of world trade.

It is claimed that a regional integration will only be successful in achieving its goal of improved economic performance and increased real income if there is a simultaneous integration at both the policy and production levels. Regional trade integration typically involves the removal, whether partial or complete, of barriers to cross-border flows of goods and services. As such, this type of integration remains relatively shallow. In contrast the regional integration of production extends to the liberalisation of barriers to cross-border flows of factors of production and technology. The policies needed for such deep form of liberalisation must necessarily go further than those policies merely designed to support the intra-regional free trade of goods and services. We can thus differentiate between *policy-led* integration and *FDI-led* integration. Policy-led regional integration is that in which the initiatives towards integration flow from national economic policies. Policy measures typically focus on reducing trade barriers between members in order to create a free trade area or customs union. Only rarely do policies go further towards the harmonisation of fiscal, monetary, industrial and other policies. The essential feature of such a process is that the institutional framework for integration precedes actual integration at the production level.

In contrast FDI-led regional integration occurs when the activities of firms (usually MNCs) drive the integrative initiative. This occurs when MNCs perceive advantages from the intra-regional integration of their operations as compared to inter-regional integration. Liberal trade policies in a region may certainly encourage firms to implement regional as opposed to global strategies but such trends may also occur in the absence of specific regional integrative policies. A minimum level of cross-border trade within a region is however likely to be present before intra-regional FDI flows begin to grow. When the integrative process is initiated by firms it is likely that pressures will exist to deepen integration at the policy and production levels.

CUSTA is an example of how early integration measures (such as the Auto Pact and years of tariff lowering) led to integration at both the policy and the production levels. The CUSTA agreement promoted FDI-based integration by including many FDI-related issues such as national treatment, performance requirements, screening procedures and trade in services. A similar process occurred in the preparation of NAFTA. It is

> thus likely that the current activities of MNCs will play a significant role
> in determining the outcome and eventual success of NAFTA. Another
> example of FDI-led integration is currently under way in the Asian region,
> even though there are hardly any accompanying policy initiatives.

Source: UN (1992).

The proliferation of the various preferential arrangements that have
been notified to GATT is often used as evidence for increased regionalisation (see Figure 17.1). More than 100 regional or preferential trading
arrangements have been notified to the GATT, although many of these do
not really belong under the category of regional trading agreements.[1] As de
la Torre and Kelly (1992) point out, only about twenty actual regional
arrangements were notified to the GATT in the period 1947–1990, these
were mainly in Africa, the Americas and Europe. Moreover, a number of
these arrangements were merely replacing earlier ones while others are no
longer operative (see Appendix 16 for the list of regional trading agreements).

While the sheer number of regional arrangements being notified to the
GATT does provide some indication as to general trends it cannot be
taken as strong evidence of growing regionalisation. A time series of intra-
regional trade flows captures the effects of integration but does not provide
rigorous evidence either. To properly evaluate the degree of regionalisation
in the world economy we would also need to take into account many other
factors which also affect the geographical distribution of a country's or
a region's trade. Some studies have already tried to more accurately
determine the effect of regional trading arrangements on the geographical
distribution of world trade (see, for example, Lloyd, 1992; Anderson and
Norheim, 1993; GATT, 1993). All these studies agree that in the absence of
more precise measures of intra-regional trade barriers their results must be
treated as broad trends. As such these results can provide only a weak
support to the claim of increased regionalisation. For example, Anderson
and Norheim (1993) argue that data in their study suggest that while the
share and intensity of intra-regional trade in the major regions has been
increasing, these regions' propensity to trade with other regions has also
been rising. On the basis of these results they conclude that the process of
multilateral trade liberalisation was strong enough to offset any possible
trade diversion effects caused by the formation of regional trading
arrangements. Similarly Lloyd (1992) argues that only weak support could
be found for the hypothesis that regional trading arrangements lead to an
increased share of intra-regional trade. It is possible that these studies
underestimate the extent of regionalisation because they exclude trade in
services and factors, both of which have been increasing relative to trade in

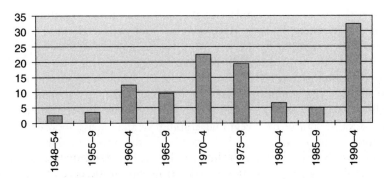

Figure 17.1 *Regional integration agreements notified to GATT, 1948–94*

Note: Data include agreements notified under Article XXIV or the Enabling Clause. A notification may include one or more related agreements involving the same group of countries. Data also include agreements which are not currently in force.
Source: WTO (1995b) p. 25 and Appendix Table 1.

goods. Although typical regional trading arrangements do not make provisions relating to these categories of trade, the Single Market, CER and CUSTA, which comprise large proportion of world trade, have all either fully liberalised this trade or plan to do so in the near future. The effect of liberalisation in this area must therefore also be accounted for in determining the extent of regionalisation.

Notwithstanding the weak empirical support for the regionalisation hypothesis we must still accept the possibility that this trend may increase in the future and that it eventually may hinder the progress of global integration. This outcome is less likely now after the successful conclusion of the Uruguay Round. Even though in the past regionalism has not significantly affected the progress of global trade integration, however, it may still have had adverse effects on world welfare. While more complex modelling is needed to establish the sign and magnitude of these welfare effects Srinivasan, Whalley and Wooton (1993) have surveyed some of the studies that measure the welfare effects of regional trading arrangements. Their conclusions correlate with the general impression that empirical results are not conclusive. However they, somewhat reluctantly, suggest that on the basis of available measurements welfare effects are more on the side of trade creation. The trouble with the Vinerian concepts of trade creation and trade diversion is that while they are useful as a description of the changes in the patterns of trade, they are not very useful in a normative sense. The Vinerian framework is thus not very well suited to the quantification of welfare effects. This is particularly true for the second generation of regionalism which is viewed as being unlikely to alter regional trading patterns in the global economy. This claim is made because the new regionalism is thought to be motivated by factors different from purely integrationist desires. The motivations behind the new regionalism range from the search for safe market access by smaller countries to the frustration felt by some larger countries with the lack of progress in multilateral liberalisation. Perhaps the most important motivation of all is the common belief that regional trading arrangements may facilitate faster growth in world trade than the more difficult multilateral talks. Indeed, if the new regional trading arrangements focused on the dynamic components of global trade and the more rapidly growing portions of the world economy they would certainly be welfare-improving. In general the welfare effects of regional trading arrangements from the viewpoint of the outside world therefore seem to be more positive, even though there are some concerns about 'beggar-thy-neighbour' terms of trade effects. However the outside world should still be able to benefit from the growth effects in the integrated region which should offset any initial terms of trade losses.

17.3 Regionalism and multilateralism: coexistence or conflict?

The central issue in this whole debate is whether the increased tendency towards regionalism endangers the established principles of multilateralism and therefore threatens to restrict the growth of world trade. The relationship between regionalism and multilateralism is of a conflicting nature, but they are not mutually exclusive. After all, they have coexisted throughout the GATT governance of post-war world trade. The conflict arises from the very nature of a trading system based on regional trading arrangements and multilateralism. Regional trading arrangements are by definition discriminatory while the multilateral system is based on a non-discriminatory most-favoured-nation (MFN) clause. There are also other conflicting features of the two systems. Regionalism depends upon the principle of (bilateral) reciprocity while multilateralism uses a very broad definition of reciprocity. Furthermore, the regionalism-based system tends to follow the so-called result-oriented approach, while the multilateral system operates primarily by following the rule-oriented approach (see also Bhagwati, 1991, Chapter 1). These conflicting features are often used as the basis for the conclusion that regionalism contradicts multilateralism and therefore must be an alternative to it.

However there are still some grounds for arguing that these two can and should act as complements and that the discriminatory nature of regional trading blocks is not necessarily harmful to world trade. To explore this possibility we must examine other aspects of the relationship between regionalism and multilateralism. There are at least three factors which should be considered. The first concerns the possibility that regionalism may lead to retaliatory action, non-cooperative trade relations or trade wars. The second aspect concerns the possibility that the various regional trading arrangements may converge towards global free trade through the process defined as coalescence (Lloyd, 1992). The third aspect relates to the impact that the implementation of preferential schemes for outside countries may have on the relevance and importance of the multilateral non-discriminatory system.

One of the biggest concerns surrounding the rise in regional trading blocs is the possibility of an outbreak of trade restrictions between blocs leading to retaliatory actions or trade wars. This possibility would become very threatening if world trade polarises into the so-called Triad comprising the three blocs centred around the EU, the Americas and Japan. In such a case the three blocs would see each other as competitors. If this occurs there is a real possibility it could lead to trade wars. From the literature on the strategic trade policies of individual countries we know that this result is very likely to be welfare-reducing for all the groups involved. However this may not be enough to prevent non-cooperative trade relations from beginning, particularly when we bear in mind that the size of the bloc is important in determining the outcome. As Kennan and Riezman (1990) have demonstrated, larger blocs could win trade wars at the expense of small blocs or countries. However, just as when we discussed the strategic trade policies of individual countries, we should point out that these results are sensitive to the assumptions used. For example the models of trade wars all assume the ability to retaliate which is not realistic under the system based on GATT rules. In addition these models implicitly assume that governments act so as to maximise national welfare rather than acting in the interests of particular groups.[2] Nevertheless these models do provide an insight into the importance of terms of trade effects and, correspondingly, of the importance of the size of the blocs and their policies towards external tariff protection.

Many commentators in this area emphasise that the international community has become interested in regionalism because it is seen as a faster route to reaching global free trade than the multilateral negotiations. Lloyd (1992), based on Kemp and Wan (1976), develops an interesting view on this issue. He argues that trading blocs can in fact extend progress towards the freeing of global trade by extending country coverage and in some cases by the merging of the blocs or through joint membership. This result is called coalescence. Real-world examples are the expansion of the EC from six original members into ten, twelve and then fifteen and also the creation of the EEA by 'merging' with EFTA. Thus, in principle, one or several trading blocs could be seen as expanding both geographically and in terms of the categories of trade covered until the world economy is one single bloc. Lloyd calls this result the 'grand coalition', which is necessarily beneficial for all. This was demonstrated by Kemp and Wan (1976) when they showed that it is always possible for a regional integration formed among an arbitrary group of countries to restructure itself in such a way as to make member countries better off without making any of non-member countries worse off. This type of regional bloc would then provide a strong incentive for new members to join, until eventually no country is left outside the bloc.

It is not uncommon for regional trading arrangements to have a separate set of preferences for non-member countries. For example, the EU operates a scheme through which most non-member countries are able to gain some form of preferential treatment. This is the Lomé IV Convention which covers more than 60 countries (see p. 503). Other schemes include the General Scheme of Preferences of the EU, the cooperation agreements with North African countries, and various types of agreements with the former socialist countries of Eastern Europe and the SU. Other existing blocs operate similar systems of preferential arrangements. The impression exists that this network of preferences has been continuously spreading. In this sense, the discriminatory nature of the regional trading arrangements has been diminished, leading countries to necessarily adhere to the non-discrimination principle of the multilateral system of world trade. Thus, in this way, trading blocs may provide a disincentive for a commitment to multilateralism.

However we should not disregard the argument that individual countries are more receptive to regional trading arrangements than multilateral ones (Jones, 1993). This is demonstrated by the high degree of liberalisation in trade, services and factor movements achieved within some trading blocs: the EU and CER are prime examples. It is obvious that these same countries would hardly tolerate a similar degree of freedom among factor movements on a world-wide basis. Nevertheless, these regional agreements' treatment of trade in services and factor flows could be used as blueprints for multilateral negotiations.

We must also note the fact that countries are inclined to form coalitions, but with partners of their own choice. Typically they choose countries which are similar in terms of development, economic policies and political systems.[3] This choice is not possible in the framework of multilateral negotiations. However, a multilateral system of trading is still necessary to provide a framework for liberal trade among blocs and countries which are not members of any trading arrangement. Such a framework will become more important as trading blocs increase both in number and their coverage of world trade.

In summary, it is quite likely that the world economy in the future will rely upon both regional trading blocs and the multilateral trading system (WTO). This 'two-way' commitment of individual countries to the liberalisation of trade through regional arrangements *and* through multilateral negotiations may push the world economy further down the path towards the free trade than would sole reliance upon multilateral negotiations. However it should be not forgotten that this could still result in the waste of some resources as compared to a more gradual freeing of trade without regional blocs (for more on these issues see Bhagwati, 1993).

17.4 The WTO and regional preferential agreements

The WTO was established on 1 January 1995. Out of 104 countries which signed the Agreement Establishing the WTO in 1994 in Marrakesh, 79 ratified it and became the members of the WTO on its first day. There are some 50 other countries at various stages of completing their ratification procedure, and a number of countries currently negotiating their membership. Thus potentially the WTO will have larger membership than GATT (128 in 1994). Given the number of agreements reached under the Uruguay Round (see Appendix 17, p. 523), the WTO will also have much broader scope than the GATT, extending it to cover trade in services and trade in intellectual property too.

The basic functions of the WTO are the following (WTO, 1995a, p. 4):

• administering and implementing the multilateral and plurilateral trade agreements
• acting as a forum for multilateral trade negotiations
• actively seeking to resolve trade disputes
• cooperating with other international institutions involved in global policy making.

WTO is to adhere to the same fundamental principles of the multilateral trading system established by the GATT: non-discrimination, liberalisation, fairness of competition and encouragement of development and economic reform.

With respect to non-discrimination, Article I of the GATT binds the signatories (member states) to grant to the products of other members treatment no less favourable than that accorded to the product of any other country. Therefore, no one country should give special trading preferences to another. All countries should be competing on an equal basis. This principle remains a cornerstone of the current multilateral trading system. However as the GATT before it, the WTO now permits departures from this principle in the following situations:

(1) *countervailing duties* are allowed against foreign subsidies and as *anti-dumping measures* aimed at offending parties (Article VI)

(2) developing countries in general receive *special and differential treatment* such as preferentially lower tariffs in GATT-member DCs (Part IV)
(3) *customs unions* and *free trade areas* (Article XXIV)
(4) *economic integration* in the area of trade in services (Article V of the General agreement on trade in services, GATS).

In the context of this chapter our primary interest is in the last two categories of departures from the principle of non-discrimination, although the other categories represent equally important issues. In area of 'goods', the WTO takes over existing GATT provisions (Article XXIV, the Enabling Clause and other relevant decisions) supplemented by the Uruguay Round Understanding of Article XXIV. The original Article XXIV permits departures from the MFN obligation for preferential trading arrangements provided that: (1) other members are notified of the details, (2) such arrangements do not on the whole increase trade barriers against other members, and (3) such arrangements cover 'substantially all trade' between partners and commit them to reduce barriers to intra-regional trade within a reasonable length of time. This third condition requires additional explanation. In fact, it implies that Article XXIV allows for preferential agreements as long as they go all the way towards eliminating tariffs (that is, 100 per cent liberalisation). From today's perspective such a condition is not justified, as we know from the theory of second best that preferential agreements with less than a full liberalisation of trade are more likely to increase welfare.[4] This theoretical insight was discovered less than ten years after the incorporation of Article XXIV in the GATT. However the Article has not yet been changed to take this into account. Bhagwati (1993, p. 25) suggests three factors that explain the rationale behind this Article. First, it was believed that regional arrangements which allowed for the full elimination of trade barriers would result in a quasi-national unit with free trade and factor movements and should therefore be exempt from the MFN obligation towards other members. Secondly, it was taken for granted that since the number of these agreements with the full elimination of barriers would be limited, this condition would preclude the outbreak of all kinds of partial preferential agreements. Thirdly, and perhaps most importantly for the current debate, the architects of the GATT recognised that such arrangements could provide a complementary and practical method of achieving the universal free trade which was the ultimate goal of GATT. However, in practice Article XXIV has not been strictly observed. First it was weakened by the 1979 Enabling Clause which enabled developing countries creating preferential agreements among themselves to bypass Article XXIV. There were also some ambiguities in the language of the Article that have permitted different interpretations. The treatment of the EU was an important test for the fate of Article XXIV. For political reasons GATT members decided not to issue a formal ruling on the Treaty of Rome and its compatibility with the conditions of Article XXIV. This set the *modus operandi* with respect to the examination of preferential trading arrangements. Of the more than 70 regional trading arrangements (including amendments to existing agreements) which were notified to the GATT for examination up to 1990, only four were declared to be fully compatible with Article XXIV. These four were all small arrangements of non-OECD countries.[5] However no arrangement has been formally declared incompatible with the Article. This indicates the Article's lack of enforcement.

Notwithstanding the lax implementation of Article XXIV there is a broad agreement that preferential trading arrangements have not, at least until now, hindered the process of global liberalisation (with the obvious exception of the EU's CAP). This is because the rounds of multilateral negotiation that took place until the mid-1980s were successful both in terms of cuts in tariffs and in the speed of negotiation. On top of this there were some unilateral liberalisation actions which increased the level of trade liberalisation world-wide. However, with the recent surge in preferential trading arrangements there is a justified concern that something must be done to ensure the furthering of free trade across the globe. Since it is very unlikely that the interest in regional arrangements will fade, it is necessary to ensure that such arrangements cannot harm the global economy. To ensure this the Uruguay Round established a new world trade institution, the WTO. In addition, the Uruguay Round signatories agreed on an Understanding on clarifying several aspects of the operation of Article XXIV, but those changes fell short of what was in fact needed to ensure transparent and enforceable rules on regional agreements. Preceding the Uruguay Round Understanding many commentators in the area asked for radical changes in this area. De Melo, Panagariya and Rodrik (1993) called for free trade agreements to be taken out of Article XXIV so that only customs unions were allowed. The rationale behind this is that customs unions require a common external tariff (CET) to be set. Since WTO members have their tariffs 'bound' this would ensure that all tariffs were reduced to the level of the lowest prevailing tariff in the union at the time of creation. What happened to Spain, Greece and Portugal's tariff when they joined the EU is often quoted in support of this proposal. In addition customs unions do not require the quasi-protectionist rules of origin required in free trade areas. The problem with this proposal is the type of barriers it deals with. Tariffs have already been reduced significantly and it is non-tariff barriers (NTBs) that are most often used to protect local producers. Thus in tandem with the suggested revision of Article XXIV there would be a need to strengthen Articles VI and XIX in order to minimise the use of non-tariff barriers at the regional level.

To improve transparency, the Understanding requires that all agreements notified under Article XXIV be examined by a working party. The Understanding also asks for biennial reporting by members of regional agreements. More light is shed on the relationship between the invocation of the dispute-settlement provisions of the WTO, and the examinations of agreements under Article XXIV. The Understanding, however, falls short of addressing some of the more difficult issues. According to the WTO (1995b, p. 20) the requirement of 'substantially all trade' was not satisfactory clarified.[6]

On the other hand, there is a general sentiment that the Understanding has done a much better job in clarifying some other aspects of Article XXIV – for example the requirements about the height of the CET and other barriers imposed by a newly formed regional agreement. The Understanding provides guidelines for assessing the level of new protection focusing on a weighted average of tariff rates and custom duties collected, using applied rates (WTO, 1995b, p. 19). This still falls short of what McMillan (1993, p. 306) proposed by using the Kemp–Wan–Vanek theorem for the purpose of assessing whether regional agreements could be beneficial to global trade. The test he suggests is simple: does the agreement result in less trade between member countries and outsider countries? If the answer is negative than the agreement is compatible with the idea of global free trade and will not hurt the global economy. Winters (1996) however claims that the Kemp-Wan theorem has been misinterpreted and that it cannot be used for analysing changes in non-member countries' welfare. In contrast, he suggests that the focus should be turned to these countries' imports and the terms of trade changes.

■ *17.5* Summary

In this chapter we have studied two different forces at work in the international (world) trading system. Multilateralism, based on the GATT 1947 rules and their extensions, implies that countries will agree to and abide by the same trading rules with all of their trading partners. By any standards so constructed multilateral trading system served the world well. After the implementation of all the agreements of the Uruguay Round, the average tariffs on industrial goods will be a small fraction of what they were before countries began multilateral negotiations. Moreover, trade in other areas, including agricultural products, services, intellectual property and similar will be more liberal and also governed by universally accepted rules. Regionalism, whose resurgence coincided with difficulties encountered in completion of the Uruguay Round, implies either discriminatory or open integration of a subset of countries in the world economy through formation of any form of regional preferential agreements. The number of such agreements notified to the GATT in the 1990s was steadily increasing and this can be used as one, although not a very reliable, indicator of increased regionalisation of the world economy.

The central issue that we addressed in this chapter was the impact of increasing regionalism on the multilateral trading system; whether the proliferation of regional preferential agreements will hurt world welfare, and how likely the 'peaceful' and mutually beneficial coexistence of regionalism and multilateralism is. Although we found that regionalism may not necessarily be trade-diverting, more and more evidence shows that in fact it is likely to cause significant trade diversion (Bhagwati, 1993; Hindley and Messerlin, 1993; WTO, 1995b) and global welfare loss. Moreover, Krueger stresses that even if, in the long run, regional preferential agreements 'should evolve in ways consistent with multilateral liberalisation, the distraction of attention during WTO's formative phase must surely be counted as a significant cost' (Bhagwati and Krueger, 1995, p. 32).

■ *APPENDIX 17* THE URUGUAY ROUND

The Uruguay Round was officially launched in 1986 although the negotiation process had started already in 1982 at the GATT Ministerial meeting in Geneva. It took eight years to finally conclude this eighth Round of multilateral negotiations with the signing of the Final Act on 15 April 1994 in Marrakesh. At the same time the Agreement Establishing the World Trade Organisation (WTO) was made. Of the 125 countries which took part in negotiation of the Round, 111 signed the Final Act and 104 signed the WTO Agreement.

Table 17.1 *Multilateral trade rounds, 1947–94*

Year		Subject	No. of countries
1947	Geneva	Tariffs	23
1949	Annecy	Tariffs	13
1951	Torquay	Tariffs	38
1956	Geneva	Tariffs	26
1960–1	Dillon Round	Tariffs	26
1964–7	Kennedy Round	Tariffs and anti-dumping measures	62
1973–9	Tokyo Round	Tariffs, non-tariff measures and 'framework' agreements	102
1986–94	Uruguay Round	Tariffs, non-tariff measures, rules, services, intellectual property rights, dispute settlement, textiles and clothing, agriculture, establishment of the WTO and others	123

Source: WTO (1995a, p. 9).

It is hoped that the successful conclusion of the Uruguay Round will result in a substantial strengthening of the multilateral trading system. The reason is found in this Round's much broader coverage. In particular, the Uruguay Round: (1) provides much more detailed rules to govern the application of a number of trade policy measures, (2) devises new multilateral trade rules in the areas of intellectual property and trade in services, (3) goes further with tariff liberalisation in goods trade, (4) reduces the discriminatory aspects of regional trade agreements, (5) links together the various agreements concluded within a formal, institutional framework (i.e. WTO) and subjects them to an integrated dispute-settlement mechanism (UNCTAD, 1994, pp. 119–21). Perhaps more importantly the sheer fact that the Round was completed has added to the confidence about the future of the multilateral trading system and its relationship with the regional arrangements.

Three of the more relevant areas of the Uruguay Round are summarised below.

■ *Trade liberalisation*

There are four most important agreements: the general agreement on tariffs, that on agriculture, that on textiles, and that on government procurement which contributed the most to the significant cut in tariffs by 40 per cent (on average) achieved in this Round. The agreement on agriculture itself is a big success given the resistance of some of the major players (such as the EU and Japan) in the world arena to proposals to include agriculture in the trade talks in the first place. The agreement calls for significant reductions in export subsidies and also some reductions in domestic subsidies over a six-year period. It also requires NTBs to be transformed into equivalent tariffs which in turn are subject to a 36 per cent cut compared to 1986–90 level. However the developing countries are given easier conditions in terms both of the extent of tariff cuts and the time period within which they have to be completed (see Table 17.2).

For the last thirty years trade in textiles and clothing was treated by the GATT as an exceptional case and was subjected to the rules of the Multifibre Arrangement (MFA; see also Chapter 9). The provisions of the Uruguay Round ensure that the trade in textiles and clothing will return under the auspices of the WTO, although in several stages over a period of ten years. A specific transitional safeguard mechanism allows members to impose restrictions against individual countries if serious damage to the relevant domestic industry in an importing country could be proved.

Table 17.2 *The Uruguay Round's average tariff cuts for industrial goods*

Country/ group	Imports from MFN origins (bn $)	Trade-weighted average tariff (%)		Average tariff cut (%)
		Pre-UR	Post-UR	
DCs	736.9	6.3	3.9	38
Canada	28.4	9.0	4.8	47
EU	196.8	5.7	3.6	37
Japan	132.9	3.9	1.7	56
USA[a]	420.5	4.6	3.0	34
Developing countries[b]	305.1	15.3	12.3	20
Economies in transition	34.7	8.6	6.0	30

Note:
UR   Uruguay Round.
a   Based on data provided by USTR.
b   Based on bound rates, not applied rates.
Source: Hoda (1994) as cited in Schott (1994, Table 7, p. 61).

The new Agreements on government procurement ensures more open access to a broad range of government contracts and extension of the coverage of its obligations to certain specified services and to subnational entities (see also Chapter 9). Most of the commitments are extended on a reciprocal basis and do not apply to all signatories of the Uruguay Round.

Tariffs on industrial goods are cut more radically than in the previous Rounds. Also the Agreement binds maximum rates for about 60 per cent of developing countries products and almost all industrial country tariffs. Overall tariff reduction will reach a trade-weighted average of almost 40 per cent (see Table 17.2). In addition, the major trading countries will eliminate tariffs altogether for a number of products as a result of the so-called 'zero-for-zero' sectoral negotiations (Schott, 1994, pp. 10–12).

■ Trade rules

The most important agreements in this area are agreements on dumping and anti-dumping, subsidies and countervailing measures, and protection from imports in the form of 'safeguards'. Contrary to hopes of 'free trade' believers, the Uruguay Round still allows members to apply anti-dumping measures under almost the same conditions as before. It is true that the

Agreement provides for greater clarity and more detailed rules in relation to the determination of dumping and it also clarifies the role of dispute-settlement panels in disputes relating to anti-dumping actions taken by WTO members. However on the basis of economic criteria about desirability of anti-dumping measures this is one of the least successful Agreements of the Round.

The agreement on subsidies and countervailing measures is seen as an improvement upon the previous decisions in this area. The reasons are found in new anti-subsidy rules, and in the expanded list of proscribed practices. Although concerns have been raised about the potential for expanding subsidies in the so-called 'non-actionable' categories of subsidies, there is also allowance for imposing countermeasures against such practices.

The agreement on safeguards has become 'famous' for banning voluntary export restraints (VERs). Some other selective safeguards are allowed, however, in cases where serious injury of domestic industry can be proved. In such cases, a safeguard measure may be applied only to the extent necessary to prevent or remedy serious injury and to facilitate adjustment by the industry concerned. Safeguard measures are not applicable to products from developing countries as long as their share of imports of the product concerned does not exceed 3 per cent, and that such developing country members' collective import share accounts for no more than 9 per cent of total imports of the product concerned.

■ *New issues*

For the first time, multilateral trade negotiations covered rules for trade in services and in intellectual property, as well as trade-related investment measures. The General Agreement on Trade in Services (GATS) provides a framework for liberalising continuously increasing world trade in services. The agreement contains three elements: a framework of general rules and disciplines; annexes addressing special conditions relating to individual sectors; and national schedules of market access commitments. There are several novelties in this agreement compared to the GATT. Perhaps the most interesting is the introduction of a new concept of trade. For the purposes of regulating trade in services, this trade has been defined to include four modes of supply: supply through cross-border movement, the movement of consumers, commercial presence and the presence of natural persons. The agreement adapts the basic GATT principles, such as national treatment and non-discrimination, but places them in a different context.

The Agreement on Trade-related Intellectual Property Rights (TRIPS) establishes new trade disciplines with regard to patents, trademarks, copyrights, industrial designs and protection of undisclosed information and builds upon the provisions of existing World Intellectual Property Organisation (WIPO) instruments. The Agreement is seen as a possible efficient barrier for the intellectual property legislation of member states to become just one of NTBs.

The Agreement on Trade-related Investment Measures (TRIMs) was perhaps most difficult to conclude due to the strong opposition by developing countries and attempts by the DCs to use negotiation in this area to achieve some other objectives. As a result, the Agreement on TRIMs does not introduce new disciplines but prohibits those TRIMs which are inconsistent with some GATT principles related to national treatment (Article III) and quantitative restrictions (QRs) (Article XI).

List of Acronyms

ACP	African, Caribbean and Pacific (nations)
AEC	African Economic Community
AFTA	ASEAN free trade area
ANCOM	Andean Common Market
APEC	Asia–Pacific Economic Cooperation
ASEAN	Association of Southeast Asian Nations
BFT	bilateral free trade
CACM	Central American Common Market
CAP	Common Agricultural Policy
CARICOM	Caribbean Community
CBI	Caribbean Basin Initiative
CEAO	West Africa Economic Community
CEEAC	Economic Community of Central African States
CEFTA	Central Europe Free Trade Agreement
CEPGL	Economic Community of the Great Lake States
CER	Closer Economic Relations Agreement (Australia–New Zealand)
CET	common external tariff
CGE	computable general equilibrium
CMEA	Council for Mutual Economic Assistance
COMECON	*See* CMEA
CRS	constant returns to scale
CUSTA	Canada–US Free Trade Agreement
DC	developed country
DRC	domestic resource costs
EAEG	East Asia Economic Group
EC	European Community
ECO	Economic Cooperation Organisation
ECOWAS	Economic Community of West African States
ECSC	European Coal and Steel Community
ECU	European Currency Unit
EEA	European Economic Area
EEC	European Economic Community
EFTA	European Free Trade Association
EOS	economies of scale
ERP	effective rate of protection
EU	European Union

Euratom	European Atomic Energy Authority
FDI	foreign direct investment
FPE	factor-price equalisation
FTA	free trade area
GATS	General Agreement on Trade in Services
GATT	General Agreement on Tariffs and Trade
GCC	Cooperation Council for the Arab States of the Gulf
GDP	gross domestic product
GNP	gross national product
HOS	Heckscher–Ohlin–Samuelson (model)
HOT	Heckscher–Ohlin theorem
HOV	Heckscher–Ohlin–Vanek (theorem)
ILO	International Labour Organisation
IRS	increasing returns to scale
ISI	import-substitution industrialisation
ITC	International Trade Commission (US)
LAFTA	Latin American Free Trade Area
LAIA	Latin American Integration Association
LDC	less developed country
LTA	Long Term Arrangement Regarding Trade in Cotton Textiles
MAGHREB	Union of the Arab Maghreb
MERCOSUR	Common Market of the South
MFA	Multifibre Arrangement
MFT	multilateral free trade
MFN	most-favoured-nation (treatment)
MNC	multinational corporation
MRU	Mano River Union
NAFTA	North American Free Trade Agreement
NIE	newly-industrialised economy
NRP	nominal rate of protection
NTB	non-tariff barrier
OECD	Organisation for Economic Cooperation and Development
OECS	Organisation of Eastern Caribbean States
OEEC	Organisation for European Economic Cooperation; *see* OECD
OMA	orderly marketing arrangement
PPF	production possibility frontier
PTA	preferential trading arrangements
QR	quantitative restriction
R&D	research & development
RFE	Ricardian Factor Endowment (theorem)
RIA	regional integration agreement
RTA	regional trading agreement

SACU	South African Customs Union
SADCC	Southern African Development Cooperation Conference
SEZ	Special Economic Zone (China)
SFT	sectoral free trade
SST	Stolper–Samuelson theorem
TR	transferable rouble
TRIMS	Agreement on Trade-related Investment Measures
TRIPS	Agreement on Trade-related Intellectual Property Rights
UDEAC	Central African Customs and Economic Union
UFT	unilateral free trade
UNCTAD	United Nations Conference on Trade and Development
USTR	United States Trade Representative
VER	voluntary export restraint
VIE	voluntary imports expansion
WHFTA	Western Hemisphere Free trade Area
WIPO	World Intellectual Property Organisation
WTO	World Trade Organisation

Glossary of Terms

Absolute advantage   The greater efficiency in terms of input requirements that one country may have over the rest of the world in the production of a particular good.

Ad valorem tariff   A tariff equal to a given percentage of selling price.

Anti-dumping duties   An *ad valorem* tariff imposed specifically on dumped imports. It is used when dumping is causing or threatening to cause material injury to an import-competing industry.

Armington assumption   Assumes that otherwise 'identical' products are imperfect substitutes for one another only because they are produced in different countries.

ASEAN Free Trade Agreement (AFTA)   The ASEAN countries announced in 1992 their intention to establish a free trading area among themselves, AFTA.

Asia–Pacific Economic Cooperation (APEC)   Launched in 1989 with 12 original members (the six members of ASEAN, the USA, Canada, Japan, South Korea, Australia and New Zealand). In 1991 China, Hong Kong and Taiwan joined the group. The policy of open regionalism, whose main thrust is non discriminatory, makes the APEC different from other regional blocs.

Assimilative capacity   The capacity of the environment to absorb or tolerate pollutants. The lower it is, the more enviromental damage will be caused by the emission of a given amount of pollutants.

Association of Southeast Asian Nations (ASEAN)   Founded in 1967 mainly out of concern for political security in Southeast Asia. The original member states Brunei, Indonesia, Malaysia, the Philippines, Singapore and Thailand were joined by Vietnam in 1995.

Autarky   The absence of international trade; closed national economy.

Bastable's test   Requires the protected industry to be able to pay back the national losses incurred during the period of protection. *See also* Mill's test.

Bertrand model   A model of oligopoly (duopoly) based on the assumption that neither firm expects its rivals to react to price changes.

Bias of the trade regimes   Measured as the ratio of the effective rate of protection of importables and the effective rate of protection of exportables. When the ratio is equal to one, trade regime is *neutral*. If the ratio exceeds one, then the regime favours importables.

Bilateralism   Preferential trading agreement between two countries.

Binding of tariffs   Tariff rates included in a country's schedule of concessions. Once a tariff is bound, it may not be increased unless affected parties are compensated.

Brain drain   The migration of educated and highly skilled labour from poorer (in principle, developing countries) to richer countries (most often the USA).

Canada–US Trade Agreement (CUSTA)   The bilateral agreement between Canada and the USA signed in 1988 with the objectives of eliminating trade barriers in goods and services, facilitating fair competition, liberalising investment conditions and establishing a joint mechanism to resolve trade disputes.

Cartels   An (international) organisation of oligopolistically competitive firms set up with the purpose of maximising their collective profits (also known as collusion).

Cascading or escalating tariffs   Progressively higher tariff rates as the stage of processing of goods advances, resulting in high effective rates of protection of final products.

Cecchini report   A study by a group of experts chaired by Paolo Cecchini on the costs and benefits of the creation of the Single Market (or 'Europe 1992') without internal frontiers in which the free movement of goods, persons, services and capital is ensured in accordance with the provisions of the Rome treaty.

Central European Free Trade Agreement (CEFTA)   A free trade agreement of 1993 linking the Czech Republic, Slovakia, Hungary, Poland and Slovenia. The main objective is to eliminate trade barriers among the countries concerned but also to weaken the anti-intra-area trade which developed during the transition process.

Ceteris paribus assumption   The assumption that all other relevant factors are held constant when examining the influence of one particular variable in an economic model.

Chinese Economic Area   This area developed rapidly after the mid-1980s and, while centering on Hong Kong, includes Taiwan and China's special economic zones (SEZs).

Closer Economic Relations Agreement between New Zealand and Australia (CER) This agreement, which replaced the 1966 New Zealand–Australia Free Trade Agreement, came into force in 1983 and was reviewed twice afterwards, in 1988 and 1992. It is seen as a hybrid between a free trade area and a common market.

Coalescence Trading blocs extend progress towards the freeing of global trade by extending country coverage and in some cases by the joining of the blocks or through joint membership.

Common Agricultural Policy (CAP) The common system of agricultural price supports and grants adopted by the EU.

Common market Transcends a *customs union* as it also entails the free movement of labour, capital and other factors of production as well as free movement of enterprises among member countries.

Comparative advantage The greater *relative* efficiency in terms of input requirements that one country may have over the rest of the world in the production of a particular good.

Computable general equilibrium methods (CGE methods) They use models that are theoretically rigorous but then the parameters may be chosen by using ad hoc methods, such as calibration.

Concertina method Reduction of the highest tariff rates to a specified level, while leaving all lower rates intact. *Extended* concertina method implies in addition to the cuts in the highest rates also the rise in the lowest tariff rates.

Cone of diversification Factor endowments of a country that lie in between the factor intensity ratios of the two sectors, enabling this country to produce both goods (that is, to diversify) by fully employing factors in these two sectors. If the total factor endowment lies outside this cone, the country has to specialise in one good only.

Consumption possibility frontier A locus of all possible combinations of two goods that a country can consume, given the relative prices of goods and technology for production.

Contract curve The set of all the efficient allocations of goods among individuals in an exchange economy. Each of these allocations has the property that no one individual can be made better off without making someone else worse off.

Countervailing duties A tariff introduced by an importing country with the objective of raising the prices of the subsidised products.

Cournot model A model of oligopoly (duopoly) based on the assumption that neither firm expects its rivals to react to changes in output.

Current account   An account in the balance of payments. Includes transactions such as exports and imports of goods and services, interest receipts and payments and other income, and current transfers.

Customs union   Involves the suppression of all intra-area trade barriers among member countries and the establishment of a common set of external tariffs (CETs) on imports from non-members.

De-industrialisation   A development in a national economy towards an increasing share of domestic output and employment being created by economic activities other than activities of an industrial (manufacturing) sector. In most cases activities such as services account for an increasing share of employment and gross domestic output.

Deadweight loss   The net cost to society of distorting the domestic free trade price. Also known as *efficiency loss*.

Deepening   The evolution of an economic integration by means of increased economic and political integration of existing member states.

Differentiated products   Products that are considered to be similar because they belong to the same industry or the general product group (and are produced by using similar factor intensities) but have such characteristics that it is possible for consumers to distinguish the product (variety) of one producer from its competitor's product (variety). Examples include different varieties of soft drinks, beer, cigarettes, or trade books!

Dispute settlement   The process by which members settle trade problems through negotiated means or with the help of a WTO (previously GATT) panel of experts which rules on legal questions and recommends solutions.

Domestic distortion argument   Is in favour of using trade restrictions to offset the impact of already existing market failures or distortions in goods and/or factor markets.

Dumping   A situation where a firm sells its product at a lower price in its export markets than in its domestic market.

DUPs or directly unproductive profit-seeking activities   Activities which are profitable but do not directly produce any goods or services. Since they use up resources but do not contribute towards national product, they are seen as wasteful.

Dutch disease   A phenomenon by which the profitability of one sector is squeezed as a result of a boom in other traded sectors of national economy. The phenomenon got the name after the development in the Netherlands' gas industry by which the relative competitiveness of the Dutch traditional industrial sector was reduced as a result of the appreciation of the Dutch florin caused by the growth of the Dutch natural gas industry.

Dynamic comparative advantage The pattern of international specialisation shifts depending on countries' overall factor endowments and technological changes.

Dynamic economies of scale See *Learning-by-doing* below.

Dynamic effects Are seen as one of many ways through which a customs union, or economic integration in general, may influence the rate of growth of those countries participating, such as economies of scale, increased competition, the stimulation of investment and technical change.

Econometric methods By using these methods and techniques it is possible to estimate all parameters by positing very simple models or by focusing on only a few endogenous variables.

Economic integration The discriminatory removal of all trade impediments between participating nations, often accompanied by the establishment of certain elements of cooperation and coordination such as the partial or full harmonisation of economic policies in one or more areas. Economic integration can take many different forms such as a *free trade area*, a *customs union*, a *common market*, an *economic union* or *total economic integration*.

Economic union A *common market* where national economic policies such as trade, monetary, fiscal and welfare policies are harmonised.

Economies of scale A production process exhibits EOS over a particular range of output per unit of time if average costs over this range decline as output increases.

ECU Abbreviation for the European currency unit, made up of a basket comprising different proportions of the currencies of each member state of the EU.

Effective protection A measure of the difference between value added in domestic industry and value added at world prices expressed in percentage terms. The extent of this difference is influenced by tariffs and other trade restrictions.

Engine of growth The view that rising exports led to rapid growth and development of the economies of the regions of recent settlement in the nineteenth century.

Entrepôt trade Refers to the importing of commodities for the purpose of re-exporting them after they have been repacked and relabelled for the final destination.

Environmental dumping It is claimed that countries with lax environmental policies have lower costs of production and therefore an unfair trade advantage. Known also as *eco-dumping*.

Equivalent tariff   The tariff rate which reduces imports to the same level as they occur under a quota.

Euro   The name of the future single currency in the EU. The first coins and notes of Euro are expected to be put into circulation in 2002.

Europe Agreements   These are the agreements signed between the EU and the individual Central and Eastern European countries (transition economies) setting a new framework for their mutual economic relationships. The agreements' major provisions include: the introduction of free trade in industrial goods within a period of ten years; improved access for agricultural products; a commitment to harmonise economic legislation with that in the EU; EU financial and technical assistance, and possibly introduction of free trade in services. Among the transition economies it is widely accepted that Europe Agreements are used as stepping stones to membership in the EU.

European Economic Area (EEA)   An agreement to create full freedom of movement for goods, services, capital, persons, and enterprises throughout Europe.

European Free Trade Area (EFTA)   Created in 1960 by Austria, Denmark, Norway, Portugal, Sweden, Switzerland and the UK with the objectives of establishing free trade in industrial goods among members and negotiating a comprehensive trade agreement with the EU.

Ex ante studies   Aim to predict the effects of trade liberalisation on prospective integrations or existing integrations which are to enlarged.

Ex post studies   Aim to evaluate the effects of integrations which already exist. This method involves examining the changes in trade patterns which have taken place as a result of a integration and comparing them with a hypothetical situation where the integration does not exist.

Ex-post or implicit tariff   Calculated as the ratio of the total customs collections for a particular product and the total value of imports of this product; this rate measures the actual protection rate.

Export bias   A case where a growth in factor endowments causes disproportionate change in the country's production mix so that it favours production for export.

Export condition   A country will export a good if and only if its relative wage rate is low enough to offset any possible absolute cost disadvantage in producing that good.

Export pessimism   A belief that DCs would not be able to absorb the increased exports of primary products from the developing countries. This is the so-called old export pessimism argument. The new export pessimism argument is based on fears of losing access to the DCs markets due to raising import barriers to the products from developing countries.

Export promotion   Efforts to expand the volume of exports through export incentives and other means such as export credit insurance or marketing boards.

Export promotion strategy   The policy that involves increasing the output of export goods relative to non-traded goods or import substitutes. Often identified with *outward oriented strategy*.

Export subsidy   Direct or indirect payments from government to a domestic producer/exporter enabling him or her to sell goods abroad at lower prices than in the domestic market.

Export-led growth   National economic growth being driven by fast and steady increases in national exports.

External debt   The debt owed to foreigners. A country accumulates debt by borrowing finance or importing goods and services against an obligation to pay later.

External economies of scale   The firm's average costs decrease with the size of the industry and the firm's output alone has no effect on its average costs. Hence, large firms have no advantage over small firms within the same industry.

Externality or external (dis)economy   An effect of one economic agent on another that is not taken into account by normal market behaviour. Externalities arise because of market failure; most often such a failure is related to inability to define and enforce property rights.

Factor abundance   The relative quantities of factors of production in a country. It can be also defined in terms of the relative prices of the factors. It is used as a basis for the Heckscher–Ohlin explanation of the pattern of trade. Also known as *factor endowment*.

Factor content of trade   The amounts of each factor that are used to produce exports and imports. It is a modified way of defining the relative factor endowments.

Factor intensity   Refers to the proportion of factors used in the production of any one good. Also known as *factor proportions*.

Factor intensity uniformity   An assumption that the same factor-intensities will be used in the production of the same goods across countries. In other words, factor intensity reversals are assumed away.

Factor-intensity reversal   Refers to a situation where a good is classified as being intensive in one factor (say, capital) at one level of relative factor prices, and then at the changed level of relative factor prices it becomes intensive in the other factor (that is, labour). The absence of factor intensity reversals requires that a good remains intensive in the same factor at *all* relative factor prices.

Factor-price equalisation theorem   Postulates that under the assumptions of no factor-intensity reversals and no complete specialisation, free trade in goods will equalise both absolute and the real factor prices across countries.

Factor-price frontier   Locus of possible equilibria comprising the portions of the *iso-price curves* that lie furthest from the origin. In equilibrium the elasticity of this frontier reflects the ratio of the shares of output going to the two factors.

Factors of production   The resources, such as labour, capital, land and entrepreneurship a country uses in the process of production.

FDI-led integration   Occurs when the activities of firms, predominantly multinationals, (MNCs) drives the integrative initiative.

First mover advantage   Firm that makes 'the first move' (such as introduction of a new product, new advertising approach, new technology or similar) often ends up having a substantial advantage (in a long run) over other firms in the same industry. Typically that advantage materialises as an ability to charge high prices and retain substantial market share.

Footloose manufactures   Products whose production is not linked to particular locations by specific requirements. Consequently, such a production can be established anywhere.

Foreign direct investment   Transactions that provide the investor with an equity position in a company, made with the objective of obtaining a lasting interest. The recipient company is considered to be a direct investment company if a foreign direct investor owns 10 per cent of the ordinary shares or voting power.

Free trade area   All tariff restrictions among participating countries are removed but each country retains its own national tariff barriers against non-members.

Gains from trade   Most simply, an increase in the level of welfare of the whole country (or world) resulting from opening up international trade. It can be expressed as an increase in real income for the country's (or world's) given input of factors or as the same real income achieved by a lesser input of factors. The gains are split into two categories depending on the source of origin: gains from exchange (trade) and gains from specialisation.

Gastarbeiter   Foreign workers from less developed (southern) European countries who were invited to temporarily move to Germany (and later

Austria, and Switzerland) to ease the problem of shortage of mostly unskilled labour in the 1960s.

General Agreement on Tariffs and Trade (GATT) An international agreement signed in 1947 to set out the rules of conduct for international trade relations and to provide a forum for multilateral negotiations regarding trade liberalisation.

Generalised system of preferences (GSP) A scheme accepted through *UNCTAD* by which the DCs agreed not to charge any duty on imports from developing countries, while maintaining duties on imports from other DCs, therefore giving a preference to a trade with developing countries. With time more and more goods were excluded from the scheme so that its effectiveness was significantly reduced.

Globalisation The global integration of the world economy through MNCs and foreign direct investment (FDI).

Growth-led exports A view arising from a new growth theory where the source of fast rising exports in the East Asian economies is found in dynamic national growth which is in turn based on internalisation of dynamic investment, knowledge and similar effects.

Harberger triangles Triangles that approximate the size of the cost of the imposition of the tariff (that is, deadweight loss).

Headquarters services Services such as management, accounting, marketing, R&D which a multinational corporation 'produces' in the home location and uses in all other locations it operates in.

Heckscher–Ohlin theorem States that each country exports the commodity which requires for its production relatively intensive use of the factor in relative abundance in that country.

Heckscher–Ohlin–Vanek theorem Postulates that a country will export services of factors of production in which it is abundant, and import the services of factors of production in which it is scarce.

Homothetic preferences or tastes When consumers exhibit homethetic taste they purchase all goods and services in the same proportion at all levels of income (i.e. indifference curves do not rotate as the consumer's level of income changes but have the same slope along any line from the origin).

Horizontal integration The production of a differentiated product in foreign subsidiaries when the same product is also produced domestically.

Human capital Refers to investments (in the form of education, on-the-job-training, or improved health) in workers which increase their productivity.

Immiserising growth   Refers to the case where an increase in production of an output leads to a such strong terms of trade effects that a country's economic welfare is diminished.

Imperfect competition   A generic term which refers to any form of market structure other than perfect competition (i.e. monopoly, monopolistic competition and oligopoly).

Implicit tariff   A differential between the post-quota domestic price and the world free trade price.

Import bias   A case where a growth in factor endowments causes disproportionate change in the country's production mix so that it favours production for substitution of imports.

Import quota   A maximum amount of imports of a good allowed to enter the country during some specified time period.

Import substitutes   Goods and services that a country produces domestically but also imports.

Import substituting industrialisation (ISI) strategy   Set of policies which as a common objective have a reduction of imports and their substitution by domestically produced goods and services. Also known as an *inward looking strategy*.

Incidence of protection parameter   The effect of import and export protection on the price of non-traded goods.

Increasing opportunity costs   The amount of good (say, A) whose production has to be forgone to obtain one more unit of another good (say, B). Increases as the process of transformation of production from one good (A) to another good (B) is continued.

Increasing returns to scale   A technology exhibits increasing returns to scale over a particular range of output per unit of time if an equiproportional increase in all inputs results in a more than proportionate expansion of output.

Indebtedness   The financial obligation to make payment in cash, goods or services to a creditor in accordance with contractual arrangements.

Infant industry argument   Finds the reason for protection in the belief that some industries require temporary protection in order to develop into internationally competitive industries.

Infant industry protection   Trade protection granted to an industry during its infancy to protect it against competition from already established and efficient foreign firms. It is shown in the text that there are other policies (such as production subsidy) which assist the domestic infant industry at lower social cost.

Input–output table   A table (in a matrix form) showing the origin and destination of each product in the economy.

Intermittent dumping   Disposal of occasional surpluses by exporting them at exceptionally low prices without any plans to eliminate competition. Known also as *sporadic dumping*.

Internal economies of scale   The firm's average costs decline as its own output increases. Hence, large firms have a cost advantage over smaller firms even when they belong to the same industry.

Intertemporal trade   A view of international capital movements as a way for countries to trade over time: the country with a capital inflow is in effect trading future goods in exchange for present goods. Such a country runs a current account deficit (a capital account surplus) at the present time.

Intra-industry trade   Trade in differentiated products that belong to the same industry or broad product group.

Iso-cost line   It links the various combinations of two inputs that can be purchased with a certain amount of money.

Iso-price curve   It links those combinations of wage rates and rental rates which are consistent with zero profits at a given commodity price.

Kemp–Wan theorem   It is always possible for a regional integration formed among an arbitrary group of countries to restructure itself in such a way as to make member countries better off without making any of the non-member countries worse off.

Labour theory of value   Any theoretical framework proposing that the value or the price of any good or service is determined on the basis of the labour input, direct or indirect, required in its production.

Large country   A country which has some influence over the world price of the imported or exported product.

Learning curve   A relationship showing a decrease in unit costs as a function of cumulative number of units of output produced. Alternatively, it can relate cumulative average output per worker/week to the cumulative output.

Learning-by-doing   Increases in efficiency (as measured by reduced production costs) arise from actual production experience, where experience is measured as the sum of all past outputs. The more a firm has produced, the lower its unit costs tend to be, all else being equal. It is also referred to as *dynamic economies of scale*.

Leontief paradox   The empirical finding by W. Leontief that in 1947 the capital-labour ratio in US imports exceeded that in US exports. The result contradicted the predictions of the HO theorem that the United States, a capital-abundant country, should export capital-intensive goods.

Leontief technology   A technology where factors (say, capital and labour) must be used in the fixed proportions to produce output.

Lerner paradox   A situation in which the terms of trade of a large country imposing a tariff worsen instead of improving.

Lerner symmetry theorem   States that in general equilibrium an across the board export tax has the same effect as one on imports of the same *ad valorem* rate.

Locational advantages   A group of reasons put forward to explain the existence of multinational corporations. Essentially the question is of comparative advantage, and it can be explained by the difference in resources, existence of transport costs and barriers to free trade.

Long-run   A period of time over which all factors of production can be varied by the producer (but not sufficiently long to change the technology of production). In terms of our analysis the long run corresponds to free intersectoral factor mobility.

Love for variety   An assumption that individuals prefer to consume some goods (i.e. differentiated goods) in many varieties so that utility increases with a number of varieties consumed.

Made-to-measure tariff   A tariff which would equalise the price of imports to domestic price so as to allow a domestic producer to stay in the market. Because it is supposed to equalise marginal costs to marginal benefits in each industry, it is said to be delivering the policy goals (often non-economic) at minimum cost to society. Known also as *scientific tariff*; the terms were introduced by Corden (1974).

Magnification effect   The result (related to the Stolper–Samuelson and Rybczynski theorems) that the price of a factor (the output of a good) changes more than proportionately in response to a change in the price of a good intensive in that factor (in an endowment of a factor intensively used in that good).

Marshall Plan   The programme of US assistance for a European economic recovery after the Second World War proposed by General George Marshall. The assistance consisted of shipments of goods, provision of services and loans which financed public investment projects.

Maximum revenue tariff   An amount of tariff that results in a maximum revenue.

Metzler paradox   A situation in which the tariff-imposing country's terms of trade improve by so much that its domestic relative price of importables in fact falls as compared to the free trade level.

Mill's test The requirement that the industry eventually becomes internationally competitive. This is one of the two requirements necessary for the infant industry protection to be socially beneficial. *See also* Bastable's test.

Monopolistic competition A market structure characterised by a large number of firms, product differentiation based on increasing returns, and easy entry/exit.

Monopoly A market structure where one firm produces a product with no close substitutes, and where there is no immediate possibility of entry by other firms.

Most-favoured-nation (MFN) rule The requirement that members of the WTO shall extend unconditionally to all other contracting members any advantage, favour, privilege or immunity affecting customs duties, charges, rules and procedures that they give to products originating in or destined for any other country.

Most-favoured-nation status (MFN) A country agrees not to charge tariffs on another country's goods that are any higher than those it imposes on the goods of any other country.

Multilateralism Has the objective of achieving non-discriminatory free trade for all countries.

Multinational corporation (MNC) Typically a large corporation having a headquarters in one country but operating subsidiaries in other countries.

National treatment Treating imported goods and services no less favourably than domestic goods and services with respect to internal taxes, regulations and other requirements.

Net resource transfer The difference between the amount of fresh loans and the amount of payments towards interest and principal and any other outflow of capital from the debtor country.

Nominal protection Measures an amount by which protection increases the domestic price of the protected good above the world price.

Non-economic arguments for protection Justify the imposition of trade barriers for non-economic reasons, that is, to achieve an objective that is not directly related to economic welfare. Examples include goals related to national defence, national pride and national foreign policy.

Nontraded goods The goods that do not enter international trade but are produced and consumed domestically by each country (such as personal services by local factors, i.e. haircut or surgery).

North American Free Trade Agreement (NAFTA)   A trilateral free trade zone between Mexico, Canada and the USA implemented in 1994. With a population of 360 mn and a GNP of over US$7,000 bn, this is the world's largest free trade zone.

Numeraire   A unit of account or a standard of value. Typically money is used as a numeraire by which different commodities' values are comparable.

Offer curve   A curve that shows the quantity of imports a country demands to be willing to supply various quantities of its exports at given world prices.

Oligopoly   A market structure characterised by a small number of mutually interdependent firms in terms of their choice variables (for example, sales, prices, or investments). Products may be either homogeneous or differentiated.

Open regionalism   Regional economic integration without discriminating against non-member countries and led predominantly through market processes not government policies.

Openness   An indicator of *outward orientation* determined by the ratio of foreign trade to national GDP. The higher such a ratio, the more open an economy is.

Opportunity costs   A cost of one good expressed in the amount of a second good that must be given up to release sufficient resources to produce one more unit of the first good.

Optimum tariff   The amount of a tariff that raises the welfare of a tariff-imposing country by the greatest amount relative to free trade welfare levels.

Outward oriented strategy   The strategy that encourages *free trade* including free movements of factors of production and foreign direct investment, and a free flow of information. It is also known as implying a support to the country's industries revealing actual or potential comparative advantage.

Pareto optimality   A state when the economy's resources and output are allocated in such a way that no reallocation can make anyone better off without making at least one other person worse off.

Persistent dumping   A long-term continuous selling of export goods at a lower price than in the domestic market; a price policy known as the *international price discrimination*.

Petro-dollars Deposits in banks and financial institutions arising from OPEC trade surpluses.

Polarisation The accentuation of regional differences due to the inter-regional migration of factors of production. If all factors concentrate in the advanced regions, growth rates will diverge between the different regions of the integration.

Policy-endogenous DUPs Their objective is to influence the government in its decisions with respect to the level and type of protection. This influence could be achieved by *lobbying* and by *strategic behaviour*.

Policy-exogenous DUPs Activities which take a given (trade) policy as fixed and focus on redistribution of revenues or rents generated by this policy. Examples of such activities are *rent-seeking, revenue-seeking* and *smuggling*.

Policy-led integration Occurs when the initiatives towards integration flow from national economic policies focusing on the reduction of trade barriers between members.

Political economy Study of the economic process focusing on the inter-relationship between the practical aspects of political action and the pure theory of economics.

Pollution haven hypothesis Holds that firms will relocate their production operations in countries with weaker environmental standards. Evidence does not support this hypothesis.

Portfolio investments The purchase of financial assets without an objective to gain control. Usually arranged through banks and other financial institutions.

Prebisch–Singer hypothesis The argument that primary-product export orientation of the developing countries results in a secular decline in their terms of trade.

Predatory dumping Occurs when foreign suppliers set prices below costs with the objective of driving domestic producers out of business.

Pro-competitive effects Effects from increased competition when free trade is introduced in the presence of imperfect competition.

Product cycle hypothesis The hypothesis that new products introduced by highly innovative industrialised countries and produced initially with a high proportion of skilled labour eventually become standardised and can be produced in other nations (imitators) with less skilled labour.

Production possibility frontier or transformation curve   The locus of the alternative combinations of two goods that a country can produce by fully utilising all resources and using the best available technology.

Profit shifting   The effect of trade on the distribution of profits between countries when there is imperfect competition such as oligopoly.

Prohibitive tariff   The tariff which increases domestic price by an amount so as to equalise domestic demand with domestic supply, thus making imports unnecessary.

Protective effect   The quantity by which domestic producers are able to increase their production due to tariff protection.

Rationalisation effects   Effects arising from reorganisation of production to take advantage of economies of scale; typically there are fewer firms in a market each producing larger volume.

Reaction functions   In a Cournot duopoly the reaction functions specify for each firm the optimum amount of output given the amount of output chosen by its competitor. More generally, the reaction function specifies an optimum value for a choice variable for any firm, given the value of that variable chosen by competitors.

Real wages   Wage rates that are expressed in terms of good(s) the workers can buy.

Reciprocal dumping   A situation where dumping by the two firms comprising an international duopoly leads to intra-industry trade in an identical product (also known as cross-hauling).

Reciprocity condition   States that the effect of an increase in a commodity price on a factor return is exactly the same as the effect of an increase in the corresponding factor endowment on the output of that commodity.

Reciprocity principle   Requires that all contracting parties of GATT (WTO) grant each other terms as favourable as they give to any other country with respect to imports and exports of products. Known also as *quid pro quo.*

Regionalisation   The apparent increase in the importance of regional trade arrangements.

Regionalism   Preferential trading agreements among a subset of countries in the world.

Regression analysis   An analysis which involves the fitting of a formally expressed relationship (a regression equation) to a set of data for the purposes, for example, of testing economic hypothesis.

Relative price The price of one good (service, factor) expressed in terms of the price of another good (service, factor). When speaking about goods, relative price is equal to the opportunity cost of one good and can be read off as the slope of the PPF.

Rent-seeking Process of wasting resources by chasing politically created scarcity premiums or rents.

Resource movement effect Contraction of output in non-booming sectors of an economy. It is a result of the boom in one sector of the economy which causes the marginal productivity of labour to rise and thus attracts labour away from the other sectors. This is one of the effects occurring in Dutch disease. Another possible effect is the spending effect.

Results-based trade policy An approach in setting trade regulations wherein trade negotiations and trade restrictions can be targeted to achieve certain specific objectives. Commentators in this field cite the trade policy formulation in the USA in the 1990s as an example.

Revenue effect The amount of revenue accruing to a government from a tariff (or any other similar policy instrument).

Revenue-seeking Process of pre-empting of the revenues of tariffs or other taxes.

Round A series of multilateral trade negotiations such as the Uruguay Round.

Rules of origin Restrict the freedom of intra-area trade in products which incorporate certain proportions of imported products or undergo certain transformation process in member countries.

Rules-based trade policy Each country commits itself to obeying international norms agreed through the GATT/WTO in setting its trade regulations.

Rybczynski theorem States that at constant commodity and factor prices, an increase in one factor endowment will cause the output of the good intensive in that factor to increase by a greater proportion, and will reduce the output of the other good.

Safeguards Emergency action taken by a government to restrict the quantity of imports which are causing or threatening to cause serious injury.

Secondary tariffs Additional taxes being imposed on imports; may be called import surcharge, equalisation tax or stamp duty.

Short run   A period of time over which some the level of utilisation can be changed only for some, so-called, variable factors of production, while the rest of the factors or production are regarded as being fixed. In terms of our analysis the short run corresponds to factor specificity.

Small country   A country that cannot affect the world price of goods.

Smuggling   Illegal activities seeking to evade trade policy, such as import duties or prohibition of imports.

Social dumping   Claims that industries in countries with lower labour standards (including denial of basic rights) have an unfair advantage over industries in countries with higher labour standards.

Social indifference curve   An indifference curve that gives all alternative combinations of two commodities which, if distributed optimally among the members of the society, produce the same amount of welfare. This social indifference curve has all the standard properties of an individual indifference curve and is known as *Samuelson's* social indifference curve. There are other definitions and types of social indifference curves (cf. Samuelson, 1956).

Social welfare function   A hypothetical device that records societal views about equity among individuals. Therefore it does not only reflects efficiency concerns (that is, maximisation of welfare requires an equalisation of marginal rates of substitution for all individuals) but also distributional ones (that is, more equitable distribution increases welfare).

Specific factors   Factors are known to be fixed in a particular sectoral usage for some time. In such a case, factors are not mobile between sectors within national economy. This is common for most factors in the short run, while for some factors (such as agricultural land) the specificity of their usage can be long-term in nature.

Specific tariff   A tariff equal to a fixed amount of money per unit of measurement of goods.

Specificity rule   The most efficient form of intervention to achieve a given objective is the one which attacks the target directly.

Spending effect   A higher real income from the boom in the export sector induces greater expenditure which causes the prices of non-traded goods to rise, which may cause the output of non-traded goods to rise too. Thus this effect works in the opposite direction from the resource movement effect.

Spread effects   Involve the diffusion of technology and externalities throughout the integration because the fast growth of the centre increases the demand for other regions' products leading therefore to higher growth in those areas as well.

Static effects Revealed by a comparison of the magnitude of the trade creation and trade diversion effects.

Stoper–Samuelson theorem States that when both factors remain fully employed, an increase in the relative price of a good will unambiguously increase the real return to the factor used relatively intensively in the production of that good, while the real return to the other factor will be reduced in terms of both goods.

Strategic arguments for protection Based on new insights from the theory of trade policy when prices depart from marginal costs and when there is a potential strategic role for government action in shifting the terms of trade to the benefit of domestic firms.

Strategic trade policy An idea that an activist trade policy in markets characterised with oligopolistic competition and increasing returns can improve national welfare.

Sunset industry argument Is in favour of granting some temporary protection to mature industries on the ground that, given enough time, they will be able to re-equip and regain competitiveness.

Tariff dispersion Range of tariff rates within a country's tariff schedule.

Tariff factories Direct investment made by a company from a low-cost country into a country or economic integration characterised by higher costs of production to avoid high import tariffs and supply this market domestically.

Tariff redundancy or 'water in the tariff' A phenomenon occuring when a tariff has no impact on the level of imports because of some other policy being superior to the tariff. For example, a tariff of 10 per cent on the imports of heroin has no impact on the quantity imported since there is a ban on imports of this product.

Tariffication Replacement of quantitative restrictions or other non-tariff barriers with approximate tariff equivalents.

Technological gap model Exports of new goods is based on technological gap between countries. A country leading in knowledge and innovation (but having an expensive labour force) becomes exporter of new goods since other countries lack this knowledge of the technology. When the knowledge becomes widespread production shifts to new locations characterised by low wages. Export of the product becomes based on low cost of production.

Terms of trade In a two-good model, the ratio of the price of the exported good to the price of the imported good (also known as commodity terms of trade).

Terms of trade effect   The extra revenue collected from foreign suppliers who are willing to share the tariff burden with domestic consumers by reducing price.

Theory of second best   If there are distortions existing in an economy that prevent it from functioning under perfect competition, then it may be best for government to use policies that add more distortions.

Total economic integration   Implies the full unification of national economic policies as well as the establishment of a central authority whose decisions are binding for all member countries.

Trade creation   Represents the substitution of inefficient (higher-cost) domestic production by efficient regional partner country production.

Trade deflection   The entry of imports from the rest of the world into the low-tariff member of a free trade area to avoid the higher tariffs of other members.

Trade diversion   Shifts the trade flows from non-member countries to member countries in response to the tariff discrimination produced by the customs union formation.

Trade modification   The change in the pattern of trade between member countries and the outside world due to the replacement of one set of tariffs by another.

Trade suppression effect   Cheaper supply from abroad is replaced by more expensive domestic supply.

Trade triangle   Tells the amounts a country is willing to trade (sides of the triangle) at a particular world price (hypotenuse of the triangle).

Trade-related intellectual property rights (TRIPs)   Establishes minimum standards for protecting such property rights as patents, copyrights, trademarks or similar.

Trade-related investment measures (TRIMs)   Foreign investment measures or regulations which restrict or distort trade.

Transferable rouble   An accounting currency unit (TR) introduced in the CMEA in 1963 for the settlement of trade balances between member countries. It never gained convertibility into either a soft or a hard currency.

Transition   A progression from a socialist planned economy to an open market-oriented economy.

Treaty of Rome   The treaty by which the governments of Belgium, France, Germany, Italy, Luxemburg and the Netherlands agreed to establish the EEC (1957).

Tripolar trading system   Based on the trade blocs centred around three blocs the USA, the EU and Japan.

True rate of protection   The difference between the post-protection price of the product and the post-protection price of the inputs used in its production, reflecting the effect of protection on the efficiency of resource allocation.

UNCTAD   United Nations Conference on Trade and Development, first held in 1964 under the auspices of the United Nations. A vehicle for advancing the demands of developing countries to improve the operation of the international economic system to better facilitate their own development.

Unequal exchange   In strict 'Marxian' sense, the supply of the products of the developing countries at prices below their labour values in exchange for the products of the developed countries at prices above their labour values (implying exploitation of developing countries by the developed countries).

Unit-value isoquant   A curve connecting all the input combinations that can be used to produce an output whose value (price) is equal to 1.

Uruguay Round   The multilateral trade negotiation that took place between 1986 and 1993. It is best known for bringing agriculture and services into GATT, for trying to reverse the trend of rising non-tariff barriers to trade and to improve dispute settlement mechanism through the establishment of the World Trade Organization (WTO).

Utility function   A functional relationship that assigns numbers to consumption bundles (assuming that all four axioms of consumers' preferences are satisfied).

Value added   The difference between the price of the final product and the cost of the intermediate goods and inputs used in its production.

Value of marginal product of a factor   The price of the product multiplied by the marginal product of the factor input, such as labour, capital or land.

Vertical integration   Backward (to supply its own inputs and raw materials) and forward (to foster its own sales and distribution) expansion of a firm.

Vinerian description   The notion that the net effect of a custom union is dependent on the relative strengths of the *trade creation* and *trade diversion* effects.

Voluntary export restraint (VER)   An agreement between importing and exporting countries for the latter to (willingly) restrain exports.

Widening   The evolution of economic integration by absorbing new member countries.

World Trade Organization (WTO)   A new international organisation established in 1995, this organisation is the embodiment of the Uruguay Round results and the successor to the GATT in that it becomes the legal and institutional foundation of the multilateral trading system.

Endnotes

☐ 1 The Ricardian Model and Extensions

1. It should be pointed out from the outset that the 'Ricardian model' is not identical to 'Ricardo's' theory. As more advanced students may already know, the version of trade theory that is normally used as an entrée in trade textbooks is named after David Ricardo (1772–1823) and his 'brilliant run' (as Evans, 1989, calls Ricardo's contributions to trade theory), *but* does not completely reflect Ricardo's model of trade as he built it throughout the *Principles* (not only in Chapter VII) and other his works. The 'textbook' Ricardian story has, however become generally adopted as a superior pedagogical device for examining the role of comparative advantage in determining the pattern of production and trade and consequently of gains from trade. See also Maneschi, (1992).

2. A reader may be tempted to make comparisons with Ricardo's own model in the process of development of the 'Ricardian model', but this is not our primary interest. In our initial textbook model, we assume inputs of labour only, and very often we assign the same assumption to Ricardo himself. However, the careful reader of his *Principles* will find out that Ricardo explicitly or implicitly assumed employment of capital (both fixed and circulating) and land in addition to labour.

3. To see this, take a point on the PPF, such as point E. From point E the production of food can be increased (say for an additional AG) only after reducing the production of cloth (by EA). However, from any point inside the locus (such as point A) the production of at least one good can be increased without causing the production of other good to contract (thus, such a point does *not* satisfy the conditions for Pareto efficiency). Such a production therefore represents an inefficient allocation of labour. We will assume that our economy always operates along its PPF.

4. The slope of the PPF is given by the marginal rate of transformation:

$$-(dC/dF) = (L/a_{LC})/(L/a_{LF}) = a_{LF}/a_{LC}$$

It is also true that:

$$a_{LF}/a_{LC} = (1/a_{LC})/(1/a_{LF}) = MP_C/MP_F = MC_F/MC_C$$

5. At the later stage we will see that it is not only the number of goods that matter but also their attributes. In Chapter 5 we formally introduce demand for variety (that is, demand for differentiated products). For now, we keep things very simple and we assume that (1) all goods are homogeneous; and (2) there are no corner solutions – that is, both goods are consumed with and

without trade. This latter assumption is somewhat unrealistic because it implies that there is no time lag between pre-trade completely specialised production and post-trade consumption of both goods. We ignore this and similar problems throughout this book.

6. This result is a consequence of our particular 'textbook version' of a labour theory of value, that is, the relative price of a good exactly corresponds to a relative labour contents, since homogeneous labour is assumed to be the only single input in timeless production. In general, a labour theory of value should include both immediate and accumulated quantities of labour embodied in goods for determination of those goods' relative prices. Once the accumulated labour in terms of capital or produced inputs are introduced, the one-to-one correspondence between relative prices and relative labour contents breaks down.

7. A country is said to have an absolute advantage in the production of a good if it needs less labour to produce a unit of that good than another country. It is then beneficial for each country to specialise in the production of such good and to import good(s) in which it has an absolute disadvantage. The 'law' of absolute advantage was first enunciated by Adam Smith (1723–90). This idea of specialisation and division of labour on a global scale was an important step forward in understanding the potential of international trade and in particular, in showing that trade is not a zero-sum game. However, since the law of absolute advantage required that each country produce at least one good with an absolute advantage to be able to engage in the gainful 'game', it was realised that many countries (even at that time) would, according to that law, remain outside the trading circle. It fell to Torrens, and particularly Ricardo, to develop these ideas further into what we now call the principle or law of comparative advantage. That has been the prevalent explanation of international trade until the revival of Smith's concepts through some of the 'new trade theory'. (For details see Chapters 4–5.)

8. We can also speak in terms of *disadvantages* or, rather, *least disadvantages*. For example, Home should specialise in the production of a good in which it has the smallest disadvantages relative to Foreign.

9. This assumption is not relevant except that it enables us to concentrate on the difference in productivity as the sole reason for trade. However, when we do assume that Foreign is 'about the same size' as Home,

$$L^* \approx L \tag{i}$$

and if we want that absolute quantities of outputs differ:

$$L/a_{LF} > L^*/a^*_{LF} \tag{ii}$$

and

$$L/a_{LC} < L^*/a^*_{LC}$$

then we must also assume that each country is assigned an absolute advantage in one of the goods:

$$a_{LF} < a^*{}_{LF} \qquad\qquad\qquad \text{(iii)}$$

and

$$a_{LC} > a^*{}_{LC}$$

It follows then that Foreign in our example will be able to offer smaller (larger) potential quantity of food (cloth) than Home, since Foreign is not larger than Home, and is absolutely and relatively less (more) productive in the food (cloth) sector.

10. This was first explicitly done by J. S. Mill (1848), who introduced an equation of international demand; and later by Marshall with his theory of reciprocal demands. However, it should be noted, some analysts hold to an alternative view that the Ricardian theory is absolutely capable of handling the problem of terms of trade determination without explicitly introducing elements of demand. We are not in position here to elaborate on this view, but interested students are referred to Negishi (1982).

11. It is easy to show that if both countries specialise in a comparative disadvantage good, that is, Home in cloth and Foreign in food, world production will be at point *m* which is the most Pareto *inefficient* point consistent with full employment and given technology.

12. J. S. Mill, for instance, made such assumptions. See Chipman (1965, section 1.2).

13. Thus, in effect, we can conduct a *partial* equilibrium style of analysis for what is really a general equilibrium problem.

14. Total world oncome may be defined as the value, at prevailing world prices, of total cloth and food produced. For any given terms of trade, p^T, we can define a set of iso-income lines whose slopes are $-p^T$. For an equilibrium with terms of trade p^T, it is obvious that point R is on the highest attainable iso-income line; and so R represents maximum world income measured with p^T as the 'standard of (relative) value.'

15. This actually means that for any point inside the frontier it is possible to find a point on the frontier that implies at least the same of the one good and more of the other good.

16. Of course, it will often be argued that given sufficient investments and time, any country can produce some quantity of any good provided it is not a natural resource. However geographic, climatic or other considerations may still mean a very substantial absolute disadvantage.

17. Of course, our results would be influenced by introducing considerations of (a) changes in tastes, and (b) negative external effects in consumption once a country has started to trade.

18. It is assumed that a reader is familiar with the concept of the 'social indifference curves' and all of the problems involved. For some basic background reading see Caves, Frankel and Jones (1993, Chapter 2); Tower (1979), or the original source, Samuelson (1956).

19. If the PPFs of both countries have the same marginal rate of transformation this area (i.e. gains from trade) shrinks to zero.

20. This is not the place to go into the host of possible reasons for change in the terms of trade. However, it is important to keep in mind that social welfare effects depend on the nature of the change.

21. When the conditions of production change (say, to increasing returns to scale) size can play very important role in providing a country with large enough production run to be cost competitive. For now, size does not matter for cost level.

22. We do not express wages in monetary units so as to escape from complications arising from having different currencies and exchange rate limits. If we were to 'monetise' these rates, it is clear that a country could use exchange rate policy in addition to wage modifications to change its 'price competitiveness'.

23. Note, however, that at this relative wage all the gains from trade accrue to Foreign (who has the comparative advantage in cloth). To see this, look at the world PPF in Figure 1.5. When both countries produce cloth, the world relative price must coincide with Home's autarky price (segment AR) implying that after-trade consumption will still be on Home's segment of the PPF (or that with-trade real income in Home will not change).

24. In this way we have got the so-called 'double-factoral' terms of trade, that is, the terms of trade adjusted for productivities in both countries. These terms of trade reflect the exchange ratio of Home's labour for Foreign labour, and vice versa. If this index increases in time, it means that a country's gains from trade are increasing.

    There are other concepts of terms of trade, too. For instance, the income terms of trade are defined as commodity terms of trade multiplied by a quantity index of exports and are supposed to express overall export-based capacity to import goods. Or, single-factoral terms of trade are commodity terms of trade adjusted only by an index of productivity in export industries. All three are conceptually important, particularly for developing countries. However, they can be rarely precisely determined since actual statistical data are often not good enough.

25. This assumes, of course, that international competition is 'open markets' and price-based as in this simple model, which is hardly the general rule (nor ever has been).

26. This is known as 'unequal exchange', a concept advanced by Emmanuel (1972). According to his view, only a situation in which the double-factoral terms of trade would equal one will be categorised as 'equal exchange'.

27. Dornbusch, Fischer and Samuelson (1977).

28. This specialisation is efficient (in a sense of being on the frontier) and characterised by the boundary good $Z(\omega)$ and a relative price structure. The relative price structure is determined by cost minimisation. From Dornbusch, Fisher and Samuelson (1977, p. 824), the relative price of any good z in terms of good z' (both produced at Home) is:

$$p(z)/p(z') = wa(z)/wa(z')$$
$$= a(z)/a(z')   \text{for } z, z' \leq Z$$

The relative price of Home's good z in terms of good z'' produced in

Foreign is:

$$p(z)/p(z'') = wa(z)/w^*a^*(z'')$$
$$= \omega a(z)/a^*(z'') \quad \text{for} \ z < Z < z''$$

29. The $B(.)$ schedule can be also interpreted as the locus of trade balance equilibria (see more on p. 825 of the original Dornbusch–Fischer–Samuelson article), equating the values of exports and imports.
30. In terms of interpreting the $B(.)$ schedule as the trade balance, a relative increase in Home's size causes it to run a trade deficit with Foreign; this requires Home's relative wage to drop so that it can export relatively more.
31. Cf. Krugman and Obstfeld (1991, p. 36).
32. It is typical in undergraduate trade texts to assume costless movement of goods (and factors) between countries. If transport and other costs (transaction costs, etc.) are mentioned at all, the explanation for their exclusion from the analysis is similar to one given in Pomfret (1991, p. 13):

> Transportation costs should be broadly conceived as the costs of doing business internationally as well as of physically moving goods. Little will be said in this book about transportation costs because their role is obvious and for the most part theoretically uninteresting. High transportation costs reduce the volume of trade and shift its composition in favour of goods whose bulk is small relative to their value. In some respects they can be viewed as natural trade barriers with similar effects to the government-imposed trade barriers.

> On the other hand, the cost of shipping goods (transportation costs included) is one of the central issues of the some of the recent work done by the 'new' trade theory economists. As an example see Krugman (1991).

33. This model assumes Ricardian *interpersonal* trade. Each individual is different in terms of productive skills and by specialising in the good in which s(he) has the comparative advantage, s(he) necessarily gains from interpersonal exchange.
34. Note again that each type of labour may have an absolute advantage in the production of one good, but this is not necessary. As in the basic model, skilled labour here could have an absolute advantage (higher productivity) in the production of both goods, but unskilled labour could still have a comparative advantage in one of them.
35. Again, the reader may recognise this statement as the Stolper–Samuelson Theorem to which we will return in Chapter 2, and which states that an increase in the relative price of the labour-intensive good must increase real wages and lower real rents.

☐ 2 The Heckscher–Ohlin–Samuelson Model

1. Eli Heckscher and Bertil Ohlin have never actually teamed up to develop the now famous Heckscher–Ohlin theorem. Their original works are put together in Heckscher and Ohlin (1991), trans. and introduced by Harry Flam and M. June Flanders.

2. Capital is treated here more as land, that is, it is given as a non-produced stock which does not depreciate with usage.
3. Given smooth isoquants there is a continuum of techniques to choose from.
4. The Lagrangian expression for the given cost function and $Q_C = 1$ is:

$$L = wa_{LC} + ra_{KC}$$

which gives the simple first order conditions:

$$\partial L/\partial a_{LC} = w$$
$$\partial L/\partial a_{KC} = r$$

or

$$\partial a_{KC}/\partial a_{LC} = w/r$$

5. Note that if the isoquant shows that there is no substitution between factors, in other words we have Leontief technology, the corresponding iso-price curve is linear. Conversely, if the factors are perfect substitutes, as in case of linear isoquants, the corresponding iso-price curve is L-shaped. Generally, the iso-price curve is convex towards the origin. This can be seen by looking at the slope of the iso-price curve which is given as the capital–labour ratio (2.2.9). Since the capital–labour ratio is an increasing function of relative factor prices the iso-price curve must be convex towards the origin. Also, the greater the degree of substitutability of factors, the more curved the iso-price curve will be.
6. If, for some commodity prices, the two iso-price curves do not intersect, the economy will produce only that good with the higher iso-price curve. Factor prices will then be determined by the point at which the slope of that particular iso-price curve is equal to the overall capital–labour ratio (Mussa, 1979).
7. This situation could be presented as the corner solution in the Edgeworth box diagram, the derivation of which follows in the next section.
8. There is actually no difference between the Edgeworth box diagram and the Lerner–Pearce diagram, except for the placement of the industries' isoquants. In the Edgeworth box, for example, the isoquants are placed back-to-back. In the Lerner–Pearce diagram, the isoquants are placed with respect to the same point as the origin. We use this equivalence when plotting *both* countries in Figure 2.14 in Box 2.2.
9. It must be true with trade, as well as it was without trade, that for each good the price of the commodity equals the cost of producing that commodity. Thus, the increase in the relative price of cloth in Home shifts the unit cost curve CC outward from the origin, while the FF curve remains in the same position (in a diagram such as Figure 2.4). A new intersection of the CC and FF curves determines the new factor prices at which capital is relatively more expensive as compared to its price without trade. This of course has an implication for hiring decisions not only in the food industry, but also in the cloth industry.

10. There is still no universally accepted and exact definition of an industry. Different criteria are used in grouping goods together into a single entry in statistical terms. Most often economists use (a) the degree of substitution in production, (b) the degree of substitution in consumption, and (c) identical or very similar methods of production as the main criteria with which to classify goods into industries. The problems of definition are not the only problems related to either the measurement of inter-industry trade or distinguishing it from intra-industry trade. We discuss these and related issues when dealing with intra-industry trade in Chapters 4 and 5.

11. Dixit and Norman (1980) and Helpman and Krugman (1985) have built on Samuelson's (1949, p. 14) parable of a world where 'all factors were perfectly mobile and nationalism had not yet reared its ugly head'. Such a world has been replicated in an 'integrated world economy'.

12. This theorem appeared as the discussion on income-distributional effects of tariffs in Stolper and Samuelson (1941). According to Jones (1987, p. 622) this article must be ranked a classic not only for giving us the theorem, 'but because it is one of the first concrete developments of the ideas of Heckscher and Ohlin in the explicit format of a two-factor, two-commodity, general equilibrium model'. Despite the original reference of the article to the effects of protection (tariff), it is commonly accepted that the SST refers to the income-distributional effects of international trade in general.

    We cannot avoid mentioning that in November 1991 the world (of economists at least) celebrated the 50th anniversary of the SST. Almost all famous economists took part in the Symposium organised for that occasion. Here we quote the introductory paragraph of the speech given by one of them, Jagdish Bhagwati:

    > I know of no major international economic theorist today who would not trade an arm and a leg and a sizeable fraction of his own research output for the authorship of this [i.e. the SST] result. The Stolper–Samuelson theorem has all the virtues of a major scientific construct in economics. It has the power of a paradox: it demonstrated, contrary to earlier intuition, that one could unambiguously infer changes in real wages, resulting from goods price changes, without having to discover who consumed what. Then again, by critical test of marginal productivity, it has been a roaring success: it has produced an unceasing flood of research, as scores of us have followed where the masters led. (Bhagwati, 1991b, p. 1)

13. What are we actually assuming is $p_F^T/p_C^T < p_F/p_C$, where $p_F^T = p_F$, and $p_C^T > p_C$.

14. This is obtained from the following comparisons. From Figure 2.13 we have:

$$(rr^T/Or) = (EB/OE) \qquad \text{(i)}$$

Then if $EE^T < EB$ it must be that:

$$(rr^T/Or) > (EE^T/OE) \qquad \text{(ii)}$$

15. $dp_C/p_C = (dw/w)(a_{LC}w/p_C) + (dr/r)(a_{KC}r/p_C)$ (2.5.3a)

   $dp_F/p_F = (dw/w)(a_{LF}w/p_F) + (dr/r)(a_{KF}r/p_F)$ (2.5.3b)

   The relative changes in goods prices (dp/p) and factor prices $(dw/w$ and $dr/r)$ in the two equations above are denoted with a hat '^' in the text's equations (2.5.3) and (2.5.4). In those equations, the shares of each factor's earnings in the total industry's earnings are given by θ (see Caves, Frankel and Jones, 1993).

16. When the comparison is made between free trade and autarky, and under the assumption that only one factor is owned by each person, there is no difference between real wages and real incomes. If a comparison is, however, made between trade with (non-prohibitive) protection and autarky, real incomes need not coincide with real wages because of the potential tariff revenue earnings that can be redistributed back to factor owners (see Bhagwati, 1959).

17. On this issue Rybczynski (1955, p. 338–9) has written:

> 7. . . . To find the new point of production and consumption equilibrium when the quantity of Factor X is increased, . . . [r]equires the derivation of the new 'production possibility' curve and its analysis in relation to the indifference curve system. Each will be examined below.
> 8. Now in virtue of our proposition that the maintenance of the same substitution rate in production, after Factor X has increased, requires an absolute increase in the output of the X-intensive commodity, and an absolute reduction in the output of the Y-intensive commodity, it follows that the slope found at R on the production curve SM [Fig. 2] must, on the production curve ZN, lie below RT where less of L is produced. We shall suppose that it lies at R.
> 9. So much for the shape of the new 'production possibility' curve.

18. The locus of such points would have to correspond to a contract curve in a box diagram whose dimensions are given with the changed factor amounts. In other words, for each point on the new contract curve we find a corresponding point of the PPF keeping the factor prices, commodity prices, and factor intensities fixed. Is it at all possible to construct the new contract curve while keeping the commodity prices, factor prices and factor intensities constant, i.e. could we speak about *efficient allocation* of a disproportionately increased amount of resources at prices which have been determined on the basis of the previous amount of resources? Therefore it would be more appropriate to call this locus the Rybczynski locus. However, we shall go along with what traditionally has been assumed, that is, that this locus satisfies the properties of the PPF.

19. Since a neutral growth assumes a proportionate increase in *both* factors, it is not possible to directly link this type of growth to the proper Rybczynski case which discusses only one–factor–increase effects

20. Much of this section follows Young (1993).

21. In his follow-up paper on the immiserising growth, Bhagwati (1968) shows that immiserising growth can arise whenever growth occurs subject to

distortions. In the case presented in our Box 2.3, where the terms of trade effect outweigh the primary growth effect, the distortion comes from the fact that this country in fact has monopoly power in trade and ought to have an optimal tariff. Instead it has free trade which then causes distortion. Similarly, growth can immiserise a small growing country if it imposes a tariff barrier instead of pursuing free trade. There are other interesting cases of immiserising growth related to foreign direct investment, immigration, lobbying etc.

22. Factor-intensity reversal cannot occur without the large difference in the elasticity of substitution of factors, labour and capital, in the production of the two goods. With a high coefficient of elasticity of substitution of labour for capital in the production of food, Foreign will produce food with labour-intensive techniques because its wages are low (Foreign being labour-abundant relative to Home). Thus, following the same line of reasoning, Home will produce food using capital-intensive techniques. If, on the other hand, the elasticity of substitution of labour for capital is very low in the cloth production, Foreign and Home will have to use the similar techniques in production of this good although they could widely differ in terms of their factor prices.

23. The explanation for the difference in shape is found in the different overall factor endowments. For Home we assume that the endowment point would be located close to the ray Or in Figure 2.26 (or close to the diagonal in the Edgeworth box diagram), while for Foreign we assume that factor endowment is given by the point distant from the ray Or.

24. The first research was conducted by Minhas (1962). This was followed by Leontief (1964) and by Ball (1966).

☐ 3 *The Augmented Heckscher–Ohlin–Samuelson Model*

1. This model also goes under the name of the Ricardo–Viner model, coined by Samuelson (1971). See Maneshi (1992, pp. 422–3) for a discussion on the appropriateness of this term.

2. The specific-factors model is often seen as the short-run variant of the HOS model. In this case the factors, in particular capital, are assumed to be immobile. This assumption is relaxed for the long run. In fact both assumptions are extreme. In reality there is always some degree of factor mobility even in the short run, and there is no such thing as perfect factor mobility, not even in the long run.

3. Ruffin and Jones (1977) show that there is a presumption that protection will reduce real wages in the specific-factors model. This result is not unambiguous, as it is in the HOS model.

4. This section draws heavily on Kierzkowski (1987) and Deardorff (1984b, 1985).

5. The factor 'land' could include any form of natural resources or agricultural capital specific to agriculture (Deardorff, 1984b).

6. The material in this subsection depends upon Ethier (1988).

7. If the extractive sector uses relatively little labour the adjustments in terms of the output fall in other sectors will not be very significant.

8. Since we have assumed that this country is small, the terms of trade are given. We can thus apply Hicks' theorem, grouping all the traded goods together and treating them as a single good.

☐ 4 *Modern Theories of Trade – 1: External Economies of Scale*

1. The same result can be expressed more elegantly in terms of derivatives. The key property is the increasing returns to scale in the production of C:

$$d(d_C/dL_C)/dL_C > 0 \tag{i}$$

The economy has a single factor, labour and $L = L_F + L_C$. We know that along the PPF $dL = 0$ (or $dL_F = -dL_C$). This means that:

$$dL = (dL_C/dC)dC + (dL_F/dF)dF = 0 \tag{ii}$$

and

$$dC/dF = -(dL_F/dF)/(dL_C/dC) \tag{iii}$$

or

$$dF/dC = -(dL_C/dC)/(dL_F/dF) \tag{iv}$$

Now, because the production of F exhibits constant returns to scale:

$$dL_F/dF = \text{ constant, say } k \tag{v}$$

we have

$$dC/dF = -k(dC/dL_C) \tag{vi}$$

that is, the slope of the PPF increases in magnitude as the output of C increases since $d(dC/dL_C)/dC > 0$.

2. Consider a single-product firm which produces output q using an input x. Its production function $q = f(x)$ exhibits EOS at x if for $k > 1$, $f(kx) > kf(x)$. That is, a small proportionate increase in input x increases output more proportionately. Such EOS are internal to the firm – its AC depends upon the output of the firm itself. For the EOS to be external to the firm, its production function has to be of a form such as:

$$q = f(x, Q) \tag{i}$$

where Q is the output of an industry that the firm belongs to. Then for $k > 1$, $f(kx, Q) = kf(x, Q)$. That is, we have constant returns to scale at the level of a single firm, while returns to scale at the industry level are increasing. To see this, note that an industry output is:

$$Q = \Sigma q_i = \Sigma f(x, Q) \tag{ii}$$

where n is the number of firms in the industry, and i is a firm's index. Since $f(x, Q)$ is homogeneous of the first degree in x, then assuming that all firms are identical and are price takers in both goods and factor markets, we have:

$$Q = f(\Sigma x_i, Q) \tag{iii}$$

and

$$Q = f(X, Q)$$

where X is the total input used by the industry. Finally, we can write the industry production function as:

$$Q = g(X) \tag{iv}$$

where $g(kX) > kg(X)$, for $k > 1$ reflects EOS at the industry level.

3. More generally, EOS need not be restricted to national industry size (that is, the size of the national market). Countries with smaller national markets can also develop economies of large-scale production by supplying to a large international market. This is indeed what was underlying Adam Smith's emphasis on the increased size of the market permitting a greater degree of specialisation and therefore higher productivity (see Appendix 4, p. 175). As national economies become more integrated via trade, the size of international rather than national industry increasingly forms the basis for external EOS. However, important country-specific factors (such as public intermediate inputs – roads, railways, telecommunications, etc.) will continue to play an important role in the determination of external EOS.

4. More mathematically inclined students, of course, realise that one of the further conditions required for strict equivalence is that an industry production function must be homothetic, otherwise EOS can exist even if the production function does not everywhere display IRS. Note, also, that changes in input prices are not considered here.

5. The price line is tangential to the PPF only if there is no difference in IRS between the two industries. Because we assume constant returns in food, and increasing returns in cloth, the price line cannot be tangential to the PPF in this case.

6. Both countries are assumed to have the same homothetic preferences, assuring that the autarkic relative price of the EOS good is smaller in the larger country. To prove this, it must be shown that for a fixed output ratio F/C, the marginal rate of transformation within the larger country is less than the marginal rate of transformation within the smaller country. This is so because EOS make marginal labour requirements for the production of cloth lower in the larger country. For a formal treatment see Markusen and Melvin (1981).

7. Note also that the world production of food and cloth has increased with no change in the overall usage of resources. Thus, by reallocating resources, trade achieves the same effects as would be achieved by technological progress. Again, we assume no adjustment costs in the process of resource reallocation.

8. Alternatively, we can say that both countries will gain from trade as long as the small country's relative price of the exported good increases with trade, relative to autarky. This can happen only if trade decreases the price of the EOS good produced in a large country and that, in turn, is ensured if a large country's production of the EOS good with trade is larger than the production of either country in the absence of trade.

9. Markusen and Melvin (1984) suggested that a sufficient condition for gains from trade in such cases is that trade has a certain rationalising effect on production. In other words, if surviving industries (food in our example) expand output more than proportionately in comparison with the number of EOS industries lost due to the opening of trade, losses need not occur.

10. In his (1923) article. For a more formal treatment see Ethier (1982) and Helpman and Krugman (1985, Chapter 3).

☐ 5 *Modern Theories of Trade – 2: Imperfect Competition*

1. It should be noted that causes of trade other than comparative advantage have been considered long before this surge in the 'new trade' literature. Ohlin himself tended to rank the 'advantages of specialisation' and 'large-scale production' on an equal footing with comparative advantage as the prime causes of trade (see Heckscher and Ohlin, 1991, p. 26). There were also different approaches to explaining trade, such as Linder's theory (Linder, 1961), Vernon's product cycle theory (Vernon, 1966), etc. All such ideas based on non-competitive market structures were labelled 'alternative' trade theories, for the simple reason that they were not rigorously formalised (rigorous in neoclassical terms, of course). Today some of these theories, presented in a more formal language, are finding their place in the (mainstream) 'new' trade theory.

2. See, for example, Helpman (1990), Grossman and Helpman (1989) or Grossman and Helpman (1991).

3. Of course, if the plant is producing only one product, these EOS become identical to the product-specific economies of scale that were so important to Adam Smith and his views on trade. The greater the output of a product, and trade is supposed to cause an increase in output, the more narrowly workers can specialise in specific tasks, therefore increasing their productivity.

4. Naturally, EOS are not the sole determinant of market structure, but they are very important. Other factors that should be taken into consideration are government policy, growth and chance. See Scherer and Ross (1990, Chapter 4).

5. For a true maximum, a second order condition must be satisfied as well. The second order condition is $(\partial^2 R/\partial B^2) - (\partial^2 C/\partial B^2) < 0$.

6. Whenever monopoly is not established on superior productivity, it is considered inefficient. Standard microeconomic texts would list several basic sources of inefficiency: the waste of resources through rent-seeking behaviour, contrived or artificially imposed scarcity of monopolised goods relative to other goods, and the X- inefficiency which causes a monopolist to fail to minimise costs.

7. The economy will still be able to operate at the PPF. Because we assume that our monopolist has no monopsonistic power, he cannot influence factor

markets. His presence, together with perfectly competitive industry elsewhere, is therefore compatible with an economy operating at (and not below) the PPF, that is, on the efficiency locus.

8. Bear in mind that a monopoly distorts relative prices in autarky. Due to the monopoly, the domestic relative price of buses is artificially high, and Home appears to have a comparative advantage in cloth. In other words we have $MC_C/MC_B = p_C/p_B > p_C/p_B < MC_C/MC_B$. This does not give us sufficient information to determine whether Home is really the lower-cost producer of cloth, although free trade will cause Home to export it.

9. Trade may result in a contraction of a monopolised output (this is in fact the traditional result). This would happen if the bus monopoly was originally producing more than the output given by T (i.e. if his cost disadvantage relative to foreign bus producers was quite large).

10. Note, however, that compared with the relative price of buses in a hypothetical case where the competitive equilibrium is given by A, the with-trade price has risen. This indicates that the monopoly is cost superior relative to the rest of the world.

11. There is an EOS basis for trade, but we disregard it here, instead concentrating entirely on the market structure as the basis for trade.

12. Note that when these curves intersect, the Home firm's reaction curve is steeper than the Foreign firm's reaction curve.

13. In fact, if we allow for free entry into bus industry, the price and output levels would become identical to the price and output levels of pure competition.

14. Recall that one of the means of identifying substitutes is through the cross-elasticity of demand. The cross elasticity between two goods that are substitutes is expected to be positive, as well as being larger than between two goods that are not substitutes.

15. Here we consider horizontal product differentiation (which occurs where products share certain basic or core attributes but combine them in different proportions). The two types briefly mentioned in the text are based on Spence (1976), Dixit and Stiglitz (1977) and Lancaster (1980, 1984). There is also vertical product differentiation, which refers to differences in the quality of goods (Falvey, 1981).

16. The concept of monopolistic competition was first developed by Chamberlin (1933).

17. The measure of monopoly power is given by the ratio of average revenue to marginal revenue, while the degree of EOS is measured by the ratio of average cost to marginal cost (Helpman and Krugman, 1985, p. 134).

18. It is also true that the total manufacturing output ($m' \times n'$ in Home and $m^{*'} \times n^{*'}$ in Foreign) is larger with trade than without trade. This implies that the reduction in the number of firms is relatively smaller than the increase in the output of each of the remaining firms. This effect can again be seen as the 'technical progress illusion' because the same amount of resources now produces a larger output.

19. Here we need the help of Samuelson's angel:

> But the factors of production [in the integrated economy] grew arrogant, daring to challenge heaven, and an angel descended and divided them into nations. Capital from one nation could henceforth work only with labor

from the same nation – and the angel did not divide the capital and labor equally. What were the chastened factors of production to do? (Krugman, 1991, p. 73).

20. Note that this is true when the same demand patterns are assumed, and when there are no large differences in factor endowments between countries.
21. There are some exceptions to the growth rates that are connected with a change in the prices of traded goods. For instance, with the two oil-price shocks, it was noted that the value of the trade between developed and developing countries was growing. But it was only nominal growth.

6 Commodity Trade Flows: Methodological Appraisal and the Evidence

1. Note that the causality flows from the comparative advantage to the share of the export market, not the other way around. The measure of 'revealed' comparative advantage which takes the existing export share to then show the comparative advantage should thus be viewed with some caution.
2. According to Dollar (1993) any particular technology is destined to become an international public good in the long run. Differences in technology can therefore provide a satisfactory explanation only for *short-term* comparative advantage. In the long run the source of comparative advantage could be the ability to generate new technology on an ongoing basis. See also p. 230 on technology-based trade theories.
3. These studies were MacDougall *et al.* (1962), Stern (1962), and Balassa (1963). Deardorff (1984) provides a systematic review of empirical tests on the Ricardian and other trade models.
4. Note that Leontief was able to perform his calculations only for competitive imports. Imports of products such as bananas, coffee, and other goods not produced in the USA were not accounted for in his tests.
5. For the developing countries see Havrylyshyn (1985). For examples from Eastern Europe and the former Soviet Union see Stolper and Roskamp (1961), Rosefielde (1974).
6. For example Kreinin (1965) states that this superiority in efficiency could be around 20–25 per cent, but certainly not 300 per cent.
7. For example Baldwin (1971) and Fels (1972).
8. If factor prices differ between countries it is possible that two industries sharing identical production functions (i.e. technology) will use different factor intensities.
9. Note that the rank correlation coefficient varies between 1, when the two rankings are identical, to −1, when they are completely opposite. A coefficient of 1 would rule out factor-intensity reversals, while a coefficient of −1 would mean that no industries in the two countries had the same or even similar technology.
10. The authors state: 'The postulate that factor intensities of industries are the same in all countries (even in the weak sense of an ordinal equivalence) is clearly refuted by the evidence compiled here' (p. 179).

11. The authors did attempt to find an explanation for their results and it seemed that the assumption of identical technologies across countries simply does not hold.
12. The fourteen countries were chosen randomly. The countries chosen were: Brazil, Cameroon, Colombia, Congo, Greece, Ivory Coast, South Korea, Nigeria, Norway, Pakistan, Paraguay, Peru, Philippines and Thailand.
13. In teaching international trade we also include the specific-factors model of Chapter 3; however this has not attracted any empirical testing.
14. Grubel and Lloyd noted:

> the mean is a biased downward measure of intra-industry trade if the country's total commodity trade is imbalanced or if the mean is an average of some subset of all industries for which exports are not equal to imports . . . This is an undesirable feature of a measure of average intra-industry trade which is due to the fact that it captures both trade imbalance and the strength of the intra-industry trade. (1975, p. 22).

15. The best known adjustments of the basic formula accounting for the trade imbalance problem were developed by Aquino (1978) and Bergstrand (1983). For a detailed analysis of adjustment to the aggregate trade imbalance see Greenaway and Milner (1986) or Tharakan (1983).
16. Krugman (1990, p. 258) notes:

> In the theory an 'industry' is a group of products produced with similar factor intensities, so that trade within an industry cannot be explained by conventional comparative advantage. Whether this concept of an industry has anything to do with a three-digit Standard International Trade Classification category – the unit to which the analysis in each case applied – is anybody's guess.

17. Among the studies examining these issues the best known are Caves, 1981; Balassa and Bauwens, 1987; Marvel and Ray, 1987.
18. Chemicals, manufactured goods classified mainly on the material base, machinery and transport equipment and other manufactures.

☐ 7 *International Factor Movements and Multinational Corporations*

1. Lindert (1991, p. 39) looks at this 'paradox' in a different way. He says that what matters is the definition of the total population of a country. If we use consistent definitions of each country in terms of their total population (native + migrants) before and after labour movements, the changes in income *per capita* should become consistent with the changes in total income. For example, in the receiving country when we use the broader (narrow) definition which includes (excludes) migrants, the income *per capita* before migration is lower than after migration. However for the sending country the changes in income *per capita* differ depending on the definition. When the narrow definition is used, the income *per capita* is higher before than after emigration

so that the sending country loses in terms of *per capita* income and in terms of total income. When, on the other hand, the broader definition is used, the income *per capita* is lower before than after migration indicating that sending country gains in terms of income *per capita* with emigration!

2. The following paragraphs draw partly upon Mikić (1989).

3. According to Friedman *et al.* (1984), the responsibility for the debt crisis is solely that of the lenders. For example, they state that the solution to debt problems is 'to require the people who make the loans to collect them. If they can, fine, and if they can't, that's their problem' (1984, p. 38).

4. A very good summary of the main issues involved in the creation of the strategy for solving the debt crisis of the 1980s is in Guitian (1992, Chapter III).

5. It took Mexico's 1982 action and other countries declarations of inability to repay for creditors to realise that they had on their hands a different type of problem as compared to the occasional short-term liquidity problems in the post-war period. The debtors, mostly LDCs, were facing long-term problems of 'insolvency'. But it was still not the same type of problem that banks were used to dealing with concerning insolvent corporations. For the first time since the 1930s the banks had to face the risk of massive sovereign debtors' insolvency or sovereign default. See for more detail about LDCs' default, Eaton and Gersovitz (1981); Eaton, Gersovitz and Stiglitz (1986).

6. We have to agree with Walter Wriston's dictum about countries, unlike firms, never going bankrupt because their external debts would exceed national wealth only under exceptional circumstances.

7. Indeed there is a casual support to this link. Looking at the countries facing external debt problems almost all of the highly indebted former socialist countries have problems with a lack of internal financial discipline (in terms of a soft budget constraint to domestic firms, consumers and even commercial banks).

8. There is, however, more to the issue of sovereign default than the enforce-ability of debt. The real problem the sovereign debtors face is the trade-off between debt service and the performance of their economies. When debt servicing becomes a heavy burden, that is, when net resource transfers becomes negative, the economic performance of the debtor country is adversely affected. It is therefore a matter of the *ability to pay* in an economic sense as well as the political ability or a willingness to depress living standards that determines for how long external liabilities will be met. In this view default is the last resort, taken only when governments decide that further resource transfers to creditors would seriously impede their own country's economic growth. Readers will realise that this view of the LDCs' debt crisis as a development problem is in contrast with the pure willingness to pay approach which concentrates on property rights and does not pay any attention to a country's economic adjustment.

☐ 8 *Economic Analysis of Tariffs*

1. In general this wedge is equal to the amount of a tariff. There are, however, exceptions. For example, when the country imposing the tariff is a large country the domestic price of the imported good need not increase by the whole amount of the tariff.

2. We therefore ignore the Armington assumption. This assumption states that consumers treat otherwise identical goods produced in different countries as different; these goods are therefore not perfect substitutes. This assumption is frequently used in empirical work.
3. We assume that these concepts are familiar to students. Consumer surplus measures the amount a consumer gains in terms of increased utility from the purchase of a good at a price lower than he or she would have been willing to pay. Similarly producer surplus measures the gains to a producer from the sale of a good at a higher price than he or she would have been willing to accept. To roughly approximate, producer surplus represents profits.
4. On the production side output valued in terms of world prices falls short of the free trade value of output. On the consumption side even with distorted production consumers consume on a lower indifference curve than they were previously. This is shown in panel (c). On this diagram there are consumption points to the right of point D_t, along the world price line $p*$, which would have provided higher levels of welfare.
5. Recall that we assume that consumer income arises from the ownership of output.
6. Here we imply net tariff revenue generated in the system of taxes and subsidies.
7. For example for the economy producing cloth and food at the competitive equilibrium, the movement along the frontier implies:

$$0 = p_F dP_F + p_C dP_C \text{ or}$$
$$0 = (p_F/p_C)dP_F + dP_C \tag{i}$$

In mathematical terms this represents the first order condition for maximisation. In graphical representation this is obtained by the tangency between the production frontier and the relative price line, $dP_C/dP_F = -(p_F/p_C)$.
8. The same result can be obtained by using expenditure and national income functions. Staring with the expression, already given in (8.3.8), describing the post-tariff level of utility:

$$e(p^t, u^t) = y(p^t) + (p^t - p^*)(D_t - P_t)$$

By using $p^t = (1+t)p^*, (D_t - P_t) = M$, we can rewrite the above expression as follows:

$$e(p^t, u^t) = y(p^t) + tp^* M \tag{i}$$

Differentiating with respect to the tariff rate t gives:

$$[(\partial e/\partial p^t)(dp^t/dt)] + [(\partial e/\partial u^t)(du^t/dt)] =$$
$$(\partial y/\partial p^t)(dp^t/dt) + tp^*(dM/dt) + M[d(tp^*)/dt]]$$

Recall the basic properties of the expenditure and national income functions through which we have $(\partial e/\partial p^t) = D_t$ and $(\partial y/\partial p^t) = P_t$. Also from $p^t = (1+t)p^*$ it follows that $dp^t/dt = (dp^*/dt) + [d(tp^*)/dt]$. Substituting these into (ii) gives:

$$D_t\{(dp^*/dt) + [d(tp^*)/dt]\} + [(\partial e/\partial u^t)(du^t/dt)] =$$
$$P_t\{(dp^*/dt) + [d(tp^*)/dt]\} + tp^*(dM/dt) + M[d(tp^*)/dt)]$$

By again using $M = (D_t - P_t)$ we obtain:

$$(\partial e/\partial u^t)(du^t/dt) = -M(dp^*/dt) - M[d(tp^*)/dt] +$$
$$tp*(dM/dt) + M[d(tp^*)/dt)]$$

Finally, the welfare effect of a change in a tariff is given as:

$$(\partial e/\partial u^t)(du^t/dt) = -M(dp^*/dt) + tp^*(dM/dt) \qquad \text{(iii)}$$

The first term on the right-hand side is the terms of trade effect while the second term is the volume of trade effect.

9. Terms of trade gains are a negative function of the tariff rate increase, while volume of trade or efficiency loss is a positive function of the tariff rate increase. This is why at low tariff rates the marginal gains are greater than marginal losses. These two effects equalise at the volume of trade determined by the optimum tariff rate.

10. Any tariff that would shift Home's offer curve so as to cut Foreign's offer curve between the points E and E on the TIC^E would improve Home's welfare as compared to the free trade level.

11. As Johnson has shown when both countries possess monopoly (monopsony) power in world markets, Foreign country retaliation to Home's imposition of a tariff will not necessarily reduce Home's welfare as long as Home imposes an optimum tariff in the first place. It can be shown that, starting from an optimum tariff in each country, both countries can gain by negotiated reciprocal reduction until at least one country is a free trader. However it is not necessarily true that both would gain from the restoration of free trade.

12. Richardson (1992) claims that one of the four traditional trade policy maxims is that the most-favoured-nation non-distcrimination clause has dominant strategic value.

13. Bhagwati (1992) and (1991) explains in detail the difference between the *national* and *cosmopolitan* case for free trade with respect to reciprocity. From the former it implies that reciprocity does not matter, while the later centres all attention to it.

14. We will discuss this in more detail in Chapter 10.

15. See n.7 above.

16. Under the assumptions that the number of firms is fixed and that all firms minimise costs.

17. As Helpman and Krugman (1989, p. 27) state, it is not very realistic to assume the complete lack of competition in one market and perfectly competitive structure for an identical industry in the world market; it is more likely that both the domestic and the world market will be charac-terised by a similar type of competitive structure for identical industries. Our

assumption, however, helps us to identify the effects of tariffs on competition in the domestic market.

18. We have already mentioned that this assumption is known as the Armington assumption. See n.2 above.

19. There are more complex forms of imperfect competition under which the ranking of tariffs and other barriers can be reversed. For interested readers the comprehensive reading on this is Helpman and Krugman (1989).

20. The reason is that for linear demand curves the slope of their associated marginal revenue curves will be twice the slope of demand curves themselves. Thus the area between *MR* curve, price and vertical axis, *tBDc* will be twice as much as the area between demand curve, price and vertical axis, p^tTAp. If the triangle *TFA* (deadweight loss) is small, as it will be for small tariff rates, the tariff will have a positive net effect.

21. The first best policy for extracting the rents from a foreign monopoly would be a price ceiling on the imported good (Helpman and Krugman, 1989, pp. 50–3). This is however an unusual instrument in the area of foreign trade.

☐ 9 *Economic Analysis of Non-tariff Barriers*

1. UNCTAD (1983) distinguishes between non-tariff measures and non-tariff barriers. The term 'non-tariff measures' is broader since it encompasses all the instruments which can be used to restrict trade, that is, function as barriers to trade. On the other hand, such measures may not have restrictive effects. Although the differentiation of these two terms is important (see Laird and Yeates, 1990, pp. 16–36), for the purposes of this chapter it does not matter if we use them interchangeably.

2. Quotas can be combined with tariffs to form a separate measure called a tariff quota. With this measure imports within a quota amount are subject to a low tariff rate, while imports above this quota are allowed at much higher rate.

3. Quotas can of course be modified by the government. By presumption this would require longer than the self-adjustment led by signals from the market.

4. When foreign supply is not perfectly elastic the increase in import demand by Home will also result in a higher price.

5. Orderly marketing arrangements (OMAs), which are government-to-government agreements and involve no industry participation in either bargaining or administration, have no important theoretical or practical difference from VERs.

6. MFA I was just a continuation of the managed trade in textiles and clothing already being put in place by the Short Term Cotton Textile Arrangement and the Long Term Arrangement Regarding International Trade in Cotton Textiles (LTA) negotiated under GATT auspices in 1961 and 1962 respectively. The LTA was a multilateral document but it functioned as a set of bilateral agreements.

7. If buyers in the importing country were monopsony they would be able to extract this rent from the exporters. It can also be captured in whole by the foreign government if it auctions the rights to export.

8. The term 'voluntary import expansion' was first introduced by Bhagwati (1987).

9. GATT's Article VI identifies dumping as a sale abroad at less than the normal value, where the normal value refers to the price of home sales.

10. If this firm were selling only in its domestic market, the pricing policy would involve equalising MC with MR and the firm would maximise profits by selling Q at price p.

11. The reader should keep in mind that monopoly will never produce at the portion of demand curve which is inelastic (or marginal revenue negative). Thus this formula makes sense only if the coefficient of elasticity is less than -1.

12. The Home market of the exporter is generally used to determine the normal or fair market value if sales in that market exceed 5 per cent of total non-US sales.

13. It seems that prices of kiwifruit dropped despite this action because of the huge expansion in production by other producers in the years following the anti-dumping action.

14. The difference between the small and the large country is of course in the effects subsidy has on the country's terms of trade.

15. These are so-called sanitary and phytosanitary measures, which refer to a requirement of governments to protect human, animal, or plant life or health from the risks arising from the spread of pests or diseases or from additives or contaminants found in food, beverages, or feedstuffs.

16. For example, in 1987 GATT ruled that a cigarette import ban by Thailand which was not accompanied by a corresponding production limit on the state cigarette monopoly could not be justified as 'necessary' under Article XX(b) (Uimonen, 1992).

17. Virtually all GATT signatories support the need for a change in the existing GATT rules regarding health-related trade restrictions. Currently under these regulations member countries have the right to adopt any measure deemed necessary to protect human, animal or plant health. However the rules are so vague that many countries use health-related requirements as actual barriers to trade.

18. Examples are numerous. For instance, the USA used to drew their health regulations in such a way that beef imported from Argentina could not possibly comply. The EU imposed an embargo in 1989 on imports of beef containing growth hormones (mostly coming from the USA). In the mid-1980s Japan moved to ban foreign-made skis from the domestic market claiming that were unsafe because Japanese snow differed from snow in countries where the skis were manufactured. In 1987 a GATT panel ruled that a cigarette import ban by Thailand could not be justified by Article XX (which allows for measures necessary to protect human, animal and plant life and health) because Thailand failed to introduce corresponding measures to limit production of the state cigarette monopoly.

19. The never born predecessor of the WTO, the International Trade Organization, was going to treat labour standards and employment as one of the major issues. Article 7 of Chapter 11 of the Havana Charter reads: 'The members recognise that unfair labour conditions, particularly in the production for exports, create difficulties in international trade, and accordingly each

member shall take whatever may be appropriate and feasible to climinate such conditions within its territory' (Charnovitz, 1987, pp. 566–7).

☐ 10 Arguments for Trade Barriers

1. The worsening of welfare relative to the autarky level is not the necessary outcome. If the production mix is not changed a lot from the autarky point *P*, it would be still possible for the free trade consumption to lie on the indifference curve above the autarky one. The reader is invited to draw such an outcome as an exercise.
2. In other words, the wage differentials prevent an economy from reaching the efficiency locus (contract curve) since the efficiency condition requires that the marginal rate of technical transformation, that is, the ratio of marginal productivities of the two factors of production must be equal in both sectors and equal to the factor-price ratio.
3. There are circumstances when governments try to make their citizens 'more patriotic' by asking them to buy more of the imported goods. For example, in the mid-1980s when the US pressure on Japan with respect to their mutual trade imbalance started, the Prime Minister of Japan was put in the position of advertising Italian ties or Swiss cheese. The whole advertising machinery was employed to convince the Japanese to spend more on imported goods thus enabling the rest of the world to buy more from Japan.
4. In fact strategic trade policy arguments have added a new flavour to this old argument. See p. 376 on import protection as export promotion where protection is supposed to support a development of an infant export industry.
5. This is how the infant industry argument is related to domestic distortions – they have common causes.
6. The names of these tests are due to Kemp (1970).
7. With respect to the impact of this import protection on the existing export sectors recall the Lerner symmetry theorem which teaches us that in the general equilibrium framework import tariffs discourage exports. In general equilibrium an across the board export tax has the same effect as one on imports of the same *ad valorem* rate. This theorem arises from the idea that in general equilibrium only relative prices matter: that is, favouring one sector implicitly means disfavouring the rest of the economy.
8. The model also allows for constant marginal costs with the average cost falling as higher output gives better 'learning-by-doing' effects, or as higher output justifies more R&D funding supplied by government. See Krugman (1984) for details.
9. There have been several simulations that produced results consistent with this 'import protection as export promotion' hypothesis. See for example Krugman (1987). There could however, be a bias in a selection of industries for simulation based on the industries were the actual targeting was relatively successful, such as the case with (Japanese) semi-conductors. On the other hand Dick (1994) found not much empirical support for this policy in the USA.
10. It is assumed that the duopoly sector accounts for only a small proportion of Home and Foreign outputs, so that the partial equilibrium analysis can be used.

☐ *11 The Measurement of Protection*

1. Development of the concept of the effective rate of protection is attributed to Corden (1966).
2. This is correct under the following assumptions: (a) the country cannot influence world prices, that is, the country is small; (b) all goods are traded before and after the imposition of tariffs; (c) physical input coefficients are constant; (d) there are no non-traded inputs except for the factors of production such as labour and capital; (e) there are no other distortions in the economy.
3. There is a considerable confusion in connection with the measurement of the effective rate of protection when the value added at the final stage of production is negative. From our formula it is obvious that in such a case the denominator is negative thus making the rate of effective protection appear as a negative number. However in this case the negative rate does not really mean 'dis-protection'. On the contrary, the industry in question would not be operating at all if the protection were not heavy.
4. There is another measure, the domestic resource costs (DRC) which provides an even broader measure than the effective rate of protection. DRC reflects the social opportunity cost of an industry because it estimates the value of domestic resources used in producing a particular product when all inputs are valued at world prices and all factor inputs are valued at their true opportunity cost prices. More specifically, DRC is obtained by dividing the value added expressed in local currency by the net foreign exchange earnings. The higher the DRC ratio, the more expensive it is to produce locally as compared to importing the product. DRC ratios interpreted in this way could be used as indicators of comparative advantage.
5. For a survey on empirical studies and measures of protection the reader should see Krueger (1984) or Greenaway and Milner (1993).
6. The estimation of the cost of protection (or gains from its removal) for a large country is more complicated since the effects on the world prices must be taken into account.
7. Such as de Melo (1988), de Melo and Tarr (1990), Greenaway and Milner (1993).

☐ *12 The Political Economy of Trade Policy*

1. This part of the section is based heavily on Vousden (1990, pp. 76–81).
2. Economists (who also vote) of all people should know where protectionism leads. But Frey *et al.* (1984) found that while 79 per cent of American economists believe that protection reduces welfare, the proportion is only 70 per cent in Germany, 47 per cent in Switzerland, 44 per cent in Austria and 27 per cent in France. One wonders if this is the consequence or the cause of the higher level of protection Europe has compared with the USA.

☐ *13 Trade Policy, Transition and Economic Development*

1. Despite their belief in the benefits of free trade, not many DCs followed the path of unilateral trade liberalisation.

2. The most influential works of these two authors were: Prebisch, R. (1950) and Singer, H. W. (1950).

3. According to Sachs (1997, p. 20) openness has proved to be the most decisive for fast growth (other factors being the differences in initial conditions, in demographic changes and in resources and geographic location). Open economies (of East and South-East Asia) grew 1.2 per cent annually faster than the closed economies of other regions, *ceteris paribus*, in the period 1965–90.

4. Nor could the experiences from the developing countries have been transposed directly. In contrast to trade liberalisation episodes in the developing countries, trade liberalisation in the transition economies required the steps not typically taken in other (market) economies. While a couple of countries (Poland and Hungary) freed the trading systems during the 1980s by more widely distributing trading rights, in the others trade liberalisation had to begin with the abolition of the state monopoly in foreign trade. All of them had to replace the system of implicit (and often very efficient) trade controls by the system of *explicit* trade controls such as quotas, licensing or tariffs. They had to establish an adequate exchange rate policy, to introduce currency convertibility and to create the legal and institutional framework for foreign direct investment (FDI).

5. We will define what trade liberalisation in fact implies in the following section. Here it suffices to say that the programmes are based on liberal trade policies which have to be designed from scratch since most of these countries did not have trade policies in the sense that market economies have. Hence when we talk about liberalising the previous administrative regulation of foreign trade that in fact means introducing trade policies that would be first neutral and secondly as liberal as possible given the state of these economies.

6. Trade liberalisation is just a part of a much broader programme of transition. There are many issues related to the position of trade liberalisation in the overall programme, for example, should trade liberalisation await stabilisation, or what the relationship is between privatisation and trade liberalisation. It would take us too far from the main theme to go into these concerns. It suffices to say that the most important support to trade liberalisation should come from: (1) privatisation and the elimination of soft budget constraints (this is essential to provide incentives to respond to foreign competition), and (2) the stabilisation of fiscal and monetary imbalances. The latter is important because inflation creates uncertainties, and government deficits usually lead to the current-account deficits. There is however no agreement whether trade liberalisation should await macroeconomic stabilisation or should occur simultaneously. It is nevertheless clear that the success of trade liberalisation will be limited or nonexistent if other distortions in the domestic economy are not (being) removed.

7. Measures of openness in terms of import (export) shares of GDP are not able to reflect to what extent the actual trade orientation or policy influences trade flows. These measures are more determined by the economy's size and structure and the type of trade policy. Thus, based on this measure, a large country would be in principle 'less open' than the small country irrespective of how restrictive the trade barriers they have.

8. The fact is that previous socialist regimes had utilised administrative, non-tariff barriers more extensively than tariffs. As a consequence (average nominal) tariffs are low and would be increased by conversion of the existing quantitative restrictions into tariff-equivalents. But for the countries that are already members of GATT it is very complicated to raise tariffs, even when it is in the temporary phase within the trade liberalisation process.

9. Differentiated intermediate goods could also be included, particularly when a net effect on producers discussed.

10. Alternative to this 'transitional protection' may be to resort to 'normal' trade liberalisation (i.e. with relatively low average nominal tariffs across the board) and to resort to government support for sectors (activities) that are hurt the most. This would serve the purpose of forestalling the huge dislocation costs equally well as the transitional protection. However past experience with subsidies in these countries does not give much cause for optimism with respect to the ability of governments to phase out the subsidy scheme in a timely manner either.

11. For example, in Hungary this was a loosening of monetary conditions (late in 1992) needed to finance the growing state budget deficit but also triggered by difficulties coming from attempts to neutralise the impact on the money supply of large capital inflows (EBRD, 1995). In contrast, in the Czech Republic the main factor for the increasing trade deficit seems to be a sharp deterioration in competitiveness.

☐ 14 The Theory of Economic Integration

1. In addition to the types of integration listed here there is also a form known as a *preferential trade agreement*. This involves a number of countries engaged in mutual trade at rates of protection lower than those applying to trade with countries outside the group. A good example of this type of preferential trading agreement is the British Commonwealth and the associated Commonwealth Preference System. This type of preferential agreements is actually outlawed by GATT.

2. For a detailed discussion on the role of the formation of a customs union within a sovereign nation state as a prelude to multilateral trade negotiation see Irwin (1993).

3. In fact the first post-war integration was established among the Eastern European countries and the Soviet Union in 1948 and was called the Council for Mutual Economic Assistance (CMEA or COMECON). More will be said about this integration in Chapter 16.

4. Article XXIV has provided a very large loophole for a wide variety of preferential agreements which contradict the most-favoured-nation clause (MFN) (Jackson, 1992, p. 141). For a discussion about the rationale behind the inclusion of this Article in the GATT see Chapter 17. See also Bhagwati (1993, pp. 25–8).

5. This conclusion does not hold if member countries are lower-cost producers than non-member countries.

6. Note that this effect is similar but not identical to the trade creation effect. Although the possibility of obtaining good *A* at a lower unit cost in Foreign is a consequence of the creation of trade with Home, this is not actually a

movement to a cheaper source of supply from a member country but rather the cheapening of the domestic source of supply.

7. For an extensive survey of the welfare effects of FTAs in general and compared to other forms of regional integration, see de Melo, Panagariya and Rodrik (1993, section 2).

8. This is because Article XXIV of the GATT requires that the external tariff be no higher than the average of the tariffs in the member countries before the formation of the union.

☐ 15 *Empirical Analysis of the Effects of Integration*

1. This section is based on Srinivasan, Whalley and Wooton (1993).

☐ 16 *Economic Integration in Practice*

1. Although the EU did not exist in its present form until January 1994 when it replaced the EC, we shall use terms 'the EU' and 'Union' in referring to all levels of integration as they emerged from early 1950s until the present time.

2. A full economic report on the implications of the 'Europe 1992' programme is given in the Commission of the European Communities (1988).

3. Note that Finland joined the EFTA as an associate member in 1961 and as a full member in 1986.

4. The significance of the difference between integrations at the production level and at the policy level is briefly discussed in Chapter 17 (Box 17.1, p. 513). Integration at the production level is ensured by free FDI and the activities of enterprises among member countries. This is supposed to imply deeper forms of integration than simply preferential trade.

5. The literature on the CMEA is extensive. Some of the more recent writings include Csaba (1990), van Brabant (1989) and Holzman (1987).

6. The following countries had observer status: Afghanistan, Angola, China, Ethiopia, Laos, Mozambique, Nicaragua, North Korea and South Yemen. Cooperation agreements were signed with Finland, Iraq and Mexico.

7. Countries were found to be maximizing their bilateral deficits with partners with whom they had agreed to settle balances in convertible currencies.

8. According to Kornai (1992, p. 358) the idea was to 'devise "a price basis of its own" starting out from the average costs in the member countries. This never happened, because the export prices payable on the capitalist market, or the export prices attainable there, exercise too great influence on the governments of certain member countries'.

9. The structural bilateralism was thus not a feature of Soviet trade with the individual members of the CMEA.

10. In terms of absolute gains, Asia was the most dynamic regional partner.

11. Many countries, such as Canada, the USA, Russia and other former Soviet Asian states, Central and Latin America, and Indo-China are thus excluded from the analysis. The role of Canada, the USA and Mexico in expanding regionalism was discussed in the previous section. Some other countries are partially covered in the section on APEC.

12. This agreement was preceded by the New Zealand–Australia Free Trade Agreement (NAFTA) which was signed in 1965 and was initially intended to last ten years. It involved the removal of tariffs on a specified 'non-sensitive'

products. This agreement was not successful in promoting trans-Tasman trade at all, in fact the share of bilateral trade in the products covered by the agreement was the same a decade after the agreement was signed.

☐ 17 Regionalism and Multilateralism

1. According to the WTO (1995b) report on *Regionalism and the World Trading System*, there were 98 regional integration agreements notified to the GATT from 1947 to 1994 under Article XXIV and 11 agreements notified under the 1979 Enabling Clause (Appendix Table 1, p. 77).
2. Grossman and Helpman (1993) provide an interesting but advanced reading on trade wars where the international objectives of governments are determined by domestic politics.
3. Only recently with the widening of the EU to the relatively lesser developed countries such as Portugal, Greece and Spain and, more importantly, with the creation of NAFTA, have trading blocs been established between quite diverse countries. In this analysis we have disregarded arrangements that were established for purely political reasons such as the US–Israel free trade area.
4. As Lipsey (1960, p. 507) argues: 'when only some tariffs are to be changed, welfare is more likely to be raised if these tariffs are merely *reduced* than if they are completely *removed* (emphasis in the original).'
5. They were the South Africa–Rhodesia Customs Union (1948), the Nicaragua–El Salvador Free Trade Agreement (1951), Nicaragua's participation in the Central American Common Market (1958) and the Caribbean Common Market (1973). See de la Torre and Kelly (1992, p. 43).
6. This is the common element of both Article XXIV of the GATT relating to goods and Article V of the GATS relating to services.

References

Aitken, N. and W. Lowry (1972) 'A Cross Sectional Study of the Effects of LAFTA and CACM on Latin American Trade', *Journal of Common Market Studies*, 11, 326–36.

Akamatsu K. (1962) 'A Historical Pattern of Economic Growth in Developing Countries', *The Developing Economies*, 3–25.

Anderson, J. and J.P. Neary (1994) 'Measuring the Restrictiveness of Trade Policy', *The World Bank Economic Review*, 8, 151–69.

Anderson, K. and Blackhurst, R. (eds) (1993) *Regional Integration and the Global Trading System* (New York: Harvester Wheatsheaf).

Anderson, K. and Norheim, H. (1993) 'History, Geography and Regional Economic Integration', in Anderson, K. and Blackhurst, R. (eds), *Regional Integration and the Global Trading System* (New York: Harvester Wheatsheaf).

Appleyard, D. and A. Field (1992) International Economics (New York: Irwin).

Aquino, A. (1978) 'Intra-industry Trade and Inter-industry Specialization as Concurrent Sources of International Trade in Manufactures', *Weltwirtschaftliches Archiv*, 114, 756–62.

Balassa, B. (1961) *The Theory of Economic Integration* (London: Allen & Unwin).

Balassa, B. (1963) 'An Empirical Demonstration of Classical Comparative Cost Theory', *Review of Economics and Statistics* 45, 231–8.

Balassa, B. (1966) 'Tariff Reductions and Trade in Manufactures Among the Industrial Countries', *American Economic Review*, 56, 466–73.

Balassa, B. (1967) 'Trade Creation and Trade Diversion in the European Common Market', *Economic Journal*, 77, 1–21.

Balassa, B. (1979) 'Intra-industry Trade and Integration of Developing Countries in the World Economy', in H. Giersch (ed.), *On the Economics of Intra-industry Trade* (Tübingen: J.C.B. Mohr).

Balassa, B. (ed.) (1982) *Development Strategies in Semi Industrialized Economies* (Baltimore: Johns Hopkins University Press).

Balassa, B. and L. Bauwens (1987) 'Intra-industry Specialisation in a Multi-country and Multi-industry Framework', *Economic Journal*, 97, 923–39.

Balasubramanyam, V.N. and Greenaway, D. (1993) 'Regional Integration Agreements and Foreign Direct Investment', in Anderson, K. and Blackhurst, R. (eds), *Regional Integration and the Global Trading System* (New York: Harvester Wheatsheaf).

Baldwin, R. (1971) 'Determinants of the Commodity Structure of US Trade', *American Economic Review*, 61, 126–46.

Baldwin, R.E. (1969) 'The Case Against Infant-industry Tariff Protection', *Journal of Political Economy*, 77, 295–305.

Baldwin, R.E. (1982) 'The Political Economy of Protectionism', in J. Bhagwati (ed.), *Import Competition and Response* (Chicago: University of Chicago Press).

Baldwin, R. E. (1992) 'Measurable Dynamic Gains from Trade', *Journal of Political Economy*, 100, 162–74.

Baldwin, R. E. and A. J. Venables (1995) 'Regional Economic Integration', in G. Grossman and K. Rogoff (eds), *Handbook of International Economics, Vol. III* (Amsterdam: Elsevier Science).

Ball, D. S. (1966) 'Factor Intensity Reversals: An International Comparison of Factor Costs and Factor Use', *Journal of Political Economy*, 74, 77–80.

Bano, S. and P. Lane (1991) 'Intra-industry International Trade: The New Zealand Experience 1964–87', University of Waikato, Department of Economics, *Working Papers in Economics*, 91/7.

Barro, R. J. (1991) 'Economic Growth in a Cross Section of Countries', *Quarterly Journal of Economics*, 101, 407–3.

Beghin, J. *et al.* (1994) 'A Survey of the Trade and Environment Nexus: Global Dimensions', *OECD Economic Studies*, 23, 168–87.

Bensel, T. and B. T. Elmslie (1992) 'Rethinking International Trade Theory: A Methodological Appraisal', *Weltwirtschaftliches Archiv*, Band 128, Heft 2, 249–65.

Bergstrand, J. H. (1983) 'Measurement and Determinants of Intra-industry International Trade', in P. K. M. Tharakan (ed.), *Intra-industry Trade: Empirical and Methodological Aspects* (Amsterdam: North-Holland).

Bhagwati, J. (1958) 'Immiserizing Growth: A Geometrical Note', *Review of Economic Studies* 25, 201–5.

Bhagwati, J. (1959) 'Protection, Real Wages, and Real Incomes', *Economic Journal*, 69, 733–48.

Bhagwati, J. (1965) 'On the Equivalence of Tariffs and Quotas', in R. E. Baldwin *et al.* (eds), *Trade, Growth and the Balance of Payments* (Chicago: Rand McNally).

Bhagwati, J. (1968) 'Distortions and Immiserizing Growth: A Generalization', *Review of Economic Studies*, Vol. 35, 481–5.

Bhagwati, J. (1971) 'The Generalized Theory of Distortions and Welfare', in J. Bhagwati *et al.* (eds), *Trade, Balance of Payments and Growth: Essays in Honor of Charles Kindleberger* (Amsterdam: North-Holland).

Bhagwati, J. (1980) 'Lobbying and Welfare', *Journal of Public Economics*, 14, 355–63.

Bhagwati, J. (1982) 'Directly Unproductive, Profit-seeking (DUP) Activities', *Journal of Political Economy*, 90, 988–1002.

Bhagwati, J. (1987) 'Outward Orientation: Trade Issues', in V. Corbo *et al.* (eds), *Growth Oriented Adjustment Programs* (Washington DC: IMF and the World Bank) 257–90.

Bhagwati, J. (1987) 'VERs, quid pro quo DFI and VIEs: Political–economy–theoretic Analysis', *International Economic Journal*, 1–14.

Bhagwati, J. (1988) *Protectionism* (Cambridge, MA: MIT Press).

Bhagwati, J. (1989) 'Is Free Trade Passé After All?', *Weltwirtschaftliches Archiv*, 125, 17–44.

Bhagwati, J. (1990) 'Departures from Multilateralism: Regionalism and Aggressive Unilateralism', *The Economic Journal*, 100, 1304–17.

Bhagwati, J. (1991) *The World Trading System at Risk* (Princeton, NJ: Princeton University Press).

Bhagwati, J. (1991b) 'The Stolper–Samuelson Theorem: Then and Now', Columbia University, *Discussion Paper Series*, 606 (November).

Bhagwati, J. (1992) 'Fair Trade, Reciprocity and Harmonization: The New Challenge to the Theory and Policy of Free Trade', Discussion Paper Series No. 604, Department of Economics, Columbia University.

Bhagwati, J. (1993) 'Beyond NAFTA: Clinton's Trading Choices', *Foreign Policy*, Summer, 155–62.

Bhagwati, J. (1993) 'Regionalism and Multilateralism: An Overview', in J. de Melo and A. Panagariya (eds), *New Dimensions in Regional Integration* (Cambridge and New York: Cambridge University Press).

Bhagwati, J. (1993a) 'The Case for Free Trade', *Scientific American* (November), 42–9.

Bhagwati, J. (1993b) 'Trade and the Environment', *The American Enterprise* (May–June), 43–9.

Bhagwati, J. and A. O. Krueger (1995) *The Dangerous Drift to Preferential Trade Agreements* (Washington, DC: The AEI Press).

Bhagwati, J. and Srinivasan, T. N. (1975) *Foreign Trade Regimes and Economic Development: India* (New York: National Bureau of Economic Research).

Bhagwati, J. and Srinivasan, T. N. (1980a) 'Revenue-seeking: A Generalization of the Theory of Tariffs', *Journal of Political Economy*, 88, 1069–87.

Bhagwati, J. and Srinivasan, T. N. (1980b) *Lectures in International Trade* (Cambridge, MA: MIT Press).

Blackhurst, R. (1977) 'International Trade and Domestic Environmental Policies in a Growing World Economy', in R. Blackhurst *et al.* (eds), *International Relations in a Changing World* (Leiden: Sijthoff).

Bollard, A. and D. Mayes (1992) 'Regionalism and the Pacific Rim', *Journal of Common Market Studies*, 30, 195–209.

Borjas, G. (1995) 'Assimilation and Changes in Cohort Quality Revisited: What Happened to Immigrant Earnings in the 1980s?', *NBER Working Paper*, 4866.

Bowen, H. P., E. E. Leamer and L. Sveikauskas (1987) 'Multicountry, Multifactor Tests of the Factor Abundance Theory', *American Economic Review*, 77, 791–809.

Brada, J. C. (1993) 'Regional Integration in Eastern Europe: Prospects for Integration Within the Region and With the European Community', in J. de Melo and A. Panagariya (eds), *New Dimensions in Regional Integration* (Cambridge: Cambridge University Press).

Brander, J. (1981) 'Intra-industry Trade in Identical Commodities', *Journal of International Economics*, 11, 1–14.

Brander, J. A and P. A. Krugman (1983) 'A "Reciprocal Dumping" Model of International Trade', *Journal of International Economics*, 15, 313–21.

Brander, J. A. and B. J. Spencer (1984) 'Tariff Protection and Imperfect Competition', in H. Kierzkowski (ed.), *Monopolistic Competition and International Trade* (Oxford: Blackwell).

Brander, J. A. and B. J. Spencer (1985) 'Export Subsidies and International Market Share Rivalry', *Journal of International Economics*, 18, 83–100.

Brecher, R. A. and Choudhri, E. U. (1982) 'Immiserizing Investment from Abroad: The Singer-Prebisch Thesis Reconsidered', *Quarterly Journal of Economics*, 97(1), 181–90.

Brown, D. K. and Stern, R. M. (1988) 'Computational Analysis of the US-Canada Free Trade Agreement: The Rate of Product Differentiation and Market Structures' in Robert C. Feenstra (ed.), *Empirical Methods for International Trade* (Cambridge, MA: MIT Press).

Caves, R. E. (1981) 'Intra-industry Trade and Market Structure in the Industrial Countries', *Oxford Economics Papers*, 33, 203–23.

Caves, R., J. Frankel and R. Jones (1993) *World Trade and Payments: An Introduction*, 5th edn (New York: HarperCollins).

Cecchini, P. (1988) *The Costs of Non-Europe* (London: Wildwood House).

Cecchini, P. M. and A. Jacquemin (1988) *The European Challenge, 1992: The Benefits of a Single Market* (Aldershot: Wildwood House).

CEPR (1994) *New Trade Theories: A Look at the Empirical Evidence* (London: CEPR)

Chamberlin, E. (1933) *The Theory of Monopolistic Competition: A Re-orientation of the Theory of Value* (Cambridge, MA: Harvard University Press).

Charnovitz, S. (1987) 'The Influence of International Labour Standards on the World Trading Regime: A Historical Review', *International Labour Review*, 126, 565–84.

Chipman, J. E. S. (1965) 'A Survey of the Theory of International Trade', Part 1 and 2, *Econometrica*, 33, 477–519, 685–760.

Chipman, J. E. S. (1966) 'A Survey of the Theory of International Trade, Part 3', *Econometrica* 34 (January) 18–76.

Cline, W. R. (1984) *International Debt: Systematic Risk and Policy Response* (Washington, DC: Institute for International Economics).

Commission of the European Communities (1988) 'The Economics of 1992', *The European Economy*, 35.

Cooper, C. A. and Massell, B. F. (1965) 'Towards a General Theory of Customs Unions for Developing Countries', *Journal of Political Economy*, 73, 461–76.

Corden, M. (1990) 'Integration and Trade Policy in the Former Soviet Union', UNDP/World Bank Trade Expansion Program, mimeo.

Corden, M. and J. P. Neary (1982) 'Booming Sector and De-industrialization in a Small Open Economy', *Economic Journal*, 92, 825–48.

Corden, W. M. (1966) 'The Structure of a Tariff System and the Effective Protective Rate', *Journal of Political Economy* 74, 221–37.

Corden, W. M. (1971) *The Theory of Protection* (Oxford: Oxford University Press).

Corden, W. M. (1972) 'Economies of Scale and Custom Union Theory', *Journal of Political Economy*, 80, 465–75.

Corden, W. M. (1974) *Trade Policy and Economic Welfare* (Oxford: Clarendon Press).

Corden, W. M. (1984) 'The Normative Theory of International Trade', in R. W. Jones and P. B. Kenen (eds), *Handbook of International Economics*, Vol. I (Amsterdam: North-Holland).

Corden, W. M. (1987) 'Protection and Liberalization: A Review of Analytical Issues', *IMF Occasional Paper*, 54 (Washington, DC: International Monetary Fund).

Corden, W. M. (1990) 'Strategic Trade Policy. How New? How Sensible?', *Working Paper Series* (Washington, DC: World Bank).

Csaba, L. (1990) *Eastern Europe in the World Economy* (Cambridge: Cambridge University Press).

Dalziel, P. and R. Lattimore (1996) *The New Zealand Macroeconomy: A Briefing On the Reforms* (Melbourne: Oxford University Press).

Davis, D. (1992) 'Intra-industry trade: A Heckscher–Ohlin–Ricardo Approach', Harvard University *mimeo*, quoted in Dollar (1993).

de la Torre, A. and Kelly, M.R. (1992) *Regional Trade Arrangements*, Occasional Paper 93, International Monetary Fund.

de Melo, J. (1988) 'Computable General Equilibrium Models for Trade Policy Analysis in Developing Countries: A Survey', *Journal of Policy Modelling*, 10, 469–503.

de Melo, J. and A. Winters (1993) 'Do Exporters Gain from VERs?', *European Economic Review*, 37, 1331–49.

de Melo, J. and D. Tarr (1992) *A General Equilibrium Analysis of US Foreign Trade Policy* (Cambridge, MA: MIT Press).

de Melo, J. and Panagariya, A. (eds) (1993) *New Dimensions in Regional Integration* (Cambridge: Cambridge University Press).

de Melo, J., A. Panagariya and D. Rodrik (1993) 'The New Regionalism in Trade Policy: A Country Perspective', in J. de Melo and A. Panagariya (eds), *New Dimensions in Regional Integration* (Cambridge and New York: Cambridge University Press).

Dean, J.M., S. Desai and J. Riedel (1994) 'Trade Policy Reform in Developing Countries Since 1985 – A Review of the Evidence', *World Bank Discussion Papers* 267, (Washington, DC: World Bank).

Deardorff, A. (1980) 'The General Validity of the Law of Comparative Advantage', *Journal of Political Economy*, 88, 941–57.

Deardorff, A.V. (1982) 'The General Validity of the Heckscher–Ohlin Theorem', *American Economic Review*, 72, 683–94.

Deardorff, A.V. (1984a) 'Testing Trade Theories and Predicting Trade Flows', in R.W. Jones and P.B. Kenen (eds), *Handbook of International Economics*, Vol. I (Amsterdam: North-Holland).

Deardorff, A.V. (1984b) 'An Exposition and Exploration of Krueger's Trade Model', *Canadian Journal of Economics*, 17, 731–46.

Deardorff, A.V. (1985) 'Developments in International Trade Theory', in T. Peeters, P. Praet and P. Reding (eds), *International Trade and Exchange Rates in the Late Eighties* (Amsterdam: North-Holland).

Dick, A.R. (1993) 'Does Import Protection Act as Export Promotion: Evidence from the United States', *Oxford Economic Papers*, 46(1), 83–101.

Dinopoulos, E. and Kreinin, M. (1990) 'An Analysis of Import Expansion Policies', *Economic Inquiry*, 99–108.

Dixit, A. (1985) 'Taxation in Open Economies', in A.J. Auerbach and M.S. Feldstein (eds), *Handbook of Public Economics I* (Amsterdam: North-Holland).

Dixit, A. and V. Norman (1980) *Theory of International Trade* (London: Cambridge University Press).

Dixit, A.K. and J.E. Stiglitz (1977) 'Monopolistic Competition and Optimum Product Diversity', *American Economic Review*, 67, 297–308.

Dollar, D. (1986) 'Technological Innovation, Capital Mobility, and the Product Cycle in North–South Trade', *American Economic Review* 76, 177–90.

Dollar, D. (1993) 'Technological Differences as a Source of Comparative Advantage', *American Economic Review*, 83, 431–5.

Dorfman, R., P. E. A. Samuelson and R. E. M. Solow (1958) *Linear Programming and Economic Analysis* (New York: McGraw-Hill).

Dornbusch, R. (1992) 'The Case for Trade Liberalization in Developing Countries', *Journal of Economic Perspectives*, 6, 69–85.

Dornbusch, R., S. Fischer and P. E. A. Samuelson (1977) 'Comparative Advantage, Trade, and Payments in a Ricardian Model with a Continuum of Goods', *American Economic Review*, 67 (December), 823–39.

Duncan, I., R. Lattimore and A. Bollard (1992) 'Dismantling the Barriers: Tariff Policy in New Zealand', *Research Monograph*, 57 (Wellington: New Zealand Institute of Economic Research).

Eaton, J. and G. M. Grossman (1986) 'Optimal Trade and Industrial Policy Under Oligopoly', *Quarterly Journal of Economics*, 101, 383–406.

Eaton, J. and M. Gersovitz (1981) 'Debt with Potential Reproduction: Theoretical and Empirical Analysis', *Review of Economic Studies*, 48, 289–309.

Eaton, J., M. Gersovitz and J. Stightz (1986) 'The Pure Theory of Country Risk', *European Economic Review*, 30.

EBRD (1992) 'Regional Initiatives', *Annual Economic Review*, 26–30 (European Bank for Reconstruction and Development).

EBRD (1994) *Transition Report 1994* (London: European Bank for Reconstruction and Development).

EBRD (1995) *Transition Report 1995* (London: European Bank for Reconstruction and Development).

ECE (1994) *Economic Bulletin for Europe*, 46 (New York and Geneva: United Nations).

Edwards, S. (1993) 'Openness, Trade Liberalization, and Growth in Developing Countries', *Journal of Economic Literature*, 31, 1358–93.

Eichengreen, B. (1993) 'Discussion on Multilateral and Bilateral Trade Policies', in J. de Melo and A. Panagariya (eds), *New Dimensions in Regional Integration* (Cambridge and New York: Cambridge University Press).

El-Agraa, A. M. (1989) *International Trade* (London: Macmillan).

Emmanuel, A. (1972) *Unequal Exchange: A Study In the Imperialism Of Trade* (London: New Left Books).

Esty, D. C. (1993) 'GATTing the Greens, Not Just Greening the GATT', *Foreign Affairs*, 72, 5, 32–6.

Ethier, W. (1979) 'Internationally Decreasing Costs and World Trade', *Journal of International Economics*, 9, 1–24.

Ethier, W. (1982a) 'The General Role of Factor Intensity in the Theorems of International Trade', *Economic Letters*, 10, 337–42.

Ethier, W. (1982b) 'Decreasing Costs in International Trade and Frank Graham's Argument for Protection', *Econometrica*, 5, 1243–68.

Ethier, W. (1984) 'Higher Dimensional Issues in Trade Theory', in R. W. Jones and P. B. Kenen (eds), *Handbook of International Economics*, Vol. I (Amsterdam: North-Holland).

Ethier, W. (1988) *Modern International Economics*, 2nd edn (New York: Norton).

Ethier, W. and Horn, H. (1984) 'A New Look at Economic Integration', in H. Kierzkowski (ed.), *Monopolistic Competition and International Trade* (Oxford: Clarendon Press).

Evans, H. D. (1989) *Comparative Advantage and Growth* (New York: St Martin's Press).

Falvey, R. E. (1981) 'Commercial Policy and Intra-industry Trade', *Journal of International Economics*, 11, 495–511.

Falvey, R. E. (1994) 'Revenue Enhancing Tariff Reform', *Weltwirtschaftliches Archiv*, 130, 175–89.

Falvey, R. E. and H. Kierzkowski (1987) 'Product Quality, Intra-industry Trade and (Im)perfect Competition', in H. Kierzkowski (ed.), *Protection and Competition in International Trade* (Oxford: Basil Blackwell).

Feenstra, R. (1992) 'How Costly is Protectionism?', *Journal of Economic Perspectives*, 6, 159–78.

Feenstra, R. (1995) 'Estimating the Effects of Trade Policy', in G. Grossman and K. Rogoff (eds), *Handbook of International Economics*, Vol. III (Amsterdam: Elsevier Science).

Fels, G. (1972) 'The Choice of Industry Mix in the Division of Labour Between Developed and Developing Countries', *Weltwirtschaftliches Archiv*, 108, 71–121.

Finger, J. M. (1975) 'Trade Overlap and Intra-industry Trade', *Economic Inquiry*, 13, 581–9.

Finger, J. M. (1992) 'Dumping and Antidumping: The Rhetoric and the Reality of Protection in Industrial Countries', *The World Bank Research Observer* 7, 121–43.

Fishlow, A. (1988) 'Alternative Approaches and Solutions to the Debt of Developing Countries', in S. Borner (ed.), *International Finance and Trade in a Polycentric World* (London: Macmillan).

Foroutan, F. (1993) 'Regional Integration in Sub-Saharan Africa: Past Experience and Future Prospects', in J. de Melo and Arvind Panagariya (eds), *New Dimensions in Regional Integration* (Cambridge: Cambridge University Press).

Forstner, H. and R. Ballance (1990) *Competing in a Global Economy* (London: Unwin Hyman for UNIDO).

Francois, J. F. *et al.* (1995) 'Assessing the Uruguay Round', in W. Martin and L. A. Winters (eds), *The Uruguay Round and the Developing Economies* (Washington, DC: World Bank).

Frey, B. and H. Weck-Hannemann (1996) 'The Political Economy of Protection', in David Greenaway (ed.), *Current Issues in International Trade* (Basingstoke: Macmillan).

Frey, B. *et al.* (1984) 'Consensus and Dissension Among Economists: An Empirical Inquiry', *American Economic Review*, 74, 986–94.

Friedman, M. *et al.* (1984) *Politics and Tyranny: Lessons in the Pursuit of Freedom* (San Francisco: Pacific Institute for Public Policy Research).

Globerman, S. and J. W. Dean (1990) 'Recent Trends in Intra-industry Trade and their Implications for Future Trade Liberalization', *Weltwirtschaftliches Archiv* 126, 25–49.

Graham, F. (1923) 'Some Aspects of Production Further Considered', *Quarterly Journal of Economics*, 37, 199–227.

Gray, H. E. P. (1986) 'Non-competitive Imports and Gains from Trade', *The International Trade Journal*, 1, 107–28.

Greenaway, D. (1993) 'Liberalizing Foreign Trade Through Rose-tinted Glasses', *The Economic Journal*, 103, 208–22.

Greenaway, D. and C. Milner (1983) 'On the Measurement of Intra-industry Trade', *The Economic Journal* 93, 900–908.

Greenaway, D. and C. Milner (1986) *The Economics of Intra-industry Trade* (Oxford: Basil Blackwell).

Greenaway, D. and C. Milner (1987) 'Current Perspectives and Unresolved Issues', *Weltwirtschafliches Archiv* 123, 39–57.

Greenaway, D. and C. Milner (1988) 'Intra-Industry Trade: Current Perspectives and Unresolved Issues', *Kyklos*, 39–57.

Greenaway, D. and C. Milner (1989) 'Nominal and Effective Tariffs in a Small Industrialising Economy: The Case of Mauritius', *Applied Economics*, 21, 995–1010.

Greenaway, D. and C. Milner (1990a) 'The Estimate of 'True Protection': A Comment on the Smeets Procedure', *Journal of Development Studies*, 26, 330–4.

Greenaway, D. and C. Milner (1990b) 'Industrial Incentives, Domestic Resource Costs and Resource Allocation in Madagascar', *Applied Economics*, 22, 805–2.

Greenaway, D. and C. Milner (1993) *Trade and Industrial Policy in Developing Countries* (London: Macmillan).

Greenaway, D. and D. Sapsford (1994) 'What Does Liberalization Do for Exports and Growth?', *Weltwirtschaftliches Archiv*, 130, 152–75.

Greenaway, D. and P. K. M. Tharakan (eds) (1986) *Imperfect Competition and International Trade* (Brighton: Wheatsheaf Books).

Grossman, G. (ed.) (1992) Imperfect Competition and International Trade (Cambridge, MA: MIT Press).

Grossman, G. and E. Helpman (1989) 'Product Development and International Trade', *Journal of Political Economy*, 97, 1261–83.

Grossman, G. and E. Helpman (1991) *Innovation and Growth: Technological Competition in the World Economy* (Cambridge, MA: MIT Press).

Grossman, G. and E. Helpman (1993) 'Trade Wars and Trade Talks', *National Bureau of Economic Research*, Working Paper No. 4280, February.

Grossman, G. M. (1984) 'The Gains from International Factor Movements', *Journal of International Economics*, 17, 73–83.

Grubel, H. G. and P. J. Lloyd (1975) *Intra-industry Trade: The Theory and Measurement of International Trade in Differentiated Products* (New York: Wiley).

Guitian, M. (1992) 'Rules and Discretion in International Economic Policy', *Occasional Paper*, 97 (Washington, DC: International Monetary Fund).

Haaland, J. and V. Norman (1992) 'Global Production Effects of European Integration', in L. A. Winters (ed.), *Trade Flows and Trade Policy After '1992'*, (Cambridge: Cambridge University Press).

Hamilton, C. and P. Kniest (1991) 'Trade Liberalization, Structural Adjustment and Intra-industry Trade: A Note', *Weltwirtschaftliches Archiv*, 127, 356–67.

Hamilton, R. and Whalley, J. (1985) 'Geographically Discriminatory Trade Arrangements', *Review of Economics and Statistics*, 67, 446–55.

Hamilton, T. (1790) *Report of Manufacturers 1790. Papers on Public Credit, Commerce and Finance* (New York: Columbia University Press, 1934).

Hanson, G. (1996) 'US–Mexico Integration and Regional Economies', *NBER Working Paper*, 5425.

Harberger, A. (1964) 'Taxation, Resource Allocation and Welfare', in *The Role of Direct and Indirect Taxes in the Federal Revenue System*: a conference report of the National Bureau of Economic Research and the Brookings Institution (Princeton: Princeton University Press).

Harkness, J. and J. F. Kyle (1975) 'Factors Influencing United States Comparative Advantage', *Journal of International Economics*, 5, 153–65.

Harris, R. (1984) 'Applied General Equilibrium Analysis of Small Open Economies with Economies of Scale and Imperfect Competition', *American Economic Review*, 74, 1016–32.

Harris, R. (1985) 'Summary of a Project on the General Equilibrium Evaluation of Canadian Trade Policy', in J. Whalley (ed.), *Canada-United States, Free Trade* (Toronto: University of Toronto Press).

Harris, R. and Cox, D. (1984) *Trade, Industrial Policy and Canadian Manufacturing* (Toronto: Ontario Economic Council Research Study).

Harrison, G., T. Rutherford and I. Wooton (1989) 'The Economic Impact of the EC', *American Economic Review*, 79, 288–94.

Havrylyshyn, O. (1985) 'The Direction of Developing Country Trade: Empirical Evidence of Differences Between South–South and South–North Trade', *Journal of Development Economics*, 19(3) 225–82.

Havrylyshyn, O. and E. Civan (1983) 'Intra-industry Trade and the Stage of Development: A Regression Analysis of Industrial and Developing Countries', in Tharakan (1983), 111–40.

Hazledine, T. (1993) 'New Zealand Trade Patterns and Policy', *The Australian Economic Review* (4th quarter), 23–27.

Heckscher, E. F. and B. Ohlin (1991) *Heckscher–Ohlin Trade Theory*, trans. and ed. by H. Flam and J. Flanders (Cambridge, MA: MIT Press).

Helpman, E. (1981) 'International Trade in the Presence of Product Differentiation, Economies of Scale, and Monopolistic Competition: A Chamberlin–Heckscher–Ohlin Approach', *Journal of International Economics*, 11, 305–40.

Helpman, E. (1984a) 'The Factor Content of Foreign Trade', *Economic Journal*, 94, 84–94.

Helpman, E. (1984b) 'A Simple Theory of International Trade with Multinational Corporations', *Journal of Political Economy*, 92, 451–71.

Helpman, E. (1985) 'Multinational Corporations and Trade Structure', *Review of Economic Studies*, 52, 443–58.

Helpman, E. (1987) 'Imperfect Competition and International Trade: Evidence from Fourteen Industrial Countries', *Journal of the Japanese and International Economies*, 1, 62–81.

Helpman, E. (1989) 'The Non-competitive Theory of International Trade and Trade Policy', *The World Bank Economic Review*, Supplement, Proceedings of the World Bank Annual Conference on Development Economics, 193–217.

Helpman, E. (1990) 'Monopolistic Competition in Trade Theory', *Special Papers in International Finance*, 16 (Princeton, NJ: Princeton University Press).

Helpman, E. and P. Krugman (1989) *Trade Policy and Market Structure* (Cambridge, MA: MIT Press).

Helpman, E. and P. A. Krugman (1985) *Market Structure and Foreign Trade* (Cambridge, MA: MIT Press).

Hertel, T. *et al.* (1995) 'Liberalizing Manufacturing Trade in a Changing World Economy', paper presented at the conference on the Uruguay Round and the Developimg Economies, January 26–27, World Bank, International Economics Department, Washington, DC.

Hindley, B. and P. Messerlin (1993) 'Guarantees of Market Access and Regionalism' in Anderson, K. and Blackhurst, R. (eds) *Regional Integration and the Global Trading System* (New York: Harvester Wheatsheaf).

Hine, R. (1992) 'Regionalism and the Integration of the World Economy', *Journal of Common Market Studies*, XXX, 115–23.

Hirsch, S. (1974) 'Capital or Technology? Confronting the Neo-factor Proportions and Neo-technology Accounts of International Trade', *Weltwirtschaftliches Archiv*, 60, 535–63.

Holzman, F. (1987) *The Economics of Soviet Bloc Trade and Finance* (Boulder, CO and London: Westview Press).

Hufbauer, G. C. (1966) *Synthetic Materials and the Theory of Interational Trade* (Cambridge, MA: Harvard University Press).

Hufbauer, G. C. and J. Chilas (1974) 'Specialization by Industrial Countries: Extent and Consequences', in H. Giersch (ed.), *The International Divison of Labour: Problems and Perspectives* (Tübingen: J. C. B. Mohr).

Hummels, D. and J. Levinsohn (1993) 'Product Differentiation as a Source of Comparative Advantage?', *American Economic Review*, 83, 445–9.

Imada, P. (1993) 'Production and Trade Effects of an ASEAN Free Trade Area', *The Developing Economies*, 31, 3–23.

IMF (1995) *Direction of Trade Statistics 1995* (Washington, DC: IMF).

Irwin, D. A. (1993) 'Multilateral and Bilateral Trade Policies in the World Trading System: An Historical Perspective', in J. de Melo and A. Panagariya (eds), *New Dimensions in Regional Integration* (Cambridge and New York: Cambridge University Press).

Irwin, D. (1994) *Mismanaged Trade: The Case Against Import Targets* (Washington: American Enterprise Institute).

Jackson, J. (1992) *The World Trading System* (Cambridge, MA: MIT Press).

Johnson, H. (1958) 'The Gains from Freer Trade with Europe: An Estimate', *Manchester School*, 26, 247–55.

Johnson, H. G. (1965) 'An Economic Theory of Protectionism, Tariff Bargaining and the Formation of Customs Unions', *Journal of Political Economy*, 73, 256–83.

Jones, R. W. (1965) 'The Structure of Simple General Equilibrium Models', *Journal of Political Economy*, 73, 557–72.

Jones, R. W. (1971) 'A Three-factor Model in Theory, Trade and History', in J. Bhagwati *et al.* (eds), *Trade, Balance of Payments, and Growth: Essays in Honor of Charles P. Kindleberger* (Amsterdan: North-Holland).

Jones, R. W. (1987) 'Heckscher–Ohlin Trade Theory', in J. Eatwell, M. Milgate and P. Newman (eds), *The New Palgrave Dictionary in Economics*, (London: Macmillan), 620–7.

Jones, R. W. (1993) 'Discussion on Regionalism Versus Multilateralism: Analytical Notes', in J. de Melo and A. Panagariya (eds), *New Dimensions in Regional Integration* (Cambridge: Cambridge University Press).

Jones, R. W. and H. Kierzkowski (1986) 'Neighbourhood Production Structures With an Application to the Theory of International Trade', *Oxford Economic Papers*, 38, 59–76.

Jones, R. W., R. King and M. Klein (1992) 'The Chinese Economic Area: Economic Integration Without a Free Trade Agreement', OECD, Economics Department Working Papers, 124.

Jones, R. W. and J. P. Neary (1984) 'The Positive Theory of International Trade', in R. W. Jones and P. B. Kenen (eds), *Handbook of International Economics*, Vol. I (Amsterdam: North-Holland).

Kaminski, B. Z., K. Wang and L. A. Winters (1996) 'Foreign Trade in the Transition: The International Environment and Domestic Policy', in *Studies of Economics in Transformation*, 20 (Washington, DC: World Bank).

Keesing, D. (1966) 'Labor Skills and Comparative Advantage', *American Economic Review*, 56, 249–58.

Kelly, M. and A. K. McGuirk and others (1992) *Issues and Developments in International Trade Policy* (Washington, DC: IMF).

Kemp, M. C. (1960) 'The Mill–Bastable Infant-industry Dogma', *Journal of Political Economics*, 68, 65–7.

Kemp, M. C. (1964) *The Pure Theory of International Trade* (Englewood Cliffs, NJ: Prentice-Hall) Chapter 8.

Kemp, M. C. and H. Herberg (1969) 'Some Implications of Variable Returns to Scale', *Canadian Journal of Economics*, 3, 403–4.

Kemp, M. C. and H. Y. Wan (1976) 'An Elementary Proposition Concerning the Formation of Customs Unions', *Journal of International Economics*, 6, 95–7.

Kennan, J. and R. Riezman (1990) 'Optional Tariff Equilibria With Customs Unions', *Canadian Journal of Economics*, 23, 70–83.

Kierzkowski, H. (1987) 'Recent Advances in International Trade Theory: A Selective Survey', *Oxford Review of Economic Policy*, 3, 1–18.

Kornai, J. (1992) *The Socialist System: The Political Economy of Communism* (Oxford: Clarendon Press).

Kostecki, M. (1987) 'Export-restraint Arrangements and Trade Liberalization', *The World Economy*, (December), 425–53.

Kreinin, M. (1965) 'Comparative Labor Effectiveness and the Leontief Scarce-factor Paradox', *American Economic Review*, 55, 131–40.

Krueger, A. O. (1974) 'The Political Economy of the Rent-seeking Society', *American Economic Review*, 64, 291–303.

Krueger, A. O. (1977) 'Growth, Distortions and Patterns of Trade Among Countries', *Princeton Studies in International Finance*, 40 (Princeton: Princeton University Press).

Krueger, A. O. (1980) 'Trade Policy as an Input to Development', *American Economic Review*, 70, 288–92.

Krueger, A. O. (1984) 'Trade Policies in Developing Countries', in R. W. Jones and P. B. Kenen (eds), *Handbook of International Economics* I (Amsterdam: North-Holland) 519–69.

Krueger, A. O. (1990) *Perspectives on Trade and Development* (Chicago: The University of Chicago Press).

Krueger, A. O. (1993) 'Free Trade Agreements as Protectionist Devices: Rules of Origin', National Bureau of Economic Research, *Working Paper*, 4352.

Krueger, A. O. (1997) 'Trade Policy and Economic Development: How We Learn', *American Economic Review*, 87, 1–22.

Krugman, P. (1984) 'Import Protection as Export Promotion: International Competition in the Presence of Oligopoly and Economies of Scale', in H. Kierzkowski (ed.), *Monopolistic Competition in International Trade* (Oxford: Oxford University Press).

Krugman, P. (1987) 'Market Access and Competition in High Technology Industries: A Simulation Exercise', in H. Kierzkowski (ed.), *Protection and Competition in International Trade* (Oxford: Basil Blackwell).

Krugman, P. (1990) 'A "Technology Gap", Model of International Trade', *Rethinking International Trade* (Cambridge, MA: MIT Press).

Krugman, P. (1991) *Geography and Trade* (Leuvien: Leuvien University Press and Cambridge, MA: MIT Press).

Krugman, P. (1992) 'A Decade of the New Trade Theory', in M. G. Dagenais and P.- A. Muet (eds), *International Trade Modelling* (London: Chapman & Hall).

Krugman, P. (1992) 'Does the New Trade Theory Require a New Trade Policy?', *The World Economy*, 15 (July), 423–41.

Krugman, P. (1993) 'Regionalism Versus Multilateralism: Analytical Notes', in J. de Melo and A. Panagariya (eds), *New Dimensions in Regional Integration* (Cambridge and New York: Cambridge University Press).

Krugman, P. (1994) 'Empirical Evidence on the New Trade Theories: The Current State of Play', in *New Trade Theories: A Look at the Empirical Evidence*, CEPR Conference Report (London: CEPR).

Krugman, P. (1995) 'Increasing Returns, Imperfect Competition and the Positive Theory of International Trade', in G. Grossman and K. Rogoff (eds), *Handbook of International Economics*, Vol. III, (Amsterdam: Elsevier Science).

Krugman, P. (1997) 'What Should Trade Negotiators Negotiate About?', *Journal of Economic Literature*, 35, 113–20.

Krugman, P. and R. Lawrence (1993) 'Trade, Jobs and Wages', *NBER Working Paper* (Cambridge, MA: National Bureau of Economic Research).

Krugman, P. and M. Obstfeld (1988) *International Economics: Theory and Policy* (New York: Scott, Foresman and Co.).

Krugman, P. and M. Obstfeld (1991) *International Economics: Theory and Policy*, 2nd edn (London: HarperCollins Publishers).

Lafay, G. (1992) 'The Measurement of Revealed Comparative Advantages', in M. G. Dagenais and P. A. Muet (eds), *International Trade Modelling* (London: Chapman & Hall).

Laird, S. and A. Yeats (1990) *Quantitative Methods for Trade-barrier Analysis* (London: Macmillan).

Lancaster, K. (1980) 'Intra-industry Trade under Perfect Monopolistic Competition', *Journal of International Economics*, 10, 151–175.

Lancaster, K. (1984) 'Protection and Product Differentiation', in H. Kierzkowski (ed.), *Monopolistic Competition and International Trade* (Oxford: Oxford University Press), 137–56.

Langhammer, R. J. (1995) 'Endogenous Tariffs and Economic Transformation: The Case of Russian Trade Policies', *Intereconomics*, (March–April) 77–86.

Lattimore, R. (1987) 'Economic Adjustment in New Zealand: A Developed Country Case Study of Policies and Problems', in Sir Frank Holmes (ed.), *Economic Adjustment: Policies and Problems* (Washintgon, DC: IMF).

Lawrence, R. (1996) *Single World, Divided Nations?: International Trade and OECD Labour Markets* (Paris: Brookings Institution Press and OECD Development Centre).

Leamer, E. (1980) 'The Leontief Paradox, Reconsidered', *Journal of Political Economy*, 88, 495–503.

Leamer, E. (1984) *Sources of International Comparative Advantage: Theory and Evidence* (Cambridge, MA: MIT Press).

Leamer, E. (1992) 'Testing Trade Theory', *National Bureau of Economic Research Working Paper*, 3957 (Cambridge, MA: NBER).

Leamer, E. (1993) 'Factor-Supply Differences as a Source of Comparative Advantage', *American Economic Review*, 83, 436–40.

Leamer, E. and J. Levinsohn (1995) 'International Trade Theory: The Evidence', in G. Grossman and K. Rogoff (eds), *Handbook of International Economics*, Vol. III (Amsterdam: Elsevier Science).

Leidy, M. (1995) 'Antidumping: Solution or Problem in the 1990s?', in *International Trade Policies: The Uruguay Round and Beyond, Vol. 2, World Economic and Financial Surveys* (Washington, DC: International Monetary Fund).

Leontief, W. W. (1953) 'Domestic Production and Foreign Trade: The American Capital Position Re-examined', in J. Bhagwati (ed.), *International Trade: Selected Readings* (Harmondsworth: Penguin Books).

Leontief, W. W. (1956) 'Factor Proportions and the Structure of American Trade: Further Theoretical and Empirical Analysis', *Review of Economics and Statistics*, 38, 386–407.

Leontief, W. W. (1964) 'An International Comparison of Factor Costs and Factor Use', *American Economics Review*, 54(4), 335–45.

Lerner, A. (1936) 'The Symmetry Between Import and Export Taxes', *Economica*, 3, 306–13.

Lewis (1982) 'The Latest Battle of Politics', *New York Times*, 13 January, D1.

Linder, S. B. (1961) *An Essay on Trade and Transformation* (New York: Wiley).

Lindert, P. H. and P. J. Morton (1989) 'How Sovereign Debt has Worked', in J. Sachs and S. Collins (eds), *Developing Country Debt, Volume I: The World Financial System* (Chicago: University of Chicago Press).

Lipsey, R. G. (1960) 'The Theory of Customs Unions: A General Survey', *The Economic Journal*, 52, 496–513.

Lipsey, R. G. (1976) 'Review of Grubel and Lloyd (1975)', *Journal of International Economics*, 6, 312–14.

List, E. (1841) The National System of Political Economy (New York: Longman Green, reprinted 1904).

Lloyd, P. J. (1982) '3 × 3 Theory of Customs Unions', *Journal of International Economics*, 12, 41–64.

Lloyd, P. J. (1992) 'Regionalisation and World Trade', *OECD Economic Studies*, 18, 7–43.

Lloyd, P. J. (1993) 'Global Integration', *The Australian Economic Review*, 1993(1) 35–48.

Low, P. (ed.) (1992) 'International Trade and the Environment', *World Bank Discussion Papers*, 159 (Washington, DC: World Bank).

Lynde, M. R. (1992) 'Testing an Imperfect Competition Trade Model', in M. G. Dagenais and P. A. Muet (eds), *International Trade Modelling* (London: Chapman & Hall).

MacDougall, G. D. A. (1951) 'British and American Exports: A Study Suggested by the Theory of Comparative Costs. Part I', *Economic Journal*, 61, 697–724.

MacDougall, G. D. A. (1952) 'British and American Exports: A Study Suggested by the Theory of Comparative Costs. Part II', *Economic Journal*, 62, 487–521.

MacDougall, G. D. A., M. Dowley, P. Fox and S. Pugh (1962) 'British and American Productivity, Prices and Exports: An Addendum', *Oxford Economic Papers*, 14.

Magee, S. P. (1993) 'The Political Economy of Trade Policy', in D. Greenaway and L. A. Winters (eds), *Surveys in International Trade* (Oxford: Blackwell).

Maneschi, A. (1992) 'Ricardo's International Trade Theory: Beyond the Comparative Cost Example', *Cambridge Journal of Economics*, 16, 421–37.

Markusen, J. (1984) 'Multinationals, Multi-plant Economies and the Gains from Trade', *Journal of International Economics*, 16, 205–26.

Markusen, J. and J. Melvin (1981) 'Trade, Factor Prices, and the Gains from Trade with Increasing Returns to Scale', *Canadian Journal of Economics*, 3, 450–69.

Markusen, J. and J. Melvin (1984) 'The Gains-from-Trade Theorem under Increasing Returns to Scale', in H. Kierzkowski (ed.), *Monopolistic Competition in International Trade* (Oxford: Clarendon Press).

Marvei, H. P. and E. J. Ray (1987) 'Intra-Industry Trade: Sources and Effects of Protection', *Journal of Political Economy*, 95(6), 1278–91.

Mayer, W. (1974) 'Short-run and Long-run Equilibrium for a Small Open Economy'. *Journal of Political Economy*, 82, 955–67.

Mayes, D. (1978) 'The Effects of Economic Integration on Trade', *Journal of Common Market Studies*, 1–23.

Mayes, D. (1988) 'The Problems of Quantitative Estimation of Integration Effects', in A. El-Agraa (ed.), *International Economic Integration* (London: Macmillan).

McKenzie, L. (1955) 'Equality of Factor Prices in World Trade', *Econometrica* 23, 239–57.

McKinnon, R. (1991) 'Liberalizing Foreign Trade in a Socialist Economy: The Problem of Negative Value-added', in John Williamson (ed.), *Currency Convertibility in Eastern Europe*, (Washington, DC: Institute for International Economics) 96–115.

McMillan, J. (1993) 'Does Regional Integration Foster Open Trade?' Economic theory and GATT's Article XXIV', in K. Anderson and R. Blackhurst (eds), *Regional Integration and the Global Trading System* (New York: Harvester Wheatsheaf).

Meade, J. (1951) *The Theory of International Economic Policy, Volume 1: The Balance of Payments* (Oxford: Oxford University Press).

Melvin, J. (1969) 'Increasing Returns to Scale as a Determinant of Trade', *Canadian Journal of Economics*, 3, 389–402.

Mercenier, J. (1992) 'Completing the European Internal Market: A General Equilibrium Evaluation Under Alternative Market Structure Assumptions', Working Paper No 892, Centre de Recherche et Developpement en Economique, Univerite de Montreal.

Metzler, L. (1949) 'Tariffs, Terms of Trade and the Distribution of National Income', *Journal of Political Economy*, 57, 1–29.

Michaely, M. (1977) *Theory of Commerical Policy: Trade and Protection* (Chicago: University of Chicago Press).

Mikić, M. (1989) 'External Debt Management', in H. W. Singer and S. Sharma (eds), *Growth and External Debt Management* (London: Macmillan).

Miller, M. and Spencer, J. (1977) 'The Static Economic Effects of the UK Joining the EEC: A General Equilibrium Approach', *Review of Economic Studies*, 44, 71–93.

Milner, C. (1985) 'Empirical Analyses of the Costs of Protection', in David Greenaway (ed.), *Current Issues in International Trade* (Basingstoke: Macmillan).

Minhas, B. S. (1962) 'The Homohypallagic Production Function, Factor-intensity Reversals and the Heckscher–Ohlin Theorem', *Journal of Political Economy*, 70, 138–56.

Mussa, M. (1974) 'Tariffs and the Distribution of Income: The Importance of Factor Specificity, Substitutability, and Intensity in the Short and Long Run', *Journal of Political Economy*, 82, 1191–204.

Mussa, M. (1979) 'The Two-Sector Model in Terms of its Dual: A Geometric Exposition', *Journal of International Economics*, 9, 513–26.

Mussa, M. (1982) 'Government Policy and the Adjustment Process', in J. Bhagwati (ed.), *Import Competition and Response* (Chicago: University of Chicago Press).

Naqvi, S. *et al.* (1983) *The Structure of Protection in Pakistan 1980–81* (Islamabad: Pakistan Institute of Development Economics).

Neary, J.P. (1978) 'Short Run Capital Specificity and the Pure Theory of International Trade', *The Economic Journal*, 88, 488–510.

Negishi, T. (1982) 'The Labour Theory of Value in the Ricardian Theory of International Trade', *History of Political Economy*, 14, 199–210.

Nogues, J. J. and R. Quintanilla (1993) 'Latin America's Integration and the Multilateral Trading System', in J. de Melo and A. Panagariya (eds), *New Dimensions in Regional Integration* (Cambridge: Cambridge University Press).

Norman, V. (1991) '1992 and EFTA', in L. A. Winters and A. J. Venables (eds), *European Integration: Trade and Industry* (Cambridge: Cambridge University Press).

OECD (1993) *From Trade-driven Growth to Growth-driven Trade: Reappraising the East Asian Development Experience*, Development Centre Documents (Paris: OECD).

OECD (1994) *Integrating Emerging Market Economies into the International Trading System* (Paris: OECD).

OECD (1996) *Trade, Employment and Labour Standards: A Study of Core Workers', Rights and International Trade* (Paris: OECD).

Ohyama, M. (1972) 'Trade and Welfare in General Equilibrium', *Keio Economic Studies*, 9, 37–73.

Papageorgiou, D., M. Michaely and A. Choksi (1991) *Liberalizing Foreign Trade, Vol. 7, Lessons of Experience in the Developing Countries* (Oxford: Basil Blackwell).

Pohl, G. and Sorsa, P. (1992) 'European Integration and Trade with the Developing World', The World Bank, *Policy and Research Series*, 21.

Pomfret, R. (1985) 'Categorical Aggregation and International Trade: A Comment', *Economic Journal*, 95, 483–5.

Pomfret, R. (1991) *International Trade: An Introduction to Theory and Policy* (Cambridge, MA: Blackwell).

Posner, M. V. (1961) 'International Trade and Technical Change', *Oxford Economic Papers*, 8, 323–41.

Prebisch, R. (1950) *The Economic Development of Latin America and its Principal Problems* (New York: United Nations).

Ratnayake, R. (1993) 'Political Economy of Protection to Australian Manufacturing: Further Results', *Economic Analysis & Policy*, 23, 29–44.

Ratnayake, R. (1993b) 'Factors Affecting Inter-industry Variation of Foreign Ownership of Manufacturing Industry', *Applied Economics*, 25, 653–9.

Ricardo, D. (1911) *The Principles of Political Economy and Taxation* (London: Dent).

Richardson, J. D. (1989) 'Empirical Research on Trade Liberalization with Imperfect Competition: A Survey', *OECD Economics Studies*, 12, 8–51.

Richardson, J. D. (1992) ' "New", Trade Theory and Policy a Decade Old: Assessment in a Pacific Context', *National Bureau of Economics Research Working Paper Series*, 4042.

Roberts, R. D. (1994) *The Choice: A Fable of Free Trade and Protectionism* (Englewood Cliffs, NJ: Prentice Hall).

Robson, P. (1987) *The Economics of International Integration*, 3rd edn (London: Allen & Unwin).

Rodrik, D. (1995) 'Comments', in A. O. Krueger (ed.), *Trade Policies and Developing Nations* (Washington, DC: Brookings Institution).

Romer, P. (1989) 'Capital Accumulation in the Theory of Long Run Growth', in Barro, R. (ed.), *Modern Business Cycle Theory* (Cambridge, MA: Harvard University Press) 51–127.

Rosefielde, S. (1974) 'Factor Proportions and Economic Rationality in Soviet International Trade 1955–1968', *American Economic Review*, 64, 670–81.

Ruffin, R. E. J. (1984) 'International Factor Movements', in R. W. Jones and P. B. Kenen (eds), *Handbook of International Economics, Vol. I* (Amsterdam: North-Holland).

Ruffin, R. E. J. (1988) 'The Missing Link: The Ricardian Approach to the Factor Endowment Theory of Trade', *American Economic Review*, 78 (September), 759–72.

Ruffin, R. E. J. (1990) 'The Ricardian Factor Endowment Theory of International Trade', *International Economic Journal*, 4 (Winter), 1–19.

Ruffin, R. E. J. and R. Jones (1977) 'Protection and Real Wages: The Neoclassical Ambiguity', *Journal of Economic Theory*, 14, 337–48.

Rybczynski, T. M. (1955) 'Factor Endowments and Relative Commodity Prices', *Economica*, 22, 336–41.

Sachs, J. (1997) 'Nature, Nurture and Growth', *The Economist*, 14 June, 19–21.

Sachs, J. and H. Shatz (1994) 'Trade and Jobs in US Manufacturing, *Brookings Papers on Economic Activity*, (Washington, DC: The Brookings Institution).

Samuelson, P. (1948) 'International Trade and the Equalization of Factor Prices', *Economic Journal*, 58, 163–84.

Samuelson, P. (1949) 'International Factor-Price Equalization Once Again', *Economic Journal*, 59, 181–97.

Samuelson, P. (1953) 'Prices of Factors and Goods in General Equilibrium', *Review of Economic Studies*, 21, 1–20.

Samuelson, P. (1954) 'The Transfer Problem and Transport Costs: Analysis of Effects of Trade Impediments', *Economic Journal*, 64, 264–89.

Samuelson, P. (1956) 'Social Indifference Curves', *Quarterly Journal of Economics*, 70, 1–22.

Samuelson, P. (1971) 'Ohlin was Right', *Swedish Journal of Economics*, 73, 365–84.

Sapir, A. (1992) 'Regional Integration in Europe', *Economic Journal*, 102, 1491–506.

Sapir, A. (1993) 'Discussion on The European Community: A Case of Successful Integration?', in J. de Melo and A. Panagariya (eds), *New Dimensions in Regional Integration* (Cambridge: Cambridge University Press).

Savosnick, K. M. (1958) 'The Box Diagram and the Production Possibility Curve', *Ekonomisk Tidskrift*, 60, 183–97.

Scherer, F. M. (1992) *International High-Technology Competition* (Cambridge, MA: Harvard University Press).

Scherer, F. M. and D. Ross (1990) *Industrial Market Structure and Economic Performance* (Boston: Houghton-Mifflin).

Schott, J. (1994) *The Uruguay Round – An Assessment* (Washington, DC: Institute for International Economics).

Scitovsky, T. (1958) *Economic Theory and Western European Integration* (London: Allen & Unwin).

Scollay, R. (1992) 'North American Free Trade: An Australasian Perspective', *Seminar Paper*, Department of Economics, The University of Auckland.

Siebert, H. (1991) 'A Schumpeterian Model of Growth in the World Economy: Some Notes on a New Paradigm in International Economics', *Weltwirtschaftliches Archiv*, 127, 800–12.

Simpson, A. (1996) 'No: Jobs and National Interests are at Stake', *Insight* (19 February, 21 and 23).

Singer, H. W. (1950) 'The Distribution of Gains Between Investing and Borrowing Countries', *American Economic Review*, 40, 473–85.

Sjaastad, L. A. and K. W. Clements (1981) 'The Incidence of Protection: Theory and Measurements', in L. A. Sjaastad (ed.), *The Free Trade Movement in Latin America* (London: Macmilllan).

Smith, A. (1994) 'Imperfect Competition and International Trade', in D. Greenaway and A. Winters (eds), *Surveys in International Trade* (Oxford: Blackwell).

Smith, A. and A. J. Venables (1988) 'Completing the Internal Market in the European Community: Some Industry Simulations', *European Economic Review*, 32, 1501–25.

Smith, A., A. J. Venables, and M. Gasiorek (1992) '1992: Trade and Welfare – A General Equilibrium Model', in L. A. Winters (ed.), *Trade Flows and trade Policy After '1992'*, (Cambridge: Cambridge University Press).

Sorsa, P. (1995) 'Environmental Protectionism, North–South Trade, and the Uruguay Round', *Working Paper of the International Monetary Fund*, 6 (January).

Spence, H. (1976) 'Product Selection, Fixed Costs, and Monopolistic Competition', *Review of Economic Studies*, 43, 217–36.

Spraos, J. (1980) 'The Statistical Debate on the Net Barter Terms of Trade Between Commodities and Manufactures', *Economic Journal*, 90, 107–28.

Srinivasan, T. N., J. Whalley and I. Wooton (1993) 'Measuring the Effects of Regionalism on Trade and Welfare', in K. Anderson and R. Blackhurst (eds), *Regional Integration and the Global Trading System* (New York: Harvester Wheatsheaf).

Stern, R. M. (1962) 'British and American Productivity and Comparative Costs in International Trade', *Oxford Economic Papers*, 14.

Stern, R. M. (1975) 'Testing Trade Theories', in P. B. Kenen (ed.), *International Trade and Finance* (London: Cambridge University Press).

Stern, R. M. and K. E. Maskus (1981) 'Determinants of the Structure of US Foreign Trade, 1958–1976', *Journal of International Economics*, 11, 207–24.

Stolper, W. and K. Roskamp (1961) 'Input–output Table for East Germany with Applications to Foreign Trade', *Bulletin of the Oxford University Institute of Statistics*, 23, 379–82.

Stolper, W. and P. Samuelson (1941) 'Protection and Real Wages', *Review of Economic Studies*, 9, 58–73.

Takacs, W. (1990) 'Options for Dismantling Trade Restrictions in Developing Countries', *The World Bank Research Observer*, 5, 25–46.

Tanzi, V. (1991) 'Tax Reform and the Move to a Market Economy: Overview of the Issues', *The Role of Tax Reform in Central and Eastern European Economies* (Paris: OECD), 19–34.

Tatemoto, M. and S. Ichimura (1959) 'Factor Proportions and Foreign Trade: The Case of Japan', *Review of Economics and Statistics*, 41, 442–6.

Tharakan, P. K. M. (1985) 'Empirical Analyses of the Commodity Composition of Trade', in D. Greenaway (ed.), *Current Issues in International Trade* (London: Macmillan).

Tharakan, P. K. M. (ed.) (1983) *Intra-industry Trade: Empirical and Methodological Aspects* (Amsterdam: North-Holland).

Tharakan, P. K. M. and J. Kol (eds) (1989) *Intra-industry Trade: Theory, Evidence and Extensions* (London: Macmillan).

Thomas, V. and J. Nash and Associates (1991) *Best Practices in Trade Policy Reform* (Oxford: Oxford University Press).

Tower, E. (1979) 'The Geometry of Community Indifference Curves', *Weltwirtschaftliches Archiv*, 115, 680–99.

Trela, I. and J. Whalley (1990) 'Global Effects of Developed Country Trade Restrictions on Textiles and Apparel', *Economic Journal* 100, 1190–1205.

Truman, E. (1975) 'The Effects of European Economic Integration on the Production and Trade of Manufactured Products', in B. Balassa (ed.), *European Economic Integration* (Amsterdam: North-Holland).

Tybout, J. R. (1993) 'Internal Returns to Scale as a Source of Comparative Advantage: The Evidence', *American Economic Review*, 83, 440–4.

Tyler, W. G. (1985) 'Effective Incentives for Domestic Market Sales and Exports: A View of Anti-export Biases and Commercial Polices in Brazil 1980–81', *Journal of Developments Economics*, 18, 219–42.

Uimonen, P. (1992) 'Trade Policies and the Environment', *Finance & Development*, (June) 26–7.

UNCTAD (1983) *Nontariff Barriers Affecting the Trade of Developing Countries and Transparency in World Trading Conditions*, (TD/B/940) (Geneva: UNCTAD).

UNCTAD (1994) *Trade and Development Report, 1994* (New York and Geneva: United Nations).

United Nations (1981) *Commodity Indexes for the Standard International Trade Classification, Revision 2*, Statistical Papers Series M, 38/Rev., Vol. II.

United Nations (1992) *World Investment Report 1992* (New York: United Nations).

United Nations (1992) *World Investment Report 1992: Transnational Corporations as Engines of Growth* (New York: United Nations).

van Brabant, J. M. (1989) *Economic Integration in Eastern Europe* (London: Harvester Wheatsheaf).

van Brabant, J. M. (1994) 'Alternative Trade Regimes and the Economics of Transition', *Russian and East European Finance and Trade*, January–February, 32–52.

Vanek, J. (1959) 'The Natural Resource Content of Foreign Trade 1870–1955 and the Relative Abundance of the Natural Resources in the United States', *Review of Economics and Statistics*, 41, 146–53.

Vanek, J. (1965) *General Equilibrium of International Discrimination: The Case of Customs Unions* (Cambridge, MA: Harvard University Press).

Venables, A. (1985) 'Trade and Trade Policy with Imperfect Competition: The Case of Identical Products and Free Entry', *Journal of International Economics*, 19, 1–20.

Verdoorn, P. (1954) 'A Customs Union for Western Europe: Advantages and Feasibility', *World Politics*, 6, 482–506.

Vernon, R. (1966) 'International Investment and International Trade in the Product Cycle', Quarterly Journal of Economics, 80, 190–207.

Vernon, R. (1979) 'The Product Life Cycle Hypothesis in a New International Environment', *Oxford Bulletin of Economics and Statistics*, 41, 255–67.

Viner, J. (1950) *The Customs Union Issue* (New York: Carnegie Endowment for International Peace).

Vousden, J. (1990) *The Economics of Trade Protection* (Cambridge: Cambridge University Press).

Wade, R. (1990) *Governing the Market* (Princeton: Princeton University Press).

Waverman, L. (1992) Editorial Introduction to a Mini Symposium on 'Modelling Free Trade in North America', *The World Economy*, 15, 1–100.

Whalley, J. (1985) *Trade Liberalization Among Major World Trading Areas* (Cambridge, MA: MIT Press).

Whalley, J. (1993) 'Regional Trade Arrangements in North America', in J. de Melo and A. Panagariya (eds), *New Dimensions in Regional Integration* (Cambridge: Cambridge University Press).

Whalley, J. (1994) 'Agreement on Textiles and Clothing', *The New World Trading System – Readings* (Paris: OECD).

Williamson, J. (1994) 'In Search of a Manual for Technopols', in J. Williamson (ed.), *The Political Economy of Policy Reform* (Washington, DC: Institute for International Economics) 9–28.

Winters, L. A. (1993a) 'The European Community: A Case of Successful Integration?', in J. de Melo and A. Panagariya (eds), *New Dimensions in Regional Integration* (Cambridge: Cambridge University Press).

Winters, L. A. (1993b) *International Economics* (London: Routledge).

Winters, L. A. (1996) 'Regionalism and the Rest of the World: The Irrelevance of the Kemp-Wan Theorem', Discussion Paper No. 1316, Centre for Economic Policy Research, London.

Wolf, T. A. (1988) *Foreign Trade in the Centrally Planned Economy* (London: Harwood Academic Press).

Wonnacott, P. and R. Wonnacott (1981) 'Is Unilateral Tariff Reduction Preferable to a Customs Union? The Curious Case of the Missing Foreign Tariffs', *American Economic Review*, 71, 704–14.

Wood, A. (1994) 'Give Heckscher and Ohlin a Chance!', *Weltwirtschaftliches Archiv*, 130(1) 20–49.

Wooding, P.(1987) 'Liberalizing the International Trade Regime', in A. Bollard and R. Buckle (eds), *Economic Liberalization in New Zealand* (Wellington: Allen & Unwin).

World Bank (1987) *World Development Report 1987* (Oxford: Oxford University Press).

World Bank (1988) *World Development Report 1988* (Washington, DC: World Bank).

World Bank (1989) *World Development Report 1989* (Oxford: Oxford University Press).

World Bank (1990) *World Development Report 1990* (Oxford: Oxford University Press).

World Bank (1992) *World Development Report 1992* (Oxford: Oxford University Press).

World Bank (1995) *Global Economic Prospects and the Developing Countries* (Washington, DC: World Bank).

World Bank (1996) *From Plan to Market, World Development Report 1996* (Oxford: Oxford University Press).

WTO (1995) *Regionalism and the World Trading System* (Geneva: WTO).

WTO (1995a) *International Trading Trends and Statistics* (Geneva: WTO).

WTO (1995b) *Trading into the Future* (Geneva: WTO).

Yamazawa, I. (1992) 'On Pacific Economic Integration', *Economic Journal*, 102, 1519–1529.

Young, A. 'Learning by Doing and the Dynamic Effects of International Trade', *Quarterly Journal of Economics*, 106, 369–405.

Young, L. (1993) 'International Economics', in 'Readings in Economics' (unpublished manuscript Department of Economics and Marketing, Christchurch, New Zealand: Lincoln University).

Index

599